C0-ARW-596

APPROACHES TO THE STUDY OF POLITICAL SCIENCE

CHANDLER PUBLICATIONS IN

POLITICAL SCIENCE

Victor Jones, Editor

Approaches to the Study of Political Science

Edited by

Michael Haas and Henry S. Kariel
University of Hawaii

CHANDLER PUBLISHING COMPANY
An Intext Publisher · Scranton, Pennsylvania 18515

COPYRIGHT © 1970 BY CHANDLER PUBLISHING COMPANY
ALL RIGHTS RESERVED
INTERNATIONAL STANDARD BOOK NO. 0-8102-0022-8
LIBRARY OF CONGRESS CATALOG CARD NO. 70-83280
PRINTED IN THE UNITED STATES OF AMERICA

Previously published and copyrighted materials are reprinted with the permission of authors, publishers, or copyright owners as listed below:

From *The Political System,* by David Easton. Copyright 1953 by Alfred A. Knopf, Inc. Reprinted by permission of the publisher.

Karl W. Deutsch and Leroy N. Rieselbach, "Recent Trends in Political Theory and Political Philosophy," *Annals,* CCCLX (July 1965), 139-162. Reprinted, with revisions, by permission of the publisher.

Theodore L. Becker, "Judicial Structure and Its Political Functioning in Society," *Journal of Politics,* XXIX (March 1967), 302-333. Reprinted, with revisions, by permission of the publisher.

Norman Meller, "Legislative Behavior Research" and " 'Legislative Behavior Research' Revisited: A Review of Five Years' Publications," *Western Political Quarterly,* XIII (#1, March 1960), 131-153; XVIII (#4, December 1965), 776-793.

From Philip M. Hauser and Leo F. Schnore, *The Study of Urbanization,* pp. 115-156. Copyright © 1965 by John Wiley & Sons, Inc. Reprinted by permission of the publisher.

From Michael Haas, "Bridge-Building in International Relations. A Neotraditional Plea," *International Studies Quarterly,* XI (December, 1967), 320-338, by permission of the Wayne State University Press.

David Easton, Presidential Address, 65th Annual Meeting of the American Political Science Association, September, 1969, by permission of the American Political Science Association.

JA
71
.A66

For HAROLD D. LASSWELL, *who opened alternatives*

ALMA COLLEGE
MONTEITH LIBRARY
ALMA, MICHIGAN

Contents

Preface

With everyone engaged everywhere in making things easier, someone was needed to make them difficult again.—*Søren Kierkegaard*

The layman tends to regard political science as a field containing scholars concerned with matters of public policy. In times past, political scientists indeed did focus on issues not far removed from the realm of current events, while academically attempting to frame their task in the broader context of ethics and historical processes. However, particularly since World War II, the behavioral movement presented a program for change. Political scientists urged one another to build broad theories, to assemble data to test specific hypotheses, and to disregard values. A concomitant of the McCarthyism era was a generation of scholars who, silent on values, appeared to believe that there was no further need for political ideology in an affluent America. If the 1950's were the heyday of theoretical, formalistic behavioralists, the apogee of empirical behavioralism was the 1960's. A behavioral political science has surely become established at the center of the discipline.

As we enter the 1970's, a time for evaluation and reflection on the state of the discipline seems to be in order. Having succeeded in producing a scientific mood in political science, behavioralists have been debating among themselves on the scope of theoretical advancements and empirical outputs, asking what stage is next in the development of the field. Meanwhile, prophets of an "end to ideology" have proved to be premature, if not downright incorrect: fundamental questions of public policy are dramatically and embarrassingly reemerging. Voting studies in the past two decades shuffled "don't know" responses into reject pockets of counter-sorters, thus failing to anticipate the intensity of ideological militancy growing up within ghettos of American cities. Scholars in international studies face escalatory moves in whatever may be our current military venture without being able to use their more scientifically grounded wisdom in order to secure a just resolution of the conflict. It also cannot be said that the basic crisis of authority was predicted—not to say explained—by those constrained by our fashionable methodologies.

The purpose of this volume is threefold. First, we seek to review the field of political science from the past to the immediate present. Second, we shall note the paradoxes and predicaments resulting from the success of behavioralism in political science. Third, we shall inquire not only where we will be heading if we project past and present trends into the future, but also toward what objectives political science ought to be developing in the 1970's.

For this task we have assembled sixteen essays. The introductory chapter looks at the history of political science and the rise of subfields of study within the discipline; it then reconstructs the logic of modern political analysis and recommends a revitalizing of the field that will be more in accord with scientific canons and social problems. Chapters 2 through 15 are surveys on each of the six traditional subfields of political science. The impact of behavioralism is assessed within the framework of the older sixfold structuring of political science along two major facets—theory and research. The final two chapters scrutinize the crystal ball most thoroughly, linking prebehavioral opponents of the behavioral persuasion with postbehavioral scholars who seem to reunite the age-old concern for values with the ongoing quest for a science of politics. The new synthesis, called *multimethodologism* by the authors of Chapter 16, would have been impossible without the behavioral revolution—just as behavioralism needed something called traditionalism to focus its plea. And just as many traditionalists in due course became behavioral, so many behavioralists are becoming multimethodologists, pursuing the optimizing strategy proposed by David Easton in the last chapter of the volume.

However, one sign that the multimethodological revolution remains incomplete is the absence of a new generation of scholars prepared to expose its flaws. In a decade or so, we anticipate a volume similar to ours which will assess postbehavioral achievements. In the meantime, confronting the present and its perplexities, we can do little more than confess to a Kierkegaardian humility.

Michael Haas
Henry S. Kariel

Honolulu, Hawaii
April, 1969

I

INTRODUCTION

1 The Rise of a Science of Politics

MICHAEL HAAS, University of Hawaii

Had I been present at the creation, I would have given some useful
hints for the better ordering of the universe—*Alonzo X*

I. INTRODUCTION

The artist, Picasso has insisted, must come to terms with classical
forms of expression; he must be taught classical art in order to understand its fallacies and reject its errors. However, classicism, whether in art
or in politics, can have a logic and an elegance all its own. It can render
reality comprehensible by a broad-brush synthesis and a grasp of wholes
so compelling that subordinate parts need not be filled in with tedious
detail. As one penetrates the interstices of one's subject, discovering new
facets and contours, the parts become the prime focus, and any sense of
organic unity vanishes. What is gained in return? Are we learning more
and more about less and less?

Political science may be unique as an academic discipline in that it
has two classicisms—or perhaps orthodoxies—not one. As the study of
politics achieved a state of self-consciousness in nineteenth-century
Europe, it blended moral philosophy, jurisprudence, and history. Unconcerned with epistemological questions which Bacon and Kant had posed
for the natural scientists, the earliest political scientists provided one
form of classicism simply by focusing upon statecraft, applying moral
absolutes to public issues, and suggesting new structural forms to
make government operations more orderly and promotive of a capitalist society that increasingly departed from laissez faire. The second
classicism is more recent, dating from the 1930's. It has been preoccupied with an application of social-scientific canons of inquiry to
the empirical investigation and theoretical explanation of phenomena
that would not have seemed "political" at all to students of earlier
generations. Yet this second classicism has been content with narrow
perspectives, while being complacently unconcerned about whether the
findings it derives so rigorously might ever percolate up (or trickle
down) to policy makers.

3

The curious bifurcation between pure and applied science had indeed been the aim of advocates of the second form of classicism, of the self-defined behavioralists. At least one effect of the sudden achievement of their goals has been a call for new syntheses, for applications of knowledge to resolve pressing domestic and international problems. The specter of a new watershed has thus been raised. On the one hand, political science may today become fragmented and specialized, breaking into so many small compartments that the primeval sense of unity would disintegrate. Alternatively, the maturing of both classicisms into full-fledged antitheses might give rise to a transcending synthesis.

The editors of this volume, as well as the contributors, hope for the latter alternative and feel that it is possible to gain increased empirical knowledge within the context of ever-broadening theoretical perspectives. The task on which we embark, however, is not the easiest to accomplish. A cautious humility best accompanies a quest for sketching out vistas and mapping paths to our destination, for we have not arrived—we have merely started, and perhaps occasionally faltered, as we looked for the appropriate doors. The questions we have sought to ask include the following: How has politics been defined? What aspects of politics may be studied autonomously as subfields? What models are appropriate? What methods of analysis are useful in assembling data about political phenomena? What new theoretical directions are at present visible?

The balance of this introductory essay supplies an overview of each of these problems. Each contribution in this book looks at a particular subfield from the standpoint of theoretical and research strategies. The concluding essay attempts to bring together the various major dilemmas of contemporary political analysis, with suggestions for their resolution.

II. EPISTEMOLOGY IN POLITICAL SCIENCE

To obtain an overview of the discipline of political science it seems inescapable to ask how knowledge about politics has been acquired and why. With regard to the latter question, one could interpret the development of the field as a set of responses to a series of newly perceived social problems. To resolve successive practical and normative dilemmas, it was considered necessary to redraw boundaries for the spheres of politics and government. One by one, each of some six subfields arose and found its place within the discipline of political science—political theory, public law, comparative government, politics, administration, and international relations. For about a half century the sixfold division by and large has persisted as the main framework for political-science department curricula. In establishing jurisdictional limits as well as rallying points for scholars, the effect of this fragmentation has been to wall off similar modes of analysis from one another. Indeed, the organizational scheme for this volume, which attempts a critical survey of the current and future status of political science, may seem most meaningful and manageable in terms of six relatively autonomous subfields, both from the standpoint of the reader and the authors. At the same time, there are clear signs that the six-pillar framework is crumbling. One explanation could be that the student of a highly limited form of government may have found the traditional separation and division suitable, but the student in an expansive welfare state sees the artificiality of the six scholarly fiefdoms erected so long ago as impeding the construction of theory as well as the application of knowledge.

In advancing the view that a sixfold division within political science is outmoded, the main argument is that a science should be structured so as to facilitate communication among scholars working with similar problems, tools, and theories.[1] In order to comprehend the inherent stultification of any such sixfold framework, a brief consideration of the major epistemological alternatives may point out why such a chasm between older and newer approaches has been developing and why it will continue to widen.

The two main theories of knowledge are realism and idealism. *Realists,* thinkers such as Aristotle, assume that the task of acquiring knowledge consists of locating a one-to-one correspondence between declarative statements and direct and vivid observations of reality. *Idealists,* notably Kant, argue that reality is neither vivid nor experienced in a direct manner but is instead decoded in accordance with various categories that the mind is able to conceive. For the idealist the quest for truth consists in developing sensitive classifications for decoding, locating individual items into a framework of categories, and organizing images of reality therefrom. The issues in the realist-idealist debate are complex, but the most relevant implication is that realists distrust models, which they feel obstruct knowledge of reality, whereas idealists contend that reality is knowable only through models, though they do not consider models to be "real." Realism, in a very naive form, is likely to be the customary view of the man in the street and of the political decision maker, both of whom find themselves coping with practical problems in an incremental manner. Idealism has become one of the main bases for modern science since the gradual acceptance of the perspectives of such thinkers as Percy Bridgman and Alfred North Whitehead.[2]

Academic political science, as it arose in the late nineteenth century, has been wedded to realism, while the major import of the recent behavioral revolution has been the self-conscious acceptance and application of models, both analytically in constructing theory and empirically in guiding research. Though a thorough study of political theorists from Plato to Marx would be incomplete without a study of models, political scientists were traditionally concerned with concrete, everyday events and preferences. As David Easton demonstrates in Chapter 2 of this volume, students of political theory have tried to explain away the analytical genius of an Augustine or a Hobbes as proceeding from merely intellectualized representations of naked self-interest. The idealist would say that traditionalists made and studied models without knowing that they were doing so. Posttraditionalists seek to make underlying models explicit and testable so that more sophisticated models can be developed.

In order to determine what sorts of models are more sophisticated or less sophisticated, it is necessary to be more formal at this point and to define a "model." A model is not the same thing as a metaphor or an analogy. An assertion that A is B is a use of *metaphorical* language, as in Stephen Bailey's "Congress is the last frontier." [3] In *analogy,* the function of A is likened to the function of B, as when the assertion is made that political parties in national politics perform the same function (aggregation) as do alliances in international politics. To employ a *model* is to go far beyond static similarity in form or function and to seek out situations in which similar laws operate within or among different phenomena. Modeling consists of finding an A that is isomorphic with a B. For example, a miniature electric train could be developed by reducing dimensions of all features of the actual train to a smaller scale in order to study such relations as the probability of derailing when speed, temperature, freight load, and angles of turns are varied. If the miniature exhibits the same relations among variables as does the actual train, we can assert that A is isomorphic with B, and that B is isomorphic with A: the miniature is a model of the train, and the train is a model of the miniature.[4] Modeling consists of at least four intellectual tasks: (1) start with an A about which very little is known, (2) search for a B about which a great deal is known, (3) compare relationships between A and B, and (4) discard B's that are not isomorphic for more sophisticated (that is, more isomorphic) models. More precisely, B's are usually referred to as *paradigms;* A's, as *referent models.* The task of theory is to develop deductively a body of declarative statements about referent models by working with paradigms.[5] At the present time, metatheories and approaches probably are gaining more attention than they may deserve in the future, for they tend to aggregate several paradigms together somewhat loosely albeit heuristically.[6] The need to develop concepts and to merge paradigms into a unified framework may stimulate much research, but in time a more parsimonious treatment of the basic relationships within political science will probably be achieved by reversion to the building blocks of theory—paradigms. As paradigms become more refined, which has been the main thrust of the behavioral revolution in political science, theory becomes gradually more formal. In physics, for example, advances in Newtonian mechanics led to the use of wave and corpuscular paradigms in the study of light (a referent model) until the rise of a more mathematically descriptive theory, which in its present form is referred to as quantum theory.

Long before quantum, corpuscular, or even wave theory were applied in research on light, some sort of conceptual and theoretical closure must have been imposed in order for the subject of light to have emerged as a distinct area for study. In other words, *light* had to be distinguished as somehow different from heat, sound, or electricity, even though at a later time modeling might succeed in reducing laws operative with respect to one of these "elements" to the laws of other "elements."[7] In a similar manner, light could only be viewed as a field for study when it was realized that similar laws might apply to such subtypes of light as daylight, twilight, blue light, yellow light, and prismatic light. Primitive man conceived reality to consist of discrete elements, each operating in accordance with very different, unique patterns, controlled by deities. The rise of science has been associated with intuitive suppositions that seemingly different phenomena were in actuality special cases of some sort of generic referent model, suppositions that science could test by modeling. For macroreferent models the term *mode of analysis* may be used. Theoretical science has grown as higher-order modes of analysis have been constructed to subsume the microreferent models of the past. Such a subsumption depends upon the refinement of paradigms through the testing of hypotheses.

An explication of such elementary concepts as model and mode of analysis is useful in assessing the development of any science, whether physics or political science. In accordance with such a formulation, we can assert that the number of subfields within a discipline, whether six or sixty, necessarily must represent a provisional enumeration of modes of analysis until human knowledge begins to embrace even larger spheres of reality. Therefore, the resistance to change—over the past half century—of the onetime sixfold division either might indicate stagnation within political science or could attest an arrival at some benign penultimate stage.[8] Certainly the behavioral movement has not been revolutionary in altering the structure of fields: it has simply retitled some of them. A discipline composed of political thought, judicial behavior and process, comparative politics, organizational behavior, political behavior, and international behavior scarcely seems to have acquired anything more than a new facade. The same modes of analysis remain: political theorizing, the legal and judicial aspect of a polity, the functioning of political structures as a whole, bureaucratic settings, the maneuverings of political party leaders vis-à-vis interest groups and the public, and the realm of foreign policy. These six are regarded as so distinct and analytically separable as to continue to constitute different modes of analysis in political science, such that behavioral and traditional researchers in any one of the subfields can pride themselves on their familiarity with sociology or psychology, yet remain strangers to the majority of work in the discipline of political science as a whole.[9]

A thesis of this introductory chapter is that the behavioral movement in political science, which has brought modeling into the discipline as an indispensable analytical tool, will eventually result in the restructuring of the discipline into a threefold division among decision theory, development theory, and conflict and integration theory. In order to understand some of the difficulties in effecting the transition in modes of analysis, it will be useful to provide a historical account of the rise of each of the traditional subfields. Just as the six modes of analysis emerged in response to various dilemmas, now the practical limitations of such a division are becoming a new dilemma. Nevertheless, some of the moral problems that occasioned the rise of new areas for study within political science are still present today. It may be fruitful to examine sociological and ideological foundations for each of the six subfields in order to understand sources of resistance to such a change. A second objective of this chapter is to discuss the older and newer paradigms that have been applied within each subfield; interpretive empirical codifications and theoretical inventories of trends in political science up to the present are discussed in subsequent chapters in this volume. The final section consists of a sketch of three orientations that are likely to constitute the structure of political science in the immediate future. Generations of scholars yet unborn may find a new restructuring appropriate in the 1980's, but our immediate concern in this volume is with the continuity between past, present, and foreseeable futures.

III. ORIGINS OF POLITICAL SCIENCE

Dawn of Political Consciousness

The notion of a separate political sphere of life possibly first occurred to an individual whose position of privilege and status was threatened by a power-seeking ruler. Whether we accept such a threat theory as an explanation for the dawn of political consciousness—which is counter to the more historically influential social-contract theory as advanced by Hobbes, Locke, and Rousseau—or embrace yet another alternative, we would undoubtedly agree that political science as a discipline became possible only when man fully realized that the idea of politics implies the concept of a nonpolitical life.[10] Consciousness of politics began when man speculated that the sphere of politics or of government was too broad (or too narrow) in relation to his own interests, values, or ideals. Similarly, the various definitions of politics and distinguishable subfields within the discipline of political science have been reformulated whenever normative dilemmas of various kinds have prompted a refocusing of earlier perspectives. The introduction of new conceptual and theoretical orientations may serve to demarcate stages in the development of political science as an autonomous field of inquiry.

Political Theory

The earliest writings on the subject of politics, such as the code of Hammurabi and the Talmudic legends, bear a decidedly religious character. The operations of government were grasped in terms of laws and edicts of rulers. As long as government was conducted by elites who relied upon religious myths to justify their rule, it was virtually sacrilegious to reflect upon the desirability of various political arrangements. When a much smaller political unit, the *polis,* arose among the Greeks, a more secular orientation toward politics became manifest. Insofar as these new forms of government allowed a wider degree of popular participation, the study of politics could become self-conscious. Men such as Socrates, Plato, and Aristotle found a ready audience for speculative discussions of the proper role of man vis-à-vis the state. The broad scope of politics in Hellenic Greece is traceable etymologically: the Greek *politikos* would be rendered as social and political in our own idiom. [11] The vast range of topics covered in Plato's *Republic* presents an even more vivid image of a lack of division between polity, economy, and society. It is perfectly understandable that the subject matter of politics, intertwined as it was with economics and sociology, became an integral part of what we now refer to as moral philosophy. Although Aristotle did in fact direct an extensive research project concerning constitutions, his research-oriented approach to politics was bypassed by later thinkers, with the exception of Polybius. Hence, in retrospect, political theory could be called the first subfield of political science, though the Greeks and Romans considered empirical theorizing about politics to be simply one part of philosophy. There was as yet no need to recognize politics as an autonomous subject of inquiry.

The students of schools established by Plato and Aristotle lived in a world dominated first by the Macedonians and later by the Romans. As a result of the decline of the polis, politics became very far removed from the ordinary citizen. Even in Rome, which developed and codified law in a truly original way, philosophic political speculation was virtually limited to a discussion of maxims and a translation of Greek thought into eloquent Roman prose. As Frederick Pollock hyperbolically asserts of the most notable Roman writer on politics, "Nobody that I know of has yet succeeded in discovering a new idea in the whole of Cicero's philosophical or semiphilosophical writings." Pollock continues:

> ... the scientific study of politics became extinct. It was a sleep of many centuries that followed, broken only by half-conscious stirrings in the Middle Ages. There were brilliant attempts and notable precursors. But there was no serious revival of interest in the theory of politics until the Renaissance; and the definite new birth of political thinking, and its consecutive growth in forms adapted to the civilization of modern Europe, may fairly be dated from Hobbes, and at most cannot be put back earlier than Machiavelli. [12]

Public Law

When articulate and self-conscious political speculation returned, the legacy of Roman legalistic conceptions provided a new lens for interpreting and ultimately resolving the contest between the papacy, the

Holy Roman Emperor, and the power of rising national states. The legal principle that the papacy and the Empire each had jurisdiction over all of Christendom, though in two different spheres—known as the Doctrine of the Two Swords—socialized men in the Middle Ages to the view that government is divinely ordained in secular matters. However, once the papal view that there are matters which cannot be touched by political agencies was accepted throughout Europe, a redefinition of such a division between politics and nonpolitics began to be seen as useful by ambitious rulers of national states in France and Germany. The papacy attempted to preserve the power of the church, but such sanctions as excommunication were no longer so effective or meaningful after the Reformation. Because the rise of secular states was conceived in legal terms and justified by the concept of sovereignty, much subsequent thinking about politics had a legal frame of reference; the main issues of the early modern period were phrased in terms of the rights, duties, and powers of rulers as well as citizens within particular states. In this sense the study of public law, under the label "jurisprudence," could be considered the second distinct subfield to emerge in political science, as Kenneth Vines's essay points out. Even today, in many countries, instruction on the subject of politics is obtained mainly in law schools, especially in the countries of Latin America. Early legalists saw the powers of rulers and of branches of government under constitutions as determined by weighing the principles of natural law against the specific provisions of legal documents. The later study of public law maintained a similar emphasis, as Kenneth Vines's essay recounts. Theodore Becker in Chapter 6 seeks to present a thorough reconceptualization.

Comparative Government

A third subfield, comparative government, appears to have been stimulated more by the philosophic than by the legal tradition of political speculation, though Robert Packenham reviews both elements in his survey of the literature on political development. Within multistate Europe from the seventeenth century onward, different governments tried a variety of political arrangements. Some states were ruled by absolute monarchs; others, notably Holland and Venice, allowed for a degree of popular sovereignty. The examples of a wide range in degrees of public participation in government decisions encouraged Locke, Rousseau, and especially Montesquieu to compare the merits and defects of various forms of government. In so doing, they advanced the cause of the aristocracy against the prevailing absolutism of the divine-right monarchies. Such thinkers as Kant and Rousseau even proposed that Europe as a whole erect an international agency modeled on their own ideas of the most practicable form of government. At one point Locke felt called upon to design or to propose constitutions for newly colonized territories where monarchs could have only indirect control. The birth of American political science probably can be dated from the time of the

Constitutional Convention, in which the experience of thirteen colonial
and independent governments was compared and assessed before selecting
arrangements that would meet the approval of men of property and
gentility. The comparative approach continued in the nineteenth century
through the writings of Alexis de Tocqueville, Walter Bagehot, Leopold
von Ranke, Lord Bryce, and John Burgess.[13] In the same century, the
industrial revolution resulted in the emergence of a middle class much
less cosmopolitan in outlook than the European aristocracy. Such a class
tended to hold a more nationalistic conception of the problems of
politics, and the comparative approach was replaced or supplemented by
a new mode of analysis.

Politics

The rise of capitalism led to the argument that special conditions
within an industrializing state demand remedial legislation to free the
entrepreneur from cumbersome legal restrictions. Because England industrialized earlier than did other countries, a comparative mode of analysis
was considered reactionary by Benthamite innovators. French capitalists
wishing to promote the diffusion of English practices to their own
country could not—for fear of being regarded as anglophiles—use the
argument that a law was good if it worked in England. Bourgeois
reformers in each land had to seek justifications in more nationalistic
terms: the rhetoric was that a law was good because it promoted the
national interest. The utilitarian view of politics, in which means are
weighed to achieve instrumental goals, tended to negate the concern
among political theorists with ultimate goals, abolish the legal and jurisprudential image of natural law as the proper source for legislation, and
nullify the once-popular comparative approach. National politics was to
be studied in its own terms. *Political economy* was one of the first
forms that the movement assumed, and many countries influenced by
French culture retain this emphasis today. The favorite type of inquiry
undertaken by the new breed of political scientists espousing the study
of politics qua politics focused upon various group or informal forces
marshaled to secure the passage of legislation. Captains of industry, who
had definite needs to bring about government arrangements favorable to
business interests, relied on such knowledge for their own purposes, while
many political scientists viewed the group struggle from a muckraking
point of view. One of the main questions was how to make government
relevant to entrepreneurial development. Because of the practical character
of this "how-to-do-it" research, many students of politics saw no purpose
for maintaining formal ties with cognate subjects, such as economics,
sociology, and history; thus separate academic departments of political
science began to appear in this period. Arthur Bentley, Woodrow Wilson,
A. Lawrence Lowell, and Henry Jones Ford spearheaded the drive to
replace the formalist character into which the comparative and legalist
approaches had fallen with a more "realistic" treatment of the actual

operations of governments. After all, contrary to the so-called literary theory of constitutions, legislators were more powerful than executives in the later nineteenth century, and they functioned amidst interest groups, political parties, and machine politics. Each national, state, and local government operated within a unique configuration of such forces.

The "realists," however, found that their preferences for a more empirically based political science were much harder to bring to fruition than they had supposed. Part of the explanation for their difficulties may have been a lingering distrust of "dirty politics" on the part of those with an aristocratic background. English political scientists, for example, declined to follow up the implications of Bagehot's suggestions for conducting more research in the real world and less in the armchair, thus freezing development of the field on that side of the Atlantic. Norman Meller, William Crotty, and Wallace Sayre and Nelson Polsby sketch the older and newer approaches to this subfield—politics—in Part V of this volume.

Public Administration

The field of public administration may also be regarded as a product of the industrial revolution. Administrators viewed businesses as organizations aiming to satisfy a clientele and to use available scarce resources efficiently and economically, and felt such a standard particularly applicable to governments, whose role should be limited as far as possible, except to allow for a more convenient economic system. According to the tenets of Jacksonian democracy in the early nineteenth century, every citizen was equally qualified to carry out the functions of government, as long as he was faithful to the party in power. But the more technical character of capitalist society was viewed as necessitating some selectivity in order to insure that efficient, competent persons would serve as public officials. Gradually the concern with organization charts, a carry-over from the institutional approach of the static comparative-government subfield, was superseded by the scientific-management movement, as described in William Gore's essay in this volume. Frederick Taylor's focus upon ways of increasing productivity led to schools of business at major universities. However, the field of public administration, as initially conceived, arose largely because the sphere of the nonpolitical was expanded: things administrative were conceived by such influential political scientists as Frank Goodnow to be analytically and empirically related to things political. Many departments of "government" date from this era, for such a label would denote the presence of students both of politics and of administration. Later, when the artificiality of such a distinction was recognized, "political science" appeared to be a more appropriate term. Nevertheless, public administration and politics were regarded as modes of analysis distinct enough to be taught separately by persons familiar with different phenomena and paradigms. In Chapters 12 and 13, William Gore and Robert Golembiewski present some of the newer formulations which transcend this distinction.

International Relations

A sixth subfield, international relations, emerged immediately after World War I. As the essay by Michael Haas states, the failure of the European balance of power to prevent the war, the conscription of a mass army, and the beginning of the practice of total war meant that international events were perceived as being very close to the everyday activities of citizens. The old diplomacy, which was conducted in secret by persons of a more refined education, was abandoned in principle. The new norm was for more popular control of foreign policy, and a new diplomacy of open covenants, mass propaganda, and publicity began. From the standpoint of the ordinary citizen, the sphere of politics widened to include matters of foreign policy; and the goal of international relations scholars was to find ways for insuring that warfare would cease to be an instrument of statecraft. The pioneering of such prewar scholars as Paul Reinsch came to fruition when the subject matter of international relations was regarded as sufficiently comprehensive and distinct to merit the status of an autonomous subfield within political science. Many new courses were offered on diplomatic history, international law, and international organization. Separate departments of international relations were occasionally formed on the premise that international affairs can best be understood on a truly interdisciplinary basis.

Behavioralism

Once mistakenly regarded as a seventh subfield, the behavioral movement has pervaded all of the traditional subfields of political science, with its exponents urging and practicing scientific canons of inquiry. Just as each of the six subfields arose in response to new ideologies and problems in governing, the behavioralist movement that began before World War II can be viewed as having a fundamentally moral basis. Such a conclusion stands out most clearly in the writings of Harold Lasswell.[14] Many American political scientists serving as public officials during the war were astonished to discover that advice rendered by psychologists and sociologists was implemented very readily whenever it was based upon a body of theory and research conducted by persons of differing normative perspectives but similar scientific scruples; political scientists, in contrast, were not regarded as having scientific competence, and their advice was unheeded in many cases. Immediately after the war many political scientists felt alienated from the garrison state that seemed an inevitable counterpart of the "power school" in international relations. They wished to change this state of affairs, but they knew how difficult it would be to demonstrate the dangers of a lessening respect for individual freedom. Similarly, the confused, amateurish manner in which the American welfare state was operated with respect to public health, transportation, and foreign policy alerted political scientists to the consequences of conceiving of politics solely in terms of pressures and interests. The attack against a continuation of an elitist, a priori political science was most compellingly stated by Lasswell, who had been one of the proponents of power analysis before the war and one of the more important political scientists employed in Washington during the war. In order for the advice of a political scientist to carry more weight, the behaviorists advocated the use of scientific methods in tackling policy problems. Proponents advanced that, as a result of a behavioral political science, government officials would be able to select the most appropriate means for accomplishing specific policies. But the behavioralist movement went one step beyond seeking to foster governmental efficiency, for many scholars ventured into the field to ascertain the opinions, attitudes, and what Charles Merriam calls the *miranda* of the public. With such knowledge about citizen preferences, they have been able to demonstrate that public officials have been unresponsive to the electorate. This democratic potential in the behavioralist approach has been slow to achieve expression, as argued in Chapter 16 of this volume, and so far has been perceived more by the friendly critics than by the practitioners of behavioral research.

The behavioral persuasion, in other words, has prepared the way for an iconoclastic political science, though the moral implications of many particular studies employing scientific methods have yet to be drawn. Opponents of behavioralism have launched attacks based on their own ideological perspectives. Three such groups may be identified; conventionalists, establishment critics, and populists. Some antibehavioralists are *conventionalists* who prefer the limited government model or who feel that political scientists are venturing into peripheral areas, leaving them strangers to the substance of policy determinations.[15] Other critics, quite naturally, are now in positions of influence vis-à-vis policy makers, and they have attempted to fend off behavioralists as persons who may ultimately be employed as public officials and be treated as much more knowledgeable. Such *establishment* critics espouse a power approach, which was advanced as the wave of the future in the 1930's.[16] Their characteristic argument has been that newer paradigms are not needed, since the old ones have been useful enough. A third group opposing behavioralism regards the current welfare-state model as much too conservative an arrangement for solving the problems of man, because dispensing more social services does nothing to alleviate fundamental sources of social unrest: welfare benefits can only delude citizens into being content with the status quo, rather than supplying socially disadvantaged persons with means for achieving personal dignity. Such *populists* would like to bring about more democracy, even if the various nondemocratic features of political systems are found to be functional to the system. Henry Kariel presents such a position in Chapter 4 of this volume.[17] The reader may reflect that the three recent antibehavioral attacks have a chronological sequence, noting particularly that behavioralists have become more conservative whenever they have attained greater access to decision-making circles. However, insofar as science develops by discarding old paradigms and referent models, it may be argued that the theoretical vistas behavioralists have opened have a permanent, built-in revolutionary character. This point is demonstrated most eloquently and concretely in the chapter by Karl Deutsch and Leroy Rieselbach.

The examination of models, primarily a theoretical and analytical task, has led to a consideration of alternative methodological tools. Some methodological monism has arisen from time to time, but, as Chapter 16 of this volume argues, a multimethodological stance seems inescapable. Just as the framing of hypotheses logically precedes the selection of a particular research technique, so theory has generally enjoyed primacy over method among behavioralists. The behavioral revolution has been innovative with respect to theory, resulting in a new and more imaginative use of older research tools.[18] Political scientists have begun only recently to come to grips with the complicated research strategies for operationalizing paradigms borrowed from other disciplines. In order to assess how truly revolutionary behavioralism has been as an analytically innovative movement, a survey now follows of early and newer paradigms used by political scientists.

IV. EARLY PARADIGMS

Paradigms and Metatheories

So far this chapter has abstained from precise definitions for a number of terms that usually receive a cursory treatment in essays on the scope and method of political science. "Political science," "politics," and "government" have had such a variety of meanings over time that an attempt to provide yet another set of boundaries with a fleeting existence evokes an image of Sisyphus.[19] There is another reason for timidity in matters of definition. The scope of what political scientists study is determined not so much by objective lexical exercises as by the modes and paradigms used for analysis. A *mode of analysis* is a frame of reference for housing similar sets of "real-world" phenomena. In the previous section of this chapter the emergence of newer subfields was linked with reorientations of earlier modes of analysis on the assumption that subfields such as theory, law, politics, or administration have constituted distinct real-world phenomenal realms. A *paradigm* consists of a parsimonious set of relationships among elements of a prototypic behavioral situation (which could also be called the analytical model) such as a fight, a game, or a debate.[20] A paradigm, thus, goes hand in hand with a *conceptual scheme*, namely, an ordered set of concepts used to represent the analytic components of a paradigm. In building theory, the generic action situation is applied for understanding or examining a particular subtype or case falling within the domain of a mode of analysis; the procedure in modeling is to match each prototypic element with appropriate real-world phenomena. Marx, for example, interprets the history of social classes in terms of a *dialectical* paradigm: the thesis in nineteenth-century Europe was capitalism, and the antithesis was communism. A dialectical model can be applied in understanding intellectual trends within political science itself, as Chapter 16 in this book attempts to do.

After matching each component in the paradigm with real-world phenomena, the investigator proceeds to specify hypotheses based on his knowledge of the paradigm. *Metatheory* arises when logical interconnections exist between declarative or factual statements about parts of the reality or referent system being examined by means of paradigms, thus integrating one or more modes of analysis, paradigms, or conceptual schemes. The most satisfactory metatheory is likely to be useful for many modes of analysis and to blend many paradigms, so in any discipline the quest for achieving knowledge inevitably involves searching for more transcendent models. Imagination and craftsmanship must be combined with rigor in order to abandon simplistic modes of analysis and paradigms. A survey of some of the earlier paradigms may suffice to present more vividly the nature of the scientific problem in selecting among alternative paradigms. The year 1945 will be used as an approximate cutting point to divide traditional paradigms from more recent innovations.

Historicism

One task of political theory has been to explicate modes of analysis and various normative and empirical propositions contained in the writings of political philosophers. To date the exegetic analysis of writings by many of these thinkers has been quite superficial, however. As David Easton points out in Chapter 2 of this volume, the traditional study of political theory by political scientists gradually degenerated into a historical survey of the alleged social underpinnings of normative positions, which Easton refers to as *historicism.* The historical determinism of William Dunning, George Sabine, and others, involves the use of optical images: moral and intellectual views are seen as mere reflections of their times, and new ideas are thus explained away as mirrors of self-interest or self-perception. Man is unable to see or even to conceive of a state of affairs differing from what appears before his eyes: he can make an intellectual contribution only by constructing a formal model of how social reality operates. The genius of Hobbes, for example, is reduced to the fact that the turbulence of English civil wars in the seventeenth century called for a theory that would make the stability of authoritarian rule seem acceptable. The specific elements in the historicist paradigm are the perceived importance of types of social conditions, value prescriptions, and intellectual constructs. Such constructs are merely representations of social reality based upon value preferences and climates of opinion. Marx's view that ideas and political arrangements are super-structures erected by ruling classes to preserve dominance is the basis for much current historicist thinking.

Naturally a certain amount of historicism may enable us to fathom the background (another optical element) to which a thinker reacts. Indeed, a historicist description appears in the second section of Easton's essay. Another such discussion appears in connection with the attractive-ness of various metatheories in international relations in Chapter 15 of this volume; it is an effort to comprehend how intellectual fads might be linked to changes in social and political realities, thus suggesting hypothe-ses for those disposed toward testing theories concerning intellectual history. But it is the complacency of an unabashed, strictly verbal reductionism that is likely to repel a serious student today, for the reduction of a referent model to a paradigm requires the collection of a vast amount of data in order to demonstrate that the laws of the paradigm are isomorphic in every respect to the laws discovered in the phenomena falling under the rubric of a mode of analysis. It is very unlikely that so multifaceted a subject as politics will easily collapse into a framework in which values may be relegated to the role of dependent variables. [21]

Debates

In the field of public law, which is now referred to as "judicial behavior" by the behavioralist, the most persistent paradigm has been the debate. Legalists have preferred to avoid being classed as normative thinkers, and they have viewed judicial decisions as debates, either within juries or between juries and litigants. Deciding exactly which law is appli-cable and determining whether precedent is clear on a particular case are seen as exercises of the rational faculties of men. In Chapter 12, William Gore further develops this idea of law as a rational overlay for minimiz-ing or channeling societal debate. The apothecary image of the legalist, who is supposed to weigh evidence, persists even in our own day. Particularly among Anglo-Saxon political scientists, the spectacle of adver-saries arguing pro and con over formal issues in a courtroom assumes a nearly sacred character. The aim of a debate, which is conducted between persons who recognize one another's rationality and accept a set of rules governing the order of presentation or rules of evidence, is either to outwit the opponent or to persuade a third party of the wisdom of one's position.

The debate model has been employed with similar fervor outside of law. Elections are portrayed by teachers of civics courses and by some political scientists as grand debates to persuade an uncommitted, rational electorate. The outcomes of international conferences and negotiations for treaties are seen as the product of forceful debate and rational reflection, according to the cognitive-rationalist theorists described in Chapter 15 of this volume. A rational debate, however, is not the same thing as a normative trial. The victor in a debate is the more persuasive, rather than the more just, speaker.

Formal Potency

A second paradigm often used in the field of public law became more popular than debate in the comparative analysis of governments. This paradigm locates structures, such as officeholders, and the legal limits set upon their actions. As traditionally undertaken, such a legal-institutional analysis consists of a description of the powers, functions, duties, and constitutional constraints upon the occupants of various institutional positions. "Congress can do this and cannot do that" is a characteristic manner in which formal-potency statements are expressed, and the familiar graphic representation is an organization chart of agencies and subagencies, each connected by direct lines to subordinate and super-ordinate structures. The emphasis is on what a public official is empowered to do and what prohibitions or checks are imposed against him. Using such a paradigm, one can assess whether the legislature or executive in one country is relatively more or less powerful than its counterpart in another country by examining the range of potency set forth in a country's constitution.

The attraction of this model has been so great that such countries as France have drafted an entirely new constitutional document to encapsulate demands for changes in regime, and Maurice Duverger continues to argue that a two-party system is the consequence of a "single member district plurality" system. [22] The fact that structure does provide certain potentialities for polities is reiterated in an entirely new light in the chapter by Fred Riggs in this volume, but in the context of a much broader framework and in juxtaposition with an entirely different set of paradigms.

Organism

In reaction to the formalistic- and legalistic-potency model, which Woodrow Wilson called "literary theory," students of the subfield politics decided that it was time to ascertain the real and effective locus of power in government. [23] The fact that the English monarch possesses the power to veto a bill passed by Parliament yet chooses not to exercise such power and the hypertrophy of power in the hands of standing committees of Congress in Wilson's day had to be taken into account. Similarly, the activity of interest groups and political parties has been far more influential than their extraconstitutional status would have suggested according to the potency model.

If a political system begins with a formal constitution specifying powers and functions but later the range of power for each official changes in character, the obvious question to pose is how such a change takes place. In the heydey of Social Darwinism a biological explanatory model which analogized the state with an organism that grows, adapts to new conditions, and occasionally dies, appeared useful. Accordingly, informal practices were viewed as evolving constantly, with the most persistent elements having the deepest roots and the more evanescent arrangements withering when no longer able to cope with the environment. For a government to survive over time, its structures need to be adapted to changing conditions, according to the organismic model. And since each government was said to exist in a unique environment, organismic political analysis proved to be noncomparative.

An organismic paradigm has been used to account for the role of precedent in court decisions and to link nineteenth-century intergovernmental organizations with the League of Nations. Also, the organic metaphor often creeps into contemporary discussions on political development. The organismic paradigm constitutes the basis for genetic theory in international relations and for the longitudinal analysis of organizations, as explicated in this volume by Michael Haas and William Gore, respectively.

Mechanism

The organismic model could certainly have provided some satisfaction for ruling classes in the early part of the nineteenth century. The capitalist class viewed itself as having naturally evolved into positions of power, and the captains of industry supposed that nothing could be done to alter such a state of affairs, inasmuch as the most fit would be most likely to survive. For observers who were less content with the dominance of a public-be-damned bourgeoisie, a Newtonian model seemed more applicable. According to the conceptions of Arthur Bentley, Peter Odegard, and others, the political arena consists of various group forces and pressures, each vying to secure rewards from government. [24] Agriculture and labor groups formed in order to counter the strength of business interest groups, which in turn sought legislative prohibitions concerning strikes. When contending groups are relatively evenly matched, a condition not handled by the organismic paradigm in a satisfactory manner, the mechanical model suggests that the dividends for each group are proportional to their relative strength, with the most powerful group receiving the largest share of the benefits. Indeed, the rationality and clocklike order of the mechanical paradigm beckon formal government machinery to await extralegislative agreements worked out among representatives of interest groups themselves. Submission of a bill to a legislature would thus entail a pro forma ratification if all relevant groups have engaged in prior give-and-take bargaining.

In politics, the mechanical analogy explains compromise and victory in group struggles, as the Meller and Sayre and Polsby essays describe. In public administration, the advent of the scientific-management movement indicated a desire to see government as efficient in its operations as a machine with finely meshed gears. In international relations, power theory applies a mechanical model in asserting that state power may push a nation into the forefront of the power struggle or may deprive a nation of the ability to participate actively in it. [25] What is most significant in the mechanical paradigm is the end product, for acceptance of such a model is most comforting to those who believe that governmental and administrative actions should be as routine and depoliticized as possible.

Process

Sequential paradigms were probably the most sophisticated within traditional political science. Some of the earlier models were based upon the notion of seasonal change—from summer to fall, winter, spring, and back again to summer. Plato's remarks about the succession of governments, from monarchy to tyranny to aristocracy and eventually back to monarchy again, is an example of such a cyclical process paradigm, though his suggestion has yet to be studied by either behavioral or traditional scholars. [26] Instead of a sequential model, a "stages-of-development" notion, which may be traced to Turgot and Comte, gained popularity within political science. Henry Maine spoke of dichotomous stages, from "status" to "contract," while some users of the organismic paradigm tended to trace the birth, infancy, adolescence, maturity, and death of political institutions. But such metaphorical descriptions of events or classes of events were taken less seriously than the idea that everything in political reality is in flux. The task of identifying individual stages through the application of explicit criteria was not attempted.

The civics-textbook orientation "Congress makes the law, the President executes the law, and the Courts adjudicate the law" is based upon a sequential view of a governmental process flowing through a number of distinct stages. Indeed, one of the criticisms of the structural functionalism of Gabriel Almond has been that in practice it does not depart radically from this old-fashioned paradigm. [27] The essay by Fred Riggs in this volume aims toward a broader formulation so as to make the new structural-functional paradigm more purely nonprocess.

A second enduring process paradigm is from the subfield of public administration, where the mnemonic symbol POSDCORB was used as an organizing framework in the 1940's. Although many of the terms—planning, organizing, staffing, coordinating, reporting, budgeting, and directing—could be reapplied within a rigorous structural-functional paradigm, their original use was as labels to identify a sequence of activities that together were conceived to comprise the administrative process. [28] The "stages" conception of processes assumed that each stage could only start when the previous one had concluded, and the process would start again only after it had cycled through to completion. The "functional" aspect of the process paradigm looked upon political history as flowing through various channels; streams, tributaries, and paths were traced by using the jargon of fluid mechanics. Process models were developed as alternatives to the organismic paradigm for studying phenomena longitudinally.

Conclusion

Each of the six paradigms treated so far provided a source for some metaphorical rhetoric within political science up to about 1945. Although employed as ways of looking at reality, none of the paradigms was involved in an effort to engage in modeling scientifically. Case studies, in which aspects of reality were likened to features of the model, flooded the literature of political science. The focus was on particular facts, rather than on relations between variables or on comparisons across cases. [29]

The six major paradigms of prebehavioral political science might have been among the first to be scrutinized in a scientific manner when systematic theory and methods began to receive a more proper and thorough emphasis. Instead, the behavioral revolution since World War II has utilized newer paradigms. These newer paradigms were largely borrowed from other disciplines, and the unwillingness of many traditional scholars to accept the appropriateness of many of the new adaptations was shared by the most self-conscious innovators, [30] who felt that the way to determine incongruities was by empirical testing of relationships. For, recalling the four tasks in modeling presented in the first part of this chapter, one would not need to model at all if one were satisfied with the present level of knowledge on a particular subject. It was the amorphous sense of dissatisfaction with the way welfare states have been operating today, coupled with the realization that few tested propositions in political science could guide a policy maker toward bringing a better polity into being, that propelled behavioral scholars to look beyond their own discipline to locate paradigms which might enable researchers to focus their attention on meaningful sets of variables and hypotheses.

V. NEWER PARADIGMS

From Positivist to Theoretical Behavioralism

Alongside the six paradigms popular in political science before World War II was a stream of thought that we may characterize as *positivist behavioralism*. [31] The quantitative, hyperfactual tradition of Stuart Rice, Harold Gosnell, and others with a grasp of various methods of analysis then being perfected in sociology and psychology was opposed to models, modeling, and theory. For the positivist behavioralists, who are realists in epistemology, political life was to be examined in terms of concrete, manifest behavior, with no intermediate conceptual or theoretical lenses to magnify true-to-life happenings into analytic sense. For the positivist, verbal symbols are a source of confusion, and theories may beguile by representing reality in terms of false analogies. As a result, scholars writing before World War II, who are regarded today as forerunners of behavioralism, lacked inspiration and produced studies with no particular aim except to "do that which has not been done before." But we should not speak entirely in the past tense, because some current behavioralists continue in the earlier tradition insofar as they engage in insolated studies, albeit with complicated research designs, that do not lead to growth in a body of scientific knowledge. Their findings are unconnected with efforts in theory building, one of the points to be considered in Chapter 16 of this volume, which supplies more specific examples. The most influential innovators in the behavioralist movement have been guided by theory.

Most of the models associated with what we may call theoretical behavioralism have been attempts to apply concepts from general systems theory, cybernetic theory, and derivatives thereof. Whereas the positivist penchant for particulars was a flight from semantic confusions, systems analysts desire to cast any problem in the social and natural sciences in words that have a common meaning. Systems theorists shun verbal symbols that are merely analogies across various fields of inquiry, preferring concepts with identical meaning within all disciplines. The task of general systems theory is to discover whether relationships between elements in one type of system are isomorphic with patterns observed in other systems. If some in the behavioralist movement spurn earlier modes of analysis because the analogies are too crude, many behavioralists have adopted models that are not intended to be analogies at all, even though their initial use has been in one of the other social sciences or even within the natural sciences. We must examine each of these new paradigms to determine whether such claims can be maintained. To establish a historical ordering of the newer paradigms is difficult and perhaps superfluous; instead, a seriatim list will be presented. Since the number of models in current use is numerous, the list will necessarily be selective, concentrating on paradigms that have been employed within most of the traditional subfields of political science.

Ends-Means Chains

Arnold Brecht deserves credit for formalizing the instrumentalist ends-means paradigm, which has proved a successor to the historicist analysis of normative values and political theory.[32] Values are placed on an infinite chain of means leading to goals, which in turn are means for higher goals. The paradigm relies on John Dewey's view that deductions based upon transcending moral absolutes are unlikely among social engineers, who are primarily concerned with how particular objectives can be achieved. Hence, political scientists are assumed to be so attached to the polities in which they reside that they will not question ultimate or higher values; instead, they look upon goal seeking as the search for effective and efficient means. Reform and reorganization of a political system is abandoned in favor of an incremental, single-issue orientation.

There is a second use of the ends-means paradigm—the construction of causal models. An ends-means chain of this sort is presented by Warren Miller and James Stokes in suggesting a "funnel of causality" to account for electoral choice. [33] One advantage provided by explicit models of causal chains, stochastic processes, and probability trees is that the narrow perspective of single-issue instrumentalism can be transcended and a macroview of social systems is more manageable.

Such early political scientists as Woodrow Wilson may have urged changes in the structure of Congress or the establishment of an association among nations for the peaceful settlement of disputes, but prescription within political science has never really rescaled the heights of a Plato or a Marx. Nevertheless, it is in this direction that Henry Kariel (Chapter 4) urges us to proceed. His message is not phrased as a plea for the revival of traditional political science, but takes for granted the ability of behavioral political science to accumulate a large body of knowledge about political reality. Behavioralists who consider that their efforts could facilitate an immense degree of benign change in statecraft may find normative speculation to be exciting and sobering at the same time. One implication of Kariel's argument is that it is useless to retain a separate subfield of political theory in which normative thinking can somehow be bottled up and forgotten by everyone else; for only a specialist with a rich theoretical and vivid substantive understanding of his subject can know how his own knowledge can and cannot be applied. If normative tasks are assumed to be part of a behavioralist's everyday operations, the effect of taking on a normative role might be to encourage research into more socially meaningful directions. While knowledge about instrumental relationships mounts, it is possible to ascend ends-means chains. In keeping with this vision of a new, applied science of politics, Robert Packenham's essay (Chapter 7) deals with the means for bringing about a political science capable of leading to "good polities," which he characterizes as "developed."

Games

A highly rational poker player is apt to randomize his strategy to win an extra margin of the stakes of the game by bluffing. The game model, as developed by John von Neumann and Oskar Morgenstern, may be seen as appropriate when opponents possess something of interest to each other. [34] A settlement, or a "deal," is likely to hinge on whether both parties find suitable options. The tendency of the Democratic Party to nominate a President and a Vice-President from a southern and a northern state or from two border states is probably the most well-played "ticket-balancing" game in American politics. Similar games have been analyzed in courts, in local communities, and in coalitions formed within legislatures. [35]

The game paradigm, as transferred from economics to political science, has eclipsed the earlier attention to debates. The outcome in a political encounter is conceived of as involving victory for the most rational or resourceful player, or for players who choose to collaborate, rather than as a ratiocinative deliberation over issues. Nevertheless, the exclusive use of a game paradigm in the study of judicial behavior leads to the neglect of precedent and fails to account for unanimous court decisions, a point developed in Chapter 16 of this volume. Moreover, misuses of game analysis in the strategy of nuclear deterrence have been described by Phillip Green as "deadly logic."[36] Much explanatory power for grasping relationships may be derived by fitting aspects of the real world into a game paradigm, but some tempering of such a model seems warranted before rushing to applications. For this reason, Bruce Russett urges case studies on deterrence in Chapter 14: the game paradigm in international relations has outrun Kariel's call for normative applications because not enough is known about the limits of propositions about game situations within the wider context of the means for bringing about peace. The game paradigm may also have to be supplemented by other models, including the debate paradigm, in order to render all of the multifaceted aspects of political reality more fully comprehensible.

Field

One of the more inclusive paradigms to become accepted within political science is the image of reality as consisting of multiple grids and forces tugging decision makers or states in various directions. In contrast with the notion that constitutional restraints check the power of government leaders, held by exponents of formal potency analysis, the field paradigm depicts actors as surrounded by a series of informal influences that effectively constrict the range of choice. The field model is used in exploring the sources socializing particular responses from political entities, thus accounting for different patterns of behavior in empirically distinct contexts.[37]

Field theory, as used in the biological approach to psychology, considers such elements as human intelligence to be influenced by two main factors, hereditary potential and environmental conditions. Intelligence is determined by the position an individual occupies with respect to a two-dimensional field—the extent to which chromosomes contain a potential for high intelligence and the extent to which an individual's social atmosphere is conducive to top intellectual performance. The task of a field analyst is to discover which factors with some potentiality for an impact are most crucial in particular types of situations.

Field analysis has been applied in many ways. The more obvious attention to political socialization of children and alternative explanations for political alienations could be regarded as special cases of the broadest field paradigm yet constructed, namely, the decision-making approach of Richard Snyder.[38] Although there is a delineation of many categories, which is often regarded as the central aspect of Snyder's contribution, the underlying paradigm is of an individual whose occupancy of multiple roles subjects him to influences on his behavior that continually tax his group loyalties, constitutional prerogatives, information-processing capabilities, and psychological dispositions. Thus, role theory is necessarily field oriented. Heinz Eulau's analysis of legislators vividly reveals the utility of such an approach within a particular formal decisional setting; Robert Golembiewski studies human relations within bureaucracies, as outlined in Chapter 13, in the same light; Richard Cyert, James March, and Herbert Simon use the field paradigm in studying administrative structures and economic firms.[39] Because role requirements and expectations may differ according to the type of issue, setting, and structural framework, one of the analytical challenges presented by field analysis is to establish a taxonomy of mutually exclusive and exhaustive types of fields. Robert Dahl and James Rosenau, for example, have delineated a set of issue areas among which role patterns differ, while Hayward Alker and Bruce Russett have located, through factor analysis, empirically distinct issues in United Nations voting.[40] In other words, field analysis is essential in any effort to draw boundaries around the scope of one's assertions, saying that a set of findings applies to contexts A, B, and F, but not to C, D, E, and G, for example. Field theory would determine boundaries between contexts, thus enabling modes of analysis to become delimitable through research investigations.

The field paradigm can be regarded as content free, since a field analyst can only hope to find noncorrelated domains. The image of a university, with distinct fields and a tacit rule that a member of one discipline ought not to poach into the domain of another, conveys rather clearly the nature of the field paradigm. Because it was long assumed that laws of human behavior would differ from relationships discovered in the natural sciences, separate departmental divisions seemed a useful means for bringing related specialists together and yet maintaining the autonomy and identity of bodies of knowledge. With systems analysis aiming to crash through such barriers to uncover isomorphisms, a field paradigm that assists in separating real from artificial disciplinary boundaries seems indispensable for the years ahead.

Input-Output

Whereas the organismic paradigm assumes that political entities operate in accordance with an inner logic of their own, the most orthodox form of input-output analysis completely bypasses internal characteristics. Particular stimuli are linked with specific responses, and the relationships are regarded as independent of the nature of the organism:

$$Stimulus \rightarrow Organism \rightarrow Response$$

Hence, the O in this SOR formulation is an unexamined component, or a "black box." The adaptation of input-output analysis from physics by psychologists James Watson and B. F. Skinner sought knowledge without having to pry open the elusive human psyche, a venture that they believed would lead nowhere. Within political science, input-output paradigms have been applied to psychological decision making by Robert North, but the earliest innovation within political science was the black-boxing of social factors in formulations by Karl Deutsch.[41] For Deutsch, a given level of social mobilization should suffice to predict whether separate countries will merge politically or will be torn asunder by revolution. Processes intervening between the two variables of communication patterns and political cohesion, which may not have appeared to be connected at all before *Nationalism and Social Communication* (1953), are left for analysis by adherents of other paradigms for studying different modes of analysis. This view does not constitute a negation of the substance of politics but instead is a recognition of the applicability of one paradigm to macrotrends in communication and another paradigm for intervening processes; Deutsch regards the former paradigm as more predictive.

Classical input-output analysis within political science dates from Taylorism in the field of public administration. The most notable study, the Hawthorne experiment, was an attempt to correlate changes in working conditions with the output of employees in a back room of a General Electric plant. As William Gore reports in his study of administrative behavior in Chapter 12, the finding that any alteration—whether an improvement or even a discomfort—led to increased output baffled the researchers until they realized that the attention received by the employees had affected something within the blackboxed O, namely, their morale.[42] However, the human-relations orientation which then emerged within the study of administrative systems, as evidenced in the essays of Robert Golembiewski and William Gore, would not seem to be negated by the more recent popularity of input-output paradigms. There are two reasons for attributing a freshness to the paradigms of North and Deutsch. First, the human-relations approach simply modifies an SR formula into an SOR paradigm and still proceeds to correlate inputs with outputs; personal and social intervening variables are added to the paradigm as control factors in order to refine the original model, not to cast that model aside. Separate analyses of SO's and OR's are undertaken from time to time but are refitted into the more modern three-factor paradigm in integrating knowledge. Such an eventual step is by no means foreclosed by either North or Deutsch, who are only embarking on their search for SR relations, and who in practice describe their O's in their writings and public lectures. The second aspect of their approach is more novel: they hope to go beyond the verbal rationale for political actions to locate objective prerequisites for particular political conditions. For, as Sidney Verba has argued, human relations appear far less salient in explaining the outcome of political processes, which take place in a highly formalized setting and involve task-oriented persons whose educational and class back-grounds place them within the stratum least likely to react independ-ently of the information that they receive.[43]

For analytical convenience, input-output analysis thus renders the debate paradigm a nullity. Rational calculations and socialization influences are counted only in terms of volumes and types of mes-sages, rather than being examined in the manner in which decision makers themselves have traditionally conceived of choices between substantive alternatives. A decision-making input-output analyst focus-ing on a specific country would assume that social communication patterns, cultural characteristics, and even the psychological drives of a decision maker are constant throughout a decision cycle. Such factors as volume, speed, and complexity of information processing are used to predict whether an eventual decision is more or less likely to be inadequate in resolving the occasion for the decision, to initiate war hastily, or to postpone consideration of a problem.

Symmetry

A fifth major paradigm in current use throughout political science depicts systems as tending toward a state of balance. This symmetry model posits inequalities, conflicts, heterogeneities, and the like as problems that a group or an individual finds so vexing that he will orient his behavior to resolve asymmetries. Marx's notion of internal contradictions in capitalism is one of the most notable forerunners of the current symmetry paradigm, and it is still influential among students of conflict. According to Marx, the historical process revolved around how capitalists undertake to solve overproduction crises, how the bourgeoisie fruitlessly attempts to underpay the proletariat, and how market expansion is necessary to maintain an economic system based on the profit motive.[44]

A variety of disciplines have used symmetry models. In sociology, Émile Durkheim uses suicides to index breaches in the "social equilibrium." A contemporary sociologist, Johan Galtung, argues that a state ranking high on one power base but not so high in other categories will respond to this "rank disequilibrium" by initiating war to rectify the asymmetric situation.[45] Social psychology uses several symmetry models as well. When a chiliastic religious sect predicts that the world will end on June 9, 1969, but no such event takes place, the cognitive-dissonance paradigm of Leon Festinger is advanced to account for the sect's course of action in reconciling the failure of the prophecy; similar paradigms in sociometric choice situations have been elaborated by Theodore Newcomb and Fritz Heider.[46] In anthropology, Gregory Bateson has examined schismogenesis, and, in collaboration with psychiatrist Jurgen Ruesch, has presented a view of psychological problems arising from asymmetries in communication.[47]

Within political science, Morton Kaplan is a pioneer in suggesting the utility of a cybernetic-based homeostatic conception of the asymmetry paradigm.[48] His analysis of international systems focuses on how stability and equilibria are maintained within a system. Departures from steady-state levels and the return to old levels, or the establishment of new equilibrium points, guide much current research investigating the relative advantages of bipolar as opposed to multipolar world-power distribution, as Chapter 15 outlines.

Since the distribution of resources among members is regarded as an asymmetrical situation that is bound to lead to strain in a system, the "distributive" conception that Lasswell builds into his analysis of influence resources is another important example of the asymmetry paradigm in political science.[49] In addition, Sidney Ulmer has examined courts for homeostatic tendencies.[50]

Within the subfield of comparative government, stability has long been a preoccupation, especially for students of French politics. Concern with development involves an analysis of time changes, which may be called temporal asymmetry.[51] Fred Rigg's ingenious definition of political development centers around the symmetry paradigm in a more systemic context, for he argues that structural development (differentiation) is optimal when increasing capabilities of a government to regulate the political constituency are balanced with efforts to maintain an integrated, supportive populace. Too much emphasis on enlarging the ambit of governmental effectiveness can evoke revolutionary sentiments, and overattention to popular consultation might result in piecemeal governmental measures, rather than comprehensive and internally consistent planning by competent persons.[52] In short, Rightist and Leftist, like the farmer and the cowman in *Oklahoma,* should learn to be friends.

Party stability has also been studied in symmetry-asymmetry terms. Whereas the game paradigm focuses on techniques for bargaining and negotiation, the effect of a stable arrangement of direct and side payments is to solidify the basis of support for majority parties and minority party winning in coalitions, as William Crotty describes in Chapter 10. Machine politics, which Wallace Sayre and Nelson Polsby state are maintained by reciprocated exchanges of votes for welfare benefits, thus had its demise in the United States when governments began to provide social services to all citizens without regard for their political leanings.

Metatask

Process models, finally, have been superseded by the metatask paradigm. The functionalism of Luther Gulick, L. Urwick, and James Mooney is merely a labeling of specialized tasks that must be performed in a particular sequence. As technology becomes more complex, Mooney suggests, the number of tasks increases and the identifiable stages in an administrative process will be more detailed, more specialized, and of course more numerous.[53] The metatask paradigm, on the contrary, posits a fixed number of generic tasks that may be performed in any order, but all of which are necessary for the persistence of a system or its operation at some optimal level.

The main proposition of the metatask paradigm is that a system survives only when it performs all of the requisite metatasks, which calls to mind the image of necessary and sufficient conditions for the creation of water molecules from distinct atomic elements. Though the metatask paradigm is best known in its structural-functional applications within the subfield of comparative politics, even the most insistent critics of structural-functionalism employ the metatask paradigm. J. David Singer, for example, refers to data collection as a sine qua non in the research process, a remark that would be meaningless unless he has in mind a series of generic and indispensable tasks for conducting research.[54]

Talcott Parsons is the most influential proponent of the metatask paradigm, and his functions of goal attainment, adaptation, pattern maintenance, and integration are utilized in Chapters 3 and 15 of this volume.[55] But it is through the writing of David Easton that most political scientists have become acquainted with metatask analysis. Easton's original formulation of inputs, withinputs, and outputs resembles the process model perhaps too vividly; his later *A Systems Analysis of Political Life* (1965) presents a more detailed specification of operations required within each of the "stages."[56]

The contribution of Gabriel Almond consists of supplying a much more precise list of political metatasks that are performed in the input, withinput, and output stages.[57] Because Almond tends to depart from the Parsonian functions without an explicit justification, at least one alternative delineation of functions has grounded its perspectives in the original fourfold formulation, notably that of Robert Holt.[58]

The research question that a metatask analyst wishes to answer is what sorts of styles of function performance lead to which types of governmental outputs. Most metatask analysts use the term "style" to refer to how structures perform particular functions. But coherent definitions of types of structures have not been advanced, a deficiency that Theodore Becker and Fred Riggs seek to repair in Chapters 6 and 8. Such a focus goes beyond the mere "system-survival" concern of early metatask paradigms to ask which structures are best suited for achieving functions that lead to political development. The historical tracing of differentiation of structures in a polity, which is the province for a longitudinal symmetry paradigm, is thus differentiated from the very separate problem of specifying which among the many possible equivalent arrangements for executing metatasks are the most efficient, democratic, or successful in the long run.

Metatheory

In attempting to lift some of the newer paradigms to the status of metatheories, one can readily appreciate how superior they are to the older paradigm models of political science. Indeed, in the discussion of some paradigms it has been difficult to avoid overstepping the domain of a paradigm and entering the realm of full-fledged approaches and metatheories. Because there is some confusion about the meaning of these terms,[59] it may now be appropriate to articulate formal definitions.

A *paradigm* has been defined as a prototypic behavioral situation, consisting of generic components whose interrelationships are already known in some other field of inquiry. A *conceptual scheme* is a set of mutually exclusive, exhaustive categories; metaconceptual schemes are not mere taxonomies or checklists, but are developed deductively to classify every element within some aspect of reality.[60] An *approach* consists of a paradigm and a conceptual scheme that has been worked out for handling aspects of one or more paradigms within a particular mode of analysis; an approach is, thus, an *applied* paradigm.

Hence, O. R. Young's ethnographic description of extant approaches in *Systems of Political Science* (1968) may be broken down into its respective paradigms. *Structural functionalism* is composed of categories for functions, structures, and styles of function performance centered around the metatask and, occasionally, the input-output paradigms. The *communication* approach classifies types of communications within an input-output paradigm and locates communication arenas, where a field analysis prevails. The *distributive* approach consists of categories of values that may be allocated asymmetrically plus the asymmetry production-reduction paradigm. *Group* theory is based on the mechanistic paradigm and contains various categories for types of groups. *Systems* analysis supplies an all-encompassing vocabulary and a logic for inquiry that can be used within any approach, though the more specific derivatives are structural functionalism and the communication approach.[61]

An approach differs from a metatheory in two respects. An approach is entirely analytic *but* restricted in application to only a few empirical domains. A metatheory contains a body of tested propositions that are organized in terms of one or more paradigms and conceptual schemes, but generalized far beyond the scope of a single mode of analysis. Of course, a body of knowledge need not be organized analytically, but without theory the import of empirical findings cannot be fathomed; facts do not speak for themselves but beg to be pieced together in a manner as coherent as reality itself. In other words, the fugitive insights of hyperfactual positivist behavioralists entail a fragmented corpus of isolated studies, as Norman Meller concludes in his survey of legislative behavior research in Chapter 9. Metatheories, when adequately developed, enable practitioners to apply knowledge in order to bring about the good life toward which Henry Kariel and Robert Packenham encourage political scientists to orient themselves, in keeping with the main tradition of science as a quest for liberating man from his own ignorance of how to effect conditions that accord with his value preferences but avoid as yet unanticipated consequences.

Metatheories in political science are only in an embryonic form at present. Alternative paradigms, conceptual schemes, and approaches have had their advocates, who have on occasion debated, wrangled, and engaged in guerrilla warfare to gain supremacy or a status of intellectual leadership within the profession. The apparent absurdity of this dispute has stimulated many younger political scientists to engage in research irrelevant to any of the major approaches, resulting in a gap in generations as well as in integrated knowledge, a point to be developed in Chapter 16 of this volume. Nevertheless, methods must be employed to test analytical formulations, or the disputes will remain at a verbal level. The claim that positivist behavioralists provide an exclusive key to reality or are innovators with respect to research techniques cannot be supported, however. Most of the research methods used today were available to political scientists in the 1920's; they have been perfected incrementally in recent years and refocused to handle the newer paradigms.

VI. METHODS OF ANALYSIS

The earliest behavioralists tinkered with content analysis and survey and experimental techniques, as Kenneth Vines and Norman Meller document in Chapters 5 and 9. Without a theoretical thrust to their efforts, such uses of research tools were sporadic and brutely empirical. Without the order that theory can impose upon empirical efforts, the use of specific tools can only be exhibitionistic. Accordingly, the theoretical spurring of increased methodological rigor since World War II is the subject of this section of the chapter.

Content Analysis: Qualitative to Quantitative

Verbal symbols constitute the most elementary form of social data. Until the nineteenth century, however, the analysis of the content of communications was entirely qualitative. Political theorists interested in what is said in an essay by Aquinas or Kant employ the technique of textual exegesis. Those who use the debate paradigm place statements in a syllogistic form for purposes of analysis; legal scholars endeavor to locate the manifest import of abstractly worded documents, either individually or in a historical progression, in terms of the formal-potency paradigm.

The first use of systematic content analysis in political science appears in Harold Lasswell's study of propaganda in World War I, but the quantitative counting of words, themes, or other units of communication awaited the formulation of the notion of "focus of attention."[62] As spelled out by Lasswell and his associates of the RADIR Project, the field-analytic principle that an individual's behavior is controlled by his location in a web of potential influences became transformed into the proposition that as a decision maker divides his attention among competing foci, so does he commit himself behaviorally and ideologically. The RADIR studies of symbols of internationalism, democracy, and other abstract ideas were followed by Robert North's use of content analysis to detect trends in decision makers' perceptions of such inputs as hostility, frustration, and perception of the magnitude of conflict, and more recently by Richard Merritt's temporal tracing of symbols of American community.[63] The proliferation of studies employing content analysis, which is probably the most expensive research technique in terms of man-hours, can only be explained by the attractiveness of newer paradigms—Lasswell's psychopathological field, North's inputs and outputs, and Merritt's search for increasing symmetry in identifications. The existence of computerized information-retrieval systems, such as the General Inquirer, heralds an era in which content analysis can be pursued more cheaply and reliably. Through the validation of lists of words as indicators of specific psychological states or moods one can even envision an "opening" of blackboxed psychological processes that have hitherto eluded the grasp of social scientists.[64]

Case Analysis: From Uniqueness to Comparative Analysis

One implication of the mechanistic model was that a series of case studies would have to be conducted to demonstrate how the outcomes of political struggles always result in the victory of the stronger groups. Studies by E. E. Schattschneider and S. K. Bailey and even some of the Inter-University Case Program monographs have such a purpose, though the latter largely aim to provide as much vicarious "experience" as possible to the fledgling bureaucrat, based on an organismic notion that each case is unique and only a succession of cases will enable the student to appreciate the complexity and variety of political life.[65] Criteria for what constitutes a "case" remain unarticulated, however.

With the use of the game paradigm, which supplies its own critieria for delimiting beginning and terminal points in events, a much more systematic basis for aggregating case studies has been established. Glendon Schubert's Supreme Court "games" are undoubtedly the best-known instances.[66] Deterrence, which is usually conceived as a gaming situation, has been treated in a rigorous comparative case-analysis framework by Bruce Russett, who urges the extension of comparative case analysis to many other situations (Chapter 14). William Crotty's report (Chapter 10) on the comparative analysis of political parties and party systems emphasizes the need for starting from comparable definitions and research questions as a basis for cumulative payoff.

Research in comparative politics has been geared most self-consciously toward testing propositions through cross-national investigations, and one of the main purposes of the metatask paradigm is to provide a framework for meaningful comparisons between political styles of many countries, an impossibility as long as the formal potency and process models, which highlight idiosyncratic features of governments, were utilized. The shift from longitudinal studies of single cases to cross-sectional comparisons of large numbers of countries in just one year is not without its costs, however. Most of the critical political problems have historically been concerned with change within a particular polity, so the implementation of policy implications from cross-sectional research is likely to be precarious unless it is accompanied by the intensive analysis of single cases. Comparisons between parallel longitudinal case analyses point toward one way of resolving the need for broadly comparative theory and the desire for nonprocrustean applications of knowledge to individual situations.[67]

Interviewing and Observation: From Polls to Surveys and Experiments

Woodrow Wilson's injunction that political scientists ought to observe the scene of political activity directly, an admonition which Wilson actually did not practice while he was an academician, encouraged students of politics to ask questions of political figures. In the early twentieth century, however, the questions were asked of a very narrow stratum, and asked in the way that a newspaper reporter digs up news with a minimum of productive effort. Such polls did yield some limited responses, and political scientists were content to have whatever information could be derived.

Only when political scientists desired to go behind manifest opinions to ascertain underlying explanatory factors did employment of the sample survey seem to be necessary. Sociologist Paul Lazarsfeld's studies of electoral voting in fact made political scientists aware of the enormous payoff that surveys can provide in terms of theory. Using a field paradigm, Lazarsfeld was able to assert that he could explain 95 percent of the votes cast in Elmira County in 1940 on the basis of only three variables—residence, socioeconomic status, and religion.[68] Probably more is now known about American voting behavior than about any other subject in political science,[69] and the study of community power structure seems impossible without sending interviewers into the field to elicit direct responses from a random and representative sample of a population. Comparative political socialization within five countries has been investigated by means of surveys in *The Civic Culture* (1963) by Gabriel Almond and Sidney Verba.

The most recent development, which promises to enable researchers to exercise more control over variables, is the small-group experiment. Harold Gosnell's field experiment on how to diminish nonvoting constitutes the first use of experiments in political science.[70] But his failure to account for many intervening factors is to be contrasted with the possibility of selecting matched groups of subjects and varying each element systematically from one group to another, which controlled experiments permit. Organization theory today depends in large part on such small-group experimental tests, as Robert Golembiewski's contribution (Chapter 13) to this volume attests.[71] Surveys may be used as checks upon the findings of experiments, which in turn can be used to validate the findings of survey studies. One early organization theorist, Harold Guetzkow, who has recently begun to simulate international processes by building in real-world factors, sacrifices control for results that can be extrapolated to the world outside the laboratory, and his efforts have encouraged rigorous tests of game paradigms in deterrence theory.[72] Since the cases for study in the so-called real world are often too few to permit definitive conclusions and are difficult to unravel in terms of reliable and valid data, experimental settings offer a unique opportunity for generalizing beyond the findings of a particular investigation.[73] Not until political scientists sought to assert generalizations about relationships between variables of particular paradigms, however, did either surveys or experiments seem useful.

Statistics: Univariate to Multivariate

The term "statistics" is used conventionally to refer to figures describing such phenomena as an aggregation of persons, electricity-generating stations, votes, or foreign trade. Population censuses, one of the most familiar procedures for deriving aggregate statistics, have been conducted for centuries; economic data of various kinds have been utilized by political writers since Marx took his daily trips to the British Museum. The early statistics have one characteristic in common: They are univariate, that is, concerned only with the magnitude of a single datum or with trends of an individual variable over time. However, there seemed little else to do with such data when one only sought that which seemed, at face value, to be "interesting." The paradigms of inputs-outputs, fields, and symmetries raise much sharper problems for measurement; a search for correlations between variables presupposes a process of selecting some aggregate indicators rather than others, a choice that can only be justified in terms of a specific model concerned with how political reality basically operates—or how it might operate in an ideal world.

Some of the most familiar bivariate analyses attempt to isolate cohesive voting groups in deliberative bodies, such as in the Supreme Court, the Congress, and the United Nations.[74] Insofar as these efforts merely seek to derive nominal classifications of distinct clusters that vote somewhat differently from one another, they reveal no major methodological innovation compared with Stuart Rice's earlier indices;[75] however, they obtain more precision in the studies reviewed by Vines, Becker, and Meller in this volume. Field-analytic propositions dealing with an explanation of voting patterns based on various background characteristics provided an initial impetus for more refined bivariate investigations. Julius Turner's interest in legislative behavior led him to study the impact of constituency characteristics; V. O. Key traces the nature of electoral support for political parties through census-tract data on counties.[76] A mere classification of cases, however, is far from satisfactory in handling complex paradigms, where the variables themselves need to be dimensionalized as indicators of asymmetries or metatasks, linked into causal chains, while spurious relationships are winnowed out. Thus, bivariate analysis is being superseded by multivariate procedures which will enable researchers to test entire paradigms in one fell swoop. Some multivariate techniques, such as smallest-space analysis, cluster analysis, and factor analysis, are useful in making preliminary explorations into the dimensions and independent fields within a large number of variables, but these techniques, which have a somewhat earlier vintage, have set the stage for contemporary causal modeling—as reviewed in William Crotty's essay (Chapter 10) on political parties—by means of which the path of causation within a system of variables may be tested.[77] But only our ability to postulate complex social processes will enable us to proceed, for the most complicated mathematical procedures do not have a built-in ability to converge on meaningful solutions independently of the models constructed by the investigator. Mathematical assumptions underlying various types of factor analysis, for example, strictly determine the answers. In multivariate analysis, in short, reality is not something "out there" awaiting representation. Instead, an intuitive feeling about what reality looks like guides the selection of variables, and the particular indicators will have to be chosen on the basis of conceptual formulations. At the highest level of methodological sophistication, the explicit use of paradigms becomes most essential, since causal modeling can determine which among several alternative political development strategies or of asymmetry reduction best fits the data. Causal-modeling procedures at once catapult paradigms and their respective concepts into metatheories. Because the inputs to causal modeling could come from content analyses, codings of case studies, surveys, and experiments, as well as from aggregated statistics, causal modeling constitutes a direction in which all researchers will be heading in the years to come. In the process of doing so, they will have to be more explicit with respect to their own paradigms.

VII. BEYOND SUBFIELDS OF POLITICAL SCIENCE

In reviewing a number of changes that have taken place within political science over the last century, the reader may welcome the comforting conclusion that in some sense he has arrived at Valhalla. Indeed, such is the message in Robert Dahl's famous "epitaph" to behavioralism, in which he observes that as a protest movement behavioralism can now disappear inasmuch as it has succeeded so eminently.[78] If Dahl's observation were correct, however, the various codificatory chapters in this book would be much more sanguine. Instead, because of a number of persistent fetishes and shortsighted formations of schools of thought within behavioralist circles, one finds the movement betrayed by many who don the now-respectable trappings of behavioralism. The specific counts in this indictment—and some current efforts to remedy the situation—are delineated in Chapter 16.

However, let us assume that some sort of behavioral-traditional synthesis develops and that political scientists embark upon a quest to establish their discipline as a vigorous contributor to the development of a theoretical science of human behavior that is able to bring about a richer life for humanity. If we take the theoretical aspects of behavioralism seriously, what will happen to the structure of political science?

As Robert A. Dahl recounts, many departments regarded behavioralism as a seventh field but soon awoke to find that behavioralists were quite content to enter the six prevailing subfields, though in some cases the names were changed: public law was renamed judicial behavior; public administration is now referred to as administrative behavior; and comparative government became comparative politics. However, if the behavioralist searches for broader theory, does he not ultimately find himself constrained by the existence of earlier modes of analysis that arise as distinct subfields? Should such domains remain secure from poaching? A general theory of human behavior, to which many behavioralists give lip service, might be studied more appropriately within an entirely new framework. One utopian solution is to disband political science departments and form cosmopolitan associations devoted to various problems that are studied in all the social sciences. But such a move can be successful only so long as other disciplines also disarm in this structural sense. It is much more likely that the traditional six or more subfields within political science will disappear. For example, the case for abandoning an autonomous political theory subfield is hinted at by Henry Kariel in Chapter 4, whereas the isolation of Richard Snyder's decision-making approach from the study of judicial process and behavior, which also involves decisions, seems artificial and wasteful.

What, then, would the new divisions resemble? Traditional political science seems to have devoted its attention within each of the various subfields on structurally distinct *entities:* local, state, national, foreign, and international politics were assumed to constitute such diverse domains of inquiry that little knowledge would spill over from one to another. And bureaucratic activities were even believed to exhibit different processes and behavioral regularities from political happenings. At a later stage, political scientists felt that a distinction between politics and administration was abandoned; a subfield called politics arose from the merger of the formerly separate fiefdoms of local, state, and national politics. Today, students of comparative government are attempting to break down artificial barriers even further in order to undertake cross-level comparisons among national governments with different structures and cultural settings, and a comparative study of international systems seems in the offing. Hence, the basis for specialization within political science in the future is not likely to be one's particular level of analysis: *what* the investigators want to compare will become central, and the most generic *problems* of political science will provide a framework for future unity. Methodology can hardly provide a series of integrating rubrics. Reorganizing the divisions within political science along the various paradigms discussed in the present chapter would freeze schools of thought and close minds to the possibility of new images. Instead, metatheoretical political problems, together with their appropriate strata of concepts and variables, seem capable of uniting persons with common interests.[79]

The influence of such schematizations of politics as David Easton's *A Systems Analysis of Political Life* would appear to point toward a three-fold division in modes of analysis within contemporary political science. Conceiving of politics as involving three phases which are at once stages in a process and required metatasks, Easton develops a relatively simplistic typology of inputs, withinputs (or throughputs), and outputs. Outputs, of course, include feedback loops leading back to inputs. Such a presentation occurs in fields as diverse as judicial behavior (Theodore Becker, Chapter 6) and international relations (Michael Haas, Chapter 15), as well as within comparative government and politics, where it has been almost an orthodoxy.

Examining Easton's schema more closely, we can see that one focus uniting researchers in each of the present subfields is how inputs are linked to withinputs: that is, how do political pressures of various sorts move from the stage of mere proposals to become adopted as official policies. This problem may be referred to as the concern of political decision-making theorists. But the conversion of political inputs into administrative outputs raises a new question of whether the aim is to return to a past state of affairs or to move forward to new models. A second question that needs attention is the content of policy and its linkage with over-all objectives, a problem that may be referred to as one of political development. A third focus might be to ascertain the impact of such outputs upon the body politic or society at large, especially insofar as new sources for eventual political inputs are affected, mitigated, or ignored. This third mode of analysis focuses on conflict and integration. The prefix "political" will serve to differentiate the three new foci from similar problem orientations in other disciplines for purposes of identification only, and should in fact dramatize the need for political scientists to discover isomorphisms within psychological decision making, economic development, and conflict or integration theories. But, first, the content of each orientation needs to be clarified.[80]

Decision Making

Decision making as a mode of analysis focuses on political systems as composed of actors engaging in such processes as opinion formation, electioneering, legislative deliberation, administrative policy formation, and adjudication. Processes, procedures, and the calculation of strategies for reaching goals are the core elements of such a microanalytic view of politics, and all involve decisions.

A concern for determinants of judicial decisions pervades the analysis of judges and courts, as surveyed by Kenneth Vines in Chapter 5. The reviews in the subfield of politics all focus on the channels between and the power relations among political decision makers and the general public as expressed in interest-group lobbying and electoral activity. William Gore and Robert Golembiewski wish to design decision processes that will permit wide consultation with subordinates and a high degree of effectiveness of programs in achieving goals. Deterrence theory, which Bruce Russett explicates in Chapter 14, has even attempted to build bridges with decision theory as studied by economists and cognitive psychologists.

A decision making expert would study formal and informal aspects of authority, collegiality, and hierarchy as devices for arriving at decisions on the national, state, or local levels, and in such nongovernmental organizations as the nuclear family, the club, the large corporation, and the public or private international organization. If decision processes are empirically different within these settings, only comparative analyses for cross-level replicated propositions will yield answers. Among the specific questions that are likely to unite such researchers is how to locate ways of democratizing political negotiations and processes, or how to make decisions more rational and efficient. However, just as many of the relationships between variables in city council decision making are likely to operate in foreign policy decision making, so also isomorphisms between political negotiations, economic bartering, social decisions within families, and psychodynamic processes within schizophrenics need to be explored with a variety of methods and paradigms.

Development

The present concern among political scientists with guiding the outcomes of decisions in ways that are beneficial to the body politic seems to suggest a separate problem area oriented around the concept of political development. The welfare state into which most of the younger behavioralists were born has not settled problems concerning minority subcultures. In addition, about half of the sovereign states of the world achieved political independence after World War II. Attempts by their leaders to achieve a better life for their peoples have been thwarted by a number of common characteristics of their polities. The desires to weld a national spirit, to stimulate popular interest in political participation, and to streamline former colonial political machinery are shared by most political elites, but they have been difficult to engineer. Moreover, development may be positive under some circumstances, negative under others; and political development might even be negatively related to economic development.

A consideration of political development as such would absorb the comparative approach into theoretical and practical speculation concerning the problems of social mobilization, economic growth, bureaucratic planning, and political modernization within both the old and the new states of the world. International development—such as technical assistance provided by advanced countries or by representatives of international organizations—would be studied under such a designation along with a concern for such problems as health, agriculture, education, and industrialization.

The need for studies on non-Western settings is particularly acute and is receiving much current attention among judicial behavioralists, whose very concepts restrict their ability to generalize about judicial roles or processes beyond the small number of countries with an Anglo-Saxon legal heritage. Within the United States, moreover, the range in levels of political development is wide enough to facilitate the comparative investigation of political change as a dependent or an independent variable.[81] Variations across city councils and state legislatures, local trial courts and state supreme courts, and one-party states and multiparty states might well be a function of levels of development. International development is in an inchoate stage at present, but theoretical vistas opened by Morton Kaplan and Richard Rosecrance beckon a comparative analysis of the factors accounting for transformations in power and alliance configurations within international and regional systems.

Conflict and Integration

Decision-making analysts focus on factors surrounding incremental actions, whereas development theorists look at the performance of polities in the aggregate. A third form of analysis is needed to interrelate various levels of structures and to ascertain how well the parts of a political system function together. Indeed, it is the very tendency for societies to break down and to be unable to solve problems informally that results in the resort to political means. One can thus study both the antecedents of conflict and the mechanisms of durability of various forms of conflict resolution. *Integration,* that is, the smooth functioning and structural linkage of parts within political systems, is not an antonym of *conflict* but describes a situation in which channels of communication between persons are open and used by all. Cooperation is the opposite of conflict, whereas fragmentation is the opposite of integration.[82]

The problems of conflict and fragmentation are common to all political systems and are mentioned by each of the authors in this volume. Political philosophers have often sought means for mitigating or legitimizing conflict, and political systems have been seen as capable of being reintegrated in order to achieve a higher level of cooperative activity. In Chapter 4 Henry Kariel cautions the political scientist against undertaking research which merely reenforces existing forms of political integration, for any such system will tend to make some kinds of conflict appear more resolvable and thus more "legitimate." We can easily see that when poverty-stricken residents of the ghetto, or college students lacking civil liberties or a forum for the expression of grievances, are not able to engage in gentlemanly discourse about conflicts affecting their very existence, their resort to violent outbursts may be a reflection of political disintegration, rather than an inadequate socialization to conventional processes of political conflict resolution; one cannot effectively bargain if one's role is assumed to be hierarchically subordinate to the individuals who have established an oppressive system that integrates what is convenient to superordinate elites alone.

The chapters on judicial politics view the courtroom as an important arena for incremental types of conflict resolution, whereas international relations is concerned very often with conflict escalating toward Armageddon solutions. The concern for integration within the new states of Asia and Africa entails determining how persons residing within certain territorial borders can perceive themselves as a single people. Students of comparative government and politics have noted that overattention to nation building as a social problem, however, can interfere with the goal of rapid economic and political modernization; the dichotomous choice between these two emphases may be so critical that power is seized in bloodless coups or violent revolutions. Cooperative behavior is manifest within legislatures when political parties join in coalitions with one another, but such cooperative behavior often is of such short duration that it fails to provide an integrated basis for lasting political leadership or the acceptance of a common ideology. In Chapter 11 we learn that political machines within American cities served the role of integrating the immigrant into his adopted homeland, and boss rule as a result was able to hold the reins of government. Integration is a prevalent theme within research and theory on organizations, as surveyed by William Gore (Chapter 12) and extended by Robert Golembiewski (Chapter 13).

Overlap

There is reason to suspect that the three programmatic foci may serve as major modes of analysis toward which political scientists will increasingly gravitate and polarize in the years ahead. But a threefold division into an analysis of process, product, and adaptation should not be conceived as yet another set of mutually exclusive categories with impenetrable boundaries. The goal of having current political theorists, public-law men, comparativists, students of political processes and behavior, administrative behavioralists, and international-relations specialists in communication with one another would be a satisfactory outcome of replacing the present six categories with three. A complacent provincialism might reassert itself. Hence, the description of the decision-making, development, and conflict-integration orientations presented above is deliberately discursive in order to facilitate possibilities for overlap and comparisons that have been ignored within political science. Our future advice to leaders of governments may, for example, differ little from knowledgeable recommendations now being made by economists to heads of corporations. Political scientists need to prepare for an eventual merger with opposite numbers in other disciplines who are studying psychotherapy, economic development, and acculturation as well as schismogenesis. As other academic departments come into closer contact with political scientists, the fiction of a completely autonomous, separable something called "politics" or "economics" may be recognized more fully, and modeling in the behavioral sciences will be freed from barriers that once contributed to parochial views of social reality. This volume has been conceived in order to initiate further momentum in the endless quest of science as the servant of man's noblest aspirations.

NOTES

1. See Ernest Nagel, *The Structure of Science* (New York: Harcourt, Brace & World, 1961); Thomas Kuhn, *The Structure of Scientific Revolutions* (Chicago: University of Chicago Press, 1964); Karl W. Deutsch, *The Nerves of Government* (New York: Free Press, 1964), Ch. I-III; Abraham Kaplan, *The Conduct of Inquiry* (San Francisco: Chandler, 1964); cf. Arthur S. Goldberg, "Political Science as Science," *Politics and Social Life,* eds. Nelson W. Polsby, Robert A. Dentler, and Paul A. Smith (Boston: Houghton Mifflin, 1963), pp. 26-36.

2. Percy W. Bridgman, *The Logic of Modern Physics* (New York: Macmillan, 1927); Anatol Rapoport, *Operational Philosophy* (New York: Harper, 1953); Alfred North Whitehead, *Science and the Modern World* (New York: Macmillan, 1925). The idealism-realism distinction is not the same as the customary dichotomy between rationalism and empiricism but, instead, is presented as the epistemological consequence of adopting the ontological positions of realism and nominalism, respectively.

3. Martin Landau, "Due Process of Inquiry," *American Behavioral Scientist,* IX (October 1965), 4-10; Landau, "On the Use of Metaphor in Political Science," *Social Research,* XXVIII (Autumn 1961), 331-354; Max Black, *Models and Metaphors* (Ithaca: Cornell University Press, 1962); cf. Harvey Nash, "The Role of Metaphor in Psychological Theory," *Behavioral Science,* VIII (October 1963), 336-345.

4. Black, op. cit., Ch. XIII; May Brodbeck, "Models, Meaning, and Theories," *Symposium on Sociological Theory,* ed. Llewellyn Gross (New York: Harper & Row, 1959), pp. 373-403.

5. Black, op. cit., pp. 224-230; John G. Kemeny, "Models of Logical Systems," *Journal of Symbolic Logic,* XIII (March 1948), 16-30; Marc Belth, *Education as a Discipline* (Boston: Allyn & Bacon, 1965); Herbert A. Simon, *Models of Man* (New York: Wiley, 1957).

6. Metatheories, paradigms, and approaches are distinguished more fully in Section III of this essay. For an essay on approaches, see Oran R. Young, *Systems of Political Science* (Englewood Cliffs: Prentice-Hall, 1968). Metatheory is the subject of Charles A. McClelland, *Theory and the International System* (New York: Macmillan, 1966) and of Chapter 15 of the present volume.

7. *Reduction* sometimes thus represents a positive step in the development of a science *if* there are laws governing phenomena previously thought to require separate forms of analysis. The view that two "elements" are separable is replaced by an assertion that they are but subsets of a single phenomenal realm. *Reductionism* involves premature analogizing of concrete phenomena to abstract paradigms before applicability has been demonstrated empirically. For example, it is an empirical question whether "politics" can be reduced meaningfully to "nonpolitics," or to paradigms that have emerged in other disciplines. Cf. Brodbeck, op. cit.

8. In some departments of political science or government a seventh field is American national government, an eighth is state government, and a ninth is local government. These fields have tended to be absorbed within the rubric "politics." James G. March, address to the International Studies Association, Western Branch, Reno, March, 1966. The six subfields, it should be recalled, are written into the Constitution of the American Political Science Association; as this volume goes to press, proposals for change are being entertained.

9. Behavioralist Heinz Eulau regards it as "fascinating" that in 1967 he was able to count 27 fields of specialization while the fifth edition of the *Biographical Directory* of the American Political Science Association was being compiled. Eulau apparently is not disturbed at this fragmentation into even smaller areas of interest. See his "Quo Vadimus?" *P.S.: Newsletter of the American Political Science Association,* II (Winter 1969), 12-13.

10. William Y. Elliott and Neil A. McDonald (eds.), *Western Political Heritage* (New York: Prentice-Hall, 1949), Part I.

11. See Aristotle, *Politics,* trans. Ernest Barker (New York: Oxford University Press, 1962), pp. lxiv-lxviii, 1-8. The term *politikos,* however, excluded the family from its scope. With increased politicization in modern welfare states, the term politics has been returning to its original usage; meanwhile, political scientists are benefiting from the legacy of Aristotle's conceptual genius by using categories of functional analysis, which are discussed below in this chapter.

12. Frederick Pollock, *An Introduction to the History of the Science of Politics* (Boston: Beacon, 1890, 1960), pp. 32-33.

13. Albert Somit and Joseph Tanenhaus, *The Development of Political Science* (Boston: Allyn & Bacon, 1967), Ch. II.

14. Harold D. Lasswell, "The Immediate Future of Research Policy and Method in Political Science," *American Political Science Review,* XLV (March 1951), 133-142; *The World Revolution of Our Time* (Stanford: Stanford University Press, 1951); *National Security and Individual Freedom* (New York: McGraw-Hill, 1950); *The Future of Political Science* (New York: Atherton, 1963).

15. See Hedley Bull, "International Relations: The Case for a Classical Approach," *World Politics,* XVIII (April 1966), 361-377; Alfred Cobban, "The Decline of Political Theory," *Political Science Quarterly,* XLVIII

(September 1953), 321-337; Leo Strauss, "What Is Political Philosophy? The Problem of Political Philosophy," *Journal of Politics*, XIX (August 1957), 343-355.

16. See David G. Smith, "Political Science and Political Theory," *American Political Science Review*, LI (September 1957), 734-746; Hans J. Morgenthau, "The Purpose of Political Science, *A Design for Political Science*, ed. James C. Charlesworth (Philadelphia: American Academy of Social and Political Science, 1966), pp. 63-79.

17. See Christian Bay, "Politics and Pseudopolitics: A Critical Evaluation of Some Behavioral Literature," *American Political Science Review*, LIX (March 1965), 39-51; Walter Berns, "The Behavioral Sciences and the Study of Political Things—The Case of Christian Bay's *The Structure of Freedom*," ibid., LV (September 1961), 550-559; Mulford Q. Sibley, "The Limitations of Behavioralism," *The Limits of Behavioralism in Political Science*, ed. James C. Charlesworth (Philadelphia: American Academy of Political and Social Science, 1962), pp. 69-93; Michael Parenti, "The Underlying Political Values," *P.S.*, II (Summer 1966), 284-286.

18. David Easton, "Alternative Strategies in Theoretical Research," *Varieties of Political Theory*, ed. Easton (Englewood Cliffs: Prentice-Hall, 1966), Ch. I.

19. Cf. O. R. Young, *Systems of Political Science* (Englewood Cliffs: Prentice Hall, 1968). Ch. I.

20. One of the most carefully worked-out discussions of alternative paradigms is presented by Anatol Rapoport, *Fights, Games, and Debates* (Ann Arbor: University of Michigan Press, 1961).

21. See Arthur Stinchcombe's treatment of the historicist paradigm in his *Constructing Social Theories* (New York: Harcourt, Brace & World, 1968).

22. Maurice Duverger, *Political Parties*, trans. Barbara and Robert North (2nd ed.; New York: Wiley, 1959); cf. Aaron Wildawsky, "A Methodological Critique of Duverger's Political Parties," *Journal of Politics*, XXI (May 1959), 303-318.

23. Woodrow Wilson, *Congressional Government* (New York: Meridian, 1885, 1956); Walter Bagehot, *The English Constitution* (London: Oxford University Press, 1867, 1928). The most explicit organismic formulation is in A. Lawrence Lowell, *Essays on Government* (Boston: Houghton Mifflin, 1889); Henry Jones Ford, *The Natural History of the State* (Princeton: Princeton University Press, 1915).

24. Arthur F. Bentley, *The Process of Government* (Chicago: University of Chicago Press, 1908); Peter Odegard, *Pressure Politics* (New York: Columbia University Press, 1928). Mechanistic theory is formalized on the basis of a rich case-study literature in Earl Latham, *The Group Basis of Politics* (Ithaca: Cornell University Press, 1952); David B. Truman, *The Governmental Process* (New York: Knopf, 1951); James G. March, "The Power of Power," *Varieties of Political Theory*, ed. Easton, op. cit., pp. 49-65.

25. Hans J. Morgenthau, *Politics Among Nations* (3rd ed.; New York: Knopf, 1963). Morgenthau explicitly builds upon the foundations of Max Weber, especially Marianne Weber, *Max Weber* (Tübingen: Mohr, 1926).

26. This point has been suggested by Harold Lasswell, class discussion, Yale University, Spring, 1960. The notion of "political generations" has been

studied in Maurice Zeitlin, *Revolutionary Politics and the Cuban Working Class* (Princeton: Princeton University Press, 1967), Ch. IX; Daniel Goldrich, *Sons of the Establishment* (Chicago: Rand McNally, 1966); and is advanced in Chapter 15 of this book as a possible explanation for changing meta-theoretical foci in the field of international relations.

27. See Gabriel A. Almond and G. Bingham Powell, Jr., *Comparative Politics* (Boston: Little, Brown, 1966). Almond's orientation is that of *metatasks,* a paradigm to be discussed below. It is interesting to note the explicit switch in paradigms from process to metatask in the various editions of one of the most widely used comparative-government textbooks, Samuel H. Beer and Adam B. Ulam, *Patterns of Government* (New York: Random House, 1958, 1962). For a recent "stages" treatise, see A. F. K. Organski, *The Stages of Political Development* (New York: Knopf, 1965).

28. Luther Gulick, "Notes on the Theory of Organization," *Papers on the Science of Administration,* eds. Luther Gulick and L. Urwick (New York: Institute of Public Administration, 1937), pp. 12-14. The categories are advanced as "phases of the job of the chief executive" on p. 13. For a similar presentation, see Harold D. Lasswell, *The Decision Process* (College Park, Md.: Bureau of Governmental Research, 1956).

29. See Edwin A. Bock (ed.), *Essays on the Case Method in Public Administration* (Brussels: International Institute of Administrative Sciences, 1962). A program for integrating the case approach into rigorous comparative analyses is outlined by Bruce Russett in Chapter 14 of this volume.

30. Many of the newer paradigms were hinted at before World War II, since they were being used more systematically in other disciplines. Some behavioralists, however, used paradigms without such a self-conscious awareness of their true role in the scientific process. See Landau, "Due Process of Inquiry," op. cit., and Chapter 16 in this collection of essays by Michael Haas and Theodore L. Becker.

31. Easton uses the term "hyperfactualism" to refer to this period. David Easton, *The Political System* (New York: Knopf, 1953).

32. Arnold Brecht, *Political Theory* (Princeton: Princeton University Press, 1959); see also Robert A. Dahl and Charles E. Lindblom, *Politics, Economics, and Welfare* (New York: Harper, 1953).

33. Warren E. Miller and Donald Stokes, "Constituency Influence in Congress," *American Political Science Review,* LVII (March 1963), 45-56. See also Manus Midlarsky and Raymond Tanter, "Toward a Theory of Political Instability in Latin America," *Journal of Peace Research,* IV (#3, 1967), 209-227. See below, n. 77.

34. John von Neumann and Oskar Morgenstern, *Theory of Games and Economic Behavior* (3rd ed.; New York: Wiley, 1953). Game theory has long since gone beyond the limitations of the zerosum model, especially in Thomas C. Schelling, *The Strategy of Conflict* (New York: Oxford University Press, 1963); Kenneth E. Boulding, *Conflict and Defense* (New York: Harper, 1962); and Martin Shubik (ed.), *Game Theory and Related Approaches to Social Behavior* (New York: Wiley, 1964). Anatol Rapoport breaks game theory down into its alternative paradigms in an essay with Melvin Guyer, "A Taxonomy of 2 x 2 Games," *Peace Research Society, Papers,* VI (1966), 11-26. In Chapter 15 of this volume the game paradigm is identified as the basis for "strategy theory" in international relations.

35. Glendon A. Schubert, *Quantitative Analysis of Judicial Behavior* (Glencoe: Free Press, 1959); Norton Long, "The Local Community as an Ecology of Games," *American Journal of Sociology,* XLIV (November 1958), 251-261; William H. Riker, *The Theory of Political Coalitions* (New Haven: Yale University Press, 1962).

36. Phillip Green, *Deadly Logic* (Columbus: Ohio State University Press, 1966); see also Anatol Rapoport, *Strategy and Conscience* (New York: Harper, 1964).

37. See Kurt Kewin, *Field Theory in Social Science* (New York: Harper, 1951); Quincy Wright, *The Study of International Relations* (New York: Appleton-Century-Crofts, 1955), Ch. XXIII.

38. Richard C. Snyder, H. W. Bruck, and Burton Sapin (eds.), *Foreign Policy Decision Making* (New York: Free Press, 1962); Snyder, "A Decision-Making Approach to the Study of Political Phenomena," *Approaches to the Study of Politics,* ed. Roland Young (Evanston: Northwestern University Press, 1958), pp. 3-38.

39. John Wahlke et al., *The Legislative System* (New York: Wiley, 1962); James G. March and Herbert A. Simon, with Harold Guetzkow, *Organizations* (New York: Wiley, 1958); Richard Cyert and James G. March, *The Behavioral Theory of the Firm* (Englewood Cliffs: Prentice-Hall, 1963).

40. Robert A. Dahl, *Who Governs?* (New Haven: Yale University Press, 1961); James N. Rosenau, "Pre-Theories and Theories of Foreign Policy," *Approaches to Comparative and International Politics,* ed. R. Barry Farrell (Evanston: Northwestern University Press, 1966), pp. 27-92; Hayward R. Alker, Jr., and Bruce N. Russett, *World Politics in the General Assembly* (New Haven: Yale University Press, 1949). An attempt to develop field theory on the interpersonal level appears in Robert E. Lane, *Political Ideology* (New York: Free Press, 1962).

41. Robert C. North et al., *Content Analysis* (Evanston: Northwestern University Press, 1963); Ole R. Holsti, Richard A. Brody, and Robert C. North, "Affect and Action in International Reaction Models," *Journal of Peace Research,* I (#3-4, 1964), 170-190; North, "The Analytical Prospects of Communications Theory," *Contemporary Political Analysis,* ed. James C. Charlesworth (New York: Free Press, 1967), pp. 300-316. North uses an SRSR paradigm, bringing in the notion of process. See also Karl W. Deutsch, *The Nerves of Government* (New York: Free Press, 1963); *Nationalism and Social Communication* (New York: Wiley, 1953).

42. F. J. Roethlisberger and W. J. Dickson, *Management and the Worker* (Cambridge: Harvard University Press, 1930).

43. Sidney Verba, "Assumptions of Rationality and Non-Rationality in Models of the International System," *The International System,* eds. Klaus Knorr and Sidney Verba (Princeton: Princeton University Press, 1961), pp. 93-117.

44. See Michael Haas, "Societal Approaches to the Study of War," *Journal of Peace Research,* II (#4, 1965), 308-309; Karel Kára, "On the Marxist Theory of War," ibid., V (#1, 1968), 1-27.

45. Émile Durkheim, *Suicide,* trans. John A. Spaulding and George Simpson (Glencoe: Free Press, 1951); Johan Galtung, "A Structural Theory of Aggression," *Journal of Peace Research,* II (#2, 1964), 95-119.

46. Leon Festinger, *A Theory of Cognitive Dissonance* (Evanston: Row,

Peterson, 1957); Leon Festinger, Henry W. Riecken, and Stanley Schachter, *When Prophecy Fails* (Minneapolis: University of Minnesota Press, 1956); Theodore M. Newcomb, Ralph H. Turner, and Philip E. Converse, *Social Psychology* (New York: Holt, Rinehart & Winston, 1965), Ch. V; Fritz Heider, *The Psychology of Interpersonal Relations* (New York: Wiley, 1958).

47. Gregory Bateson, *Naven* (2nd ed.; Stanford: Stanford University Press, 1958); Jurgen Ruesch and Gregory Bateson, *Communication* (New York: Norton, 1951): Ruesch, *Disturbed Communication* (New York: Norton, 1957).

48. Morton A. Kaplan, *System and Process in International Politics* (New York: Wiley, 1957). Kaplan's ideas are derived from W. Ross Ashby, *Design for a Brain* (2nd ed.; New York: Wiley, 1960), and are developed further by Richard N. Rosecrance, *Action and Reaction in World Politics* (Boston: Little, Brown, 1963). See also David Easton, "Limits of the Equilibrium Model in Social Research," *Political Behavior,* eds. Heinz Eulau, Samuel J. Eldersfeld, and Morris Janowitz (Glencoe: Free Press, 1956), pp. 397-404.

49. Harold D. Lasswell, *Politics: Who Gets What, When, How* (New York: Meridian, 1936, 1958); Harold D. Lasswell and Abraham Kaplan, *Power and Society* (New Haven: Yale University Press, 1950); O. Young, op. cit., Ch. V.

50. S. Sidney Ulmer, "Homeostatic Tendencies in the United States Supreme Court," *Introductory Readings in Political Behavior,* ed. S. Sidney Ulmer (Chicago: Rand McNally, 1961), pp. 167-188.

51. An inventory of types of asymmetries is presented in Michael Haas, "Types of Asymmetry in Social and Political Systems," *General Systems,* XII (1967), 69-79; cf. Panos D. Bardis, "Synopsis of Theories of Social Change," *Social Science,* XXXVII (June 1962), 181-188.

52. Fred W. Riggs, "The Theory of Political Development," *Contemporary Political Analysis,* ed. Charlesworth, op. cit., pp. 337-349.

53. James D. Mooney, *The Principles of Organization* (rev. ed.; New York: Harper, 1947). The term *metatask* is from Kaplan, op. cit.

54. J. David Singer and Melvin Small, "The Composition and Status Ordering of the International System," *World Politics,* XVIII (January 1966), p. 250, n. 17.

55. Talcott Parsons and Neil J. Smelser, *Economy and Society* (New York: Free Press, 1956).

56. David Easton, "An Approach to the Analysis of Political Systems," *World Politics,* IX (April 1957), 383-400; Easton, *A Systems Analysis of Political Life* (New York: Wiley, 1965).

57. Almond and Powell, op. cit.

58. Robert A. Holt and John E. Turner, *The Political Basis of Economic Development* (Princeton: Van Nostrand, 1966). See also Michael Haas, *International Conflict* (Indianapolis: Bobbs-Merrill, forthcoming), Ch. X.

59. O. Young, op. cit., Ch. I., reports the confusion but unfortunately does not identify the respective elements of metatheories versus approaches versus paradigms.

60. Michael Haas, "Comparative Analysis," *Western Political Quarterly,* XV (June 1962), 294-303.

61. I have used the word "analytic" in such phrases as *field analytic* or *asymmetry analysis* to denote that a paradigm enables the student to break down phenomena into components. *Field analysis* becomes *field theory* when

those parts have been subjected to empirical operations that yield tested propositions. Thus, the word "theoretic" applies at the level of a metatheory rather than to approaches or paradigms.

62. Harold D. Lasswell, *Propaganda Technique in the World War* (New York: Smith, 1938); this book was Lasswell's doctoral dissertation. He develops quantitative indices for "focus of attention" studies in Harold D. Lasswell, Nathan Leites, and associates, *Language of Politics* (New York: Stewart, 1949) and especially in his *The Comparative Study of Symbols* (Stanford: Stanford University Press, 1952). The latter publication emerged from the RADIR Project.

63. North, et al., op. cit.; Richard L. Merritt, *Symbols of American Community, 1735-1775* (New Haven: Yale University Press, 1966); see also Robert C. Angell, Vera S. Dunham, and J. David Singer, "Social Values and Foreign Policy Attitudes of Soviet and American Elites," *Journal of Conflict Resolution*, VIII (September 1964), 329-401.

64. Philip J. Stone et al., *The General Inquirer* (Cambridge: MIT Press, 1966). See also Michael Haas, "Image and Mood Content Analysis" (Stanford: Stanford Studies on International Conflict and Integration, ditto, 1962).

65. Bock, op. cit.; Hedda Bolgar, "The Case Study Method," *Handbook of Clinical Psychology*, ed. Benjamin B. Wolman (New York: McGraw-Hill, 1965), pp. 28-39. Elmer E. Schattschneider, *Politics, Pressures, and the Tariff* (New York: Prentice-Hall, 1935); Stephen K. Bailey, *Congress Makes a Law* (New York: Columbia University Press, 1950).

66. Schubert, op. cit.

67. See Michael Haas, "Aggregate Analysis," *World Politics,* XIX (October 1966), 106-121.

68. Paul F. Lazarsfeld, Bernard Berelson, and Hazel Gaudet, *The People's Choice* (New York: Duell, Sloan Pearce, 1944).

69. See Campbell et al., op. cit.

70. Harold F. Gosnell, *Getting Out the Vote* (Chicago: University of Chicago Press, 1927). Technically his research design is that of a "quasi-experiment."

71. See Cyert and March, op. cit.

72. Harold Guetzkow (ed.), *Simulation in Social Science* (Englewood Cliffs: Prentice-Hall, 1962); Harold Guetzkow et al., *Simulation in International Relations* (Englewood Cliffs: Prentice-Hall, 1963); Richard A. Brody, "Some Systemic Effects of the Spread of Nuclear Weapons Technology: A Study Through Simulation of a Multi-nuclear Future," *Journal of Conflict Resolution,* VII (December 1963), 663-785. See also Theodore L. Becker, *Political Behavioralism and Modern Jurisprudence* (Chicago: Rand McNally, 1965).

73. See C. West Churchman, *Theory of Experimental Inference* (New York: Macmillan, 1948).

74. Schubert, op. cit.; C. Hermann Pritchett, *The Roosevelt Court* (New York: Macmillan, 1948); David B. Truman, *The Congressional Party* (New York: Wiley, 1959). Thomas C. Hovet, *Bloc Politics in the United Nations* (Cambridge: Harvard University Press, 1950).

75. Stuart A. Rice, *Quantitative Methods in Politics* (New York: Knopf, 1928); cf. Herman C. Beyle, *Identification and Analysis of Attribute Cluster*

Blocs (Chicago: University of Chicago Press, 1931).

76. Julius C. Turner, *Party and Constituency* (Baltimore: Johns Hopkins Press, 1952); V. O. Key, *Politics, Parties, and Pressure Groups* (5th ed.; New York: Crowell, 1964); V. O. Key, with Alexander Heard, *Southern Politics in State and Nation* (New York: Knopf, 1949).

77. Simon, op. cit.; Hubert M. Blalock, *Causal Inference in Nonexperimental Research* (Chapel Hill: University of North Carolina Press, 1964); Otis Dudley Duncan, "Path Analysis: Sociological Examples," *American Journal of Sociology,* LII (July 1966), 1-16; Stinchcombe, op. cit.; Dennis J. Palumbo, "Causal Inference," *Statistics,* ed. Michael Haas (Evanston: Northwestern University Press, forthcoming), Ch. XIX.

78. Robert A. Dahl, "The Behavioral Approach in Political Science: Epitaph for a Monument to a Successful Protest," *American Political Science Review,* LV (December 1961), 763-772.

79. Walter Goldschmidt, *Comparative Analysis* (Berkeley: University of California Press, 1966); Donald T. Campbell, "Ethnocentrism of Disciplines and the Fish-Scale Model of Omniscience," *Problems of Interdisciplinary Relationships in the Social Sciences,* ed. Muzafer Sherif (Chicago: Aldine, in press); James G. Miller, "Living Systems: Structure and Process," *Behavioral Science,* X (October 1965), 337-379; Miller, "Living Systems: Cross-Level Hypotheses," ibid., pp. 380-411.

80. Many graduate programs within political science departments seem to be moving in this postbehavioral direction. One of the more recent efforts is in a brochure, *Graduate Study in Political Science at the University of Hawaii,* which lists four programs—systems of political thought, decision making, political development, and international relations.

81. See Kenneth Sherrill, "The Attitudes of Modernity," *Comparative Politics,* I (January 1969), 184-210.

82. Michael Haas, "Types of Asymmetry in Social and Political Systems," *General Systems Yearbook,* XII (1967), 69-79.

POLITICAL THEORY

2 Classical Theory

DAVID EASTON, University of Chicago

> But there have not been wanting brave souls who have taken the historical faith quite seriously and have actually attempted to make the historical point of view replace or supersede all independent method or standpoint of valuation.—*Morris R. Cohen*

[The] point was made that rational inquiry into systematic theory requires intimate knowledge of the moral frame of reference within which the research takes place and that such knowledge is attainable only through a constructive approach to moral problems. [We shall now] continue this discussion by asking just how well prepared political scientists are to explore their moral premises in this way. In answer, I shall suggest that the study of political values in American political science during the last fifty years or more has failed to provide the student of political life with the skills and knowledge necessary to explore fully his own moral preconceptions.

The study of value theory has traditionally fallen to political theory, although . . . this need not be the only task of political theory. Implicitly political theory has dealt with causal as well as value theory. Nevertheless, in the division of labor among political scientists, it is customary to attribute to political theory an exclusive interest in philosophical, normally meaning moral, problems. However much this may unnecessarily narrow the scope of theoretical thinking in political science, the fact is that research into political theory is now equated with the study of value theory. Our question, therefore, concerning the adequacy of value theory for helping political scientists to reveal their moral convictions must be directed to political theory.

■ This chapter from *The Political System* (New York: Knopf, 1953) is offered as a historical document illustrating an interpretation of the condition of political theory as late as the mid-1950's. At that time, it will be noted, political theory still referred almost exclusively to philosophical or moral theory. Today, due to the impact of the thesis of *The Political System,* political theory refers to empirical theory as well. This broadening in nomenclature is itself an index of the deep transformations that have taken place in political theory in the 1960's. The essay by Deutsch and Rieselbach describes the new kind of empirical theory.

1. DECLINE INTO HISTORICISM

With certain exceptions that definitely lie outside the main pattern, political theory has been devoted to a form of historical research that has robbed it, as it has descended to us in the European tradition, of its earlier constructive role. In the past, theory was a vehicle whereby articulate and intelligent individuals conveyed their thoughts on the actual direction of affairs and offered for serious consideration some ideas about the desirable course of events. In this way they revealed to us the full meaning of their moral frame of reference. Today, however, the kind of historical interpretation with which we are familiar in the study of political theory has driven from the latter its only unique function, that of constructively approaching a valuational frame of reference.

An examination of some classic American works in the study of theory over the last half-century, such as those by Dunning, McIlwain, and Sabine, will uncover a vital source of the contemporary decline in constructive moral inquiry in the United States and, therefore, of its inadequacy as a tool for helping political scientists lay bare their moral premises. In the past, theory was approached as an intellectual activity whereby the student could learn how he was to go about exploring the knowable consequences and, through them, the ultimate premises of his own moral outlook. He studied the history of theory in much the same way that Rousseau, for example, might have inquired into the work of Aristotle: as a means to inform himself of the way in which others viewed standards of right so that he might himself be better able to solve the same problems to his own satisfaction.

Scrutiny of the works by the American political theorists just mentioned reveals that their authors have been motivated less by an interest in communicating such knowledge than in retailing information about the meaning, internal consistency, and historical development of past political values. There are, of course, others who are genuine exceptions to this trend, but they are a mere handful among the vast majority that confines itself to this kind of historical interpretation.

As it has been practiced by the majority, the historical approach has managed to crush the life out of value theory. Not that the historical treatment of political ideas need in itself produce this result; rather, it is the kind of history, which can be described as historicism, that, having seized the minds of theorists in the last half-century, must bear the blame.

It is with considerable hesitation and reluctance that I describe this approach as historicist. Like so many other concepts current in philosophy, it has assumed a variety of meanings and its use here, unfortunately, must add another. On the one hand, historicism has normally been used to suggest the hypothesis that all ideas are historically conditioned and, therefore, that all ideas, both moral and causal, are purely relative. There can be no universal truths except perhaps the one truth that all ideas are a product of a historical period and cannot transcend it.[1] On the other hand, some have called this view historism or sociologism—the sociology of knowledge carried to an extreme—and have reserved the term historicism for a different purpose.[2] In this case, historicism is defined as the belief that history is governed by inexorable laws of change and that human actions are guided by permanent ultimate purposes.

As I have indicated, historicism in the present discussion does not go so far as the meaning attributed to it in either of these two contexts. Historical interpretation in political theory today does not necessarily lead to the belief that universal generalizations are impossible or that history is governed by inevitable laws of evolution. Instead, the contemporary historical approach [1953] is historicist solely because it believes that very little more can be said about values except that they are a product of certain historical conditions and that they have played a given role in the historical process. Political theory today is interested primarily in the history of ideas. This preoccupation with problems of history, rather than with problems of reflection about the desirability of alternative goals, is what gives contemporary research in political theory its special significance.

The historical approach to values, which I am calling historicism, has led theorists to concentrate, first, on the relation of values to the milieu in which they appear; second, on a description of the historical process through which such ideas have emerged; and third, as part of these two objectives, on the meaning and consistency of the ideas expressed. In political theory, students have been devoting themselves to what is essentially an empirical and a logical, rather than a value, problem, at least in terms of the prevailing disjunction between facts and values. They have been learning what others have said and meant; they have not been approaching this material with the purpose of learning how to express and clarify their own values. They have in effect assimilated political theory into empirical and causal social science and have thereby abandoned its genuinely moral aspect.

True moral reflection would not, of course, neglect the history of value theory. Such history would be invaluable as a source for appreciating the nature of other kinds of moral standards. Since the meanings of words depend upon the culture and its historical moment, full understanding of a moral idea, as of any other, requires an investigation into its meaning in the light of the cultural conditions under which it arose and was in use. The sociology of knowledge, which seeks to reveal the ties between knowledge and the historical circumstances, would provide vital material for a moral inquiry into earlier political theory. But even though moral research would include history, it would use the latter for purposes entirely different from those of historicism. History would be a means for informing the inquirer of alternative moral outlooks with the

hope that this would aid him in the construction of his own political
synthesis or image of a good political life.

Although there is solid unity in the disregard for constructive moral
inquiry, differences do exist in the general approach which each theorist
has adopted towards the role of ideas in the historical process. There are
at least three main points of view. Some attention to these will serve to
bring out the intrinsic nature of the prevailing historicist approaches and,
thereby, the main reasons for their effective disablement of theory. It
will show how theory has come to lose its utility for training students of
political life in the knowledge and skills necessary for understanding
those moral premises within the matrix of which they conduct political
research.

2. THE HISTORICISM OF DUNNING

In a very broad sense, W. A. Dunning in his three volumes entitled *A
History of Political Theories,*[3] published in the first two decades of this
century, set the tone for research in political theory. His training as a
historian furnishes the key to his work; he approaches political theory
with a primary interest in problems of historical change and seeks to
reveal the role of political ideas in this process. History, he assumed, is a
product of the interplay between social practices or institutions and
political ideas. An adequate understanding of historical change will
require investigation into the way in which each of these aspects of the
historical process influences the other. As a result, political theory, for
Dunning, becomes a historical account of the conditions and consequences of political ideas. He seeks to uncover the cultural and political
conditions which generate and shape the prevailing political conceptions
of an age and to isolate the influence of these ideas, in turn, on the
social conditions.

This interpretation of the function of theory recurs as the major
unifying theme throughout his writing. "The only path of approach to
an accurate apprehension of political philosophy," he writes in the opening pages of his first volume, "is through political history,"[4] "The criterion of selection," he writes in the same vein, "will be a pretty definite
and clearly discernible relationship between any given author's work and
the current of institutional development."[5]

Dunning is clearly historicist, therefore, in his conception of political
theory, but he goes even further in helping to divert attention from
moral reflection. Relentlessly he rejects the value of dealing with moral
problems even in a purely historical context. For him, political theory is
essentially historical research into views that derive from observation of
political facts and practices, especially as they are related to the legal
form of political life. Later, with the growth of political realism,[6] his
disciples broadened this interest in legal ideas to the history of all
empirically based theories of political activity.[7] But, as for Dunning,

there was no doubt that so far "as discrimination and selection are inevitable, the present history will prefer those lines of development in which political ideas appear as legal rather than as ethical."[8]

He does tolerantly accept the possibility, it is true, of writing about political theory from a variety of points of view, each of which may have its own justification and among which ethical analysis might hold an important place. He was undoubtedly thinking of the moral emphasis of Paul Janet's *Histoire de la science politique dans ses rapports avec la morale,* one of the prominent texts in use at the time, which Dunning's work was to displace in a few years. Dunning's catholicity, however, was only nominal. In his own work he rejects the utility of historically scrutinizing the varieties of moral views about political life, except perhaps as an accidental by-product of the analysis of empirical ideas. Moral views, for him, were "dogmas, with endless varieties of shading and detail."[9] Implicitly he views moral premises as the product of mere caprice or whim, dogmas without warrant and therefore scarcely worth analyzing or interpreting. To the extent that they must be included in a history, they can be treated only with regard to their place as a variable in the historical process.

In Dunning's hands, therefore, the study of political theory is virtually converted into the history of factual ideas and theories. There can be no objection, of course, to including the history of causal theory in the tasks of political theory as a field of specialization within political science. In fact, in the concluding chapter [of *The Political System*] I shall urge the need for the inclusion of causal theory in the general study of political theory. From the point of view of the present discussion, however, Dunning's was a sin of omission. He would exclude from political theory the treatment of moral ideas even as a variable in the historical process. Confronted with the task of writing three volumes about political ideas, in practice he did find it impossible to banish all reference to moral views; they are too intertwined with factual statements in any political theory. Nevertheless, he sought consciously and successfully to locate moral ideas in the penumbra of his work.

It is symptomatic of the general attitude towards moral questions in the early part of this century that Dunning's interpretation of political theory should have been acceptable. It is equally reflective of the premises of contemporary political science that with important, although not fundamental, modifications (especially with regard to the place of moral ideas), his approach continues to color research in theory today.

Although he directed theory towards a historical examination of the interaction between ideas and the social environment, it was impossible for him to neglect entirely other aspects. He did pay considerable attention to the meaning and logical consistency of ideas; without logical analysis of a theory the relation to the times could scarcely be explored. Further, in spite of the fact that his critics universally noted that "the most striking characteristic of the *opus magnum* was its dispassionate and objective quality, its detached point of view,"[10] his readers could not fail to discover that Dunning favored representative democracy, even though moral views found only a grudging place in his thinking. And where a theorist offered an idea that could be checked against known facts, Dunning did not hesitate to express his opinion about its validity. But in spite of these excursions into logic, moral interpretation, and empirical verification, his motivating concern in writing his three volumes was for the interaction of factual ideas with institutions in the historical process.

It would be saying too much to isolate Dunning as the source of contemporary historicism in American political theory. Rather, he reflected social conditions which formed the hospitable soil in which such a conception of theory could flourish. But if personal responsibility can be fixed in a complex historical process, Dunning must accept a large share of the blame for establishing a pattern from which research today still shows few signs of departing. Subsequent works differ in emphasis, and later histories of theory often show greater depth of scholarship and perception, but they do not fundamentally broaden the limits imposed on the study of political theory by its early historical orientation at the hands of Dunning.

3. THE HISTORICISM OF McILWAIN

The Growth of Political Thought in the West by C. H. McIlwain,[11] one of the most inspiring teachers of theory in this century, illustrates a second variation on the historical theme. Whereas Dunning had turned to history because he saw political ideas as a possible influence on the course of events, McIlwain adopts historical research because for him a political idea is an effect rather than an influential interacting part of social activity. Being virtual ciphers in the changing patterns of actual life, ideas can have meaning only as part of a history of theories in which ideas may condition subsequent ideas, but in which they leave no impact upon action. McIlwain comes to history, it will appear, primarily because there is in his understanding of the nature of theory as a set of ideas no other meaningful way in which it can be discussed.

As the title of this volume indicates, the purpose underlying his study is historical; it seeks to show the way in which Western political thought has emerged from antiquity to the end of the medieval period.[12] Ideas, he assumes, have a history, and it is necessary to inquire into this history. The question here, however, is just why he feels he should make a historical study.

McIlwain's conclusions about the place of ideas in social life help to explain why his attachment to history in the realm of political theory was not simply a matter of caprice. To put in its bald form a view that he puts consciously, but more subtly, a political theory for him is normally a rationalization, not a determinant or influential condition of action. Ideas for him are epiphenomena, the mere froth on the ocean, as it were, that has little effect on the movement of the waves. They justify behavior but are scarcely instrumental in influencing political activity. Verbally at any rate—for his actual practice and even a few of his comments would indicate a contrary view—he does not conceive that ideas have even the power of a myth in persuading men to act.

This view is, as I have suggested, the product of a conscious judgment, not the derivative of a hidden assumption. In the very concluding chapter of his work, McIlwain carefully draws attention to his reflections on the subject. "But as we have seen," he writes, "it is almost a law of the development of political thought that political conceptions are the by-product of actual political relations, and oftentimes in history these relations have changed materially long before this change attracted the notice even of those most affected by it, or became a part of their unconscious habits of thought, much less of their political speculation, when they had any."[13]

Although he speaks here with conviction, McIlwain is not completely at one with himself. Sometimes, in passing, he is reluctant to do more than pose as an empirical question, to be answered for each time and place, the extent to which ideas and practices interact.[14] At other times he states without reservation that "the constitutional doctrines concerning the basis of the Emperor's authority, and the ideas political and religious that gathered about his person or his office, had effects upon both the theory *and the practice* of monarchy in the later western world...."[15] However much the actual writing of his history may have compelled a less extreme view about the effectiveness of ideas, his own conception of their role served at least to provide for him a justification for his way of dealing with theory.

Although McIlwain explicitly rejects the conclusion that ideas can influence action, in doing so he does not mean to imply that they are totally devoid of effect. They may be influential, but their influence lies exclusively in the realm of ideas. When men search for a justification or rationalization of a particular act or set of institutions, McIlwain does not hold that they cut their ideas out of whole cloth. They adopt, modify or elaborate the arguments of their predecessors, in this way contributing to the development of these ideas. The fact, however, that ideas have a history does not convert this history into a causal element in the whole historical process. For McIlwain, it merely shows that political ideas in Western civilization have some kind of continuity and this provides a good reason for tracing their development. Without the possibility of ideas leaving some kind of impact on succeeding ideas, there would have been little occasion for a book dealing with "the *development* of our ideas about the state and about government."[16]

With these clear assumptions about the role of political theory, as sets of ideas, we can understand why McIlwain should not feel compelled to question the historical pattern of research already popularized in the

United States by Dunning. If political ideas follow upon practices, then an examination of moral criteria prevalent in other ages, as an aid in formulating our own, would seem to have little utility in and of itself. This does not mean that McIlwain must summarily reject any criterion other than the historical for judging political thought; for that matter, as we saw, neither did Dunning. But the point at issue here is not what other variety of tests or modes of examination an author could conceive as legitimate, but what prompted him to adopt his own as the most meaningful context for the study of theory. McIlwain's explanation is unambiguous. Since research reveals the inconsequential nature of political theories, he who wishes may explore them as a means to help him to understand his own moral standards; but for McIlwain, research into the continuity of ideas yields the richest rewards for scholarship.

This interpretation of ideas as a reflection of activity leads to certain consequences for the study of the history of theory. It transfers the emphasis of history from a causal study of the contribution ideas make to the actual process of social change, as it had been conceived by Dunning, into an exploration of the historical conditions surrounding the emergence of an idea. These are the bounds that McIlwain sets for himself. As he phrases his task, when discussing the reasons for the decline of the Western Roman Empire, "the chronicler of the growth of political thought is concerned *only* with the changes in men's conception of the state produced by the new political conditions that accompanied and followed this decline."[17] In effect, political theory is here construed as a branch of the sociology of knowledge, which deals primarily with the circumstances shaping knowledge as it has varied over time. The task of the political theorist is to show the way in which a social milieu molds and shapes political thought. It is concerned with the exclusively empirical task of uncovering the determinants of ideology.

In spite of this reduction of political theory to the study of an aspect of history, there was imbedded in McIlwain's approach to the history of theory a respect for moral views that saved them from the utter eclipse they had suffered in Dunning's work. For McIlwain, a theory includes more than propositions anchored in observation. He prefers rather an inclusive history of theory, one that does not neglect any aspect of a political idea that seeks to justify political practices and institutions. And the moral justification appears to him primary. In fact, his very formulation of the kind of ideas which constitute the subject matter of a history of theory suggests his initial concern for men's views on the good political life, rather than their conclusions about the way in which men do act. " 'Man is born free and everywhere he is in chains. . . .What can make it legitimate?' It is the central question of all political thought."[18] With this moral question from Rousseau as the opening comment of his work, he sets as his task the history of men's reflections about the moral basis of political obligation.

McIlwain thus selects moral ideas for special attention not only because they are in fact the preoccupation of theorists, but also because in his own interpretation they have special significance in men's lives. He leaves the definite impression that moral views are worth discussing and affirming. For example, in the light of his own values, there is little doubt that the moral premises associated with contemporary democracy, especially when viewed as a constitutional order, are of paramount significance and that a person would be eminently rewarded in discussing them. In a sense, the inspiration behind his whole volume is an attempt to depict the early origins of these moral convictions.[19]

Since McIlwain attributes such special significance to moral judgments, it might appear inconsistent to characterize his historical work as historicist. If he felt that a person ought to assert his allegiance to a particular set of moral ideals, then this might appear to be the basis for a direct inquiry into the way in which we go about formulating such ideals. McIlwain, however, does seem to be strongly influenced by an interpretation of the nature of moral judgments that bars him from approaching theory in anything but a historical context.

Let us look for a moment at his conception of the nature of values to trace its influence on his thinking. This conception is nowhere unambiguously set forth. Inference from his scattered comments does lead to the conclusion, however, that he considers values to be a product of the individual's response to his environment. Moral standards, he holds, are essentially unprovable. Political theory, he argues, cannot be discussed without penetrating to the philosophical premises underlying a theory, that is, to the attempts to "solve the mysteries of existence and knowledge."[20] But he holds that in the past some of these "profoundest assertions remained unproved because in their nature unprovable."[21] Presumably, the most perplexing of these mysteries concerns the purposes of men. If it is true that these purposes are indeed unprovable, then our values cannot be a matter of cognition. They can be only expressions of a point of view or personal opinion. To this extent his interpretation of the nature of values does not vary substantially from that common to modern social science—values are an emotional response to experience. While differences in refinements may exist, the essential point is that McIlwain aligns himself with those who see moral experience as subjective in origin and nature.

This subjective view is conclusively upheld when McIlwain finally asserts that when a person's duty is at stake, "the individual opinion or conscience is the ultimate test in all cases."[22] If we could know what our moral obligations were in the same way that we know about the existence of a fact, manifest evidence, not individual conscience, would be our guide. Conscience sets our moral purposes when, because of the nature of moral judgments, the latter are considered to be the product not of rational inquiry but of responses to social circumstances.

This relativistic interpretation of the nature of values raises a dilemma which we shall meet again in Sabine's work .... If moral judgments are subjective and relative, then how are we to justify ourselves in adopting one set of preferences as superior to all others? Although McIlwain makes no attempt to answer this question, it is clear that he does believe decidedly in the need to affirm one's moral premises. And yet, in spite of this belief, he does not avoid one of the consequences that is often said to flow from moral relativism; namely, that if all moral beliefs are a product of the life-experience of each individual, then no one belief can lay claim to any higher worth than any other. There is, therefore, so the argument runs, little use in discussing values; let each man simply set forth his own with the knowledge that the values of any other person are just as good as his.

Historicism is a natural outgrowth of this kind of reasoning. If we begin with a belief in the equal value of all moral judgments, then there is little use in inquiring into such judgments; whatever our moral convictions, they are no better than the standards held by anyone else. Accordingly, if we must deal with moral problems, the only approach that has any meaning is the historical one. It instructs us in the analysis both of the meaning of terms and of their relation to the historical process. In the matter of moral issues comprehension in historical terms alone makes sense.

Obviously McIlwain, from the standpoint of his conscious convictions, would not agree with this sequence of reasoning. His belief in the superior moral worth of his own outlook does subtly assert itself. But the fact that he does not go beyond a historical analysis is equal evidence that he has not avoided entirely the consequences of this kind of reasoning. In fact, his historicism, in practice, indicates the firm grip that this interpretation of the consequences of moral relativism has upon his study of political theory. There is a possible interpretation of relativism, to be examined later, that can help us to restore the study of moral theory to its natural place in political science. The fact that McIlwain confines himself to historicism, however, indicates that he has not availed himself of this alternative conception of the meaning of moral relativism.

When we join his view of the nature of values to his conviction that ideas can have little consequence for practical human affairs, we can understand why his work in the realm of ancient and medieval political theory should have been so hospitable, in its basic assumptions, to historicist research. In spite of his undoubted conviction that it is worth while to affirm moral views, his conception of the role of ideas in general bars him from advocating anything other than a historicist treatment. We must infer that moral views, being a species of ideas and, indeed, being in his own interpretation the central part of a theory, are really not influential in the course of history. Logically, he cannot escape from the inference that, like all ideas, moral views are products, not interacting causes in historical change. As such we can say no more about moral theories than we can about ideas in general. We can speak of their meaning and of the circumstances molding them, but beyond this, little can be said. We are therefore forced to conclude that McIlwain never makes clear why it really is worth while to assert one's moral views vigorously; presumably they do not guide action. We can understand, however, why he should be led to history as the most meaningful mode for interpreting moral ideas.

4. THE HISTORICISM OF SABINE

A third type of approach to the history of political theory is represented by G. H. Sabine's *A History of Political Theory*.[23] Without doubt this brilliant volume has exercised deeper influence over the study of political theory in the United States during recent years than any other single work. With Dunning and McIlwain, Sabine does not pause to question whether a historical study of theory is an appropriate approach to the subject matter. It is true, he does show exceptional insight into his own method. He is able to explain, however, only what his historical research involves, not why it is justified. We are left with the impression both from his work and from his own description of his method, that a historical study of theory provides its own self-evident justification. The very nature of Sabine's understanding of moral judgments seems to point to no other kind of useful approach.

In his attitude towards the history of theory, Sabine falls into a category separate from that of Dunning or of McIlwain. He combines elements from the approaches of both. With the former he agrees that the examination of political thought merits attention because it is an aspect of the political process that interacts with and influences social action. With the latter he maintains the necessity of describing and analyzing the moral judgments in each theory. Through this blend he lays the basis for a serious inquiry into the values of various thinkers. For Sabine, moral judgments need not be viewed as mere rationalizations of activity; rather they may be influential factors in history. As a subject matter they are not inferior to factual proposition, as by implication Dunning insisted. Thus, while in his basic interpretation of the relation of ideas to action, Sabine does not go beyond Dunning, his conception of the nature of the history of political theory does differ in the emphasis he gives to the role of ethical judgments.

Every political theory, Sabine points out, can be examined from two points of view: as social philosophy and as ideology.[24] In the latter aspect theories stand as psychological phenomena and, as such, their truth or falsity is not in question. Regardless of their validity or verifiability, theories are beliefs, "events in people's minds and factors in their conduct."[25] They are, therefore, influential events in history. As Sabine writes, "political theory is itself a product of, or factor in, politics."[26] For this reason, the task of the historian is to determine the extent to which the theories have helped to shape the course of history.

But a theory can be scrutinized for its meaning rather than for its impact on human actions. When it is viewed in this light, Sabine suggests that it contains two kinds of propositions: factual and moral. Although we can inquire into the logical consistency of both kinds, Sabine adopts the conception of values traditional to social science and argues that it is possible to warrant by evidence only those statements that refer to factual conditions. Moral statements cannot be described as either true or false. They just are. Values, he states, in complete awareness of his own position, are "always the reaction of human preferences to some state of social and physical fact."[27] Values are not *deducible from* facts; moral laws cannot be rationally discovered either in the actual course of events or in the nature of man.[28] Nor are they *reducible to* facts; they are expressions of emotions.

Nevertheless, Sabine holds that since a political theory invariably includes some statements of preference, and indeed since the exposition of preferences is the occasion for the development of a theory, value judgments lie at the heart of a theory and are the very reason for its existence. The moral element seems to him so to color a political theory that he considers the latter primarily a moral enterprise. This is why, in spite of the obvious factual propositions within a theory, Sabine did not feel it anomalous to conclude, in the light of his premises about the nature of a value judgment, that "taken as a whole a political theory can hardly be said to be true."[29]

From Sabine's careful exposition of the nature of a theory, the tasks of a history of political theory become quite clear. In such a study we ought to isolate the influence of a theory on the actions of men; this is its psychological aspect. We can analyze the factual statements implicit in any theory and set them against the facts as we know them today. In this respect, political theory is concerned with empirical truth. This is clear from Sabine's own history of theory in which he feels free to pass judgment on the validity of various causal theories and factual assertions. The history of theory, in this respect, is a stimulus for reflection on the truth of empirically oriented propositions.

Sabine is less sanguine, however, about the utility of the study of theory for moral reflection. We can and ought to examine the logic of the statements embodying value judgments and comment on their compatibility; we can and ought to reveal the full meaning of statements of preference. And yet, while the study of theory may help us to make up our minds on the validity of causal theories, apparently it is no important part of its task to help us to formulate our views on moral matters. In this respect the study of theory is reduced to historical narration.

If Sabine's interpretation of the meaning of value judgments had led him to believe that any one man's moral preferences was equivalent in worth to another's then his reduction of moral research to pure history would have been understandable. It is true, he calls himself a social relativist.[30] But he does not feel it is inconsistent with this position to affirm vigorously the superior value of one moral position.[31] He feels free to offer a forcible defense of his own values. It is undeniable that he believes firmly in the reality and meaningfulness of ethical predicates.

In spite of this deep conviction about the merit of personal self-expression in the realm of values, historicist preconceptions nevertheless do govern the execution of his history of theory. In his work, moral inquiry does not use the history of political theory for purposes other than of historical understanding. This historicism becomes quite apparent when we ask the question: What can a student of theory learn about the tasks of research into value theory from Sabine's *History?* He can learn how to describe a variety of value systems that have emerged in the past and how to inquire into their meaning and possible consequences. He can learn about the need to demonstrate their historical continuity, and perhaps he can indicate the path of growth of certain ideas of importance, such as liberalism or democracy. He can discover categories for describing the social and psychological conditions which influenced the growth and form of ideas and contributed to their diffusion and perpetuation or decline. In fact, the student would be taught that a complete study of political theory must inquire into all these problems. But a question would remain: To what end?

There can be no doubt about the purpose behind the clarification of a theorist's empirical propositions. Here, as we saw, the student is permitted and encouraged, by Sabine's example, to pass judgment, where it is relevant, on the empirical validity of a part of a theory. But when we approach values, there is little to guide the student of history with regard to what he is to learn from his research that passes beyond a mere report of a theorist's moral speculation. The student may always indicate the presence of logical incompatibilities; the assumption is that inconsistency violates good reasoning even where it involves values. It is even possible to argue from what Sabine says that the historian of values may evaluate a moral system in terms of its acceptability to himself, as long as this judgment is undertaken consciously and clearly. With Max Weber, Sabine recognizes that although knowledge in any science "is independent of moral values ... such values are [nevertheless] involved in its origin and in its use."[32] However, beyond the description of the social conditions molding values, the analysis of their meaning and a comparison with his own or other values, the student is never encouraged to interpret the study of value theory as the examination of a process of valuation that may instruct him in the nature and problems of this process. The analysis of a theory appears to be a prerequisite primarily to an understanding of the theory's place in history, not to its use in helping one formulate his own moral outlook. Any help it may give appears to be largely accidental and incidental.

I have inquired into the approach of these three truly distinguished historians of political theory because there can be little doubt that in the United States today they are representative of research in this field. Political theorists are primarily historicist in their orientation. They do not use the history of values as a device to stimulate thought on a possible constructive redefinition of political goals. Their fundamental outlook prevents this.

In political theory today [1953], if these authors are representative, there lurks a conception of values that prevails in social science, a misconception as I shall maintain. According to this view, all a social scientist can legitimately and significantly say about moral propositions is that they have a certain meaning and logical coherence and that they are a part of a historical situation to which they may contribute something and from which they take their character. It is true, of course, that McIlwain, and especially Sabine, believe that their interpretation of the nature of moral judgments, which is relativistic, does not stand as a bar to a strong attachment to and affirmation of these judgments, or indeed to their elevation as a superior moral frame of reference for all men. It is nonetheless apparent that, in the exclusive place they give to the historical study of values, they do not feel that moral judgments are really worth talking about directly, *qua* moral judgments.

The fact is that political theorists have so construed the consequences flowing from their conception of values that they are forestalled from attempting a radical reconstruction of their moral heritage. They are driven to assume that, aside from historical description, their major task in moral matters is to clarify, like extreme semanticists, and not to reconstruct, like imaginative moral architects. As I mentioned at the outset of this discussion of historicism, these two tasks are not, of course, unrelated; formal clarity and historical perspective are obviously prerequisites for any intelligible formulation of views about the good political life. But they are not ends in themselves.

As a result of this preoccupation with historicism in moral matters, the study of political theory . . . is manifestly unsuited for training political scientists in the skills and knowledge of genuine moral clarification. Without such clarification, a research worker is unable to estimate the full extent to which his moral frame of reference might limit and distort his efforts towards the construction of systematic theory. To permit exhaustive inquiry into moral premises, political science is compelled to revise its approach to value theory and to set as one of its central objectives the study of moral problems as such, and not their history largely for the sake of narration.

5. THE SOURCE OF DECLINE

To this point, the objective of the discussion about the moral premises of research has been, first, to show that knowledge of these premises is vital to any empirically oriented research, especially with respect to the construction of systematic theory; and second, to indicate that today political theory, which in political science assumes responsibility for research in moral matters, has in fact failed to help research workers in achieving a full understanding of their moral frame of reference. Effective moral clarification requires a constructive rather than a historicist approach to values.

We must now look for a moment at some of the reasons for the decline of theory and research into historicism. These need to be stated, for they indicate the path that research in value theory might well follow if it is to prove useful in helping research workers to understand their moral frames of reference. Since the reasons go beyond the circumstances particular to the United States, they must be viewed in the context of value theory in the Western world. My theme will be that moral historicism, of the kind described here, has emerged from three sources: the proneness of political scientists, for broader social reasons, to conform to the moral presuppositions of their own age; the general misconstruction of the consequences of a relativistic interpretation of values; and finally, the very historical epoch, stretching back a century, out of which we are just now passing.

Most students of political theory today accept, as given, the moral premises of Western civilization. The assumption is that they must be considered eternally right. For this reason, when we insist upon a research worker revealing his values, we need only ask him to clarify, avow, or affirm them. The task is simple because there does not appear to be any real conflict over what is desirable in the long run. Presumably research workers agree on ultimates even if they may disagree violently about means. Whether this is genuinely true could not be determined, of course, without closer examination; but the feeling that it is true has important consequences for the role of research into value theory. It inhibits students of moral theory from making a radical exploration into their values. Such an inquiry would demand the assumption that something new can be said about what is desirable and that the prevailing moral theories are not necessarily the last word. It may be that they are, but only by beginning with the contrary assumption could a theorist hope to prove to himself that no other alternative is more acceptable.

This tendency toward moral conformity is both a symptom of and a cause contributing to the lack of a constructive approach; therefore it prevents the very kind of inquiry necessary for a thorough understanding of the values underlying research. By indicating that a student can discover his values merely by postulating or clarifying them through avowal or affirmation, political science thereby places its imprimatur on the going values. To avow or affirm implies that a research worker knows what he wants to express or that what he wants can be easily uncovered. We do not ask mathematicians to *avow* a solution to a problem; we merely require them to avow their axioms, a less difficult task. Where there is a problem, we ask them to *think out* or worry about a solution.

Value clarification is normally placed at the same level as a declaration of axioms. The assumption is that it is a relatively simple task to uncover and make known one's preferences; hence a research worker does not need to worry through this problem. And a significant reason for this assumption is found in the prevalence of a feeling that values are well-known. But when we ask just what values are well-known we see that normally they must be the commonly accepted ones. Because we are very familiar with them, we feel we know their meaning well and no longer need bother to explore them in depth. The exhortation, therefore, that a research worker need only avow his preferences, in effect makes the assumption that he need not go beyond the accepted values of the day.

Since political science is thus operating on the assumption that it needs only to avow what it knows, the problem that remains to challenge it is not inquiry into the merit, that is, acceptability, of these moral goals, but at most an examination of their origins, development, and social impact. There seem to be few operations political theory can perform on moral views except to explore their apparent meaning and to trace their history. The irony of this procedure, however, lies in the fact that through it political research is rapidly caught up in a vicious circle. Once it traces the history of moral ideals, the fact that they have a long and respected ancestry associates them with all the glamor and sanctity of tradition. And although in general history we have long ago given up the idea that the world inevitably progresses from worse to better, in the realm of moral history we still feel that our moral premises have been enriched over the ages. What we believe today appears to have moral worth exceeding that of most earlier ages. History, therefore, reinforces the tendency in political research to conform to current moral ideals, and conformity, in turn, leads political science to history as the only approach useful in moral research.

We have numerous examples today of this appeal to history that well illustrate how this predilection in political research for adopting the going values ultimately converts moral clarification into a study of historical roots. This approach to history differs in its purposes from the three modes of historicism which we have discussed earlier, although even in the work of those political theorists, the present kind of outlook towards history is present in varying degrees.

The history stemming from conformity begins with the deliberate choice of contemporary values and then seeks to understand their meaning more fully by examining their growth through a special tradition, such as the Machiavellian in some few cases, or the liberal and democratic in most. It uses history to illuminate the meaning and to establish the worth of contemporary moral postulates, whereas other historians of political ideas emphasize the objective description of growth. In effect, the first kind of approach to political theory assumes, in Burke's traditionalistic vein, that the political values which have evolved through trial and error of a civilization over the centuries have thereby acquired a sanctity and truth which no re-analysis can fundamentally impair or radically modify.

A recent work by A. D. Lindsay, *The Modern Democratic State,*[33] well represents this approach. Although this example is not drawn from an American work, nevertheless for two reasons it is permissible and desirable to turn to it as representative. First, it is well-known and used in the study of political theory in the United States; and second, it provides a mature and self-conscious use of the method and for this reason lends itself to a less complicated and briefer analysis.

In the very first chapter of *The Modern Democratic State,* Lindsay clearly demonstrates that he uses history to place the stamp of approval on his interpretations of conventional values in a democratic society. In this chapter he maintains that at his best the theorist must confine himself to an attempt to understand the "operative ideals"[34] which have proved effective in determining men's political relations. From this starting point, the subject matter of theory consists of the beliefs and purposes which actually operate at any time to help determine men's relations to the law, to authority, and to the kind of political organizations they establish.[35] Since these ideals, he holds, differ with each time and place, the task of a student of theory is to decide upon the culture he wishes to study, to identify the operative ideals, to make these "explicit"[36] so that men will "understand what their purposes and will regarding the state actually are";[37] finally, the student must discuss "how this type of state [and ideals] came into being."[38]

Lindsay is, therefore, exceptionally clear about his intentions and about the place of political theory as an area of research. He does not intend to inquire into a theory of a good political system that may serve succeeding generations as well as our own; as the title of his work indicates, he intends to restrict himself to *modern* demo-cratic ideas. After clarifying them and as part of the process of making them explicit, he will trace their historical development. "This volume," he writes, "is not about a general ideal called democracy but an historical type called the modern democratic state. . . ."[39] He therefore devotes himself to the explanation of what he conceives to be the true meaning of contemporary ideals, in terms of which men seem to act, as they have been handed down and modified through the centuries.

In the execution of this work he is forced, of course, to inter-pret contemporary democratic ideas, since there is no clear unanimity about their content and meaning. Furthermore, in no more than half of his book does he really adhere to his initial commitment; instead, he attempts in limited measure to redefine democratic premises. But in terms of his avowed approach, which describes accurately an important rationale of contemporary historical research into theory, the reformulation must be considered secondary and incidental to his main purpose: the attempt to present a historical understanding of what we seem to cherish today.

This essentially uncritical commitment to prevailing values as necessarily the most acceptable to the present and immediately succeeding generations, while a distinct source of current historicist tendencies, has strengthened the hold of tradition. It aborts any attempt on the part of students of theory to think in terms of new formulations of their moral goals. No one could argue that historical research is solely to blame for the lack of what, to parody Robert Lynd, might be called outrageous moral hypotheses.[40] But since research into moral theory presumably could give intellectual leader-ship here, the failure of political theory to do so must leave theory with a share of the blame for an almost casual resignation to our moral traditions.

Conformity in moral theory has been the more easily accepted because of a widespread misconstruction of the consequences that flow from the usual relativistic view of values adopted by social scientists. This relativism constitutes a second factor contributing to the current preoccupation of theory with history.

In the long span of time, ranging from its birth in ancient Greece to the middle of the nineteenth century, ending perhaps with Hegel and Marx, political theory was more than a mere offshoot of politi-cal history. As we have had occasion to observe repeatedly, in that long epoch, political inquiry, which in retrospect we misname politi-cal theory,[41] began and adhered to an elemental question for which people, as laymen, have always sought an answer; namely, what criteria ought one to use in evaluating the variety of social programs offered by groups competing for political power? . . . [The] resulting concern of political science with social policy led to innumerable questions. But in the whole field of political science, contemporary political theory has undertaken, as part of its task, to engage in research into standards within the framework of which practical policy might be established.

As long as men thought it possible to arrive at some moral standards in terms of which a future political system could be conceived, there was sufficient incentive for a constructive examination of past moral ideas. But once the conclusion was drawn in the nineteenth century that all values are the expression of individual or group preferences and that these preferences, in turn, reflect the life-experience of the individual or group, then the impetus for the constructive study of values disappeared. If values are only the expressions of sentiments, then there seemed to be no ground upon which a person or an age could argue for the superiority of his or its moral views. Varying preferences were construed to be neither better nor worse than others, simply equal in moral worth. Social scientist A could say to his colleague B that his, A's, preferences were just as good as those of B; if B was a relativist, it appeared that he had no grounds for denying this. However strongly he might believe in his own moral position, there was no rational evidence that he could present to demonstrate that A's views were inferior. At most he could say only that his moral views differed. If no one preference could be proved to be better than another, then it seemed, if not a waste of time, at least a purely aesthetic and, therefore, politically meaningless task for scholars to devote themselves to the constructive elaboration of value systems.

This interpretation and conclusion, as I shall try to show in a moment, was quite incorrect and misleading. The adoption of a correct conception of moral relativism need not in itself have led to the decline of the critical appraisal of values. Yet, however illogical this conclusion was, since its truth was accepted, its effect was to turn political theorists to a study of the source, origin, and historical importance of moral ideas as the most meaningful way of dealing with them. The hitherto constructive functions of theory promptly evaporated.

This belief in the ultimate equal worth of all moral views is the product, however, not of logic, but of preference itself. To say that a moral position is relativistic need not mean more than that it stems from the life-experiences of an individual and that by factual evidence no one value can be proved to be superior to another. To borrow Mannheim's term, it means that a preference is relational;[42] it relates to the social conditions in which it appears. The vital fact about this meaning of relativism is that the description of the conditions surrounding the emergence of moral preference does not by itself necessarily imply any opinion about the merit or demerit of these preferences. It does not demonstrate values to be either equal or unequal in worth. It merely indicates that they are equal in their origins, in the sense that they are each a product of historical circumstances. If we wished, we could of course compare them with regard to other qualities such as their moral worth. This would however be a separate and independent task. To do so we would need first to establish an acceptable moral standard in terms of which varying preferences could be compared. But barring agreement on such a standard, two differing value judgments can be said to be neither better nor worse when each stands by the side of the other. They just differ and are incommensurable until some third standard of comparison is adopted.

Let us assume, for example, that we know clearly what we mean when we talk about the desirability of freedom and of security. We can talk about the relativism of these moral preferences. When we say they are relative, we need only mean that we happen to accept them as desirable and that this acceptance can be explained in terms of our response to the historical circumstances in which we live. If we were to argue, however, that in terms of their varying life-experiences, one person considers freedom preferable and another person, security, and, therefore, that each statement of preference is equal in worth to the other, such an argument would carry us beyond the bounds of good reasoning. The mere fact that each expression of a preference is equally relative to circumstances does not in itself mean that we must necessarily conclude that they are equally valuable. Whether freedom is considered superior, inferior, or equal in moral worth to security depends obviously upon some prior moral standard or preference in terms of which these two preferences are themselves evaluated. The relativism of freedom and security implies no statement about the merits of these two goals. The position which holds that because preferences are relative, they are by virtue of that fact of equal value is itself an evaluation and I shall call it equalistic relativism. Equalistic relativism is a moral position; it argues that because no value judgment can be proved superior, all values must be treated as equally good. Moral relativism, or properly, relationism, is a statement of fact; it simply declares that all value judgments are responses to historical conditions.

Yet, however untenable the conclusion of equalistic relativism, it has been implicit in most social science; as I have already suggested, this invalid interpretation succeeded in converting the study of moral ideas into the history of these ideas. Without identifying equalistic relativism by name, we have already witnessed its impact on political theory, as for example, in the work of McIlwain and Sabine. There its influence was indirect but nonetheless present. Although, as we saw, Sabine and McIlwain verbally would reject the idea of equalistic relativism, in the execution of their work they are unable to escape its consequences, so prevalent is this outlook in our age. A moral problem for them is therefore primarily one of historical description, not of constructive inquiry.

The preoccupation of theory with the history of values can be traced, finally, to a third source, the very historical conditions out of which it has emerged. The ultimate reason for the deliquescence of the hitherto constructive functions of theory can be attributed to the historical circumstances of the last hundred years. With the recent change in these conditions, any historical justification for the refusal publicly to re-evaluate moral frameworks must now be considered destroyed.

In the latter half of the nineteenth and in the early twentieth centuries, there was undoubtedly sufficient agreement in western Europe for the indifference to value reformulation to have little important meaning in every-day political affairs. There were no deep cleavages in ethical opinion that could so sharply divide antagonistic groups as to require a choice among fundamentally irreconcilable and competing values. Since there was this greater unity in moral outlook than we know today, it did not seem inconsistent or neglectful for contemporary and later value theorists to devote their energies largely to the history of moral ideas. Since men did not feel that these ideas could be fundamentally disputed, there was little left to do but to explore their history.

With the growth of fascism, however, at the end of the First World War and the subsequent spread of totalitarianism in the West, the fact that Nietzsche had foreseen decades earlier, and which is now popularized through social anthropology, namely, that men can act on the basis of widely divergent ethical standards, has become all too apparent. And this realization that the Western moral heritage, however we may describe it, is not universally or eternally acceptable must gradually lead to a reconsideration of the need, not only to analyze and describe historically but also to question prevailing political values and their institutional implications. The fact is that, unlike [the thinkers of] the nineteenth century, we do feel the need for some conscious guidance for our conduct in practical matters. In our period of conflicting value patterns, reinforced by almost irreconcilable power relations, the mere adoption of the values of our ancestors begins to pall unless they are seriously subjected, before acceptance, to critical analysis and imaginative reconstruction. In its approach to moral problems, however, theory still operates on the assumptions of the nineteenth century; hence it is reluctant to abandon its historical orientation.

These are a few of the more important reasons for the decline in the study of theory today as compared with its earlier days. While helping to explain the source of captivation with historicist research today, at the same time these reasons do suggest part of the remedy if research workers are to receive the training necessary for genuine moral self-clarification. There can be little doubt that research workers need to be sharply aware of the historical position in which they now find themselves. Mere avowal or affirmation of preferences was satisfactory for an earlier period when ultimate moral assumptions appeared to be clear and settled. Conformity to prevailing values involved fewer dangers than it does today. Research workers could even afford the luxury of misconstruing the nature of moral relativism to mean moral indifference. Social purposes had not been substantially and profoundly challenged. Now, however, if purposes are to receive full clarification, historical perspective itself opens our mind to the need for a deeper kind of moral inquiry, one that is freed from commitment to prevailing values just because of their prevalence or to relativism as a moral position rather than as a descriptive concept.

The discussion . . . has therefore sought to show that research into empirical theory must be inadequate unless it is undertaken with a full awareness on the part of the research worker of his own moral premises. These premises are not easy to identify. Special competence is required for this purpose. We might have assumed that training for this competence was available in political (value) theory, but examination of the contemporary historicist approach indicates the deficiency of theory in this respect. Political theory [has become of little] aid [to] political scientists in going beyond a formal clarification of their values. The very needs of work in systematic theory, therefore, demand the rejuvenation of political theory. Without the knowledge of how to go about clarifying their moral premises through a constructive approach, political scientists can scarcely expect to be able to acquire the competence necessary to detect the influence of moral views on their research in systematic theory.

NOTES

1. Consult especially the work of Wilhelm Dilthey and Karl Mannheim.
2. K. R. Popper, [*The Open Society and Its Enemies,* rev. ed. (Princeton: Princeton University Press, 1950)], esp. chapter 12; see also a series of articles by the same author in 11 and 12 *Economica,* New Series, (1944 and 1945), which appraises historicist methodology.
3. (New York: Macmillan, 1902, 1905, and 1920).
4. W. A. Dunning, *A History of Political Theories,* Vol I. pp. 1-2.
5. Ibid., pp. xviii-ix.
6. [Defined in] chapters 6 and 7 [of *The Political System*].
7. C. E. Merriam, *American Political Ideas* (New York: Macmillan, 1920), writes in his Preface: "The purpose of the writer is to trace the broad currents of American political thought in their relation to the social, economic and political tendencies of the time. Sometimes these ideas have been best expressed in political institutions; sometimes in laws, judicial

decisions, administration, or customs; again, in the utterances of statesmen and publicists or leaders of various causes; sometimes by the formal statements of the systematic philosophers. . . . This study is the outgrowth of investigations begun in the Seminar on American political philosophy given by Professor Dunning, in Columbia University, 1896-97, and the writer wishes to acknowledge his deep sense of obligation for the inspiration then given, and for subsequent encouragement in the prosecution of this work."

8. W. A. Dunning, op. cit., Vol. I, p. xxi; see also pp. 302-3.

9. Ibid., Vol. III, p. 422.

10. C. E. Merriam in "News and Notes," 16 *American Political Science Review* ([November] 1922), 689-94, on p. 694.

11. (New York: Macmillan, 1932).

12. Ibid., p. v.

13. Ibid., p. 391.

14. See, for example, ibid., p. 201.

15. Ibid., p. 132. Italics mine [Easton's].

16. Ibid., p. v., italics in original; see also p. 131.

17. Ibid., p. 167. Italics mine [Easton's].

18. Ibid., p. 1.

19. Ibid., pp. 1-3.

20. Ibid., p. 97.

21. Ibid.

22. Ibid., p. 369.

23. (1st ed., New York: Henry Holt, 1937).

24. Ibid. (2nd ed., 1950), p. 704; also G. H. Sabine, "What Is a Political Theory," [*1 Journal of Politics* (February 1939), 1-16].

25. "What Is a Political Theory," p. 10.

26. G. H. Sabine, "Logic and Social Studies," [*48 Philosophical Review,* #2 (1939)], p. 170.

27. *A History of Political Theory* (1st ed.), p. viii.

28. Ibid., esp. in chapters 29 and 32.

29. Ibid., p. vii.

30. Ibid., p. viii.

31. Ibid., 2nd ed., p. ix; 740-9; 908-9; and "Beyond Ideology," 57 *Philosophical Review* ([January] 1948), 1-26.

32. "Beyond Ideology," p. 2.

33. (New York: Oxford University Press, 1943).

34. Ibid., pp. 37-8.

35. Ibid., p. 47.

36. Ibid., p. 47.

37. Ibid.

38. Ibid., p. 51.

39. Ibid., p. 1.

40. R. S. Lynd, *Knowledge for What?* (Princeton: Princeton University Press, 1939).

41. See [*The Political System*], chapter 12.

42. K. Mannheim, *Ideology and Utopia* [New York: Harcourt, Brace, 1949], p. 70.

3 Empirical Theory

KARL W. DEUTSCH, *Harvard University*

LEROY N. RIESELBACH, *Indiana University*

I. THE NATURE OF POLITICAL THEORY

The terms "political theory" and "political philosophy" represent two distinct but overlapping aspects of a single intellectual task. Political theory is concerned with the search for a coherent image of the political system. It seeks an over-all picture of the workings of the subsystem of each society that deals with influencing or controlling human behavior through politics, that is, through the interplay of limited habits of compliance and limited probabilities of organized enforcement. Where other branches of political science may concentrate their attention on partial forecasts or partial descriptions of the political process, or of particular political phenomena, it remains the task of political theory to search for an orderly picture of the entire political system and of its chief interrelations with the other major subsystems of society, as well as with personalities and value systems.

Whenever the emphasis of our inquiry is placed on the understanding of what *is* or exists in politics—on the web of "if . . . then" relations that can be verified regardless of the preferences and values of the observer—we are inclined to speak of *political theory*. By contrast, when our interest is focused on what we think *ought* to be in politics—on the effects of political practices or institutions on the normative aspects, the values and the personalities of people *including those of the observer*—then we tend to speak about *political philosophy*. In the first case, we tend to see ourselves in the role of detached observers, and, in effect, in the role of social scientists. In the second case, we tend to see ourselves in the role of political philosophers.

■ This is an updated revision of our paper "Recent Trends in Political Theory and Political Philosophy," *Annals*, CCCLX (July 1965), 139-162, reprinted with the permission of the American Academy of Political and Social Science.

It is almost impossible for most of us not to oscillate between these two roles. Any scientific statement about the effect of an action or decision upon a personality system or social system of which the actor himself forms a part inevitably has normative implications. Ethics here appears as another way of looking at the science of seeking and identifying non-self-destructive actions and systems—a science to which it then adds the dimension of motivation to adopt at least one of the "good" paths of actions so identified— that is, a path that is not destructive either to oneself or to the human community of which one forms a part. Conversely, any ethical statement about a proposed action has obvious scientific implications, since it implies some consequences that are expected to follow from it. Even Kant's pure "good will" implies the obligation to get the best information about the probable consequences of one's action that is obtainable at the time and place of one's decision.

In a survey of recent writings in political theory, reported later in this study, we found that writers with a normative emphasis felt sure that they were dealing with some aspect of reality, and also that they shared many needs and values with their fellow men. And all writers working in the scientific mode of thought did so with an explicit or clearly implied concern for values, usually beginning with truth and knowledge but leading on to many others. Both kinds of writers were continuing the time-honored patterns of political science, but in doing so some of them were going on to new departures.

The purpose of political theory is similar to that of all theory. To the Greeks, *theoria* meant the passionate contemplation of reality; to the modern scientist, theory means an abstract, symbolic image or model of relevant aspects of reality—a model which may or may not be capable of being imagined in visual terms, but which permits the orderly retention and recall of relevant memories from the past, and the forming of relevant and dependable expectations for the future. Every theory is in principle an engine for the selection of information as well as for its storage and retrieval, and for the making of predictions. If it is an open theory, it will also be an instrument to start or extend the search for new information, and for the dissociation and recombination of old and new information into new patterns by means of which the original theory itself may be extended, transformed, or replaced by a new one. And, if it is a scientific theory, it will be susceptible to testing by operational evidence obtained by standardized and impersonally reproducible procedures.[1]

The above remarks—except for the last sentence—apply to all political theories as well, and the last sentence applies also to the subclass of political theories that are intended to be scientific.[2] It is this class of theories that show more recent developments, without upsetting, however, the traditional unity of political science as a discipline and political theory as a subfield.

II. POLITICAL THEORY AS A FIELD

Political theory is not only a field of inquiry conceived in abstract thought. It is also an organized body of human activity. It is a society of political theorists, of scholars united by common concerns—both similar and interlocking—and by at least limited habits of mutual attention and communication. It involves a body of records, such as a literature, and of specific communication channels, such as journals or sections within journals. With the help of such personnel and facilities, it forms a social instrument of inquiry, including a pool of common memories, a pool of more or less expert referees and reviewers, and an explicit or implied set of standards of quality and relevance for judging new work. In all these respects, political theory is an established discipline, in contrast to a mere ad hoc field of interdisciplinary collaboration where topic-oriented investigators may join forces from time to time, without any more permanent and substantial structure of communication, work habits, memories, and personnel.

Political theory as a field has an established structure, and each such structure or social system, as Talcott Parsons has suggested, requires effort to be *maintained* at least in its basic patterns. It also requires effort to be *adapted* to changing conditions in its social, intellectual, and scientific environment; additional effort to *attain* or approach whatever *goals* are implied in its structure as a system; and still further efforts to *integrate* all these different functions and activities, so as to keep them coherent and mutually supportive, rather than incoherent or mutually frustrating. Pattern maintenance, adaptation, goal attainment, and integration are, according to Parsons, the four basic functions of every social system; and they offer an illuminating schema for analyzing the distribution of recent efforts in the field of political theory.[3]

During the period from 1955 through 1964 a total of 440 books were reviewed in the "Book Notes" of the *American Political Science Review* (APSR) under the explicit heading of "Political Theory, History of Political Thought, and Methodology." Another 588 books were reviewed during the same period in the lead review section of the *Review,* without explicit designations as to the degree, if any, of their relevance to theory. In fact, we judged that almost three-quarters, or 154 out of 211 books singled out for lead reviews, between 1960 and 1964, were wholly or partly relevant to theory; nevertheless, we propose to treat the lead reviews as indicative of the general interest in the field of political science as a whole. Each book reviewed in either section—lead reviews or "Political Theory"—was then coded by us in accordance with what we considered its predominant emphasis in terms of one of the four Parsonian functions.

Under the heading of Pattern Maintenance were coded studies which mainly continued one or more of the traditional concerns of political science, such as descriptions or normative discussions of political theories, practices, institutions, or events—ranging, of course, in the normative preferences of their authors from the radicalism of C. Wright Mills to the conservatism of Willmoore Kendall. Works devoted to a substantial degree to adapting political theory to changes in the findings, concepts, or methods of social sciences, either as outright discussions of new theories or by using some new methods for drawing general theoretic inferences from the study of particular cases, were coded under Adaptations. Books mainly devoted to improve political science so as to make it a better guide to prediction or prescription, or alternatives to the good life, were coded under the heading Goal Attainment. Those works, finally, which attempt to integrate the various strands of political science, or to integrate political science with one or more of the other social sciences, were coded under Integration. To obtain an estimate of trends, the period 1955 to 1959 is contrasted with 1960 to 1964 (Table 1).

TABLE 1. Shifts in Interest in General Political Science
and in Political Theory[a]

	Number of Books Reviewed	Percentage of Books Devoted to				
		Pattern Maintenance	Goal Attainment	Adaptation	Integration	Total Percentage
General Political Science[b]						
1955-1959	377	79	14	7	0	100
1960-1964	211	59	34	6	1	100
Net Change		-20	+20	-1	+1	0
Political Theory, History of Political Thought and Methodology[c]						
1955-1959	240	74	22	4	0	100
1960-1964	200	55	29	14	2	100
Net Change		-19	+7	+10	+2	0

[a]Based on works reviewed in the *American Political Science Review,* 1955-1964, in percentages.
[b]Lead reviews.
[c]Reviews in "Book Notes" section.

As the figures show, the interest in pattern maintenance was by far the strongest in both periods, but it declined from about four-fifths in the late 1950's to about three-fifths in the early 1960's for books receiving lead reviews; and from about three-quarters to about one-half for the books reviewed in the "Book Notes" section. This decline was parallel within both political theory and general political science, but in both periods the specific political-theory field seemed slightly less dominated by traditional preoccupations. In both fields, there was a marked increase in adaptation, but in the theory field part of the shift of interest went into an increase in books devoted largely to "goal attainment." In both fields, books devoted to integration of our intellectual efforts were a rarity.

If one were to speculate about the possible distribution of efforts in political theory during the next five or ten years, using the present table as a starting point, it would seem reasonable to expect a further moderate decline of interest in pattern maintenance, perhaps roughly to the 40-percent level, accompanied by a rise to about the same level in the number of works devoted to "adaptation," together with a limited rise of interest in "goal attainment" and in "integration" to take up jointly the remaining 20 percent.[4]

Thus far, our survey has been couched in gross quantitative terms. What about the kinds of work that have attracted the most interest or seemed to hold the greatest promise, and what about the particular works that made the most significant contributions?

III. BETWEEN PAST HISTORY AND CURRENT THEORY

The great tradition of political theory, from the fourth century B.C. until the beginning of the nineteenth century A.D., has consisted largely of original works, ranging from Plato and Aristotle to Rousseau and Burke. All writers have combined normative and realistic considerations focused on the concept of justice—and from the Greek Sophists to Machiavelli and Hobbes, with a more exclusively realistic or pragmatic emphasis on the concept of power.

From the beginning of the nineteenth century, however, the major preoccupation of political theorists has been not the development of their own theories but the explication of the ideas of their predecessors. Proponents of new ideas, such as John Stuart Mill, Karl Marx, Vilfredo Pareto, and Max Weber, have been in the minority, and none considered himself, or was considered by others, primarily a theorist of politics. Since the rise of an organized profession of political science at the beginning of the twentieth century, the overwhelming preoccupation of students of political theory has been with history, exegesis, and methodological conservatism. This is in striking contrast to other fields in the natural and social sciences. Current contributions in theoretical physics, philosophy, literary criticism, and economic theory are clearly distinguished from the history of past theories in these respective disciplines.

IV. PATTERN MAINTENANCE: WORKS STEMMING FROM THE CLASSICAL TRADITION

In recent political theory, on the contrary, some of the most distinguished writings in the great tradition have combined concern for ideas from the past with efforts to apply them to intellectual, moral, and practical problems of the present. Leo Strauss's *On Tyranny* and *What Is Political Philosophy?* are written in this mood, and so—with a stronger emphasis on the present—are Sheldon Wolin's *Politics and Vision,* Dolf Sternberger's *Grund und Abgrund der Macht,* Hans Morgenthau's *Politics in the Twentieth Century,* and Kenneth Thompson's *Political Realism and the Crisis of World Politics.*[5]

A number of writers draw on the classic tradition as well as on contemporary thought for their discussions on the concept of democracy. Notable among these are the contributions of Leslie Lipson, C. W. Cassinelli, Giovanni Sartori, David Spitz, Thomas L. Thorson, and Hanna Pitkin.[6]

Work on significant figures in the history of political thought in the setting of their times has been carried in such studies as those of John Harrington by Charles Blitzer, of James Mill by Joseph Hamburger, of Gaetano Mosca by James Meisel, and of John Locke by Richard Cox. Larger numbers of thinkers have been surveyed by Leo Strauss and Joseph Cropsey, and in greater depth and breadth in a two-volume work, *Man and Society,* by John Plamenatz. Horace B. Davis has surveyed carefully and lucidly the complex encounters of early Marxist theorists with the rising nationalist movements of their time.[7]

An attempt to combine the insights of the great traditions—including both a concern for ethics and a continuing interest in such concepts as the balance of power—with sociological considerations marks Raymond Aron's *Paix et Guerre entre les Nations,* Stanley Hoffmann's editorial notes in his reader *Contemporary Theory in International Relations,* and Hoffmann's more recent essays in *The State of War.* The analysis of world politics and international organization is blended with political theory in Inis Claude's *Power and International Relations* and in George Liska's *Nations in Alliance.* Insights into history, psychology, and culture are effectively combined in a volume edited by Louis Hartz, *The Founding of New Societies,* and particularly in Hartz's own sections of the volume. Selectively perceived elements of the historical record are used as background, foil, and springboard for Hannah Arendt's *On Revolution,* and another set of ideas linking original speculations to a great tradition is found in Bertrand de Jouvenel's *Sovereignty* and *The Pure Theory of Politics.* Major studies in the borderland of history and large-scale theory are rare in the United States, but an outstanding contribution of this kind is Barrington Moore's *Social Origins of Dictatorship and Democracy.*[8]

Another bridge between the great intellectual traditions of classical philosophy, nineteenth and early twentieth century, has been developed by a number of imaginative German scholars including T. W. Adorno, Ralf Dahrendorf, Jurgen Habermas, and Alexander Mitscherlich.[9]

A number of interesting variations on themes from Marxist philosophy have been developed by writers from both Western and Eastern Europe as the Marxist intellectual tradition grew more diverse in the 1950's and 1960's.[10]

V. INTEGRATION: MAJOR ATTEMPTS AT SYNTHESIS

Several works attempt a broad synthesis of political thought and political description, together with an effort to build intellectual bridges from the world of pattern maintenance to that of the adaptation of political thought to the result of recent empirical research and to the development of the other social sciences. Leslie Lipson aims at such a synthesis for a portion of political theory in *The Democratic Civilization.* Arnold Brecht tries more specifically to link political theory, the philosophy of science, and normative concerns in *Political Theory.*[11]

The broadest and most thoroughgoing effort at a synthesis of classic political theory and of the newer empirical research in political science and other social sciences is offered in Carl J. Friedrich's *Man and His Government*—the most important work of its kind to appear during the last several decades. The broadest effort at a synthesis of political theory from the viewpoint of empiricism is George Catlin's *Systematic Politics.*[12]

A far more empirical summary, though not a synthesis, is furnished in Bernard Berelson's and Gary A. Steiner's *Human Behavior,* which lists over one thousand propositions about human conduct that the authors consider more or less verified by empirical evidence from repeated studies.[13] This is not a book about political theory, and it makes few direct comments about politics. It is primarily based on the experiments and findings of social psychologists, with sociology, psychiatry, anthropology, and biology making secondary but substantial contributions. Neither political science nor any of its major concepts rates a chapter heading; only "political institutions" get a subheading covering less than 20 of the over 650 pages of the book; very few professional political scientists are represented in the bibliography, their works furnishing less than 2 percent of the total. Nonetheless, this is a book of findings about human conduct, and thus indirectly about human nature. The references to particular research papers and to specialized studies are extremely valuable, and the final chapter, "The Findings and the Image of Man," should interest students of political thought.

A briefer overview of findings has become available through Otto Klineberg's *The Human Dimension in International Relations.* This work to some extent supersedes Klineberg's earlier *Tensions Affecting International Understanding.*[14] Both books draw primarily upon the work of social psychologists.[15] Klineberg's surveys are highly relevant to any political theory that makes assumptions about the conduct of individuals and groups, and particularly about their motivations and perceptions. A more general survey of behavioral research, largely of the work of social psychologists, is James C. Davies' *Human Nature in Politics.*[16] Despite the identity of its title with that of earlier work by Graham Wallas, Davies' book builds most of its useful intellectual bridges from one side of the river: There are rich and varied citations from the fields of social psychology, and to a lesser degree, of sociology, but there are scant references to the obviously relevant literature in political science. Davies' book thus appears as a contribution to a continuing effort in which much of the work of mutual discovery and confrontation—a confrontation of the particular work of political scientists on each major problem with the corresponding studies of the same problems by scholars from other disciplines—still has to follow. In the meantime, a collection of research concepts from the social-psychological sciences entitled *Human Behavior and International Politics* has been edited by J. David Singer with an explicit view of their relevance to international politics.[17] Christian Bay has attempted to apply the insights of modern psychology to problems of classical political theory.[18]

Within more limited fields, such as international relations, works toward broad surveys have been initiated by political scientists. Noteworthy here are: the volume edited by Klaus Knorr and Sidney Verba, *The International System,* with significant chapters by Charles McClelland, Fred Riggs, J. David Singer, and Sidney Verba; the survey by Richard C. Snyder, "Some Recent Trends in International Relations Theory and Research" in Austin Ranney's volume *Essays on the Behavioral Study of Politics;* a volume edited by Roger Fisher, *International Conflict and Behavioral Science: The Craigville Papers;* and, for the field of comparative politics, the survey by Robert A. Packenham, "The Study of Political Development," in the present volume.[19] The adaptive trend in all these works by political scientists seems unmistakable, together with a growing concern with better goal attainment for their discipline.

VI. ADAPTATION TO SPECIFIC NEW METHODS OR FINDINGS

The summaries, by Berelson and Steiner, and by Klineberg, all pose sharply to political theorists the task of continuing adaptation of their work to the growth of other social sciences. Except for the broad syntheses by Friedrich and Catlin, and to some extent by Brecht, all such adaptation has taken part in regard to particular fields or subjects.

Personality and Politics

The adaptation of political theory to the growing body of findings of psychology and psychiatry was pioneered more than thirty years ago by Harold Lasswell in such books as *Psychopathology and Politics*—reissued with a fifty-page essay on "Afterthoughts" in 1960—and *World Politics and Personal Insecurity.* Lasswell himself in 1948 continued this interest in *Power and Personality,* and recently in his joint work with Arnold Rogow on *Power, Corruption and Rectitude.* A somewhat parallel development has been the increase in the interest in the political implications of Sigmund Freud's thought, such as in the notable work, *Freud,* by Paul Roazen.[20]

Another interest is in psychologically oriented biographies of political leaders and decision makers. This interest was strengthened in 1956 by Alexander and Juliette George's *Woodrow Wilson and Colonel House,* and still more by Erik H. Erikson's already classic *Young Man Luther* in 1958. Arnold Rogow contributed to this trend his biography of James Forrestal, and Erikson's forthcoming biography of the young Gandhi promises to develop the application of this approach to cross-cultural research.[21]

Erikson has contributed significantly to the further development and modification of Freudian psychology by stressing the crucial importance of the period of childhood and adolescence for personality development.[22] Erikson's ideas were summarized by Lucian Pye, who also applied them to present-day problems in a study of Burma as a possibly representative case for a number of developing countries.[23]

The concepts of political choice and political commitment were further developed under the impact of the ideas of the psychology of personality, and of the depth-interview methods elaborated by clinicians. Such work requires a scholar's learning in political theory and in psychology, a scientist's respect for evidence, the perceptiveness of a clinician, some of the imagination of a poet, and the sense of reality of a professional student of political practice. Each of these ingredients is perceptible in Robert E. Lane's *Political Ideology,* which breaks new paths after Lane's earlier book, *Political Life,* a summary of research results on political attitudes, voting, and political participation.[24]

The tradition behind studies on psychological factors in politics goes back in its roots at least as far as Rousseau. It rests upon the notion that the individual by entrusting his fate to a government or to a political group is identifying himself with it, gaining a new image of himself or acting out and reinforcing an old one, and that he is in any case reaching out for a strengthened sense of personal identity and worth. But whereas past theorists were concerned with similarity among people, modern psychologists and political theorists find it necessary to pay attention to the differences among personalities even within a seemingly uniform industrial nation and culture.

This modern tradition was conspicuous in two path-breaking works. In *The Authoritarian Personality,* T. W. Adorno and his associates made partial use of questionnaire data; Brewster Smith, Jerome Bruner, and Robert White combine extended interviews and standardized psychological tests in *Opinions and Personality.*[25] It is this tradition which has been carried forward and deepened in Lane's work and in a number of articles by Robert Agger and his associates, and by Charles Farris, Herbert McClosky, and other researchers on the identification and measurement of particular attitudes and values relevant to political theory.[26]

The effects of this concern for the psychological basis of political behavior are visible in the theoretical section of the study by Angus Campbell, Philip Converse, Warren Miller, and Donald Stokes in *The American Voter.* The act of voting, and of the choice of a political party, the authors suggest, is not so much like the choice of a brand of consumer goods, which is largely influenced by expected satisfactions; rather, it is a choice of a role, an identity in the eyes of oneself as well as of others. People vote and act in politics, these theorists say, less for what they want to get than for what they want to be.[27]

If so much of a person's self-image and sense of identity may come from his choice of a political group—or a religious, social, or cultural group—with which he affiliates and identifies himself, then choosing such a group is a truly existential choice for every individual, and it should be possible to construct a theory of democracy based upon the opportunity of individuals to choose their small-group affiliations with a considerable degree of freedom, and thus indirectly to choose the future development of their own personality structures and personal identities. Such a theory in fact has been constructed by Hermann Weilenmann, an author who has combined the stature of a scholar in his special field with that of a leader in Swiss citizenship and education.[28] A comparison of Weilenmann's thinking with a major direction in American political theory reveals a striking case of convergence of a theory built upon careful historical and descriptive work with the results of behavioral science.

Another instance of convergence of theoretical approaches is "Patterns of Individuation and the Case of Japan: A Conceptual Scheme" by Masao Maruyama. The essay presents a conceptual scheme with two variables—the associative or dissociative attitudes of individuals toward one another, and their "centripetal" or "centrifugal" attitudes toward political authority. Though seemingly simple, the scheme generates many combinations, and these are connected with specific historical, social, and biological evidence from the various stages and cycles of the political development of Japan. The scheme has promising possibilities of comparative application to the politics of other countries.[29]

Group Theory, Political Socialization, and Political Culture

The results of much of the recent research on small groups are summarized and evaluated for their political significance in Sidney Verba's *Small Groups and Political Behavior.* Another survey is Robert T. Golembiewski's *The Small Group.* James David Barber has applied many ideas derived from small-group research in laboratory studies of political officials, specifically members of town boards of finance in Connecticut.[30]

Another set of adaptations of political thought has been elicited by advances in the study of group behavior. Groups, small and large, not only have their own communications patterns, organization, and dynamics, but often also their peculiar political culture or subculture into which adolescents are initiated and where they may learn most of their habits of action within the larger political system of their country. Studies of group formation, political culture, and political socialization thus can be studies of the body politic in *statu nascendi.* In substance they deal with the origins of political loyalty and of the sense of civic obligation, as Aristotle, Hobbes, and Rousseau dealt with the subject in their time. A major recent work in this field is Gabriel Almond and Sidney Verba's *The Civic Culture,* which develops some of the ideas of political culture in Almond and Coleman's *Politics of the Developing Areas.*[31] Other relevant studies, summarizing considerable bodies of research, are Herbert Hyman's *Political Socialization,* Richard E. Dawson's article of the same title, and William Kornhauser's *The Politics of Mass Society.* Earlier, focused applications of relevant knowledge upon particular political problems were offered in the 1956 study by Morton Grodzins, *The Loyal and the Disloyal,* and, in combination with extended interview data, in Almond's *The Appeals of Communism.*[32] More recent examples of the political-culture approach are Edward C. Banfield's *The Moral Basis of Backward Society* and, in some aspects, Margaret Mead's *Continuities in Cultural Evolution.*[33]

The general culture pattern shared by a population at a particular time and place, and particularly their political culture, become even more salient in the study of non-Western politics. Here the great issue that concerned theorists from Aristotle to Montesquieu—to what extent is human nature uniform in politics, and to what extent is it shaped by the spirit of times and of countries or peoples?—has become crucial in the work of present-day students of politics. The studies edited by Almond and Coleman on developing countries, studies by David Apter of Ghana and of the Buganda kingdom, by James Smoot Coleman of *Nigeria,* the work of Lucian Pye on Burma and on *Guerrilla Communism in Malaya,* the parallel studies of Japan and Turkey edited by Robert E. Ward and Dankwart Rustow, and the studies of *Political Parties and National Integration in Tropical Africa,* edited by Coleman and Carl Rosberg[34] —all these raise again, explicitly or by implication, the basic theoretical questions about the culture or spirit of a body politic, a people, or a state; about the ways such a culture or spirit can be recognized and studied; about the difference this culture or spirit will make to the actions and the fate of populations informed by them; and about the process through which such a political culture, national character, or spirit of the times—in short, such a configuration of memories, attention patterns, and value orientations—come into being or pass away.

Communication Studies

The theory of communication and control—sometimes also called cybernetics, that is, the theory of steering or of government—arose in the late 1940's and the 1950's in science and technology. Some of its intellectual implications have been spelled out in the work of Norbert Wiener, Claude Shannon and Warren Weaver, John von Neumann, W. Ross Ashby, George A. Miller, Colin Cherry, Herbert Simon and Allen Newell, and others.[35] Some inferences have been drawn from this body of thought to the theory of government and politics.[36] This general conception is of a configuration of communication channels in a society; of language and culture as habits of complementary communication; of the media of mass communication, their content and their control; the memories held by individuals and groups; and the visible and invisible filtering mechanisms influencing the selective perception, transmission, and recall of information in large populations or small social groups or within the minds of individuals. Communication theory further permits us to conceive of such elusive notions as consciousness and political will as observable processes. It defines the latter as the process by which postdecision information is so selected and censored as to subordinate it to the outcome of the predecision messages that "hardened" into the decision. Independent evidence for this process of subordinating postdecision or postcommitment messages has been presented recently within another theoretical framework by Leon Festinger and his associates.[37]

From the viewpoint of communications theory, the content of message flows and of memories is crucial. It is the content of memories, recalled for purposes of recognition of items in current messages from the outside world, that often determines which messages will be recognized and transmitted with special speed and attention, and whether other messages will be neglected or rejected.

The consonance or dissonance of messages, of memories, and of several projected courses of action is thus decisive for behavior. The dissociation of items from old memories and their recombination to new patterns is seen from this viewpoint as an essential step in the processes of initiation, of innovation, and of essential human freedom. Communication channels do have an influence upon the composition of message flows and memories, and on the content of their ensembles, but the content of messages may change the operating preferences and priorities—that is, the values—of the system.

Stanley Hoffmann's observation that the communications approach tends to neglect the content of the information transmitted or stored in the system is thus inapplicable to anything that is essential to theories of this type.[38] On the contrary, their essential thrust is toward taking ever greater account of the content of the messages with which the students of political communication are concerned. Nonetheless, the criticism points to an element of truth. In practice, writers have tended either to concentrate upon the content of messages and memories, giving less attention to the configuration of communication channels and of the communication system; or else they have tended to spend most of their time on studying the channels and the system, with not much attention to spare for the content of the information processed by it. Perhaps one-sidedness was initially necessary to permit any progress at all: gains of knowledge in one particular sector often are only later balanced ,by advances in another. To insist on complete balance at all times may often result in standing still.

In fact, lively contributions have been made in each sector. Concern for the images carried in the minds of individuals and transmitted and preserved by social institutions has led to Kenneth E. Boulding's *The Image,* and the concern about the effect of political stereotypes and images has been carried forward in such studies as those in *International Political Behavior,* edited by Herbert Kelman.[39]

The study of the content of messages has been receiving a strong impetus from the development of computer content analysis, lending powerful technological support to the long-standing interest in content analysis pioneered earlier in the RADIR studies by Harold Lasswell and his associates.[40] The Studies in International Conflict and Integration, under the leadership of Robert C. North, Richard Brody, and others, is making extensive use of content analysis by computer, within a communications-oriented framework of concepts.[41]

Several recent major studies have stressed channel configurations and political-communication systems. They have done so, however, usually in combination with an effective concern for the content of the messages transmitted and remembered, and of the value changes produced in the course of time. Studies of this kind appear in the volume edited by Lucian Pye on *Communications and Political*

Development; Daniel Lerner's *The Passing of Traditional Society;* and the volume by Raymond Bauer, Ithiel Pool, and Lewis Dexter, *American Business and Public Policy.* [42]

Insofar as the analysis of communications involves the analysis of messages, it leads to a concern with semantics. Insofar as it involves the analysis of communication channels and networks, it soon enters common ground with the theory of organizations. Logical analysis may be relevant for either of these two concerns; for logical analysis clarifies the content and meaning of messages and theories, and logical conjunctions and disjunctions—the "ands" and "ors" of logical discourse—often may correspond to the switching points or points of decision in communication networks or organizations.

Semantics has been developed in ways relevant to political theory and to the analysis of values by Charles Morris, Arne Naess, Charles E. Osgood, and in the semantic portions of the political writings of Anatol Rapoport.[43] Symbolic logic has been used as a tool of political analysis by Robert Dahl in his *A Preface to Democratic Theory* and more recently by Felix E. Oppenheim in his *Dimensions of Freedom.*[44]

Theories of Organization and Decision Making

Herbert Kaufman has compared modern theories of organization with formulations of traditional political theory, and has noted a number of "totally unexpected" parallels in their findings.[45] His analysis confirms the high relevance of organization theory—and of role theory as developed by sociologists—to the theory of politics. Political scientists, such as James March and Herbert Simon, have also been leaders in the field of organization theory. March and Simon's joint volume on *Organizations,* and Simon's *Models of Man* and his article "On the Concept of Organizational Goal" contain important potential contributions to political thought.[46] The application of role theory to the study of organizations is stressed by Peter M. Blau, a political sociologist. And a cross-disciplinary approach, with a distinct vocabulary, has been proposed by Fred W. Riggs.[47]

The common thrust of much of this writing is to do away with the oversimplification of the "rational" actor in politics, government, or business—similar to Machiavelli's prince or Adam Smith's businessman—whose skills and values are almost independent of his social environment, and who neatly maximizes some clearly defined value on the basis of complete information and unlimited capacity to think and calculate at no cost in resources or delay. At the same time, this stream of research has been demolishing desperate or cynical views that have presented the stream of major decisions in politics, administration, and business as the blind outcome of irrational passions, trivial intrigues, or absurd accidents. Simon has replaced the notion of "optimizing" with that of a "satisficing" decision process in which decision makers, with limited time and incomplete knowledge, try to substitute relatively better outcomes for less preferable ones, but which often fall short of optimal results. Jacob Marschak has added some explicit considerations concerning the cost of additional predecision information and the price which it would be rational to pay for it, and the same kind of reasoning could be extended to the costs and acceptable prices of additional time to think, or of additional personnel and computing resources for calculation.[48]

A specific approach to foreign-policy decision making, treating the decision process as the crucial element in organization theory and in politics, has been developed by Richard C. Snyder and his associates, utilizing both theoretical analysis and the study of an actual case.[49] A more philosophical analysis, involving a critique and "rehabilitation" of utilitarianism, is presented in David Braybrooke and Charles E. Lindblom's *A Strategy of Decision,* where a method of "disjointed incrementalism" is put forward. A number of empirically and historically oriented studies of major policy decisions and decision failures have been published by Allen Whiting, Robert J. C. Butow, Roberta Wohlstetter, and others, so that further theoretical discussions of decision making will have more data to draw upon.[50]

General Systems Theory, Game Theory, and Mathematical Models

Communication theory, organization theory, and the study of decision processes all share the characteristics that they are not limited to any single discipline and that their reasoning and their results often can be expressed in mathematical language. All these approaches imply that the processes and structures with which they deal have many important aspects in common, not only from field to field, but across system levels between small and large groups or organizations, and at lower and higher echelons within them. An original historical and analytical study by Masao Maruyama, "Thought and Behavior Patterns of Japan's Wartime Leaders," has important implications for the model of a national foreign decision system producing outcomes different from those intended by most of its participants.[51]

In general systems theory, such assumptions are made explicit. General systems theory largely drew upon the early collaboration of biologists, mathematicians, and medical and social scientists.[52] In time, their interests came to overlap and converge with the originally nonmathematical concepts of a social system developed by Talcott Parsons and his collaborators; with the interest of David Easton in the study of a political system; with Kenneth Boulding's interests in organization and economics; and with the interests in communication theory and cybernetics developed by Norbert Wiener and W. Ross Ashby.[53]

During the period under review herein, 1955 to 1964, the general-systems approach was being actively developed. In 1962, an important article was authored by Parsons on the possibility of an emerging two-party system in international politics, with the United States and the Soviet Union in the roles of leaders of the contending parties, and the developing countries in the role of the electorate. Parsons' concepts were applied to *The American Polity* by William C. Mitchell, and David Easton completed *Systems Analysis of Political Life*.[54] Works on the international political system were published by Morton Kaplan, George Liska, Anatol Rapoport, Richard Rosecrance, J. David Singer, and others.[55] Applications of the systems approach to the American scene have also been undertaken.[56] The present-day interdisciplinary use of general-systems concepts, and in particular by political theorists, has been surveyed recently by Oran Young.[57] In addition to the specific concepts and terms of systems theory, however, there has been a rising interest in studying and confronting the political systems of large countries as a whole, in such works as Zbigniew Brzezinski's and Samuel Huntington's *U.S. and USSR;* the writings of Walt W. Rostow; and Anthony Down's effort at analyzing politics in the manner of economic theory.[58]

The interest of political scientists in game theory was aroused in the early 1950's, almost a decade after the appearance of John von Neumann and Oskar Morgenstern's well-known book.[59] Since that time, the limits of the game-theory approach have become better understood, and a literature including both development and criticism has arisen. William Riker published *The Theory of Political Coalitions,* and Glendon Schubert included elements of game theory in his *Quantitative Analysis of Judicial Behavior*.[60]

The main application of game theory, however, has been in the field of international politics, where it has been applied particularly to the analysis of deterrence and to the theory of threats. Major intellectual contributions in this respect have been made by Thomas C. Schelling's *The Strategy of Conflict* and by Kenneth Boulding's *Conflict and Defense*. The main criticism of the use of game theory in this context has come from Anatol Rapoport's *Fights, Games and Debates,* and from his more recent *Strategy and Conscience*. Perhaps even more significant in the long run may be the turning of game theory into an experimental science in the large-scale experiment with the "prisoner's dilemma" game by Anatol Rapoport and his associates.[61] More general theoretical concerns are also found in the recent critical analyses of deterrence theory and policy by J. David Singer and by Glenn Snyder.[62] However, many strategic studies, discussing the possibilities and prospects of various deterrence and defense policies, command and control systems, safeguards against accidental war, and the proliferation of nuclear weapons, have been, for the most part, oriented toward policy rather than theory.[63]

Game situations and political systems can be represented, at least in principle, by means of mathematical models. In practice, variables used in such models often seem to be too few to be realistic, too many to be easily managed, too vague or subtle to be measured, and too controversial to be estimated by the agreement of experts. The same often holds for the relations between them, and often the mathematical tools seem to be lacking by which particular social or political relationships could be adequately represented.

Despite these difficulties, progress has been made, thanks to several intellectual tools, such as the consistent use of the concept of probability rather than determinism, the use of stochastic processes in which deterministic and probabilistic elements are combined, and the quickly improving resources of the electronic high-speed computer. Interest in mathematical models has been carried forward by Herbert Simon, by the revival of interest in the work of Lewis F. Richardson, and particularly by the rise of serious efforts at simulating the behavior of groups of voters, whole electorates, and even of national or international political systems.[64]

Actual simulation of processes sometimes has been attempted sometimes by means of the automatic manipulation of programmed computer data, sometimes simply by having human actors play assigned roles in a political game, and sometimes by combinations of men and machines. All-human simulation exercises have been discussed by Herbert Goldhamer and Hans Speier, by Lincoln Bloomfield and Norman Padelford, and by Bernard C. Cohen. Man-machine combinations have been used by Harold Guetzkow, Richard Brody, and others. Automatic simulation methods—which, of course, require a great deal of hard political thinking in the form of their design and programming—have been developed most significantly by Ithiel Pool and Robert Abelson, but other efforts are in progress.[65]

The eventual aim of these and other efforts is to develop ways of organizing past information as to how voters and groups of opinion-leaders have reacted to certain recurrent issues in the past; what has been the distribution of their responses when two or more issues or appeals impinged at nearly the same time; and what the likely distribution of their responses might be if certain contingencies should come to pass, or if certain actions or policies were chosen by their government or by some political leader. The attainment of this goal is still a fair number of years away, but several steps can be taken, perhaps sooner than expected.

The first of these steps would be to project a particular series of changes—such as the proportions of members of the nonagricultural work force, or of wage-earners, or of city dwellers, or of literate adults, or of high-school graduates, or of persons born after 1930—into the future for ten or twenty years, using as a basis the past rate of change of the relevant variable in the same country during the preceding one or two decades, and correcting the estimate perhaps in the light of corresponding rates of change observed in other comparable countries. This could be done not only for other subgroups of the mass public, but also for various elite groups. If something is known of the political propensities of any such group and of expected changes in its composition, and if it is known to what extent individuals tend to retain these propensities as they grow older, estimates of potential popular or electoral receptivity toward certain policies or issues can be made for some periods ahead, and it can be estimated how much political and propagandistic effort might have to be made ten years in the future if some particular policy—such as limited supranational integration, or lower farm subsidies, or more public spending on education—is to be accepted by the public.

Another series of rough estimates might deal with the stability of images and attitudes. How large a portion of the population is likely to change an opinion on some major political question in response to the impact of some spectacular event? If we know the approximate frequency of such events in the past, and the approximate shift in opinion one or more of these events are likely to produce, we could estimate both the secular trend of opinion, at least on some issues, and the range of variance likely to be produced by the impact of sudden changes under various contingencies.[66]

A third method would then involve tracing the range and speed of such secular changes through the content analysis of samples of comparable documents drawn from different decades of the past, and comparing the results with those of the other methods. Still another method would be then to compare and to correlate the results of many series from many variables and from several different methods, moving gradually toward the richness of a model for more nearly full-fledged simulation of some major political attitudes and modal responses of a population, so that the results thus gained could be then criticized and evaluated by confronting them with the expectations derived from political intuition and judgment of a more historical and literary style of thought.

To make any substantial progress in this direction, much empirical data are needed. It is possible to design mathematical models with dummy variables, by assuming arbitrarily, say, a fairly rich country with an annual gross national product of $1,500 per capita and with an agricultural work force of 90 percent of the total—but there are no such countries in the real world, nor are there likely to be. In order to know what assumptions have at least a chance of being approximately realistic, we need tested propositions. We need to know about social and economic relations and proportions, about the distribution of incomes and other values, about attitudes, and about rates of change. The increasing interest in such theoretical questions has logically led political and social scientists to undertake the largest and most systematic efforts to gather quantitative data so far attempted.

Testing Causal Theories and Models

While this is not the place to explore methodological developments in political science,[67] many of which have taken place independent of theory building, one such development is related intimately to theory and, thus, is worth noting here. We refer to what has come to be called the Simon-Blalock causal-model analysis.[68] This technique enables the researcher "to make causal *inferences* concerning the adequacy of causal models, at least in the sense that [he] can proceed by eliminating inadequate models that make predictions that are not consistent with the data."[69] Through the use of correlational methods, it becomes possible to make empirical choices as to which causal model best describes the causal relationships among a set of variables, that is, to decide which independent variables, operating in what sequence, best account for behavior of a given dependent variable. In short, the Simon-Blalock method permits movement beyond simple covariation in the direction of causal orderings among variables.

For example, Cnudde and McCrone apply this technique to the question of whether Congressmen's personal policy preferences or their perception of the attitudes of their constituents is most crucial to their roll-call votes. They conclude that "constituencies do not influence civil rights roll calls by selecting Congressmen whose attitudes mirror their own. Instead, Congressmen vote their constituencies' attitudes (as they perceive them) with a mind to the next election." In other words, the causal sequence runs from constituency opinion through Congressmen's perception, to which Congressmen's preferences are adjusted, and thence to roll-call vote.[70] The same authors have applied the same mode of analysis to causes of political development, whereas Goldberg has used it to discern the determinants of individual voting behavior.[71]

The difficulty in much of this important work on causal modeling is that it assumes either a one-way flow of influence, or at least a relatively strong asymmetry in interaction. Many systems in the real world, however, are characterized by feedback relations in which one-way causation is difficult to assign and fails to give an adequate description. Do chickens cause eggs, or do eggs cause chickens? Which link in the circuits of a thermostatically controlled heating system causes the output of the system? Eventually, an array of models and analytic methods will have to be evolved, which will be particularly suited to the comprehensive and realistic mapping of feedback systems in their performance over time, and which can be applied to the inputs, outputs, and performance characteristics of political and social systems.

A Response to Theory: The Collection and Analysis of Quantitative Data

The systematic collection and comparison of politically interesting quantitative data is at least as old as Sir John Petty's *Political Arithmetick* of 1672. Indeed, it was political science as the "science of the state" which in the eighteenth century gave to the discipline of statistics the name it bears today. Nonetheless, the efforts of the last few years in the field of political science have been different, in quantity and quality, from most of the work that has gone before.

Between 1950 and 1960, it has been estimated, the volume of statistical data reported by national governments to the United Nations has increased about tenfold. The quality of these data has improved considerably through the adoption of more uniform standards of reporting and through the United-Nations-aided training of statistical officers in many countries. The political and social relevance of many of these data has been stressed in the periodic United Nations *Survey of the World Social Situation* and in other United Nations publications.[72]

More searching analysis of many kinds of data, and of their correlations with dichotomized (either-or) qualitative descriptions of political characteristics for countries, is given in Arthur Banks' and Robert Textor's *Cross-Polity Survey*. More systematic estimates of the probable error margins of data, and somewhat more sophisticated methods of mathematical analysis and projection, characterize the *World Handbook of Political and Social Indicators* by Bruce Russett and his associates.[73] Another important volume is *Comparing Nations*, which discusses the critical evaluation and use of such data.[74]

These books are merely the first results of the rise of large facilities for the gathering and analysis of quantitative political and social data. At Williams College, the Roper Center of Public Opinion Research holds currently about eight million punched cards of public-opinion data, contributed by over seventy opinion-polling organizations in more than forty countries. At the University of Michigan, the Institute of Social Research, cooperating with the Inter-University Consortium of more than one hundred graduate departments of political science, holds several million data cards, with considerably larger facilities for their interpretation and analysis. Other centers are developing at the University of California at Berkeley, at the Universities of Chicago and of North Carolina, and elsewhere. The Yale Political Data Program specializes in techniques of data analysis, interpretation, and application, in the manner of a laboratory rather than that of an archive—recognizing, however, that the data-gathering and storage function of a repository must to some extent go hand in hand with the more active processing and exploitation of data for the purpose of a continuing and fruitful dialogue between theories and data.[75]

Though its roots are as international as political theory itself, the "data movement" first gained momentum in the United States. Now, however, it is spreading overseas. With the cooperation of the United Nations Educational, Scientific, and Cultural Organization and of the International Social Science Council, social and political data centers are currently being established in one form or another at Paris, Cologne, Amsterdam, and Buenos Aires. Similar developments for Rio de Janeiro, Tokyo, Calcutta, and perhaps Mexico are under consideration.

VII. UNDERREPRESENTED FUNCTIONS: GOAL ATTAINMENT AND INTEGRATION

In contrast to the wealth of writings attempting to develop some aspect of political theory in adaptation to advances in other sciences, natural and social, there have been only a very few works devoted to the tasks of moving political theory closer toward attaining its stated goals, or setting new goals for it, or integrating its various branches. The chief exception was Harold Lasswell's *The Future of Political Science.* Another relevant contribution is Bertrand de Jouvenel's *The Art of Conjecture,* which reminds political theorists of their task to assist human foresight in politics, as economists have done, often with no better equipment.[76]

De Jouvenel has not remained alone in his initiative. A whole series of studies has now appeared pointing to future developments in the United States and in other countries. The efforts at such projections build a bridge between theory and empirical science. They are based on images of present-day political and social systems and on data about their changes in the past; and they extrapolate these with more or less plausible assumptions about future contingencies, so as to sketch a path which these societies and political systems seem likely to follow for some limited period of the future. Here projection becomes similar to simulation, whether this simulation is carried out with abundant data and adequate programs on a large computer, or with sketchier data in the mind of an imaginative scientist, or finally by some combined work of men and machines.[77]

At present, political theory is not a well-integrated field, nor does it seem well oriented toward a prominent goal. Yet some such goals are perhaps beginning to emerge, and they may yet come to fulfill an orienting and unifying function for our field.

The first of these goals, or key problems, is that of a political theory of peace—a theory that would point the way to political institutions and practices by means of which groups, races, and nations may preserve the integrity and dignity of their basic values and traditions, and yet avoid destroying themselves and mankind in nuclear conflict or eroding their own values in the endless tensions at the brink of nuclear disaster.[78]

A second problem is that of enunciating a more adequate theory of political development that would permit the developing countries to chart their own courses with fewer dismal choices among stagnation, chaos, and oppression, and help them to preserve and to enhance human life and freedom during each stage of their rise from poverty.[79]

The third problem might be that of finding a political theory for the self-transforming society which is arising in our most highly developed countries—the countries that are reaching beyond the stage of high mass consumption, not only toward a technology of ample nuclear energy, automation, and capabilities of interplanetary transportation, but also toward a transformation of their settlement patterns, their occupational and educational structures, their human relations, their culture, and their value orientations. Such a society might indeed learn to learn, to transform itself continuously, to economize for greater abundance for all, and to govern itself for the ever greater freedom of each individual.

There are no political theories today adequate to the attainment of these goals even in thought, much less in the world of action. Yet these goals are implied in much that men think and do today, and it is possible that some future historian of political thought, at a time when political theory and practice will be far more effective and will have come much closer to these goals, will look back to our period for the beginnings of their rapid growth.

NOTES

1. See Anatol Rapoport, "Various Meanings of 'Theory,'" *American Political Science Review*, LII (December 1958), 972-988; and Rapoport, "The Use of Theory in the Study of Politics," *Essays in Political Science*, ed. Edward H. Buehrig (Bloomington: Indiana University Press, 1966), pp. 3-36. See also David Easton (ed.), *Varieties of Political Theory* (Englewood Cliffs: Prentice-Hall, 1966).

2. See James B. Conant, *Science and Common Sense* (New Haven: Yale University Press, 1954); Ernest Nagel, *The Structure of Science: Problems in the Logic of Scientific Explanation* (New York: Harcourt, Brace & World, 1961); Karl W. Deutsch, "On Scientific and Humanistic Knowledge in the Growth of Civilization," *Science and the Creative Spirit*, ed. Harcourt Brown (Toronto: University of Toronto Press, 1958), pp. 3-52; Deutsch, "On Theories, Taxonomies, and Models as Communication Codes for Organizing Information," *Behavioral Science*, XI (January 1966), 1-17; and Ernest Topitsch (ed.), *Logik der Sozialwissenschaften* (3rd ed.; Cologne and Berlin: Kiepenheuer & Witsch, 1966). For two different critical approaches, see Jürgen Habermas, "Zur Logik der Sozialwissenschaften," *Philosophische Rundschau*, Supplement 5 (February 1967); and Wilhelm Hennis, *Politik und Praktische Philosophie* (Neuwied: Luchterhand, 1963).

3. See Talcott Parsons, Robert F. Bales, and Edward Shils, *Working

Papers in the Theory of Action (Glencoe: Free Press, 1953); Talcott Parsons and Neil J. Smelser, *Economy and Society: A Study in the Integration of Economic and Social Theory* (Glencoe: Free Press, 1956); and Parsons, "An Outline of the Social System," *Theories of Society: Foundations of Modern Sociological Theory,* eds. Talcott Parsons, Edward Shils, Kaspar D. Naegele, and Jesse K. Pitts (New York: Free Press, 1961), pp. 30-80. For a discussion see Chandler Morse, "The Functional Imperatives," and Parsons, "The Point of View of the Author," *The Social Theories of Talcott Parsons,* ed. Max Black (Englewood Cliffs: Prentice-Hall, 1961), pp. 100-152, 311-363. See also William C. Mitchell, *Sociological Analysis and Politics: The Theories of Talcott Parsons* (Englewood Cliffs: Prentice-Hall, 1967). For recent developments in Parsons' thinking, see his *Sociological Theory and Modern Society* (New York: Free Press, 1967).

4. Examination of the first ten numbers of the APSR published since December 1964 partially confirms these speculations. Lead reviews published from March 1965 through June 1967 divided as follows: 50 percent pattern maintenance, 43 percent adaptation, 6 percent goal attainment, and 1 percent integration. Within "Book Notes," both pattern maintenance and adaptation gained—the former to 59 percent, the latter to 36 percent, at the expense of goal attainment and integration.

5. Leo Strauss, *On Tyranny: An Interpretation of Xenophon's Hiero* (rev. ed.; New York: Free Press, 1963); Strauss, *What Is Political Philosophy? and Other Studies* (Glencoe: Free Press, 1959). Dolf Sternberger, *Grund und Abgrund der Macht: Kritik der Rechtmassigkeit heutiger Regierungen* (Frankfurt: Insel-Verlag, 1962); see also Sternberger, *Der Begriff des Politischen* (Frankfurt: Insel-Verlag, 1961). Sheldon S. Wolin, *Politics and Vision: Continuity and Innovation in Western Political Thought* (Boston: Little, Brown, 1960). Hans J. Morgenthau, *Politics in the Twentieth Century;* Vol. 1: *The Decline of Democratic Politics;* Vol. 2: *The Impasse of American Foreign Policy;* Vol. 3: *The Restoration of American Politics* (Chicago: University of Chicago Press, 1962). Kenneth W. Thompson, *Political Realism and the Crisis of World Politics: An American Approach to World Politics* (Princeton: Princeton University Press, 1960). Michael Oakeshott, *Rationalism in Politics and Other Essays* (London: Methuen, 1962).

6. Leslie Lipson, *The Democratic Civilization* (Oxford: Oxford University Press, 1964); C. W. Cassinelli, *The Politics of Freedom: An Analysis of the Modern Democratic State* (Seattle: University of Washington Press, 1961); Giovanni Sartori, *Democratic Theory* (Detroit: Wayne State University Press, 1962); David Spitz, *Democracy and the Challenge of Power* (New York: Columbia University Press, 1958) and *The Liberal Idea of Freedom* (Tucson: University of Arizona Press, 1963); Thomas L. Thorson, *The Logic of Democracy* (New York: Holt, Rinehart & Winston, 1962); Hanna Pitkin, "Obligation and Consent," *American Political Science Review,* LIX (December 1965), 990-1000; LX (March 1966), 39-52. See also Charles S. Hyneman, with the collaboration of Charles E. Gilbert, *Popular Government in American Foundations and Principles* (New York: Atherton, 1968); Michael L. Walzer, "The Obligation to Disobey," David Spitz (ed.), *Political Theory and Social Change* (New York: Atherton, 1967), pp. 185-202; Judith N. Shklar, *Legalism* (Cambridge: Harvard University Press, 1964).

7. Charles Blitzer, *An Immortal Commonwealth: The Political Thought*

of James Harrington (New Haven: Yale University Press, 1960); Joseph
Hamburger, *James Mill and the Art of Revolution* (New Haven: Yale Univer-
sity Press, 1963); James H. Meisel, *The Myth of the Ruling Class: Gaetano
Mosca and the Elite* (Ann Arbor: University of Michigan Press, 1958); Leo
Strauss and Joseph Cropsey (eds.), *History of Political Philosophy* (Chicago:
Rand McNally, 1963); John Plamenatz, *Man and Society;* Vol. 1: *Machiavelli
Through Rousseau;* Vol. 2: *Bentham Through Marx* (New York: McGraw-
Hill, 1963); Horace B. Davis, *Nationalism and Socialism: Marxist and Labor
Theories of Nationalism to 1917* (New York: Monthly Review Press, 1967).
See also Hanna Pitkin, "Hobbes's Concept of Representation," *American
Political Science Review,* LVIII (June 1964), 328-340; (December 1964),
902-918; and Pitkin, *The Concept of Representation* (Berkeley: University of
California Press, 1967).

  8. Raymond Aron, *Peace and War: A Theory of International Relations,*
trans. R. Howard and A. B. Fox (New York: Doubleday, 1966); Aron, *Essai
Sur les Liberties* (Paris: Calmann-Levy, 1965); Stanley Hoffmann (ed.), *Con-
temporary Theory in International Relations* (Englewood Cliffs: Prentice
Hall, 1960); Hoffmann, *The State of War: Essays in the Theory and Practice
of International Politics* (New York: Praeger, 1965); Inis L. Claude, *Power
and International Relations* (New York: Random House, 1962); George
Liska, *Nations in Alliance: The Limits of Interdependence* (Baltimore: Johns
Hopkins Press, 1962); Louis Hartz (ed.), *The Founding of New Societies:
Studies in the History of the United States, Latin America, South Africa,
Canada, and Australia* (New York: Harcourt, Brace & World, 1964); Hannah
Arendt, *On Revolution* (New York: Viking, 1963); Bertrand de Jouvenel,
Sovereignty: An Inquiry into the Political Good (Cambridge: Cambridge
University Press, 1957); de Jouvenel, *The Pure Theory of Politics* (New
Haven: Yale University Press, 1963); Barrington Moore, Jr., *Social Origins of
Dictatorship and Democracy: Lord and Peasant in the Making of the Modern
World* (Boston: Beacon, 1966). See also James Meisel, *Counter-Revolution:
How Revolutions Die* (New York: Atherton, 1966).

  9. Theodor W. Adorno, *Aspekte der Hegelschen Philosophie* (Berlin:
Suhrkamp, 1957); Adorno, *Negativ Dialektik* (Frankfurt: Suhrkamp, 1966);
Ralf Dahrendorf, *Marx in Perspektive* (Hannover: Dietz, n.d.); Dahrendorf,
Für eine Erneuerung der Demokratie der Bundesrepublik (Munich: Piper,
1968); Jürgen Habermas, *Strukturwandel der Offentlichkeit* (Neuwied:
Luchterhand, 1963); Habermas, *Theorie und Praxis: Sozialphilosophische
Studien* (Neuwied: Luchterhand, 1963); Alexander der Mitscherlich, *Auf dem
Weg zur Vaterlosen Gesellschaft* (Munich: Piper, 1963); and Mitscherlich, *Die
Unfähigkeit zu Trauern* (Munich: Piper, 1967). Note also several collections
of essays, such as Iring Fetscher, *Karl Marx und der Marximus: Von der
Philosophie des Proletariats zur proletarischen Weltanschauung* (Munich:
Piper, 1967); Heinz Weisbrock (ed.), *Die Politische und Gessellschafthche
Rolle der Angst* (Frankfurt: Europäische Verlagsanstalt, 1967); and the
posthumous collection of Theodor Geiger (ed.), *Demokratie Ohne Dogma:
Die Gesellschaft zwischen Pathos und Nüchternheit* (Munich: Szczesny, n.d.).
See also the anonymously edited collection of critical essays, *Über Theodor
W. Adorno* (Frankfurt: Suhrkamp, 1968).

  10. See Ernst Bloch, *Naturrecht und menschliche Würde: Erläuterun-
gen zu Hegel* (Frankfurt: Suhrkamp, 1961); Bloch, *Das Prinzip Hoffnung,* 2

vols. (Frankfurt: Suhrkamp, 1959); and the anonymously edited collection, *Über Ernst Bloch* (Frankfurt: Suhrkamp, 1968), including an interview with Bloch about unsolved tasks of socialist theory. See also Leszek Kolakowski, *Toward a Marxist Humanism*, trans. Jane Peel (New York: Grove Press, 1968); Adam Schaff, *Marxismus und das menschliche Individuum* (Vienna: Europa-Verlag, 1965); Schaff, *Sprache und Erkenntnis* (Vienna: Europa-Verlag, 1964); Ota Sik, *Plan und Markt in Sozialismus* (Vienna: Molden, 1965). See also the posthumous publication of Max Adler, *Die Solidarische Gesellschaft* (Vienna: Europa-Verlag, 1964).

11. Lipson, op. cit.; Arnold Brecht, *Political Theory: The Foundations of Twentieth Century Political Thought* (Princeton: Princeton University Press, 1959).

12. Carl J. Friedrich, *Man and His Government: An Empirical Theory of Politics* (New York: McGraw-Hill, 1963). George E. G. Catlin, *Systematic Politics: Elementa Politica et Sociologica* (Toronto: University of Toronto Press, 1962). See also the review by Charles S. Hyneman, *American Political Science Review*, LVII (December 1963), 956-957.

13. Bernard Berelson and Gary A. Steiner, *Human Behavior: An Inventory of Scientific Findings* (New York: Harcourt, Brace & World, 1964). For an earlier and far more abstract effort, see Roy Grinker (ed.), *Toward a Unified Theory of Human Behavior* (2nd ed.; New York: Basic Books, 1966).

14. Otto Klineberg, *The Human Dimension in International Relations* (New York: Holt, Rinehart & Winston, 1964), and *Tensions Affecting International Understanding: A Survey of Research* (New York: Social Science Research Council, 1950).

15. Berelson and Steiner, op. cit., pp. 493-522.

16. James C. Davies, *Human Nature in Politics: The Dynamics of Political Behavior* (New York: Wiley, 1963).

17. J. David Singer, *Human Behavior and International Politics: Contributions from the Social-Psychological Sciences* (Chicago: Rand McNally, 1965). See also, Herbert C. Kelman (ed.), *International Behavior: A Social-Psychological Analysis* (New York: Holt, Rinehart & Winston, 1965).

18. Christian Bay, *The Structure of Freedom* (Stanford: Stanford University Press, 1958); Bay, "Politics and Pseudopolitics: A Critical Evaluation of Some Behavioral Literature," *American Political Science Review*, LIX (March 1965), 39-51.

19. Klaus E. Knorr and Sidney Verba (eds.), *The International System: Theoretical Essays* (Princeton: Princeton University Press, 1961); Richard C. Snyder, "Some Recent Trends in International Relations Theory and Research," *Essays on the Behavioral Study of Politics*, ed. Austin Ranney (Urbana: University of Illinois Press, 1962); Roger D. Fisher, *International Conflict and Behavioral Science: The Craigville Papers* (New York: Basic Books, 1964); Robert A. Packenham, "The Study of Political Development," Ch. VII of the present volume.

20. Harold D. Lasswell, *Psychopathology and Politics* (New York: Viking, 1960); Lasswell, *World Politics and Personal Insecurity* (Glencoe: Free Press, 1950); Lasswell, *Power and Personality* (New York: Norton, 1948); Arnold A. Rogow and Harold D. Lasswell, *Power, Corruption, and Rectitude* (Englewood Cliffs: Prentice-Hall, 1963). Paul Roazen, *Freud: Political and Social*

Thought (New York: Knopf, 1968). See also Philip Rieff, *Triumph of the Therapeutic: Uses of Faith After Freud* (New York: Harper, 1965).

21. Alexander L. George and Juliette L. George, *Woodrow Wilson and Colonel House: A Personality Study* (New York: Day, 1956); Erik H. Erikson, *Young Man Luther: A Study in Psychoanalysis and History* (New York: Norton, 1958); Arnold A. Rogow, *James Forrestal: A Study of Personality, Politics, and Policy* (New York: Macmillan, 1963); and E. Victor Wolfenstein, *The Revolutionary Personality: Lenin, Trotsky, Gandhi* (Princeton: Princeton University Press, 1966). A more controversial contribution has been the belated publication of a combined study, *Thomas Woodrow Wilson, Twenty-eighth President of the United States: A Psychological Study* (Boston: Houghton Mifflin, 1967), by Sigmund Freud and William C. Bullitt. Freud's contributions to the study were largely secondary since he depended almost completely on Ambassador Bullitt's report of Wilson's policies at the Versailles Peace Conference, and they were written during the early years of Nazi rule in Germany when Freud was exposed to considerable psychic and perhaps material pressures. See also the reviews by Erik H. Erikson and Richard Hofstadter in *The New York Review of Books*, VIII (#2, February 9, 1967), 3-8. For two important biographies with less explicit psychological orientation, see Chalmers Johnson, *An Instance of Treason: Ozaki Hotsumi and the Sorge Spy Ring* (Stanford: Stanford University Press, 1964), and Stuart Schram, *Mao Tse-Tung* (New York: Simon and Schuster, 1966). See Bruce Mazlish (ed.), *Psychoanalysis and History* (Englewood Cliffs: Prentice-Hall, 1963). Erwin C. Hargrove has examined presidential leadership in the light of personality theory in his *Presidential Leadership: Personality and Political Style* (New York: Macmillan, 1966). For a critique of the views of one noted psychoanalyst, see John H. Schaar, *Escape From Authority: The Perspectives of Erich Fromm* (New York: Basic Books, 1961). The personality of political leaders is treated in the collection edited by Lewis J. Edinger, *Political Leadership in Industrialized Societies: Studies in Comparative Analysis* (New York: Wiley, 1967), with a notable opening essay by Alexander Mitscherlich. For a larger work by Mitscherlich, see n. 9 above.

22. Erikson, op. cit.; Erikson, *Childhood and Society* (2nd ed.; New York: Norton, 1964); and Erikson, *Identity: Youth and Crisis* (New York: Norton, 1968). Other applications of post-Freudian theories to political behavior are found in the work of such socially oriented psychiatrists as Robert Jay Lifton and John Spiegel. See Lifton, *Thought Reform and the Psychology of Totalism: A Study of Brainwashing in China* (New York: Norton, 1961); and Lifton, *Death in Life* (New York: Random House, 1968). Spiegel's recent work is contained largely in unpublished memoranda of the ten-year projection on violence at Brandeis University. For an earlier contribution of Spiegel, see Grinker, op. cit., n. 13 above.

23. Lucian W. Pye, "Personal Identity and Political Ideology," *Behavioral Science*, VI (July 1961), 205-221; Pye, *Politics, Personality and Nation-Building: Burma's Search for Identity* (New Haven: Yale University Press, 1962).

24. Robert E. Lane, *Political Ideology: Why the American Common Man Believes What He Does* (New York: Free Press, 1962); Lane, *Political Life: Why People Get Involved in Politics* (Glencoe: Free Press, 1959).

25. T. W. Adorno, Else Frenkel–Brunswik, Daniel J. Levinson, and R.

Nevitt Sanford, *The Authoritarian Personality* (New York: Harper, 1950); M. Brewster Smith, Jerome S. Bruner, and Robert W. White, *Opinions and Personality* (New York: Wiley, 1956).

26. Lane, *Political Ideology;* Robert E. Agger, Marshall N. Goldstein, and Stanley A. Pearl, "Political Cynicism: Measurement and Meaning," *Journal of Politics,* XXIII (August 1961), 477-505; Charles D. Farris, "Selected Attitudes on Foreign Affairs as Correlates of Authoritarianism and Political Anomie," *Journal of Politics,* XXII (February 1960), 50-67; Herbert McClosky, "Conservatism and Personality," *American Political Science Review,* LII (March 1958), 27-45; McClosky, "Personality and Attitude Correlates of Foreign Policy Orientation," *Domestic Sources of Foreign Policy,* ed. James N. Rosenau (New York: Free Press, 1967), pp. 51-109. For a listing of a number of instruments for personality assessment specifically relevant to political science, see John P. Robinson and Phillip R. Shaver, *Measures of Social Psychological Attitudes* (Ann Arbor: Institute for Social Research, 1969), which surveys more than 100 sources, many of which date from the late 1950's and early 1960's. M. E. Shaw and J. M. Wright, *Scales for the Measurement of Attitudes* (New York: McGraw-Hill, 1967) provides a compendium of attitude measures.

27. Angus Campbell, Philip E. Converse, Warren E. Miller, and Donald E. Stokes, *The American Voter* (New York: Wiley, 1960). In *Elections and the Political Order* (New York: Wiley, 1966), the same authors explore the implication of individual voting for the larger political system. For an intensive examination of the political behavior of the members of a specific group, see Donald R. Matthews and James W. Prothro, *Negroes and the New Southern Politics* (New York: Harcourt, Brace & World, 1966). On the relation of voters and political parties, see Seymour M. Lipset and Stein Rokkan (eds.), *Party Systems and Voter Alignments: Cross-National Perspectives* (New York: Free Press, 1967), and Robert A. Dahl (ed.), *Political Oppositions in Western Democracies* (New Haven: Yale University Press, 1966).

28. Hermann Weilenmann, "The Interlocking of Nation and Personality Structure," *Nation-Building,* ed. Karl W. Deutsch and William J. Foltz (New York: Atherton, 1963), pp. 33-55. See also Weilenmann's earlier *Pax Helvetica: Die Demokratie der Kleinen Gruppen* (Zürich: Rentsch, 1951).

29. Masao Maruyama, "Patterns of Individuation and the Case of Japan: A Conceptual Scheme," *Changing Japanese Attitudes Toward Modernization,* ed. Marius B. Jansen (Princeton: Princeton University Press, 1965), pp. 489-531.

30. Sidney Verba, *Small Groups and Political Behavior* (Princeton: Princeton University Press, 1961); Robert T. Golembiewski, *The Small Group: An Analysis of Research Concepts and Operations* (Chicago: University of Chicago Press, 1962). See also William F. Whyte, *Street Corner Society: The Social Structure of an Italian Slum,* (rev. ed.; Chicago: University of Chicago Press, 1955); M. Sherif and C. Sherif, *Intergroup Relations and Leadership* (New York: Wiley, 1962); and M. Sherif and C. Sherif, *Reference Groups: An Exploration into Conformity and Deviation of Adolescents* (New York: Harper & Row, 1964). James David Barber, *Power in Committees: An Experiment in the Governmental Process* (Chicago: Rand McNally, 1966). See also H. M. Blalock, Jr., *Toward a Theory of Minority Group Relations* (New

York: Wiley, 1967), and Theodore M. Mills, *The Sociology of Small Groups* (Englewood Cliffs: Prentice-Hall, 1967).

31. Gabriel A. Almond and Sidney Verba, *The Civic Culture: Political Attitudes and Democracy in Five Nations* (Princeton: Princeton University Press, 1963); Gabriel A. Almond and James S. Coleman (eds.), *Politics of the Developing Areas* (Princeton: Princeton University Press, 1960); Gabriel A. Almond and G. Bingham Power, Jr., *Comparative Politics: A Developmental Approach* (Boston: Little, Brown, 1966). For another anthropological approach to the study of cultural—and quite possibly of political—values, see Florence R. Kluckhohn and Fred L. Stodtbeck, *Variations in Value Orientation* (New York: Harper & Row, 1961). For a cross-cultural emphasis with numerous survey data, see Hadley Cantril, *The Pattern of Human Concerns* (New Brunswick: Rutgers University Press, 1965). David McClelland, *The Achieving Society* (Princeton: Van Nostrand, 1961) presents a more psychologically oriented approach.

32. Herbert H. Hyman, *Political Socialization: A Study in the Psychology of Political Behavior* (Glencoe: Free Press, 1958); Richard E. Dawson, "Political Socialization," *Political Science Annual,* I (1966), 1-84; William Kornhauser, *The Politics of Mass Society* (Glencoe: Free Press, 1959); Morton Grodzins, *The Loyal and the Disloyal* (Chicago: University of Chicago Press, 1956); Gabriel A. Almond, *The Appeals of Communism* (Princeton: Princeton University Press, 1954).

33. Edward C. Banfield, *The Moral Basis of Backward Society* (Glencoe: Free Press, 1958); Margaret Mead, *Continuities in Cultural Evolution* (New Haven: Yale University Press, 1964). On political socialization, see also Fred I. Greenstein, *Children and Politics* (New Haven: Yale University Press, 1965); the writings of David Easton and his collaborators, notably David Easton and Robert D. Hess, "The Child's Political World," *Midwest Journal of Political Science,* VI (1962), 229-246, and David Easton and Jack Dennis, "The Child's Acquisition of Regime Norms: Political Efficacy," *American Political Science Review,* 61 (1967), 25-38; Robert D. Hess and Judith V. Torney, *The Development of Political Attitudes in Children* (Chicago: Aldine, 1967); and Richard E. Dawson and Kenneth Prewitt, *Political Socialization* (Boston: Little, Brown, 1969). For critical reviews, see Jack Dennis, "Major Problems of Political Socialization Research," *Midwest Journal of Political Science,* XII (1968), 85-114; and Roberta S. Sigel, "Political Socialization: Some Reactions on Current Approaches and Conceptualizations," paper presented to 1966 Annual Meeting of the American Political Science Association.

34. Almond and Coleman, op. cit. David E. Apter, *Ghana in Transition* (New York: Atheneum, 1963); Apter, *Political Kingdom in Uganda: A Study in Bureaucratic Nationalism* (Princeton: Princeton University Press, 1961). Coleman, *Nigeria: Background to Nationalism* (Berkeley: University of California Press, 1958). Pye, op. cit.; Pye, *Guerrilla Communism in Malaya* (Princeton: Princeton University Press, 1956). Robert E. Ward and Dankwart A. Rustow (eds.), *Political Modernization in Turkey and Japan* (Princeton: Princeton University Press, 1964); James S. Coleman and Carl G. Rosberg, Jr. (eds.), *Political Parties and National Integration in Tropical Africa* (Berkeley: University of California Press, 1964). For a radical criticism by a Negro psychiatrist from Martinique, the late Franz Fanon, see Fanon, *The Wretched*

of the Earth (New York: Grove, 1965), and Fanon, *A Dying Colonialism* (New York: Grove, 1967). See also Robert T. Holt and John E. Turner, *The Political Basis of Economic Development: An Exploration in Comparative Political Analysis* (Princeton: Van Nostrand, 1966); and David E. Apter, *Some Conceptual Approaches to the Study of Modernization* (Englewood Cliffs: Prentice-Hall, 1968).

35. Norbert Wiener, *Cybernetics* (2nd ed.; New York: Wiley, 1961); Wiener, *The Human Use of Human Beings: Cybernetics and Society* (2nd ed.; Garden City: Doubleday, 1954); and Wiener, *God and Golem, Inc.* (Cambridge: M.I.T. Press, 1964). Claude Shannon and Warren Weaver, *The Mathematical Theory of Communication* (Urbana: University of Illinois Press, 1949). John von Neumann, *The Computer and the Brain* (New Haven: Yale University Press, 1958). W. Ross Ashby, *An Introduction to Cybernetics* (New York: Wiley, 1956); and Ashby, *Design for a Brain* (2nd ed.; New York: Wiley, 1960). George A. Miller, *Language and Communication* (New York: McGraw-Hill, 1951). Colin Cherry, *On Human Communication: A Review, a Survey, and a Criticism* (Cambridge-New York: M.I.T. Press-Wiley, 1957). See also Herbert A. Simon and Allen Newell, "Information Processing in Computer and Man," *American Scientist*, LII (September 1964), 281-300; Julian Feldman and Edward Feigenbaum (eds.), *Computers and Thought* (New York: McGraw-Hill, 1963); and D. M. Mackay, "Machines and Societies," *Man and His Future*, ed. Gordon Wolstenholme (Boston: Little, Brown, 1963), pp. 153-167, and the discussion, pp. 168-187. See also J. R. Pierce, *Symbols, Signals and Noise: The Nature and Process of Communication* (New York: Harper, 1961); Charles R. Dechert (ed.), *The Social Impact of Cybernetics* (Notre Dame: University of Notre Dame Press, 1966); Georg Klaus, *Kybernetik und Gesellschaft* (Berlin: VEB Deutscher, 1964); Klaus, *Kybernetik und Erkenntnis Theorie* (Berlin: VEB Deutscher, 1966); and Warren S. McCulloch, *Embodiments of Mind* (Cambridge: M.I.T. Press, 1965).

36. Karl W. Deutsch, *The Nerves of Government: Models of Political Communication and Control* (New York: Free Press, 1963). Cf. *Nationalism and Social Communication* (2nd printing; Cambridge: M.I.T. Press, 1962). For a recent discussion, see Robert C. North, "The Analytical Prospects of Communications Theory," *Contemporary Political Analysis*, ed. James C. Charlesworth (New York: Free Press, 1967), pp. 300-316.

37. Leon Festinger, *Conflict, Decision and Dissonance* (Stanford: Stanford University Press, 1964), for example, pp. 30-31, 97-100, 152-158. See also Festinger, *A Theory of Cognitive Dissonance* (Stanford: Stanford University Press, 1957); and Festinger et al., *When Prophecy Fails* (Minneapolis: University of Minnesota Press, 1956).

38. Hoffmann, op. cit. pp. 45-47.

39. Kenneth E. Boulding, *The Image: Knowledge in Life and Society* (Ann Arbor: University of Michigan Press, 1956); and Kelman, op. cit.

40. For example, Harold D. Lasswell, Daniel Lerner, and Ithiel de Sola Pool, *The Comparative Study of Symbols* (Stanford: Stanford University Press, 1952); Pool et al., *The Prestige Papers* (Stanford: Stanford University Press, 1952); Pool, *Symbols of Internationalism* (Stanford: Stanford University Press, 1951). The first of a proposed series of revised and updated editions has recently appeared. See Harold D. Lasswell, Nathan Leites, and

associates, *Language of Politics: Studies in Quantitative Semantics* (Cambridge: M.I.T. Press, 1965).

41. Philip J. Stone et al., *The General Inquirer: A Computer Approach to Content Analysis* (Cambridge: M.I.T. Press, 1966); Robert C. North et al., *A System of Automated Content Analysis of Documents* (Stanford: mimeographed, 1963); Ole R. Holsti, Richard A. Brody, and Robert C. North, *Theory and Measurement of Interstate Behavior: A Research Application of Automated Content Analysis* (Stanford: mimeographed, 1964); North, Holsti, and Brody, "Perception and Action in the Study of International Relations: The 1914 Crisis," *Quantitative International Politics,* ed. J. David Singer (New York: Free Press, 1968), pp. 123-158. Cf. North et al., *Content Analysis: A Handbook with Applications for the Study of International Crisis* (Evanston: Northwestern University Press, 1963); and Ithiel de Sola Pool (ed.), *Trends in Content Analysis* (Urbana: University of Illinois Press, 1959). See also Manfred Kochen, "System Technology for Information Retrieval," *The Growth of Knowledge: Readings on Organization and Retrieval of Information,* ed. Manfred Kochen (New York: Wiley, 1967), pp. 352-372. For an interesting application, see David J. Finlay, Ole R. Holsti, and Richard R. Fagen, *Enemies in Politics* (Chicago: Rand McNally, 1965).

42. Lucian W. Pye (ed.), *Communications and Political Development* (Princeton: Princeton University Press, 1963); Daniel Lerner, *The Passing of Traditional Society* (Glencoe: Free Press, 1958); Raymond A. Bauer, Ithiel de Sola Pool, and Lewis A. Dexter, *American Business and Public Policy: The Politics of Foreign Trade* (New York: Atherton, 1963). See also Wilbur Schramm, *Mass Media and National Development: The Role of Information in the Developing Countries* (Stanford: Stanford University Press, 1964); Leonard Doob, *Communication in Africa* (New Haven: Yale University Press, 1961); James N. Rosenau, *National Leadership and Foreign Policy: A Case Study in the Mobilization of Public Support* (Princeton: Princeton University Press, 1963). Important theoretical ideas, such as that of communication overload, are developed in Richard L. Meier, *A Communication Theory of Urban Growth* (Cambridge: M.I.T. Press, 1962), and James G. Miller, "The Individual as an Information Processing System," *Information Storage and Neural Control,* eds. William S. Fields and Walter Abbott (Springfield: Thomas, 1963), pp. 301-328.

43. See Charles Morris, *Signification and Significance: A Study of the Relations of Signs and Values* (Cambridge: M.I.T. Press, 1964); Morris, *Varieties of Human Value* (Chicago: University of Chicago Press, 1956). Arne Naess, *Democracy, Ideology and Objectivity: Studies in the Semantics and Cognitive Analysis of Ideological Conflict* (Oxford: Blackwell, 1956). Charles E. Osgood, G. J. Suci, and P. H. Tannenbaum, *The Measurement of Meaning* (Urbana: University of Illinois Press, 1957). Anatol Rapoport, *Fights, Games and Debates* (Ann Arbor: University of Michigan Press, 1960), Part III, "The Ethics of Debate," pp. 245-358; Rapoport, *Strategy and Conscience* (New York: Harper, 1964), Part III, "The Two Worlds," pp. 199-288.

44. Robert A. Dahl, *A Preface to Democratic Theory* (Chicago: University of Chicago Press, 1956); Felix E. Oppenheim, *Dimensions of Freedom* (New York: St. Martin's, 1961).

45. Herbert Kaufman, "Organization Theory and Political Theory," *American Political Science Review,* LVIII (December 1964), 5-14.

46. James G. March and Herbert Simon, *Organizations* (New York: Wiley, 1958); Simon, *Models of Man: Social and Rational* (New York: Wiley, 1957), and "On the Concept of Organizational Goal," *Administrative Science Quarterly,* IX (June 1964), 1-22. See March's survey, "Some Recent Substantive and Methodological Developments in the Theory of Organizational Decision-Making," *Essays on the Behavioral Study of Politics,* ed. Ranney, op. cit., pp. 191-208. See also Mason Haire (ed.), *Modern Organization Theory* (New York: Wiley, 1959), and A. H. Rubenstein and C. J. Haberstroh (eds.), *Some Theories of Organization* (Homewood: Dorsey and Irwin, 1960).

47. Peter M. Blau and W. R. Scott, *Formal Organizations: A Comparative Approach* (San Francisco: Chandler, 1962). For the direct application of role theory to legislatures, see John C. Wahlke, Heinz Eulau, William Buchanan, and Leroy C. Ferguson, *The Legislative System: Explorations in Legislative Behavior* (New York: Wiley, 1962). Fred W. Riggs, *Administration in Developing Countries: The Theory of Prismatic Society* (Boston: Houghton Mifflin, 1964).

48. See Simon, *Models of Man,* op. cit., pp. 165-182 and 241-273; Jacob Marschak, "Efficient and Viable Organizational Forms," *Modern Organization Theory,* ed. Haire, op. cit., pp. 307-320.

49. Richard C. Snyder, H. W. Bruck, and B. Sapin (eds.), *Foreign Policy Decision-Making* (New York: Free Press, 1962); and Glenn D. Paige, *The Korean Decision* (New York: Free Press, 1968). For a recent statement of the decision-making perspective, see James A. Robinson and R. Roger Majak, "The Theory of Decision-Making," *Contemporary Political Analysis,* ed. Charlesworth, op. cit., pp. 175-188. For some critical commentary see James N. Rosenau, "The Premises and Promises of Decision-Making Analysis," ibid., pp. 189-211.

50. David Braybrooke and Charles E. Lindblom, *A Strategy of Decision: Policy Evaluation as a Social Process* (New York: Free Press, 1963); Allen S. Whiting, *China Crosses the Yalu: The Decision to Enter the Korean War* (New York: Macmillan, 1960); Robert J. C. Butow, *Japan's Decision to Surrender* (Stanford: Stanford University Press, 1954); Roberta Wohlstetter, *Pearl Harbor: Warning and Decision* (Stanford: Stanford University Press, 1962). See also the earlier attempt to develop a calculus for the possible decision of foreign powers to surrender to the United States, suggested by Paul Kecskemeti, *Strategic Surrender: The Politics of Victory and Defeat* (Stanford: Stanford University Press, 1958).

51. Masao Maruyama, *Thought and Behaviour in Modern Japanese Politics,* ed. Ivan Morris (New York: Oxford University Press, 1963), pp. 84-134.

52. The term "general systems theory" was introduced in 1932 by Ludwig von Bertalanffy, a biologist, and the idea was taken up in 1951, in collaboration with him, by the Committee on Behavioral Science at the University of Chicago, which included Robert Crane, Ralph W. Gerard, Jacob Marschak, James G. Miller, Anatol Rapoport, and others. In 1954 the Society for General Systems Research was founded. See the yearbook of the Society, *General Systems.* See also Mihajlo D. Mesarović (ed.), *Views on General Systems Theory* (New York: Wiley, 1964), especially Kenneth E. Boulding, "General Systems as a Point of View," pp. 25-38. For a recent statement of the general-systems viewpoint by one of its major proponents, consult James G. Miller, "Living Systems: Basic Concepts," "Living Systems: Structure and

Process," and "Living Systems: Cross-Level Hypotheses," *Behavioral Science,* X (July 1965), 193-237; (October 1965), 337-379; and (October 1965), 381-411.

53. Parsons and Smelser, op. cit.; David Easton, *The Political System: An Inquiry into the State of Political Science* (New York: Knopf, 1953); Kenneth E. Boulding, *The Organizational Revolution* (New York: Harper, 1953); Wiener, *The Human Use of Human Beings;* Ashby, op. cit. See also Walter F. Buckley, *Sociology and Modern Systems Theory* (Englewood Cliffs: Prentice-Hall, 1967).

54. Talcott Parsons, "Polarization of the World and International Order," *Preventing World War III: Some Proposals,* eds. Quincy Wright, William M. Evans, and Morton Deutsch (New York: Simon & Schuster, 1962). Cf. Bruce M. Russett, "Toward a Model of Competitive International Politics," *Journal of Politics,* XXIV (May 1963), 226-247. William C. Mitchell, *The American Polity* (New York: Free Press, 1962); David Easton, *Systems Analysis of Political Life* (New York: Wiley, 1964); Easton, *A Framework for Political Analysis* (Englewood Cliffs: Prentice-Hall, 1965).

55. Morton A. Kaplan, *System and Process in International Politics* (New York: Wiley, 1957). Liska, op. cit.; Liska, *International Equilibrium: A Theoretical Essay on the Politics and Organization of Security* (Cambridge: Harvard University Press, 1957); Liska, *Europe Ascendent* (Baltimore: Johns Hopkins Press, 1964). Anatol Rapoport, *Fights, Games and Debates,* Part I; Richard N. Rosecrance, *Action and Reaction in World Politics: International Systems in Perspective* (Boston: Little, Brown, 1963). J. David Singer, "The Level of Analysis Problem in International Relations," *The International System,* eds. Knorr and Verba, op. cit., pp. 77-92; Bruce M. Russett, *Community and Contention: Britain and America in the Twentieth Century* (Cambridge: M.I.T. Press, 1963), and Russett, *International Regions and the International System: A Study in Political Ecology* (Chicago: Rand McNally, 1967).

56. Richard F. Fenno, Jr., *The Power of the Purse: Appropriations Politics in Congress* (Boston: Little, Brown, 1966); Leroy N. Rieselbach, "Congress as a Political System," in *The Congressional System: Notes and Readings,* ed. Rieselbach (Belmont, Calif.: Wadsworth, 1970); and Berle L. Crowe and Charles G. Mayo, "The Structural-Functional Concept of a Political Party," *American Political Parties: A Systemic Perspective,* eds. Crowe and Mayo (New York: Harper & Row, 1967), pp. 1-36.

57. Oran R. Young, "A Survey of General Systems Theory" and "The Impact of General Systems Theory on Political Science," *General Systems,* IX (1964), 61-80 and 239-253. For later discussions of the systems perspective, see Morton A. Kaplan, "Systems Theory," *Contemporary Political Analysis,* ed. Charlesworth, op. cit., pp. 150-163, and Herbert J. Spiro, "An Evaluation of Systems Theory," ibid., pp. 164-174. See also Oran R. Young, *Systems of Political Science* (Englewood Cliffs: Prentice-Hall, 1968).

58. Zbigniew K. Brzezinski and Samuel P. Huntington, *Political Power: US/USSR* (New York: Viking, 1964). Walt W. Rostow, *The United States in the World Arena: An Essay in Recent History* (New York: Harper, 1960); Rostow, *The View From the Seventh Floor* (New York: Harper, 1964); as well as Rostow, *The Stages of Economic Growth: A Non-Communist Manifesto* (New York: Cambridge University Press, 1960). Anthony Downs, *An*

Economic Theory of Democracy (New York: Harper, 1957). See also, Bruce M. Russett (ed.), *Economic Theories of International Relations* (Chicago: Markham, 1968).

59. John von Neumann and Oskar Morgenstern, *Theory of Games and Economic Behavior* (3rd ed.; New York: Wiley, 1953). Cf. Martin Shubik (ed.), *Readings in Game Theory and Political Behavior* (Garden City: Double-day, 1954); Shubik (ed.), *Game Theory and Related Approaches to Social Behavior: Selections* (New York: Wiley, 1964); Shubik, "The Uses of Game Theory," *Contemporary Political Analysis,* ed. Charlesworth, op. cit., pp. 239-272. Richard C. Snyder, "Game Theory and the Analysis of Political Behavior," *Research Frontiers in Politics and Government: Brookings Lectures, 1955,* ed. Stephen K. Bailey (Washington: Brookings, 1955), pp. 70-103. T. C. Schelling, "What is Game Theory?" *Contemporary Political Analysis,* ed. Charlesworth, op. cit., pp. 212-238. For a critique of game theory as a tool of political analysis, see Deutsch, *The Nerves of Government,* pp. 57-72.

60. William H. Riker, *The Theory of Political Coalitions* (New Haven: Yale University Press, 1962); Glendon A. Schubert, Jr., *Quantitative Analysis of Judicial Behavior* (Glencoe: Free Press, 1959). See also James Buchanan and Gordon Tullock, *The Calculus of Consent: Logical Foundations of Con-stitutional Democracy* (Ann Arbor: University of Michigan Press, 1962).

61. Thomas C. Schelling, *The Strategy of Conflict* (Cambridge: Harvard University Press, 1960). Kenneth E. Boulding, *Conflict and Defense: A General Theory* (New York: Harper, 1962). Rapoport, *Fights, Games and Debates,* Part II, "The Logic of Strategy," pp. 107-242; Rapoport, *Strategy and Conscience* (New York: Harper, 1964); see also Phillip Green, *Deadly Logic* (Columbus: Ohio State University Press, 1966). Anatol Rapoport and Albert M. Chammah, *Prisoner's Dilemma: A Study in Conflict and Co-opera-tion* (Ann Arbor: University of Michigan Press, 1965); Rapoport, *Two Person Game Theory: The Essential Ideas* (Ann Arbor: University of Michigan Press, 1966). See also Finley, Holsti, and Fagen, op. cit., n. 41 above.

62. J. David Singer, *Deterrence, Arms Control, and Disarmament: Toward a Synthesis in National Security Policy* (Columbus: Ohio State University Press, 1962); Glenn H. Snyder, *Deterrence and Defense: Toward a Theory of National Security* (Princeton: Princeton University Press, 1961).

63. For example, see Bernard Brodie, *Strategy in the Missile Age* (Prince-ton: Princeton University Press, 1959); Morton H. Halperin, *Limited War in the Nuclear Age* (New York: Wiley, 1963); Herman Kahn, *On Thermonuclear War* (Princeton: Princeton University Press, 1960); Kahn, *On Escalation* (New York: Praeger, 1965); Henry A. Kissinger, *The Necessity for Choice* (New York: Harper, 1961); Oskar Morgenstern, *The Question of National Defense* (New York: Random House, 1959); Samuel P. Huntington, "Arms Races: Prerequisites and Results," *Yearbook of the Graduate School of Public Administration,* eds. Carl J. Friedrich and Seymour Harris (Cambridge: Harvard University Press, 1958), pp. 41-86; Albert Wohlstetter, "The Delicate Balance of Terror," *Foreign Affairs,* XXXVII (January 1959), 211-234; W. W. Kaufmann, *The McNamara Strategy* (New York: Harper & Row, 1964). See also Martin C. McGuire, *Secrecy and the Arms Race* (Cambridge: Harvard University Press, 1965); Jeremy J. Stone, *Containing the Arms Race: Some Specific Proposals* (Cambridge: M.I.T. Press, 1966); and Robert S. McNamara,

The Essence of Security: Reflections in Office (New York: Harper, 1968).

64. Kenneth J. Arrow, Samuel Karlin, and Patrick Suppes (eds.), *Mathematical Methods in the Social Sciences, 1959* (Stanford: Stanford University Press, 1960). Herbert A. Simon and Allen Newell, "Models: Their Uses and Limitations," *The State of the Social Sciences,* ed. Leonard D. White (Chicago: University of Chicago Press, 1956), pp. 66-83; Simon, *Models of Man.* Lewis F. Richardson, *Statistics of Deadly Quarrels* (Chicago: Quadrangle, 1960); Richardson, *Arms and Insecurity* (Chicago: Quadrangle, 1960). Anatol Rapoport, "Lewis F. Richardson's Mathematical Theory of War," *Journal of Conflict Resolution,* I (September 1957), 249-299. Richard R. Fagen, "Some Contributions of Mathematical Reasoning to the Study of Politics," *American Political Science Review,* LV (December 1961), 888-900. Rufus P. Browning, "Computer Programs as Theories of Political Processes," *Journal of Politics,* XXIV (August 1962), 562-582. Hayward R. Alker, Jr., "The Long Road to International Relations Theory: Problems of Statistical Non-Additivity," *World Politics,* XVIII (July 1966), 623-655. See also Joseph L. Bernd (ed.), *Mathematical Applications in Political Science,* II (Dallas: Southern Methodist University Press, 1966); and Bernd (ed.), *Mathematical Applications in Political Science,* III (Charlottesville: The University Press of Virginia, 1967).

65. Herbert Goldhamer and Hans Speier, "Some Observations on Political Gaming," *World Politics,* XII (October 1959), 71-83. Lincoln P. Bloomfield and Norman J. Padelford, "Three Experiments in Political Gaming," *American Political Science Review,* LIII (December 1959), 1105-1115. Bernard C. Cohen, "Political Gaming in the Classroom," *Journal of Politics,* XXIV (May 1962), 367-381. Harold Guetzkow, Chadwick F. Alger, Richard A. Brody, Robert C. Noel, and Richard C. Snyder, *Simulation in International Relations: Developments for Research and Teaching* (Englewood Cliffs: Prentice-Hall, 1963); Guetzkow (ed.), *Simulation in Social Science: Readings* (Englewood Cliffs: Prentice-Hall, 1962). Ithiel de Sola Pool, Robert P. Abelson, and Samuel Popkin, *Candidates, Issues and Strategies: A Computer Simulation of the 1960 President Elections* (Cambridge: M.I.T. Press, 1964). Andrew M. Scott, with William A. Lucas and Trudi M. Lucas, *Simulation and National Development* (New York: Wiley, 1966).

66. Karl W. Deutsch and Richard L. Merritt, "Effects of Events on National and International Images," *International Behavior,* ed. Kelman, op. cit., pp. 132-187.

67. Karl W. Deutsch, "Recent Trends in Research Methods in Political Science," *A Design for Political Science: Scope, Objectives, and Methods,* ed. James C. Charlesworth (Philadelphia: American Academy of Political and Social Science, 1966), pp. 149-178, surveys recent methodological developments. See also Johan Galtung, *Theory and Methods of Social Research* (New York: Columbia University Press, 1967).

68. See Simon, *Models of Man,* and Hubert M. Blalock, *Causal Inference in Nonexperimental Research* (Chapel Hill: University of North Carolina Press, 1964).

69. Ibid., p. 53. Cf. Otis Dudley Duncan, "Path Analysis: Sociological Examples," *American Journal of Sociology,* LII (July 1966), 1-16.

70. Charles F. Cnudde and Donald J. McCrone, "The Linkage between Constituency Attitudes and Congressional Voting Behavior: A Causal Model,"

American Political Science Review, LX (March 1966), 66-72.

71. Donald J. McCrone and Charles F. Cnudde, "Toward a Communications Theory of Democratic Political Development: A Causal Model," *American Political Science Review,* LXI (March 1967), 72-79; Arthur S. Goldberg, "Discerning a Causal Pattern Among Data on Voting Behavior," ibid., LX (December 1966), 913-922. Cf. Hubert J. Blalock, "Causal Inferences, Closed Populations, and Measures of Association," ibid., LXI (March 1967), 130-136. For other considerations of the causality question, see Hayward R. Alker, Jr., "Statistics and Politics: The Need for Causal Data Analysis," paper presented at the 1967 Annual Meeting of the American Political Science Association; Alker, *Mathematics and Politics* (New York: Macmillan, 1965); and Raymond Tanter, "Toward a Theory of Political Development," *Midwest Journal of Political Science,* XI (May 1967), 145-172.

72. United Nations, *Report on the World Social Situation* (New York: Columbia University Press, 1957, 1961); United Nations, *Compendium of Social Statistics,* 1963 (New York: Columbia University Press, 1963); and an unpublished study of United Nations statistics by Madeleine Gross, University of Pennsylvania, 1962.

73. Arthur S. Banks and Robert Textor, *A Cross-Polity Survey* (Cambridge: M.I.T. Press, 1963); Bruce M. Russett, Hayward R. Alker, Jr., Karl W. Deutsch, and Harold D. Lasswell, *World Handbook of Political and Social Indicators* (New Haven: Yale University Press, 1964); Charles Lewis Taylor (ed.), *Aggregate Data Analysis* (Paris: Mouton & Co., 1968); Cf. Raymond A. Bauer (ed.), *Social Indicators* (Cambridge: M.I.T. Press, 1966); Bertram M. Gross (ed.), "Social Goals and Indicators for American Society," *Annals of the American Academy of Political and Social Science,* CCCLXXI (May 1967), CCCLXXIII (September 1967); N. Ginsberg (ed.), *Atlas of Economic Development* (Chicago: University of Chicago Press, 1961); and Rudolph Rummel, Jack Sawyer, Raymond Tanter, and Harold Guetzkow, *Dimensions of Nations* (forthcoming). For general discussions of problems of data analysis, see Clyde H. Coombs, *A Theory of Data* (New York: Wiley, 1964); and Raoul Naroll, *Data Quality Control: A New Research Technique* (New York: Free Press, 1962).

74. Richard L. Merritt and Stein Rokkan (eds.), *Comparing Nations: The Use of Quantitative Data in Cross-National Research* (New Haven: Yale University Press, 1965). See also Douglas Price, "Micro and Macro Politics: Notes on Research Strategy" (forthcoming).

75. Karl W. Deutsch, Harold D. Lasswell, Richard L. Merritt, and Bruce M. Russett, "The Yale Political Data Program," Yale Papers in Political Science, No. 4, 1962. Stein Rokkan in collaboration with Karl Deutsch and Richard Merritt, "International Conference on the Use of Quantitative Political, Social and Cultural Data in Cross National Comparisons," *Social Science Information,* II (December 1963), 1-20. Cf. Warren E. Miller and Philip E. Converse, "The Interuniversity Consortium for Political Research"; Robert E. Mitchell, "The Survey Research Center, University of California, Berkeley"; and Philip K. Hastings, "The Roper Public Opinion Research Center," *International Social Science Journal,* XVI (#1, 1964), 70-76, 86-89, 90-97. See also Ralph L. Bisco, "Social Science Data Archives: A Review of Developments," *American Political Science Review,* LX (March 1966), 93-109.

76. Harold D. Lasswell, *The Future of Political Science* (New York:

Atherton, 1964); Bertrand de Jouvenel, *The Art of Conjecture,* trans. Nikita Lary (New York: Basic Books, 1967). Cf. Daniel Bell, "Twelve Modes of Prediction—A Preliminary Sorting of Approaches in the Social Sciences," *Daedalus,* XCIII (Summer 1964), 845-880.

77. See, among others, the symposium, "Toward the Year 2000: Work in Progress," *Daedalus,* XCVI (Summer 1967); Herman Kahn and Anthony J. Wiener, *The Year 2000: A Framework for Speculation on the Next Thirty-Three Years* (New York: Macmillan, 1967); and Fritz Baade, *Der Wettlauf zum Jahre 2000* (Oldenburg: Stalling, 1962).

78. See, for instance, J. W. Burton, *Peace Theory: Preconditions of Disarmament* (Cambridge: Cambridge University Press, 1962), and Michael Haas, *International Conflict* (Indianapolis: Bobbs-Merrill, forthcoming).

79. In addition to the works by Almond, Riggs, and Packenham, cited above, see Samuel P. Huntington, "Political Development and Political Decay," *World Politics,* XVII (April 1965), 386-430; Huntington, *Political Order in Changing Societies* (New Haven: Yale University Press, 1968); and Chalmers Johnson, *Revolutionary Change* (Boston: Little, Brown, 1966). Huntington's Stimson Lectures at Yale are soon to be published by the Yale University Press.

4 Normative Theory

HENRY S. KARIEL, University of Hawaii

Reason must indeed approach nature with the view of receiving information from it—not, however, in the manner of a student who listens to all his master chooses to tell him, but in that of judge who compels witnesses to reply to those questions which he himself thinks fit to ask.—*Immanuel Kant, Critique of Pure Reason*

I. INTRODUCTION

Discussions on both the functions and the meanings of theory abound in the study of politics. Carl J. Friedrich, for example, has usefully distinguished between theories, types, and models in his *Man and His Government: An Empirical Theory of Politics* (1963). George Kateb has offered a concise statement in *Political Theory: Its Nature and Uses* (1968). Anatol Rapoport has delineated a variety of theoretical approaches to an understanding of politics and has provided persuasive definitions.[1] More broadly, Abraham Kaplan has defined models and theories in *The Conduct of Inquiry* (1964). I do not presume either to add to their helpful accounts or to reduce the diverse usages now in vogue to some common denominator, in the manner of the lexicographer. Instead, I should like to draw on some of my own previous writing and argue for employing normative theory as an instrument for moving beyond prevailing theoretical and practical closures.

It would seem best, first of all, to clear the air by noting that one mode of political speculation is near collapse today. Those forms of idealism which presume to derive public policies from a realm of transcending absolutes have been undermined by linguistic analysis and by a more general skepticism. Whether traditional political philosophy is actually dead, as widely reported, is perhaps best answered in the spirit of the man who, asked if he believed in baptism, replied that he certainly did, having seen it performed many times. In the same sense, traditional political philosophy is still being offered, though much of it has become a species of historicism—as David Easton shows in Chapter 2 of this volume. That it remains viable has been affirmed by Dante

Germino's *Beyond Ideology: The Revival of Political Theory* (1967). Yet it may be doubted that it continues to compel belief. There may be pathos in this situation; still, one need not be saddened by the decline of idealist political philosophy. It may be disconcerting that the new research frontiers are being settled on the one hand by empiricists whose studies remain abbreviated, and on the other by mystics, theologians, literary critics, psychologists, journalists, and novelists, writers who either fail to disclose the distinctively political dimensions of problems or else deal only *ad hoc* with the crises and hysterias of the moment.

Empiricists whose work shows them to have made their peace with prevailing systems have been less concerned with creating new possibilities than with communicating what are said to be "findings." Rather than breaking boundaries, they have been ratifying them.[2] As if in reaction to this needlessly one-dimensional empiricism, writers whose commitment is not to political science—but who nonetheless are deeply concerned about the condition of politics—have made themselves publicly heard.[3] I do not know if the work of such social commentators engages the best students in the discipline of political science, but my impression is that students whose moral drive is more intense than their affection for the taught methodologies of contemporary political science frequently fail to find relevant values in the professional literature.

It would be foolish to deprecate the efforts to come to terms with contemporary politics made by writers who are not duly accredited professionals. Yet precisely the most engaging of social commentators fail to relate their insights in terms relevant to the underlying issues which confront us. Although concerned with the values of public life, they scarcely face up to the specific organizational and technological imperatives of the modern era. Their conceptual systems, their metaphors, and their idiom fail to order the relevant facts. Insofar as the forces behind our political experience elude these writers, we are left at loose ends. A positivistic empirical orientation relates successfully to the status quo, but the antipositivists and the nonprofessionals too often offer what seem to be irrelevancies. They tend to rely on spongy abstractions ("polymorphic perversity"), on homely pleas for decentralized government ("refertilizing the grass roots of central city"), on eloquent challenges ("the fire next time"), on rhetorical intonations ("the root is man"), or on exhortations to "transcend man's alienation by a new industrial communitarianism." Complicating the picture further, the more astute of the nonprofessional observers do succeed in unearthing all manner of potentially relevant facts. But the political scientist is not *professionally* moved by their vision—if indeed his exhausting labors allow him to consider it even during his leisure hours. And nonprofessionals, as has been noted frequently, rarely read the writings of political scientists.

If this divorce of normative and empirical work is unsatisfactory, what would change the situation? What are the possibilities for relevant political thought? More specifically, how might normative political theory properly function today?

II. THE UTILITY OF A POSITIVIST EMPIRICISM

Considerable skepticism exists today about the desirability of distinguishing between normative and empirical theory. In the best of all scholarly worlds, it may be argued, theories—indeed all propositions referring to experienced reality—become significant only insofar as they serve some human purpose. True, there are theories which do not. The terms of such theories are not presumed to refer to experienced reality; their terms do not signify. Not describing, not symbolizing, they may be said to be "pure." Theories composed of such terms are generally regarded as analytic, whether they are purely logical or mathematical. They are not, literally speaking, "significant"—however much they may become significant when someone has the power to apply them to reality, using them to identify and relate specific elements of experience. Thus analytic theories are *potentially* significant.

Because men purposefully direct their political theories at some selected aspect of reality (namely, the aspect they define as political), political theories may be thought of as normative. They cannot be said to be "pure," or free from purposes, ideals, values, and interests. And because so-called empirical theory is thus normative and never exclusively descriptive, the conventional distinction between normative and empirical political theory cannot hold. This conclusion may be arrived at in another way; namely, by treating so-called normative theories as empirical ones to be tested, the test determining experimentally to what extent action based on them is actually life-enhancing or conducive to well-being. In that case, too, the conventional dichotomy between empirical and normative realms is misleading and untenable.

An untenable distinction, I realize, may yet be functional, and I would suggest that the prevailing normative-empirical dichotomy functions ideologically and psychologically: it protects political scientists from various social and personal troubles. Given the distinction, political scientists committed to the development of so-called empirical theory can assert but need neither justify nor significantly delimit the basic norms which direct their work; they can avoid exposing the normative component of their work to empirical tests. Political scientists committed to the development of so-called normative theory can similarly protect themselves against testing specific values experimentally. If it is desirable, however, to make one's basic norms explicit *and put them to the test*—always at the risk of revealing that one's work protects special interests—the dichotomy between normative and empirical theory ought to be transcended.

Because this result can scarcely be achieved by exhortation, I think it may be best to relax and abide by the prevailing distinction and seek to spell out some of the implications of what on the one hand is an *empirical approach* (concerned with experienced reality) and on the other a *normative approach* (concerned with the elucidation of norms for empirical work).

An authentic empirical approach to understanding politics should need no defense, though it may be useful to be clear about the specific form it has assumed. Intent on gaining systematic knowledge, an appreciable part of contemporary political science seeks to chart the manifest behavior of voters and nonvoters, pressure groups and congressional committees, civic leaders and Supreme Court justices, weapons systems, and developing nations. The research preoccupation is with what is given, with what exists; the hope is to make intelligible the experienced facts of politics—to order them and thereby to make them appear as parts of a rational order.

In relation to the political events that depress or exhilarate us, or in relation to contemporary happenings which involve us as human beings, the results of this academic research often seem to be irrelevant. Some results are, but the points made, for example, in V. O. Key's *Public Opinion and American Democracy* (1961) about the amount of consensus necessary to maintain democratic institutions are in no sense trivial.[4] Not only can such research lead to wiser public policy (inasmuch as it shows us that we do not actually require as many consensus-building rituals as we think we do), but it also can help identify our limitations, compulsions, fatuities, and addictions; it can identify our various nonpolitical enclosures.[5] At its best, research can help us discover how much of our conduct is in fact repetitive, conditioned, and compulsive. Focusing on our behavior, we can derive empirically confirmed generalizations about the world as it presents itself. Even when empiricists remain naive about their assumptions and when they claim to offer no point of view and presume merely to describe objectively what things are really like (or, worse, what things really *are*), they may nevertheless disclose relationships where we formerly believed things to be unrelated, accidental, or mysterious. They may thereby enable us to observe ourselves more fully and to enlarge our self-knowledge.

Research focusing on our political behavior may provide us, then, with tested generalizations, generalizations that remain positivistic insofar as they reveal what is manifestly present in a situation, what is palpably there, and what can be systematically accounted for in a descriptive, naturalistic behavioral theory. And when such generalizations are integrated into broader theoretical frameworks, it becomes possible to transcend data and to ask about the broader meanings of research.

Despite a growing polemical literature, there is not much serious professional discussion today about the normative implications of such empirical political theory.[6] By this I do not mean that the research methods commonly employed are immune to professional criticism, but rather that even the most vociferous criticism tends to be attenuated: While a behavioral approach to understanding public life is generally accepted, it is accepted in its present form. One result of the lack of radical debate is that behavioralism fails to develop its considerable possibilities. Its practitioners, though commendably ambivalent toward the operations of the physical sciences, have remained confined by the realm of the practicable. Careful not to strain for far-out conclusions (apart from asides in footnotes), they keep their work abbreviated. And it is precisely in this abbreviated form that the work tends to be respected. More significantly, its very elegance, restraint, and discipline prevent it from taking risks and pushing ahead. Preempting the field of rigorous political speculation, it leads us to believe that whatever is is necessary and that we have arrived at the end of ideological conflict—when in fact we have merely ceased to become active in areas where conflict remains inarticulate and repressed.

III. THE DISCIPLINE OF NORMATIVE THEORY

Given this situation, it becomes important to recall the functions of normative theorizing and remain hospitable to open-ended modes of political speculation. If acceptable behavioral theory readily affirms what exists—if it arrestingly exposes the fixed relationships among political events—a more venturesome approach would employ procedures for severing these relationships. Such an approach begins by disavowing and disowning theoretical connections, deliberately introducing incongruities. Detaching the imagination from the institutions and ideologies at hand, it enables us to gain what Kenneth Burke, in discussing Nietzsche, called "perspective by incongruity."[7]

To engage in such activity is to express oneself dialectically and discursively, offering denials after each affirmation, multiplying meanings, and exploding reifications. The appropriate style is unavoidably literary, for whatever conclusions are offered are found not at the end but in the totality of the work. Attempting to describe, to draw out what a position entails, such work subverts reality insofar as it remains attentive to the complexity of the data and alert to needless closures.

Confronting the inescapable ironies of our existence, this orientation deprives us of our easy sophistication, our "findings" and "conclusions." It challenges prevailing settlements, contracts, and establishments by calling attention to unfelt purposes, unexpressed interests, and unregistered aspirations. It does so by leading us into a world of symbols in which we exist unfulfilled and disquieted,

unredeemed by the prevailing institutional structure. It shows us for-
ever off-balance. One test of its success is its ability to furnish
accounts of our public life which strike us as pathetic or comic. A
further test is its ability to inspire action-oriented empirical work
that would pay off insofar as it would make our social environment
less embarrassing.[8]

The initial thrust of such an approach, it should be evident, is
destructive. But if it is negative, it is so in behalf of unrealized
goods, of intimated but unachieved goals, and of sensed but inarticu-
lated purposes. Thus it finally aims to move us to a higher plateau
and to establish our existence not on the basis of what is now
embraced as given, but on the basis of what we might yet achieve.
It seeks to make us conscious not only of what we now do (the
way we divide our labor, spend our free time, or permit ourselves to be
governed), but of what we might yet do.

In view of such an approach, we can see more precisely how
much contemporary theorizing fails to fulfill its promise. To welcome such an approach is to recall that our intellectual task is not
merely to solve predefined problems—to provide solutions and
resolutions—but also to give full symbolic expression to our problems,
and thereby to frame our inarticulate dilemmas, to delineate predicaments beyond those designated by convention, to define the gaps
between what we profess and what we do, and to reveal the way
our lives are burdened by rationalization, ideology, or mythology.

If political theorists were to move along these lines, they would
first have to become fully sensitive to what is said to be reality and
then drive the prevailing rhetoric to its inherent conclusions, revealing
the dead end to which it leads. Moreover, they would have to become
ineluctably attentive to what is done—literally to take note of our
behavior—and then to project it into the future, elucidating its probable results. By logically extrapolating, they would help those involved
in public life understand what they are doing, making them see the
worrisome, unanticipated outcomes of their decisions. Abstracting and
building political models, political theorists would make others aware of
their conduct, compelling them to act with more concern for alternatives.

This method has been employed by writers as diverse as Weber,
Schumpeter, Veblen, Arendt, and Lasswell—all fastidious ironists who
have sought to depict our environment so precisely and elaborately
that their work was bound to jeopardize the hopes of established
elites, altering conventional perceptions. Weber on bureaucracy, Schumpeter on capitalism, Veblen on our economic conventions, Arendt on
man's labor, and Lasswell on the state as a garrison have pointed to
inversions and perversions of public life not ordinarily perceived. Focusing on our immediate surroundings, these writers have rigorously
extrapolated, exposing contexts and consequences and exploring fuller

meanings of the prevailing balance. Initially engaged by what they saw as most upsetting, they ultimately sought to articulate the patterns, tendencies, potencies, and movements of the age.

A concern for the present and the near-at-hand does not mean a disregarding of the past or the geographically distant. On the contrary, one would wish to reexamine past political alternatives—especially those which have met defeat. A review of Rousseau and de Tocqueville, for example, is justified because they express clearly and fully what goes through our own minds. Furthermore, they become useful precisely because they are distant: The strangeness of their idiom protects us, at least temporarily, from resenting their reflections. It is easier, after all, to assess Plato's idealism or Comte's antilegalitarianism than to assess either of these in the confused and impure versions that are ours.

Finally, the classic political philosophers have faced up to problems in all their dimensions, dimensions which are apt to escape us. Thus, Hume really confronted the issue of consensus in social-contract theories. Rousseau—more consistent than we—included civil religion in his discussion of the social contract. Hobbes—more explicit and passionate than we—diagrammed a state quite devoid of human depravity and redemptive love, a state in which to be realistic meant to obey only such laws as men succeed in making for themselves.

IV. THE TASK OF NORMATIVE THEORY

I have suggested that we should appreciate not so much the solution of defined problems as their full expression, and this in order to make progressively more of our experience clear to ourselves. But to what questions should normative theory address itself today?

It would be presumptuous to respond in anything but the most formal terms: to provide a specific agenda for inquiry is to suppose that others lack the moral sensibilities to perceive and to rank specific problems for themselves. Accordingly, I should like to insist only that we resolutely challenge every order of facts and allocation of values said to be "given" or "authoritative" or "official," beginning with those which are most overpowering. The function of normative theory, in this view, is to enable men to develop and to govern themselves. Freeing men from the grip of established conceptions of reality, it should enable them to think of their environment as something that they might progressively appropriate and govern by compelling it to serve their purposes and bending it to their will.

It follows that we must always assume our enclosures—schools, prisons, academic departments, corporations, and bureaucracies—to be more open than past experience indicates, and that we must certainly not assume them to be as closed as claimed by those who profit by closure and feel secure in the seats of power. To the extent that we (and not some presumed order of facts) are sovereign, our efforts to test existing organizational boundaries are certain to have the effect of changing them, at best enlarging the realm of politics and satisfying a wider range of human needs.

Using what power we have to structure "the facts" and make them relevant to our needs, we change boundaries and definitions which have become conventional. Definitions—whether of a "developed" nation, a "corrupt" society, or a "mature" individual—can thus be seen as dependent upon our present and prospective needs, and as immune to invalidation by "the facts," past experience, or the "conclusions" of a positivistic empiricism.

Insofar as we can handle the facts, including and excluding them as it suits us, we bestow legitimacy on our boundaries and definitions. Creatively redesigning reality and putting our new designs to the test, we humanize the world we inhabit. Our empirical tests *make* the world valuable. There is indeed no other defensible way of legitimizing our environment, for until the final set of definitions is universally accepted and the last boundary conclusively drawn, until all our mortgages are burned and all our promises redeemed, there are always more possible relationships that men can experience. Until nothing further becomes possible—or everything becomes possible at will—a potentially meaningful future still impinges on the present. As long, then, as the future continues to be open—to the extent that it is open at present—men can draft and enforce the laws of social science; they can theorize and proceed to implement their theories, thereby giving life to them.[9]

In this view, political scientists are professionally committed to an unattained future, regarding man's usual business and politics as always incomplete ventures. Their concern is not with specific causes but all causes; it is with the partiality of truths and all parties. The decision about how much reality to encompass and make intelligible is therefore not properly determined by what happens to be certified as real at the moment—the experience *now,* controlled by men *now* in charge. Which possible order of facts to make visible and which to leave invisible is not to be decided by groups in power. Such decisions must be seen to rest on a standard transcending present experience, a standard which (when applied) will change into a critical situation whatever situation men happen to know and control. Our imperative is to make known experience appear problematical. Constituting a criticism of familiar conditions, it prepares the ground for changing known states of affairs.

Assuming that institutional boundaries are not settled, we must reject the notion that our intellectual problem is to derive general laws (and, ultimately, casual laws) from the life lived within the boundaries. We must therefore realize that there are limits to systemic analysis, that is, to efforts to index aggregates of behavior within systems and

efforts to pyramid generalizations into a body of empirical propositions. We must recognize that such generalizations are not about open-
ended systems, about men as agents, or about consciously purposeful
action. I am assuming, in other words, that there is something more
than immediately describable reality, that there are unacknowledged
additional resources, that these might yet be used to satisfy our
need to remain alive to undescribed possibilities, and finally that
norms might be posited to discover and develop latent potentialities.
Insofar as behavioral research confronts what Camus termed the
"absurd," normative theorists can dramatize and thereby redeem such
absurdities.

Consequently, what we call "research" may, first of all, be
directed by our interest in creating options, our interest in introducing complexities into our lives. This requires stressing the defects
and the excesses of all modi vivendi, ceaselessly qualifying, amending,
overturning, and negating. We must insist on imbalance when balance
is comforting and supported by research foundations. We must seek
to expose the things designated as significant—not because nothing is
finally significant, but because the order of significant experiences
may always be enlarged. We must realize that to demythologize
venerable institutions (such as the American high school or the
Supreme Court) is not necessarily to annihilate them; demythologizing
may expose a higher order of bearable complexity.

Thus normative theory properly serves to challenge the existing
reality-organizing principles. None being wholly acceptable, they constitute problems. Our problems, it should be clear, are posed not by
an intractable reality (for reality, when we are empowered to *do*
social science, may turn out to be tractable enough), but rather by
our constructs, definitions, and methods. Our organizing principles
pose a problem precisely to the extent that they fail to make
reality yield.[10] The norms that direct testing can be regarded as
adequate only insofar as they make reality more various, forcing the
powerful to open their strongholds. Until our concepts and instruments destroy closed systems and literally move the population into
open-ended ones, they remain problematical.

It follows that our problems are preeminently posed by our
conceptual frameworks, present as well as future ones. Introductory-
course lectures notwithstanding, the primary problem is not conveying
more knowledge about the existing political reality but formulating
reality-organizing principles in such a way that they enable us to
know and to govern a progressively larger reality. *The relevant professional and scientific question is how much manageable reality our
discipline incorporates.* How inclusive is it? How successfully does it
cope with life's oddities? What is the scope and depth of the
experience on which it touches? How much conflict do the models
of political science tolerate?[11] Because things of value can be

established only by acting on principles of explanations, modes of conceptualizing, research designs, and conventions for verification, these precisely constitute the problem for scientific inquiry. They direct our attention to what is central, notable, and noteworthy—that is, of value.

Since normative theories, however exuberantly advanced, function to set limits, none can be presumed to take exhaustive account of reality. They are indispensable for giving meaning, and yet are never adequate. If, then, we wish to multiply meanings and expand awareness, our theories must be ever subject to reformulation. Because we are inclined to relax and to accept the prevalent order of things, we must welcome whatever environments induce us to create theories which, when acted on, create new realities.

V. NEGATIVISM, EMPIRICISM, IDEALISM

I do not wish to make it appear that I am underwriting an exercise in demolition. It may seem that normative political theory, defined in my terms, would be in no position to help us formulate constructive policy prescriptions. Yet even though the edifice of idealism may have collapsed, I am not contending that criteria for making practical judgments are discredited. True, some kinds of theorizing are no longer possible. They rest, to put it too simply, on metaphysical, epistemological, and ontological premises that we are unable to justify. We cannot appeal to an immanent or transcendental Spirit, Reason, Truth, or Natural Law to give authenticity to our judgments. We are compelled—to use language not now congenial even to theologians—to talk sense. In short, we must move modestly, not claim divine sanction for our projects, not expect new certainties from political theory, and not permit outselves to succumb to that sense of loss and nostalgia characteristic of certain existentialist thinkers who know there are no absolutes left and yet yearn for the certainties of classical political philosophy for life that has God-given Meaning, enduring Significance, and a divinely vouchsafed Purpose.

Even though the powers of idealism have been shaken, all is not lost. We may still offer policy options. Why should we not be skeptical about ultimates—and yet affirm specific alternative goals of public action? Moreover, why should we not accept an affirmative case for a negative approach to public life and public philosophy? There is nothing paradoxical in advocating such negativism as a positive ideal. We need to promote both a critical dialogue and the civil, social, economic, and industrial institutions likely to perpetuate it. We need merely to keep in mind what is central to the procedures for meaningful philosophical discussion and, at the same time, seek to provide for the political practices likely to facilitate such discussion and to keep discussion alive and inconclusive.

This approach demands a commitment to the traditional method of rational discourse, a discipline which enables individuals to consider the contexts and consequences of alternative policy recommendations. It also demands a commitment to a political order that preserves enough peace—but no more—to allow individuals to identify and test their own various interests. In the absence of final sanctions for our policies, it is still possible for us jointly to make our way by designing the kind of environments and encouraging the kind of leadership which will protect the individual and which, by fostering habits of civility, will clear space for freely competing communities.

Explicit expression is given to this approach to the extent that political theory is vigorously analytical and radical, compelling public policy to meet the only test to which everyone can be shown to subscribe: Will the policy tend to preserve the inconclusiveness of our human enterprise? The question is whether it is likely to maintain the tension between private ideals and public possibilities, between what Max Weber called the ethics of absolute ends and the ethics of responsibility.

In sum, normative activity opens our existence to new experiences and new styles of life by creating plausible futures. Narrowly conceived and rigorously executed positivistic theory is indispensable in this activity, but it is insufficient when it merely reinforces the status quo. What we need is a commitment to creative negativism, denial, and skepticism, which are at the heart of the empirical tradition. What is required is a positive commitment to those scientific institutions and practices which make the critical, negative temper of an unconstrained empiricism a going concern.

NOTES

1. See Anatol Rapoport, "The Meanings of 'Theory,'" *American Political Science Review,* LII (December 1958), 983; and Rapoport, "The Use of Theory in the Study of Politics," *Essays in Political Science,* ed. E. H. Buehrig (Bloomington: Indiana University Press, 1966), pp. 3-36. See also May Brodbeck, "Models, Meaning, and Theories," *Models in Social Science,* ed. Llewellyn Gross (New York: Harper & Row, 1959), pp. 373-403.

2. I have tried to make this point in *Open Systems: Arenas for Public Action* (Itasca, Ill.: F. E. Peacock, 1969).

3. Promiscuous name-dropping may help make my point: Eric Hoffer, David Riesman, Marshall McLuhan, Paul Goodman, James Baldwin, Norman Mailer, B. F. Skinner, Harold Rosenberg, Erich Fromm, C. Wright Mills, Edmund Wilson, Oscar Lewis, Reinhold Niebuhr, Lewis Mumford, Dwight Macdonald, Paul Tillich, R. D. Laing, Paul Baran, Frantz Fanon, Norman O. Brown, and others.

4. Equally pertinent are the analyses provided by two works which merit singling out: Robert E. Agger, Daniel Goldrich, and Bert Swanson, *The Rulers and the Ruled: Political Power and Impotence in American Communities* (Chicago: Wiley, 1964); and Robert Rubenstein and Harold D. Lasswell, *The*

Sharing of Power in a Psychiatric Hospital (New Haven: Yale University Press, 1966). See also the strategy proposed by Aaron Wildavsky and Vincent Ostrom in *Political Science and Public Policy,* ed. Austin Ranney (Chicago: Markham, 1968).

5. A positivistic empiricism which disregards man as purposeful actor may be useful precisely because it does *not* presume to focus on distinctively political phenomena. Curiously, this proposition tends to be denied both by those who reject and by those who favor positivistic approaches. It is instructive to puzzle out what "politics" must mean to someone who believes that "an adequate explanation of a great many human *actions* can be made with no reference at all to motives, particularly when the individual is acting in a highly structured social situation—the usual case in much of *politics.*" I would submit that behavior can indeed be explained without reference to motives and that it occurs precisely in highly structured situations; but I would also argue that oppressive situations which tolerate no choice are to that extent best regarded as nonpolitical, and that nonpolitical situations are the very ones amenable to behavioral study. The point simply is that at particular times some men behave and some act—and that one cannot tell who does what merely by looking at them. Similarly, some men intentionally act on the political stage while others just cannot help themselves—and mere observation cannot enable us to distinguish between the two types. The quotation, with my emphasis, is from Eugene J. Meehan, *Contemporary Political Thought* (Homewood: Dorsey, 1967), p. 81. The logical impossibility of explaining purposeful action in terms of scientific correlations or such concepts as cause and effect is shown by Richard Taylor, *Action and Purpose* (Englewood Cliffs: Prentice-Hall, 1966); see also A. R. Louch, *Explanation and Human Action* (Oxford: Blackwell, 1966).

6. See, however, Charles A. McCoy and John Playford (eds.), *Apolitical Politics: A Critique of Behavioralism* (New York: Crowell, 1967); William E. Connolly, *Political Science and Ideology* (New York: Atherton, 1967); and Henry S. Kariel (ed.) *Frontiers of Democratic Theory* (New York: Random House, 1970).

7. To free ourselves from our immediate pressures, Kenneth Burke has urged that we seek dialectically to oppose whatever seems to dictate our fate, attempting to gain knowledge by viewing our situations from incongruous points of view. *Attitudes Toward History* (New York: New Republic Books, 1937), I, 213; II, 82.

8. For an example, see Rubenstein and Lasswell, op. cit.

9. See Alan Gewirth, "Can Men Change Laws of Social Science?" *Philosophy of Science,* XXI (July 1954), 299-341.

10. A survey of public opinion, for example, which does not *change* opinions, and which, competing with other mass media, fails to create a new awareness by failing to counteract the existing opinion-molding instruments, constitutes a *problem* for normative political science.

11. These questions are recognized as the centrally relevant ones for the physical sciences by Joseph Schwab, *The Teaching of Science as Enquiry* (Cambridge: Harvard University Press, 1964), p. 39.

PUBLIC LAW AND JUDICIAL BEHAVIOR

5 Judicial Behavior Research

KENNETH N. VINES, *State University of New York at Buffalo*

I. EARLY STUDIES OF PUBLIC LAW

At the beginning of political science as a self-conscious discipline, judicial studies were subsumed under the rubric of public law, a conception that was at the very core of the discipline. Indeed, public law and political science were closely interrelated in the development of political science, a state of affairs that, as Glendon Schubert has noted, was reflected in the name given to the Columbia University department where parturition occurred, "The Department of Public Law and Jurisprudence."[1] Such early political scientists as John W. Burgess and Frank Goodnow held joint appointments in the law school, students took instructions in both law and political-science departments, and the theory and methods of law were firmly impressed on the younger discipline. The study of the judiciary was christened "public law," and the term still commands popular support.

Public-law scholars were frequently trained in the law, and it was customary to imitate legal case compendia in public-law textbooks, to structure courses along legalistic lines, and to place theoretical and research problems within a legal framework. In short, the field of public law was tied to the elements of the legal subculture in a way characteristic of no other field, not even political theory in its relationship with philosophy. The difficulty obstructing academic research and development was that legal professionalism looked at judicial institutions from a narrow and intellectually constricting point of view. It examined as data primarily the published decisions of courts and treated them as a corpus of law, structured by legal principles. The judicial process was regarded as a set of deductive premises and philosophical axioms, understood by the legally trained, and expertly administered by the courts—the higher the court, the more expert the administration. Jurisprudence specialized in theoretical and philosophical speculation and presented sampling of conflicting definitions and views of the law. Often insightful on specific problems of the history and development of law, jurisprudential works offered no framework suitable for a political science of the judiciary and suggested few lines of empirical research and social-science inquiry.[2]

Political scientists in the field of public law had claimed an important area of political science, including one of its major institutions (the judiciary), a group of its most important decision makers (judges), and one of its leading political processes (the judicial process), and perceived it in terms largely suitable for the training of legal professionals.

In practice, public-law scholars specialized in much the same kind of research found in law journals and frequently published in them. Legal principles were traced through evolutionary studies, legal problems were briefed through research on cases, and occasional normative pieces evaluated the course of decisions. Given the immersion of public law in legalism, it is remarkable that any research emerged that was concerned with political behavior, power, or the political process. However, vivid, carefully documented biographies were written of Supreme Court justices that suggested the behavioral basis of decision making and hinted at empirical explanations.[3] In historical tradition, judicial biographies never generalized to political explanations, but were content with coloring the legal principles that their subjects manufactured on the courts. Another line of research in public law was concerned with the exposition of constitutional history and development.[4] Sometimes viewing the development of law against its environment, such works did not venture theoretical explanations to account for the interrelationships. In another vein, Edward S. Corwin wrote during the exciting times of the Supreme Court's conflict with the New Deal; skeptical toward so-called legal principles announced by the Court, his critical evaluation did much to lay the foundations for a more empirical analysis of the judiciary by looking critically at legal processes and conceptions.[5]

In such surroundings, fundamental development in both theory and research lagged. Particularly lacking were statements of the political identity and significance of the judiciary, conceptualizing it as a political institution, its activities as political behaviors, and its decisional outputs in terms of political power and political impact. Instead, the judiciary was conceived in special legal terms, quite apart from the rubrics of political power, decision making, and political processes characterizing other political institutions. Had the legal subculture been institutionalized in an empirically and theoretically oriented school, matters doubtless would have been different. But such was not the case. Intellectual ferment occurred largely in philosophical investigations into the origin and nature of law. Nevertheless, writings on sociological jurisprudence and legal realism did bring fresh viewpoints, questioning the conventional legal myths and thus providing theoretical support for later social-science investigation.[6] Even the most iconoclastic writings, however, led neither to research nor systematic documentation.

Not surprisingly for a field with such linkages, public law became increasingly marginal to the discipline of political science, even though tradition decreed its formal inclusion on state occasions. In assessments of the state of the discipline, the position of public law was usually ambiguous, and assessors were unsure how to project the future of the field.[7] Political scientists gave the field low ratings, graded in terms of its contributions to a systematic knowledge of politics. A contemporary evaluation of the fields of political science by practicing political scientists sees public law and political theory "running neck and neck ... for last place."[8]

II. INNOVATIVE EFFORTS

While a nonempirical restrictive approach typified the mainstream of public-law presentation of judicial studies, a few studies of courts and judges were more experimental and innovative in conceptual framework and empirical in purpose and presentation. These studies, some conducted by other than political scientists, had little impact on the development of public law and little effect on the presentation of the field. Nevertheless, such pioneering efforts served to illumine the limitations of the traditional public-law approach as well as to point the way to other studies that would be undertaken by political scientists in the future.

A work published in 1919 was one of the most remarkable of the experimental works. Titled quaintly "The Human Element in Justice,"[9] the study examined differences in judicial behavior among the 42 judges of the New York Magistrates Court, on the supposition that "peculiarities of temperament" among the judges were not "charmed away by the donning of judicial robes." Variations found in judicial behavior were wide, and their distribution assumed a step-like regularity suggestive of a scalar model. The theme was distinctly modern in its conviction that similar comparisons of judges in other courts would show diversity in behavior and reflect the "temper" of communities as well as "personal" qualities of judges. Beneath the old-fashioned language was a rather modern theory of judicial behavior, not yet made quite explicit. Conclusions were generalized, but the implications of the findings were stated in terms of a reformist ethic: "by the publication of these records the magistrates will come to a better understanding of their own work." A generation later the study was replicated in some studies of sentencing behavior, which used somewhat more sophisticated analysis but discovered substantially similar patterns of behavior.[10]

Comprehensive statistical analysis of the judiciary was embodied in a remarkable work by Felix Frankfurter and James Landis, *The Business of the Supreme Court* (1928).[11] The work showed what could be known about the federal court through a quantitative examination of statements of their activities, but also interwove materials on judicial history and institutional characteristics to make its points.

Although based on legalistic assumptions, it explicitly suggested a suprisingly modern systemic theory of the judiciary and indicated an awareness of the political character of both the Supreme Court and the lower federal courts and of their interrelationships.

The relationship of attributes of judges to their decision making was investigated in a study by Rodney Mott and others.[12] Various characteristics of state and federal judges were combined into a "personal index," and scores on the index were related to the prestige of the courts as measured by their citation by other courts. In its reliance on prestige, job performance, and personnel indices, the study was more like a public-administration personnel study than an investigation of the relationship of socialization to decision making. Despite theoretical inadequacies, however, the study demonstrated the utility of investigations of judicial attributes.

Also reformist in its conclusions was Edward Martin's study of judicial selection.[13] One of the most thorough judicial-recruitment studies ever made, it is the only one ever to attempt an empirical assessment of the success of bar association endorsements in state elections. Although the study is a careful assessment of influences in a judicial election, it rests on no explicit theoretical framework and views the implications of the investigation in normative terms, hoping that the "venal effects of political considerations would be much ameliorated because the Bar, instead of the party organizations, would become the responsible agency . . . ."

More descriptive and less prescriptive was Malcolm Moos's investigation of judicial elections in Minnesota.[14] Considering the influence of ticket voting, the impact of political change, and the efficacy of partisan endorsement, the author investigated the election of judges within a broad framework of descriptive electoral theory.

Utilizing methods for data gathering and analysis that are rarely exploited even today, Oliver Field conducted a comparative study of judicial decisions in ten states.[15] Decisional information was gathered by a systematic survey of cases using a detailed code—in a day when encoding of information was conducted largely by hand and computer analysis was not used. Although Field confined the survey to cases involving judicial review, reflecting the conventions of the day, he based the analysis on a comparative presentation of data from the ten states, and raised challenging questions concerning the function of dissent, the relation of opinions to decisions, and the correlation of state political structures with decisions. Another study of local courts, involving the case-study method, was Albert Lepawsky's book on the judicial system of Chicago.[16] Even though the work expressed interest mainly in bringing conventional public-administration goals of structural soundness and procedural efficiency to the analysis of "judicial administration," the work broke new ground in its comprehensive examination of a local judicial system, its use of judicial statistics, and its attention to court interrelations.

Rodney Mott's investigation of influence among state supreme courts anticipated some modern attempts to measure judicial attributes.[17] It operationalized influence by comparing ratings of law professors, opinions reprinted in case books, and citations to opinions by other supreme courts, and finally by combining these into an index of prestige. Interesting as the recorded differences are, it was never made clear what theoretical propositions supported the investigation or what the significance of the indices was. Nevertheless, the study did demonstrate the use of quantitative methods in comparing court institutions.

Taken together, these studies proceeded along lines of investigation and followed methods of inquiry and analysis, in strong contrast to the legalistic presentations that largely dominated judicial studies in pre-World War II political science. The prevalent textbooks and expositions of the judiciary of the earlier period revealed little trace of these imaginative studies. The studies were duly noted and published in many standard sources, but the leads they furnished and the information they provided were not absorbed.

For several reasons, the innovative studies cited above did not, during their time, furnish the creative basis for the development of a judicial politics. For the most part, each work existed as a unique example of experimentation and demonstration of what could be done; seldom were any of the studies followed up, and rarely did they stimulate similar investigation. Moreover, they did not serve as the basis for a reorientation of the concepts taught and cited in the political science of that day. Rarely did any of the works proceed from a basic theoretical framework suitable for further investigation and logical implementation. When findings and conclusions were not justified by reformist apologia or normative references to a "better judiciary," they were stated in largely descriptive terms. Another reason that these works did not start a research dialectic and were not emulated was based in the general state of the discipline. Although there were prophets of behavioral political science at work, and some empirical research was being carried out, comparatively little had been written in general theory to guide the development of a science of judicial politics. As a discipline, political science was not generally receptive to an empirical politics and to behavioral procedures. Quite the contrary, formal theories and nonempirical procedures still heavily influenced the theory of institutions.

III. BEHAVIORAL DEVELOPMENTS

The impetus for the development of systematic scientific treatment of judicial politics began with the publication of C. Herman Pritchett's *The Roosevelt Court*,[18] and was particularly accelerated in Glendon Schubert's *Quantitative Analysis of Judicial Behavior*.[19] Both books outlined a method based upon a general theory of judicial politics, and both demonstrated how various research techniques could be utilized to test the more important and enduring questions of interest to the student of judicial politics. Pritchett's work, the first systematic study of voting in the courts, utilized attribute-cluster bloc analysis to describe voting patterns on the Supreme Court from 1931 to 1946. His method involved the tabulation of patterns of assent and dissent on the Court, using the association of judges in split decisions, a procedure that was helped mightily, as Pritchett himself noted, by the fact that the Court had become an increasingly dissenting institution. Schubert presented a more refined demonstration of cluster bloc analysis and also explored the application of game theory and scalogram analysis to Supreme Court decision making.

Whereas Pritchett's and Schubert's works put forward no explicit general theory of the judiciary and outlined no general program of research, their impact on the development of research in judicial politics has nonetheless been significant. Their work focused on judges as political actors and judicial decisions as political acts, and sought, through careful statistical analysis, to find regularities in the behavior of judges. Free of the impediments of legal expositions of principles and normative descriptions of opinions, their analyses sought to describe the political character of the Supreme Court by concentrating on power and voting relationships, thus pointing the way to newer conceptions of the judiciary as a political institution.

In legislative politics it is not necessary to say that state legislatures and city councils as well as Congress ought to be examined. In the field of judicial politics, because of the nonpolitical and non-empirical assumptions made in public law, it has been thought necessary to urge precisely such examination. In 1955, Jack Peltason urged that the lower federal courts be accorded the same attention as the Supreme Court.[20] He urged especially that the courts should be considered in the context of the group process of politics, a view first stated so impressively by Arthur Bentley and later by David Truman. Herbert Jacob and Kenneth Vines wrote in 1963 that state and local courts should be accorded fuller attention and examined according to accepted political analysis.[21] Other hortatory analyses that were consistent with political science but not found in conventional legal theory were Victor Rosenblum's conception of the law as policy making,[22] John Schmidhauser's investigation of the relevance of judicial recruitment to policy making,[23] Clement Vose's demonstration that interest groups successfully seek access to courts,[24] and Stuart Nagel's tests that revealed that independent variables such as ethnic background and political-party affiliations systematically affect the direction of policy.[25]

Five years after Pritchett's *The Roosevelt Court,* Peltason made the forthright declaration that the judiciary was as much a political institution as the legislature and ought to be studied as such:

Judges make decisions and write opinions. Their opinions are orders to their subordinates and explanations to their constituents. These opinions and decisions can and should be described in the same framework of analysis as the decisions made by congressmen, administrators, and other groups, governmental and non-governmental . . . . This is not the way, however, that the activities of judges are described.[26]

In the context of present-day political-science systems theory, such a statement seems to belabor the obvious; but for reasons intrinsic to the development of the field, Peltason's statement has not been recognized as valid among many scholars of the judiciary, and it is doubtful that the type of poll designed by Albert Somit and Joseph Tanenhaus would reveal majority acceptance. The explanation is suggested in the previous pages, but is also inherent in the limitations of "judicial behavioralism," the term sometimes used to describe the new approach.

Of the two main types of criticisms made of empirical studies of the judiciary, one parallels the condemnations of behavioral political science in criticizing the scientific method and social science as such. An example is John Roche's rejoinder, in the *American Political Science Review*, to Glendon Schubert's statement in favor of behavioral investigation of judicial behavior.[27] Without attempting a discussion in terms of problems of social-science methods, Roche affirms that systematic empirical treatment of judicial politics leads to results which are banal, trivial, and obvious.

A more academic line of argument takes to task the behavioral investigation of the judiciary on the grounds that it does not take account of the law or use legal methods of analysis. The best-known such critique is Wallace Mendelson's vigorous defense of law as a body of rules for explaining decision making in the courts.[28] Systematically attacking demonstrations that clash with conventional legal explanations, Mendelson posits, for example, that variations in behavior may be attributable to "vagueness in the law" rather than to behavioral forces. Quoted with special approval is a law professor's review of *The Roosevelt Court* and his objection that neither "the merits of the cases nor the reasoning of the opinions affect these statistics. In spite of the multitude of opinions, the charts record only the votes, in the manner of a voting machine."[29] In another instance, seeking to disprove the findings of a political scientist's investigation of Justice Frankfurter's judicial behavior, Mendelson gathers the opinions of ten law professors. When the law professors disagreed with the political-science findings, Mendelson considered the empirical analysis refuted.[30]

However, Mendelson is often insightful in his analysis. In the course of his discussion he comments on several interesting problems in social-science methodology as they might be applied to the study of the courts; but difficulties in analysis and methodology are regarded by him as beyond easement and solution, rather than as hardships to be overcome or problems to be solved.

An irony of the argument over the role of law as a determinative agent is that Mendelson and others do not have the support of the most sophisticated theorists in today's law schools. In the past, the works of such realists as Holmes, Cardozo, Frank, and Llewellyn have provided a substantial theoretical framework for the behavioral study of the judiciary. An even more trenchant critique of the cognitive elements of legal mythology has been provided by Eugene Rostow:

... there is an inescapable Bergsonian element of intuition in the judges' work—in their ordering of facts, in their choice of premises, in their reformulation of the postulates we call 'rules' or 'principles,' in their sense of the policy or policies which animate the trend or change it. . . . The judicial process and the academic study of the law alike become mature and responsible when both judges and academic students of the law acknowledge the legitimate interplay of these factors in the action of decision and seek to deal with them as functionally, and as directly, as the state of our knowledge permits.[31]

The behavioral study of the judiciary concerns precisely these Bergsonian elements in the "action of decision." It seeks to discover the regularities of the elements and to identify their structure and origin.

However, in a curious explanation, Mendelson asserts that empirical analysts merely adopt the legal theories of the judicial activists among the judges: "I think that neo-behavioralism has been over-influenced by the judicial activists who are, after all, essentially behavioralists . . . I suggest, in short, that modern behavioralism is a by-product of libertarian activism . . ."[32] Such a view indicates that Mendelson sees the judiciary within a framework of normative, speculative personal jurisprudence.

A newer type of critical evaluation of judicial behavioralism has emerged from the writings of Theodore Becker, who is both quantitatively and theoretically oriented, but dissatisfied with the state of the field of public law. There are strong reasons to support Theodore Becker's contention in Chapter 6 of this volume that the earlier conception of public law should be abandoned in favor of a term more consonant with modern political science. The term "public law," while important in the origins of the discipline, conveys an ambiguity concerning objectives and methods of inquiry. Moreover, the terms "political jurisprudence" and "sociological jurisprudence" suggest a somewhat speculative jurisprudence; they would be inappropriate concepts for an empirical and broad-gauged treatment of the judiciary. On the other hand, if field identification is needed, the term "judicial politics" is attuned to modern political science and elastic enough to include investigation of all politically relevant elements.

Even critics recognize that the studies of judicial behavior have constituted a main current. Not only have such works implemented the original studies made by Pritchett and Schubert, but they have also branched off into related works. As a group, the studies have much in common, both in their specific character and in their approach to the study of the judiciary. The works have examined the judiciary variously through the use of dissenting bloc analysis, of cumulative-scale demonstrations, of factor analysis, or of game-theory analysis. As studies of the judiciary, they have had the following elements in common: (1) concentration on the national Supreme Court, (2) specialization in nonunanimous decisions, (3) analysis of the data by quantitative techniques, and (4) specialization in contemporary sessions of the Supreme Court, usually those after 1948.

Following Pritchett's lead, Schubert refined dissenting bloc analysis by a more structured presentation of blocs and also through measurement by means of indices of cohesion and adhesion. Schubert also suggested the wider applicability of the technique by analysis of the bloc structures on the Michigan Supreme Court.[33]

Other systematic measurements of Supreme Court votes have been made through the use of cumulative-scale analysis. By grouping cases under certain policy headings, such as civil libertarianism and economic libertarianism, Guttman scaling techniques have been applied to ascertain the responses of the nine members of the court to the decisional questions. The advantage of cumulative scaling over more primitive methods of scale analysis lies in its location of items (judicial policies) that elicit ordinally structured responses (decisions) from the members of the group (court). Successful location of such policy areas means that the behavior of judges may be described in unidimensional terms, representing a marked advance in precision.

Several investigators report finding groups of cases that fit the scalar model, that is, are capable of unidimensional measurement among the members of the Court. Among those discovered are the E (economic liberalism) scale, the C (civil liberties) scale, the F (fiscal liberalism) scale, the B (business affairs) scale, and the W (labor relations) scale. These scales yield acceptable criteria of scalability measured by the CR (coefficient of reproduceability) and S (coefficient of scalability) indices.[34] Moreover, scaling of cases has made it possible to operationalize some subtle policy questions, such as "Where is political power on the Court?" or "Is Frankfurter really a civil-libertarian?"[35] Despite the widespread reports of successful scaling, some have questioned the usefulness of the device.

Tanenhaus, in a searching critique, has pointed out that the nature of voting on the Court builds biases into scalability criteria, thus raising serious validity questions.[36]

The use of game theory suggests a more formal method of looking at decision making on the Court. Although game theory enables the investigator to calculate relative power positions on the Court, to compare the relative power of blocs on the Court, and to analyze strategies in decision making, it does so through abstract references to real situations and not through detailed data from the situations being examined. Schubert has shown how certain political processes in the Roosevelt Court can be understood by construction of the "Hughbert" and the "Certiorari" games.[37] Krislov has demonstrated a method for calculating specific power ratios for various combinations of group voting on the court.[38] The most ambitious and advanced quantitative analysis of voting on the Supreme Court has been undertaken by using factor analysis in an extensive study of the Vincent and Warren Courts: Schubert's *The Judicial Mind* applies factor analysis to voting behavior patterns on the Court in order to analyze and to locate more precisely the structure of judicial behavior.[39] Differences and consistencies in judicial behavior, necessary for preparing data matrices as inputs, are derived by regression analysis and cumulative-scaling techniques. Correlational matrices provide the basic behavioral data for the analysis, while cumulative scales are used as criteria for the rotation of reference axes.

Schubert's findings corroborate and extend his view that voting behavior on the Supreme Court presents a structured and consistent institutional pattern. Generally, he finds, behavior on the Court is responsive to psychological factors, more specifically to a liberal ideology and attitudes and to a conservative ideology (there is no conservative attitude). In a foreword to the work, Harold Lasswell sees the research in *The Judicial Mind* as able to "bring out the residual perspective of the great revolutions of the eighteenth and nineteenth centuries."

As a whole, the quantitative investigations of the Supreme Court have become the most visible and influential examinations of judicial politics. Indeed, since political science began to turn away from legalistic methods in its examination of the judiciary, these works have constituted the leading systematic and critical research into a sector of the judicial system.

An important contribution of the quantitative studies of the Supreme Court has been to demonstrate that political-science analysis can be successfully utilized for judicial institutions and that the use of legal analysis for judicial studies is inadequate. Successful demonstrations of institutional differences and congruencies quite clearly have ruled out traditional mechanistic and syllogistic legal processes as models appropriate for a meaningful description of judicial behavior.

However, the most immediate and explicit usefulness of the judicial behavior studies has been in their institutional descriptions. For
the first time in judicial studies it became possible to delineate consistent behavior patterns that are the fundamental structure of institutions.

In recent years, some investigators have used mathematical extensions of behavioral models to predict Supreme Court outcomes.[40]
Such studies not only provide excellent checks on the reliability and
accuracy of studies of the Court's voting behavior, but they also fulfill one of the central functions of scientific effort, namely, the prediction of behavior. Simulation and experimental studies of judicial
behavior have, similarly, provided an opportunity for testing theories
of judicial behavior under rigorously controlled conditions.[41]

A more empirical analysis of the Supreme Court has been undertaken by Walter Murphy in his *Elements of Judicial Strategy*. Drawing data from the papers of several former chief justices as well as
from a variety of contemporary sources, he conceptualizes a number
of institutional functions the Court performs. By discussing such
functions as methods by which support is marshaled on the Court,
its relationship with lower federal courts, and strategies by which it
deals with other political agencies, Murphy conveys a much fuller
picture of a judicial institution than do studies of voting patterns.
His work also theorizes that the federal judiciary is a kind of
bureaucracy that is manipulated by the Supreme Court as director.
According to this bureaucratic theory of the federal judiciary, lower
courts are politically subordinate, and an important task of the
Supreme Court is to "manage" them.[42]

IV. NEW THEORETICAL DIRECTIONS

The explanatory power of quantitative studies of the Supreme
Court—despite their proliferation—has been questioned by Becker and
Jacob[43] in particular. Becker has commented that Schubert and
Spaeth find "satisfactory explanation in the coincidences of attitudes
of the judges as that factor which is responsible for described agreement and disagreement." He argues further that the judicial behavioral lists, as he calls them, "err in trying to explain behavior by
that behavior itself."

The argument over the usefulness of judicial-behavioralist studies
focuses on their disregard for sociological explanations of voting
behavior. Hypotheses about voting behavior of the Supreme Court
have been replicated on several occasions and have successfully
isolated meaningful dimensions of voting. But these judicial studies
have rarely attempted sociological explanations by linking voting
behavior with extracourt political and social variables, though, psychological linkages have been revealed in a number of studies. It is

obviously important to know whether a judge's behavior is linked to his political attitudes. Several kinds of attitudes may be used in establishing the connection. One type is a general political orientation such as conservatism or liberalism, and another concerns attitudes related to more specific behavior. Some evidence indicates that different attitude clusters are not necessarily correlated within individuals;[44] for example, persons who are generally conservative may identify with left-wing political parties. Studies of the Supreme Court have usually dealt with attitudes implied by specific behavior, with no indication of the judges' general political attitudes. It would seem possible, for example, for a judge to be generally conservative in social and political ideas yet manifest quite different ideas in his voting on the bench because of some feature of his judicial role.

A major limitation in the construction of a general theory of judicial institutions is the difficulty of generalizing from Supreme Court studies to the judiciary as a whole. The activities of the Supreme Court are so specialized that it seems hazardous to extend findings made concerning that organization to the operation of lower federal courts, state and local courts, or nonjudicial officials active in the judicial process. The implication that the courts exist in hierarchical form and function with the Supreme Court at the top of the arrangement, or the notion that the lower courts exist as a bureaucracy headed by the Supreme Court, giving form to its orders and directions, cannot be easily justified. Indeed, as Kenneth Dolbeare has pointed out, such models are misleading derivations of the "upper-court myth."[45]

Dolbeare suggests that a better model for judicial institutions would proceed from the perspective of ongoing local political processes (each with distinctive and local political culture-based approaches to the law-politics relationship) and would emphasize the discretionary power and multitude of decisions at each court level.[46] Although there is a little research experience with such a model, the theory would have the advantage of avoiding overgeneralization from the experience of the Supreme Court by suggesting variables that distinguish between types of courts. In contrast with existing literature on the Supreme Court, few examinations of lower or special federal-court decision making have been made.[47]

Equally in short supply are studies of state and local courts. We need considerably more study before an acceptable theory of that judicial subsystem can be constructed.[48] Among the few studies that have been made are those of the recruitment of state judges by Herbert Jacob,[49] of decision making in the Maryland Court of Appeals by Robert Sickels,[50] of role behavior in some state supreme courts by Kenneth Vines,[51] and of local trials by Dolbeare.[52] An over-all analysis of state courts remains a task for the future.[53]

Doubtless one of the factors retarding examination of state and local courts has been the idiosyncratic character of the operation of these agencies of government. It has not been possible to apply systematically the methods used to examine the national Supreme Court. For example, methods of analysis that utilize split opinions, such as bloc description, scalar presentation, and factor analysis, are not possible because fully three-quarters of state supreme courts have too few dissenting opinions to permit such study. In 1961 only 10 states had split votes in more than 10 percent of cases decided, and 20 state supreme courts had dissents in less than 5 percent of cases decided. Conflict within the national Supreme Court, which yields sufficient data to permit sophisticated quantitative analysis, is not manifest elsewhere in the courts of the federal system. Only the state of Pennsylvania, with its high dissent rate of about 30 percent, yields adequate information on voting behavior for an analysis of split opinions.[54]

State judges, however, are not more uniform in political behavior than other state officials or the judges of the national Supreme Court. Studies of judicial decision making indicate that differences in the backgrounds, experiences, and viewpoints of judges are reflected in the character of political behavior on the courts. However, voting patterns on the state collegial courts indicate that, unlike on the national Supreme Court, differences are not expressed in the decision votes.[55] Studies of decision making on state courts must investigate the process by which dissent is so frequently avoided and the means for reaching group consensus before the vote is recorded. Robert Sickels has suggested that something akin to legislative logrolling occurs in the Maryland Court of Appeals and that justices trade off support so that the majority-opinion writers usually command the consensual support of the justices.[56]

For somewhat different reasons, quantitative methods developed in Supreme Court studies are not very useful in studies of other federal appellate courts. A microanalysis of the appeals courts, for example, does not yield a sufficient number of split opinions for close analysis, although there are more dissents in these tribunals than in most state appellate courts.[57] Voting blocs evident in an examination of a limited period of time (one year or less) or of a particular policy area (civil liberties, for example) are not large enough for use as data in extensive quantitative analysis. Sheldon Goldman has shown that microanalysis of the appeals courts over several years can supply voting blocs for the purpose of studying judicial behavior.[58] Although useful as a general description of judicial behavior, such microanalysis does not supply a very detailed or discriminating investigation.

The panel composition of federal appeals courts poses even greater difficulties for bloc analysis.[59] Since appeals cases are heard by ad hoc committees which shift from case to case with different judges sitting on different cases, an individual judge reaches his decisions in varying contexts depending upon the composition of each panel. Judges pictured in a bloc make their decisions in different panels, unlike on the Supreme Court, where cases are decided *en banc* and judges usually decide cases in the company with the same judges. Because role factors are likely to differ considerably from one appellate body to another, voting blocs on the appeals courts must be interpreted with great caution. Bloc analysis must be supplemented by additional methods suitable to the character of decision making.

Whereas the national Supreme Court is the single most important institution in the American judiciary, trial courts on both the federal and state levels are responsible for decisions made at the most fundamental level of the judiciary. Trial courts are far more numerous than collegial appellate courts and hence affect a far greater number of persons. Not only is the number of cases initiated and settled greater in the trial courts, but also the activity carried on in these courts is decisive in structuring and defining the issues in the cases that are eventually appealed to higher courts. Thus, lack of research on these lower courts indicates a serious gap in our knowledge of judicial institutions.[60]

The tendency to focus largely on the Supreme Court has entailed a neglect of the study of trial-court judicial recruitment and institutional activities as well as of their decision-making processes. Decisions in trial courts are almost always made by individual judges; sociometric relational analysis is not, therefore, possible, and the decisions made by individual judges must be analyzed through comparison of decision making on common policies or concepts. Moreover, analysis of decision making in trial courts on the state and local levels is often not possible because such decisions are not published. Yet another problem in trial-court analysis is the large quantity of trial-court decisions, many of them on matters unfamiliar to students of constitutional law. Whereas the Supreme Court hears about 150 to 200 cases a year, many of them on major concepts of constitutional law, the federal district courts decide several thousand cases each year, many of them by jury trials and on regional and local issues. Such procedures as sampling of cases, coding of decisional characteristics, and comparative analysis are needed to render analysis of trial-court decision making meaningful research activity.[61]

Because of the amount of specialization in judicial research, and the lack of data on certain key areas, general treatments of judicial institutions are difficult to imagine. Two works, however, have successfully dealt with the judiciary as a whole and have looked at interrelationships and over-all factors. Glendon Schubert's *Judicial Policy Making*[62] examines judicial functions and relations within a framework of systems theory and relates all levels of court activity.

Herbert Jacob, in *Justice in America,* pulls together a wide variety of political and legal materials and organizes them into a politically meaningful conceptual framework.[63] Both works lack data on some crucial questions, and thus are partial theories useful only for particular areas of analysis.

As is the case within all subfields in political science, studies of the judiciary have been provincial in their reference and have generalized largely from the American experience. Judiciary scholars have been occupied with exploring sectors of the judicial system and have experimented with and perfected methods of analysis and of developing theory. Furthermore, material on non-American judiciaries has come largely from studies by anthropologists and legalists and has usually not treated the judiciary in the tradition established by political scientists, thus making comparison difficult and generalization hazardous. General treatments of comparative politics often do not deal with the judiciary at all, and when they do, treat it in formalistic and legalistic terms. The field of comparative politics has not produced any specialists in judicial institutions, and work on non-American judicial systems has tended to be an extension of the interests of scholars trained and experienced in the American judiciary.

Comparative studies have been under way for some time to broaden the scope of judicial studies, and a recent collaborative volume included studies of Japanese and Norwegian courts.[64] In 1965 a conference on cross-cultural studies of judicial institutions was held at the East-West Center of the University of Hawaii, leading to research on court systems in such countries as Australia, Japan, and the Philippines. Partly as a result of the conference, studies of the court systems of Japan, Germany, and Switzerland were included in a volume of research papers from the Shambaugh conference held at the University of Iowa in 1967.[65]

V. CONCLUDING REMARKS

The above survey of judicial-politics literature documents an exciting and forward-moving subfield in political science. One could argue, supported by the works cited above, that judicial politics, née public law, has moved rapidly and securely toward the goal of becoming a political science of the judiciary. Our mood of scholarly optimism should be tempered, however. One puzzle is the continued use of the term "public law" to identify the subfield of judicial studies on the part of traditional political scientists and, to some extent, judicial scholars themselves. The upsetting feature of this social lag in scientific terminology is that "public law" fails to capture the mood and the substance of the new scholarship in judicial politics that has made such pronounced progress, and recalls, instead, a legalistic past.

Even more disturbing is the failure of recently published work on general institutional and systems theory to include the findings of judicial politics and to extrapolate these into the theoretical structure. Such general works often simply omit judicial institutions or discuss them in traditional terms of a long-dead legalistic orientation.

Judicial studies seem to have been isolated from those of other political-science subfields for at least two reasons. As long as the analysis of judicial institutions defined judicial politics as public law, conceptualized and studied by methods endemic to the legal subculture, it developed a vocabulary and a set of methods somewhat marginal to the mainstream of political science. The turn of judicial studies to a more behavioral orientation brought new problems to light. Instead of embarking upon macroanalyses of judicial institutions, quantitative studies focused on the Supreme Court, the most visible component of judicial behavioralism, employing sophisticated methodology but a rather specialized frame of reference. More theoretically rich studies of judicial institutions have grown in number and scope in recent years. Today, different aspects of the judicial system are more frequently examined, and comparative analyses are more numerous.[66] General theories and comparative descriptions of the judicial system have accumulated, and our picture of judicial institutions becomes both more general and more informed.

NOTES

1. Glendon Schubert, "The Future of Public Law", *George Washington Law Review*, XXXIV (May 1966), 593-614.

2. See Richard Richardson and Kenneth N. Vines, *The Politics of Federal Courts*, (Boston: Little, Brown, 1969), Ch. I.

3. For example, Carl B. Swisher, *Roger B. Taney* (New York: Macmillan, 1935), and Charles Fairman, *Mr. Justice Miller and the Supreme Court 1862-1890* (Cambridge: Harvard University Press, 1939). For a more extended treatment of Supreme Court justices in relation to famous cases they decided see Rocco J. Tressolini, *Justice and the Supreme Court* (New York: Lippincott, 1963).

4. The standard work is Carl B. Swisher, *American Constitutional Development* (2nd ed.; Boston: Houghton Mifflin, 1954), in which the involvement of the Supreme Court in constitutional development is described; other courts, federal, state, and local, are hardly mentioned.

5. For example, an influential work was Edward S. Corwin, *Court Over Constitution* (Princeton: Princeton University Press, 1938).

6. Two such works were Jerome Frank, *Courts on Trial: Myth and Reality in American Justice* (Princeton: Princeton University Press, 1949), and Roscoe Pound, *Social Control Through Law* (Cambridge: Harvard University Press, 1942).

7. For example, Thomas Reed, *Report of the Committee on Policy, American Political Science Review*, XXIV (1930), supplement.

8. Albert Somit and Joseph Tanenhaus, *American Political Science* (New York: Atherton, 1964), p. 55.

9. George Everson, "The Human Element in Justice", *Journal of the American Institute of Criminal Law and Criminology*, X (May 1919), 90-94.

10. For example, Albert Somit, Joseph Tanenhaus, and Walter Wilke, "Aspects of Judicial Sentencing Behavior," *University of Pittsburgh Law Review*, XXI (June 1960), 613-619.

11. Felix Frankfurter and James M. Landis, *The Business of the Supreme Court* (New York: Macmillan, 1928).

12. Rodney L. Mott, Spencer D. Albright, and Helen R. Semmerling, "Judicial Personnel," *Annals of the American Academy of Political and Social Science*, CLXVII (September 1933), 143-155.

13. Edward W. Martin, *The Role of the Bar in Electing the Bench in Chicago* (Chicago: University of Chicago Press, 1936).

14. Malcolm Moos, "Judicial Elections and Partisan Endorsements of Judicial Candidates in Minnesota," *American Political Science Review*, XXXV (March 1941), 69-75.

15. Oliver Field, *Judicial Review of Legislation in Ten Selected States* (Bloomington: Bureau of Government Research, 1939).

16. Albert Lepawsky, *The Judicial System of Metropolitan Chicago* (Chicago: University of Chicago Press, 1932).

17. Rodney Mott, "Judicial Influence," *American Political Science Review*, XXX (March 1935), 295-315.

18. C. Herman Pritchett, *The Roosevelt Court* (New York: Macmillan, 1948).

19. Glendon Schubert, *Quantitative Analysis of Judicial Behavior* (Glencoe: Free Press, 1959).

20. Jack W. Peltason, *Federal Courts in the Political Process* (Garden City: Doubleday, 1955).

21. Herbert Jacob and Kenneth N. Vines, "The Role of the Judiciary in American State Politics," *Judicial Decision Making*, ed. Glendon Schubert (New York: Free Press, 1963).

22. Victor G. Rosenblum, *Law as a Political Instrument* (New York: Random House, 1955).

23. John R. Schmidhauser, *The Supreme Court: Its Politics, Personalities, and Procedures* (New York: Holt, Rinehart, & Winston, 1960).

24. Clement Vose, "Litigation as a Form of Pressure Group Activity," *Annals of the American Academy of Political and Social Science*, CCCXIX (June 1958), 20-31.

25. Stuart Nagel, "Political Party Affiliation and Judges' Decisions," *American Political Science Review*, LV (December 1961), 843-851; Nagel "Ethnic Affiliation and Judicial Propensities," *Journal of Politics*, XIV (February 1962), 92-110.

26. Jack W. Peltason, "A Political Science of Public Law," *Southwestern Social Science Quarterly*, XXXIV (June 1953), 51-56.

27. John P. Roche, "Political Science and Political Fiction," *American Political Science Review*, LII (December 1958), 1026-1030.

28. Wallace Mendelson, "The Neo-Behavioral Approach to the Judicial Process: A Critique," *American Political Science Review*, LVII (September 1963), 593-603.

29. Ibid., 595.

30. Ibid., 599.

31. Eugene V. Rostow, "American Legal Realism and the Sense of the Profession," *Rocky Mountain Law Review*, XXXIV (Winter 1962), 123-149.

32. Mendelson, op. cit., 603.

33. Schubert, op. cit.

34. For a summary of the work of Schmidhauser, Spaeth, Schubert, and Ulmer on scaling see: Joseph Tanenhaus, "The Cumulative Scaling of Judicial Decisions," *Harvard Law Review*, LXXIX (June 1966), 1583-1594.

35. Joel Grossman, "Role Playing and the Analysis of Judicial Behavior: The Case of Mr. Justice Frankfurter," *Journal of Public Law*, XI (#2, 1962), 285-298.

36. Tanenhaus, op. cit.

37. Schubert, *Quantitative Analysis of Judicial Behavior*, pp. 192-210.

38. Samuel Krislov, "Power and Coalition in a Nine-Man Body," *American Behavioral Scientist*, VI (April 1963), 24-26.

39. Glendon Schubert, *The Judicial Mind* (Evanston: Northwestern University Press, 1965).

40. For example, Fred Kort, "Simultaneous Equations and Boolean Algebra in the Analysis of Judicial Decisions," *Jurimetrics*, XXVIII (Winter 1963), 143-163.

41. For example, Werner F. Grunbaum, "Analytical and Simulation Models for Explaining Judicial Decision-Making," *Frontiers of Judicial Research*, eds. Joel Grossman and Joseph Tanenhaus (New York: Wiley, 1969); Theodore L. Becker, *Political Behavioralism and Modern Jurisprudence* (Chicago: Rand McNally, 1964).

42. Walter Murphy, *Elements of Judicial Strategy* (Chicago: University of Chicago Press, 1964).

43. Becker, op. cit., Ch. I; Herbert Jacob, review of Schubert's *The Judicial Mind*, *Wisconsin Law Review* (Summer 1967).

44. See Herbert McCloskey, "Conservatism and Personality," *American Political Science Review*, LII (March 1958), 27-45; Bernard R. Berelson, Paul F. Lazarsfeld, and William N. McPhee, *Voting* (Chicago: University of Chicago Press, 1954), pp. 198 ff.

45. Kenneth Dolbeare, "Urban Politics in a Federal District Court," Grossman and Tanenhaus, op. cit., 173.

46. Ibid, p. 175.

47. In addition to Dolbeare see Richard J. Richardson and Kenneth N. Vines, *The Politics of Federal Courts* (Boston: Little, Brown, 1969) and Vines, "Review, Dissent and the Appellate Process," *Journal of Politics*, XXIX (August 1967), 597-616; also Vines, "Federal District Judges and Race Relations Cases in the South," *Journal of Politics*, XXVI (May 1964), 337-358.

48. See Jacob and Vines, op. cit.

49. Herbert Jacob, "The Effect of Institutional Differences in the Recruitment Process," *Journal of Public Law*, XIII (#1, 1964), 104-119.

50. Robert J. Sickels, "The Illusion of Judicial Consensus: Zoning Decisions on the Maryland Court of Appeals," *American Political Science Review*, LIX (March 1965), 100-104.

51. Kenneth N. Vines, "The Judicial Role in the American States: An Exploration," Grossman and Tanenhaus, op. cit.

52. Kenneth Dolbeare, *Trial Courts in Urban Politics* (New York: Wiley, 1967).

53. Kenneth N. Vines, "Courts as Political Governmental Agencies"; Herbert Jacob and Kenneth Vines, *Politics in the American States* (Boston: Little, Brown, 1965), 239-291.

54. On voting behavior in state courts see Henry Glick and Kenneth N. Vines, *State Courts* (forthcoming).

55. Ibid.

56. Sickels, op. cit.

57. Richardson and Vines, "Review, Dissent and the Appellate Process."

58. Sheldon Goldman, "Voting Behavior on the United States Court of Appeals," *American Political Science Review,* LX (June 1966), 374-383.

59. Richardson and Vines, *The Politics of Federal Courts,* Ch. VI.

60. For implementation of this point see the works of Dolbeare already cited.

61. See the methodology in Richardson and Vines, *The Politics of Federal Courts.*

62. Glendon Schubert, *Judicial Policy Making* (Chicago: Scott, Foresman, 1965).

63. Herbert Jacob, *Justice in America* (Boston: Little, Brown, 1965)

64. Schubert, *Judicial Decision Making.*

65. Grossman and Tannenhaus, op. cit.

66. See, for example, the collection in David Danelski and Glendon Schubert (eds.), *Comparative Judicial Behavior* (forthcoming).

6 Judicial Theory

THEODORE L. BECKER, University of Hawaii

> Might not the catastrophe of Charles I have been prevented by the mere transposition of words? —*Jeremy Bentham*

I. INTRODUCTION

One of the principal objects of this essay is to dramatize a past and current narrowness and shallowness in the work of many political scientists professionally committed to the study of the law and courts. By and large these scholars have been limited by the questions they have posed, the materials they have chosen to study, and by the approaches to knowledge they have employed. Up to now, their orientation has permitted them to define and thus to delimit the field of public law.

The main body of subject matter of the field of public law has been, and continues to be, a presentation and analysis of appellate-court decisions, principally those of the Supreme Court of the United States, and some description of the judicial structure of the federal government and, occasionally, state governments. The overriding emphasis is on the American system.

By analogy, the field of public law would resemble the field of international relations if *that* field consisted exclusively of two courses: one on American Foreign Policy (using a case approach) and one called Organization and Procedures of the American State Department. This is not to say that such courses do not belong in a field of international relations; but they could by no means be said to comprise its central part.

In the past fifteen years or so, such political scientists as Harold Lasswell, C. Herman Pritchett, Jack Peltason, Henry J. Abraham, Victor Rosenblum, Kenneth Vines, Walter Murphy, and Glendon Schubert made contributions to the study of courts in politics that

■ An earlier version of one part of this essay appeared in "Judicial Structure and Its Political Functioning in Society," *Journal of Politics*, XXIX (March 1967), 302-333. This essay, in much the same form, will be published as the Introduction to *Comparative Judicial Politics* (Chicago: Rand McNally, 1970).

went far beyond legalistic case analysis and the legal structural description mentioned above. Moreover, a rapidly growing group of younger political scientists follows in their footsteps.[1] Yet, it seems to me, that the steadily increasing weight of the body is still too heavy for all these extra legs to move it very far. The trouble is that many of the first wave of innovative political scientists in this field were actually bound more than they thought by traditional ways and by traditional fascinations. In other words, they were liberal rather than radical.[2] Had they been radical, an equivalent force of their number and of the ranks of their followers might have wrought a more significant and important change in direction. Today it seems even more appropriate to suggest a reconceptualization of the field, that is, to suggest alterations capable of qualitatively broadening the traditional concerns. The main point is that we *must* drop the label "public law" immediately. It is not particularly euphonious; it hardly evokes nostalgia; it misleads the uninitiated; and it has absolutely no relationship to the development of any theory whatsoever.

A few words about the process of reconceptualizing a field or subfield of study are appropriate at this point. I believe that the criteria established to guide the process of formulating or reformulating concepts should be the same as those employed in the natural and social sciences; for where goals are similar (that is, the development and redevelopment of conceptual tools to improve teaching and to further empirical research in a discipline), the sciences and their procedures are excellent models to follow. First of all, each new or redefined concept must refer to observable, distinguishable phenomena. Second, operations involving quantification should be devised. Third, each concept must have substantial lexical grounding.[3] To put this latter point another way, it is desirable to avoid the kind of in-group jargonizing which creates ill will, duplication of effort, and confusion in the literature. Coining of words ought to be kept to a minimum; traditional concepts ought to be used with as close an adherence to their general usage as is consistent with a maximum degree of precision. To subscribe to these criteria is to favor the fostering of eventual understanding of the world about us through making (1) the relationship between the world and our vocabulary as clear as possible and (2) the relationship between our past and present efforts at gaining knowledge as cooperative as possible. I realize that I am simply calling for the performance of a task that has been underway for some time now in other areas of political science. Also, I am aware of the fact that several theoretical frameworks have been advanced recently concerning the subject matter traditionally conceived as being that of public law.[4] Unfortunately, although they have all been highly sophisticated they have suffered from one basic flaw. Each of them, again fascinated by traditional concern, has used the United States Supreme Court as the central area of concern. Though a theory of the Supreme Court would be a step in the right direction, it is also quite limited. An even further step would be a theory about courts in general—*judicial theory*, as it were. More specifically, it is our lot to come up with a theory of the interrelationships between judiciaries (of all kinds and at all levels) and the entire political system.

I suggest that we redefine the field of public law, at least partially, in terms of "courts," "the judicial structure," or "the judicial process" as that phenomenon interacts with "politics." I claim no originality in using and combining these words. Murphy and Pritchett have employed these concepts in the title of their reader, *Courts, Judges, and Politics,* in which they note:

The attention of most lawyers and scholars of the law has been primarily on the law produced, not on the process by which it was produced... But political scientists have sought more and more to develop an approach to the judicial process which would give activities of the courts new meaning by placing them within the mainstream of political relationships.[5]

Although Murphy and Pritchett and others have utilized and interrelated these general concepts, they have presented the linkage implicitly and unsystematically and, as I have noted, with an acute case of American myopia. To be sure, they have discussed interconnections between some of their abstractions, but they have taken only one step on a long journey. What follows is a second step—an explication of each of the main concepts (as I see them) and of some of the mechanics of their interrelationship.

II. THE CONCEPTS OF FUNCTION, STRUCTURE, AND COURT

The concept judicial function is frequently employed synonymously with the concept of court, but the description of that function entails so much that is turns out to describe very little. Some time ago, Frank Goodnow stated that the judicial function is really only part of the law-enforcement function. And in 1944 Charles Beard said that "from another point of view the judiciary may be regarded as an executive organ engaged in the interpretation, application and enforcement of the law."[6] Recently, a widely used book in current political-science introductory courses pointed out that the judicial function is the "enforcement of law through legal or court process[es]."[7] The same book also notes, as do so many others, that the judiciary is a policy maker; and policy making is ordinarily considered to be the function of the legislature and the executive. Indeed, the courts' function as policy maker has now been widely

accepted by political scientists. Therefore we find the courts functioning in forming policy, enforcing it, and interpreting it. Apparently,
courts and other judicial institutions perform nearly all of the
customary governmental functions. It should be noted that writings in
political science contain many similar formulations concerning legislatures and executives. All too often we find that the executives, the
legislators, and administrative agencies are described as engaging in, or
being defined by, the functions of making, interpreting, and enforcing
policy. These words utterly fail as primary definitional terms insofar
as they fail to discriminate between separate phenomena.

   Political scientists also tend to interchange the words "branch" and
"power" with "function." Accordingly, I believe them to be dealing
implicitly in a functional type of definition. Certainly if "branch,"
"power," and "function" are not being used synonymously, no one
bothers to specify the differences. A representative example of the
intermingling of these particular concepts is found in a recent edition
of a widely used textbook written by Alpheus T. Mason and William
M. Beaney:

Our fundamental law separates and limits power, even as it confers
it. Congress is endowed with "legislative" *power:* it may not, therefore
(except as a result of a specific grant or by implication), exercise
executive or judicial *power.* The same restrictions apply to the other
branches of the national government: the terms judicial *power* and
executive *power,* like legislative *power,* have a technical meaning. In
the exercise of their respective *functions,* neither Congress, President
nor Judiciary may, under the principle of separation of *powers,*
encroach on fields allocated to the other *branches* of government.[8]

   One is forced to conclude that there is either a fundamental confusion in conceptualization or no distinctive governmental phenomena
to study. Do all branches have all powers and all functions? Surely,
our concepts should be isomorphic with an empirical reality; there
ought to be considerable correspondence between our concepts and
their empirical referents. If all is indeed such confusion in reality,
then confusion in our conceptualization is understandable, if not
justifiable. I do not happen to think this is true. In other words, I
believe that there are distinguishable governmental phenomena in the
societies of the world that can be separated for purposes of conceptual clarity. For example, I think that there are distinguishable
phenomena that can be called courts, councils, or whatever, but that
words like branch, function, law enforcement, or policy making are
quite inadequate for making such distinctions as traditionally and
presently employed. Much politico-juridical theory rests upon the
assumption that there are structural differences in various governmental phenomena; but the traditional-legalistic usage of such terms
as structure, function, branch, and power has been less than helpful

in our search for knowledge on the interaction and consequences of these phenomena.

Perhaps a look from another perspective will provide a clearer comprehension of my concern. When a committee of Congress is listening to witnesses in a hearing or an investigation, what goal is served by referring to this panel as being "quasi-judicial" or as having a "quasi-judicial function"? Do the Congressmen *really* constitute a court? Or, are they a half-court? A semicourt? Perhaps they are a pseudocourt? Were Gestapo inquests "courts"? Is a "kangaroo court" situation best defined by using the word "court"? Or are all of the above designations sloppy uses of the English language? Did the man wearing a black robe and called "Judge" Thayer, and the man called the "district attorney," and the "jury" that tried Sacco and Vanzetti *really* constitute a court? Were the "proletarian courts" of 1919 Soviet Russia or are today's People's Courts in the USSR (when they interpret the Anti-Parasite Law) *really* courts? Are the men who hear some of the sit-in demonstration cases against Negroes in the South *really* "judges"? Several ACLU lawyers reported a proceeding in 1963 in which a man came out of a chamber marked "Judge" wearing a pistol over a black robe and carrying a copy of the decision—before the argument was made. Was such a proceeding "quasi-judicial," "semijudicial," or "almost judicial"? After all, he was wearing a black robe, he was inside a "courtroom," and he did present an argument and a decision.

The above set of questions might be so construed as to categorize the author as a Platonist. This would be in error because there is no assumption made that these questions deal in what Hermann Kantorowicz has called "verbal realism,"[9] which is very similar to what usually is called real or true definitions. Although I employ the word "really," I do not claim that one can know that the "essential" court exists or what the "real" definition of the word "court" is. What I mean is that it is useful to separate in one's mind various political phenomena existing in the world from other social-political phenomena, with the aid of a series of verbal symbols. Whether these phenomena have any importance in understanding politics can only be revealed by study. One such phenomena frequently is defined as "court," and this phenomenon can be distinguished from others labeled "legislature," "inquisition," and the like. As I have noted above, political-science jargon has obscured differences between what is frequently termed in its lexicon as "court," from the phenomena often termed "legislature" and "inquisition," under a mass of prefixes and qualifications and through a tautological usage of the concept of "function."

As a result of this confusion, the understanding and testing of politico-juridical theory has been hindered, and the development of wider and more comprehensive and incisive political-juridical theory has been retarded. Sadly, we have conducted very little research into the structural nature of "courts" and into what results they can and do achieve. My first job, then, must be to isolate a politically relevant reality through precisely defining "judicial structure" or "judicial process" or "court." These concepts, together with that of function," seem to me to have great potential in helping us understand and redevelop past and present politico-juridical theory.

At the outset, I must confess that I think it will be most parsimonious *and* fruitful to adopt the sociological concepts of structure and function in our effort to develop judicial theory. I also think that little would be gained for the purpose of this volume by engaging either Kingsley Davis[10] or Irving Louis Horowitz[11] in a polemic over the value of structural-functional analysis of undertaking a more philosophical discussion on structural-functionalism with such scholars as Carl Hempel and Ernest Nagel.[12] However, several points made in a recent essay by Walter Goldschmidt seem worth treating, for his arguments, made to persuade social scientists to abandon structural-functional analysis, have some merit, and help to clarify my limited goals.

One of Goldschmidt's major points is that the attempt to compare structures and institutions cross-culturally is doomed to failure, as it is an attempt at a "comparison of incomparables."[13] According to Goldschmidt, there is not a substantial enough similarity in institutions from society to society: "What is consistent from culture to culture is not the institution; what is consistent are the social problems. What is recurrent from society to society is solutions to these problems."[14] He suggests that the best approach is one he calls *comparative functionalism*—since all societies have the same problems to solve, these problems should be basic units for comparative analysis, for the methods toward solution (that is, institutions, structures) vary so greatly.

Goldschmidt's contention is persuasive. Still, I am not so certain that it should sway political scientists at this stage in the development of the discipline and particularly those who would pursue the development of judicial theory or the study of judicial politics. Sciences must grow as they can grow, given their peculiar circumstances. Sometimes it may be necessary to use a conceptual device that can guide and stimulate the collection and analysis of information in order to test some durable, though possibly confusing, theories. In the study of case-law and courts, concepts akin to those of structure and function as used in sociology and anthropology have a peculiar pervasiveness in the existent theory. It is for this reason that I believe structural-functional analysis as practiced in sociology and anthropology will help to illuminate gaps and resolve ambiguities in that theory as well as to provide a framework by which much important information that can be relevant to subsequent testing of hypotheses can be gathered. The question may be asked, and correctly, "Must you make the same mistakes?" My answer must be "Yes," for in this case it is primarily important to ask questions in a way that will be understood, and to motivate field research where heretofore there has been very little. What may be a fatal mistake to an old man may be priceless help to an adolescent.

There is one further reservation to Goldschmidt's argument. Goldschmidt's solution appears to be vulnerable to the same charge he makes against structural-functional analysis. Why should one, for instance, accept the assumption that social problems (the focus of comparative functionalism) are more precisely classifiable than the attempted institutional solutions? The so-called needs of man are, at this point in time, so intricately mixed into the cultural solutions as to make them next to indistinguishable. Furthermore, so long as researchers remember that the culturally bound conceptualizations they employ in structural-functional analysis are simply verbal conventions and flexible approximations, there would seem to be little damage done to the collection of data or the analysis that follows. Of course structures vary from place to place and over time—but there may well be come core structural phenomena that are classifiable and that do have great multicultural existence. Why not study where that core exists and where it does not? Why not study the variations of phenomena around that core; that is, variations in the structure? In other words, though Goldschmidt's alternative is appealing, it is not compelling.

For our teaching and research purposes, then, I think it would be fruitful to use the term *structure* when there is a reasonably close correspondence between, on the one hand, defined and expected formal and informal behavior patterns set by rule, custom, and law, and on the other hand, some actual adherence by participants within a system. In other words, structure, whether *systemic* or *procedural,* is a pattern of consistent behavior observed between the laws *and* customs (rules, statutes, constitutions) of a group, association, or society, and the human behavior within that system. If the norms of custom and law differ, there may be no structure. That would depend on behavioral patterns. If behavior is substantially consistent with either law or custom, the expectancy-behavioral convergence would comprise the extant social structure in that system. In light of the tendency towards merger of custom (as expected behavior) and most people's behavior in that customary or legal system, there is some difference between my concept of structure and that employed by Fred Riggs. He states:

A structure is defined as any pattern of behavior which has become a standard feature of a social system. Thus, a government bureau is a "structure," or rather a whole set of structures consisting of the many things the officials in the bureau do regularly: the decisions they make, the people they see, the papers they sign. The structure is not composed of the people and things themselves, but *of their actions.* It does not include all their actions, but only those actions which relate to the goals and work of the bureau. The bureau also includes relevant actions of "outsiders" with whom it interacts on the normal course of business, its *clientele* or "audience." They may be served or regulated by it; they may be the subjects as well as the objects of its activity.[15]

The difference between Riggs' usage and my own lies simply in the fact that I choose to take behavioral-expectation, particularly custom or laws, into account whereas Riggs does not. Riggs is not at all concerned with formalized or traditional expectations. My concern with such expectations is the effect of their violation on the superego, for such violation undermines (makes invisible or unstable) prior or latent structural-behavioral regularities. I am also willing to take such psychological concepts as belief systems and attitude patterns into account as elements in structure or at least as strong indicators of it. The concept of structure, then, as I define it, is closely akin to Marion Levy's concept of "analytic" structure in contrast with "concrete" structure.[16]

The sociological concept of *function,* as contrasted with the civics type discussed above, is one which some modern political scientists ostensibly have adopted to assist them in the behavioral study of politics. In fact, in its new garb, one might say that the concept of function is now fashionable on the political science scene. It seems to me, however, that such political scientists as David Easton[17] and Gabriel Almond[18] may have misapplied the notion of function to which they seem oriented, for they appear to define it differently from a sociological consensus that seems to exist on the content of that term. They too have equated the word "function" to what political science institutionalists call "branch." Perhaps they have refined the concept of branch a bit, and surely they have broken down that which government does into a myriad of components. Yet modern political science's concept of function seems much the same as the traditional political science concept, and resembles the sociological term only barely.

Robert Merton discusses the term "function"—and this is important to understand—in the following way:

It is the fifth connotation which is central to functional analysis as this has been practiced in sociology and social anthropology. Stemming in part from the native mathematical sense of the term, this usage is more often explicitly adapted from the biological sciences, where the term function is understood to refer to the vital or organic processes considered in the respects in which they contribute to the maintenance of the organism.[19]

Merton then goes on to say:

Radcliffe-Brown is the most often explicit in tracing his work conception of social function to the analogical model found in the biological sciences. After the fashion of Durkhein, he asserts that the function of a recurrent physiological process is thus a correspondence between it and the needs (i.e., the necessary condition of existence) of the "organism." And on the social sphere where human beings, "the essential units," are connected by networks of social relations with an integrated whole, the function of any recurrent activity, such as the punishment of crime, or a funeral ceremony, is the part it plays in the social life as a whole and therefore the *contribution* it makes to the maintenance of the structural continuity.[20]

Now, Merton does not really *define* function, although some cite his statement, "social function refers to observable, *objective consequences* and *not* to subjective dispositions,"[21] as a definition. It seems to me, however, that what Merton, Radcliffe-Brown and others have said quite clearly is that structure is one thing, *effect* of structure quite another. In other words, function as a concept referring to something structural or processlike does not exist in a static state. We can only speak of nonexistence ("X is not functioning"), and shades of existence of an actual functioning relationship ("X is not functioning to peak capacity, and a repair in structure is needed to maximize the effect that is desired."). As Riggs would have it: "Thus a function is a ... *relationship between variables.*"[22] In linking this concept of function with those of structure and system, Robert Holt states:

It is typical for those who have made important contributions to functionalism to define function more or less explicitly as an *effect*. Merton speaks of functions as "observed consequences"; Radcliffe-Brown refers to "functions of any recurrent activity"; Levy, more explicit than most, defines function as "a condition or state of affairs resultant from the operation of a structure through time." Hempel points out with devastating simplicity, however, that the term *function* cannot be used synonymously with the term *effect*. He presents the following statement for consideration: "the heartbeat has the function of producing the heart sounds; for the heartbeat has that effect." No functionalist would accept this proposition. Function is not a synonym for effect; it is a subtype of effect. Functions are system relevant effects of structures. The term has meaning, therefore, only if the terms of structure and system relevant are explicitly defined and if the system under study is explicitly identified.[23]

Thus, it seems to me that Almond's and Coleman's idea of a governmental (judicial) function being to "interpret the rules" falls more comfortably within the concept of structure. After all, is this not simply a description of a pattern of behavior of certain men playing certain roles? So it would be with "apply the rules," "policy-making," and "judicial review." Categorization of such activities as "functions" is something that Glendon Schubert, too, seems to have misunderstood, since he discusses the "function" of judicial review to be "to *consider* the constitutionality of acts."[24] This error finds persistent and widespread acceptance. Kenneth Dolbeare has also noticed the fact that judicial scholars use the concept of function as being a synonym of decision making, that is, "interpret the laws."[25] Another recent illustration of this usage is in "The Judicial Process" chapter of Alexander Dragnich and John Wahlke's *Government and Politics.*[26] Therein one discovers the "political functions" of the "legal system," and they, as usual, include judicial review, which is simply a type of rule-interpretation, and thus a structural variation.

III. DEFINITION OF THE CONCEPT "COURT"

A good place to locate widely accepted definitions of a concept in any field is in an introductory textbook. Dell Hitchener and William Harbold, for instance, describe the "essential nature" (verbal realism) of a "court," as follows: (1) it "administers justice" (a functional type of relationship); (2) it is "the provision by the state of an impartial judge to decide a cause" (structural factor involving normative, formal expectation), and (3) "the third characteristic of the judicial process is its conduct by determinate standards that causes disputes to be resolved according to law. It is this feature of the proceedings which gives the qualities or order and predictability to the disposition of individual interests..." (structural and functional).[27] Similarly, but more lengthily, we have political scientist Herman Finer's structural notion:

The Courts of Justice: ... their whole procedure has been built up on the basis of impartial umpireship between two parties. They have had no personal interest in the result, for they are irremovable, exempted from suit for any fault; there is little question of promotion; and the acceptance of gifts is forbidden .... Procedure makes the discovery and presentation of all evidence fully possible, and gives all parties the opportunity of stating their case with expert help. Proceedings are public; reports are published; records are kept; and precedents have weight. Moreover, the principles of the law, as they are taught, include these things, and they are revered ... counsel comes before a court with strict etiquette, presided over by justices who jealously guard the traditional morals of the profession. These things produce definite principles which all may know with considerable certainty, and a process and convention on impartial and impersonal attention to the claims of the parties.[28]

And, according to a prominent jurist,

... the conclusive reason why judicial independence is necessary is that without it there can be, properly speaking, no judgment and no judge.[28]

A fuller examination of the relevant materials would take us little further, for I believe the above excerpts contain the ingredients of that mixture known as a "judicial structure" or a "court." A *court* is (1) a man or body of men (2) who have power to decide a dispute, (3) where the parties or advocates or their surrogates present the facts of the dispute and cite existent, expressed, primary normative principles (in statutes, constitutions, rules, and previous cases) that (4) are applied by that man or those men, (5) who *believe* that they should listen to the presentation of facts and apply such cited normative principles "impartially," "objectively," or with detachedness" ("judicial role," "bungageli"),[30] and (6) that they may so decide, and (7) as an "independent" body.

Two of the concepts used above will require some explication at this point because (1) they serve as important boundary points as to what constitutes a court (if they are not present in reality, the decision-making institution will not be classified as a court), and (2) once present, as they vary, they comprise a structural shading (in degree or kind) of that particular court. The concepts are those of "impartiality" and "independence." In both cases, in order for the observer to include a particular man or decision-making body of a given society within the confines of the concept "court" (contrasted with non-court) there must be a visible manifestation that the society expects (and in interaction with this, the relevant decision makers themselves expect) a measure of impartiality in the decision makers, and/or that the body have a measure of independence. Vilhelm Aubert, a noted Norwegian sociologist, in his own recent conceptualization of "court," had this to say: "The nature of the particular 'service' which judges contribute, its origin in a conflict between two parties, implies that the service can only be contributed when an atmosphere of objectivity prevails."[31]

A manifestation or indicator of "impartiality" can be (I simply make a stipulation at this point of research) simply a formulized, visual norm (for example, a constitutional provision, a law, or a ritual), or it could be made ostensible through the existence of some trappings of political insulation. Some actual objective *behavior* must be discovered, however, before we know that impartiality exists—at least to a minimal degree—in other words, that it is possible because it has happened.

Perhaps a few words about the usage of "impartiality," "objectivity," and "detachedness" might be in order. At this point, I intend to use the terms interchangeably, though it may become necessary in the near future to make distinctions. For instance, employing the term "impartiality" runs a risk if a scholar confuses the decision-making process with its output. Torstein Eckhoff, a well-known Scandinavian scholar, asks how a judge who strictly applied Nazi laws to Jews could be considered impartial (from the pro-Jewish point of view).[32] Since the law was highly partial to this group, the resulting decisions could not be considered impartial. In the study of judicial politics—from my perspective—*impartiality* will be conceived of as only applying to the decision-making process; it is tantamount to the concept of "objectivity." It might be easier on the nerves of some to say that a judge can objectively (rather than impartially) apply a partial law—but it is no clearer once one recognizes that we are primarily concerned with structure and process when we speak of impartiality.

Independence in decision making, it seems to me, can be manifested by some decisions which are clearly in opposition to other politically significant decision makers in society. Only one such instance need be found in order to classify the decision maker as "independent" and the structure as a court. It would have, at that point, only the minimum degree of independence. Of course, the degree of independence of courts varies greatly from society to society. Finally, "independence" as used in relationship to the advocates is not meant to imply that the parties themselves or their relatives may not argue the case.

Several elements of this definition are arbitrary. Items number three and five above include the structural factors of the presentation and application of some normative principles—formal or informal—but extant and theoretically compelling. This inclusion is probably best explained by the fact that the author is a product of the Anglo-American law school tradition. This tradition is based on the assumption that both of these structural factors may be incorporated into any societal decision-making situation in the hope that they will provide for a measure of impartiality in the authoritative allocation of values for the society. It is this requirement of impartiality in judgment that is necessary in my working concept of the judiciary.[33]

Nevertheless, it is equally clear that there are ways that impartiality can be accomplished other than by the presentation and application of law and custom. Impartiality also can be achieved by reliance on chance factors just as well as on the use of reason in the application of law.[34] After all, the person desiring judicial impartiality who is hauled before a court for judgment need be concerned with the fact that the judge's own biases *toward him* do not dictate his decision making in the name of society. A judge who is free to vent personal animosities to a litigant is a feared instrument, and an impartial determination of innocence or guilt is valued highly in many societies. Obviously the application of generally applicable, rigidly applied normative rules is only one way for this impartiality to be guaranteed. Man has devised other ways such as trial by ordeal and trial by combat. Also, E. Adamson Hoebel has described the Eskimo "song duel" as a "juridical form" which would not be a court within our definition.[35] Hoebel notes that victory in this proceeding is the result of "singing skill," which would then exclude the song duel as a "court" within my definition, as it has a basis of impartiality other than that of application of a primary normative principle.

A few words about the concept of "expressed, primary normative principles" are also in order because this phrase has a few ambiguities that would best be eliminated. Solomon, as King, in the famous "cut-the-baby-in-half" parable, was not acting as a judge (was not a "court" in a legal sense) because he was not applying or interpreting any *expressed* normative principles. What principles were actually involved? The whole decision-making process in the fable was little more than a gimmick; it was a guess; it was a clever prediction about the "true" response of "motherly love." The only "law" involved was a behavioral one rather than a normative one, about the reaction of a mother under certain conditions. There was surely no specific rule applied. A different situation that would also have to be classified as one without expressed rules is the one in which the early Soviet "judges" were empowered to interpret "the interests of the proletariat." The interpretative leeway was so great here for each "judge" that only the most amorphous sort of subjectively defined "justice" could really be applied. There were no guides for the decision maker. There was no precedent and no tradition to apply to those words. A *judge* (a judicial decision maker) interprets reasonably definite, expressed prescriptions, and if the words are extremely vague, one would have to find at least some historical fact that guides the judge as to specific applications. I think that Alf Ross, the noted Scandinavian jurisprudent, is in accord with me. He put it this way:

The judge shall not be like the Homeric king who received his *themistes* direct from Zeus, or like the Oriental cadi who makes his decision out of an esoteric wisdom. The idea of the supremacy of law makes us react against the tendency in the totalitarian states to authorize the judge, disregarding all fixed rules, to decide according to the "sound legal consciousness of the people" or "the interests of the proletariat"—which we look upon as a denial of the very idea of law. [36]

IV. THE CONCEPT OF "POLITICS"

Harold D. Lasswell, in one of his enduring and celebrated works, has defined the practice of politics as "who gets what, when, how." [37] In the same work, he defines the study of politics as the "study of influence and the influential." Implicitly crucial to both of these definitions is the concept of "values." Values are the "what" in the first Lasswell definition and are what one wants to wield influence for in the second. Of course, there are many values—and Lasswell has been in the process of refining his typology for many years. In the early 1960's, Lasswell's value classification scheme was as follows:

1. Wealth
2. Power (for example, a higher office or a voice in a party council)
3. Respect (favorable publicity)
4. Well-being (luxurious entertainment)
5. Affection (acceptance in a family circle)
6. Enlightenment (inside dope)
7. Skill (access to advanced training)
8. Rectitude (moral support from a cynical group)[38]

This specific set of values might be helpful in our explication of the concept of politics, since it is reasonably extensive and specific.

David Easton has offered what is probably the most widely professionally quoted and professionally accepted definition of politics—or at least of the concept "the political system." I mention it here to emphasize the place of the concept of value in a definition of politics. According to Easton, politics is "the authoritative allocation of values for a society."[39] Unfortunately, Easton says little here about values as such. No typology is advanced; no detail is supplied.

On the other hand, Dahl and Lindblom have worked out an intricate adaptation of Lasswell's delineation:

The important prime goals of human beings in Western societies include existence or survival, physiological gratification (through food, sex, sleep and comfort), love and affection, respect, self-respect, power or control, skill, enlightenment, novelty and many others. These are the ultimate criteria by which we would like to test alternative politico-economic devices. But to use criteria of this kind would force one to a level of specificity that would require an encyclopedia of particular techniques.

On the other hand, there are seven goals that govern both the degree to which these prime goals of individuals are attained and the manner of deciding who is to attain his goals when individuals conflict in their goals seeking .... These seven instrumental goals are freedom, rationality, democracy, subjective equality, security, progress, and appropriate inclusion.[40]

The specificity of the value systems afforded by Dahl, Lindblom, and Lasswell helps us see certain problems more clearly. For instance, keeping these more specific list of values in mind and thinking about what courts (for instance in the U.S.) ordinarily do, the realms of *courts* and *politics* become wider than commonly conceived:

1. When a court grants a divorce, this is an authoritative allocation of freedom and perhaps also of well-being. Is this decree of divorce a

political act by the court? Should political scientists be interested in this type of subject matter?

2. When a court acquits a defendant in a burglary case, it again is authoritatively allocating well-being and reinforcing the value of freedom and well-being to the defendant. Should the political scientist be interested in this type of decision as such (that is, without raising any due process or similar issues)? What about a court's decision in favor of a tenant in an eviction case? Is this "political"?

3. When a court awards a plaintiff money in a tort case, is it authoritatively allocating wealth? Is that politics? Political scientists almost totally ignore such subject matter—at least traditionally. Yet political scientists would be interested in a decision by a court which held a corporation merger to be the creation of a monopoly. But is not that tort case an authoritative allocation of wealth? Why does political science emphasize the values of power—economic power (different from wealth?)—in the monopoly case? Under scrutiny, has this distinction any conceptual foundation? If wealth and economic power are indeed so different, would a court's decision on the validity of an election of a board of directors of a corporation then be considered to be within the bailiwick of political science? Surely that is an authoritative allocation of the value of power in the society as well as on the behalf of society.

4. When the Supreme Court holds that a state statute prohibiting a Negro from going to the state law school is unconstitutional, the court is authoritatively allocating (potential) skill. Is this decision political?

The list of these situations could proceed endlessly, yet I think that these four make the point fairly clear. A combined Dahl-Easton-Lasswell definition would allow us to treat *everything* that the court finally did to be subject to study by political science, since by its very nature it is authoritatively allocating a value allocated by the political system. Precisely at this point the individual teacher-researcher must make his own definitional choices. What is his research interest? What does he wish to include in his syllabus? A scope broad enough to include all of the specific situations discussed above is surely justifiable when one defines government as the monopolized force of society organized to distribute authoritatively all the values and to maintain internal order. As such, a divorce decree as well as a major constitutional statement is a political output. As such it is certainly relevant to the study of political science. The choice of where to cut the definitional line depends *only* upon the nature of the theory the teacher-researcher favors as a course-organizational device or as an over-all framework upon which he can hang his research; no *a priori* reason seems to exist in its own right. But it would appear that to date the line has been drawn very narrowly by political scientists. It is rare that a political science course or research design on the judiciary exercises the kind of elbow room that this definition allows. It might be interesting to ask, for instance, why political scientists studying courts and cases draw their line of study in much the same manner as law schools used to distinguish between private and public law. What could be more "political" than the entire "law of wills" and probate? This area of law, according to some political theorists, is the very essence of political inequality and deprivation of opportunity.

Now that I have somewhat explicated the concept that might add up to "judicial politics," it is appropriate to demarcate the general boundaries of a conceptual scheme that I believe necessary to guide the teaching and research programs important for the future of this field.

V. THE CONCEPTUAL SCHEME AND A PARADIGM

I use the notion "conceptual scheme" rather than that of "theoretical framework" because I define them differently and that difference matters here. In my view this verbal distinction relates to two different degrees of closeness between words and their empirical referents. Quite simply, the former concept is just one step further removed from material reality than the latter, that is, I take the phrase *conceptual scheme* to mean a lesser relationship to empirical data and induction than the phrase "theoretical framework" suggests. The former is more a product of the mind allowing itself to roam at will within the confines of two or more high-level concepts: it is systematic interrelationship at the same level and deduction to a lower, more explicit level. Its cardinal function is to guide research in a new area. The phrase *theoretical framework,* on the other hand, is taken to mean a scheme which is rooted more in some tested and verified (or diversified) proposition. There are data and propositions, and "island of theory,"[41] which are placed in a framework primarily as inventory and only then as help to guide further, more advanced research.

Since I choose to operate at a high level of abstraction in this undertaking because of the dearth of data and low-level theory on judicial politics phenomena, a few words on political *metatheory* may be helpful for following my line of development. It seems to me that almost all major theoretical constructs involved in a field of political science can be placed within one of three or so "phases" of theory. These phases can be theorized to interrelate, even at their highest level of abstraction.

James Robinson has worked out a splendidly simple but inclusive model of all political theories in his attempt to develop a case for a general strategy for future political science research.[42] After discussing the general set of boundary problems for political science, he discusses "the intervening and independent variables":

When we try to translate political factors or political units into more specific form for studying their impact on public policy, we are seeking to identify the independent and intervening variables related to our dependent variable . . .

FIGURE 1. Political Units and Policy

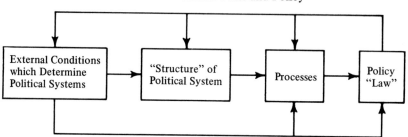

The arrows show relationships among these factors or variables. Moving from left to right, some external conditions give rise to some type of political system which adopts some kind of processes for making and executing policies. Hypothetically, there may be high correlations between external conditions and policy, as indicated by the longest arrow at the bottom of the diagram. Political systems may also be directly related to policy, or process to policy, as indicated by the shorter arrows at the bottom. However, what one would expect to be more likely is that conditions and systems are mediated by process. Furthermore, policy may well have reciprocal impact on the other variable as noted in the "feedback loops" at the top of the diagram. Most noticeably, one would expect policy outcomes.[43]

For my purposes here, the word "structure" would replace "system." System and procedure are easily conceived as being two subareas under structure.

Another recent attempt to create a research strategy included a similar political-metatheoretical pattern. Robert Cahill and Harry Friedman, in arguing for the "merits of a strategy for the comparative study of local government," discuss five questions which they deem central to almost all (if not all) "Western tradition of political inquiry":

1. What kinds of alternative political arrangements are *conceivable and/or possible?*
2. What kinds of alternative political arrangements can actually be *discerned to exist or to have existed?*

3. What are the underlying causes of alternative kinds of political arrangements?
4. What are the consequences of alternative kinds of political arrangements for other aspects of human life?
5. What are the respective *advantages and disadvantages* of alternative kinds of political arrangements?[44]

It is not too drastic a leap to liken the notion "political arrangements" with that of "political structure," or "causes" with that of "external conditions," or "consequences" with that of "policy" and/or "policy," "structure," and "process feedback onto external conditions." In other words, the perceived over-all pattern of theory in political science by Robinson, Cahill, and Friedman is very much the same, and I believe that this model can guide efforts to establish a general conceptual scheme for the field of judicial politics.

Our interest centers on "courts" or "judiciaries" and their relationship to "politics." The key phase of any potential theory in this area is that of structure, that is, the judicial structure, together with system and procedures; this is the variable which can well serve as the core of the field. The real, observable phenomena bounded by my conceptualization might prove to have no explanatory value, or my conceptualization may be found to relate to no phenomena in no orderly way. However, this is not a flaw at this point. It is the very essence of the scientific enterprise, the key point of the exploration, to formulate a conceptualization of reality and then to look into reality to see if it is at all isomorphic—if it is at all consistent with reality. As Easton says:

We do not need to conclude from this generalized description of what is involved in the delineation of boundaries that, once established, they are eternally fixed. If it should turn out that owing to some mistaken interpretation or lack of insight, in order to improve our understanding of the political system we must include within it some element previously assigned to the environment, we are faced with no crisis. *We simply redefine the system to meet our analytic needs.* Each time that we enlarge our system we simultaneously shrink the environment. If this seems to introduce an element of indeterminancy into our conceptualization, I can only refer to our discussion of what we mean by a system. *It is a device to help us to understand a defined and redefinable area of human behavior, not a strait jacket to imprison analysis permanently within a preconceived mold or model.*[45]

Within this suggested reconceptualization and metatheoretical position, I submit that a new field of knowledge awaits development. Political scientists can stake out a relatively undisputed virgin area that needs creative exploitation. It only takes a pinch of zest, an ounce of playfulness, and a teaspoonful of science.

The questions which await answer, if indeed there are any answers, may be usefully placed into several major categories. First of all, there is the question of whether or not such a phenomenon as I have defined as "court" or "judicial structure" exists at all in the world. And, if it does, its very dynamic needs extensive examination. It is within this context that we must pursue the inquiry into judicial role and into the mechanics of the judicial decision-making process. Actually, most of the so-called "judicial behavioral" work falls comfortably within this category, but by failing to conceptualize what "judicial" was, it failed to ask the right questions. Thus, much of its output will be found to be irrelevent and immaterial despite its competence.[46]

Another major question involves the isolation and description of societies that are "courtless." In other words, we must find those societies which do not have the type of structure for settling disputes that was conceptually labeled judicial structure or court in the body of this essay. These societies must then be described. Thereafter, the task is twofold. First of all, it will be necessary, within the dictates of the theoretical model, to determine what, if any, factors are associated with the existence of this structure. Second, we must ask what are the functions (actual effects) of the bare existence of this structure or of the nonexistence of this structure? Are courts necessarily related to order? to the maintenance of the societal status quo? to the administration of justice? to the maintenance of democracy? There is much lore and implicit theory on this topic. The time has come to be explicit in our theory and then to observe the real world systematically. Perhaps there will be corroboration, perhaps not.

The next major category posits the existence of judicial structure in society and the host of questions which involve the vast array of differences in judicial structure that exist and have existed in the world. Using slightly different terms, I suggest that many societies have judicial structure of one sort or another. Political scientists interested in the policy-science and system-science aspects of gaining knowledge must seek answers to questions that arise as to the consequences of these variations upon the social system of which the courts are but one part. How can we best explain the development of the English court system from the thirteenth to the fifteenth centuries? How can we explain the use of the particular trappings employed by the Ghanians in the twentieth century? Why do some judiciaries have more independence than others? How can we explain the specific consequences (the function) of the use of judicial review (as a structure) in a democracy—why not employ legislative committees with no structures of political isolation? Is France less democratic because it has no jury system? These, too, are questions which theorists have only implicitly answered—and rarely without internal inconsistency. Again the theory must be explicit, and a systematic and rigorous look must be taken—for the first time.

For far too long political scientists have played alien roles concerning their interest in the court system. They have played the roles of: lawyer, in attempting case analysis; historian, in sketching judicial biographies and constitutional developments; philosopher, in pondering problems of jurisprudence; and statistician, in describing judicial decisions with quantitative exactitude. Yet the main area of the field remains almost barren in terms of analysis and study, and it is this field that is peculiarly their own. It is time to develop judicial theory; it is time to do the research that can lead to a large body of scientifically collected, comparatively based knowledge; it is time we pulled the field of judicial politics together.

The twentieth century may be distinguished in the future as that time when a large, scientifically oriented group of men began to inquire openly, seriously, and objectively into their institutions and those of others—as to both cause and effect. The social sciences, as a major system of social thought underlying this inquiry, have their roots in the nineteenth century and before, but the force, size, and technological competence of this search are uniquely of the twentieth. Its hope is in the past, its momentum is contemporary. I interpret William Golding's *Lord of the Flies* to mean that man's institutions are delicate and that the flaws in man's nature will drive him to his own destruction by fire. If this is correct, then of course there is little for us to worry about. The social sciences, as men currently practice them, involve a faith that something *can* be done by man himself. The twentieth century has become an era when man has thought much and done much about changing his institutional environment on a scale qualitatively different than ever before. One major area that has been substantially overlooked by researchers, however, has been the political and societal significance of the judicial structure and process. I believe that it is potentially far too important an area to continue to ignore, even if the ultimate conclusion may turn out to be that the existence of or variations in judicial systems and structure were of little social value or social consequence whatever. One primary role of the political scientist is to pursue answers to time-honored questions that have been dishonored by neglect.

NOTES

1. Instead of producing a lengthy footnote containing the names of all of these scholars and their books, I would simply refer the reader to Kenneth Vines's discussion of research in the present volume.

2. My first argument that the behavioral movement in the study of the judiciary has not been much of a revolution was set forth at

length in *Political Behavioralism and Modern Jurisprudence* (Chicago: Rand McNally, 1965). See the Introduction and Ch. I.

3. I rely heavily on Carl C. Hempel, *Fundamentals of Concept Formation in Empirical Science* (Chicago: University of Chicago Press, 1952).

4. Walter Murphy, *Elements of Judicial Strategy* (Chicago: University of Chicago Press, 1964), especially Ch. II; Glendon Schubert, *Judicial Policy Making* (Chicago: Scott, Foresman, 1965) especially Ch. V; Joel Grossman, "Social Backgrounds and Judicial Decisions: Notes for a Theory," *Journal of Politics*, XXIX (May 1967), 334-351.

5. Walter Murphy and C. Herman Pritchett, *Courts, Judges and Politics* (New York: Random House, 1961), p. vii.

6. Charles A. Beard, *American Government and Politics* (New York: Macmillan, 1944), p. 194.

7. Austin Ranney, *The Governing of Men* (New York: Holt, 1958), Ch. XX.

8. Thomas A. Mason and William B. Beaney, *American Constitutional Law* (3rd ed.; Englewood Cliffs: Prentice Hall, 1964), p. 12. Emphasis added. Another offender is R. M. MacIver, *The Modern State* (London: Oxford University Press, 1926), especially Ch. XII.

9. *Definition of Law* (Cambridge University Press, 1958), pp. 1 ff.

10. Kingsley Davis, "The Myth of Functional Analysis as a Special Method in Sociology and Anthropology," *American Sociological Review*, XXIV (December 1959), 757-773.

11. Irving Louis Horowitz, "Sociology and Politics: The Myth of Functionalism Revisited," *Journal of Politics*, XXV (May 1963), 248-264.

12. Carl G. Hempel, "The Logic of Functional Analysis," *Symposium on Sociological Theory*, ed. Llewellyn Gross (Evanston: Row, Peterson, 1959); Ernest Nagel, *The Structure of Science: Problem in The Logic of Scientific Explanation* (New York: Harcourt, Brace, & World, 1961).

13. Walter Goldschmidt, *Comparative Analysis* (Berkeley: University of California Press, 1966), p. 28.

14. Ibid., p. 31.

15. Fred R. Riggs, *Administration in Developing Countries* (Boston: Houghton Mifflin, 1964), p. 20. Emphasis added.

16. Marion J. Levy, *The Structure of Society* (Princeton: Princeton University Press, 1962).

17. David Easton, *Framework for Political Analysis* (Englewood Cliffs: Prentice-Hall, 1965).

18. Gabriel Almond and James S. Coleman (eds.), *The Politics of Developing Areas* (Princeton: Princeton University Press, 1960).

19. Robert N. Merton, *Social Theory and Social Structure* (rev. ed.; Glencoe: Free Press, 1957), p. 21.

20. Ibid., p. 27. Emphasis added.

21. Ibid., p. 24.

22. Riggs, op. cit., p. 20. Emphasis added.

23. Robert T. Holt, "A Proposed Structural-Functional Framework for Political Science," *Functionalism in the Social Sciences*, ed. Don Martindale (Philadelphia: American Academy of Political and Social Science, 1965), pp. 86-87.

24. Glendon Schubert, *Judicial Policy Making* (Chicago: Scott, Foresman, 1965).

25. "The use of the term 'functions' with reference to courts is a frequent one in the literature, but it almost always is as a label only and not as a means of linkage to other elements in the system; it is another way of saying that courts decide cases—their 'function' is to interpret laws, for example." Kenneth M. Dolbeare, *Trial Courts in Urban Politics* (New York: Wiley, 1967), p. 10. Dolbeare indicts Vines as well as Schubert. See Kenneth Vines, "Political Functions of a State Court," in Kenneth Vines and Herb Jacobs, *Studies in Judicial Politics* (New Orleans: Tulane Studies in Political Science, VIII, 1963). Cf. Donald Kommers' definition of functionalism in his "Professor Kurland, The Supreme Court, and Political Science," *Journal of Public Law*, XV (#2, 1966), 230-252.

26. Alexander N. Dragnich and John Wahlke, *Government and Politics* (New York: Random House, 1966), pp. 372 et seq. The argument might be made that "introductory texts" are simply straw men. I would dispute that— in this case at any rate. Indeed, the chapter on "The Judicial Process" is more sophisticated in its rhetoric and choice of materials than some of the more specialized political-science monographs on the courts.

27. D. G. Hitchener and William H. Harbold, *Modern Government: A Survey of Political Science* (New York: Dodd, Mead, 1962).

28. Herman Finer, *The Theory and Practice of Modern Government* (rev. ed.; New York: Holt, 1949), p. 114.

29. Henry T. Lummis, *The Trial Judge* (Chicago: Foundation Press, 1937), p. 10.

30. Max Gluckman, *Judicial Process Among the Barotse of Northern Rhodesia* (Manchester: Manchester University Press, 1954).

31. Vilhelm Aubert, "Courts and Conflict Resolution," *Journal of Conflict Resolution*, XI (March 1967), at p. 42.

32. Torstein Eckhoff, "Impartiality, Separation of Powers, and Judicial Independence," *Scandinavian Studies in Law*, IX (1965), 9-52.

33. This theoretical requirement is frequently cited. See, for instance, David H. Bayley, *Public Liberties in the New States* (Chicago: Rand McNally, 1964), p. 129.

34. See Vilhelm Aubert, "Chance in Social Affairs," *Inquiry*, II (#1, 1959), p. 1 ff.

35. E. Adamson Hoebel, *The Law of Primitive Man* (Cambridge: Harvard University Press, 1954), p. 9.

36. Alf Ross, *On Law and Justice* (London: Stevens, 1958) p. 281. See also Sir Henry Maine, *Ancient Law* (London: Dene, 1917), Ch. I.

37. Harold D. Lasswell, *Politics: Who Gets What, When, How?* (New York: McGraw-Hill, 1936).

38. Harold D. Lasswell and Arnold Rogow, *Power, Corruption and Rectitude* (Englewood Cliffs: Prentice-Hall, 1963), p. 133.

39. David Easton, *The Political System* (New York: Knopf, 1951) p. 129. His current definition is very much the same. In *A Framework for Political Analysis*, Easton defines politics indirectly by discussing the "essential variable" in the political system. (1) "Making and execution of decisions for a society," and (2) "their relative frequency of acceptance as authoritatives or binding by the bulk of society." (Englewood Cliffs: Prentice-Hall, 1955), pp. 96-97.

40. Robert A. Dahl and Charles E. Lindblom, *Politics, Economics and Welfare* (New York: Harper, 1953), p. 28.

41. This phrase is often used by Harold Guetzkow. I like it because it seems more apt than that of "some theory," since it implies that one can have ostensibly independent, but invisibly connected, areas of theory. The connection is that afforded by a bedrock of data—some of which has not yet reached a general-theory "surface."

42. "Problems in Political Science," *Politics and Public Affairs*, ed. Lynton K. Caldwell (Bloomington: Indiana University, 1962).

43. Ibid., pp. 172-173.

44. Robert S. Cahill and Harry J. Friedman, "A Strategy for the Comparative Study of Local Governments." *Philippine Journal of Public Administration*, VI (July 1965), 1-34.

45. *A Framework for Political Analysis*, p. 67. Emphasis added.

46. The most current bibliography on this material is contained in the footnotes to the articles in a symposium on "Social Science Approaches" to the study of courts published in the *Harvard Law Review*, LXXIV (Summer 1966).

IV

COMPARATIVE GOVERNMENT AND POLITICS

7 Political Development Research

ROBERT A. PACKENHAM, Stanford University

I. INTRODUCTION

The term "political development" has been used increasingly in recent years by scholars, government officials, and others. "Economic development" has been part of the lexicon of economics for a longer period, and courses in the subject—for example, The Theory of Economic Development—have proliferated. There are doubtless fewer courses in the theory of political development, and political scientists feel (as they should) less comfortable with this concept than economists do with "economic development." Nevertheless, the idea of political development appears much more now than it used to both in the academic literature and in the councils of government, especially with reference to the so-called emerging nations or developing areas.

One obvious reason for this usage within American political science is the growing role of the United States in world affairs, which has propelled Americans out of their traditional isolation into involvement in the political affairs of other nations. Thus involved, the United States has had to consider questions of political change in these countries. Another reason is the transition, after World War II, from the colonial to the postcolonial epoch, with the corresponding expansion of interest by the developed countries in the politics of developing areas. Yet another factor is the analogy with economic change; that is, if basic, positive economic change is called "economic development," why not call basic, positive political change "political development"?

Despite—perhaps because of—its increasing usage, "political development" is an ambiguous concept for many people. One scholar in the field recently noted ten different, though overlapping, meanings attached to it.[1] His list could perhaps be extended. Some argue that the economic analogy is very deceptive, and that the notion of political development should be abandoned altogether.

My position is that the economic analogy is deceptive, but this does not mean that the concept should be abandoned. Political development is a more elusive concept than economic development. This is partly because political development is more controversial in normative terms, and more difficult to measure in empirical, operational terms, than

169

economic development. Nevertheless, we believe that reasonable men with varying normative orientations can agree that some political systems are more developed than others, and that differences between such systems can be identified and measured with some precision. The progress in the literature on political development since the concept first became widespread is already impressive. We still do not know very much about political development, but we know much more than we did twenty years ago.

All concepts or theories of political development that I know about or can conceive of are both normative and non-normative (existential). Development means not only change, but implies change for the better, which makes it normative.[2] Hence any concept of political development unavoidably has a normative aspect; but it must also be, in some measure, existential as well, insofar as it specifies or implies the empirical nature and characteristics of the good political system, and perhaps the conditions of such a system. Briefly and roughly, all concepts of political development may be regarded as normative insofar as they deal with the ends of and the justifications for good political systems; and they may be regarded as existential insofar as they define the characteristics and specify the conditions of good (developed) political systems. Though all political-development concepts and theories may be seen as both normative and existential;[3] they vary in the amount of attention devoted to these dimensions.

Normative theorists stress that a political system develops as it approaches the good political order. They devote most of their attention to specifying the ends of, justifications for, and perhaps the characteristics of good political orders. They devote less attention to systematic statements of the conditions which give rise to and maintain political development, and are often more concerned with specifying the ends and justifications of political development than elucidating its characteristics.

Existential theorists devote relatively little attention to the normative premises on which their theories are based and which motivate them to do their work. They spend less time on spelling out the ends of and justifications for the good political system and more time on specifying the characteristics of what they regard as politically developed systems and the conditions and processes which give rise to them.

The literature of political development produced since World War II is mainly existential theory in the above sense. However, this emphasis is not only a postwar phenomenon; it reflects a tendency in Western social science that goes back to the eighteenth century, at least.[4] My review of this literature suggests the conclusion that political-development theorists need to improve both the existential *and* the normative dimensions. Especially lacking is sophisticated normative theory to balance the significant achievements in existential theory.[5] I shall return to this point later in the essay.

In Sections II and III, I shall indicate what seem to be the main ways in which political-development theorists have conceptualized their topic, the main types of propositions contained in this literature, and some of the strengths and weaknesses of these writings. Such a review and synthesis is necessarily abstract, and inevitably involves some oversimplification. Nevertheless, the writings on political development are not so divergent and discordant as they may at first appear, and greater clarity may result from a distillation of research to date. This review is thorough but not fully comprehensive. More attenwill be devoted to treatments of political development as an independent or intervening variable than to those writings treating it as a dependent variable.

II. POLITICAL DEVELOPMENT AS A DEPENDENT VARIABLE

Most of the literature up to about 1964 or 1965 treated political development as a dependent variable. Those who explicitly defined it at all usually were rough and subjective in their classifications of some political systems as more developed than others. The criteria of political development most frequently relied upon were political modernization and/or political democracy. Political modernization was defined as rationalization, participation, and integration; sometimes the measures used were precise, but more often they were not very precise. Political democracy was variously defined as political competitiveness, pluralism, polyarchy, legitimacy of elections, or "subsystem autonomy." Measures of democracy were also usually rough and subjective.[6]

Scholars writing about political development devoted relatively little attention to specifying political-development utopias. In addition, they tended to assume that the ends of the political order in developing countries were political modernization and, if possible, political democracy. They did not spend much time or energy in justifying such definitions of political development in normative terms, nor were they very attentive to or precise in specifying the substance of political development so defined. Probably it would not be an exaggeration to say that they believed that modernization and democracy were self-evidently the goals for the political systems of peoples in the third world. Perhaps this belief also helps explain why they were usually so imprecise about defining political development, for it was assumed that everybody knew in some intuitive way what political development was.

Apparently more interesting to these writers was the question of the *conditions* of political development, so defined. It was to this question that the scholars devoted most of their attention. My review and synthesis of the literature as of 1964 found five different approaches to the study of political development. Each approach contained a fundamental proposition, as well as many subsidiary ones, about the conditions of political development.[7] The five approaches, stated in the form of the fundamental proposition embodied in each, are:

1. Political development is mainly a function of (that is, it varies with)[8] the *legal-formal apparatus* of government, prescribing such features as equal protection of the law, the rule of law, regular elections by secret ballot, federalism, the separation of powers, single-member or proportional representation, and the like.[9]

2. Political development is mainly a function of a *level of economic development* sufficient to serve the material needs of the members of the political system and to permit a resonable harmony between economic aspirations and satisfactions.[10]

3. Political development is mainly a function of the *administrative capacity* efficiently and effectively to maintain law and order and to perform governmental output functions rationally and neutrally.[11]

4. Political development is mainly a function of a *social system* that facilitates popular participation in governmental and political processes at all levels, and helps bridge regional, religious, caste, linguistic, tribal, or other cleavages.[12]

5. Political development is mainly a function of a *political culture* —that is, fundamental attitudinal and personality characteristics—among the members of the political system, such that they are able both to accept the privileges and to bear the responsibilities of a modern, democratic political process.[13]

The literature summarized by these five propositions represents a major achievement in the study of comparative politics. Three decades ago, the modal approach to comparative politics was the legal-formal one. The emergence of new nations, along with many other factors, expanded the horizons of political scientists, and they began to question old orthodoxies and old knowledge. More importantly, new hypotheses began to emerge and old hypotheses gained new support.

The venerable idea that politics is largely a function of economics was reemphasized and provided with a firmer empirical base. S. M. Lipset's article on "Some Social Requisites of Democracy: Economic Development and Political Legitimacy" had a major impact on students of political development.[14] Moreover, it is probably as true today as it was in 1959 (when Lipset published his article) that there is a correlation, although far from a perfect one, between level of economic development and degree of political democracy.

It was equally apparent, however, that economic development and political development were not perfectly correlated.[15] Some economically underdeveloped countries were highly developed politically (such as India), whereas some economically developed countries were poorly developed politically (such as Argentina or France). By pointing out that political systems and political development have roots also in the social-structural fabric, the administrative capacity, and even the attitudinal and personality structures of society, and by specifying more carefully and comprehensively than ever before the characteristics of such roots, these writings dramatically increased understanding of the conditions of political development. One way to index the change that had occurred is to compare any pre-World War II comparative-government textbook with contemporary ones.

The literature utilizing these approaches also has shortcomings, however. Although it cannot be denied any longer that social, economic, administrative, and politicocultural variables are relevant to political development, many of the propositions contained in this literature have not been tested adequately. The relative weights to be assigned to each—in order to predict political development under varying circumstances—have not been determined. Many of the concepts are so poorly operationalized that they are not amenable to weighting and testing. Even if they were, much of the data necessary for testing them would be lacking.

Some other weaknesses could be noted, but I shall confine myself to two. One is the paucity of attempts to justify and defend these notions of political development in normative terms, a weakness already noted and to which we shall return. The other is that political development might profitably be looked at in a radically different way. The literature just described conceptualizes political development as a dependent variable—as political phenomena *caused by* something else. Another way to conceptualize political development is to see it as an independent variable—as phenomena that *cause* something else. In other words, instead of asking, "What are the social and economic conditions of political development, defined as political modernization and democracy?" one might ask, "What are the political conditions of over-all modernization and economic development?" Recently, an increasing number of scholars have done just that.

III. POLITICAL DEVELOPMENT AS AN INDEPENDENT AND INTERVENING VARIABLE

Among writers who have treated political development as a dependent variable, there has been a strong tendency to neglect such variables as the will and capacity of political actors and institutions. Political development was seen as something determined by massive socioeconomic and psychological forces. Individual or group choice, skill, and capacity were, for the most part, left out of the analysis.

Recently, and especially since about 1965, writings on political development have increasingly stressed just these latter variables. There has been a strong tendency to view political development as will and capacity to cope with the issues, demands, and needs of society (or polity) that are cast up by the force of, or the imputed desire for, modernization. In this perspective, political development has been conceptualized as either an independent and/or an intervening variable.[16] (For our purposes, we can treat political development as both an independent and an intervening variable, although for other purposes it may be desirable to separate these uses of the concept.) Writers employing this approach have avoided seeing political development as some fixed-end state; rather, they have seen it as a continuing process—in Halpern's terms, "a persistent capacity for coping with a permanent revolution." This approach goes by various names: "will and capacity" is the generic name that I shall give to it, although others use such terms as "problem-solving capacity," "institutionalization," and "ability to sustain new goals." Examples of this approach are the works of Diamant, Halpern, Eisenstadt, Hirschman, Holt and Turner, Ilchman and Ilchman and Bhargara, Nye, Huntington, and Deutsch.[17]

One of the most stimulating efforts along these lines has been Samuel P. Huntington's article "Political Development and Political Decay." Huntington defines political development as "the institutionalization of political organizations and procedures." His concept "liberates [political] development from [socioeconomic] modernization," so that countries like India, which are very underdeveloped socioeconomically, are considered highly developed politically, and countries like Argentina, which have high socioeconomic development, are considered poorly developed politically. Another virtue of Huntington's concept is that it avoids the implication, so deeply rooted in much of the previous literature, of unilinearity, or movement only toward development (and never toward decay). As Huntington points out, "institutions . . . decay and dissolve as well as grow and mature." Finally, and most significantly, Huntington's concept focuses attention on the "reciprocal interaction" between the ongoing social processes of modernization on the one hand, and the strength, stability, or weakness of traditional, transitional, or modern political structures on the other.[18]

Interestingly, such definitions of political development as "will and capacity" were not so prominent among writings treating political development mostly as a dependent variable; however, some of them have now shifted their emphasis. For example, Almond and Powell, building upon but somewhat modifying Almond's earlier analysis, define political development as "the increased differentiation and specialization of political structures and the increased secularization of political culture." They continue: "The significance of such development [that is, differentiation and secularization] is, in general, to increase the *effectiveness and efficiency* of the performance of the

political system: to increase its *capabilities.*" In this formulation, differentiation and secularization intervene between "various environmental
pressures and internal aspirations," including socioeconomic and psychological forces, and "the effectiveness and efficiency of the performance
of the political system," that is, "its capabilities."[19] Another example
is David Apter, who argues that political development may be seen as
either an intervening or an independent variable:

> ... political groups can be defined as intervening variables between
> stratification and government and as independent variables acting on
> both. . . . One needs to be able to see that, in concrete applications of
> authority, the instrument of authority turns into an independent variable.
> Without such a view, political analysis is simply residual to some other
> form.[20]

One of the weaknesses of this literature is the imprecision of the
definitions. Diamant says:

> A political system is said to be developing when there is an increase
> in its ability to sustain successfully and continuously new types of social
> goals and the creation of new types of organization.[21]

Halpern defines political development as the relationship between "the
structural changes and demands set loose by the uncontrolled forces
of transformation" and "the will and capacity of political authority"
to cope with these changes and demands.[22] Eisenstadt defines it as
"an institutional framework capable of continuous absorption of
change."[23] It appears that these writers intuitively have grasped
something important for the study of political development; but
much work needs to be done to refine definitions and to make
them more operational. It should be noted, incidentally, that these
concepts are vague for understandable reasons: concepts like "ability,"
"will," "skill," and, to a lesser extent, "capacity" are difficult to
define operationally. This does not mean that they should be discarded, but they should be made more precise and more operational.
    Huntington is an important exception to the generalization that
definitions of political development as "capacity" are imprecise. After
defining political development as "the institutionalization of political
organizations and procedures," Huntington further refines this concept
by defining institutionalization in terms of the "adaptability, complexity, autonomy, and coherence of its organizations and procedures."
He then suggests a great variety of promising ways to operationalize
these four concepts in order to measure level of institutionalization,
or political development.[24] Both the concept and the measures
deserve the serious attention of students of political development.[25]
    If political development usually is defined somewhat vaguely by
the "will and capacity" writers, so too is the dependent variable—

perhaps more so. Usually, this variable is called "modernization." Though it can be operationalized in various ways, most conveniently in terms of indicators of economic development, such as per capita income and industrialization, often it is not. A common strategy seems to be to leave the dependent variable "open" and allow it to be defined and operationalized more precisely in context. This strategy has some virtues, to be discussed below; but one cost is that it is difficult to test the hypotheses generated by this approach because the investigator has no operational dependent variable. All he has is "modernization" or some more precise indicator to be defined in context. So long as the dependent variables are not operational, there can be no testing of hypotheses, only the exploratory generating of hypotheses to see how they fit one's intuitive sense of reality. Now that many writers seem to have chosen "will and capacity" as a useful way to define political development, it may be time to begin to "close" the dependent variables to see how the hypotheses generated thus far stand up in the light of systematic evidence.

Huntington, who defines political development rather precisely, also operationalizes his dependent variable more than most other writers. He defines it as "strength of political organizations and procedures," or "stability." Although he does not elaborate the meaning of "strength" or "stability" as much or as well as his concept of "institutionalization," he does use several indicators such as the number of coups d'etat.[26] Since operational indicators of stability are not so hard to come by, and defining "institutionalization" is much more difficult, his emphasis is probably well placed.

Another common weakness in the literature that uses the "will and capacity" approach is an overlap between definition and explanation. That is, variables used to define political development and those used to explain it are seldom clearly distinguished from one another. (The same weakness is present in the literature that treats political development as a dependent variable.) This overlap occurs, or so it seems to me, even in the work of such able scholars as Diamant and Eisenstadt. For example, in Diamant's article, it is difficult to distinguish political development—"ability to sustain successfully and continuously new types of social goals and the creation of new types of organization"—from some of his suggested explanatory "theories," such as equilibrium and input-output analysis and, especially, cybernetic models. After defining political development in terms of "an institutional framework capable of continuous absorption of change" and of "institutional ability," Eisenstadt uses "initial patterns of institutionalization of modern political frameworks," also defined as "basic political symbols and political and legal frameworks" and "initial modern political frameworks," as one of three broad types of explanatory variables. It is not clear in what ways these defining and explanatory variables are different.[27]

Whether political development is treated as an independent or a dependent variable, it is necessary to define it and the other variables, even if only vaguely. Most theorists do this. Then there are two possibilities: (1) If political development is treated as a dependent variable, then one presumably seeks to discover variables explaining it. (2) If political development is treated as an independent variable, then the intellectual task is to see whether it explains something else, that is, the dependent variable. To state the obvious: when political development is conceptualized as an independent variable, one does not try to explain it; if an independent variable is explained, then it is one no longer. For example, when Lipset finds that economic development and political legitimacy are conditions of democracy, he is treating the former as independent variables and the latter as his dependent variable. If he were defining the conditions of economic development and political legitimacy—a perfectly reasonable task—then they would no longer be independent variables, but dependent or intervening variables. Of course, such definitions are highly abstract, and there is almost always, in reality, interaction and influence in both directions among such variables; but it is precisely such abstraction that is necessary in order to test hypotheses that enable us to understand reality.

All this reasoning is that of elementary social science. However, the literature does not always conform to these simple rules. As noted, when political development is treated as an independent variable, one presumably is concerned with defining it, identifying and defining what variable or variables are supposed to explain it, and then seeing whether one's hypotheses work. One does not seek to explain an independent variable. Yet one finds theorists treating political development as an independent variable and then devoting much attention to possible explanations of it. For example, Diamant rejects "for present purposes" the strategy of conceptualizing political development as a dependent variable;[28] he elects to treat it as an independent variable. He concedes that his choice is arbitrary and abstract, but argues that it is the more useful way to deal with the phenomenon of political development in the "new states." He writes:

In the process of modernization . . . the political system undergoes transformation both in what it does for the society as a whole and in the manner in which it transacts its business and is organized. In this transformation the relations between the polity and the society are both autonomous and interdependent . . . The dynamic of political development is, in the present view, autonomous; it proceeds along lines distinguishable from economic, social, or other forms of change. Furthermore, the political system in a modernizing society deals with an ever wider range of problems, for it has become the generalized problem-solver for the entire society, unfettered by ascriptive-traditional elements which, in the traditional society, cope with the limited range of problems that arise according to ascriptive criteria. The political system is, of course, not the only problem-solver even in a modernizing society, but for present purposes and because of conditions in new states, the principal emphasis is on government.[29]

Then he states his definition of political development, which was noted above. After taking this approach, he addresses most of his essay to a review of the literature in order to answer the question of "how it [political development] comes about," or "what are the minimum preconditions for political development."[30] Although he explicitly rejects the notion of considering political development as a dependent variable, he uses it implicitly as such throughout most of the essay. As for his stated dependent variable—"modernization"— Diamant writes: "At this point it should not be necessary to define precisely what is meant by modernization, except to say that it is the sort of transformation which we have come to know in Europe and North America and in less complete forms in other parts of the world. The details might vary, but there is little disagreement on the types of goals involved."[31]

The point here is not to criticize all of Diamant's essay, which is only one illustration among several possibilities. However, he has defined both of his stated key variables—"ability to sustain new goals and organizations" (independent variable) and "modernization" (dependent variable)—only in the vaguest terms. Just about the only proposition contained in the article that treats political development as an independent variable is the one that emerges from the definitions, namely, that the "ability to sustain..." is a condition of "modernization." If he were to reply to the criticism by stating that personality variables (from Hagen, McClelland; see footnote 32), structural-functional analysis, or cybernetics models are part of his definition of political development and help account for "modernization," that would only be to call this literature by another name, since most of it in fact treats economic or political development as a dependent variable. Moreover, such a reply would also illustrate the criticism already made, namely, that definitions and explanations often overlap. As he writes in his summary, "We have *identified* the political system as the general legitimizing system for a society and have *thus* identified the subsystem of a society which *generates* political development..."[32]

Now we can summarize briefly. First of all, in defining political development, scholars using the "will and capacity" approach seem to be more explicit than, and usually as precise as, those who treat it as a dependent variable. Both groups of scholars are fairly rough and subjective in defining political development; the latter group, in contrast to the former, often does not define political development at all explicitly. Second, "will and capacity" writers have been extremely vague, in general, in defining their dependent variables. Perhaps it is time to begin to close these definitions. Third, in order for this literature to gain in conceptual clarity, greater care should be taken in distinguishing definitions from explanations. Fourth, if one treats political development as an independent variable, then he should maintain that strategy—which means using political development to explain something else. Thus, both political development and what is to be explained need to be specified with sufficient clarity so that it is possible to test concrete hypotheses. If one chooses to treat "will and capacity" as a dependent variable, that research strategy is also legitimate. However, it is a different one, and researchers should realize the difference.

IV. NORMATIVE ASPECTS OF POLITICAL DEVELOPMENT

Studies treating political development as an independent variable tend to be relatively weak as regards normative theory. If political development is the ability to sustain new types of social goals, or the capacity to cope with transformation, then what are the goals, and what the ends of transformation? The general answer is "modernization"; but explicit, operational answers to these questions are seldom offered.

The reasons why social goals and the ends of transformation are not spelled out by these writers are understandable, for the approach has its advantages.[33] This intellectual strategy enables one to focus on the independent variable, and to leave "open" the dependent variable. The operational meaning of the dependent variable—vaguely defined as general "modernization"—is to be determined contextually by what the people, leaders, or politically articulate groups want. Such an approach avoids arbitrary specification of goals, and seems to avoid normative questions by allowing goals to be determined by what people, leaders, or groups want. Since the latter questions are (or seem to be) empirical, it seems possible to skirt the normative ones.

This strategy is attractive and fruitful and its advantages deserve to be exploited. However, the matter cannot be entirely resolved in this fashion. First, in most developing societies all social groups are not politically articulate. (Politically inarticulate groups are also found, though to a lesser extent, even in relatively democratic and apparently developed societies—for example, the Negroes in the United States.) Even among those groups that are articulate, it is no easy matter to know what they want. Hence, decision makers make—and must make—normative decisions about who gets what. Second, even if decision makers know what persons and groups want, they will not be able to satisfy all the demands made upon them, which is especially true in developing countries, where resources are especially limited. Choices have to be made about who gets what, which hurt some and help others. These choices necessarily involve setting priorities regarding the allocation of scarce resources. Third, even if priorities are set and justified in normative terms, the problems of defining and measuring the "outputs" and "outcomes" of government decisions remain. Political decisions allocate wealth, which is relatively easily measured. But they also allocate such values as influence, justice, and liberty,[34] which are much more difficult to operationalize. Usually the data available to measure them are much more scarce and inferior in quality than data on wealth. Thus far, few political-development theorists have seriously confronted these problems.

An interesting and important partial exception to the foregoing generalization is, again, Huntington. His treatment of the normative dimension is necessarily brief, but he devotes almost a third of his article (a section entitled "Mobilization vs. Institutionalization: Public Interest, Degeneration, and the Corrupt Polity") to spelling out his vision of the good political order and to justifying his notion of political development in terms of it. It is instructive that in this section, in contrast to all the rest, his citations are more from political philosophers (Plato, Aristotle, Lippmann) than from contemporary social scientists, and even from a contemporary novelist (William Golding, author of *Lord of the Flies*). To be sure, this section, as well as the one following on "Strategies of Institutional Development," contains much with which one might quarrel. Huntington identifies "the public interest" with "strength of political organizations and procedures" or "stability."[35] For him, the "public interests" of the United States, the USSR, and the developing countries are served, respectively, by the Presidency, the Communist Party of the Soviet Union, and strong political parties, whether communist or noncommunist. I personally find the exclusive stress on stability in developing countries, and the idea that the American President represents the public interest in the United States more than any other institution, extreme and objectionable in some of their implications. However, relevant to this discussion is how much thoughtful attention Huntington pays to these normative issues and the sophisticated defense he offers for his position. Compare, by contrast, the dearth of similar discussions in the works of such scholars as Holt and Turner, Eisenstadt, and Diamant.[36]

Also embedded in the studies treating political development as an independent variable seems to be the norm of a "moving equilibrium"[37] between the "forces of change" and "capacity to cope." Almost invariably, the contention seems to be that capacity to cope should keep pace with, or be just ahead of, social change. There may be some disequilibria in the short run; but the notion appears to be that over the long run the forces of change should never become stronger than the capacity to cope with them. This idea is seldom called into question in the literature, and little attention is devoted to explicit defenses of it.

In my view, this position has substantial merit. Stability is valued not for its own sake, but only if stability is "moving," that is, if it is occurring within the context of broader social change. However, this norm, by postulating long-run equilibrium even if allowing short-run disequilibria, tends to neglect the benefits of cataclysmic, radical social change, where "capacity to cope" is overwhelmed by socio-economic transformation. The approach, in short, tends overwhelmingly to deny the utility—for the realization of humane values—of revolution, in the sense of a violent economic and sociopolitical upheaval.

Embodied, though seldom explicit, in this approach seems to be a calculus that the over-all (not just economic) costs at the individual level of revolution are greater than the costs incurred if revolution does not occur. The bang of a revolutionary course toward moderni-zation is seen to be more costly than the whimpers of the countless souls who die slow deaths along gradualist paths.

Only a minority of American scholars—indeed, of Western scholars —challenges this calculus; probably relatively few seriously entertain any other. The most notable recent dissent from these assumptions comes from Barrington Moore, Jr. Toward the end of a comparative historical analysis of modernization in England, France, the United States, China, Japan, and India, Moore writes:

For a Western scholar to say a good word on behalf of revolutionary radicalism is not easy because it runs counter to deeply grooved mental reflexes. The assumption that gradual and piecemeal reform has demon-strated its superiority over violent revolution as a way to advance human freedom is so pervasive that even to question such an assumption seems strange. In closing this book I should like to draw attention for the last time to what the evidence from the comparative history of moderniza-tion may tell us about this issue. As I have reluctantly come to read this evidence, the costs of moderation have been at least as atrocious as those of revolution, perhaps a good deal more.[38]

Moore's conclusions are doubly discouraging: If "the gradualist argu-ment seems shattered ... the revolutionary argument also collapses," he writes, citing the repressive policies and unfulfilled promises of Russian and Chinese communism. The sad conclusion, for him, is that "both Western liberalism and communism (especially the Russian version) have begun to display many symptoms of historical obsoles-cence. As successful doctrines they have started to turn into ideolo-gies that justify and conceal numerous forms of repression." Conse-quently, Moore holds that it is "dubious in the extreme" that the "oppressive tendencies of both systems" can be overcome.[39]

Moore himself does not go very far into the profound normative (and empirical) question of what kind of political system is most appropriate under varying circumstances for maximizing modernization while minimizing oppression. However, his analysis surely provides sober grist for the intellectual mills of those who would go further.

V. POLITICAL-DEVELOPMENT RESEARCH

General Remarks

Various data, variables, and perspectives relevant to political development have been relatively neglected in the literature. Some of them, such as violence and revolution, have been mentioned already; but there are many others. Until recently, historical materials have been neglected—a curious omission in the study of political development.[40] Ideology has not been stressed much as a variable relevant to political development, although this emphasis also may be changing.[41] Some say that the neglect of history and ideology is characteristic of American social science generally.[42] Political rights and freedoms have been very little studied in the developing countries— again an amazing omission, especially for political scientists.[43] This neglect is particularly surprising and lamentable given the conflicting claims which pervade the literature about the appropriateness or inappropriateness of democratic, autocratic, or totalitarian political systems as models for modernization. The relationship of the international environment to domestic political development has been much neglected; it is now receiving more attention, although most of it is at the theoretical, rather than the empirical, level.[44] Political structures—legislatures, adjudicating agencies, political executives, political parties, bureaucracies, political-interest groups, and the military— were neglected for a time as the surge of behavioral studies pulsed through the literature on the politics of the developing areas. Some political structures have been studied more extensively than others: My impression is that legislatures, courts, and executives have received less attention than parties, and that the military, interest groups, and bureaucracies have been studied even more than parties. However, most of the literature on political structures is rather thin, especially in terms of theoretically rich treatments as contrasted with descriptive accounts.[45] The tradition of studies of political economy seems to be returning after a long absence.[46]

Each of these neglected variables and perspectives could be discussed at some length, and still others could be added. I would like to say a little more about two other neglected areas: studies of leadership and studies of policy relevance.

Leadership Studies

There is a woeful lack of theoretical knowledge about political leadership in developing countries. Indeed, the situation is much the same even with respect to leadership in the United States, where political life is studied much more intensively. In a recent essay, James D. Barber was able to state only two very general propositions about political leadership that seem strongly supported by available evidence. These propositions are: (1) Leadership is not a fixed set of qualities possessed or even sought by all leaders everywhere. The characteristics relevant for leadership vary with the situation. (2) Leaders choose among alternative behaviors, and these choices have important impacts on public policy.[47] These propositions probably apply also in developing countries; but they are not very powerful tools for understanding the role of political leadership in political development.

A logical source for helpful hypotheses about political leadership would seem to be the "elite studies." They provide much descriptive information about the socioeconomic backgrounds of elites, or leaders; but, with very few exceptions, they do not provide data on the political attitudes or performance of leaders.[48] Since they fail to link socioeconomic-background material to political variables, their use in theorizing about political development is very limited. This state of affairs is perhaps illustrated by the fact that one of the relatively few theoretically rich treatments of political leadership in the context of development is by an economist, Albert O. Hirschman.[49]

Is it possible to generate more fruitful hypotheses about political leadership? It is impossible to say; but the effort should, I believe, be made more than it is. In this spirit, I propose the following very tentative, crude hypothesis: *Successful political leaders in developing countries tend to be skillful politicians who also are receptive to applied scientific expertise.* Several terms require brief definitions. *Leaders* refers to those with the most power; in the illustrations to follow, the term refers only to those individuals assumed to be most powerful in some national political systems. *Successful leaders* are those who (1) maintain acceptance of their *government* until the end of their term (in constitutional regimes) or until they wish to leave (in unconstitutional regimes), and (2) promote per capita income, industrialization, and/or any other reasonable measure or measures of modernization. *Skilled politicians* are those who maintain acceptance of their political *community* and *regime* during their tenure in office and generate popular and elite support or enthusiasm for the policies of their government.[50] *Applied scientific expertise* refers simply to those persons with the attitudes and skills commonly thought to be associated with modernization; examples include experimental, man-over-nature attitudes and competence in applied economics or engineering. Note that *applied scientific* here includes applied social science, especially applied economics.

These definitions are still crude, but they may help. Let us try to "test" the hypothesis with some impressionistic evidence. The hypothesis suggests a four-cell table (see Table 1).

TABLE 1. Political Skill

		High	Low
		Cell 1 Betancourt Frei Belaunde Terry Ayub Khan Nehru, Shastri Fidel Castro early Mao Tse-tung	**Cell 2** Castello Branco Porfirio Díaz
Receptivity to Applied Scientific Expertise	High		
	Low	**Cell 3** early Nkrumah early Peron early Sukarno later Mao Tse-tung Nasser	**Cell 4** later Nkrumah later Peron later Sukarno João Goulart Rojas Pinilla

This crude tabling would seem to lend tentative support to the hypothesis. Leaders in Cell 1 seem to have been more successful: in general they have impressive records in promoting modernization, and at this writing only two of them (Belaunde Terry and Ayub Khan) may be classified among those who left office by other than natural death or established procedures. By contrast, the leaders in Cell 4 all left office alive, but prematurely; and the economic and political disarray they left behind them suggests that they were not successful leaders.

The point of this illustration is not really to test the hypothesis, or even to argue very strongly for it. Besides being extremely impressionistic and post hoc, it perhaps violates Barber's warning against the hopeless search for "*the* essential traits shared by all leaders in all situations." However, Barber also cautions against "a trap of a different sort: The conclusion that every leadership situation is unique."[51] I believe that even hypotheses of this very general type may serve as useful starting points toward discovering uniformities in political leadership. Such knowledge is much needed in political-development research.

Policy Relevance

A second relatively neglected perspective in the political-development literature is the view that this literature should be useful to policy makers. There are some serious efforts by students of political development to make their work useful to policy makers, but the efforts are relatively rare,[52] and even more rarely successful.

A study conducted in 1962-1963 of political-development doctrines in the American foreign-aid program found that political development was not a salient operational concern of foreign-aid administrators; that these officials tended to be relatively insensitive to many of the ideas contained in the political-development literature; and that they were not very much aware of or interested in this literature.[53] The salience of political development has probably increased since then, and probably sensitivity to and interest in the literature has increased as well. Yet policy makers still do not find this literature very useful for their needs. Why not?

Some of the reasons for this lack of usefulness have to do with the practitioners themselves.[54] Here, I shall consider only the reasons inherent in the literature, and of the community of scholars producing it, which may help us understand why this literature is not perceived as more useful than it is. This discussion purposefully omits, therefore, treatment of the ways in which it is useful and might be more so if there were changes on the part of the officials.

One reason why officials do not find the theoretical literature useful is that the theory is so imperfect. It is not powerful theory: it is not a well-integrated set of definitions and axioms yielding hypotheses of high predictive potential. There is some power in these writings, to be sure—more than the policy makers use. Much of the literature treating political development as a dependent variable, and Huntington's article treating political development as institutionalization, are examples. However, even these contributions are very imperfect; although they are among the best we have, the policy makers (correctly) do not perceive them as *very* powerful and therefore do not regard them as very useful.

A second reason is that the scholars have not, by and large, focused their attention on variables which seem, to the policy maker, to be amenable to control or manipulation by them. For example, policy makers find such variables as mass political culture, systems of social stratification, or voluntary-association structure difficult to affect and control in a purposive, directive way. Probably the main reason for the scholars' focus is that they have operated, or tried to operate, mostly in the social system of pure science; in general they have not operated in the social system of applied social science.[55]

The norms of the social system of pure science are that knowledge should be discovered and extended for its own sake, without regard for its immediate or even predictable policy relevance, even though it is usually assumed that knowledge produced in this manner will ultimately have some policy relevance. In this sense, social scientists in the social system of pure social science write for, and receive gratification from, other social scientists in the same social system. If policy makers do not find it useful, that is no matter.

The norms of the social system of applied social science are very different. Gouldner has specified them sufficiently for our limited needs. According to him, the criteria for the selection of variables in the social system of the applied social sciences include: (1) the extent to which they are susceptible to control or manipulation; (2) how much they violate or are consistent with his values or goals; (3) how much it costs to manipulate them; and (4) often, whether they are related to leadership, which is a "presumably efficient locus of intervention" or control.[56]

In the long run, political-development research produced in the social system of pure social science will probably have greater utility for policy makers than it has so far. For this reason, and because scholars will (and should) be allowed to do what they want to do anyway, it would be unrealistic and unwise for anyone to demand that political-development researchers all redirect their efforts to make them more policy-relevant. On the other hand, the fact remains that the short-run and predictable utility of most political development research has been, is, and probably will continue to be relatively low so long as the vast majority of it is produced in the social system of pure social science.

It seems that there may be at least two ways to make research on political development more useful to policy makers. One is for pure social scientists to maintain their current reference groups, but within that social system to consider the advantages of pure social-science knowledge directing more attention to policy-relevant variables. Gouldner succinctly states the case for this approach:

It is likely . . . that even the most inveterate of pure theorists will profit from examining the hiatuses between the needs of applied fields and the accomplishments of the basic ones. For it may be that these gaps signalize, not only a handicap of the applied social scientist, but also an unnecessary defect in pure theory itself.[57]

In this way the needs of pure and applied social science may both be served at the same time. In my view, the trend to treat political development as an independent variable, and especially Huntington's contribution, exemplify this possibility.

Another way is for a larger proportion of those scholars doing political-development research willingly to adopt, in some larger measure, the norms of the social system of applied social science.

This adoption would involve individual choices and allocations of resources which many might find distasteful and unwise. In any case, to the extent that pure social scientists refuse to accept such norms, they reduce in part the validity of complaints that their work is neither used nor perceived as useful by policy makers.

My own position is that effort along both of these lines is appropriate at this time. However, I have not written these final paragraphs in order to propose exact solutions. My purpose is to try to identify why the political-development literature has not been seen as more useful than it is by policy makers. Greater attention to these factors might allow students of political development to evaluate their own stances more clearly. Moreover, it might help members of the disciplines concerned to arrive at their own formulas for more appropriate ways to define and to allocate their responsibilities.

NOTES

I wish to thank Richard Brody, Heinz Eulau, G. Bingham Powell, Sidney Verba, and Michael Haas for their helpful comments on an earlier draft of this essay.

1. Lucian W. Pye, *Aspects of Political Development* (Boston: Little, Brown, 1966), Ch. II.

2. "Develop: "1. to cause to become gradually fuller, larger, better, etc. 2. to bring into activity, as an idea. 3. to expand, as in business . . ." *Webster's New World Dictionary of the American Language, Concise Edition.* (Cleveland: World Publishing Company, 1956), p. 207.

3. So, it would seem, is most or all political theory in general, not just political-development "theory." See Harold Lasswell and Abraham Kaplan, *Power and Society* (New Haven: Yale University Press, 1957), pp. xiii, 118n.

4. Bert F. Hoselitz, "The Social Sciences in the Last Two Hundred Years," *A Reader's Guide to the Social Sciences,* ed. Bert F. Hoselitz (Glencoe: Free Press, 1959), pp. 9 ff. and passim.

5. This and earlier reviews of the literature suggest a more general conclusion. The sharp separation of fact and value that has become relatively well established in American social science has led not only to the analytic separation of these dimensions, but also to a functional division of labor among academic practitioners. Often neither social scientist nor social philosopher is equipped to perform the tasks of the other. Thus the adoption of the fact-value distinction, while important, has not been an unmixed blessing. The functions of the social scientist and the social philosopher overlap more than is commonly recognized. A greater understanding by each group of the corpus of generally accepted findings of the other, a greater propensity to make both existential and normative assumptions explicit, and a greater sensitivity to the issues at the frontiers of their respective fields would do much to make the labors of each group of theorists more satisfying.

6. For discussions (with citations) of this literature, which specify the meanings of the concepts used in this paragraph, see Samuel P. Huntington, "Political Development and Political Decay," *World Politics,* XVII (April

1965), 386-393; and Robert A. Packenham, "Political-Development Doctrines in the American Foreign Aid Program," *World Politics,* XVII (January 1966), 195-199.

7. For a more detailed elaboration of these five approaches, with citations, see Robert A. Packenham, "Approaches to the Study of Political Development," *World Politics,* XVII (October 1964), 108-120. For examples of "subsidiary" hypotheses that may be subsumed under these five approaches, see Robert A. Dahl, *Modern Political Analysis* (Englewood Cliffs: Prentice-Hall, 1964), pp. 77-92, and Barrington Moore, Jr., *Social Origins of Dictatorship and Democracy: Lord and Peasant in the Making of the Modern World* (Boston: Beacon, 1966), pp. 430-432. Dahl's hypotheses are about the conditions for peaceful adjustment of conflict, Moore's about the conditions for democracy.

8. "Function" here is used in the mathematical sense of "varies with." Thus, in this view, political development varies with the legal-formal apparatus of government. Further, although not all writers are explicit, most of them imply that political development "is caused by" the legal-formal apparatus. The same usage of "function" applies in the other four approaches to be noted.

9. Theodore D. Woolsey, *Political Science or, The State: Theoretically and Practically Considered* (2 vols.; New York: Scribners, Armstrong, 1878); Woodrow Wilson, *The State: Elements of Historical and Practical Politics: A Sketch of Institutional History and Administration* (Boston: Heath, 1892); John W. Burgess, *Political Science and Comparative Constitutional Law* (2 vols.; Boston: Ginn, 1891); Gwendolyn Carter, John H. Herz, and John C. Ranney, *Major Foreign Powers* (New York: Harcourt, Brace, 1957); Taylor R. Cole et al. *European Political Systems* (New York: Knopf, 1959); Austin Macdonald, *Latin American Politics and Government* (New York: Crowell, 1954); Miguel Jorrin, *Governments of Latin America* (New York: Van Nostrand, 1953).

10. Seymour Martin Lipset, *Political Man: The Social Bases of Politics* (Garden City: Doubleday, 1960), Ch. II; James S. Coleman, "The Political Systems of the Developing Areas," in *The Politics of the Developing Areas,* eds. Gabriel A. Almond and James S. Coleman (Princeton: Princeton University Press, 1960), pp. 538-534; Everett E. Hagen, "A Framework for Analyzing Economic and Political Change," *Development of the Emerging Countries: An Agenda for Research,* eds. Robert E. Asher et al. (Washington, D.C.: Brookings, 1962), pp. 1-8; and Phillips Cutright, "National Political Development: Measurement and Analysis," *American Sociological Review,* XXVIII (April 1963), 253-264.

11. Zbigniew Brzezinski, "The Politics of Underdevelopment," *World Politics,* XI (October 1956), 55-75; Guy Pauker, "Southeast Asia as a Problem Area in the Next Decade," *World Politics,* XI (April 1959), 342-345; Howard Wriggins, "Foreign Assistance and Political Development," *Development of the Emerging Countries,* eds. Asher et al., op. cit., pp. 181-214; John H. Badgley, "Burma's Political Crisis," *Pacific Affairs,* XXXI (December 1958), 350-351.

12. James S. Coleman, *Nigeria: Background to Nationalism* (Berkeley and Los Angeles: University of California Press, 1960); Karl W. Deutsch, *Nationalism and Social Communication* (New York: Wiley, 1953); Deutsch, "The

Growth of Nations," *World Politics,* V (January 1953), 168-196; William Kornhauser, *The Politics of Mass Society* (New York: Free Press, 1959); Selig Harrison, *India: The Most Dangerous Decades* (Princeton: Princeton University Press, 1960); Robert E. Scott, *Mexican Government in Transition* (Urbana: University of Illinois Press, 1959); Myron Weiner, *The Politics of Scarcity: Public Pressure and Political Response in India* (Chicago: University of Chicago Press, 1962); and Rupert Emerson, *From Empire to Nation: The Rise to Self-Assertion of Asian and African Peoples* (Cambridge: Harvard University Press, 1960).

13. Gabriel A. Almond and Sidney Verba, *The Civic Culture: Political Attitudes and Democracy in Five Nations* (Princeton: Princeton University Press, 1963); Edward Banfield, *The Moral Basis of a Backward Society* (Glencoe: Free Press, 1958); Nathan Leites, *On the Game of Politics in France* (Stanford: Stanford University Press, 1959); Daniel Lerner, *The Passing of Traditional Society* (Glencoe: Free Press, 1958); Lucian Pye, *Politics, Personality and Nation Building* (New Haven: Yale University Press, 1962).

14. S. M. Lipset, "Some Social Requisites of Democracy: Economic Development and Political Legitimacy," *American Political Science Review,* LIII (March 1959), 69-105. The impact of this article is indexed by the frequency of citations to it in the scholarly literature.

15. As Lipset himself recognized; see ibid., p. 70.

16. Note that once political development is defined, it can be treated as either a dependent, independent, or intervening variable. It happens that writers defining it as democracy or political modernization have tended to treat it as a dependent variable, and that writers defining it in terms of will and capacity have tended to treat it as an independent or intervening variable. However, these ways of handling definitions conceptually, and generating hypotheses from them, are not logically necessary. For example, one could treat will and capacity as a dependent variable, seeking to identify conditions under which elites with high and low will and capacity to cope occur.

17. Alfred Diamant, "Political Development: Approaches to Theory and Strategy," *Approaches to Development: Politics, Administration and Change,* eds. John D. Montgomery and William J. Siffin (New York: McGraw-Hill, 1966), 15-48; Manfred Halpern, "Toward Further Modernization of the Study of New Nations," *World Politics,* XVII (October 1964), 157-181, at p. 177; S. N. Eisenstadt, "Modernization and Conditions of Sustained Growth," *World Politics,* XVI (July 1964), 576-594; Albert O. Hirschman, *Journeys Toward Progress* (New York: Twentieth Century Fund, 1963); Robert T. Holt and John E. Turner, *The Political Basis of Economic Development* (Princeton: Van Nostrand, 1966); Warren F. Ilchman, "Foreign Aid and Political Stability: The Case of India," paper delivered at the American Political Science Association Annual Convention, New York City, September 6-10, 1966; Warren F. Ilchman and Ravindra C. Bhargava, "Balanced Thought and Economic Growth," *Economic Development and Cultural Change,* XIV (July 1966), 385-399; Joseph Nye, "Corruption and Political Development," *American Political Science Review,* LXI (June 1967), 417-427; Huntington, op. cit.; Karl W. Deutsch, *The Nerves of Government* (New York: Free Press, 1963).

A crucial assumption of some of these writers is that modernization unleashes demands by the masses which tax the capacities of governing elites and thus threaten to bring about political decay. This assumption needs to be examined more carefully. For example, some evidence from Latin American countries suggests that modernization, defined mainly as urbanization, has not very markedly increased *political* demands nor the incidence of radicalism. See Daniel Goldrich, "Toward the Comparative Study of Politicization in Latin America," *Contemporary Cultures and Societies of Latin America*, eds. Dwight B. Heath and Richard N. Adams (New York: Random House, 1965), pp. 361-366, William Mangin, "Latin American Squatter Settlements: A Problem and a Solution," *Latin American Research Review*, II (Summer 1967), 65-98, especially pp. 82-85.

18. Op. cit., pp. 393 ff. See also Huntington, *Political Order in Changing Societies* (New Haven: Yale University Press, 1968), passim. Except where indicated otherwise, subsequent references to Huntington refer to his 1965 article (see n. 6 above).

19. Gabriel A. Almond and G. Bingham Powell, *Comparative Politics: A Developmental Approach* (Boston: Little, Brown, 1966), pp. 105, 216-217. See also Almond, "Political Systems and Political Change," *American Behavioral Scientist*, VI (June 1963), 3-10, and "A Developmental Approach to Political Systems," *World Politics*, XVII (January 1965), 183-214.

20. David E. Apter, *The Politics of Modernization* (Chicago: University of Chicago Press, 1965), p. 231. See also p. 223. On pp. 181-182, Apter suggests how political parties may be seen as either independent, intervening, or dependent variables.

21. Diamant, op. cit., pp. 25-26.

22. Op. cit., p. 177. On "uncontrolled forces," see n. 17 above.

23. Op. cit., p. 583. Eisenstadt here uses the term political "modernization," but for him, as for many (though not all) authors, political "development" and political "modernization" appear to be synonymous. For example, see his "Bureaucracy and Political Development,"*Bureaucracy and Political Development*, ed. Joseph LaPalombara (Princeton: Princeton University Press, 1963), pp. 96-119, at p. 96. This essay contains references to many other writings by Professor Eisenstadt.

24. Op. cit., pp. 394-405.

25. One of the very few works of empirical research which measures institutionalization, over time and with hard data, is Nelson W. Polsby, "The Institutionalization of the United States House of Representatives," *American Political Science Review*, LXII (March 1968), 144-168. Polsby's concept of institutionalization and the measures he uses are similar to but somewhat simpler than the ones proposed by Huntington. Even so, Polsby found the task of operationalizing the concept a formidable one; despite his own diligence and imaginativeness, he remarks that "the operational indices I am about to suggest [and use] . . . may strike the knowledgeable reader as exceedingly crude; I invite the ingenuity of my colleagues to the task of suggesting improvements." Ibid., p. 145. Polsby's experience suggests that using Huntington's more elaborate formulation at the more complex level of the whole national polity would be extremely difficult. I do not know any easy way to resolve the problem, but efforts toward resolution would be very worthwhile.

26. Op. cit., pp. 394, 407-408, 427.

27. Diamant, op. cit., pp. 25, 28-38; Eisenstadt, "Modernization and Conditions of Sustained Growth," quotations at pp. 583, 593, 587, 589, 593, respectively.

28. Diamant, op. cit., pp. 15-28, explicitly on pp. 25-26.

29. Ibid., p. 25.

30. Ibid., pp. 28, 26; the review of the literature is on pp. 28-46.

31. Ibid., p. 25.

32. Ibid., p. 47; emphasis added. See Everett E. Hagen, *On the Theory of Social Change: How Economic Growth Begins* (Homewood: Dorsey, 1962); David C. McClelland, *The Achieving Society* (Princeton: Van Nostrand, 1961).

33. See Packenham, "Political-Development Doctrines," p. 204.

34. For a good discussion of this point, see J. Roland Pennock, "Political Development, Political Systems, and Political Goods," *World Politics,* XVIII (April 1966), 415-434.

35. Op. cit., pp. 394, 405-417 and passim. For another thoughtful treatment of the normative dimension of political development, see Pennock, op. cit. Pennock's discussion of political "goods"—security, justice, liberty, and welfare—deserves more attention than we give it here.

36. Opera cit.

37. I originally found this term in Nye, op. cit., p. 419, but it is also used by Ralf Dahrendorf to describe "functional theory." Dahrendorf adds that "American values are characterized by the desire to preserve progress rather than any particular state of affairs. But this attitude is nonetheless conservative for its progressiveness . . . this is an attitude ill prepared for radical change. . . . Like every conservatism, that of American values is vulnerable to the exigencies of history, and betrays traces of anxiety and insecurity." "European Sociology and the American Self-Image," *Archives Européenes de Sociologie,* (#2, 1961), 364.

38. Op. cit., p. 505. See also Ch. VI (the title of which is "Democracy in Asia: India and the Price of Peaceful Change"), especially 406-410; Ch. VII-IX; and the Epilogue, especially pp. 505-508.

39. Ibid., pp. 506, 508. Compare W. Arthur Lewis, *Politics in West Africa* (New York: Oxford University Press, 1965), and Charles C. Moskos, Jr., and Wendell Bell, "Emerging Nations and Ideologies of American Social Scientists," *The American Sociologist,* II (May 1967), 69. It is of interest that among the eighteen countries Moskos and Bell cite as having political systems "with public liberties and competitive parties," virtually all but India have relatively small populations.

40. The points made in this paragraph and the rest of this section about neglected areas are matters of judgment, and it is impossible to document my judgments adequately in the space available. Therefore, I shall note only some illustrations of my points, or exceptions to the rule, or both. Obviously, students of political development always have had to rely to some extent on historical data. However, there has been until recently a stress on comparisons at single points in time using quantitative data, rather than historical comparisons using more qualitative data. Some recent examples of the latter include the already cited works by Almond and Powell, Moore, and Holt and Turner, and also S. N. Eisenstadt, *The Political Systems of Empires* (Glencoe: Free Press, 1963); Reinhard Bendix, *Nation-Building and Citizenship* (New York: Wiley, 1964); S. M. Lipset, *The First New Nation* (New York: Basic Books, 1963); and Samuel P. Huntington, "Political Modernization: America vs. Europe," *World Politics,* XVIII (April 1966), 378-414.

41. In a generally favorable review of L. W. Pye and S. Verba (eds.), *Political Culture and Political Development* (Princeton: Princeton University Press, 1965), Aristide Zolberg wrote that "unexplainably, the only thing that seems to be systematically excluded from the domain of 'political culture' is the explicit set of organized political concepts usually encompassed by the terms 'political thought' and 'political ideology.' " *American Political Science Review*, LX (March 1966), 121. For some recent works with emphasis on ideology in the context of political development, see David Apter, *The Politics of Modernization*, Ch. IX; and Apter (ed.), *Ideology and Discontent* (New York: Free Press, 1964).

42. Dahrendorf, op. cit., pp. 357-358; Moskos and Bell, op. cit., pp. 71-72.

43. One of the very few treatments of this topic is David H. Bayley, *Public Liberties in the New States* (Chicago: Rand McNally, 1964), which contains a short bibliography.

44. Almond and Powell, op. cit.; also Irving Louis Horowitz, *Three Worlds of Development* (New York: Oxford University Press, 1966).

45. See Fred W. Riggs, "Systems Theory: Structural Analysis," Ch. VIII in the present volume; Robert A. Packenham, "Legislatures and Political Development," *Legislatures in Developmental Perspective*, eds. Allan Kornberg and Lloyd Musolf (Durham, N.C.: Duke University Press, in press).

46. See especially the works of Ilchman, Holt and Turner, and Hirschman cited in n. 17 above; William C. Mitchell, "The Shape of Things to Come: From Political Sociology to Political Economy, *American Behavioral Scientist*, XI (November-December 1967), 8-20, 37.

47. James D. Barber, *Political Leadership in American Government* (Boston: Little, Brown, 1964), pp. 5-10.

48. The two best critiques of elite studies I have seen are Dankwart A. Rustow, "The Study of Elites," *World Politics*, XVIII (July 1966), 690-717, and Lewis J. Edinger and Donald D. Searing, "Social Background in Elite Analysis: A Methodological Inquiry," *American Political Science Review*, XLI (June 1967), 428-445. An innovative study which *does* link motivational and socioeconomic variables to political behavior is James David Barber, *The Lawmakers* (New Haven: Yale University Press, 1965).

49. Op. cit. See also "Philosophers and Kings: Studies in Leadership," *Daedalus*, XCVII (Summer 1968), especially the Introduction by Dankwart A. Rustow.

50. The distinctions between *political community* (existing territorial arrangements), *regime* ("rules of the game"), and *government* (those in power) are borrowed from David Easton, "An Approach to the Analysis of Political Systems," *World Politics*, IX (April 1957), 383-400. Where Easton speaks of "support," I use "acceptance"; thus my use of "support" in "generate popular and elite support or enthusiasm" implies a more specific meaning than that suggested by Easton.

51. *Political Leadership in American Government*, p. 6.

52. For some of the main exceptions, see the items cited in Packenham, "Political-Development Doctrines," p. 205, n. 34. Two recent efforts which, in my judgment, deserve the attention of policy makers—not only in the United States, but also (and perhaps especially) in the developing countries—are Huntington, op. cit.; and Giovanni Sartori, "Political Development and

Political Engineering," *Public Policy,* XVII (1968), 261-298. There is much potential utility for policy makers in Huntington's essay even for those like myself who may have misgivings about his normative premises.

53. Packenham, "Political-Development Doctrines."

54. Ibid., pp. 229-235.

55. The distinction used here between pure and applied social science in terms of the social systems of the two enterprises rather than their characteristics per se borrows, I hope accurately, from Norman W. Storer, *The Social System of Science* (New York: Holt, Rinehart & Winston, 1966); Herbert A. Shepard, "Basic Research and the Social System of Pure Science," *Philosophy of Science,* XXIII (January 1956), 48-57; Alvin W. Gouldner, "Theoretical Requirements of the Applied Social Sciences," *American Sociological Review,* XXII (February 1957), 92-102; and, especially Kathleen Archibald, "The Social Structures of Pure and Applied Social Science" (Santa Monica: unpublished paper, 1967).

56. Gouldner, op. cit., as reprinted in Warren G. Bennis, Kenneth D. Benne, and Robert Chin (eds.), *The Planning of Change: Readings in the Applied Behavioral Sciences* (New York: Holt, Rinehart & Winston, 1961), pp. 83-95, at pp. 88-90.

57. Ibid., pp. 94-95.

8 Systems Theory: Structural Analysis

FRED W. RIGGS, University of Hawaii

> The fact remains that some form of functionalism is the only current alternative to Marxism as the basis for some kind of general theory in political science. . . . But its usefulness must be assessed by the value of the explanatory propositions to which it guides the investigator of a particular problem. It may, if nothing else, provide a framework for the comparative discussion of different political systems, for which the vocabulary of traditional political theory is no longer adequate. It may direct attention to causes and effects which would otherwise pass unnoticed. . . . It is only as a would-be general theory that it becomes more likely to be misleading than helpful, and to by-pass the search for the rigorous and testable statements of cause and effect out of which a political science is to be constructed.—*W. G. Runciman* [1]

I. THE CONTROVERSY IN COMPARATIVE GOVERNMENT

In recent years structural-functionalism and system theory have made a striking impact on political science, notably in its new sub-fields of comparative politics and comparative public administration—subfields which might well be reconnected through the traditional field of comparative government.

Much criticism has been provoked by this borrowed theoretical framework, borrowed in the sense that it has been taken largely from sociology and anthropology. A sharp, even peevish, debate has ensued. In this essay I propose, not to review the controversy as such, but to reconsider it in the light of our need for a theoretical perspective to help us understand governmental phenomena (both political and administrative) in the vastly expanded array of "sovereign" states that have made their appearance in the aftermath of the last great war. Following Runciman, as quoted above, I shall argue that, as an analytic framework, system theory and structural-functionalism can be very helpful—provided the word "structure" is weighted as heavily as "function"—but that, as a doctrine alone, it is misleading and treacherous.

It was precisely the need for a fresh analytic framework to enable political science to deal more systematically with the phenomena

194

exhibited by the new Afro-Asian states that made structural-functionalism so appealing. Familiar and well-established institutional categories—parliament, president, federal and unitary systems, monarchy, republic, executive, legislature, judiciary, one-, two-, and multiparty government—seemed to lose their generic utility. Functionalism was seized upon as a welcome solution. It seemed to make little difference what the institutional structures of a political system might be. More important were the common purposes of any polity, its functional requisites. Whereas the patterns of government appeared to vary and change with kaleidoscopic indeterminateness, the new concept of a political system offered a reassuring sense of stability. Under the superficial appearance of change one could detect an ineluctable order: every political system had to solve a limited set of problems in order to survive. It mattered not what concrete structures of government, what formal institutions, were chosen to satisfy these needs. The important thing was to identify a few basic needs, and then observe with what infinitely varied fecundity proliferating polities generated means to satisfy these needs.

The Preoccupation with Functions

The writings of Gabriel Almond best illustrate this trend. They have been clear and much-quoted, and they represent some consensus among members of the influential Committee on Comparative Politics. As formulated in the opening essay of the Almond-Coleman volume,[2] published almost a decade ago, seven essential functions of any political system were classified, under the broad headings of "inputs" and "outputs."

Subsequently Almond and the other members of the Committee on Comparative Politics rephrased their functional conceptualization in terms of political change. Thus in 1965 Almond published an essay urging that political systems be viewed in a developmental context. Using a biological analogy, he suggested that just as an amoeba and a vertebrate resemble each other insofar as they perform basic physiological functions but differ in the structures by which these functions are performed, so simple and complex political systems share common functions but differ in their structural characteristics, the latter becoming more differentiated and interdependent.[3] In this essay Almond also added to his classification of functions, suggesting that the seven input-output functions belonged to a larger category of *conversion* functions, to which should be added two additional large categories—*capabilities* and *system maintenance and adaptation* functions—each of which was analyzed into a set of component elements. Although recognizing the importance of structures, this essay did not specify their characteristics, whether in simple or complex systems.

In 1966 this framework of comparative politics was further

expanded by reference to four types of problems faced by political systems in the process of development. Almond and Powell wrote:

The first of these is the problem of penetration and integration; we refer to this as the problem of *state building*. The second type of system-development problem is that of loyalty and commitment, which we refer to as *nation building*. The third problem is that of *participation,* the pressure from groups in the society for having a part in the decision making of the system. And the fourth is the problem of *distribution,* or welfare, the pressure from the domestic society to employ the coercive power of the political system to redistribute income, wealth, opportunity, and honor.[4]

It is inherent in system theory, nevertheless, that any system, by definition, contains a set of objects that are related to each other. In social systems, the nature of the relationships is that of inter-actions. Almond himself implicitly recognizes that these component parts of a political system are structures, and that their reciprocal relations as they affect the system are functions. Clearly, therefore, if we are to use the conversion, capability, and system-maintenance functions of a political system as a basis for analysis, we must identify the structures which perform these functions and discover how they are related to each other. Almond and Powell direct attention to this subject when they write that "political development has been defined as the increased differentiation and specialization of political structures and the increased secularization of political culture."[5] Yet a certain vagueness pervades their book whenever the subject of political structures is discussed. We learn that the solution to the problem of state building is "essentially a structural problem. That is to say, what is involved is primarily a matter of the differentiation of new roles, structures, and subsystems which penetrate the countryside."[6] Concretely, this problem seems to be linked to the emergence of centralized bureaucracies. By contrast, the problems of participation are "usually associated with, or have the consequence of producing, some form of political infrastructure—political groups, cliques, and factions, and representative legislative assemblies."[7]

It is interesting to find that bureaucracies are discussed in the Almond-Powell volume primarily under the functional category of rule application, political parties under interest aggregation, legislatures under rule making, and courts under rule adjudication. The authors say that each of these structures performs other functions as well, and that other structures perform each of the functions just mentioned. However, I fail to find definitions in the book for any of the governmental structures mentioned, except for bureaucracy, which is described as a "group of formally organized offices and duties, linked in elaborate hierarchy, subordinate to the formal rule makers." Even this definition uses a functional category, rule making, to identify the apex of the bureaucratic hierarchy.

In their discussion of bureaucracies, Almond and Powell draw on a five-fold classification of "types of bureaucracies" suggested by Merle Fainsod, namely, representative, party-state, military-dominated, ruler-dominated, and ruling bureaucracies.[8] It is significant that even here the criteria used are not structural characteristics of different kinds of bureaucracies but, rather, diverse political settings of bureaucracies, as Almond and Powell themselves point out. In the absence of explicitly structural criteria for the definition and classification of structures, we find a curious vacillation between the view that structures are somehow either unifunctional or omnifunctional. Although it is frequently asserted that any given structure can and does perform a variety of functions, unifunctionalism is implicit in the tendency to discuss structures in connection with a salient function, and omnifunctionalism is implicit in a preoccupation with functionalism which often gives the impression that almost any structure could perform the functions which are requisite for system survival.

In my view, a given structure may perform several, but not all, functions, and a limited number of structures may be capable of performing the key functions of a political system. Later in this essay I shall describe a structural framework which may be used in hypotheses about how given functions can or cannot be performed.

In thus drawing attention to the importance of structure I do not claim originality. A similar, though more extreme, view is taken by Joseph LaPalombara, himself a leading member of the Committee on Comparative Politics, who writes:

... while the so-called structural-functional approach to the comparative study of political systems has served to cut away the parochialism of Western scholarship and perhaps alerted us to dimensions of political organization and behavior that might have been otherwise overlooked, I do not at all feel that it provides the key to a general theory of political systems. I think it is now fair to say that a number of us drank deeply of the promise of this particular approach only to awaken with an enormous intellectual hangover.[9]

LaPalombara discerns a trend against structural-functionalism, and cites Morroe Berger, Robert Presthus, and Carl Beck as evidence. These authors, however, direct their attack primarily against the legal-rational model of bureaucracy expounded by Max Weber, and it is not clear to me that they necessarily reject structural-functionalism as such, although I suspect that some of them are essentially adherents of a logical form of positivism, which directs attention primarily to the behavior and attitudes of individual actors rather than to the characteristics of social systems containing a plurality of actors.

By linking functionalism with the input side of the political-system model, LaPalombara seems to imply that the increased focus on outputs by Almond and other members of the Comparative Politics committee, reveals a rejection of structural-functionalism. Yet it was in the context of this framework that outputs were first presented as a set of functions. Perhaps the confusion arises because outputs are linked with *governmental* structures, whereas inputs are associated with *nongovernmental* processes. The corrective required is not simply a stress on outputs—although I agree that this stress is needed—but also an emphasis on structures, defined in their own terms, and then related to the various political functions, including outputs as well as inputs.

Nevertheless, I do agree with LaPalombara in thinking that structural-functionalism, *as adapted to comparative politics,* has proven a heady brew that has both numbed and stimulated. What is needed now is not its rejection but a new synthesis. Such a synthesis, I submit, can be generated if we give as much attention to the *structural* characteristics of political systems as we have heretofore given to their *functional* aspects. In other words, we need a systematically constructed framework for dealing with governmental structures, based on criteria essentially different from the functional requisites of social and/or political systems. With such a framework, I believe, we might overcome some of the difficulties inherent in a predominantly functionalist approach.

An Antidynamic Bias

Another pitfall of system theory and structural-functional theory involves its allegedly nondynamic qualities. Almond himself refers to this point, recognizing the paradox involved in trying to use it for the analysis of political change. "Systems theory," he writes, "does have a static, 'equilibrium' bias. . . . The only answer to this criticism," he continues, "is that this seems to be the way sciences develop—not by orderly, systematic progression, but in a dialectical process involving overemphases and neglects. If we are to come to grips more effectively with political change, we shall have to redress this imbalance, adapt systems theory in a developmental direction . . . ."[10]

Yet the question must be raised whether system theory is inherently static, as alleged. Is it necessary to reject system theory in order to find some other ordering framework within which to deal with the problem of change? Perhaps the difficulty lies in a one-sided interpretation of the meaning of system theory. Certainly in the empirical work of the sociologists who have made use of structural-functionalism we find considerable interest in problems of change. Marion Levy, for example, has recently published a lengthy work on modernization in the context of a very explicit structural-functional system model.[11]

Why should it seem so self-evident that system theory is inherently static? Perhaps the conclusion results from a failure to distinguish adequately between an analytic and a prescriptive theoretical orientation. The naturalistic fallacy implies that what is ought to be, and few political scientists would explicitly subscribe to this fallacy; yet implicitly they often seem to accept it when they employ system theory.

At one level of analysis in system theory the assertion is that *if* a system were to maintain itself over a period of time, then we could assume that its structures were able to satisfy certain functions which are required for system maintenance. This is a big *if*, however. It provides some leverage for purposes of analysis, just as the economists' assumptions of market competition and economic rationality provide such leverage, although it is well understood that actual systems in fact do change, that markets are never perfectly competitive, and that "economic man" is nonexistent. Moreover, to build an analysis by reasoning from an arbitrary assumption by no means implies that that condition is normatively desirable unless explicit policy recommendations are drawn from the analysis. We need not assume that an unchanging system is good any more than we have to assume that a purely competitive market is good, although clearly there are social theorists who make such assumptions.

Another misunderstanding arises from ambiguities in the key word *function*. In mathematics it refers to a correlation between two variables, and in system theory, to a system-relevant relation between parts. In this sense the function of a structure may be to change a system, just as much as it is its function to maintain it. However, the word is also used in a narrower sense, to refer to a relationship between a structure and a system which serves to maintain the system. When one says that something is functional, he normally means something of this kind. Marion Levy, in order to distinguish between these two meanings, proposed that the word *function* be limited to the first concept, and the neologism *eufunction* be used for the second. This distinction has not been picked up in the comparative-politics literature, leading to a serious confusion of ideas. It is falsely inferred that because a structure is said to have a function it is also a eufunction, that is to say, it serves to maintain the system. However, clearly one of the most important functions of political structures is to bring about system change.[12]

When Levy pointed out that only some functions are eufunctional, he simultaneously noted that other functions tend to be disruptive, that is, that some structures do lead to system change. Unfortunately he accepted an established term for this concept, *dysfunction,* rather than coin another neologism, and in doing so ran into another ambiguity. The prefix *dys-* carries a negative connotation, so that the idea of a function which changes a system is confused with the idea of a function which is bad or disruptive. By confusing the two ideas, many critics have unjustifiably concluded that to speak of a structure as *dysfunctional* implies hostility to change, and therefore implies a static, even a conservative, normative orientation.

This terminological difficulty led Gideon Sjoberg to coin the phrase *contradictory functional requirements.* He points out that any system may require functions which can be met only by a set of structures that are to some degree incompatible with each other. Uneasy tensions between such structures, entailing conflict or competition, may lead to system change.[13]

Sjoberg's formulation no doubt entails difficulties, but they need not detain us here. More importantly, the formulation suggests the idea that conflict may be a necessary characteristic of certain kinds of systems. It is strange that one school of thought, identified with such names as Marx and Simmel, should emphasize conflict and another, linked with Weber and Parsons, stress system, as though the two ideas were incompatible. Rather, it seems to me, system and conflict are two different perspectives for looking at the interactions of collectivities. Although it may be true that excessive conflict would lead to the collapse of a system, it is equally true that one of the essential functions of any system involves the institutionalization and channeling of conflict. Moreover, if there were no conflict, there would characteristically be no need for an interactive system. Indeed, a political system without conflict would probably lack coherence and vigor.

This idea will scarcely seem paradoxical if we think of the prevalence of opposition in a competitive-party system. The idea of majority rule implies conflict with minority demands. Also, judicial procedures institutionalize opposition between prosecutors and defendants. Our market model similarly institutionalizes competition between entrepreneurs, and game models depict conflict between sportsmen. Galbraith has made the idea of "countervailing power" central to his explanation of how American capitalism and democracy survive. In other words, it may well be that conflict between rival structures, or components of structures, in any political system is essential for the fulfillment of the functional requisites for survival of that system.

If we think of social systems as a means for institutionalizing a maximum of manageable conflict, then the allegedly antidynamic bias of system theory may be overcome. It is easy enough to see that although a conflict-free system might be antidynamic or static, one in which conflict is institutionalized may not only be dynamic but also liable to fundamental changes, especially if the existing structures prove incapable of resolving conflicts, thereby generating the need for new patterns of settlement. Whereas failure to create such patterns may lead to the breakdown of a system, success can lead to further development. From this perspective, developed political systems are seen as ones that have learned how to institutionalize and resolve more numerous and complex types of conflict than have less developed systems.

In this context, the main point of Almond's conversion functions, of the input-output matrix, is that it provides for conflict resolution. Conflicting demands are related to each other and reconciled in terms of the decision-making and decision-implementing processes of a polity. But in this respect specification of the political-system model is simply another way of phrasing the political aspects of a social system, and accordingly the integrative subsystem, to use Parsonian terminology. If we see the integrative function as a process of coordinating and harmonizing contradictory tendencies or interests within a social system, then we can view functionalism, not as a way of reducing life to a still-life composition, but rather as a way of conceptualizing its dynamic, ever-changing turbulence.

The system model leads us to ask how a political system can institutionalize conflict and conflict-resolution. This question directs our attention to the component structures of a polity, and to the overarching question: What is the political system itself?

The Unit of Analysis

In view of the preoccupation of writers on comparative politics with functionalism, it is scarcely surprising that they have defined political system in an analytic rather than a concrete sense. Thus the term refers to an aggregate of all so-called political functions performed in a given society, rather than to that society's government, defined institutionally. In this usage, we can scarcely distinguish a "political system" from a "society."

It may well be impossible to determine whether or not a political system so conceptualized has survived, and hence to discover what system maintenance implies. The only operational meaning of the term might be the survival of the society of which the political system is an aspect. In this sense, the Chinese political system survives to the present day and has been in continuous existence from the dawn of Chinese history. By contrast, the Tasmanian political system came to an end with the death of the Tasmanians.

If, however, we think of political systems concretely, as institutions of government, then we can give a precise meaning to the idea of functional requisite, because we can determine whether or not a given form of government survives. For example, during much of Chinese history government took the form of bureaucratic empires, which flourished intermittently, separated by interdynastic periods of fragmented or feudalistic anarchy. It is possible to determine with some precision the necessary conditions for the survival of this form of government, and to point exactly to the date of its collapse, for the last time, in 1911.

Some contend that the present Communist regime in China is a revival, functionally speaking, of the old Chinese empire; but this is to use the word "empire" for two different types of government, illustrating the basic ambiguity of much of our conventional political terminology. Characteristics which the Communist regime has that no previous Chinese bureaucratic empire had are the presence of a political party, an electoral system, and an elected national assembly. It will simplify our analysis to use a single expression for the *composite structure which includes one or more party, elections, and an elected assembly.* I propose to call this structure a *constitutive system.* All contemporary Western governments have a constitutive system, and almost all contemporary non-Western governments have also established, within the last half-century, a constitutive system. So important is this concrete structure of government that its presence may be used as a touchstone of modernity. For convenience of reference, I shall speak of any government with a constitutive system as a *tonic* polity, and any government lacking a constitutive system or knowing nothing about the possibility of having such a system as *nontonic.* [14]

It now becomes clear that Chinese bureaucratic empires were a variety of the nontonic species, whereas the Chinese Communist regime is a variety of the tonic species. More generally, all modern and most modernizing states have tonic polities, whereas all traditional forms of government were nontonic.

Expanding the structural criteria, we can specify different varieties of government with considerable precision. For example, let us identify the Chinese Communist regime as a variety of tonic polity by classifying its constitutive system as noncompetitive. If opposition parties are permitted to nominate candidates for election to an assembly, and if some of them succeed in being elected, then a constitutive system is competitive; otherwise it is noncompetitive. We can then call any tonic polity with a competitive constitutive system a *contratonic* polity, and any tonic polity with a noncompetitive constitutive system an *anatonic* polity. [15]

TABLE 1. Some Basic Types of Government

Type of Government	Tonic		Nontonic
	Contratonic	Anatonic	
Constitutive system	yes	yes	no
Competitive constitutive system	yes	no	no

A constitutive system by definition includes one or more political parties, an electoral system, and an elected assembly.

A constitutive system is defined as competitive if one or more political parties can secure the election of candidates to the elective assembly.

The Chinese Communist regime, therefore, may be an anatonic polity, whereas the Western democratic regimes have contratonic polities. It is interesting to note that contratonic polities have arisen in societies in which feudalism formerly prevailed, and anatonic polities have arisen mainly in societies which once had imperial bureaucratic forms of government.

Significantly, contemporary studies in comparative politics have focused attention mainly on behaviors related to constitutive systems, while paying very little attention to other major components of government, notably the office of the chief executive or head of state, and the hierarchy of offices under the authority of the executive. I shall refer to this hierarchy of offices as the *bureaucracy*. Note that this is an extension of normal usage, for it includes cabinet-level positions, and military as well as civilian offices. Both tonic and nontonic polities can be classified according to the characteristics of their bureaucracies. Indeed, the key differences between governments in modernizing societies and those in the "modern" societies probably lie in the structure of their bureaucracies rather than in their constitutive systems.

We may well discover structural requisites to be more significant than functional requisites in the analysis of political and administrative systems. A *structural requisite* may be defined as a necessary, though not a sufficient, structural condition for the accomplishment of a given effect, or for the performance of a given function. The input-output or conversion functions identified by Almond may be performed well only in tonic polities, and insofar as they are performed in nontonic polities, they are performed spasmodically and ineffectually.

If we take a concrete structure, government, as our basic unit of analysis, rather than an analytically defined aspect of society, the political system, I think we can overcome the preoccupation with functions associated with structural-functional theory. Moreover, since governments do not eliminate conflict, but furnish institutional means of structuring and resolving conflict, we can dissolve the antidynamic bias often attributed to social-system theory.

Setting, Context, and Environment

A serious limitation of most structural-functional analysis is its preoccupation with a whole-system framework, yet this limitation is certainly not necessary. The distinction involved here is related to but different from the familiar dichotomy between an "open" and a "closed" system. A closed-system framework is useful in mechanics and other applications, but it has been widely recognized that social systems are typically, if not always, open. Consequently problems of boundary maintenance and cross-boundary relations are typically included in a complete discussion of system theory.

This consideration leads to ecological and contextual frameworks for the study of constraints placed on a system by its environments, and also of the ways in which a system changes its environment. Such frameworks are essential for system theory and may suggest better hypotheses for explaining political behavior than the analysis of intrasystem structures and functions.

It is necessary to distinguish two large subcategories of a system's *environment*. We may draw here on a concept taken from general-systems theory, namely the "order of interaction." Different systems may be of similar or different orders. Let us refer to all other systems of the same order as the system under analysis as its *context*. By contrast, we can speak of all other systems of a different order from the system under analysis as its *setting*.

If the system under analysis is a government, then all other governments compose the context of a given government. If we think of all governments as together constituting a system, such as an international system, then any particular government may be regarded as a subsystem or component of that larger system. To examine the interactions between a government and its context is, therefore, to make a *contextual analysis*. Such an analysis includes a study of how the context influences the system, and also how the system influences its context.

In this sense a national government may be viewed not only as an actor in an international system, but also as a subsystem, and hence in part a product of the international system. In other words, in relation to the international system, a polity may be treated both as a dependent and as an independent variable. Similarly, any component of a national government, such as an elective assembly or a bureaucracy, can be treated contextually as being shaped by a larger system of which it is a part, and also as constituting a contributing element to that larger system.

It is sometimes convenient to use the expression *partial-system analysis* in place of contextual analysis. This labeling involves treating any system as a subsystem of some larger system that contains other systems of the same order. Since the definition of a system is never absolute, but relative, we can treat any given set of interacting parts as a *whole system,* viewed from the outside looking in. The same system can also be seen as a *partial system* in relation to its context, viewed from the inside out.

Contextual (or partial-system) analysis differs in important respects from *ecological analysis,* which involves relations between a system and other systems of a different order, namely its setting. Thus the *physical* world of time-space, and of material resources, constitutes one ingredient of the noncontextual environment, or setting, of any social system. Another part of the setting of any social system is the *cultural* environment containing man-made traits, institutions, and currencies which are transmitted from generation to generation.

If we think of the basic unit of social systems as consisting of roles played by human actors, then we can distinguish analytically between the roles and the persons enacting them. The personal characteristics of these actors undoubtedly influence the way in which they perform the roles, but these characteristics can be treated as environmental to the role and as belonging to a different order from that of a social system. No doubt the definition of a social system could be expanded to include the individuals who enact roles in it as a part of the system, but we can achieve a substantial increase in clarity of analysis if we treat persons as part of the *human environment* of social systems. So considered, the human environment includes not only personal characteristics of individuals, but also aggregative demographic and demotypic characteristics: the numbers, distribution, growth patterns, and ascriptive attributes of human populations.

To summarize, a distinction has been made between two levels of environment that interact with social systems. One level, involving interactions between systems of the same order, is referred to as a *context.* Another level, involving interactions between systems of different orders, is called a *setting.* Interactions between a system and its context can be studied through *contextual* (or *partial-system*) analysis, whereas interactions between a system and its setting are examined by *ecological* analysis. Ecological analysis of social systems involves studying their relations with physical, cultural, and human systems. Note that in this usage the word "ecology" is not a synonym for "environment," but refers to patterned relationships between a system and part, but not all, of its environment, for it includes only that part of a system's environment which is of a different order, that is, its setting.

The distinction between contextual and ecological analysis may not be important from a general-systems perspective, where biological and mechanical systems are emphasized, but it is very important in the study of social systems because these systems involve deliberate decision making by the actors in the system. The teleological, or intentional, aspect of social action implies the presence of conscious efforts to change the environment of social systems. Such efforts take on a very different meaning when applied to systems of the same order than they do when applied to systems of a different order. In other words, for one person to try to change another person, or for one polity to manipulate another, raises questions of a different kind from those which arise when a person or polity seeks to change its setting. The latter is involved in *development,* but, I think, the former raises questions of *self-aggrandizement* and the distribution of power. Whereas an increase in the capacity of a social system to change its setting signalizes development, an increase in its capacity to change its context may actually block development. Let us look at these propositions more closely.

Ecological analysis recognizes that interactions are asymmetrical in the sense that a system may have more influence over its setting, or the setting may prove, relatively, more decisive for the system. A *characteristic, if not a defining feature, of development is the increasing capacity of a system to influence its setting.* Such phenomena as economic growth should be viewed as possible consequences of development—not as synonyms for development.

The same cannot, I believe, be said about relations between a system and its context. More developed systems probably enter into more intricate and interdependent patterns of interaction with their context, but we cannot say that this interaction involves an increase in their ability to control their context. Rather, *an enhanced ability to control a system's context demonstrates an increase in its power position.* Development probably requires that a social system become increasingly sensitive to constraints shaped by its context. Thus a polity's drive for more power may obstruct rather than enhance prospects for development in the international system.

Our interest here, however, is not so much in how a system influences its context as in how it is influenced by its context. This perspective is reinforced when we refer to contextual analysis as partial-system analysis. In other words, we must not only ask how a given system is related to its parts (whole-system perspective) and to its setting (ecological analysis), but also how it is related to the context of which it is a part (partial-system perspective).

To illustrate, we may study Congress as a whole system by looking at the relations among its branches, committees, caucuses, party groups, and the like. However, we also need to study Congress as a partial system by asking how it fits into a larger framework of government, and how this framework affects the power and behavior of Congress.

For some reason we are prone not to view social systems in context. For example, traditional community-power studies in American political science typically ask how individuals and groups within a city affect its political decisions, but not how the city's decisions are affected by the larger framework of state and national governments in which it is embedded. Similarly, we view national governments as autonomous actors on a world stage, asking how they make decisions internally, and how they influence international politics; but until recently we have failed to ask how the larger arena of world politics shapes the domestic policies of member states.

Comparative studies of non-Western polities dramatize this point by giving us absurd findings when we fail to apply a contextual framework. For example, research on an Indian city carried out in terms of a community power-structure framework may lead to the ridiculous finding that no decisions are made in the city. A contextual framework would perhaps lead to the conclusion that decisions for the city are largely made by units outside the city, such as the district, province, and union governments, and also by infra-urban units of governance within the city. Similarly, studies of a polity such as Thailand have led me to the opinion that international pressures and foreign models exert decisive influence on the outcomes of revolutions and crises within that country.

Once one is alerted to the importance of partial-systems analysis, one immediately becomes aware of the extent to which decisions made in cities and states are affected by political and social forces outside the jurisdiction under study. Similarly, even American politics at the national level is much affected by what happens in world politics, despite our presumed autonomy as an independent superpower.

The importance of contextual (partial-system) analysis has long been recognized in other disciplines. Linguists, for example, have shown that the meaning of a word is determined by the context in which it is used rather than by its abstract symbolic meaning as given in a dictionary. Similarly, psychologists have come to view the human person within a matrix of social interactions rather than as a clinically abstracted biological organism. System theory, applied to the study of government, impels us to apply a contextual framework in this field also.

Applying such a perspective, we can take a fresh look at the functional categories used by Parsons and Almond. The Parsonian concept of "goal attainment" and Almond's idea of "capabilities" strike me as particularly relevant to relations between a polity and its context. In more traditional usage, the power position of a government (or a component of government) measures the degree to which it can shape its context. Alternatively stated, weight of power varies inversely with the extent to which a political structure is shaped by its context.

This frame of reference enables us to relate system theory to conflict at the partial-system level, as we did above at the whole-system level. Just as conflict provides a reason for seeking integration (coordination) within a government, so conflict also sets the stage for interactions between a government and its context. Thus, system theory, instead of blinding us to conflict and limiting our attention to what happens within a system, should explicitly direct our attention to power struggles and manifest interactions between polities and their contexts.

Contextual analysis also suggests that more precision is needed in the way we use the word "function." No system or structure, as such, has a function. However, if we are thinking contextually, then we may say that a system performs given functions in relation to a specified context, within which it is a subsystem. Differently put, the context generates functional consequences for its subsystem; but if we are thinking in whole-system terms, we may say that a given component performs functions for the system, or that a given function is performed for the system by a specified set of parts.

Since *functions* are *system-relevant consequences of social action,* we should not apply the word to ecological interactions, although it is so applied in ordinary usage. To reduce ambiguity, it would be better to use the word *program* to refer to *governmental activities intended to accomplish changes in a setting.* Thus an agricultural program seeks to increase the productivity of the soil, and educational and population programs to shape the social characteristics of the human environment. But in Parsonian terms, the "adaptive" and "pattern-maintenance" functions are often carried out *in terms of* environmental transformations. Thus a school system may perform a pattern-maintenance function for a polity by means of its educational program. In short, the ecological analysis of social systems provides a basis for understanding development.

To summarize, system theory as commonly used in comparative politics and government has so far involved a preoccupation with functions at the expense of structures, has tended to slight the importance of conflict and change, and has narrowed the range of inquiry by concentrating on whole-system perspectives at the expense of contextual and ecological analysis. The main thrust of this essay is to argue that these defects are not intrinsic in system theory but arise from errors in its early application to the comparative study of government. More broadly construed, system theory focuses on structures of government, as well as on the functions they perform for a polity. It emphasizes not only the prevalence of, but the need for, conflict and change. It calls for both a contextual and an ecological analysis of systems, and thereby demands a study of power and development.

In the second part of this essay I shall try to spell out in more positive form some of the implications of this way of viewing system theory.

II. FUNCTIONALISM WITHOUT DOCTRINE

The objection may be raised that the view of system theory proposed in this essay is, if not heretical, at least unconventional. No doubt the ways in which functionalism has been used in political science, and especially in comparative politics and administration, differ from the stance adopted here.

As evidence we may consult a recent essay on "Functional Analysis" which distinguishes between three main approaches, identified as "eclectic functionalism," "empirical functionalism," and "structural-functional analysis."[16] By *eclectic functionalism* the authors, Flanigan and Fogelman, refer to the study of how any actor or structure contributes to the performance of a given purpose or activity. They consider this usage to be the most widespread but the least theoretically interesting form of functionalism. It treats a function as one among several characteristics of any phenomenon. In this sense, the word "function" clearly has a different meaning from that employed in this paper. It refers to a purpose or program, not to a system-relevant consequence of action. It is unnecessary to belittle this type of functionalism, but it is necessary to point out that it involves a different kind of analysis. Usually it refers to purposes or intentions of actors, and hence to a different concept. Sometimes, however, it also refers to the consequences of intentional action, without reference to their system-relevance. When this is the meaning, it would be better to use the word "consequences" instead of "function."

By *empirical functionalism* Flanigan and Fogelman refer to work by Robert Merton and others in which specific demands or needs are recognized, and structures are then characterized by their ability to satisfy these needs, whether consciously or unconsciously. The concept of functional requisite is not employed. Functional analysis is the central orienting concept, but no theory of social action is implied thereby. I believe this use of the word "function" corresponds to the meaning intended in this paper, but empirical functionalism does not specify the systems for which action is relevant, and it does not provide a coherent framework for classifying and understanding the types and roles of structures found in various kinds of systems. Also, it does not imply contextual and ecological perspectives.

A third approach identified by Flanigan and Fogelman is associated with the names of Parsons and Levy. "The promise of *structural functionalism*," they write, "is nothing less than to provide a consistent and integrated theory from which can be derived explanatory hypotheses relevant to all aspects of a political system." Almond, Apter, and Mitchell are listed as political scientists who have embraced this approach, although clearly with marked individual differences.[17] It seems to me that the structural-functional framework used in these formulations is helpful for whole-system analysis as usually applied, but fails to provide guidance for the study of conflict and for the contextual and ecological analysis which I think should be required by system theory. Moreover, in suggesting that explanatory hypotheses can be deduced from the framework, they seem to embrace a doctrine which contains many difficulties. It is these doctrinal implications of functional theory that Runciman attacks with such cogency and vigor.[18]

I do not see why structural-functionalism cannot also be viewed as a nondoctrinal framework for the organization of analysis, perhaps a fourth approach which might be called a *social-system approach*. As such it suggests a range of questions to be asked. It provides a way of looking at phenomena without specifying in advance what conclusions will be reached about them. It is this approach that Runciman seems to support in the quotation given at the beginning of this essay, in which he endorses the utility of nondoctrinal use of functional theory. This framework is the one I shall use in the remainder of this essay.

The Focal Structure: Government

In discussing the preoccupation with functions in contemporary comparative politics, we need to give equal attention to the analysis of key political and administrative *structures*. This is not to say that functional analysis should be discarded in favor of traditional forms of institutional analysis, but rather that the use of system theory requires a balanced approach in which structures and functions are separately identified, and then related to each other by hypotheses, not by definitions. Unfortunately, much current terminology quite confusingly links structural and functional meanings by definition.

Consider two terms which are in common use, *legislature* and *public administrator*. Both are normally defined structurally, the first as an elected assembly, the second as a bureaucratic office. However, the words also imply functions, namely, to legislate and to administer. Separating these conjoined ideas, we can replace them by hypotheses. Thus, instead of *defining* a legislature as an elected assembly which makes laws, we offer the *hypothesis* that a normal function of elected assemblies is rule making. This hypothesis leaves open to empirical investigation the extent to which assemblies do in fact legislate. It makes it easier to deal with elected assemblies which do not legislate, and with legislation by organizations that are not elected assemblies. Similarly, instead of *defining* a public administrator as an official who administers, we *hypothesize* that the usual function of bureaucrats in a polity is administrative. We can then easily recognize that bureaucrats often perform other functions, for example, political ones, and that administrative functions are also performed by nonbureaucrats.

If we can separate, analytically, the key structures of government from the functions which they perform, then we could formulate propositions about structures independently of propositions about functions. This formulation would pave the way for hypothesizing about relationships between structures and functions in nontautological fashion. So long as we do not do this, we run the constant risk of reification, as when we identify the structures engaged in the rule-making function as "legislatures" because the word "legislature" is defined in terms of the legislative or rule-making function.

Let us now take, as our basic structural unit of analysis, the concept of government. *A government* may be defined as *a formal organization through which authoritative decisions are prescribed for a specified domain. A domain* is defined as *a geographic area with a resident population.* A government need not be sovereign in the sense of possessing exclusive jurisdiction within its domain, for the sphere of competence of governments can overlap, as in a federal system of governments. Moreover, governments may assert jurisdiction over citizens outside their domain, and a government in exile may even assert jurisdiction over a domain outside its control.

In an embryonic sense, the United Nations possesses some characteristics which might be ascribed to a world government. Cities, counties, and school boards may also be classified as governments. However, private corporations, trade unions, free churches, and professional societies, although formal organizations, are not governments. The mode of analysis presented here is probably relevant to some degree for all formal organizations, but my intention is to deal only with one subtype of formal organization, government.

Government in this sense is not coextensive with the concept of a political system as defined analytically and functionally. As pointed out above, current practice tends to make political system mean all political functions occurring within a given society, using Marion Levy's definition of society.[19] I propose a more limited usage in which a *political system* would be defined as *the processes of decision making employed in a specified government.*

In this sense, a given society is likely to contain not one but many political systems. Even nongovernmental organizations may be thought of as having their own political systems, but I shall not try to deal with them at this time.

Since it is convenient to make an analytic distinction between the administrative and political functions as they occur through governments, it is useful to speak of an *administrative system* as *the way in which the decisions made by a specified government are implemented.* Any government (and any formal organization), in other words, may be thought of as containing a political and an administrative system, or better, as exhibiting political and administrative aspects. These aspects are not concrete structures, whereas a governmental bureaucracy is a structure, defined as a formal hierarchy of offices under the head of a government or state. It normally plays a key part in any administrative system. However, nonbureaucratic roles are also involved in any administrative system, and every bureaucracy also participates in the political system of its government. Similarly, a constitutive system performs both administrative and political functions, and it is as incorrect to identify a constitutive system with the political system of a government as it is to equate bureaucracy with the administrative system. Failure to recognize this explains the tendency of many writers on politics to ignore the political influence of bureaucrats and hence to give a one-sided view of political action, and of writers on administration to ignore the administrative importance of nonbureaucrats.

It is useful to recognize yet another concept, namely *the total system of action which occurs in terms of a government.* Such a concrete system of action will be referred to as a *polity.* All analytic aspects of any social system may, therefore, be discerned in a polity, including the political and administrative. The familiar Parsonian functional requisites of pattern maintenance, goal attainment, adaptation, and integration could, if this seemed helpful, be sought in any polity. Using more conventional terminology, we can also discover economic, social, religious, educational, and other aspects of a polity.

Strictly speaking, a political system and an administrative system are analytic aspects of a polity, not of a government; but for convenience we speak of a political system "in terms of" government, thereby indicating the political aspects of a polity defined by a specified government. Government, in this usage, is not part of a polity, but part of its cultural environment. Thus we have defined a polity by reference to its setting.

Many contemporary political scientists will take exception to the use of government as a focal unit of analysis, arguing that nongovernmental phenomena also need to be considered. There are several ways of handling this objection. The first is to consider the ecological perspective and to agree that political science needs to consider how environmental constraints affect governmental structures and the operations of a polity, and also that we should investigate how polities impinge on and change their environments. Certainly, a weakness of traditional political science was that its preoccupation with governmental institutions led it to neglect these ecological relationships. Our new interest in the governments of non-Western countries now forces us to take them into account.

Second, if political science be defined in whatever way people who call themselves political scientists happen to choose, then there is no reason why we should not study anything we wish, including art, the oceans, family systems, and infant care. However, if the discipline is to be given any coherence, it requires a central focus. The historically persisting fields of political science identified by Michael Haas in the introductory essay of this book are all clearly linked to government and the polity as a touchstone.

Political theory, for example, sought to relate government to religious, philosophical, and ethical considerations; public law studied the basis and character of authoritative decisions through government; comparative government, as its name suggests, originally involved the quest for better forms of governmental organization; politics turned to a study of internal social forces affecting governmental outcomes, with a concentration on the role of elected assemblies; public administration directed attention to the problems of implementing governmental decisions, with a special focus on the role of bureaucracies;

and finally, international relations became concerned primarily with interactions between governments.

Behavioralism, not as a field of political science but as a mode of analysis within political science, directed attention to empirical behaviors within and affecting government. Thus behavioralism was an effort to shift from normative and policy-oriented types of inquiry to descriptive-explanatory theory. In the process many political scientists strayed from the original focus of the discipline on government to a study of various environmental phenomena, not as they affect government but as subjects of intrinsic interest. Yet this expansion of the range of interest of political scientists now threatens not so much to enrich the discipline as to confuse and to fragment it.

New Concerns of Political Science

In Chapter 1 of this book, Haas suggests that the impact of behavioralism may lead to a restructuring of political science around three central concerns: decision theory, development theory, and system theory. Each of these types of theory to some extent transcends a concern with government. There are undoubtedly nongovernmental institutions, such as private firms and trade unions, in which authoritative *decisions* for a collectivity are made. There are also institutions, such as markets, that are not formal organizations, but through which decisions of a different kind are made by aggregative processes. *Development* theory has no doubt received its greatest impetus from the study of economic change. *System* theory, as practiced by sociologists and natural scientists, pays little attention to government.

If these three wide-ranging modes of analysis are to be helpful to political science, they need to be related to a common focus of attention. I submit that such a focus is the historic concern of political science with government and the polity. We can, after all, ask how *decisions* are made by polities through their governments. We can examine processes of political and administrative change in polities under the heading of *development*. Finally, we can apply *system* theory in the analysis of governmental structures and processes.

With some shift in emphasis, these observations apply to the study of international relations as well as to national and subnational governments. Insofar as embryonic forms of world and regional government have arisen, they clearly fall within the range of our concern with government; but much if not most international politics still occurs outside the framework of world government. Nevertheless, it does involve relations between governments, and hence the interstate system provides a context which helps to shape, as it is shaped by, the participant states. Thus it is in the contextual framework, a framework which—as we have seen—has been largely neglected, that international politics makes a basic contribution to our understanding of government; and this context may be even more important for understanding government in the "new" than in the "old" states of the world.

Clearly there is an increasing number of relationships between and among the peoples of the world which can be studied outside of government and intergovernmental relations. These relationships constitute, on the one hand, the subject matter of the newly emergent interdisciplinary field of international studies. They also provide information needed for an ecological, as contrasted with a contextual, analysis of world government and intergovernmental relations, which is also a subject of direct interest to political science.

In sum, both the traditional concerns of political science and the newer themes which have emerged in response to the impact of behavioralism come into focus when viewed in the context of government and polity. If we are to take seriously this renewed emphasis on the importance of government and its component institutions, then where do we go next? How shall we begin our analysis of political and administrative structures?

I suggest that we might first clarify our thinking about some general characteristics of all social structures, including those of government. These characteristics can be formulated as a series of axioms, to which we now turn.

Some Axioms of Structural Analysis

First, structures tend to survive despite changes in their functions. This axiom seems tautological, for the definition of a structure is a pattern of action, which implies continuity of behavior over time. A structure cannot be a structure at a single instant in time. Action becomes a structure only when it is repeated often enough to become recognizable as a pattern. However, there are clearly differences in the length of time during which a pattern of action persists. A well-established structure becomes entrenched or enculturated. It is then reinforced by the attitudes and norms of those directly involved. When a structure becomes thus entrenched we speak of it as an *institution.* Thus institutionalization involves the relatively permanent or persistent establishment of a structure, or of a set of interrelated structures.

Over a period of time the exact way in which an action is performed tends to vary—indeed, it is never performed twice in exactly the same way. A word is an example of a structure, and the words which are used most frequently become the most highly institutionalized. If the same word is said by two speakers whom you know well but do not see, you can usually identify each speaker. Thus you will have proven that the sounds are different, yet you will recognize that both persons have spoken the same word. In this sense a given structure always changes in detail, yet retains a recognizable configuration.

Anyone who studies the United States Congress in detail can identify changes in its operations from session to session and even from day to day. Yet Congress as an institution has persisted since the promulgation of the American Constitution. No doubt the functions performed by Congress have changed more during this time than has its structure.

A more dramatic illustration is provided by the Imperial Institution of Japan, which is supposed to have lasted as a family dynasty from legendary times, but the power exercised by the Japanese emperor has fluctuated, declining drastically under the Tokugawa Shogunate, rising again with the Meiji Restoration, and declining again with the reforms that followed World War II.

How long a structure will last is not given a priori. What is asserted in the axiom is merely the remarkable tendency of structures (or of institutions) to survive in the face of changes which markedly affect their functions. This point has frequently been made about the tendency of organizations to outlast the loss of their original purposes, as when a philanthropic association achieves the goals which initially led to its creation. Governments are, in this sense, among the most persistent of organizations (institutions, structures). The various components of government also have their own history, often outlasting the forms of government with which they were once associated.

Second, although a structure normally performs a given function, there is no assurance that it will always do so. This axiom may be merely another way of stating the first, but it needs to be asserted. We have already insisted on the importance of distinguishing between structure and function, and avoiding definitions which link structure with function. The importance of the point is evident if we consider the tendency of foreign technical advisers to recommend practices which normally have a given function in the countries where they originated. In the new setting, however, a structure may be adopted, but its functions are likely to be different.

The second axiom may be tested by looking at the process of *modernization,* which means *adopting, by emulative acculturation, structures and practices that are prevalent elsewhere in societies regarded by the emulators as more advanced, that is, "modern."* The underlying assumption in these processes of modernization is that the borrowed structures will enable the emulators to accomplish results (functions) similar to those achieved by the modern country. Our second axiom warns that these results may not follow.

A reverse relationship also follows from the axiom. The persistence of a given structure offers no assurance that the functions once performed by an institution will continue to be performed by it. A familiar example of this phenomenon is the changed function of kingship which marks the transition from absolutism to constitutionalism. Limited monarchies are familiar in some of the most modern and democratic contemporary states, in which the formal institution of kingship persists almost unchanged from a distant past. However, the political and administrative functions of these kings in their polities have been drastically reduced.

An even older social structure, perhaps the oldest human institution, is the family. Despite rising rates of divorce and illegitimacy, there is little evidence that the family will disappear, notwithstanding such fantasies as Huxley's *Brave New World*. However, as with kingship, the functions performed by the family in contemporary Western societies have been substantially curtailed, and the same process is undoubtedly also taking place throughout the non-Western world.

In the light of these two axioms it is perhaps understandable that students of comparative politics should often assume that the particular set of structures found in any society is largely a matter of culture and history and presumably a matter of indifference so far as the performance of requisite functions is concerned. Indeed, one often gets the impression from this literature that almost any structure can perform the essential functions and therefore that the existing structures, whatever they are, will be able to fulfill these functions, and so do not need to be reformed or even studied.

Unfortunately, the relation between structure and function is not so casual. Let us posit a *third axiom* of structural theory, as follows: *Some functions, under the constraints of existing social technology, can only be performed by a given structure or set of structures.* This axiom rests on the assumption that certain structures may be necessary, though by no means sufficient, conditions for the accomplishment of specified functions. The third axiom is consistent with the second, since a given structure may permit the performance of a related function without any assurance that the function will in fact be performed.

Such relations are familiar in the physical world. For example, the only way in which human beings today can travel through the air at speeds greater than 500 miles per hour is by means of a jet-powered plane. Perhaps other means will be invented in the future. Perhaps angels or creatures from outer space can do it by other means, but currently available human technology offers only one solution to this problem. However, the mere possession of a jet plane by no means assures anyone that he can fly. Many other conditions must also be met, such as having a qualified pilot, a supply of gasoline, and an adequate airport. The same principle applies to social structures. There are certain political functions that can be performed only by bureaucracies, by legislatures, by elections, or by political parties, but the mere possession of these structures does not guarantee the performance of these functions.

This axiom helps to explain a perplexing phenomenon of contemporary modernization. Because the salient governmental structures found in Western countries normally perform a given range of functions, it is often assumed, by Westerners and non-Westerners alike, that these structures can be counted on to perform the same functions wherever they are found. Consequently, modernizers, whether indigenous non-Westerners or Western foreign advisers, tend to focus their energies on the transplanting of Western structures of government in the false expectation that their mere introduction will lead automatically to desired functional consequences.

Some Consequences of Area Studies and Functionalism

When the expectation that a given structure will automatically yield given functions proves illusory, a natural reaction sets in—to discredit the value of alien institutions. The argument is that the solution to political problems can only be found in culturally particularistic terms, as a natural evolution from within. The expectation arises that somehow each society can invent its own distinctive way to solve the universal problems which accompany the spread of science and the industrial revolution. This rather utopian expectation has been reinforced by two intellectual tendencies or modes of analysis that have become particularly popular in the last twenty years.

One mode of analysis has been spread under the mantle of area studies, which assumes that each society can be understood and appreciated only in terms of the totality, or Gestalt, of its own history and culture. From this holistic perspective, comparative analysis becomes suspect, and the intrusion of alien institutions and practices is deplored as disturbing to the balanced growth (or maintenance) of indigenous forms.

The second tendency, although universalistic and comparative in form, paradoxically reinforces the area approach. This is functionalism, as widely interpreted. It has been argued that if the performance of requisite functions is most important, then it does not matter much what structures perform these functions so long as they are indeed carried out. Let each society, therefore, devise its own institutions to meet its own functional requirements. Carried further, as a functionalist doctrine, we encounter a kind of Panglossian optimism, which asserts that the very existence of any structures in a given cultural context proves their functionality; and conversely that if a functional need arises, structures designed to meet these needs will automatically be improvised. What is required, therefore, is to study each historical and cultural case in its own terms to discover how it has met, and presumably will meet, its own functional needs.

The prevalence of area studies and functionalism in these forms has, I think, put the practitioner, both Western and non-Western, in a difficult position. He is given little choice between a rather naive modernizing approach in which he strives to transfer institutions and practices, hoping that they will assure the accomplishment of desired ends; and as an alternative, a functionalist or area approach which tells him that his efforts are doomed to futility, while offering no practical alternatives.

This normative dilemma compels us to examine not only the structures which may be necessary, though not sufficient, conditions for the accomplishment of specified functions, but also the additional elements which may be sufficient to achieve these desired results. In order to understand what are the sufficient as well as necessary conditions for a government to solve the political and administrative problems posed by the industrial and scientific revolutions, we need to understand governments as whole interactive systems, which includes an analysis of how their component parts are related to each other. In the third part of this essay, a structural synthesis is presented in the hope that it will provide a foundation on which to build a viable theory of political and administrative development that will avoid the paralyzing alternatives mentioned above.

III. A STRUCTURAL SYNTHESIS

Let us begin by distinguishing relationships between roles which are *symmetrical* from those which are *asymmetrical.* Patterns of action involving exchange or reciprocity illustrate the former; those involving the exercise of power and authority illustrate the latter. Symmetrical exchanges of goods and services, whether mingled with personal respect and affection, or with fear and hostility, are primitive and protean, and they persist in a myriad forms in all contemporary societies.

Asymmetrical relationships involve recognition by some of a generalized obligation, within narrow or wide limits, to obey others, to provide goods and services without expectation of direct or specific benefits. These relationships appear to derive from symmetrical patterns, and to be limited in number. Blau has explored quite persuasively a variety of ways in which symmetrical relationships can become asymmetrical, normally requiring that those who gain power and authority succeed in performing unrequited or unrequitable services for those over whom they secure eminence.[20] For present purposes we need not examine this question. Let us rather concentrate on the varieties of asymmetrical relationships, for clearly all governmental structures are marked by role asymmetry. If decisions are to be made by a few on behalf of many, as they are in all polities, then we must examine the structures involved in such decision making.

Simple and *complex* asymmetrical relationships can be distinguished. In the former, one person exercises authority over a group of others, or a group collectively makes decisions which are then regarded as binding on all its members. In each case individuals find themselves obligated to act as a result of decisions by others. Such decisions are not merely a result of dyadic exchanges with other individuals. In order to make these distinctions clearly, without redundant repetition of cumbersome phrases, we must use some arbitrary terms whenever no commonsense expression is available. Let us therefore refer to *an individual who asserts nondependent authority over a group of persons* as an *autocrat,* and refer *to one who accepts the authority of a group to make authoritative decisions governing his behavior* as a *democrat.* Authority is *nondependent* if it is not conferred on one by a hierarchic superior.

Complex Asymmetry: Hierarchy and Polyarchy

Simple asymmetrical relationships are probably salient in the emergent governments of folk societies, but contemporary civilizations require far more complicated patterns of complex asymmetry. These patterns may be classified under two broad headings, "hierarchy" and "polyarchy."

A *hierarchy* involves *a structure of authority in which subordinate roles are dependent on the authority of a superior, yet exercise authority over others.* We can use the word *hierarch* technically to refer to *a role characterized by the exercise of authority over other roles, plus the derivation of this authority from a superior role.* Thus a hierarchy consists of a set of authoritatively linked hierarchs. A *pyramid* includes an autocrat, hierarchs under the authority of the autocrat, and subjects under the authority of the hierarchy.

This terminology may seem arbitrary, but, as we shall see, it is important to be able to distinguish between autocrats who do not derive their authority from another superior role, and hierarchs who do. A two-tiered pyramid would contain an autocrat and subjects, but no hierarchs, and hence it would not contain a hierarchy. Only pyramids having three or more *echelons,* therefore, contain a hierarchy.

A *polyarchy* is also *a pyramidal structure of authority,* but it is one *in which superior roles act collectively on the basis of authority delegated to them by inferiors.* A *polyarch,* therefore, is *a role whose authority is derived from a collectivity by election, and involves participation in a collegial or voting organization.* As in our definition of hierarchy, a pyramid can include voting citizens as the base, and an elected autocrat as the apex, with a polyarchy in between.

This terminology enables us to see that only pyramids having three or more levels can contain a polyarchy. Pyramids may be hierarchic as well as polyarchic, the difference lying in the direction of flow of authority. We can refer to the heads of both polyarchic and hierarchic pyramids as autocrats, and by our definition an autocrat is neither a polyarch nor a hierarch. We can refer to the base roles in both hierarchic and polyarchic pyramids as democrats since they meet the defined criteria of accepting the authority of the collectivity. Autocrats may be elected, or they may secure office by other means, such as inheritance or coup d'etat, but not by appointment of a superior, for then they would become hierarchs. Democrats may be both citizens and subjects in the sense that they participate in voting for polyarchs and also act under the authority of hierarchs. It is possible for democrats to be subjects but not citizens, but I think it quite unlikely that they could be citizens but not subjects.

If an elected autocrat behaves responsibly and responsively, he is not autocratic in the ordinary sense. In other words, an autocrat may be autocratic or not, just as a democrat may be democratic or not.[21]

The Autocrat-Democrat Structure: Presidents and Monarchs

Let us now regard the simple form of asymmetry as a basic "autocrat-democrat" structure. By adding the two complex forms of "hierarchy" and "polyarchy" we arrive at a basic list of three fundamental structures of government: autocrat-democrat, hierarchy, and polyarchy. We can then state some historical propositions about these forms starting with the simplest.

The autocrat-democrat form emerged first, perhaps soon after the evolution of man, but not in every society. Indeed, some folk societies persisting into our times do not have this simplest form of government. Their relations continued to be governed by dyadic patterns of reciprocity and exchange. These are the "stateless societies" described by anthropologists.[22]

The autocrat-democrat form of government, although very ancient, also persists into our times, and may even be found in the United States in rural self-government, notably at the township level. Here we often find a town clerk or trustee who is the local autocrat, and sometimes a town meeting at which the local democrats make collective decisions.

It is a mistake to think that there can be only one autocrat in a given polity. There may, indeed, be many autocrats, each with his own more or less clearly defined sphere of authority. We may refer to any such *group of autocrats in a given polity* as an *autocrat set.* A classic example in American politics of autocrat sets is the collection of elected officeholders found formerly, and even to this day, in many rural local governments. Each of these offices is nondependent and exercises authority directly over a particular domain in a specified subject or field. Their relations with each other are governed by symmetrical patterns of exchange or reciprocity, and they fit neither in a hierarchy nor a polyarchy of authority. Of course, they are subject to constraints imposed by officers of higher levels of government within whose jurisdiction they are permitted only a limited range of autonomy. These externally imposed constraints severely restrict the range of functions which can be performed by offices in these autocrat sets, thereby illustrating the proposition that the functions performed by persisting structures may be drastically modified.

Another kind of autocrat set which is prevalent in the American polity—as in other common-law countries—is the bench. Judges and magistrates, whether elected or appointed, operate autonomously to define the law as it applies to particular cases brought before them for trial. Although there are different ranks of judges, and higher courts may overrule decisions appealed from lower courts, it would not be accurate to describe the judges of lower courts as acting under the authority of higher-court judges. Rather, the legal parameters in terms of which they act are continuously defined and redefined by earlier court decisions, according to the principle of *stare decisis.*

In traditional societies, adjudication was frequently one of the most important functions of kings and tribal chiefs. In the processes of political development, one of the earliest functions to be transferred from the king to other offices was the judicial, and it seems natural enough that the structure to which this function was transferred should have been that of another autocrat, or an autocrat set.

Mention of kings brings us to the distinction between an autocrat claiming generalized and preeminent authority over a domain, and autocrats asserting more limited jurisdictions. Using Max Weber's term, let us call the former a *monocrat,* and the latter *restricted autocrats.* The actual weight of power exercised by a monocrat may fluctuate within a wide range, and the effective scope of a monocrat's authority may also be constitutionally limited in various ways. The central importance of a monocrat to government frequently does not lie in the weight or scope of his effective power, but rather in his legitimizing function. This function is performed variously in different kinds of government, as we shall see below.

Monocrats may be recruited in several ways. Perhaps originally they seized power by violence or by persuasive evidence of supernatural favor, but in routinized forms of government, they gain power through two main procedures—inheritance and election. *We can refer to the office of an inherited monocrat* as a *monarch,* and *a government subject to the authority of a monarch* as a *monarchy.* In this sense most traditional polities took the form of monarchies. However, elected monocrats were also found in very early times, and the Greek and Indian city-states provide classic evidence of the importance of such regimes.

An elected monocrat is referred to as a *president,* and *a government subject to the authority of a president* as a *republic.* Some political philosophers used to think of republics as a more advanced form of government than a monarchy, and they suggested that political development involved the transformation of monarchies into republics. It is now widely recognized, however, that both monarchic and republican forms of government are very old, and quite modern polities may be monarchic as well as republican. The ratio of monarchies to republics has progressively declined as polities have become larger and more complex, but this occurrence is unrelated to the level of advancement of the two forms of government.

No doubt in simple governments, where both polyarchic and hierarchic structures were lacking, whether the monocrat was elective or hereditary made considerable difference. Consequently, such words as "king" and "president" became very familiar, whereas a word to cover both types of office remained virtually unknown. Just as the word "sibling" has been coined to refer to both brothers and sisters, so we can use the word "monocrat" to refer to both presidents and monarchs. It should now be clear that the monocratic structure is one of the oldest institutions of government, and it is a structure which persists, with variable functions, in all contemporary polities.[23]

Both hierarchic and polyarchic structures of government emerged much later than the simple autocrat-democrat regimes. Moreover, they emerged at different times. *Hierarchy appeared within historical memory, about two millenia ago, whereas polyarchy became important for government only within the last two centuries.* It is true that democracy with elected officials, voting, and nonelective assemblies appeared long ago in the Greek city-states; but they did not have polyarchy as defined above. True polyarchy appeared only with the emergence of constitutive systems in modern times.

Now it is possible to make a very broad classification of forms of government under four main headings: (1) a null form, without even the simplest structure of asymmetrical relations; (2) a basic autocrat-democrat pattern, containing a monocrat; (3) a form in which a hierarchy of offices is erected under the authority of the monocrat; and (4) a system in which the exercise of authority by monocrat and hierarchy is balanced by the countervailing authority of a polyarchy. I find it convenient to use technical terms for these basic patterns of government, but readers who dislike neologisms can keep the ideas in mind by using descriptive phrases. Employing terms which I have proposed elsewhere, I shall speak of *a domain lacking any government* as an *acephaly;* of *one containing a monocrat but not a hierarchy or a polyarchy* as a *procephaly;* of *a regime with monocrat and hierarchy but no polyarchy* as an *orthocephaly;* and finally *a regime with monocrat, hierarchy, and polyarchy* as a *tonic polity.*[24] Since constitutive systems are polyarchic, this definition of tonic polity amplifies that given on p. 202.

TABLE 2. Common Types of Government

Type of Government	Tonic Polities	Orthocephaly	Procephaly	Acephaly
Monocracy	yes	yes	yes	no
Bureaucracy	yes	yes	no	no
Polyarchy (Constitutive system)	yes	no	no	no

The Hierarchic Structure: Bureaucracy and Feudalism

Having already briefly considered acephaly and procephaly as primitive forms of government, typical of folk societies and city-states, we can now turn to orthocephaly. By definition an orthocephaly contains not only a monocrat but also a hierarchy—and it lacks a polyarchy. We shall distinguish two main forms of hierarchy—bureaucratic and feudal.

The most familiar form of hierarchy—at least in modern times—is the bureaucratic. The first bureaucracies were perhaps invented as early as the dawn of history, but the best-known instances are those of the Chinese and Roman empires. Considerable research has been done on the origins of these bureaucracies so that, although documentation is necessarily fragmentary, a good deal is known about them.[25] It is unnecessary to recapitulate the historical evidence here, but it is perhaps useful to point out that quite complex and highly secularized forms of government, such as those found in the Greek and Chinese city-states, did not have bureaucracies. In the Greek city-states, for example, one found autocrat-democrat structures, and even a proliferation of autocrat sets with the election, or more usually the selection by lot, of annual officeholders charged with specific administrative responsibilities. However, these autocrat sets were not linked in a pyramid of authority and hence did not constitute a bureaucracy.

In classical times it appears that the bureaucratic principle of organization became established in the provincial military governments of the Roman republic, and later was extended by Julius Caesar and Augustus over the entire emerging empire. Thus a comprehensive functional transformation of the polity was accomplished with minimal structural change, for all the old forms of the Senatorial republic were maintained, and the imperial domain was administered as though it were a province.

In the Chinese case bureaucratic forms of government were devised for military purposes by the southern state outside the mainstream of the contending patrimonial states clustered about the great bend of the Yellow River. Subsequently, in self-defense, this pattern of governmental organization was hesitatingly and reluctantly adopted by the northern states, permitting them to aggregate power until one among them absorbed its rivals, creating the first Chinese empire two centuries before Christ.

This historical experience should help us to understand what distinguishes a bureaucracy from other forms of hierarchy. In these cases powerful instruments of an expanding royal government were built when monocrats learned how to recruit men to fill positions in a hierarchy under their control. As the size of bureaucracy grew, it became manifestly impossible for a monocrat to name all the officials under his authority, and so higher officials took over this activity, naming their own subordinates. Thus, a *bureaucracy* is a hierarchy in which the higher positions are filled by appointment from above.

The initial impact of the creation of a bureaucracy was to enhance the power of the monocrat it served; but bureaucracies were subject to their own internal dynamics. In due course bureaucrats found ways to enhance their own powers and security at the expense of their ruler's power over them, thereby reducing his ability to keep them under control. Bureaucrats were successful in making their offices hereditary, subject to transmission from father to son with only nominal authorization by the monocrat. Thereby a different form of hierarchy came into existence, which we may call a *feudal hierarchy*. Thus, *the prevalent characteristic of a bureaucracy is the appointment of men to hierarchic office, whereas the prevalent characteristic of a feudal hierarchy is the inheritance of office.*

The distinction which we find here between two forms of orthocephaly neatly parallels the cognate distinction found earlier in procephalies. In that case we found two polar types of monocrat, the monarch and the president, one hereditary and the other elective. Now we also find two forms of hierarchy, one hereditary and the other appointive; the former feudal, the latter bureaucratic. Again, historical analysis and political speculation have rarely seen that they were polar alternatives of the same basic type of government, but have tended to treat the one case under the name of Feudalism, the latter under such headings as Oriental Despotism and Asiatic Society. We need to see that they are both examples, though in different forms, of a single structure of government, the orthocephalic, a polity with a monocrat and hierarchy.

Earlier in this paper the persistence and ultimate collapse of a bureaucratic empire in China were used to illustrate the need for structural criteria in system theory as applied to the comparative study of government. We can now define a *bureaucratic empire* more exactly as an orthocephaly whose hierarchy takes a bureaucratic form. The termination of the Chinese bureaucratic empire was followed by the emergence in China of a tonic polity. Accordingly, we now turn to tonic polities.

The Polyarchic Structure: Orthotonic and Heterotonic Polities

We have just redefined a *tonic* polity as one which contains a polyarchy in addition to monocracy and hierarchy. Earlier we defined a constitutive system as a component of government containing an elected assembly, an electoral system, and one or more political parties which, by definition, nominate candidates for election to seats in the assembly. Those who are so elected satisfy the definition of a polyarch, and hence the constitutive system is a pyramid which contains a polyarchy. Thus the two definitions are substantively equivalent.

Recalling our first axiom, it should not surprise us to find that the older structures, monocracy and bureaucracy, persist despite the superimposition of a new polyarchic structure, the constitutive system. Moreover, in accord with the second axiom, we expect to find the functions performed by these older structures to be modified as a result of the addition of major new components of government. These changes include a reduction in the power position of the monocracy, and increasing functional specialization of the bureaucracy as an organ of administration rather than of politics.

In line with our third axiom, we should also be prepared to see that polyarchic structures which appear to have enhanced the ability of Western states to govern themselves and bring others under their sphere of influence or control have been borrowed by non-Western states seeking to protect themselves or gain their independence. It is also scarcely surprising that these modernizing polities should have found it difficult to establish an easy balance between the new polyarchic institutions and their own older hierarchic and monocratic structures. The result has been failure to achieve the levels of political and administrative development for which they hoped.

One of the reasons why polyarchic structures of government took so long to emerge is undoubtedly their fragile and complicated character. Polyarchies are even more vulnerable to dissolution and corruption than are hierarchies. To have a polyarchy, according to our definition, there must be a set of roles which act collectively on the basis of authority delegated by citizens. The institution of an elected autocrat is, as we have seen, an ancient one. So also is the institution of an assembly, college, council, or senate, consisting of a group of democrats acting collegially to make decisions. Such were the councils of Athens, the Senate of Rome, and the House of Lords in England.

The extraordinary innovation involved in a constitutive system was to form an assembly whose members are elected. The members of such an assembly are polyarchs, and acting collegially they form a polyarchy. In order for them to be elected there must be an electoral system, a means whereby eligible citizens can cast their ballots and have them counted. Moreover, a method is necessary by which candidates for election to the assembly can be nominated. The political parties emerged as a distinctive structure able to perform this function. We may, indeed, define *a political party* as *an organization which nominates candidates for election to an assembly.* [26]

Strangely enough, contemporary political science fails to see the essential structural unity of an elected assembly, a mode of elections, and one or more political parties. Yet this set of interactive institutions constitutes a single major component of almost all contemporary polities. Perhaps the lack of a convenient term, such as "constitutive system," has led to this curious gap in our conceptualization of governments; yet one could also argue that it is our failure to recognize the existence of such a structure which explains the lack of a name for it.

Since comparative politics and administration today are, as suggested above, almost exclusively concerned with tonic polities, it behooves us to pay particularly close attention to the characteristics of constitutive systems. In considerable measure the great tradition of studying comparative government did in fact consist largely of the analysis of constitutive systems or, more exactly, of the assemblies, electoral systems, and parties of which each constitutive system is composed.

However, when the constitutive systems of modernizing polities were first studied, it quickly became apparent that they did not work as expected. Essentially, this failure of the established models to enable political scientists to make sense of the key (polyarchic) institutions of the new states led them to seek alternative modes of analysis, and hence to embrace functionalism as a solution. What they failed to see was that the decisive difference between the modern and modernizing polities does not lie in the characteristics of their constitutive systems, but rather in the characteristics of their bureaucracies and monocrats. Once this point is grasped, it should be possible to distinguish between a variety of tonic polities by structural criteria, and so to discover when critical differences among constitutive systems are decisive for the behavior of a form of government.

Let us examine this point more closely by asking what happens to bureaucracies when constitutive systems are added to a polity. First of all, we can observe that, although constitutive systems were invented in orthocephalies which once contained feudal hierarchies, these hierarchies had already become partially bureaucratized, and after the establishment of polyarchy, bureaucratization became even more complete.

Bureaucracy: Compensated and Noncompensated

In this gradual transformation an important difference appeared. Whereas the higher levels of an orthocephalic bureaucracy are filled by appointment of the monocrat, we find in tonic polities that the positions are usually filled by persons selected through or with the consent of the constitutive system. This subtle but decisive change led, strangely enough, to a modification in the concept of bureaucracy itself. People have come to think of a bureaucracy as including only some of the positions in the pyramid of offices under the authority of a monocrat, namely, those filled by career officers, recruited and promoted from below. They have even further restricted the scope of the concept by excluding those hierarchs having military duties, thus limiting the term "bureaucracy" to the civil bureaucracy. This arbitrary curtailment of the concept was one reason why the critical importance of bureaucracy in the structure of tonic polities was not seen. Once we identify a bureaucracy with the total hierarchy of offices in a tonic polity, we can see that the mode of selection of officers at the highest levels, including cabinet members, has a basic influence on the performance of the system of government.

Political scientists who thought only of modern states took for granted the idea that the highest level (or levels) of the bureaucracy would be filled by, or on the advice of, the constitutive system. The fact that they cut back their concept of bureaucracy to exclude the offices filled in this manner reflects their implicit acceptance of this idea. However, familiarity with tonic polities in the modernizing states shows us that it is possible to have the top (cabinet) level of a bureaucracy filled by appointment from within of career officers (military and civil), and it is also possible to have not only the top but also the intermediate levels of a bureaucracy filled predominantly by outsiders named through the constitutive system. If one defines a bureaucracy in terms of its career services, then hierarchies staffed by patronage would not be classified as bureaucracies. However, using the definitions proposed in this paper, we can say that bureaucracies vary widely in the way their positions are filled, ranging all the way from a complete career service to a complete patronage system. The two principles of appointment are always combined in the governments of modern states, but one or the other may be used almost exclusively in some of the modernizing polities.

How can the two principles of appointment be combined? Let us suppose that the *highest (cabinet) level of a bureaucracy is filled through the constitutive system, and the intermediate (bureau chief) level is staffed primarily by insiders, career officers.* We can describe the structure of such a bureaucracy as *compensated* in the ordinary mechanical sense of a balancing of weights or forces. If these conditions are not met, the bureaucracy is *noncompensated.* The importance of this structural condition is suggested by the hypothesis that *a compensated bureaucracy will tend to be politically responsive and administratively capable.* A noncompensated bureaucracy may be politically responsive but will not be administratively capable, if it is predominantly staffed on a patronage or spoils basis; and it may be administratively capable but not politically responsive, if it is predominantly staffed on a career basis. In many of the modernizing tonic polities we find that the bureaucracies are noncompensated, whereas the governments in most of the modern societies have compensated bureaucracies.[27]

Monocrats: Accountable and Nonaccountable

Similar distinctions need to be made regarding the role of monocrat.[28] We have already seen that the traditional dichotomy between kings and presidents was based on the mode of selection of monocrats. In procephalies this distinction is fundamentally important. A second distinction became important in orthocephalies, namely the extent to which monocrats actually exercised power. In Japan, especially during the Tokugawa period, we see how the emperor, while retaining his monocratic title, actually lost power to a commanding hierarch, the Shogun. Similarly, in European feudalism, emperors and kings became pawns in the hands of their own hierarchic vassals. Thus the question whether a monocrat held absolute or limited power became important.

In tonic polities, although the distinctions between hereditary and elective monocrats, and between absolute and limited rulers, still persist as interesting structural variations, a third and still unrecognized distinction has become far more important. This distinction involves the extent to which a monocrat is held accountable by the constitutive system, and/or the bureaucracy. Presidents elected by a constitutive system, whether directly or through the assembly, may exercise great or little power, and kings in tonic polities may be held accountable to the assembly (parliament).

Using only the example of the modern states, in which monocrats became universally accountable to the new constitutive system, political scientists came to assume that this relation would always hold, and so they failed to recognize its importance. But in some of the modernizing polities we find monocrats who are not accountable, or become nonaccountable. This situation has important structural consequences for the constitutive system and bureaucracy, and for the performance of the government as a whole.

To restate, the implicit assumptions about governmental structure made in the traditional writings on comparative government are: the monocrat was always accountable, and the bureaucracy was compensated. Variations in the form of the constitutive system proved of fundamental importance only if these two parametric assumptions were valid. If they were not, then changes in the constitutive system have much less influence on the performance of government as a whole.

If the monocrat is not accountable, he may interfere in operations of both the constitutive system and the bureaucracy so as to disrupt their normal behavior. If the higher levels of a bureaucracy are not staffed by or with the consent of the constitutive system, it is unlikely that the bureaucracy will reflect decisions made in the constitutive system, and hence its characteristics will not prove decisive for the polity. Moreover, if the bureaucracy is inadequately staffed with experienced men, it will not be able to carry out decisions made in the constitutive system, so that again the characteristics of this polyarchy of offices will not prove decisive. In other words, a noncompensated bureaucracy can frustrate the operations of a constitutive system by being unwilling or unable to implement its decisions, and by intervening directly to obstruct the workings of the constitutive system itself.

By taking into account the distinction between accountable and nonaccountable monocrats, and between compensated and noncompensated bureaucracies, we can construct a morphology of tonic polities capable of distinguishing the most important structural differences to be found among them. In order to refer to the various types without cumbersome descriptive phrases, let us use some more prefixes to qualify tonic polities.

We may refer to any *government with a nonaccountable monocrat and a constitutive system* as a *protonic polity.* We find examples in countries like Iran, where a strong monarchy persists after the introduction of a constitutive system; and formerly in Indonesia under Sukarno's "guided democracy," where a nonhereditary monocrat had made himself president for life. Clearly both the constitutive system and the bureaucracy can be manipulated in arbitrary ways by the personal wishes of the monocrat in such protonic polities. However, their number remains small and continues to dwindle.

More important is the large category of *neotonic polities* defined as *having accountable monocrats.* Within this category let us next distinguish between neotonic polities having *compensated bureaucracies* and those with *noncompensated bureaucracies.* I shall call the former class *orthotonic polities,* and the latter class *heterotonic.* This distinction gives us a major watershed between contemporary governments, for we shall find that almost all the countries thought of as modern have orthotonic polities, whereas the modernizing countries have heterotonic (and protonic) polities.

For the purposes of this paper it is unnecessary to carry this analysis of governmental structures much further.[29] However, it is important to clarify the distinction between "contratonic" and "anatonic" polities, which was made near the beginning of this paper. It was not possible to state there what can now be simply said, namely, that these two types of government are also defined as having compensated bureaucracies. They are therefore subtypes of orthotonic polities. By making a further distinction between two varieties of contratonic polity, it is possible to provide a systematic distinction between "parliamentary" and "presidential" systems.

We can also distinguish systematically between two varieties of heterotonic polity. To make this distinction, we must clarify a point already mentioned. We have seen that in a compensated bureaucracy top positions are predominantly filled by *outsiders,* (that is, not career officials recruited from within), and that intermediate-level positions are predominantly filled by *insiders.* In an uncompensated bureaucracy, by contrast, both the top and intermediate levels must be filled by either outsiders, or by insiders. (We can rule out the logical possibility of a bureaucracy staffed by insiders at the top level and by outsiders at intermediate levels as implausible if not impossible.) Now let us say that if these key bureaucratic levels are both staffed by insiders, then the system is *closed,* if by outsiders, then *open.* Let us call any heterotonic polity in which the bureaucracy is open a *syntonic polity,* and one in which the bureaucracy is closed, *homotonic.* Examples of the syntonic polity will be found in those new states where a revolutionary movement for independence has established itself as a ruling party and, in the name of nationalism, replaced expatriate officials by indigenous partisans of the new regime. Homotonic polities are to be found in regimes where the constitutive system proved unable to maintain an adequate level of countervailing power, making it possible for career officials, both military and civilian, to staff the highest-level posts. When this occurs, the post of monocrat is likely to be seized by a bureaucrat, typically a military officer. The military coup d'etat is thus a sign of the existence of a homotonic polity.

TABLE 3.   Basic Types of Tonic Polity

Type of Government	Neotonic				Protonic
	Orthotonic		Heterotonic		
	Contratonic	Anatonic	Syntonic	Homotonic	
Accountable Monocracy	yes	yes	yes	yes	no
Compensated bureaucracy	yes	yes	no	no	no
Open Bureaucracy	yes/no	yes/no	yes	no	yes/no
Competitive constitutive system	yes	no	yes/no	yes/no	yes/no

Conclusion: Toward a Theory of Change

Let us now observe some parallels in the distinctions drawn above between subtypes of each major category of government. Taking our original autocrat-democrat structure as a basis, we can say that some regimes at every level of complexity are more strongly oriented to the autocrat pole, others toward the democrat pole.

TABLE 4. Taxonomy of Fundamental Polity Types

Structural Level	Autocrat-Oriented	Democrat-Oriented
Procephaly	monarchy	republic
Orthocephaly	bureaucratic empire	feudal system
Heterotonic polity	homotonic polity	syntonic polity
Orthotonic polity	anatonic polity	contratonic polity

Table 4, in summarizing these dichotomies, suggests two dimensions of change. Those involved in moving from procephaly to orthotonic polities are associated with the functional transformations involved in *development*. It has been suggested above that development could be defined as the increasing ability of a social system (for example, a polity) to make effective choices involving environmental transformations.[30] I have also called attention to the different dimension of change involved in *democratization,* defined as an expansion in the number of members of a social system who participate in making its decisions and share in the benefits of its operations. We can now see that, relatively speaking, the governmental structures listed under *democrat-oriented* function, at each level of government, more "democratically" than do those listed under *autocrat-oriented*. However, it may also be true—although I am less confident of this proposition— that the forms of government listed as autocrat-oriented have a higher level of capability than the democrat-oriented ones.

A number of questions now present themselves. What leads to changes from one level of government to another? Clearly the contextual influence of foreign models has had a decisive bearing on the process of modernization in the new states, inducing by various means the rapid adoption of constitutive systems within the last half century. What effect have these changes had upon the processes of development and modernization? Certainly in both instances less progress has been made than is desired by leading spokesmen for both the older and the newer states. Comparing the two, I see more interest in development than in democratization, and many leaders of the modernizing countries seem to feel that, if a choice must be made, they will sacrifice democratization for development.

Insofar as the spokesmen of these states speak for their elites, they reflect a natural elitist interest everywhere in greater capacity at the expense of equality and popular participation in government. For the spokesmen of more equality we may have to listen to the leaders of insurgent movements which seem to be growing. However, the tragic irony of revolution is that after they gain power the leaders of successful political revolutions tend to stress the elitist demand for more capacity at the expense of equality.

The quest for answers to these problems of change will require analysis going far beyond the scope of this essay. I suggest that in pursuing this inquiry, we can well take advantage of the framework for analysis suggested by system theory. Building on a structural foundation such as that presented above, one can study the processes of conflict and integration leading to change within polities viewed as whole systems. One must then go on to examine the processes of conflict and goal attainment which arise in the interactions between polities (viewed as partial systems) and their context. This examination needs to be followed by a careful analysis of the ecological transactions which occur between polities and their environment, transactions which bear heavily on the adaptive and pattern maintenance functions, and go far to explain the course and prospects of institutional change, and political and administrative development. System theory, with more stress on structures, can thereby make an important contribution to the strengthening of political science, and also provide policy guidance for statesmen and technical advisers seeking to enhance political and administrative development, and to promote democratization.

NOTES

1. W. G. Runciman, *Social Science and Political Theory* (Cambridge: The University Press, 1963) pp. 122-123.

2. Gabriel A. Almond and James Coleman (eds.), *Politics of the Developing Areas* (Princeton: Princeton University Press, 1960), pp. 26-58.

3. Gabriel A. Almond, "A Developmental Approach to Political Systems," *World Politics,* XVII (January 1965), 183-214.

4. Gabriel A. Almond and G. Bingham Powell, Jr., *Comparative Politics: A Developmental Approach* (Boston: Little, Brown, 1966), p. 35. Emphasis in original.

5. Ibid., p. 105.

6. Ibid., p. 36.

7. Ibid., p. 36.

8. Ibid., p. 149. The typology is taken from Merle Fainsod, "Bureaucracy and Modernization: The Russian and Soviet Case," *Bureaucracy and Political Development,* ed. Joseph LaPalombara (Princeton: Princeton University Press, 1963) pp. 234-237.

9. Joseph LaPalombara, "Theory and Practice in Development Administration: Observations on the Role of the Civilian Bureaucracy" (Bloomington: CAG Occasional Paper, 1967), p. 25. Prepared originally for the

Brookings Institution symposium on the theory and practice of political development, September 1966. Elsewhere LaPalombara has remarked, "once we have learned the important lesson of structural alternatives for functional performance and the multifunctionality of similar structures, little remains of structural-functionalism that is useful to political science, and much remains that can be damaging to comparative research." "Parsimony and Empiricism in Comparative Politics: An Anti-Scholastic View," *The Methodology of Comparative Research,* eds. Robert T. Holt and John E. Turner (in press), MS pp. 9-10. LaPalombara also writes in this essay that "Functionalism . . . leads one to emphasize the input side of the equation and therefore tends to push research in the direction of such problems as the political socialization of children." Ibid., MS p. 30.

10. "Developmental Approach . . .," 183.

11. Marion J. Levy, Jr., *Modernization and the Structure of Societies,* 2 vols. (Princeton: Princeton University Press, 1966).

12. The arbitrary rejection of neologisms, primarily for aesthetic reasons, stands in the way of clear thinking. In the same paragraph in which LaPalombara rejects structural-functionalism, for example, we find him writing, "the concepts and propositions that go into 'theories' of political development are so abstract and obscure, so shot through with unfortunate *neologisms,* or so clearly static rather than dynamic in their final implications as to make empirical testing either a very risky enterprise or downright impossible." (Emphasis added) LaPalombara, "Theory and Practice in Development Administration," p. 25. Yet the fundamental ambiguities that arise when the same word is used for different concepts, and when no other standard words can be found to distinguish between these concepts, can only be overcome by coining new terms, assigning restricted meanings to familiar words, or using complex expressions. Levy, among others, does both, and is often criticized for both practices. Yet the rejection of this attempt to clarify basic concepts leads to fuzzy thinking and imposes obstacles to empirical testing. Some neologisms can, of course, be criticized on aesthetic grounds as unpleasant and difficult. Moreover, some writers use neologisms unjustifiably when standard words carry the required meanings unambiguously. But the development of any science has necessarily entailed the creation of new technical terms, and comparative politics will be held back if fastidious rejection of neologisms intimidates authors into a preference for euphonic ambiguity. New words should be objected to if they do not clarify useful concepts, but to object to neologisms as such is anti-intellectual and tends to block progress in our discipline. Let us object to the use of euphemisms, periphrases, catachreses, and *unnecessary* neologisms in technical writing, but let us not avoid neologisms ritualistically when they enhance clarity and reduce ambiguity.

13. Gideon Sjoberg, "Contradictory Functional Requirements and Social Systems," *Journal of Conflict Resolution,* IV (June 1960), 198-208. The idea is further discussed in relation to the idea of political development in Sjoberg, "Ideology and Social Organization in Rapidly Developing Societies" (Bloomington: CAG Occasional Paper, 1966) pp. 4-9. In this essay Sjoberg attributes the term *dysfunction* to Merton and asserts that it carries a negative connotation of undermining a system's stability. He points out that contradictory functional requirements may be found in systems in which the resulting

tensions are normal and do not necessarily involve system change. Our difficulty might be resolved by introducing another neologism—perhaps *parafunction*—to designate a relationship between a structure and a system which leads to system change, without positive or negative evaluation of the change. Structural innovations might then be seen, for example, as leading to functions which were neither eufunctional nor dysfunctional, but parafunctional. The affected system might then not be undermined or destabilized, but developed. An inquiry into the nature of parafunctions would perhaps demonstrate how structural-functionalism and system theory could be made both dynamic in theory and normatively liberal. I shall not use this new bit of jargon elsewhere in this paper, but I mention it in a footnote to show how the poverty of our vocabulary sometimes interferes with clarity of thought.

14. A fuller explanation of the concept and terminology of "constitutive system" and "tonic polity" is presented in my essay "The Structures of Government and Administrative Reform," *Political and Administrative Development,* eds. Ralph Braibanti et al. (Durham: Duke University Press, 1969), pp. 243-250.

15. A number of new words using "tonic" as a root may be formed with prefixes, thereby designating a variety of forms of government all having constitutive systems. One of the meanings of "contra-" is "in opposition," and hence will suggest a constitutive system containing one or more opposition parties, whereas "ana-" means "backward" or "excessively" and may be used, somewhat arbitrarily, for systems without opposition parties.

16. William Flanigan and Edwin Fogelman, "Functional Analysis," *Contemporary Political Analysis,* ed. James C. Charlesworth (New York: Free Press, 1967) pp. 72-85.

17. Ibid., p. 76.

18. Runciman, op cit.

19. Marion J. Levy, Jr., *The Structure of Society* (Princeton: Princeton University Press, 1952) pp. 111-148.

20. Peter M. Blau, *Exchange and Power in Social Life* (New York: John Wiley, 1964), pp. 115-142.

21. The distinction could be made clearer if we were to use an artificial adjectival form for the properties of the role as contrasted with the behavior customarily attributed to the role. We could do this, for example, by hyphenating the word. Thus "autocrat-ic" would be defined as pertaining to any characteristics of the role of autocrat, whether beneficent or maleficent, whereas "autocratic" would refer to arbitrary and high-handed behavior. Similarly, "democrat-ic" would refer to all traits of the democrat role, whereas "democratic" would mean equalitarian and permissive behavior. Another instance of this problem involves the word "bureaucratic," which typically means obscurantist and dilatory. It should be distinguished from "bureaucrat-ic," which would refer to the characteristics of officeholders in a bureaucracy. The distinction could be made orally by placing the stress on the final syllable for the hyphenated forms. Although I think such a usage would be convenient and clarifying, I fear it would raise too many objections on aesthetic grounds, and so I shall avoid it by using circumlocutions where necessary.

22. M. Fortes and E. E. Evans-Pritchard (eds.), *African Political Systems* (London: Oxford University Press, 1940), pp. 5-6, and chapters dealing with

the Logoli, the Tallensi, and the Nuer. See also critical commentary by David Easton, "Political Anthropology," *Biennial Review of Anthropology*, I (1959), 210-62.

23. A. M. Hocart, *Kingship* (London: Oxford University Press, 1927) gives a classic analysis of the highly elaborate and well-developed structures of kingship.

24. "Structures of Government . . .," pp. 29-30. See also "The Comparison of Whole Political Systems" (Bloomington: CAG Occasional Paper, 1966); to be published in *The Methodology of Comparative Research*, eds. Robert T. Holt and John E. Turner (in press).

25. On China, see H. G. Creel, "The Beginnings of Bureaucracy in China: The Origin of the *Hsien,*" *Journal of Asian Studies*, XXIII (February 1964), 155-184. For a study of the origins of Roman Imperial bureaucracy see George H. Stevenson, *Roman Provincial Administration Till the Age of the Antonines* (Oxford: Blackwell, 1939). For a useful bibliography on bureaucracy in traditional empires, see S. N. Eisenstadt, *The Political Systems of Empires* (New York: Free Press, 1963), pp. 473-521.

26. "Comparative Politics and the Study of Political Parties: A Structural Approach," *Approaches to the Study of Party Organization*, ed. William J. Crotty (Boston: Allyn & Bacon, 1967) 45-104.

27. For further elaboration see "Structures of Government . . .," pp. 253-268. See also my "Professionalism, Political Science and the Scope of Public Administration," *Theory and Practice of Public Administration*, ed. James C. Charlesworth (Philadelphia: American Academy of Social and Political Science, 1968), pp. 32-62.

28. In earlier essays I used the word "executive" for "monocrat," but I now think the latter term is somewhat less subject to misinterpretation. See "Structures of Government . . .," pp. 246-250, 293-300.

29. Ibid., pp. 268-301, contains such an analysis.

30. Ibid., pp. 230-236.

V

POLITICAL PROCESSES
AND BEHAVIOR

9 Legislative Behavior Research

NORMAN MELLER, University of Hawaii

> Legislative theories do not develop by themselves, as if wishing
> would make them so ... Unfortunately for those who want a quick
> or easy answer, the dynamics of the legislative process do not relin-
> quish their secrets readily.—*Roland Young*

I. CHRONOLOGY

For purposes of chronology, a point of time slightly earlier than
the turn of the twentieth century looms large as a benchmark for
tracing the development of systematic investigation into legislative
behavior.[1] Influenced by Walter Bagehot's *The English Constitution,*
which cut through encrusted form to reveal the actual mechanism of
the British system, a graduate student at Johns Hopkins University in 1885 published his famous *Congressional Government.*
Ours is a "government by the Standing Committees of Congress,"
wrote the young Woodrow Wilson. "The leaders of the House are
the chairmen of the principal Standing Committees" and "each
committee goes its own way at its own pace."[2] Wilson accomplished
for the United States what Bagehot had achieved for England, an
emphasis upon the practical as distinguished from formal rule.

Following Wilson, a number of pioneers continued along the direction he had pointed out. Haynes, as early as 1895, had embarked
upon his quantitative studies in state representation,[3] and Moffett
demonstrated that irrespective of state representation in the Senate
being equal and not based upon population, in most cases the
balance of votes on selected issues would have been similar if the
state vote had been weighted by population.[4] In the following year,
Mary P. Follett published the first comprehensive work on the
Speaker of the House of Representatives, important not alone for

■ This is a revised and updated version of "Legislative Behavior Research," *Western
Political Quarterly,* XIII (March 1960), 131-153; " 'Legislative Behavior Research'
Revisited: A Review of Five Years' Publications," ibid., XVIII (December 1965),
776-793.

239

identifying the basis of that officer's political authority in three nominally parliamentary powers but also for reliance upon observation and interview.[5] Ford, in *The Rise and Growth of American Politics* (1898), likens Congress to "a diplomatic body" and defines committee action as "negotiation between diverse interests" in "diplomatic privacy."[6] Probably the work of this period exerting the greatest immediate impact was Lowell's painstaking examination of the control of parties over the work of legislative bodies both in the United States and England, and though the formulation of an index of measurement, quantitatively demonstrating the difference between party control within Congress, in selected states, and in the House of Commons.[7] This early period came to a close with Bentley's *The Process of Government* (1908), a work destined to shape the political behavioralist movement by furnishing it with an explicit theoretical formulation.[8]

The second decade of the twentieth century is of interest primarily to the chronologer. The works of this period are all dwarfed by the pioneering studies which preceded them and by the research findings published in the 1930's. The first articles that appeared in the early issues of the *American Political Science Review* at best tended to be mere descriptions of legislative structure, parties, personalities, and product. Bruncken, in "Some Neglected Factors in Law-Making," gave promise of a new approach; hypothesizing that efficiency is related to legislative subject matter, a legislative note in a 1917 issue of the *Review* contains an analysis of the Massachusetts legislative output.[9] Dodd's study of legislative procedure pushed beyond formal requirements to describe the functioning of state legislative bodies.[10] Concerned with the budding of the legislative process, Harlow showed evolution of structure and practices in relation to legislative behavior prior to 1825.[11]

In modern parlance, the decade of the 1920's signalized a "breakthrough." It opened in 1923 with an article by Burton Berry treating the influence of the factors of party and gubernatorial support upon the legislative product in Indiana.[12] In the following year, Holcombe's study of political parties in part demonstrated the relationship between the economic and regional bases of the parties in Congress and stressed the importance of sectional strength in party dominance.[13] It was followed by Roach's treatment of sectionalism in Congress through an examination of roll-call votes for the period 1870 to 1890.[14] Ford's *Representative Government,* published contemporaneously, discussed the spread of the doctrine of representation and its theoretical premises.[15] Also during these years, annual conferences on the science of politics proposed ambitious, even if somewhat primitive, designs for research in legislative behavior.[16]

In the latter half of the decade, Rice's novel statistical demonstrations suggested a number of techniques applicable to legislative-

behavior research.[17] Modestly, he later disclaimed "credit for origi-
nating a new approach to the study of political behavior" and called
attention to the fact that "contemporary with my own studies were
others of analogous types . . . by L. L. Thurstone, William F. Ogburn,
Floyd Allport, Charles Merriam and Harold Gosnell, and a number of
others."[18] Be that as it may, the quantitative approach heralded by
Lowell's pioneer study was now firmly wedded to legislative behavior
research. The results of interview methodology borrowed from the
other social sciences also began coming to the fore.[19] The decade
was rounded out with the intensive group inquiries of Odegard and
Herring into the structure and techniques of pressure groups.[20]
Nearly the full scope of interest in legislative-behavior research was
thus being anticipated in the 1920's.

Robert Luce's four volumes on the "science of legislation," relating the legislative practices of antiquity to the present, were published over a span bridging the 1920's and 1930's.[21] Replete with
insights, they nevertheless lacked a theoretical formulation. In 1931,
Winslow issued his study on Maryland and Pennsylvania committees,
the first to be written on the procedure of state committees.[22] A
few years later, Willoughby published as the last volume of his
trilogy on the principles of public administration a work dealing with
the legislature.[23] It was more concerned with legislative organization
and administration than legislative behavior, a characterization also
applicable to Walker's textbook.[24] Chamberlain's distillation of his
wide legislative experience, published at approximately the same time
as the other monographs, sought to go beyond "a mere description
of the functioning parts of the legislatures."[25] It was neither a
history such as the contemporary work by Bates,[26] nor as institutionally focused as the texts previously noted, which, moreover, lacked
the conceptualization which distinguishes Chamberlain's study. This
subtle difference is best illustrated by another work of the same
vintage, Schattschneider's treatment of pressure groups and the tariff,[27] or by contrasting Galloway's *Congress at the Crossroads* with
his subsequent book, *The Legislative Process in Congress.*[28] In the
latter he incorporates much of the former's substance, but now
recognizes that the legislative process embraces all of the elements and
forces in society influencing legislative action.

Many other works might have received acknowledgment in passing, but
they were not in the central stream of legislative-behavior research.
Griffith's lectures on the United States Congress are typical of a number
of publications on the federal legislature, mostly descriptive, usually
impressionistic, and frequently hortative.[29] Once the historical stages of
development are outlined, little is to be accomplished by insisting on
further refinements; rather, a fuller understanding of the scope of legislative-behavior research may be gained by turning attention to the focal
points for the various studies of the legislative process.

In positing the political process as a continuum from individual to decision making, and legislative-behavior research as representing an array of inquiries clustered around the role of the legislature on that continuum, the task of briefly surveying the state of legislative-behavior research becomes somewhat more tenable. The formal legislative structure, the place of the executive, the individual legislator, internal and external groups exerting pressure upon the legislature, and the influence of constituent opinion—all constitute distinct foci for surveying a disparate body of research. The artificiality of the treatment of each element in isolation from the others is best summarized by Bailey in his intensive case study of a single act. He states that legislative policy making is

. . . almost unbelievably complex . . . [and] appears to be the result of a confluence of factors streaming from an almost endless number of tributaries: national experience, the contributions of social theorists, the clash of powerful economic interests, the quality of Presidential leadership, other institutional and personal ambitions and administrative arrangements in the Executive Branch, the initiative, effort, and ambitions of individual policy commitments of political parties, and the predominant culture symbols in the minds both of leaders and followers in the Congress.[30]

II. INFLUENCE OF FORMAL STRUCTURE

Although the morphology of legislatures has long interested the political scientist, few studies seek to assay the influence of formal, structural elements. Perhaps it is because processes and structures only set the frame, and their restraining and channeling effects are difficult to detect; more likely, the pervading drive to push beneath the institutional in order to reveal underlying behavioral patterns continues to encourage attention on the informal and to neglect research on the more visible "parameters of legislative behavior."[31]

Sir John Marriott, in an early descriptive study of "upper" houses, found them to be a bulwark of conservatism.[32] Normally, the role of the second house has tended to occupy only a debater's forum in discussions on unicameralism versus bicameralism,[33] but the prospect of addressing inquiry to a single-house legislature through controlled experiment retains its appeal.[34]

The unit for representation and the basis of representation in legislative bodies have long interested political commentators, in the main because of a normative concern for democracy, but also because of their relation to the legislative product.[35] The impact of *Baker v. Carr,* and the ensuing litigation and legislation, have resulted in a veritable flood of writing on such subjects as malapportionment and reapportionment.[36] In exploring another dimension of representation, Sorauf reported that single-member districts elect candidates differing neither in legislative attitude nor role toward localism from legislators chosen from multimembered districts.[37] Blair has found that cumulative voting in Illinois' multimembered districts contributes to the reduction of legislative turnover.[38]

Staffing as a factor in the shaping of legislative product and the facilitating of legislative action remains inadequately researched,[39] and there are relatively few studies on the influence of formal legislative procedures.[40] The Wahlke-Eulau-Buchanan-Ferguson State Legislative Research Project (SLRP), which explored various aspects of legislators' roles in four state legislatures, gave only glancing attention to the nature of legislative staff as affecting representatives' specialization.[41] In his case study, Berman highlights the importance of legislative rules in setting the limits to legislative action by tracing of the enactment of the Civil Rights Act of 1960 through its successive stages;[42] and Robinson considers the range of rules granted by the House Rules Committee and the conditions under which they are employed.[43] Probably of greater moment have been the publications probing into the interrelation of the formal rules with the "rules of the game" and with legislative folkways.[44]

In contrast to the foregoing, reflection on legislative behavior has found fertile outlet in numerous studies on the committee system and the characteristics of individual committees. As first stressed by Woodrow Wilson, American legislative practice can often be "government by committee"; thus committees in general,[45] subcommittees,[46] conference committees,[47] investigating and select committees,[48] and specific standing committees[49] have each been the subject of attention. In addition, the formal and informal processes of committee assignments have been studied in considerable detail.[50]

III. EXECUTIVE AND ADMINISTRATIVE AGENCIES

The President, governors, and administrative agencies occupy a position that has been conceived of as between external pressures impinging upon the legislature and forces internal to its operations by virtue of the role of the chief executive as principal legislator, bulwarked by his veto power and the intimidation implicit in its possession.[51] In view of a chief executive's ambiguous tie to his legislative party and his overarching responsibility for directing the administrative branch, he perpetually poses a challenge to the legislature's power. Kendall attributes the tension between Congress and President, and, concomitantly, the former's interest in specifics and the latter's in principles, to the differences in character (aristocratic versus democratic) of the majorities which elect them.[52] Nelson describes the practice of Congressional consultation and advice in the area of foreign policy as a mitigant to this controversy between the two branches.[53]

Studies concerned with the detail of executive-legislative relationships have sought to determine the importance of executive agencies as initiators of legislation,[54] have treated legislative devices for administrative oversight,[55] concentrated on committee-administration relationships,[56] and have identified areas of legislative inaction, such as reluctance to exert controls in matters of national defense.[57] Scher advances hypotheses concerning individual-member proposals for committee action on administrative oversight,[58] and he also has analyzed the behavior of Congressmen in their role as overseers of an independent regulatory commission.[59] Rosenau has attempted to provide a schema useful for classifying Senatorial attitudes toward department heads.[60]

Roll-call inquiry on foreign-aid issues reveals the influence of Presidential leadership and a two-way congruent shift of parties toward opposite poles with the change of Presidents.[61] Truman concludes that there is a "functional interdependence between the majority leaders in Congress and a President of the same party" and that Congressional parties and their leaders are of limited significance "when the President is tied to a congressional minority, or when the majority on Capitol Hill is truncated, or when the congressional party is 'out of power' at both ends of Pennsylvania Avenue."[62] Less attention has been given to the state scene. In a study of a one-party state, Oklahoma legislative leaders and new members had higher rankings in support of the governor's program.[63] Research in state executive-legislative relations somehow has not had the same attraction as this variable on the federal level of government.

IV. INDIVIDUALS

Once Bentley's mechanistic approach is qualified by emphasizing that men comprise the legislature—and, as such, themselves contribute to shaping the legislative product rather than merely automatically responding to pressures applied within the legislative frame—the study of the legislator *qua* legislator assumes major importance.

Burns, in *Congress on Trial,* after denying the existence of an "average" Congressman, describes the *type genus* as a small-town lawyer in an agricultural setting, primarily committed to his district and possessing a vague set of personal ideals.[64] The composite may be grossly accurate, but is inadequate for purposes of determining the representativeness of Congress as well as relating the socioeconomic backgrounds of Congressmen to the predispositions and attitudes they bring to the legislative halls. As early as the mid-1890's, researchers were scrutinizing the age, place of birth, education, occupation, and public-office experience of legislators.[65] Since then, assays of Congress and the legislatures of the various states have reemphasized, sometimes with considerable sophistication, the finding that in composition these bodies are far from being mere reflections of constituency characteristics, and have speculated upon the importance of the variances revealed.[66]

One of the earliest findings from these surveys of legislative bodies pointed up the sharing by legislators of certain characteristics in common over time[67] and across jurisdictional boundaries. This has encouraged studies that distinguish lawyer-legislators from their colleagues,[68] analyze the effects of occupational mobility,[69] and turn attention to other components of the "legislative profile," such as age of legislators[70] and their length of tenure.[71] Matthews' probe into class origins; race, nationality, and creed; education; occupation; and associational life of United States Senators is based upon the premise that "a Senator's behavior pattern is set to some degree long before he comes to Washington."[72] The SLRP undertaking, utilizing interviews, measures state legislators' own perceptions of their political socialization—the process by which they acquired the "values, attitudes, interest or knowledge" that have influenced their roles.[73] Similarly, Barber develops a four-category typology of Connecticut legislators' self-conceptions.[74] Personality and opinion tests administered to a few of South Carolina's law-makers raise doubts concerning Lasswell's displacement hypothesis as an explanation for the political man, or at least the legislative man.[75]

Froman demonstrates through roll-call analysis that "it does make a difference in Congressional voting as to which particular Democrat or Republican holds office."[76] Approaching the importance of individual differences from another perspective, Huitt concludes in his sketching of Senator Proxmire's style that there is "no [one] role of a deviant" in the U.S. Senate but, rather, many alternative orientations which the Senate will accept.[77] Patterson, also focusing his attention on Wisconsin's legislators, but directing his inquiry to the state's representatives, conceptualized three deviant types, the "talker," the "moocher," and the "maverick."[78] In addition, various factors have been identified that may encourage individual nonconformity with legislative norm.[79]

Little systematic data exist on the flow of information to the legislator and the sources on which he depends in decision making.[80] As shown by Garceau and Silverman, a legislator's own view of the legislative process undoubtedly shapes his responses to queries probing into this area.[81] What a Congressman hears from his constituents tends to be selectively biased to conform to his own values.[82] Congressmen may welcome communications from interest groups,[83] but some have reported that they relied less on them for expert information than on committee hearings, office staffs, and other specified sources identified with the workings of legislative bodies.[84]

It is feasible to measure a legislator's actions in order to demonstrate consistency in his voting pattern,[85] but there is as yet no comparable objective scale for measuring legislative ability. In their analysis of what some Washington correspondents selected as the "ablest" Congressmen, ranked according to prescribed criteria, Carlson and Harrell conclude that to the "correspondents a Congressman's influence is not at all related to his intellectual fortitude."[86] On another tack, a statistical attempt to correlate brain weight with legislative ability came to naught.[87]

Since Congress (and many a state legislature) has long been acknowledged as a body of "distributed power and disintegrated rule,"[88] one must penetrate behind formal legislative posts in order to identify legislators occupying the positions of leadership. Conceptually such identification may be approached by studying the conduct of official, party, and charismatic leaders,[89] or by establishing criteria for distinguishing leadership roles, such as the number of observed contacts between legislators on the floor of a legislative chamber[90] or contributions to the written record.[91] Formal position may reveal legislative influence, but so will success in the passage of bills; however, the two do not relate significantly, and "high formal position success . . . is not sufficient for high general influence."[92] Formal leaders are attributed respect and affection more frequently than rank-and-file members,[93] and legislators with leadership status are likely to be identified as friends;[94] but conflicting findings have been reported when testing the "middleman" and "extremity" hypotheses for recruitment and role playing of formal and party leaders.[95]

Besides the predispositions, knowledge, and ability which the legislator himself brings to the legislative halls, the legislator's decisions also are influenced by self-perceptions of his own role and those of others, particularly of leaders.[96] In contrast to journalists' and legislators' impressionistic observations, both general and specific, about legislators,[97] the SLRP studies painstakingly delineate the nature and interrelation among a variety of roles which state legislators take, among them social and political, specialist and purposive. Of the roles legislators can assume, that of a representative has probably attracted the most careful study.[98] Pushing beyond legislators' verbal self-identification, Crane's cross-check of the Wisconsin legislators' vote on a measure subsequently submitted to referendum demonstrates a surprisingly high "delegate" component.[99] The SLRP's suggestion that the "trustee" role perception is related to constituency control, and the latter in turn to intricacy and obscurity of issues, has been questioned in two subsequent empirical studies.[100] Focusing of attention upon roles has also encouraged inquiry into their linkage with personal-background characteristics.[101] The half-century concern with the legislative profile appears to have exhausted its potential for further fruitful inquiry; the significance of its components must now be explored in relation to a whole gamut of legislative roles which has only just been sketched. In an era of group politics, the

legislator as an individual still remains an important subject for legislative-behavior research.

V. GROUPS

One theory of politics that has progressively gained prominence
posits the group as the basic political form and the legislature as
but an official group refereeing the group struggle and formalizing
the victories of the successful coalitions.[102] The concern among
social psychologists with the ramifications of small-group interaction
has been a parallel development. The two complement each other in
spanning the gamut of group involvement with legislative activity,
from coalitions of legislators internal to a legislative body to organized formal groups external to but impinging upon the legislature.

The major group for consideration is the legislative house itself.
"The Senate of the United States, just as any other group of human
beings, has its unwritten rules of the game, its norms of conduct, its
approved manner of behavior."[103] Among these Senate folkways are
such norms as apprenticeship, courtesy, reciprocity, and institutional
patriotism.[104] The "unwritten rules of the game in [state] legislative
bodies [yet] provide an almost virgin field for empirical research."[105] That there are differences between the legislative houses
was disclosed in an inquiry into constituency influences conducted in
Pennsylvania.[106] However, the SLRP study showed the "same over-all
patterns of role relationships . . . in each state's two chambers [while]
these within-state patterns of both houses varied considerably from
one state to another."[107]

Membership and group life of legislative committees have also been
subjected to systematic treatment. Propositions comparable to those
employed for explaining political behavior in other contexts have
been found applicable to the major variables in committee decision
making.[108] Fenno's study of subgroup integration as dependent upon
such group norms as specialization, reciprocity, unity, and minimal
partisanship[109] is balanced by Jones's probe into the causes of
another House committee's failure to secure integrative behavior.[110]
Truman posits that public hearings of committees have informational,
propaganda, and cathartic functions,[111] two of which are identified
by Huitt in his reporting on hearings considering the continuance of
the Office of Price Administration.[112] The effect of Senate committee membership on the reversing of the solons' prior-policy position[113] and committee cohesion evidenced in floor action[114] provide
additional dimensions for assessing the influence of a committee considered as a subgroup.

The search for other, less structured subgroups—or their absence—
has been carried forward in studies on friendship cliques,[115] sectional
and state blocs,[116] and subparty groupings,[117] the last including

both state party delegations in the Congress and informal subgroups within them. [118] Approaching the same target inversely, Rice's earlier research into legislative behavior analyzed roll calls of the whole legislature and of "leading" Congressmen in an attempt to discover and to demonstrate the existence of intra-legislative groupings. [119]

The legislative party, with its distinctive structure and norms, is the largest subgroup within the legislative body, and it has long been studied as a major element influencing the legislative process. [120] In the past, following the lead of Lowell's early findings on party voting solidarity, it has been customary to depreciate party differences in legislative decision making. [121] More recent legislative studies have tended to confirm ideological variances between the parties. [122] Truman contends that "if one seeks a reliable understanding of the Congress, it is likely to be found most readily in . . . the legislative parties," [123] and that "the party label evidently is the single most reliable indicator of Congressional voting behavior." [124] Studies of state legislatures have emphasized the role of parties as reference groups, [125] and stressed the norms of voting with one's party on procedural motions and "platform bills." [126] On the more formal side, conditions for party leadership, [127] leadership styles [128] and roles, [129] and the activities of units of the party's legislative organization [130] have received both descriptive and quantitative scrutiny. A measure for state inter-party competition has been suggested by categorizing party strength as a composite of the party affiliations of the legislature and governor. [131]

With the way pointed by Odegard and Herring, the study of organized interest groups, their techniques and influence, became an engrossing subject for the academician. [132] Thus, Riggs would distinguish the "catalytic" group from other pressure organizations. [133] Schattschneider, through analyzing the public records pertinent to the 1929-1930 revision of the tariff, erected a schema for classifying pressure-group activity. [134] Since these early studies, the organized interest group and its relation to the entire spectrum of the legislative process has undergone more realistic consideration; as a by-product, the group-focused conception of pressure politics has lost something of the éclat it enjoyed when sketched in simplistic terms of unilateral, group-to-legislator orientation. Key, in his last work on public opinion, included reference to the emptiness of the lobbyist's threat of electoral reprisal and downgraded the efficaciousness of the pressure-group "rituals." [135] Matthews reports, "the Senator is far from a passive puppet manipulated from afar." Lobbying now emerges as a matter of bargaining, a two-way flow of influence, with reinforcement and activation, rather than conversion, its major effects. [136] The contact of pressure group with legislator through the lobbyist becomes "essentially a communication process" in which techniques of communication may be differentiated from effort directed to keeping open the channels of communication.[137] State legislators are disclosed as adopting role orientations toward pressure groups, and lobbyists as doing the same toward their legislative counterparts. For the former, the SLRP research identifies "facilitators," "resisters," and "neutrals," and stresses the position of the facilitator in mediating the group struggle;[138] for the latter, "contact men," "informants," and "watch dogs" emerge as role types in an Oklahoma study, as well as tendencies for specific categories of interests to be represented by distinctive lobbying types.[139] The bulk of the literature on pressure-group activity, including representation of group interests through legislation, is ably summarized in Zeigler's recent text.[140]

VI. CONSTITUENCY INFLUENCE

What Oliver Garceau has called the "broad gauge . . . study of the constituency itself, its economy, social stratification, group organization, media of communication and party organization" remains outside the scope of this essay.[141] However, one of the major clusters of legislative-behavior research is concerned with constituency impact on the legislative process, including correlation between legislative roll calls and demographic characteristics of the constituencies, and the factors at work within the constituency affecting "career sequences" of legislators. This attention to constituency encompasses more than the study of organized pressure-group activity and questions whether constituency influence extends beyond the mere selection or rejection of candidates to affecting the legislative output.[142] To this end, variations in political styles of Congressmen from two roughly comparable Negro districts are traced to dissimilarities in their internal political systems.[143] The influence of a constituency's international ties on Senate votes has been found to be directly proportional to the weight of their economic importance within the constituency.[144] And pursuing the same approach, several studies have related the emergence of Southern isolationism in Congress to constituency causation.[145]

Building upon the hypothesis that political party differences reflect constituency differences, and that intra-party variation within the legislature may similarly be explained, Congressional inquiries have linked district demographic and electoral characteristics with Representatives' voting records.[146] Comparable studies of state legislatures found party regularity to be related to party typicalness of a member's constituency.[147] Sensitivity to constituency interest as affected by "safeness" of the constituency has also been explored, both on the national and state scenes.[148]

Turnover rates in legislative membership offer a potentially useful measure for the influence of constituency characteristics.[149] McKinney's study of Congressional turnover shows a tendency within a constituency to continue to cast votes for candidates with the same religion, a tendency even stronger than the tradition of voting for the same party. [150] A less rigorous treatment for the state of New Mexico concerned itself with comparable ethnic considerations. [151] The high turnover reported upon extensively several decades ago, and implicated in single-state studies that incidentally looked into this, [152] ought to have prompted systematic inquiry into constituency disapproval, but this remains for further investigation.

Constituency influences must also be considered in terms of the voters' very limited knowledge of their representative's actions [153] and their conceptions of the representative's role. On national issues it has been found that although constituents believe that a representative should depend least upon his own judgment, they regard it to be his chief reliance. [154] This line of inquiry currently complements the research on legislators' self-perceptions. [155]

It appears somewhat ironic that as the urban areas of the nation receive equal representation, through the intervention of the judicial process, recent legislative-behavior studies cast doubt upon the potential effects of such readjustment in the modifying of legislative action. The existence of urban-rural cleavage has been questioned in at least six states. [156] One commentator boldly generalizes that "urban-rural factionalism is not characteristic of legislative conflict in American state legislatures." [157] Jewell in his work on state legislatures attempts to explain these disquieting studies, [158] but the ambiguous findings in Oklahoma [159] probably support the most adequate evaluation which can be reached at this juncture: "It seems more likely that rural-urban differences are important, but more so in some kinds of issues than others, and more so in some parts of the country than others." [160]

VII. CONCLUSION

Legislative-behavior research is distinguishable, as is the whole behavioral approach, by an acute awareness of methodology. Frequently studies in the field are premised upon analyses of legislative roll calls, pointing up the behavior of individual legislators, "categoric groups," and clusters or blocs of coalescing legislators. [161] Many utilize indicators which were developed at the very beginning of the inquiry into the legislative process by Lowell and Rice, or variants thereof, [162] while others employ more recent statistical tools. [163] With greater sophistication, too ready a reliance upon raw legislative voting scores is being subjected to reconsideration. [164] In contrast with the early interest displayed in roll calls, the search for power indexes was somewhat later in appearing, when power was identified as the central axis of political science. Here, too, proposals attempting to quantify power have been followed up with critical appraisal. [165]

Beyond well-traveled areas of methodological interest, a whole new array of statistical techniques and measuring devices awaits demonstration of their utility when used in the study of varying legislative bodies before their automatic acceptance as standard tools of legislative-behavior research.[166]

Like raindrops on a dirty windowpane, legislative-behavior studies afford brief glimpses at a broader vision of the legislative process, but have failed to furnish a framework enabling its full comprehension. Studies are yet too disperse and lack replication; conflicting findings have not always served as stimuli for subsequent clarificatory research. Also, there has been too ready a subsuming of the basic unity of the legislative process[167] and too little attention given to the generation of an inclusive theory.[168]

A conservative illustration of the current problem in legislative-behavior research may suffice. One could select, say, 10 potentially significant attributes (such as education and occupation) of a legislator as an individual, with again an arbitrary 10 roles, functioning within a formal legislative framework (similarly 10 variables) and amidst group pressures (10), constituency influences (10), and the executive-administrative complex (10). Giving a separate paragraph to the delineation of each of these 60 variables and their relation with all of the others, both singularly and in combination, would require billions of learned journal pages. This process becomes even more unwieldy if one seeks replication in the national and each of the 50 state jurisdictions, and corroboration over time to verify findings. Such a study becomes even more encyclopedic when the research is subdivided into categories for specific legislative functions or classes of policy decisions. In short, measurements motivated mainly by convenience of legislative data must be abandoned and prolixity rigidly curtailed. The ultimate goal of formulating a theory of legislative behavior will otherwise be completely submerged in a torrent of print.

NOTES

1. This is not to imply that the peers of yesteryear were unconcerned with the behavior of legislators—Aristotle for one, stressed the role of the middle class for achieving the "best" form of political society and pointed out that Solon, Lycurgus, Charondas, and "most of the other legislators" of ancient fame traced their origins to the middle class. *Politics*, trans. Ernest Barker (Oxford: Clarendon Press, 1946), Book 4, Cl. XI, XV, pp. 182-83.

2. Woodrow Wilson, *Congressional Government* (Boston: Houghton Mifflin, 1885), pp. 56, 60, 61.

3. George H. Haynes, "Representation in New England Legislatures," *Annals of the American Academy of Political and Social Sciences*, VI (September 1895), 58 ff; "Representation in the Legislatures of the North

Atlantic States" and "Representation in the Legislatures of the North Central States," ibid., XV (March 1900), 204 ff and (May 1900), 405 ff; "The Southern States" and "The Western States," ibid., XVI (July 1900), 93 ff and (September 1900), 243 ff. Vermont, Ohio, Indiana, and Missouri are covered more impressionistically by Samual P. Orth, "Our State Legislatures," *Atlantic Monthly*, XCIV (December 1904), 728 ff.

4. S. E. Moffett, "Is the Senate Unfairly Constituted?" *Political Science Quarterly*, (June 1895), 248 ff.

5. Mary P. Follett, *The Speaker of the House of Representatives* (New York: Longmans, Green, 1896).

6. Henry Jones Ford, *The Rise and Growth of American Politics* (New York: Macmillan, 1898), pp. 221, 224.

7. A. Lawrence Lowell, "The Influence of Party Upon Legislation in England and America," *Annual Report of the American Historical Association*, 1901, H. R. Doc. No. 702, 57th Cong., 1st Sess. 321 (1902).

8. Arthur F. Bentley, *The Process of Government* (Chicago: University of Chicago Press, 1908).

9. Ernest Bruncken, "Some Neglected Factors in Law-Making," *American Political Science Review*, VIII (May 1914), 222 ff; "Legislative Activity in Massachusetts, 1916," ibid., XI (August 1917), 528 ff.

10. H. W. Dodds, "Procedure in State Legislatures," *Annals*, Supplement No. 1 (May 1918). Reinsch's 1906 study of both Congress and state legislatures had set the pattern—Paul S. Reinsch, *American Legislatures and Legislative Methods* (New York: Century, 1906).

11. Ralph Volney Harlow, *The History of Legislative Methods in the Period Before 1825* (New Haven: Yale University Press, 1917).

12. Burton Y. Berry, "The Influence of Political Platforms on Legislation in Indiana, 1901-1921," *American Political Science Review*, XV (February 1923) 51 ff.

13. Arthur N. Holcombe, *The Political Parties of Today* (New York: Harper, 1924).

14. Hannah G. Roach, "Sectionalism in Congress (1870 to 1890)," *American Political Science Review*, XIX (August 1925), 500 ff.

15. Henry Jones Ford, *Representative Government* (New York: Holt, 1924).

16. National Conference on the Science of Politics," *American Political Science Review*, XVIII (February 1924), 119 ff; XIX (February 1925), 104 ff; XX (February 1926), 124 ff. The 1932 note on governors' messages appears to be a direct response to a conference plea of the need for this type of study. "Governors' Messages and the Legislative Product in 1932," ibid., XXVI (December 1932), 1058 ff.

17. Stuart A. Rice, "The Behavior of Legislative Groups: A Method of Measurement," *Political Science Quarterly*, XL (March 1925), 60 ff; "Some Applications of Statistical Method to Political Research," *American Political Science Review*, XX (May 1926), 313 ff; "The Identification of Blocs in Small Political Bodies," ibid., XXI (August 1927), 619 ff; *Quantitative Methods in Politics* (New York: Knopf, 1928). These studies were preceded by Rice's 1924 study, *Farmers and Workers in American Politics* (New York: Columbia University Press, 1924).

18. Stuart A. Rice, " 'Quantitative Methods in Politics,' after Thirty

Years," *PROD*, I (January 1958), 20 ff.

19. See Martin L. Faust, "Results on the Split-Session of the West Virginia Legislature," *American Political Science Review*, XXII (February 1928), 109 ff.

20. Peter H. Odegard, *Pressure Politics: The Study of the Anti-Saloon League* (New York: Columbia University Press, 1928); E. Pendleton Herring, *Group Representation Before Congress* (Baltimore: Johns Hopkins Press, 1929).

21. All four were published by Houghton Mifflin Company, Boston. In the order of publication: *Legislative Procedure* (1922); *Legislative Assemblies* (1924); *Legislative Principles* (1930); and *Legislative Problems* (1935). In addition, Luce delivered a series of lectures, *Congress—An Explanation* (Cambridge: Harvard University Press, 1926).

22. Clinton I. Winslow, *State Legislative Committees, A Study in Procedure* (Baltimore: Johns Hopkins Press, 1931).

23. W. F. Willoughby, *Principles of Legislative Organization and Administration* (Washington, D.C.: Brookings, 1934).

24. Harvey Walker, *Law Making in the United States* (New York: Ronald, 1934). The same may be said for his later text, *The Legislative Process* (New York: Ronald, 1948).

25. Joseph P. Chamberlain, *Legislative Processes: National and State* (New York: Appleton-Century, 1936), p. v.

26. Ernest S. Bates, *The Story of Congress* (New York: Harper, 1936).

27. E. E. Schattschneider, *Politics, Pressures and the Tariff* (New York: Prentice-Hall, 1935).

28. George D. Galloway, *Congress at the Crossroads* (New York: Crowell, 1946); *The Legislative Process in Congress* (New York: Crowell, 1953).

29. Ernest S. Griffith, *Congress: Its Contemporary Role* (New York: New York University Press, 1951). For works on Congress, see Ronald Young, *This is Congress* (New York: Knopf, 1943); Thomas K. Finletter, *Can Representative Government Do the Job?* (New York: Reynal & Hitchcock, 1945); Estes Kefauver and Jack Levin, *A Twentieth Century Congress* (New York: Duell, Sloan & Pearce, 1947); Floyd M. Riddick, *The United States Congress: Organization and Procedure* (Manassas, Va.: National Capitol Publishers, 1949). For an example of state studies, see Hallie Farmer's series on the legislative process in Alabama: *Legislative Apportionment* (1944), *Local and Private Legislation* (1944), *Standing Committees* (1945), *Recess and Interim Committees* (1946), *Legislative Costs* (1947), and her larger work, *The Legislative Process in Alabama* (1949), all published by the Bureau of Public Administration, University of Alabama.

30. Stephen K. Bailey, *Congress Makes a Law* (New York: Columbia University Press, 1950), p. 236.

31. Borrowed from John C. Wahlke and Heinz Eulau (eds.), *Legislative Behavior* (Glencoe: Free Press, 1959), p. 5; they include both institutional objectives and procedures within the "parameters." As an illustration of research on formal elements that ignores behavioral aspects, see the job analysis of legislators' duties and responsibilities for compensation purposes in Alexander Cloner and Richard W. Gable, "The California Legislator and the Problem of Compensation," *Western Political Quarterly*, XII (September 1959), 712 ff.

32. Sir John A. R. Marriott, *Second Chambers* (Oxford: Clarendon, 1910). Compare this with the findings of Lewis A. Froman, Jr., in *Congressmen and Their Constituents* (Chicago: Rand McNally, 1963), that the U.S. Senate is more liberal than the House, which he attributes to structural and constituency factors.

33. See Alvin W. Johnson, *The Unicameral Legislature* (Minneapolis: University of Minnesota Press, 1938); John P. Senning, "Unicameralism Passes Test," *National Municipal Review*, XXXIII (February 1944), 60 ff; Roger V. Shumate, "The Nebraska Unicameral Legislature," *Western Political Quarterly*, V (September 1952), 504 ff. However, see "Bicameralism as Illustrated by the Ninetieth General Assembly of Ohio; A Technique for the Studying of the Legislative Process," *American Political Science Review*, XXXII (February 1938), 81 ff; Dorothy Schaffter, *The Bicameral System in Practice* (Iowa City: State Historical Society of Iowa, 1929), pp. 103 ff.

34. See Richard S. Snyder, "Experimental Techniques and Political Analysis," *The Limits of Behavioralism in Policical Science*, ed. James C. Charlesworth, (Philadelphia: American Academy of Political and Social Sciences, 1962), pp. 94-123, at p. 114.

35. For example, see Cortez A. M. Ewing, *Congressional Elections, 1896-1944* (Norman: University of Oklahoma Press, 1947); Robert A. Dahl, *A Preface to Democratic Theory* (Chicago: University of Chicago Press, 1956), pp. 146-147.

36. Malcolm E. Jewell (ed.), *The Politics of Reapportionment* (New York: Atherton, 1962); on the characteristics of overrepresented, equitably represented, and underrepresented districts, see Andrew Hacker, *Congressional Districting* (Washington, D.C.: Brookings, 1963), pp. 74-87; Alan L. Clem, "Measuring Legislative Malapportionment: In Search of a Better Yardstick," *Midwest Journal of Political Science*, VII (May 1963), 125 ff. Glendon Schubert and Charles Press, "Measuring Malapportionment," *American Political Science Review*, LVIII (June 1964), 302 ff. See novel proposal for assigning weighting to reflect popular support in Robert H. Engle, "Weighting Legislators' Votes to Equalize Representation," *Western Political Quarterly*, XII (June 1959), 442 ff; a theoretical application of this to congressional roll calls appears in Hacker, op. cit., pp. 89-91; for a report on a short-lived adoption see "New Mexico Tries Weighted Voting," *National Civic Review*, LIII (January 1964), 33 ff.

37. Frank J. Sorauf, *Party and Representation* (New York; Atherton, 1963), p. 133; on the subject of turnover, see Ruth C. Silva, "Compared Values of the Single- and Multi-Member Legislative District," *Western Political Quarterly*, XVII (September 1964), 504 ff; also see Howard D. Hamilton, "Legislative Constituencies: Single-Member Districts, Multi-Member Districts, and Floterial Districts," *Western Political Quarterly*, XX (June 1967), 321 ff.

38. George S. Blair, *Cumulative Voting* (Urbana: University of Illinois Press, 1960).

39. Lindsay Rogers, "The Staffing of Congress," *Political Science Quarterly*, LVI (March 1941), 1 ff; Gladys M. Kammerer, "The Record of Congress in Committee Staffing," *American Political Science Review*, XLV (December 1951), 1126 ff; Norman Meller, "The Policy Position of Legislative Service Agencies," *Western Political Quarterly*, V (March 1952), 109 ff; Max M. Kampelman, "The Legislative Bureaucracy: Its Response to Political

Change, 1953," *Journal of Politics,* XVI (August 1954), 539 ff; Kenneth Kofmehl, *Professional Staffs of Congress* (West Lafayette: Purdue University Press, 1962); Warren H. Butler, "Administering Congress: The Role of the Staff," *Public Administration Review,* XXVI (March 1966), 3 ff; Norman Meller, "Legislative Staff Services," *Western Political Quarterly,* XX (June 1967), 381 ff.

40. See, however, William H. Riker, "The Paradox of Voting and Congressional Rules for Voting on Amendments," *American Political Science Review,* LII (June 1958), 349 ff.

41. William Buchanan et al., "The Legislator as Specialist," *Western Political Quarterly,* XIII (September 1960), 636 ff. Significantly, the legislative-council movement took root and flourished in the Midwest, where the average lawmaker is a "citizen-legislator." Harold W. Davey, "The Legislative Council Movement, 1933-53," *American Political Science Review,* XLVII (September 1953), 785 ff.

42. Daniel M. Berman, *A Bill Becomes a Law* (New York: MacMillan, 1962). However, this was ground already traversed. See Howard E. Shuman, "Senate Rules and the Civil Rights Bill," *American Political Science Review,* LI (December 1957), 955 ff.

43. James A. Robinson, "The Role of the Rules Committee in Regulating Debate in the U.S. House of Representatives," *Midwest Journal Political Science,* V (February 1961), 59 ff. Also see Robinson, n. 49 below.

44. See n. 103 below and text, p. 247.

45. For example, Matthews' sketch of the U.S. Senate's "committee caste system." Donald R. Matthews, *U.S. Senators and Their World* (Chapel Hill: University of North Carolina Press, 1960), pp. 148-158. Also see Henry W. Lewis, *Legislative Committees in North Carolina* (Chapel Hill: University of North Carolina Press, 1952); Ralph K. Huitt, "The Congressional Committee: A Case Study," *American Political Science Review,* XLVIII (June 1954), 340 ff; Dean E. Mann, "The Legislative Committee System in Arizona," *Western Political Quarterly,* XIV (December 1961), 925 ff.

46. Burton L. French, "Sub-Committees of Congress," *American Political Science Review,* IX (February 1915), 68 ff; Elias Huzar, "Congress and the Army: Appropriations," ibid., XXXVIII (August 1943), 661 ff; George Goodwin, Jr., "Subcommittees: The Miniature Legislatures of Congress," ibid., LVI (September 1962), 596 ff. See Charles O. Jones, "The Role of the Congressional Subcommittee," *Midwest Journal of Political Science,* VI (November 1962), 327 ff, and its comparison of the functions of subcommittees with Fenno's findings in Richard F. Fenno, Jr., "The House Appropriations Committee as a Political System," *American Political Science Review,* LVI (June 1962), 310 ff.

47. Ada C. McCown, *The Congressional Conference Committee* (New York: Columbia University Press, 1927); "Conference Committees in Nebraska Legislature," *American Political Science Review,* XXX (December 1936), 1114 ff; Robert H. Horwitz and Norman Meller, "Land and Politics in Hawaii" (3rd rev. ed.; Honolulu: University of Hawaii Press, 1966), pp. 25-45; Richard F. Fenno, Jr., *The Power of the Purse* (Boston: Little, Brown, 1966), Ch. XII.

48. Ernest J. Eberling, *Congressional Investigations* (New York: Columbia University Press, 1928); Marshall E. Dimock, *Congressional Investigating*

Committees (Baltimore: Johns Hopkins Press, 1929); Martin N. McGeary, *The Developments of Congressional Investigative Power* (New York: Columbia University Press, 1940); V. Stanley Vardys, "Select Committees of the House of Representatives," *Midwest Journal of Political Science,* VI (August 1962), 247 ff.

49. For example, the Joint Atomic Energy Committee: Harold P. Green and Alan Rosenthal, *Government of the Atom* (New York: Atherton, 1963); H. L. Nieburg, "The Eisenhower AEC and Congress," *Midwest Journal of Political Science,* VI (May 1962), 115 ff. The Senate Foreign Relations Committee: Eleanor E. Dennison, *The Senate Foreign Relations Committee* (Stanford: Stanford University Press, 1942); David N. Farnsworth, *The Senate Committee on Foreign Relations* (Urbana: University of Illinois Press, 1961); Farnsworth, "A Comparison of the Senate and its Foreign Relations Committee on Selected Roll-Call Votes," *Western Political Quarterly,* XIV (March 1961), 168 ff. House Committee on Foreign Affairs: Holbert N. Carrol, *The House of Representatives and Foreign Affairs* (rev. ed.; Boston: Little, Brown, 1966). Rules Committee of the House of Representatives: James A. Robinson, *The House Rules Committee* (Indianapolis: Bobbs-Merrill, 1963); Robinson, "Organizational and Constituency Backgrounds of the House Rules Committee," *The American Political Arena,* ed. Joseph R. Fiszman (Boston: Little, Brown, 1962), pp. 211-218; Robinson, "The Role of the Rules Committee in Regulating Debate . . .," op. cit.; Robinson, "The Role of the Rules Committee in Arranging the Programs of the U.S. House of Representatives," *Western Political Quarterly,* XII (September 1959), 653 ff; Robinson, "Decision-Making in the Committee on Rules," *Administrative Science Quarterly,* III (June 1958), 73 ff. Also see Robert L. Peabody, "The Enlarged Rules Committee," *New Perspectives on the House of Representatives,* eds. Robert L. Peabody and Nelson W. Polsby, (Chicago: Rand McNally, 1963), p. 129.

50. Nicholas A. Masters, "Committee Assignments in the House of Representatives," *American Political Science Review,* LV (June 1961), 345 ff; George Goodwin, Jr., "The Seniority System in Congress," ibid., LIII (June 1959), 412 ff. Differences in methods of committee assignments helped explain reductions vs. restorations in budget consideration in Robert A. Wallace, "Congressional Control of the Budget," *Midwest Journal of Political Science,* III (May 1959), 151 ff. See also Loren P. Beth and William C. Havard, "Committee Stacking and Political Power in Florida," *Journal of Politics,* XXIII (February 1961), 57 ff.

51. The interest in vetoes is of long standing. See Edward C. Mason, *The Veto Power,* Harvard Historical Monograph No. 1 (Boston: Ginn, 1890); "The Presidential Veto Since 1889," *American Political Science Review,* XXXI (February 1937), 51 ff; John A. Fairlie, "The Veto Power of the State Governor," ibid., XI (August 1917), 473 ff; M. Nelson McGeary, "The Governor's Veto in Pennsylvania," ibid., XLI (October 1947), 941 ff; Frank W. Prescott, "The Executive Veto in America States," *Western Political Quarterly,* III (March 1950), 98 ff. See game-theory constructs in L. S. Shapley and Martin Shubik, "A Method for Evaluating the Distribution of Power in a Committee System," *American Political Science Review,* XLVIII (September 1954), 789 ff; R. Duncan Luce and Arnold A. Rogow, "A Game Theoretic Analysis of Congressional Power Distributions for a Two-Party System,"

Behavioral Science, I (April 1956), 83 ff. See also Sarah P. McCally, "The Governor and His Legislative Party," *American Political Science Review,* LX (December 1966), 923 ff.

52. Willmoore Kendall, "The Two Majorities," *Midwest Journal of Political Science,* IV (November 1960), 317 ff.

53. Randall H. Nelson, "Legislative Participation in the Treaty and Agreement-Making Process," *Western Political Quarterly,* XIII (March 1960), 154 ff. See also James A. Robinson, "Process Satisfaction and Policy Approval," *American Journal of Sociology,* LXVII (November 1961), 278 ff, which explored the relation to legislative satisfaction of information flow from the State Department; found also in Robinson, *Congress and Foreign Policy-Making* (rev. ed.; Homewood: Dorsey, 1967), Ch. VI.

54. Edwin E. Witte, "Administrative Agencies and Statute Law Making," *Public Administration Review,* II (Spring 1942), 116 ff; Elizabeth McK. Scott and Belle Zeller, "State Agencies and Law Making," *Public Administration Review,* II (Summer 1942), 205 ff. However, compare Harvey Walker, "Who Writes the Laws," *State Government,* XII (November 1939), 199 ff. For literature on the executive as initiator and catalyst see Harry W. Reynolds, Jr., "The Career Public Service and Statue Law-making in Los Angeles," *Western Political Quarterly,* XVIII (September 1965), 621 ff, at p. 624, n. 10. Legislative innovation of a measure as the significant variable in its successful enactment was investigated in Robinson, *Congress and . . . ,* pp. 108 ff.

55. John A. Fairlie, "The Legislature and the Administration," *American Political Science Review,* XXX (April 1936), 241 ff, (June 1936), 494 ff; Elias Huzar, "Legislative Control Over Administration: Congress and the W. P. A.," ibid., XXXVI (February 1942), 51 ff; "Executive Responsibility to Congress via Concurrent Resolution," ibid., (October 1942), 895 ff; Cornelius P. Cotter and J. Malcolm Smith, "Administrative Accountability to Congress: The Concurrent Resolution," *Western Political Quarterly,* IX (December 1956), 955 ff; J. Malcolm Smith and Cornelius P. Cotter, "Administrative Accountability: Reporting to Congress," ibid., X (June 1957), 405 ff; Joseph P. Harris, *Congressional Control of Administration* (Washington, D.C.: Brookings, 1964).

56. J. Leiper Freeman, *The Political Process: Executive Bureau–Legislative Committee Relations* (Garden City: Doubleday, 1955); Fenno, *The Power . . . ,* Chs. VI, VII, XI; Ira Sharkansky, "An Appropriations Subcommittee and Its Client Agencies," *American Political Science Review,* LIX (September 1965), 622 ff.

57. Morgan Thomas, "Appropriation Control and the Atomic Energy Program," *Western Political Quarterly,* IX (September 1956), 713 ff; see here also Raymond H. Dawson, "Congressional Innovation and Intervention in Defense Policy," *American Political Science Review,* LVI (March 1962), 42 ff; Bernard K. Gordon, "The Military Budget: Congressional Phase," *Journal of Politics,* XXIII (November 1961), 689 ff.

58. Seymour Scher, "Conditions for Legislative Control," ibid., XXV (August 1963), 526 ff.

59. Seymour Scher, "Congressional Committee Members as Independent Agency Overseers," *American Political Science Review,* LIV (December 1960), 911 ff.

60. James N. Rosenau, "Senate Attitudes Toward a Secretary of State,"

in *Legislative Behavior,* eds. Wahlke and Eulau, op cit., pp. 332-347.

61. Mark Kesselman, "Presidential Leadership in Congress on Foreign Policy," *Midwest Journal of Political Science,* V (August 1961), 284 ff.

62. David B. Truman, *The Congressional Party* (New York: Wiley, 1959), p. 317.

63. Samuel C. Patterson, "Dimensions of Voting Behavior in a One-Party State Legislature," *Public Opinion Quarterly,* XXVI (Summer 1962), 185 ff.

64. James M. Burns, *Congress on Trial* (New York: Harper, 1949), pp. 1-17.

65. Haynes, "Representation in New England Legislatures."

66. On Congress see Donald R. Matthews, *U.S. Senators and Their World;* Matthews, "United States Senators and the Class Struggle," *Public Opinion Quarterly,* XVIII (Spring 1954), 5 ff; Matthews, *The Social Background of Political Decision-Makers* (Garden City: Doubleday, 1954), pp. 20-41. For examples of multiple state studies, see Charles Hynemann, "Who Makes Our Laws?" *Political Science Quarterly,* LV (December 1940), 556 ff, and Malcolm E. Jewell and Samual C. Patterson, *The Legislative Process in the United States* (New York: Random House, 1966), Ch. V. Legislative profiles, many recent, now exist for nearly every state, as see Leonard I. Ruchelman, "A Profile of New York State Legislatures," *Western Political Quarterly,* XX (September 1967), 625 ff.

67. The permanency of various aspects of the legislative profile has been demonstrated despite a two-thirds' decrease in size resulting from Nebraska's adoption of unicameralism (Senning, op. cit.) or Hawaii's two-thirds' expansion, statehood, and reapportionment. Norman Meller, "Recent Changes in Composition of Hawaiian Legislatures," *Social Process in Hawaii,* XXV (1961-1962), 45 ff.

68. M. Louise Rutherford, "Lawyers as Legislators," *Annals,* XCV (January 1938), 53 ff; David R. Derge, "The Lawyer as Decision-Maker in the American State Legislatures," *Journal of Politics,* XXI (August 1959), 408 ff; Derge, "The Lawyer in the Indiana General Assembly," *Midwest Journal of Political Science,* V (February 1962), 19 ff; Heinz Eulau and John D. Sprague, *Lawyers in Politics* (Indianapolis: Bobbs-Merrill, 1964). Little cohesion among lawyers in Illinois was also noted by Gilbert Y. Steiner and Samuel K. Gove, *Legislative Politics in Illinois* (Urbana: University of Illinois Press, 1960), p. 3. See also the suggestion that since lawyers tend to depersonalize conflict, they may help to reduce tension in the legislature: William C. Mitchell, "Reduction of Tension in Legislatures," *PROD,* II (January 1959), 3 ff.

69. Mapheus Smith and Marian L. Brockway, "Mobility of American Congressmen," *Sociology and Social Research,* XXIV (July-August 1940), 511 ff; Heinz Eulau and David Koff, "Occupational Mobility and Political Career," *Western Political Quarterly,* XV (September 1962), 507 ff. See this study's relation of "status stables" vis-à-vis "mobiles" to legislative party competition and legislative party officeholding.

70. For instance, see Duncan and Edith MacRae, "Legislators' Social Status and Their Votes," *American Journal of Sociology,* LXVI (May 1961), 599 ff.

71. Length of service as related to influence over general-policy and specific-policy areas in Wayne L. Francis, "Influence and Interaction in a

State Legislative Body," *American Political Science Review*, LVI (December 1962), 953 ff; as associated with articulateness of rules (p. 167), expertise (pp. 206-207), friendship (pp. 223-224), and pressure-group orientation (p. 341) in John Wahlke, et al., *The Legislative System* (New York: Wiley, 1962). Neophyte action in Theodore Urich, "The Voting Behavior of Freshman Congressman," *Southwestern Social Science Quarterly*, XXXIX (March 1959), 337 ff. Length of uninterrupted legislative experience as a variable in legislators' sensitivity to constituency interest: Pertti Pesonen, "Close and Safe State Elections in Massachusetts," *Midwest Journal of Political Science*, VII (February 1963), 54 ff.

72. Matthews, *U.S. Senators and Their World*, pp. 11-46, at p. 12.

73. Heinz Eulau et al., "The Political Socialization of American State Legislators," *Midwest Journal of Political Science*, III (May 1959), 188 ff; in Wahlke and Eulau, op. cit., pp. 305-313; see also Wahlke et al., op cit., pp. 77-94.

74. James D. Barber, *The Lawmakers: Recruitment and Adaptation to Legislative Life* (New Haven: Yale University Press, 1965).

75. John B. McConaughy, "Certain Personality Factors of State Legislators in South Carolina," *American Political Science Review*, XLIV (December 1950), 897 ff.

76. Lewis A. Froman, Jr., "The Importance of Individuality in Voting in Congress," *Journal of Politics*, XXV (May 1963), 324 ff.

77. Ralph K. Huitt, "The Outsider in the Senate," *American Political Science Review*, LV (September 1961), 566 ff.

78. Samuel C. Patterson, "The Role of the Deviant in the State Legislative System," *Western Political Quarterly*, XIV (June 1961), 460 ff.

79. As see Donald R. Matthews, "The Folkways of the United States Senate," *American Political Science Review*, LIII (December 1959), 1064 ff; Matthews, *U.S. Senators and Their World*, 102-117.

80. Rowena Wyant, "Voting Via the Senate Mailbag," *Public Opinion Quarterly*, V (Fall 1941), 359 ff, (Winter, 1941), 591 ff; see also L. E. Gleeck, "96 Congressmen Make Up Their Minds," ibid., IV (March 1940), 1 ff.

81. Oliver Garceau and Corinne Silverman, "A Pressure Group and the Pressured: A Case Report," *American Political Science Review*, XLVIII (September 1954), 672 ff; Corinne Silverman, "The Legislators' View of the Legislative Process," *Public Opinion Quarterly*, XVIII (Summer 1954), 180 ff.

82. Lewis A. Dexter, "The Representative and His District," *New Perspectives on the House of Representatives* eds. Peabody and Polsby, op cit., at p. 3.

83. Raymond A. Bauer, Ithiel de Sola Pool, and Lewis A. Dexter, *American Business and Public Policy* (New York: Atherton Press, 1963), pp. 433-434.

84. Lowell H. Hattery and Susan Hofheimer, "The Legislators' Source of Expert Information," *Public Opinion Quarterly*, XVIII (Fall 1954), 300 ff.

85. Dean R. Brimhall and Arthur S. Otis, "Consistency of Voting by Our Congressmen," *Journal of Applied Psychology*, XXXII (February 1948), 1 ff; see also N. L. Gage and B. Shimberg, "Measuring Senatorial 'Progressivism,'" *Journal of Abnormal and Social Psychology*, XLIV (January 1949), 112 ff.

86. Hilding B. Carlson and Willard Harrell, "An Analysis of Life's 'Ablest Congressmen's Poll,' " *Journal of Social Psychology,* XV (February 1942), 158 ff.

87. Arthur Macdonald, "Brain Weight and Legislative Ability in Congress," 75 Cong. Rec. 8008 (1932); see S. P. Hayes, Jr., "A Note on Macdonald's 'Brain Weight and Legislative Ability in Congress,' " *Journal of Social Psychology,* VIII (May 1937), 269 ff.

88. Wilson, op. cit., p. 92.

89. For example, see "The Roles of Congressional Leaders: National Party vs. Constituency," *American Political Science Review,* XLVI (December 1952), 1024 ff; Duncan MacRae, Jr., "The Role of the State Legislator in Massachusetts," *American Sociological Review,* XIX (April 1954), 185 ff; MacRae, "Roll Call Votes and Leadership," *Public Opinion Quarterly,* XX (Fall 1956), 543 ff; Stephen K. Bailey and Howard D. Samuel, *Congress at Work* (New York: Holt, 1952), Ch. VIII.

90. Garland C. Routt, "Interpersonal Relationships and the Legislative Process," *Annals,* CXCV (January 1938), 129 ff.

91. Macdonald, op. cit.; the details of the formula, however, are not given. See also Frank H. Garver, "Leadership in the Constitutional Convention of 1787," *Sociology and Social Research,* XXI (July-August 1937), 544 ff, for a somewhat similar measure.

92. Wayne L. Francis, "Influence and Interaction in a State Legislative Body," *American Political Science Review,* LVI (December 1962), 953 ff, at p. 960.

93. Heinz Eulau, "Bases of Authority in Legislative Bodies," *Administrative Science Quarterly,* VII (December 1962), 309 ff. "Respect is probably the most distinguishing value at the base of authority in legislative bodies," p. 321.

94. Samuel C. Patterson, "Patterns of Interpersonal Relations in a State Legislative Group," *Public Opinion Quarterly,* XXIII (Spring 1959), 101 ff; confirmed in Wahlke et al., op. cit., p. 226.

95. Duncan MacRae, Jr., *Dimensions of Congressional Voting* (Berkeley: University of California Press, 1958), p. 295; Truman, *The Congressional Party,* p. 106; Matthews, *U.S. Senators and Their World,* pp. 131-132; Samuel C. Patterson, "Legislative Leadership and Political Ideology," *Public Opinion Quarterly,* XXVII (Fall 1963), 399 ff.

96. See the attempt to explain legislators' conduct in investigations in Edward A. Shils, "The Legislator and His Environment," *University of Chicago Law Review,* XVIII (Spring 1951), 571 ff.

97. See William S. White, *Citadel, The Story of the U.S. Senate* (New York: Harper, 1956); Jerry Voorhis, *Confessions of a Congressman* (Garden City: Dougleday, 1948), especially pp. 24-39; George Wharton Pepper, *In the Senate* (Philadelphia: University of Pennsylvania Press, 1930).

98. Heinz Eulau et al., "The Role of the Representative," *American Political Science Review,* LIII (September 1959), 742 ff; also Wahlke et al., op. cit., pp. 267-310. However, compare with different distribution of representative roles in Robert J. Huckshorn, "Decision-Making Stimuli in the State Legislative Process," *Western Political Quarterly,* XVIII (March 1965), 164 ff; and in Jewell and Patterson, *The Legislative . . . ,* p. 398.

99. Wilder W. Crane, Jr., "Do Representatives Represent?" *Journal of*

Politics, XXII (May 1960), 295 ff.

100. Sorauf, op. cit., at p. 133; Norman Meller, "Representational Role Types: A Research Note," *American Political Science Review,* LXI (June 1967), 474 ff.

101. For a discussion on relationship between role orientations and pressure groups, see John C. Wahlke et al., "American State Legislators' Role Orientations Toward Pressure Groups," *Journal of Politics,* XXII (May 1960), 203 ff; also Wahlke et al., *The Legislative System,* pp. 311-342.

102. See Earl Latham, *The Group Basis of Politics* (Ithaca: Cornell University Press, 1952); Bertram M. Gross, *The Legislative Struggle* (New York: McGraw-Hill, 1953).

103. Matthews, *U.S. Senators and Their World,* p. 92.

104. Ibid., pp. 92-117; see also Matthews, "The Folkways . . . "; Ralph K. Huitt, "The Morse Committee Assignment Controversy: A Study in Senate Norms," *American Political Science Review,* LI (June 1957), 313 ff.

105. Wahlke et al., *The Legislative System,* p. 168; see also Jewell and Patterson, *The Legislative . . . ,* pp. 362-381.

106. Thomas R. Dye, "A Comparison of Constituency Influences in the Upper and Lower Chambers of a State Legislature," *Western Political Quarterly,* XIV (June 1961), 473 ff; see also n. 33 above.

107. Heinz Eulau, "Comparative Political Analysis: A Methodological Note," *Midwest Journal of Political Science,* (November 1962), 397 ff.

108. Robinson, "Decision-Making in the Committee on Rules"; see also, Steiner and Gove, op. cit., at p. 69, which denies utility to a standing committee as a decision-making agency when complete agreement or disagreement exists among all the parties concerned.

109. Fenno, "The House Appropriations Committee . . . "; also see John F. Manley, "The House Committee on Ways and Means," *American Political Science Review,* LXIX (December 1965), 927 ff.

110. Jones, "The Role of the Congressional Subcommittee."

111. Truman, *The Governmental Process,* pp. 372-377.

112. Huitt, "The Congressional Committee . . . ."

113. Farnsworth, "A Comparison of the Senate . . . ."

114. Matthews, *U.S. Senators and Their World,* pp. 166-169.

115. Patterson, "Patterns of Interpersonal Relations . . . ."

116. See V. O. Key, Jr., *Southern Politics in State and Nation* (New York: Knopf, 1949); George L. Grassmuck, *Sectional Biases in Congress on Foreign Policy* (Baltimore: Johns Hopkins Press, 1951); H. Bradford Westerfield, *Foreign Policy and Party Politics* (New Haven: Yale University Press); David B. Truman, "The State Delegations and the Structure of Party Voting in the U.S. House of Representatives," *American Political Science Review,* L (December 1956), 1023 ff; Neal A. Maxwell, "The Conference of Western Senators," *Western Political Quarterly,* X (December 1957), 902 ff.

117. Kenneth Kofmehl, "The Institutionalization of a Voting Bloc," *Western Political Quarterly,* XVII (June 1964), 256 ff.

118. See, for example, Alan Fiellin, "The Function of Informal Groups in Legislative Institutions: A Case Study," *Journal of Politics,* XXIV (February 1962), 72 ff.

119. Rice, "The identification of Blocs in Small Political Bodies"; Hilding B. Carlson and Willard Harrell, "Voting Groups Among Leading Congressmen

Obtained by Means of the Inverted Factor Technique," *Journal of Social Psychology*, XVI (August 1942), 51 ff; Duncan MacRae, Jr., "The Underlying Variables in Legislative Roll Call Votes," *Public Opinion Quarterly*, XVIII (Summer 1954), 191 ff; Charles D. Farris, "A Method of Determining Ideological Groupings in the Congress," *Journal of Politics*, XX (May 1958), 308 ff.

120. See William J. Keefe, "Party Government and Lawmaking in the Illinois General Assembly," *Northwestern University Law Review*, XLVII (March-April 1952), 55 ff; Keefe, "Parties, Partisanship, and Public Policy in the Pennsylvania Legislature," *American Political Science Review*, XLVIII (June 1954), 450 ff; Keefe, "Comparative Study of the Role of Political Parties in State Legislatures," *Western Political Quarterly*, IX (September 1956), 726 ff; W. Duane Lockard, "Legislative Politics in Connecticut," *American Political Science Review*, XLVII (March 1954), 166 ff; Malcolm E. Jewell, "Party Voting in American State Legislatures," ibid., XLIX (September 1955), 772 ff.

121. American Political Science Association's Committee on Political Parties, *Toward a More Responsible Two-Party System* (New York: Rinehart, 1950).

122. Samuel P. Huntington, "A Revised Theory of American Party Politics," *American Political Science Review*, XLIV (September 1950), 669 ff; Julius Turner, *Party and Constituency: Pressures on Congress* (Baltimore: Johns Hopkins Press, 1951).

123. Truman, *The Congressional Party*, p. vii.

124. Ibid., p. 247. It should be noted that Truman carefully adds the qualification that the party label is not a "perfect indicator" (see p. vii).

125. For the effect of absence of party competition in a one-party state, see Patterson, "Dimensions of Voting Behavior . . . "; for nonpartisan legislature, see G. Theodore Miteu, *Politics in Minnesota* (Minneapolis: University of Minnesota Press, 1960), pp. 57-79.

126. Patterson, "The Role of the Deviant . . . ."

127. Lewis A. Froman, Jr., and Randall B. Ripley, "Conditions for Party Leadership: The Case of the House of Representatives," *American Political Science Review*, LIX (March 1965), 52 ff; see also Robert L. Peabody, "Party Leadership Change in the U.S. House of Representatives," ibid., LXI (September 1967), 675 ff.

128. Ralph K. Huitt, "Democratic Party Leadership in the Senate," *ibid.*, LV (June 1961), 333 ff.

129. Wahlke et al., *The Legislative System*, p. 170-192.

130. Charles L. Clapp, *The Congressmen: His Work as He Sees It* (Washington, D.C.: Brookings, 1956), pp. 297-320; Hugh A. Bone, "An Introduction to the Senate Policy Committees," *American Political Science Review*, L (June 1956), 339 ff, and "Some Notes on the Congressional Campaign Committees," p. 116; Malcolm E. Jewell, "The Senate Republican Policy Committee and Foreign Policy," *Western Political Quarterly*, XII (December 1959), 966 ff; Randall B. Ripley, "The Party Whip Organizations in the U.S. House of Representatives," *American Political Science Review*, XVIII (September 1964), 561 ff.

131. Robert T. Golembiewski, "A Taxonomic Approach to State Political Party Strength," *Western Political Quarterly*, XI (September 1958), 494 ff;

see also Malcolm E. Jewell, *The State Legislature* (New York: Random House, 1962), pp. 9-17.

132. As evidenced by the many studies published between Edward B. Logan, "Lobbying," Supplement to *Annals*, CXLIV (1929) and the issue "Unofficial Government: Pressure Groups and Lobbies," *Annals*, CCCXIX (September 1958), three decades later.

133. Fred W. Riggs, *Pressures on Congress: A Study of the Repeal of Chinese Exclusion* (New York: Kings Crown Press, 1950).

134. Schattschneider, op. cit., pp. 103 ff.

135. V. O. Key, Jr., *Public Opinion and American Democracy* (New York: Knopf, 1961), pp. 521-528.

136. Matthews, *U.S. Senators and Their World*, pp. 190, 196. See also Bernard C. Cohen, *The Influence of Non-Governmental Groups on Foreign Policy-Making* (Boston: World Peace Foundation, 1959); Wilder W. Crane, Jr., "A Test of Effectiveness of Interest Group Pressures on Legislators," *Southwestern Social Science Quarterly*, XLI (December 1960), 335 ff.

137. Lester W. Milbrath, "Lobbying as a Communication Process," *Public Opinion Quarterly*, XXIV (Spring 1960), 32 ff. Also see his *The Washington Lobbyists* (Chicago: Rand McNally, 1963).

138. Wahlke et al., "American State Legislators Role Orientations Toward Pressure Groups"; and also Wahlke et al., *The Legislative System*, pp. 311-342. Or see use of role theory in Jay S. Goodman, "A Note on Legislative Research: Labor Representation in Rhode Island," *American Political Science Review*, LXI (June 1967), 474 ff.

139. Samuel C. Patterson, "The Role of the Lobbyist: The Case of Oklahoma," *Journal of Politics*, XXV (February 1963), 72 ff.

140. Harmon Zeigler, *Interest Groups in American Society* (Englewood Cliffs: Prentice Hall, 1964), pp. 249-276. As a frame for consideration of pressure-group activity, these pages also summarize the major literature on the entire legislative process.

141. All quoted material taken out of context from Oliver Garceau, "Research in the Political Process," *American Political Science Review*, XLV (March 1951), 78 ff.

142. Warren E. Miller and Donald E. Stokes, "Constituency Influence in Congress," ibid., LVII (March 1963) 45 ff; Charles F. Cnudde and Donald J. McCrone, "The Linkage Between Constituency Attitudes and Congressional Voting Behavior," ibid., LX (March 1966), 66 ff.

143. James Q. Wilson, "The Negro Politicians: An Interpretation," *Midwest Journal of Political Science*, IV (November 1960), 346 ff. Party pressure from the constituency must be distinguished from pressure applied by Congressional or national party leadership. Avery Leiserson, "National Party Organization and Congressional Districts," *Western Political Quarterly*, XVI (September 1963), 633 ff.

144. Bruce M. Russet, "International Communication and Legislative Behavior," *Journal of Conflict Resolution*, VI (December 1962), 291 ff.

145. Charles O. Lerche, Jr., "Southern Congressmen and the 'New Isolationism,'" *Political Science Quarterly*, LXXV (September 1960), 321 ff; Malcolm E. Jewell, "Evaluating the Decline of Southern Internationalism Through Senatorial Roll-Call Votes," *Journal of Politics*, XXL (November 1959), 624 ff.

146. See MacRae, *Dimensions of Congressional Voting* pp. 256-278; Lewis A. Froman, Jr., "Inter-Party Constituency Differences and Congressional Voting Behavior," *American Political Science Review*, LVII (March 1963), 57 ff.

147. Duncan MacRae, Jr., "The Relation Between Roll Call Votes and Constituencies in the Massachusetts House of Representatives," ibid., XLVI (December 1952), 1046 ff; Dye, op. cit.; also see Sorauf, op cit., pp. 140-141.

148. MacRae, *Dimensions of Congressional Voting*, pp. 284-289; see Pesonen, op cit., replicating MacRae's study in Massachusetts, and questioning the continuing adequacy of the owner-occupancy variable to summarize socioeconomic differences. Note Robert W. Becker, et al., "Correlates of Legislative Voting: Michigan House of Representatives, 1954-1961," *Midwest Journal of Political Science*, VI (November 1962), 384 ff, where party *primary* competitiveness appears not to influence deviation in legislators' voting behavior from party position.

149. For an early attempt to establish a measure of turnover, the "percentage of fluidity," see Paul D. Hasbrouck, *Party Government in the House of Representatives* (New York: Macmillan, 1927), p. 177, and its use in Charles O. Jones, "Inter-Party Competition for Congressional Seats," *Western Political Quarterly*, XVII (September 1964), 461 ff.

150. Madge M. McKinney, "Religion and Elections," *Public Opinion Quarterly*, VIII (Spring 1944), 110 ff.

151. John C. Russell, "Racial Groups in the New Mexico Legislature," *Annals*, CXCV (January 1938), 62 ff.

152. Henry W. Toll, "Today's Legislatures," 6, 7; Charles S. Hyneman, "Tenure and Turnover of the Indiana General Assembly," *American Political Science Review*, XXXII (April 1938), 311 ff, and his "Tenure and Turnover of Legislative Personnel," *Annals*, CXCV (January 1938), 21 ff; Paul Beckett and Celeste Sunderland, "Washington State's Lawmakers: Some Personnel Factors in the Washington Legislature," *Western Political Quarterly*, X (March 1957), 180 ff.

153. Donald E. Stokes and Warren E. Miller, "Party Government and the Saliency of Congress," *Public Opinion Quarterly*, XXVI (Winter 1962), 531 ff.

154. National Opinion Research Center Poll, ibid., X (Summer 1946), 268.

155. And may result in a reformulated conceptualization. See, for example, Huckshorn, op. cit., at p. 183, and Alan Kornberg, "Perception and Constituency Influence on Legislative Behavior," *Western Political Quarterly*, XIX (June 1966), 285 ff.

156. David R. Derge, "Metropolitan and Outside Alignments in Illinois and Missouri Legislative Delegations," *American Political Science Review*, LII (December 1958), 1051 ff; also see Derge, "Urban-Rural Conflict: The Case in Illinois," in Wahlke and Eulau, op. cit., pp. 218-227. See attack in Communication of Richard T. Frost, "On Derge's Metropolitan and Outstate Legislative Delegations," *American Political Science Review*, LIII (September 1959), 792; and reply in Communication of David R. Derge, "On the Use of Roll-Call Analyses: A Reply to R. T. Frost," ibid., LIII (December 1959), 1097; H. D. Hamilton, J. E. Beardsley, and C. C. Coats, "Legislative Reapportionment in Indiana: Some Observations and a Suggestion," *Notre*

Dame L. Rev., XXXV (May 1960), 368 ff; Thomas A. Flinn, "The Outline of Ohio Politics," *Western Political Quarterly,* XIII (September 1960), 702 ff; Robert S. Friedman, "The Urban-Rural Conflict Revisited," ibid., XIV (June 1961), 481 ff; Becker et al., op. cit.

157. But also added that "further studies are needed to confirm this." Flinn, op. cit., at p. 721.

158. Jewell, *The State Legislature,* pp. 60-62.

159. Patterson, "Dimensions of Voting Behavior . . . ."

160. Ibid., p. 193, n. 7.

161. See Lee F. Anderson, Meredith W. Watts, Jr., and Allen R. Wilcox, *Legislative Roll-Call Analysis* (Evanston: Northwestern University Press, 1966), and many studies cited herein. See also John G. Grumm, "The Systematic Analysis of Blocs in the Study of Legislative Behavior," *Western Political Quarterly,* XVIII (June 1965), 350 ff.

162. See n. 7 and 17 above, and Keefe's modification of Lowell in Keefe, "Party Government and Law-making . . . " and "Parties . . . ."

163. For example, Guttman scaling and factor analysis, in Anderson, et al., op. cit. Or see such publications as Duncan MacRae, Jr., "Cluster Analysis of Congressional Votes with the BC TRY System," *Western Political Quarterly,* XIX (December 1966), 631 ff, or Aage R. Claussen, "Longitudinal Analysis of Legislative Voting," *American Political Science Review,* LXI (December 1967), 1020 ff.

164. Wilder W. Crane, Jr., "A Caveat on Roll-Call Studies of Party Voting," *Midwest Journal of Political Science,* IV (August 1960), 237 ff; Fred Greenstein and Elton Jackson, "A Second Look at the Validity of Roll-Call Analysis," *Midwest Journal of Political Science,* VII (May 1963), 156 ff.

165. The Shapley and Shubik a priori power index, which is based upon game theory—L. S. Shapley and Martin Shubik, "A Method for Evaluating the Distribution of Power in a Committee System," *American Political Science Review,* XLVIII (September 1954), 787 ff—is questioned by William H. Riker, "A Test of the Adequacy of the Power Index," *Behavioral Science,* IV (April 1959), 120 ff. See also Dahl's measurement of power in the legislative process and its critical appraisal: Robert A. Dahl, James G. March, and David Nasatir, "Influence Ranking in the U.S. Senate," paper presented at the annual meeting of the American Political Science Association, Washington, D.C., September 6-8, 1956; "The Concept of Power," *Behavioral Science,* II (July 1957), 201 ff; Andrew Hacker, "Mathematics and Political Science," *Mathematics and the Social Sciences,* ed. James C. Charlesworth (Philadelphia: American Academy of Political and Social Sciences, 1963), pp. 58-76, at pp. 61-63; Duncan MacRae, Jr., and Hugh D. Price, "Scale Positions and 'Power' in the Senate," *Behavioral Science,* IV (July 1959), 212 ff.

166. For example, indexes of overrepresentation, specialization, party effort, and so on, in Matthews, *U. S. Senators and Their World.*

167. As the pride of an impugned legislative body appears to engender activity differing in kind as well as degree from routine adoption of special or local legislation.

168. See the examination of the legislature as a functioning system of roles (Wahlke et al., *The Legislative System*), or the advancing of a "middle-range" theory of legislative behavior tying together both roles and groups in

Samuel C. Patterson, *Toward a Theory of Legislative Behavior,* Oklahoma State University Publication, LIX (February 1962); and see also Jewell and Patterson, *The Legislative* . . . .

10 Political Parties Research

WILLIAM J. CROTTY, Northwestern University

> It cannot be that axioms established by argumentation can suffice for the discovery of new works, since the subtlety of nature is greater many times over than the subtlety of argument.—*Francis Bacon*

I. INTRODUCTION

Research on political parties is noted neither for its innovative theoretical or methodological approaches nor for its systematic accumulation of reliable data on the institution and its operations. Other, and related, areas of social-science inquiry have registered impressive gains in conceptualizing their subject matter and contributing to an appreciation of its significance. To illustrate briefly: voter decision-making studies[1] have profited enormously by borrowing conceptual orientations from such fields as social psychology and consumer research and matching these with continually refined methodological investigations, such as the adaptions of panel and cross-national survey technology to national and cross-national attitudinal studies. The result has been a level of success—in understanding voter motivations and the variables that affect it—unmatched in the less sophisticated exploration of political parties. Comparative politics, in response to the challenge of accounting for developments of newer nations, has been liberated from conventional modes of thought, in the process broadening its scope of interests and reformulating its basic concepts into potentially more rewarding conceptual frameworks.

The list of developments in disciplinary subfields could be enlarged substantially. The point, however, is to contrast this abundance with the *lack* of comparable formulations in the study of political parties. Political-parties research has not benefited from a similar regeneration; nor has it undergone the fundamental reassessment of knowledge or approaches evident in other areas of social-science inquiry.

The significant role that parties are presumed to play in achieving systemic goals has long been acknowledged, although not often articulated. Parties represent "a strategically critical concept," as Leiserson

267

puts it,[2] for understanding the power distributions within a society, for aggregating and representing social demands within the political system, for socializing individuals to the system and for educating citizens to both its long-run and more immediate objectives, and as a vehicle for leadership recruitment. The major difficulty with statements elaborating the significance of parties is in empirically verifying their contentions, isolating the factors that affect party performance, and identifying the cultural variables that predetermine a party's role. Curiously, given the perceived importance of political parties, limited stores of reliable data are available with which to substantiate the points made or to identify the factors that condition performance.

This is not to argue that parties have suffered from a lack of scholarly attention. Quite the opposite is the case. There is a healthy amount of work in the area. And, for the most part, the problems isolated for analysis in the more ambitious works have proven relevant—How does the party adapt to its environment? How does it attempt to achieve its objectives and with what success? To what extent is party aggregation based on ideological attractiveness? What linkage functions does the party perform between constituency and representative? And what is the significance of political parties judged from the perspective of the total political system? Few, if any, of these questions have been satisfactorily answered.

The literature on political parties is generally nonscientific in design and content. Perhaps its chief distinguishing attribute over time has been the lively commitment to prescriptive assessment. Studies elaborate party "weaknesses," and the analyses often are accompanied by proposals designed to facilitate the achievement of the agency's imputed objectives. "Reforms" are advanced and their potential effects debated with unabashed enthusiasm. At many points, a schizophrenia—or in Eldersveld's more felecitous phrase, a "tension"[3]—appears in a writer's appreciation of the manifest functions performed by the party, accompanied by profound disillusionment with the manner in which these responsibilities are executed.

Penetrating assessments of parties have resulted from the lengthly dialog over reform, some of which enters the discussion below. These assessments, in concert with other works of the earlier periods of parties research, are superior by any standards. Nonetheless, taken as a whole, the research to date is *not* notable for its commitment to standards of scientific evaluation, its accumulation of a base of reliable empirical data, its comparative orientation, its additive or thematic exploration of related topics, nor for its particularly imaginative theoretical or multifaceted methodological approaches to its subject matter.

Little is gained from an extensive post facto dissection of generations of scholarly work by standards unrelated to their original execution. Of greater importance is that the ground has been broken and, for the most part, the relevant questions framed. Past work has much to contribute in these respects. The need at present is to push beyond the limitations of available research, to incorporate methodological perspectives and techniques that lend themselves to interrelated comparative studies, and to encourage the beginning of a theoretically, empirically, and scientifically acceptable data bank concerning political parties.

This essay will not attempt a review of the literature in any traditional sense. Balanced accounts of the work in the field are available through the 1955 review by McDonald and the more recent critical evaluations of Hennessy and Schlesinger.[4] Each makes a distinctive contribution in assessing the research executed, or in reviewing the thematic exposition of particular lines of inquiry, or in indicating substantive areas requiring attention. The objectives of this chapter will be more to evaluate developments within the field with specified criteria in mind and to indicate the adaptability of several conceptual foci to parties research. Particular attention will be given to contemporary theory as it touches on empirical parties research and to an elaboration of orientations useful for comparative analysis. The focus, then, is methodological, broadly conceived.

II. POLITICAL PARTIES AND EMPIRICAL POLITICAL THEORY

Theory and data have never had a comfortable fit in the analysis of political parties. This situation does not result from any lack of appreciation for what theory can contribute to the systematic growth of scientific inquiry. Rather, it is more the product of the failure of the imagination in conceptualizing an elusive subject matter, coupled with a conservative approach toward experimentation. No convenient theoretical perspectives adequately explain the wide variance among institutional forms and party operations in different cultural settings. For example, according to Talcott Parsons, political parties are power-mobilization agencies,[5] a characteristic common to these institutions in both authoritarian and democratic political regimes. How a party would exercise, or mobilize, power would differ from one political system to another. To borrow Almond's terminology, the emphasis in participant cultures is on input factors, or pre-policy-making, that is, on seeking consensus among coalitional groups and promoting alternative candidates and issues attractive to large segments of the voting population. In subject-oriented political cultures, greater attention is given to the post-policy-making phase, in particular to the mobilization of support for officeholders and decisions; parties are more important as institutions designed for communication and control purposes. However, the distinction is not clearcut: parties are multifunctional. Nonetheless, the extent to which different activities are performed and to which the environmental factors influence institutional priorities represent data important for an understanding of any political system and, in turn, a major barrier to comparative analysis.

Given the multitude of variables influencing parties and the general diffuseness of the subject matter, the immediate utility of theory for the parties researcher would appear great. Theory, or more realistically, theories, of party behavior when broadly employed would seek to provide a coherence and unity to research undertakings, presently unattainable, and an impetus to execute works within conceptual frameworks. The ability to generalize findings and to explore less obvious research questions and their implications, a welcome corrective for the imbalance of works resulting from short-run approaches to discrete problems, would also represent important by-products of a semirigorous theoretical focus. Individual research pieces, in addition to being imbued with broader significance, are forced into a specific elaboration of the interrelationships among theory, constructs, and data. A demand for precision in investigations and an orientation conductive to comparative scientific inquiry are further beneficial results. More formal theories may eventually contribute the predictive and deductive power associated with more mature sciences.

Most researchers accept the utility of such theoretical guidance. Tactical problems arise, however, in determining the load the theory is to carry, given the priority of research objectives. For example, accepting the present vague appreciation of party operations, it may prove of limited value to employ a high-powered theory in field investigations and conscientiously to elaborate the implications of the perspective. At the outset, the researcher may be better advised to remain flexible and to let his objectives dictate the theories, or partial theories, he borrows. In either case, Meehan's injunction that "the value of a theory will depend on its 'usefulness' to the inquiry" represents a practical criterion for selectivity.[6]

A distinction should be drawn between the rigorous criteria applied to formal theory and the weaker criteria more commonly applied to social science theory. A *formal theory* includes sets of interdependent propositions logically derived from specified common assumptions and translatable into hypotheses that are subject to empirical verification. These are few examples of such formal theories in political science, although one constructed by Downs with implications for parties exploration does receive treatment below. The second classification of theory is more precisely labeled *alternative strategies for research*. Easton reminds us that "in the social sciences as a whole, theory in any ideal sense is as yet little known." It is enough that empirical theory, or "weak" or "quasi" or whatever label one appends to the majority of those currently available, can be viewed as "programs for analysis that under appropriate conditions could develop into theories more rigorously defined."[7] These working theories can structure the initial and more primitive research efforts.

They supply a research orientation, indicate the type of questions that should be asked, and provide criteria for limiting and comparing phenomena and for interrelating findings in a generally meaningful, although still loose, manner. More elegant predictive theories can be built from continued research outputs, successive field returns providing the basis for more internally consistent inductive theories the progressively greater explanatory power.

In adopting either of the two theoretical strategies outlined, the initial approaches should be eclectic. That is, whatever works, should be employed. From these early sorties, more descriptive theoretical accounts closely related to the subject matter examined should emerge. The approach is pragmatic. The preference in the argument to follow is for limited, principally inductive theories grounded upon careful empirical investigation, although other possibilities will be discussed. A commitment to the gradual building of theories of the middle range, as described by Merton,[8] would maximize comparability and offer many of the same advantages of their more formal, and elusive, counterparts. The preference is a personal bias, and no doubt will not excite all. Still, the strengths of this orientation include a greater flexibility in structuring research questions; one is not limited to explicating the empirical implications of formally derived hypotheses, though there is an insistence on theoretical statements that rest on a solid empirical base. The latter could provide the steps toward the additive theoretical understanding desired. However limited such objectives may appear to the model builder they represent formidable goals for the contemporary parties researcher.[9]

Most of the macrotheories currently propounded fall into the "weak" or "working" theory classification. These theories hold promise for adequately realizing several of the limited objectives stipulated, in particular those of providing and relating research foci. Beyond this, and more impressively, they present a global overview for parties analysis; and they are helpful in constructing descriptive typologies along less conventional lines.

Systems theory and structural-functional analysis are the most visible of the current macrotheories.[10] Both hold potential rewards for those able to adapt them to parties research. Systems theory, as developed by David Easton, directs attention to problems of stability and adaptation of systems.[11] It encourages comparisons by freeing the analyst from the restrictions of time and geography.[12] Related developments in structural-functional analysis, the political implications of which have been propounded principally by Almond, offer similar advantages. Both systems theory and structural-functional analysis allow for a framework in which to analyze democratic and totalitarian party systems in advanced or traditional social and economic settings.

Almond and Powell have gone the farthest in discussing the applicability of their ideas to an understanding of parties.[13] The characterization is understandably loose though it provides a broad orientation that is at the same time specific enough to suggest many researchable questions. The authors direct attention to such topics as "style" of interest aggregation, fragmentation in aggregation patterns as they relate to political culture, structural factors as they affect performance, and the extent to which parties perform other functions in addition to aggregation—political recruitment, socialization, and articulation. As in Parsons' writings, the concepts developed are suggestive; interrelating them systematically with empirical data is difficult. The orientation is potentially valuable, and the promise of finding an agency, or its functional equivalent, in all societies performing distinctive patterns of duties that contribute to systemic survival needs is positively enticing. Almond and Powell write:

... all types of political systems rely heavily on the political party; totalitarian societies, as a means to mobilize support; democratic societies, as a channel to articulate and aggregate demands; and transitional societies, as an agency to create and structure new norms of behavior.[14]

Their discussion does not pretend to deal with the fundamental problems of relating the abstract to the concrete, of conceptualizing terms in an operational and empirically verifiable manner, or of clarifying the political units for analysis—the logical next steps in the analysis.

Two research efforts that borrow broad theoretical orientation may be illustrative of the difficulties involved in even partially adapting these general theories to empirical investigations. The theoretical strategies indicate questions and areas that need exploration. Articulating hypotheses of relevance to the broader perspective with the precision demanded in empirical investigations, establishing some interrelationship among these, and then shaping the constructs needed for field investigations should challenge the best of students. These working theories make no pretensions to deductive capabilities, although they do suggest relationships that invite attention.

Operationalizing theoretical propositions in a manner amenable to empirical inquiry is a particularly sensitive and crucial point in analysis. One of the many strengths in the first study to be commented on, Gatlin's testing of 12 propositions linking socioeconomic aggregation to party competition in North Carolina,[15] is at the operationalization stage. The Gatlin work combines a number of research threads. Of immediate consequence is that he chose to characterize the political party as the principal agency charged with facilitating the transmission of social demands to responsible decision makers. Yet it is noteworthy that in operationalizing and testing hypotheses relating to his general characterization of the party, Gatlin makes no attempt to order the theories of Parsons, Easton, or Almond, or some hybrid of these general theories, nor to deduce empirically researchable propositions. Rather, he permits the general orientation to supply the broader framework for his analysis. The specific propositions to be tested are drawn from, among others, James Madison, Epstein, Binkley, Lipset, Campbell and others, Berelson and others, Holcombe, and Key. In short, his propositions are developed from the traditional commentaries on parties, a contribution to the cumulative development of knowledge in the area. As he notes, however, there is no intrinsic relationship between the macrotheoretical orientation and the specific hypotheses chosen for testing. The general theoretical orientation provides for a more unified presentation and a clearer articulation of his assumptions, as well as a framework in which related studies, through research similar in conception to Gatlin's, could build toward an interrelated set of middle-range propositions posited as desirable. One other aspect of the Gatlin report that deserves comment is the conscientious enunciation of the interaction among hypotheses, data, and findings, and the use of aggregate data to test relationships that have theoretical significance.

Turning to the second study employing a general-theories orientation, we note that Harder and Ungs used a survey to construct a profile of the functions that a party is perceived to perform.[16] They derived data from a questionnaire sent to the county chairmen in five Midwestern states. The information was employed to examine the uniformities and dissimilarities in characterizations of what a party should be. A helpful addition to analyses that advances from such a base would be quantitative data on party activities and the more easily obtained demographic and electoral data available for counties. With these, indices could be developed to measure the impact of the agency in the functional areas outlined. Calculations could be made of the extent to which different attributions of party role affect performance and are conditioned by relative competitive advantage. Such data incorporated in an extended analysis could provide the basis for generating a series of tentative hypotheses on the role of political parties and the conditions that affect their success.

The gap between a macrotheory orientation and empirical investigation is difficult to bridge,[17] as these studies help to illustrate. Perhaps it is enough that the general theories in their present form serve as guides to the less obvious questions needing research attention and, in the more conjectural works, contribute broad formats in which to interpret party activities.

Another avenue of exploration, and one considerably more demanding than the macrotheory strategies discussed, is to construct formal theories applicable to party behavior that employ many of the assumptions and retain much of the logical strength of those propounded in economics. These formal theories go beyond providing research orientations to articulating basic assumptions concerning political behavior and allowing hypotheses to be deduced that permit empirical testing. Perhaps the best known of these efforts, and the one with the most apparent utility for parties research, is that advanced by Anthony Downs. He has constructed a parsimonious model of party strategy and voting behavior deduced from a series of modest assumptions. He first defines the rules of the game—democratic government, fixed elections, plurality victories, legalized opposition—and attributes objectives both to parties (winning office) and to individuals (maximizing their income).[18] Subsidiary assumptions are elaborated as Downs builds the model. Party is defined as "a team of men seeking to control the governing apparatus by gaining office in a duly constituted election."[19] Conditions limiting party action are not far removed from the practices of democratic systems. Downs proceeds from here to develop the role of the party within the model. For example, he assumes that each individual has one vote, that parties, dedicated to their own self-interest, attempt to maximize votes, that disruptive individual self-interest has definable parameters, and that parties formulate policies to win elections, which opposes the view stressed in the party-responsibility literature. Equally important, the model assumes that voters and parties act rationally to achieve their goals.

Against the charge that the assumptions in the model—in particular, the stipulation of rationality—are divorced from reality to the extent that they preclude the construction's usefulness, Downs argues that models of this nature "should be tested primarily by the accuracy of their predictions rather than by the reality of their assumptions."[20] The model is *not* intended to describe actual conditions. Yet it can have value for empirical research:

First, it proposes a single hypothesis [governments seek to maximize political support] to explain government decision-making and party behavior in general. Since this hypothesis leads to testable corollaries, it can be submitted to empirical proof. If verified, it may lead to non-obvious conclusions about the actions and development of parties, thus adding to our knowledge of reality.

Second, the model tells us what behavior we can expect if men act rationally in politics. Therefore it can perhaps be used to discover (1) in what phases of politics in the real world men are rational, (2) in what phases they are irrational, and (3) how they deviate from rationality in the latter.

In all these ways, . . . the model will help guide empirical research to investigate important issues rather than trivial ones.[21]

The model can be tested by relating it to empirical reality. It posits a relatively uncomplicated principle (vote maximization) as underlying systemic democratic behavior, and it advances guidelines by which to judge rational and irrational political actions. An application of the model's propositions to field testing could contribute to the middle-range theory, although this would not be its chief promise. An economical predictive theory of party behavior could emerge, but the model has yet to be fully applied in empirical research, which suggests difficulties that belie its simplicity. It may be too demanding for present research purposes. Internally, it is not so consistent as it first appears, and the problems implicit in operationalization are discouraging. This combination of factors has sufficed to deter anyone from undertaking the formidable tasks involved in so rigorous an approach to empirical research.

The model is explicit enough, however, to invite evaluation in light of present knowledge. Actually there are several models implicit within Down's theoretical superstructure, each with its own unarticulated assumptions and each presumably applicable to different aspects of party behavior. Donald Stokes[22] has accepted empirical utility as the gauge of the construction's value, the standard being applied here, and one that he argues is of more import within social than natural science research. Stokes interprets the model as employing an assumption of one-dimensional space with the continuum based on acceptance of relative degrees of government influence on the economy. Theoretically at least, each individual and political party within this dimensional space could be placed on the continuum relative to their belief in the efficacy of government control of the economy. If the assumption is correct, then it in turn raises several other suppositions that are difficult to accept. For example, Stokes traces the intellectual antecedents in economics of Down's model to Hotelling and Smithies. Two demands underlay Hotelling's original explanation of the geographical proximity of competing firms: the even linear distribution of consumers and inelasticity of demand. The assumptions are taken over into political discourse by substituting an ideological dimension for geographical space. Simply put, voters and parties are dispersed upon one Right-Left or Liberal-Conservative spatial dimension. Market forces act to push the parties toward the center, where most of the voters are; the assumption of inelasticity of demand is relevant at this point, and an unemotional matching of voter position with policy alternatives offers results in party support. These assumptions underlie much political conjecture.

Smithies relaxes the assumption of inelasticity and introduces the alternative of nonvoting for individuals who believe that neither party substantially represents their point of view. The 1964 election would indicate that politicians may employ this as a tactical argument in seeking nomination, but those who accept it as a political fact of life court electoral disaster.[23]

Downs violates the second assumption by stipulating that

placement along the spatial dimension is a variable by which the party system can be comparatively assessed. An elaboration of this modification permits consideration of the emergence of new parties and adds an element of flexibility to the theory. An even distribution of voters along the continuum is not assumed.

The basic equation between geographical and ideological space is untenable. Political attitudes have yet to be mapped clearly, but findings to date support a number of contentions not compatible with the model in its present form. For example, there is no evidence of a single Right-Left dimension underlying political cognitions. Ideology, which can be defined as a coherent system of beliefs justifying the exercise of political power, as it predicts to voter decision making, is a highly imperfect instrument. Any associations that emerge may be spurious. Neither Stokes nor Downs clearly develops the relationship expected between a person's ideology and his stand on issues. Ideological space is better visualized as fluid and changing in response to electoral conditions. Research on French electorates indicates that, in even more explicity issue-oriented societies than the American, the same factors prevail. [24]

The imposition of dimensionality on some issues—prosperity, corruption, peace, and brotherhood, which Stokes defines as "valence issues"—violates any sense of reality. Differences arise as to means of achieving specified ends among parties or voters, but no party or individual can be graphed on a dimension running from pro- to anti-corruption or brotherhood. The objection is more theoretical than methodological. Operationally, one could develop indices that assume homage to a principle but plot individuals on a modified social-distance scale that presents a respondent with specific alternatives. The extent to which measures of this nature are artifacts of the analysis, superimposed on the data, determines the validity of the test of hypotheses deduced from the theory.

Provisions for assumptions of multidimensionality, or nondimensionality, would strengthen the model. Concomitant implications of dimensional stability and order and generally accepted referents are difficult to sustain empirically. The substitution of an ideological continuum for a geographical one is a gross oversimplification of the political world and, more significantly, one that has limited utility for empirical research.

Converse has attempted to develop Stokes' notion of the "divergent space" occupied by party leaders and electorates. [25] His comments are based on a secondary analysis of survey returns from two multiparty systems, the French and the Finnish. The argument supports Stokes' call for multidimensionality with a particular emphasis on pro- and anticlericalism and urban-rural choices to complement a Left-Right economic continuum. Converse places the parties on a unidimensional scale based on voter preferential rankings of parties other than their own. The data are difficult to evaluate, but it appears that Converse has introduced an assumption of directionality into Down's exposition, that is, an individual located on the continuum will exhaust all alternatives in one direction before moving in the other, rather than proceeding on the basis of successive approximations of the best fit between his views and a party's. In establishing party position on the dimension, it would be interesting to place the parties on a continuum through an independent measure; for example, average party-leader scores on a policy scale or a content analysis of party appeals could be matched with orderings of voter preference. Or even more directly, the analysis could correlate voter-policy commitments with party-issue appeals and then focus on explaining the variance among choices that emerge. Converse does indicate refinements needed in the Downs model. Specifically, he posits that "the absolute length of the axes or coordinates of the perceived party spaces vary inversely as a function of political involvement and/or information."[26] The relative centrality of combinations of dimensions for individuals may systematically influence the psychological space the parties occupy for these people.

Converse develops the implications of perceived differences in the multidimensional space in which parties are located and sees the distances between them as characterized by respondents. The Downs model deals in general terms with similar problems, but a specification of qualifying conditions could lead to potentially rewarding empirical applications. Individual field investigations such as Alford's comparative assessment of cleavages within the Canadian party system,[27] support the call for a clearer theoretical development of diverse strains—social, religious, ethnic, regional, and cultural, as well as economic and ideological—in any model of party action.

The possibility exists of employing survey data to group aggregations of individuals by either building from narrow policy clusters to broader coalitions of mutual views or, alternatively, working from levels of ideological acceptance to multidimensional policy themes within electorates and relating these to party support. Converse's inability, in another research work,[28] to find substantial elements of constraint within views indicates the difficulties involved in the approach. Issue orientation may well represent a limited aspect of party attachment. The importance of nonrational factors for party affiliation, beyond differential levels of involvement, would constitute another aspect of the model needing precise development.

The "divergent space" of the party managers possibly could be explored in research centering on campaign behavior, especially in studies that concentrate on establishing the factors of importance in determining candidate strategy. The parameters of the decision-making process could be established—the relevant political norms of the area, the office sought, the peculiarities of the contest, the strengths and weaknesses of the opponents, and the organizational and individual resources at the disposal of the office-seeker. The influences that weigh on decision making could be evaluated and a judgment entered as to the soundness or "rationality" of the decisions made, as judged by the outcome or an objective reading of the electorate's mood and/or opponent's intentions as determined through interviews.[29] The perspective could permit the researcher to comment on the rationality of individual campaigns and campaign decisions; and such a research orientation would appear receptive to a rigorous structuring through hypotheses deduced from models comparable to Downs's.

In another context, Riker has developed a model of coalition building in a formal theoretical effort reminiscent of Downs. He has provided a limited illustration of its applicability to party concerns in American politics by employing it to explain the 1825 compromise.[30] Sellers has adapted the "size principle" developed by Riker to explain voting shifts between parties from 1789 to 1960 in their continual search for equilibrium.[31] The Downs, Riker, and Seller approaches order political phenomena in a more intelligible framework. Interestingly, all concentrate on one aspect of party behavior, coalitions of voters and competition between parties. In longitudinal analysis such as that exemplified by the Sellers piece, this focus is on the available data, namely, census materials and electoral returns, and thus is justified. Coalition models of various kinds, as discussed above, beckon for expansion of the research to include consideration of agencies that order priorities and determine the nature of the appeals to be carried to electorates.

One final study deserves attention, the less known work of David Braybrooke.[32] His report can be divided into two distinct parts. Similarly to the Gatlin research, Braybrooke is concerned with developing a "consensus-list" of propositions on political parties. The list is drawn from a number of prominent works—Herring's *The Politics of Democracy* (1940) and Truman's *The Governmental Process* (1953), in particular, and to a more limited extent, Key's *Southern Politics* (1949), Duverger's *Political Parties* (1951), and an abbreviated early report of Downs's model (1957). Braybrooke was not concerned with testing his propositional inventory; this testing was left for others. The propositions represented those agreed on, by the authors in question, as reflecting political realities. They do not pretend to be empirically verified assertions; they are simply assumptions accepted by the authors, or advanced by some and not challenged by others. After establishing his consensus-list in this fashion, Braybrooke isolates the divergences that occur and comments on reasoning processes that account for the majority of differences.

The propositions derived by Braybrooke can be tested, although they are not so clearly operational as those developed by Gatlin, and could be employed to construct an authority-based, if not empirically based, theoretical superstructure. They also provide a limited codification of the available knowledge. Braybrooke is aware of the general nature of the propositions and their vagueness. Still, even the broadest of the propositions "assert something to be the case which could intelligibly be supposed to be otherwise."[33] In this regard, they are worthy of attention. They do have the limitation of dealing again with restricted aspects of parties, essentially voting configurations, and in both the propositions and the axiomatic theory Braybrooke derives from them potential causal factors that condition party growth—principally the electoral arrangements that give rise to two-party and multiparty systems. Both reflect the concerns of the works they are derived from and certainly represent long-honored traditions in the parties' literature.

Braybrooke is aware of the relationship between his own work and that of Downs. The latter is seen as superimposing a rigorous theoretical framework borrowed from a more formal science on the subject matter of political science. Braybrooke perceives his own more modest efforts as working from available data sources towards the general systems of Downs. The two efforts contribute to a more rigorous science of politics and in fact are complementary:

[The] expeditions should eventually join up: general systems like Downs' undergoing modifications as they are interpreted more exactly; constructions from standard works becoming more ambitious, and particular attempts at partial systems connecting up, as more works are surveyed and further connections perceived among the parts of longer consensus-lists.[34]

In actuality, neither has moved much beyond his position since 1957, when Braybrooke wrote his work. Nonetheless, Braybrooke made his contribution to a partial rapprochement through the construction of a "miniature axiomatic theory" elaborating the relationship between political parties and electoral arrangements. The theoretical system consists of axioms selectively drawn from several of the propositions in the original consensus-list, theorems deduced from these, and proofs for each of the theorems. The axiomatic system, as Braybrooke reminds us, is comparatively low-level and restricted. It does, however, contribute to the clarification of research findings and to rudimentary theory building on a topic of direct relevance to parties research.

Over-all, the results to date indicate that progress apparently will be sporadic in developing more formal theories relevant to parties' analysis, or in adapting macrotheoretical orientations to the concerns of the researcher. Perhaps computer simulations of party operations may provide the opening wedge in developing coherent logical expositions of party behavior. Such theories, initially at least, would suffer from criticisms of generality and oversimplification, as with any type of model building, but they are subject to continual refinement through feeding in empirical data as it becomes available, testing propositions, and executing the necessary corrections.[35]

The development of initial propositional inventories of a scope well beyond anything currently available should be stimulated by Kenneth Janda's project, presently underway, to code published source materials on non-American political parties for the period 1950-1962 for purposes of systematic automated retrieval.[36] The study includes 260 parties in 92 countries and employs a code category that is an elaboration of Duverger's original typology, which has the virtue of directing attention to the party itself, its organization, membership, and activities, topics neglected in studies of competitive patterns or electoral arrangements. Simply by listing the location of extensive bibliographic source materials on parties, the project will provide a service. By ordering available information, the study contributes to a needed codification of knowledge. It should provide a spur to develop testable propositions from assertions common to many research works. One further contribution, in an area where the quality of much of the data is questionable, will be to guide researchers to what has been done, facilitating the quest for a more empirically based theoretical understanding of the institution and its operations.

III. CONCEPTUALIZING POLITICAL PARTIES FOR COMPARATIVE ANALYSIS

Challenging definitional and operational problems confront the parties researcher in comparative analysis. Research on totalitarian parties has faced the formidable task of sketching party procedures within a political system and contrasting these with democratic parties. Comparative aspects of the analysis have been blurred in studies that develop the party's role within the system, but leave its comparative functionings unexplored. The generally unfelt need to articulate the significance of parties and to develop their theoretical implications in democratic societies has resulted in a failure to construct acceptable theoretical models of parties in these systems, a further inhibition upon comparative analysis. The wide diversity of party types in democratic societies and the conceivable multitude of variables affecting them increase the difficulty of isolating common dimensions and molding them into a comparative theoretical framework. The result has been a nonrigorous approach to research in democratic party systems which utilizes available data and focuses on problems of general interest, usually political campaigns of national significance. Descriptive studies on different party systems, democratic and authoritarian, are difficult to interrelate and speak more to the provincial concerns of area specialists—on Africa, the Far East, Europe, Latin America, or the United States—than they do to comparative parties analysts. Discouragingly few studies have been initiated that do battle with the basic conceptual difficulties inherent in parties research. Conceptual models suggesting, although not developing, the relationship of sets of characteristics have been employed to characterize party types, a preliminary explication of the available knowledge. The orderings are rudimentary, although they do convey associations that less structured descriptions fail to communicate. The Coleman and Rosberg adaptation of a refined Almond typology provides an overview for their edited series of studies on African parties, and similar modifications of Duverger's orientation assist Hodgkin and Sorauf in organizing their material.[37] In these cases the descriptive purposes of the orderings are well served.

The more avowedly comparative works—and the Coleman-Rosberg volume may belong to this category—ordinarily contain a series of reports on party systems within a number of countries, with each of the contributing authors following a commonly accepted format in his exposition. These essays are principally of descriptive value and geared to the demands of those interested in specific party systems. An additional essay or two is devoted to confronting the more formidable conceptual problems that underlie comparative analysis.

The most notable of these efforts in the 1950's was the volume edited by Sigmund Neumann, *Modern Political Parties*.[38] The work was conceived of as a "preliminary pathfinder" and introduced by Neumann, in words still relevant today, as a needed exercise in a field innocent of "sharp theoretical concepts, historical depth, and the comparative data which alone could assure a substantial delineation of this crucial institution of modern political dynamics."[39] Each of the ten contributing authors treats the individual party systems in historical perspective and focuses attention on social forces that give rise to various political aggregations. The party systems range from those in long-established democracies to those of Germany and Japan, the Commonwealth countries, and the Communist parties in Russia and Eastern Europe. The concluding essay by Neumann,[40] of principal importance here, briefly reviews the problems implicit in comparative analysis and the vague conceptualizations underlying the principal means of dealing with them, the party-within-system orientation and the one-, two-, and multiparty distinctions employed in both intranational and cross-national studies. The essays on the individual party systems in Neumann's volume employ an analysis of their development both within the comprehensive framework of the total social system and as an institution that develops in response to pressures generated by the system. More recent studies of totalitarian party systems and those in the newly emergent nations focus on the role

of political parties within the system in both reacting to and effecting social change. Principal examples of this genre of single-country
monographs drawn from those on African political parties would
include Zolberg's *One-Party Government in the Ivory Coast* (1964),
an analysis of the role of the Parti Démocratique de Côte d'Ivoire
in the birth and consolidation of a "modernizing oligarchy"; Sklar's
Nigerian Political Parties (1963), a detailed account of the rise of
the party system and its response to problems of social and political
cohesion; and possibly also Apter's earlier classic *The Gold Coast in
Transition* (1955), a work that contributes to an understanding of
the role of the Convention People's Party in establishing a viable
national government.[41]

Such research maps previously unknown terrain and tentatively lays
the groundwork for cross-national comparisons while presenting a
thorough firsthand knowledge of the political system and its antecedents. A premium is placed on the ability of the analyst to sift
through data of varying degrees of quality to evaluate the contribution of political parties vis-à-vis other institutions.

The second possibility of comparatively analyzing parties based on
a judgment as to the number of major parties in the system is of
admitted convenience, but it obscures more than it illuminates. Basic
questions arise; for example: do all, or even a majority of, one- or
multi-, or for that matter two-, party systems share enough characteristics to be analyzed as members of the same class? The contention
here is that they do not. The great extent of variance within such
classifications is one of the few aspects of parties that can be richly
documented. The approach also reveals little about the factors contributing to the competitive patterns identified or the specific role
the party plays in influencing them.

Neumann rejects both orientations in favor of an evolutionary perspective that emphasizes parties as responses to stages of social development. The contemporary period is characterized by a "planned search for
a new social order" and is represented among party types by the limited
"party of individual representation" and the comprehensive "party of
integration." Parties of integration are subdivided into parties of democratic integration, for which the continental socialist parties serve as pro-
totypes, and the parties of total integration, symbolized by totalitarian
parties. Neumann outlines dimensions along which the parties can be
compared. These dimensions include the scope and inclusiveness of the
party's structure, the conditions of the individual's commitment to the
party, and the systemic influences that the party reflects. It cannot be
argued that Neumann advances a working theory of parties, or even a
reasonably precise typology with which to structure comparative descriptions. This is not the case. However, he did achieve his principal objective of putting forward in highly suggestive terms a constructive examination of the problems in comparative parties analysis.

Neumann's ideas generated discussion and are credited with stimulating a series of essays published in 1966 under the editorship of Joseph LaPalombara and Myron Weiner as *Political Parties and Political Development*.[42] The volume is one of seven sponsored by the Committee on Comparative Politics of the Social Science Research Council, each designed to explore some aspect of political development. The range of topics and countries treated is considerably broader than in Neumann's volume, although the integrative threads among the essays are less pronounced. The volume is more speculative than its predecessor, designed to raise questions—specifically, on the contribution of parties to political development—and to introduce diverse conceptualizations of potential analytic value. It is disappointing, however, in its inability to achieve conceptual precision in the few typologies advanced and its failure to deal exhaustively with any of the basic problems in comparative analysis. Most of the essays are broadly conceived treatments of given topics with limited support from empirical sources.

The volume contains two essays by the editors. The first is a selective overview of party development with an emphasis on the conditions giving rise to parties. Unfortunately, few data are offered to strengthen the analysis. The brevity and generality of the essay precludes its consideration as a definitive comparative historical assessment of party development and the lessons to be learned from it, an exercise that has yet to be executed satisfactorily.[43] The authors conclude their initial discussion by advancing a classificatory scheme. They draw the traditional distinction between "competitive" and "non-competitive" systems, and subdivide competitive systems into four classifications depending on internal party characteristics and systemic factors—specifically, in their words, "the way political power is held."[44] The first dimension the authors refer to as "turnover" and "hegemonic." In a *hegemonic* system, one party or party coalition holds power "over an extended period of time." The category, as the entire scheme, is complicated by a vagueness; for example, the authors are vague in defining what constitutes reasonably long periods of time—the United States during the New and Fair Deals would be classified under this heading. The confusion is increased when *turnover* is defined as "situations . . . where there may have been hegemonic periods, [but] there is relatively frequent change in the party that governs or in the party that dominates a coalition."[45] The second dimension along which to measure party systems is "ideological-pragmatic." The authors state that this characteristic refers to the parties themselves and reaffirm that it is of vital importance, but fail to elaborate their intentions. They do not define or illustrate key terms, nor do they offer convenient benchmarks for measuring and categorizing systems. Research ventures that might lead to clearer and more consistent classifications of problems in cross-national party comparisons are not indicated. The noncompetitive systems are subclassified into "one-party authoritarian," "one-party pluralistic," and "one-party totalitarian." Over-all, the categorization represents no great advance over Neumann's ideas and falls short of the typology developed in 1951 by Duverger.

The concluding essay by LaPalombara and Weiner[46] defines and clarifies developmental problems on which parties appear to have particular impact, such as national integration, political participation, legitimacy, and conflict management. The alternative characterizations of each of these elements are said to account for the variance among the works of the contributing authors. Similarly to the other essays in the volume, this essay indicates a series of questions, particularly in relation to the impact of parties on developmental processes, that represent promising, although not clearly interdependent, avenues of exploration.

The initial division introduced in the typology of LaPalombara and Weiner between competitive and noncompetitive systems raises more questions than it answers. Under what conditions do competitive systems emerge? Are competitive and pluralistic social and democratic systems synonymous? Whether used intra-nationally or cross-nationally, the classification of party systems in this manner abstracts parties from their total environment. The researcher can deal with either of two questions, but seldom both. What are the characteristics of competitive systems—comparatively high urbanization, mass-media penetration, literacy, per-capita income, industrialization, education, and some familiarity with traditional democratic problem-solving practices? Lipset, for one, has researched this question.[47] A second major question, and the one usually neglected, is about what contribution parties make to competitive patterns. To answer this question, the researcher is forced to consider basic conceptual problems in parties research, such as what is a political party, how can it be measured, and how can its effects be weighed. Also, once the broad categorizations are accepted, distinctions within categorizations conceivably of greater importance, for example among types of one- or multiparty systems, are blurred.

With the foregoing in mind, Sartori's essay in the LaPalombara-Weiner volume has special interest. Sartori, in a prelude to a major exploratory work,[48] accepts the restrictions implicit in competitive typologies and argues for the replacement of such categorizations with one based on distinctions between bipolar and multipolar party systems. Sartori develops models for each of the party systems that permit (1) specific discussion of problems directly associated with parties research—for example, the causes and consequences of ideological rigidity, the conditions necessary for assumptions of brokerage functions by parties, and recruitment patterns and their effect on conflict management and representation of interests, and (2) the advancing of a series of hypotheses amenable to more extended research, and hence potential contributions to testing assumptions, theorizing, and tightening the logical interrelationship among its principal assertions. For example, Sartori stipulates that a stable party system which precedes the introduction of proportional representation will result in a moderate pluralism; a fragmented party system, in extreme pluralism. Such contentions are subject to historical verification. Nonetheless, the reasoning is still broad, and the focus of the implied research needs specific elaboration before it can direct attention to the empirical and conceptual problems of comparative research that requires intensive exploration.

The developmental approach elaborated by Chambers in his essay in the LaPalombara-Weiner volume and in an earlier monograph, *Political Parties in a New Nation: The American Experience 1776-1809* (1963), contributes to empirical model building by indicating the relationship between propositions and time-series data and, thus, is appropriate for the middle-range theory being stressed here. Concentrating on the United States, Chambers, and others,[49] attempt to superimpose a developmental perspective on party evolution and extract from the American experience propositions of general utility for structuring models of party development. To date, the effort is in its preliminary stages, and the differences between the American experience and those of the newer developing nations are more striking than the similarities. Still, the possibilities are exciting, and the availability of extensive electoral data for the period from the 1820's to the present should encourage such analyses. The essays by Chambers, Burnham, and the other co-authors of *The American Party Systems: Stages of Political Development* (1967) stake out similar lines for analysis, as well as illustrate the substantive contributions such an approach can make. When a simplified theoretical model, more than likely of a working theory caliber, is backed with empirical illustration, its utility can be tested in non-American situations.

Developmental studies relevant to party concerns usually establish the meaning of the concept "political party" within the broader outlines of the approach and then concentrate on recording the evolution of parties as responses to "loads" placed on the political system or as agencies contributing to the resolution of specified problems that emerge in the course of change. The party is a dependent or independent variable, depending on the author's structuring of his materials. The approach indicates questions to be analyzed, and attempts to describe uniformities in the institutional workings across cultures during different time sequences or "stages" of development.

One problem in such analyses is to specify toward what a transitional society is developing. An author would next attempt to clarify the relative contribution of various institutions to the resolution of crises that arise during the transformation process. Pye's

writings provide a lucid presentation of the basic assumptions of
what he calls the "developmental syndrome."[50] Criteria to gauge the
developmental process of a maturing system would include three
domains of behavior: (1) the system's handling of "equality," an
analysis of mass electoral involvement, achievement standards, and
universalistic laws; (2) its "capacity," a judgment as to scope of a
government's actions and the relative efficiency and rationality of
distributive practices; and (3) systemic "differentiation," an estimation
of functional specificity within a broadly integrated framework. Developmental approaches concern themselves with such problems as the
establishment of a national identity, legitimation of authority, governmental penetration of the society, expansion of citizen participation
in political decision making, social integration, and patterns of
resource distribution. Analyses evaluate the impact of political parties
in various stages of maturation or on one or all of the problem
areas. The LaPalombara-Weiner and Chambers-Burnham volumes modify
some aspects of this outline but remain true to its essentials. The
necessity to cope with the dynamics of change in newer countries
within a meaningful comparative framework represents one stimulus to
the elaboration of the approach. Thus, both volumes develop research
questions that have contemporary field utility, as well as possibilities
for aggregate time-series analysis.

A variation on standard developmental themes is found in the
book edited by Lipset and Rokkan, *Party Systems and Voter Alignments: Cross-National Perspectives* (1967).[51] The twin objectives of
this volume as presented by the editors are to account for the
historical evolution of cleavage structures and their institutionalization
and to present deployment, within stable and competitive party
systems. The volume is an exercise in comparative sociology, and
more explicit than most in the problems addressed and the analytic
techniques and compatible data sources employed. The eleven essays
on individual party systems deal principally with the class structures
of European and Anglo-American party systems, although the chapters
on Japan, Brazil, and West Africa add perspective, with the bulk of
the analyzed electoral data drawn from the 1950's. The selections
include Linz's analysis of Spain and Dogan's comparison of stratification and party support in Italy and France.

The editors contribute an opening theoretical paper[52] in which
they construct an explanatory model of competing sociocultural forces
within specified time periods—the Reformation, the "Democratic
Revolution" (more specifically, the fight over control of mass educational outlets), and the Industrial Revolution—and analyze how the
different resolutions of each led to identifiable cleavage patterns
formalized within European party patterns. The authors are concerned
with social pressures manifest *prior* to the general spread of suffrage
rights around the 1920's. The contention is that contemporary party

systems, as distinguished from individual parties within given systems, are the culmination of forces generated before the acceptance of mass electoral involvement.

The model presents a modification of Parsons' ideas and deduces aggregations of conflict representation from alternative resolutions of problems in different evolutionary periods. The typology developed results in eight possible classifications of party systems. The authors illustrate each through reference to historical examples and suggest specific conditions that would lead to the principal exceptions to their developmental model, such as parties committed to the protection of agrarian and territorial interests. Atypical parties of this nature develop outside the pull of conventional environmental forces. Factors associated with such parties are communication barriers, identifiable sectional and cultural boundaries and minimal economic interdependence with other social groups, as also the opportunity to develop and solidify bases of voting support.

The authors deal with two stages of evolutionary growth, first, the emergence of broad focal points for conflict in different historical time periods and, second, the channeling of cleavage divisions into party systems. Their definition of political parties reflects their dual concerns: parties are conceptualized as "alliances in conflicts over policies and value commitments within the larger body politic" that serve both to emphasize conflicts within populations and, simultaneously, to promote coalitions that bridge cleavage lines.[53]

Parsons' classification of the four functional subsystems within a society provides a convenient base from which to develop their model of social conflict. Lipset and Rokkan concentrate on the internal mobilization of Parsons' "Integrative" or "I" quadrant, which they conceive to include the crystallization stage for party systems in mass democracies. They postulate two dimensions, the territorial, or center-periphery (nation-locality), geographical divisions, and the functional, absolutist "we-they" approach to political negotiation contrasted with discrete policy-bounded and essentially class-based orientations. The first, territorial consolidation under a national government, is stipulated as a necessary condition for the second, conflict over economic representation.

Lipset and Rokkan overlay these two axes with four conflicts generated in turn by the "National Revolution" and the Industrial Revolution. The National Revolution represents a threat to particularistic values and cultures, for example, localized identifications or a nationwide Church-State conflict, whose "average tendencies" can be graphed along the territorial dimension. The Industrial Revolution, with its attack on primary occupations and overtones of urban-rural and later owner-employer conflicts, cuts across territorial lines and emphasizes economic divisions. Employing both dimensions and the conflicts unleashed by each of the revolutions, the authors plot four significant cleavage areas: (1) dominant against subject cultures, (2) church against state, (3) primary against secondary economy, and (4) workers against employers. They also sketch antisystem, or nonintegrative, movements that fringe the quadrant explored, although these developments are less explicit.

The model is broad-gauged and nonrigorous. The authors recognize its weaknesses and specify their intentions as presenting "a set of analytical tools" that introduce order "into the comparative analysis of party-political developments." The model explores "the potentialities of a scheme of classification developed from central concepts in current sociological theory" and initiates discussion as to the possibilities for conceptualizing comparative historical developments in a series of different party systems.[54] Those objectives have been met. While the model is loose, it is nonetheless a promising beginning for the developmental cross-national sociological perspective it represents.

The linkages among conflict structures and party systems are explored in a three-stage model based upon European experiences (Figure 1).[55] The authors initiate the discussion by exploring a sequence of thresholds, or barriers to acceptance, with which an interest movement attempting to survive as a party must contend. These include "legitimation," the right to protest; "incorporation," electoral participation rights extended to dissidents; "representation," interests voiced through extant organizations or an independent movement; and "majority power," checks protecting minority groups against numerical majorities. Stipulating the options available, and overlaying these considerations with a dichotomous response to crises arising during specified historical periods, the authors predict the cleavage bases of eight types of party systems. Apparently explanatory power is not greatly increased nor parsimony sacrificed by the owner-worker cleavage, the fourth dimension considered; the issues it raises are included in the typology, although ramifications of the conflict are briefly investigated.

Scandinavian parties best illustrate those of category II. The majority party within the country would be committed to a dominant state church exercising influence over mass education and urban-industrial and commercial-economic policies, with opposition parties built from out-coalitions of particularistic territorial cultures, dissident non-Catholic religious groups, and landed interests. The majority conservative parties in the Scandinavian party systems exemplify the first coalition with opposition "left" parties of Agrarians, Christians, and/or Radicals. The authors elaborate on each party system in the model and present relevant examples.

The developmental model is obviously rudimentary. It represents essentially successive dichotomous responses to major social influences. The format that results serves to locate specific national party systems within a historical context common to all. The evolutionary

FIGURE 1. Developmental Model of Cleavage Consolidation
in Eight Party Systems

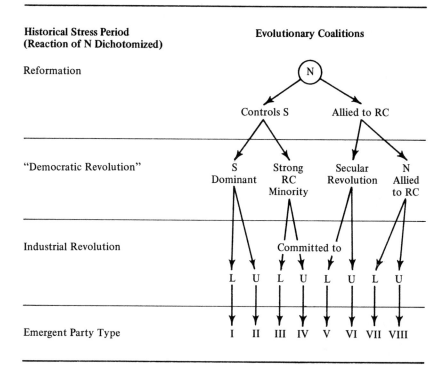

Historical Stress Period
(Reaction of N Dichotomized)

Evolutionary Coalitions

Reformation

Controls S   Allied to RC

"Democratic Revolution"   S   Strong   Secular   N
                            Dominant   RC   Revolution   Allied
                                        Minority   to RC

Industrial Revolution   Committed to

                            L   U   L   U   L   U   L   U

Emergent Party Type   I   II III IV   V   VI VII VIII

KEY   N = National Government
       S = Non-Catholic State Church
      RC = Roman Catholic Church
       L = Landed Interests
       U = Urban Interests

lines sketched can be employed to order comparative descriptions of
cleavage structures and identify variables in each locus of significance
in determining alternative choice strategies. The model stipulates certain responses that can be subjected to investigation and could serve
as a typology providing a comparative depth perspective to current
party alignments. As indicated, neither party development within a
system nor the independent contribution of parties in collating
interests and transforming these into broader coalitions is explored.
The authors' promise of a more precisely articulated model to come
indicates that this effort is in progress.

The internal processes of parties, as formalized organizations within
polities confronted by pressures that arise both from systemic
demands and their own survival needs, resolved with varying degrees

of adequacy, are not approached in analyses of cross-national cleavage lines or evolutionary developments that employ party as the dependent variable. These comments represent not so much a criticism of this strain of sociological inquiry, as an argument for research perspectives designed to assess the contributory aspects and internal priority-ordering mechanisms of parties, a research focus addressed in the next section. A developmental approach, whether evolving from the cleavage pathways elaborated by Lipset and Rokkan or the more diffuse perspectives of societies in transition, does hold the advantage of being implicitly dynamic. A tracing of party evolution and of the factors and crises that affect it stresses environmental interaction and response to change. It contains the promise of achieving verifiable predictive capabilities, and it could provide a corrective to the inherently static nature of equilibrium models and much of the research based on cross-sectional data.

IV. A PERSPECTIVE FOR COMPARATIVE ANALYSIS

Definitions of Political Party

It is difficult to find a stipulation of meaning for political parties that isolates its distinctive qualities and is of obvious applicability to comparative empirical research. Yet the attempt to bring the institution being analyzed into relief would appear a prerequisite to serious inquiry. Unfortunately, the fluid interaction of parties with their environment, their frequently diffused organizational structures, and the variety of cultural arenas in which they operate, in addition to the unusually large number of activities in which they engage, frustrate definitional efforts. Some students, in fact, argue that the search for a reliable definition is premature and, were the complications in framing one arbitrarily resolved, the result would be too restrictive for present purposes. The best definition, then, is not a definition in the traditional sense, but rather a description of reality. "The nature of parties," says Key, "must be sought through an appreciation of their role in governance."[56] Commentaries should deal with the agencies commonly accepted as political parties and should relate their activities. Authors often treat American political parties in this fashion, prefacing their works with an organizing framework which serves to integrate their materials. The most common of the distinctions introduced in this regard are those made among the party-in-the-electorate, the party-as-organization, and the party-in-the-government or the party-in-the-legislature. The approach reflects the inadequacies of the available research. It does little to encourage comparative work. The party as a vital force of independent consequence in uniting the multifaceted aspects of its behavior is dealt with obliquely, if at all. This manner of presentation has the further regrettable effect of directing attention away from problems not explored in previous studies. It deals with what has been done, which is a product of an individual researcher's interest and the corresponding availability of data—one reason for the extended concern with aggregate patterns of electoral behavior and group support.

A more positive attack on the problem would begin by specifying criteria for a minimally acceptable definition. These criteria should include the attempt to isolate, to the extent that they exist, uniformities among parties in structure and behavior, that is, the identification of dimensions common to the phenomena and the boundaries as well as the characteristics that distinguish them from other social institutions and from their environment. To paraphrase Riggs,[57] the definition should also have elasticity. That is, it should be both inclusive and selective to the extent that it distinguishes near-parties or interest groups from parties and that it comprehends all agencies people normally think about when they talk about parties, authoritarian or democratic, electorally successful or unsuccessful, and broadly representative geographical, social, or economic coalitions or not. And it should lend itself to empirical analyses, that is, it should be capable of being operationalized. Such criteria are difficult to meet. Perhaps a beginning can be made; and to the extent error occurs, let it favor too great a generality: "it is less likely to blunt the imagination."[58]

A review of the definitions put forward in the literature with these criteria in mind yields limited returns. It does convey the heterogeneity of associations made with the concept "political party." Downs's and Lipset's and Rokkan's definitions were introduced earlier, and Almond and Powell's is "the specialized aggregation structure of modern societies."[59] Burke's famous definition of the party as men united by principle and committed to promoting the national interest has served more to stimulate debate than to encourage empirical inquiry as to the nature of the ideological bonds that dintinguish parties from other groups. McClosky, Flinn, and Wirt have been concerned with the consistency of issue preferences among selected groups of party leaders and between activists and followers,[60] and the voting studies have dealt with questions of policy consensus among partisans. In general, however, Burke's statement has been taken as a base point for normative assessments of the institution. Deviations from the expected have been severely criticized.[61]

American scholars have emphasized the electoral characteristics of parties—their attempts to gain control of the government by promoting candidates and issues attractive to large segments of the voting population. The Sait, Ranney and Kendall, Schattschneider, and Hennessy definitions exemplify this strain.[62] Not unexpectedly, research concentrates on this aspect of party behavior. The perspective is useful and can be converted to comparative analyses to the extent that parties in other nations nominate candidates and contest elections. Its limitations rest in its restricted identification of party concerns and its failure to deal with the party as an independent organism with distinctive structural properties competing with other groups, but also serving the political system in more subtle ways.

An adaptation of this definition is found in legal stipulations of what constitutes a party. A certain percentage of the vote in a specified election or in a series of elections, or evidence of geographical consistency in support, serves to qualify a group as a legally recognized political party. The same type of qualifying standards could be introduced into comparative research; for example, a political party could be defined as a group that received 5 percent or more of the vote in a (or two or more succeeding) national parliamentary elections (or holds X percent of the parliamentary seats). Such a definition serves as a preliminary qualification for reducing the number of groups to manageable proportions, but does not go beyond this result in directing attention to relevant dimensions for analysis.

Duverger might be of help here. For him, the party is "a community with a particular structure." Contemporary parties "are characterized by their anatomy."[63] Duverger does not argue that structure qualifies as the most significant question in parties research; but he does proceed on the assumption that organizational considerations represent workable units for comparative investigation and that an exploration of structural attributes can provide the basis for answering fundamental questions on other complex aspects of party behavior.

Eldersveld has carried this strategy further, and in the process has directly related his conceptual definition to empirical inquiry.[64] In fact, the distinguishing characteristic of his definition is its obvious research potential and its ability to overcome the unreal quality of organizational typologies abstracted from environmental considerations, a failing which Duverger is unable to avoid.

Eldersveld argues that the party is a "social group," that its boundaries can be established, that it has internal decision-making processes and influence channels, and that it attempts to accomplish specifiable objectives. The performance of political parties has implications of broad significance for the social system of which it is part. The characteristic that distinguishes parties from other social institutions is its desire to control governmental positions and to seek such ends through electoral combat. This definition, similar to most, is an amalgam of many themes. It invites the researcher to establish empirical social and ideological boundaries of the group, strength and basis of shared membership ties, structural outlines of the organization, nature of decision making within the group, relationships between the group and other structural subsystems within the society, and activities engaged in by the organization and their functional significance. The vantage point from which to begin the analysis is the party organization; conceptualization and investigation of this organization would then be the basis on which to build an understanding of the role played by the party within the system.

With these definitional attempts as background, political parties can be defined as institutionalized agencies that share certain dimensions of behavior. These dimensions include both a common objective—to influence and, if possible, control governmental decision making—and related methods, distinguished by principally nonviolent means directed toward occupying authoritative positions. This initial stipulation should distinguish party objectives from the more limited attempts of interest groups to influence issues and policy makers in areas of direct concern to them and the minor parties, or personal collectivities, such as the Best Party, the American Christian Party, or the Socialist Labor Party. Although these groups may legally qualify as parties in the United States, their goals appear more to dramatize such issues as prohibition and bingo than to contest for office. The distinction is a matter of degree in both cases, and a minor party or an interest group, for instance, a labor movement, could emerge as a major party. The reference to peaceful means deliberately excludes revolutionary groups dedicated to overthrowing the established order through force. The distinction is one of tactics and does not encompass ideology. A communist party in Italy or elsewhere may be committed to fundamental changes within the political system, but may attempt to realize them through conventional efforts at the polls.

The dimensions of behavior common to the genus party, which might be called functions performed for the political system, would include the education of citizens to an understanding and at least partial acceptance of the political system and to the more immediate implications of policy. Even parties devoted to the reorganization of the political system, if they meet the criterion of peaceful remonstration, must first acquaint their followers with the system and the opportunities it allows for dissent. This activity represents a socializing function that parties perform, it is argued, in all countries. An understanding is beginning to emerge of the importance of parties in the United States as a socializing agent developing early affective bonds to the system. The party should fulfill a similar function in all systems. In developing nations, the party's contribution in this regard to integrative tendencies at the national level may represent its most important service.

Proceeding from the general and more diffused along the same continuum, parties may educate citizens to the policies of the government. In democratic societies, this proposition would have to be investigated by a critical evaluation of governmental activities and, for the opposition, by the promotion of a priority listing of reasonable alternatives. In nondemocratic one-party systems, the emphasis may be placed on communicating decisions, once made, to party followers and encouraging their acceptance of them. The party in these societies may serve largely as a vehicle of conflict management with a greater emphasis on familiarizing the populace with policy output than with developing intelligent alternatives and coalescing group support behind them, which is an input function.

Parties also recruit individuals into decision-making positions. The broader aspects of recruitment, including indoctrination with the political norms of the system and the promotion of a mutual commitment to established devices for problem solving, are subsumed under the educating-the-public rubric. Recruitment in the present sense would be confined to constituting the range of groups eligible to hold power and advancing and actually selecting individuals for political decision-making positions. In democratic societies, the parties nominate candidates to put before the electorate and work in their behalf in seeking election. In authoritarian one-party systems, the selection procedures are less visible, involving the rise of individuals through party ranks until they emerge as organization-supported, and hence victory-assured, nominees for any of a series of public offices at different levels of government.

And finally, political parties in all societies represent a communications network performing a crucial two-way linkage function between government and citizenry. The advancement of interests and the funneling of support and group and individual demands occur through the party apparatus, whether formally coalesced into party-endorsed programs or not. The party is an instrument sensitive to the concerns of the electorate and, alternatively, a vehicle through which the leadership can communicate their own needs and assumptions. This particular function is more informal and centers to a greater extent on the internal channels of influence within the party than on either promotion of generally supported issues or on the selection of candidates for office.

In sum, then, a political party is a formally organized group that performs the functions of educating the public to acceptance of the system as well as the more immediate implications of policy concerns, that recruits and promotes individuals for public office, and that provides a comprehensive linkage function between the public and governmental decision makers. It is distinguished from other groups by its dedication to influencing policy making on a broad scale, preferably by controlling government, and by its acceptance of institutionalized rules of electoral conduct—more specifically, capturing public office through peaceful means.

The definition could be expanded by adding complementary dimensions of behavior—that, upon examination, parties appear to perform with consistency in various political cultures. Limitations to the scope of the definition could be added by stipulating refinements that narrow the range of agencies involved and facilitate operationalization. For example, it may be convenient for a researcher to accept the idea of candidate promotion as representing a principal responsibility of parties, yet a precondition of his research would be that he articulate this idea more precisely. He could limit the dimensions by concentrating his attention on parties in democratic societies that contest for office with measurable success.

Functions of Political Parties

In developing a perspective for examining party behavior, it is helpful to conceive of the party in terms that permit weighing its impact on systemic questions. Figure 2 diagrams the connecting points between the institution and its background and indicates variables useful in empirically structuring the party's setting and in establishing both the agency's and the broader system's boundaries.

Figure 2 borrows a systems orientation to serve as a framework for interrelating the party with environmental forces. The adaption from macrotheory is causal, and employs assumptions not explicit in equilibrium models. Nonetheless, it assists in focusing on quantifiable variables that can be developed as a backdrop for party operations. The perspective links the party to broader social concerns and relates its structure and activities to environmental stimuli. It retains some advantages of the systemic orientation of Easton, Almond, Parsons, and others. The party is characterized as a structure—a set of patterned interactions among individuals—solidified into a formal organizational mold and operating within a broader context, and as a group that performs functions of consequence for the total system. The researcher's attention is attracted to the central institution. The weaknesses of systems theory adaptations that concentrate overly much on input or output aspects of the system and exclude detailed consideration of the principal conversion agencies can be avoided by employing the party organization as the principal concern through which to integrate the various research strains.

Second, the analyst is encouraged to measure the agency's impact on its environment. The complacency of explanatory approaches based on a functional perspective that delineates the party's contributions to a sophisticated and continuing system of action is rejected in favor of a rigorous empirical assessment of the causal implications of party performance. The abstractions of structural-functional analysis can be discarded, while retaining its emphasis on systemic conse-quences; The party can be conceived of as a causal agent that engages in prescribed activities of discernible import. The researcher develops a construct of party, translates it into a field situation, and attempts to gauge the scope of party activities and their impact. The party becomes the independent variable and the consequences of its

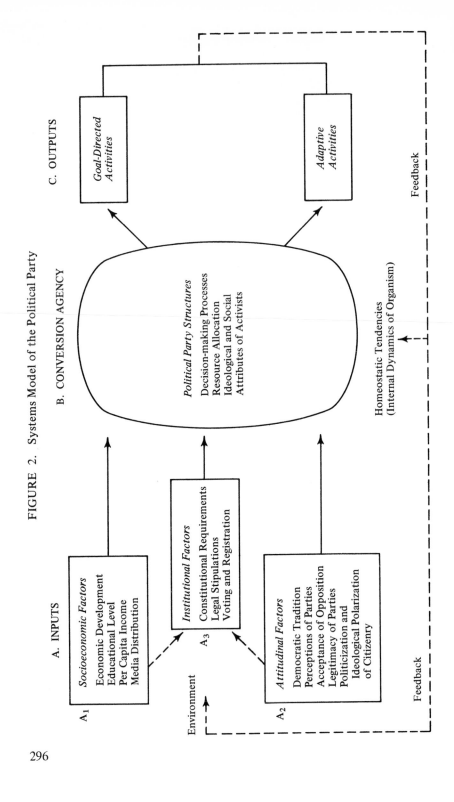

FIGURE 2. Systems Model of the Political Party

A. INPUTS

B. CONVERSION AGENCY

C. OUTPUTS

A_1

Socioeconomic Factors
Economic Development
Educational Level
Per Capita Income
Media Distribution

Institutional Factors
Constitutional Requirements
Legal Stipulations
Voting and Registration

A_3

Environment

A_2

Attitudinal Factors
Democratic Tradition
Perceptions of Parties
Acceptance of Opposition
Legitimacy of Parties
Politicization and
Ideological Polarization
of Citizenry

Political Party Structures
Decision-making Processes
Resource Allocation
Ideological and Social
Attributes of Activists

Homeostatic Tendencies
(Internal Dynamics of Organism)

*Goal-Directed
Activities*

*Adaptive
Activities*

Feedback

Feedback

296

activities the dependent variables. Formalized associations among groups of actors are postulated to arise in response to varieties of environmental demands and result in an emphasis on different activities executed with measurable degrees of success. The uniformities and dissimilarities in organization and performance are dimensions for comparative assessment. There is a circularity to the relationship between party and environment. Structural-functional theoretical approaches opt for generality in outlining the interaction between the institution and its setting; such generality is implicitly vague and confounds empirical investigations.[65] In turn, a major theoretical problem in an approach employing a causal explanatory perspective becomes one of building discrete empirical findings into acceptable middle-range generalizations. Nonetheless, concern directed toward such ends and the reorientation of attention towards the methodological problems involved in comparative investigations argue in favor of this position at this stage in the evolution of parties research.

Figure 2 suggests three sets of variables important for delineating a party's environment—demographic, attitudinal, and institutional. More immediate attitudinal data could be found in voter surveys and cross-national research on tolerance for democratic forms, as represented by the Almond and Verba five-nation study. These data serve to indicate the climate within which the parties develop. They can also contribute a gauge of party performance—to what extent and in what manner does the party cultivate the electorate? How successful is the party from the individual's perspective in representing his opinion and in providing him with attractive issues and candidate alternatives? What role do electors believe proper for the party within the system? And how much of a continuing influence is associated with a party in voter decision making, and, more importantly, in acceptance of the total system? The information collected in attitudinal surveys can be directed toward answering these questions.

Data obtained in voter surveys can also assist in establishing the group bonds. A discussion of parties as groups brought together to promote shared ideological concerns, or the conception implicit in Almond's stipulation of "aggregation" as the party's chief function, or the similar assumptions more empirically developed in the historical analysis depicting parties as socioeconomic and geographic coalitions advancing priority consensual policies need not be entered into here.[66] At a minimum, nonetheless, perceptions of and attachments to a political party held by voters assist in identifying the distinctive attributes of the group. The "image," or psychological reality, that parties have for the individual, the intensity of party ties, differential levels of participation in party activities, policy concerns and social bonds linking party members, and the relative intrusion of political parties into the affairs of individuals constitute important, if not indispensable, variables for assessing the party's interrelationships with its environment.[67] Such variables have been included in the voting studies, although their relationship to party operations has suffered from a broad conceptualization of the party in the major works and a belated and, for the most part, unexploited appreciation of the importance of the political parties in structuring voting alternatives and an individual's attachment to the broader system.[68] Studies which focus on the party organization and which work from here to clarify its impact on the adaptation to its environmental setting, should prove more successful in interrelating the party and its activities with the electorate.

The universe in which the political party operates is further indicated by the social and economic factors that, some have argued, form prerequisites for democratic development, and that others have related to party activities, electoral competition, and policy outputs.[69] Such data are necessary for establishing the context within which parties operate and for differentiating variations among the systems examined. They also serve to isolate factors influencing party performance and variables important for analyzing party effectiveness, for example, in co-opting and representing social groups within the electoral unit or in measuring the relative increments in the vote that are traceable to party efforts.

The institutional variables of political consequence that delimit the field within which parties operate have received less attention than the socioeconomic ones. One reason is the difficulty of assembling reliable data on, for example, registration figures, comparative electoral laws, magnitude of and overlap among electoral districts, ballot form, and electoral formulas such as proportional representation, plurality election, or majority vote. In a pair of articles, Donald Matthews and James Prothro[70] have related 21 socioeconomic and 10 political variables to Negro and white registration figures for 997 southern counties. The authors' statement that compiling the socioeconomic data from census and noncensus sources alone took one man-year of work gives an idea of the volume of effort involved and an explanation for the infrequency of such studies. The political factors analyzed include legal voter requirements such as literacy tests and the poll tax, party-system variables such as the influence of primaries, party factionalism and competition between parties, interest-group organization along racial lines, and racial turmoil. The authors apply multiple regression and residual analysis to develop the relationship between these variables and voter registration. The findings vary from the expected and previously well documented—an inverse ratio between Negro concentration in a county and Negro registration—to the unanticipated—the negative correlation between white educational attainment in a county and Negro registration. The 31 political and socioeconomic variables account for approximately 50 percent of the variance found in Negro-registration figures. The authors may even have a greater explanatory power than they realize. A reanalysis of the data employing stepwise regression methods might indicate that selectively few factors explain most of the variance. If so, increasingly stronger indices of forces acting on (in this case) registration could be developed. The political factors are difficult to quantify meaningfully in their analysis and would profit from considerable refinement. The over-all results, specifically the amount of difference that is explained and the ability of the political variables virtually to double the variance accounted for, are impressive and warrant further study.

A similar analysis by Stanley Kelley and associates[71] attempts to assess the variables associated with the 1960 voter registration in 104 cities in the United States and to judge the extent to which registration affects turnout in Presidential elections. The authors employ an interesting adaptation of one of Downs's assumptions to guide their analysis, namely, that an individual rationally calculates the disparity between "benefits" and "costs" before committing himself to vote. Cost factors associated with registration, the dependent variable in the analysis, include literacy tests, registration closing dates, time and location of registration, and permanent or periodic registration schedules. Other independent variables are socioeconomic factors such as age, sex, race, education, income, length of residence in the state, party competition, and residence stipulations. Employing regression analysis, 78 percent of the variance in the proportion of the eligible population voting is accounted for by registration. Put in other terms, registration is a more effective deterrent to the vote than any factors that enter the calculation after the registration stage. Election turnouts can be artifacts of rules drawn by those in positions of power. The authors hypothesize that the decline in voting turnout in the first quarter of this century may have resulted from the introduction of stringent registration requirements. Over-all, this and the previous analysis indicate the utility of their approaches. Both could be employed in more general studies to structure the setting within which parties maneuver.

A further elaboration of the relationship between election rules and party systems is drawn by Douglas Rae in his comparative exploration of the political implications of electoral arrangements.[72] The study treats ballot form, electoral-district characteristics, and election qualifications in the single-member, plurality elections and in three categories of proportional-representation systems. Data include the returns for 121 elections in 20 countries over the period 1946-1964. The findings, collated into a summary 13 positions, indicate, for example, that electoral laws overrepresent the larger parties in parliamentary seats and deemphasize the voting impact of the smaller parties, and that district magnitude is positively associated with both party fractionalization and legislative representation. Such analyses build upon available data and strive to put forward universally applicable generalizations resting on empirical analyses. They promote an understanding of the constitutional factors that condition representation and provide the beginning of an understanding of the relationship between legal prerequisites and party form. It has yet to be determined whether political parties are an intervening variable between environmental factors (socioeconomic, attitudinal, and institutional) that establish the boundaries of the social system within which the party operates, and dependent variables such as individual motivation to participate, competitive patterns among parties, registration figures, vote increments, and issue representation.

Political Parties and Organization Theory

Much of the empirical research relevant to parties contends with problems that fall within the input or output areas in Figure 2. Group aggregations of party support are analyzed, static profiles of voters are drawn, campaigns are described, and associations are examined between indices of party competition and/or economic capacity and policy outcome, as reflected in legislative roll call or proportion of a state's budget devoted to a policy area. Normally, an assumption underlies these studies that competitive party systems effectively represent lower-income groups and that this effectiveness can be measured through some judgment as to support for education, aid to dependent children, welfare, public-assistance programs, and the like.[73] At a minimum, the competitive patterns between parties are expected to account for a significant portion of the variance in state emphases. Actually, economic indicators independent of competitive practices have proven more effective predictors of the patterns of resource distribution that occur within states.

Analyses of this nature make no attempt to examine the role of principal conversion agencies, such as political parties, or the comparative effectiveness with which they collate interests, articulate their views, and then channel these to decision makers. It is conceivable that differences among conversion agencies, introduced as intervening variables between gross calculations of socioeconomic development and public expenditures, would assist in accounting for the variance in the patterns of resource allocations encountered. The comparative analysis of distributive practices among nations, as opposed to variations among the more homogeneous states within one country, would profit from an inclusion of a consideration of the political party and its role as a conversion institution in the process. In conceptualizing the transmittal agency, investigation is required of the "withinputs," as Easton labels them, or the dynamics of the party in coalescing a series of demands that arise from various groups, evaluating each and determining the rationale behind the priority assigned by the organization to the advancement of specified interests. If the reorienting function within the party could be established with reasonable precision, a beginning could be made toward inserting at least one linkage agency into the equation relating input and output variables. In turn, the relative success of parties and different combinations of structural properties associated with them in promoting policy interests could serve as a comparative variable.

A degree of quantitative precision will be sacrificed in the initial studies of aggregate variables that expand their concerns to include the party as a conversion mechanism. An increased understanding of policy-making processes should serve to justify the short-run inconveniences. The attempt to frame questions about the contribution of intervening factors in the allocation of resources would encourage the consideration of conceptual questions and field research of direct relevance to the empirical analysis of political parties.

Each of the sets of variables illustrated by Figure 2—the socioeconomic factors, the cultural-heritage and contemporary attitudinal orientations of its citizenry, and the institutional limits on party performance—helps delineate parameters of the context within which the parties operate. In response to pressures occasioned by their environment and their own organizational needs, individual parties develop distinctive structures, attract personnel, and frame goals that they hope to achieve. They engage in activities designed to realize objectives of immediate relevance to the political system, such as, contesting for office, educating citizens to policy decisions, and facilitating the organism's adjustment to its surroundings. The two classifications of effort can be labeled "instrumental," or goal-directed, and "adaptive," respectively. The activities stressed and the relative success of their execution have consequences both for the organization and its environment.

Party programs that contribute to the realization of systemic objectives, that is, those clearly related to the process of governing, are the more visible and important, and correspondingly receive the greatest attention. However, once political parties become viable entities, they develop a commitment to assuring the group's continued existence, a consideration that can interfere with the promotion of group or policy interests of restricted appeal. The exchange of a group-advocate stance for a more inclusive representative posture and the costs involved in such transformations receive their classic statement in Michels' early writings.[74]

Strains generated by the organization's will to survive and its corresponding response to pluralistic social forces can be resolved through: (1) a coalitional attempt to put forward priority items of meaning to the greatest number of electors, the American experience; (2) an accommodation designed to advance in diluted form a group's welfare or a particular strain of ideology, yet in combination with other policy interests directed at sufficient numbers of voters to enable the party to exercise substantial influence on policy making—a constraint upon the operations of European socialist parties that Michels recognized but whose resolution he deplored; and (3) a failure to compromise with other social groupings, in other words, an explicit unwillingness to change. In the last situation, the party retains its original identity, its goals intact, and its limited electoral support, and hopes for factors beyond its control to rearrange electoral forces in its favor.

The focal point for integrating an analysis of these diverse forces is the organization of the party. The institutional forms that become associated with a party reflect the accommodation reached between societal pressures and group needs. An examination of the organization of the party and a sketching of its distinctive structural attributes could be employed for distinguishing the political party from other subsystems within its environment, for evaluating its priority-ordering mechanisms, and for interrelating its activities. Comparatively, the organization of political parties could be conceptualized in a manner conducive to investigating cross-national differences in group dimensions and functions.

Party organizational analysis is not new and not without defects. This particular line of inquiry represents one of the oldest and one of the most frustrating. Parties can epitomize the "flagrantly open system" that, Katz and Kahn argue, characterize some varieties of social organization.[75] Party structures in the United States, and more than likely in the traditional political systems in which they are found to exist, would approximate this polar extreme. In such cases, boundary identification is difficult to establish, membership ties are diffuse, participation in party affairs is sporadic, and authority structures and role differentiation are unclear. The structural dissimilarities between parties and more conventional bureaucracies are clearly discernible.

The inability to approach party analysis from a conventional organizational perspective or to modify, for party organizational exploration, indices constructed to study more tightly bureaucratized groups—schools, hospitals, government agencies, military establishments, or business organizations—is an additional source of frustration to the researcher.[76] The lack of conventionally adaptable guides from studies on more highly structured groups necessitates caution in specifying the component units and their limits and requires experimentation with indices. In this regard, party research, whether approached from an organizational perspective or some other, needs an extensive development of empirical indices to encourage both comparative research and a turn toward cumulative field investigations of the institution and its operations.

Numerous studies have struggled with the difficulties inherent in organizational analysis. An exploration of the development and use of organizational measures in determining combined county and pre-cinct activity in North Carolina[77] indicates that they can account for a portion of the variance in the distribution of the vote between the contending parties. Such indices can be constructed from data collected with a modest amount of financing. The findings of this study could be employed as a basis from which to develop other studies within states or among sets of states in order to build, through comparative analysis, a generally accepted propositional inventory on middle-level party operations and their significance.

In attempting to assess the formal and informal interaction processes within organizations, and between organizational personnel and those not officially identified with the organization, political parties would be analyzed as a set of interdependent actors operating within a given group context and performing acts calculated to realize instrumental and adaptive objectives. In empirical research, the specific organizational positions investigated could vary, depending on the intentions of the researcher. For example, an investigator con-cerned with structural associations as they affect performance could focus on developing the interrelationships among formal party office-holders and the comparative differences in behavior among incum-bents. The analysis could be expanded to include informal contacts among actors and the part played by nonelected individuals in party decision making. Informal leaders who influence party affairs, yet do not hold party office, could be identified through the perceptions of organizational officers or through nomination techniques developed in the community studies.

An example of the inclusion of such considerations into a field study is provided by a 1962 analysis of party-nomination practices at the county level in Indiana.[78] The study was designed to examine the influences on the nomination process exerted by both profes-sional party activists and interested citizens within the county. Candi-dates for office in one county were interviewed concerning their own decision-making processes, the individuals who influenced these pro-cesses, and the factors they perceived as being important in the nomination fight. Party leaders were questioned about their role in the recruitment process and about those whom they consulted on party matters. And finally, community leaders were contacted and interviewed concerning their contribution to specific nomination decisions and their relationship to the formal party organization. The latter were chosen through reputational techniques commonly employed in community studies. The findings were compared with those taken from more limited investigations in fifteen other com-parable counties. The result was a balanced analysis of party opera-tions that begins to assess the complex interrelationship between formal and informal party participants.

Political Parties and Role Theory

Role theory could prove useful in conceptualizing organizational positions and developing the factors that unite an organization's personnel and shape group boundaries. Difficulties exist in adapting role theory to the analysis of political parties, difficulties that relate both to the nature of the subject matter under study and the conceptual diffuseness of the theory. The comparative variety among organizational types and, within one classification of party structures, among role relationships, is potentially great, although it remains essentially unexplored.[79] Figures 3 and 4 illustrate two polar types of organizations and, secondarily, the nature of the problems with which the researcher must contend. Figure 3 corresponds to a highly articulated organizational pattern with clear perception of duties, little overlap among roles, identifiable role and boundary lines, and a hierarchical decision-making system. This diagram would reflect the more highly bureaucratized and perhaps militant parties, such as various ideological subtypes and even the combat groups outlined by Selznick.[80] Figure 4 indicates a relaxed organizational structure with much duplication of effort, an absence of centralized direction, permeable boundaries, and, by inference, a poorly developed sense of organizational purpose. American political parties at the national level and in most of the states would approximate this extreme. Problem areas that could be elaborated for analysis include the specificity-diffuseness of roles, modal types, the parochial or universal characterizations of actor roles, the balance between individual and collective forces, self-perception as it influences role playing, attributes of personnel, motivations for and gratifications from group involvement, and other such variables. All are legitimate research concerns to the extent that they contribute to the investigator's objectives.[81] As the research expands in scope and volume, more sophisticated studies of role sets and activity patterns should emerge.

Role theory may prove of greatest utility in creating a conception of the organization for exploratory analyses that suggest questions and relationships a researcher could later explore in more detail. It may also continue to be of use for describing observed behavior or for organizing explanations in which the "roles" played are amalgams of activity patterns that result from a complex of other forces—the organization-oriented as against campaign-oriented party official.[82] For the more precise type of empirical research advocated herein, in which the party and its operations are conceptualized in terms that permit employing operational indices adaptable to comparative quantitative analyses, the contribution of role theory is less pronounced. If it is employed to supply a comparative working orientation, the emphasis should be on the activity patterns of the organizations and less on prescriptive concerns. The resulting comparisons then should

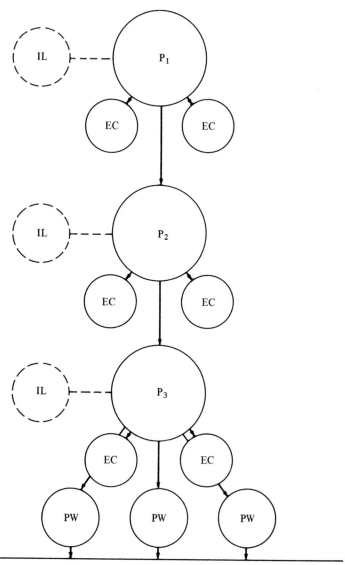

Clientele Groups (Environment)

KEY IL = Informal Leaders
     EC = Executive Committee Member
     C = Candidate
     P₁⎤
     P₂⎬= Formal Party Organizational
     P₃⎦ Positions at Different
            Hierarchical Levels
     PW = Party Workers

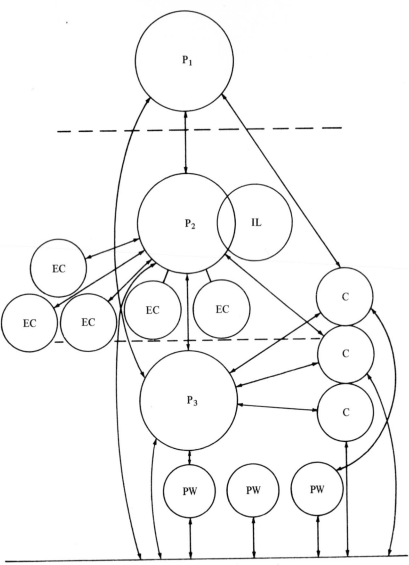

FIGURE 4. Role Relationships within Party Organizations:
Diffused Role Structure

Clientele Groups (Environment)

KEY   IL = Informal Leaders
EC = Executive Committee Member
C = Candidate
P_1 Formal Party Organizational
P_2 = Positions at Different
P_3 Hierarchical Levels
PW = Party Workers

build from actual behavior towards judging systemic impact of individual parties and relative differences among party systems.[83] The relationship between the behavior expected of role incumbents and what they in fact do in promoting candidates for office, in contacting voters, and the like, is problematical. There could well be no significant empirical relationship between the two. The burden of the argument here is that party organizations and their personnel are more profitably conceived of as responses to group and environmental pressures, which they handle in distinctive fashion. If so, there are definite limits to what an activist can do, regardless of the expectations he or others have of what he should do.

There are perhaps as many arguments against role theory as there are critics. Its difficulties need not be elaborated. It does have utility for descriptive and exploratory works as noted, and possibly, though less assuredly, for comparatively assessing party operations within cultural arenas. An investigator should be aware of the limitations of role theory and cautious in introducing it into his research; and if he does employ it, he should be precise in developing the interrelationships stressed. In addition, the systematic inclusion of validity checks should serve to minimize some of its drawbacks. Role theory, if applied in a more limited context, is less a working theory than a broadly defined data-gathering strategy that suggests group dimensions and patterns of relationship susceptible to exploration.

V. EXAMPLES OF PARTY ORGANIZATIONAL ANALYSIS

The best known of the contemporary studies that focus on party organization and empirically trace its relationship to its setting are those by Katz and Eldersveld, Eldersveld, Valen and Katz, and Rossi and Cutright.[84] Their research focuses on party structure, or aspects of it, and attempts to quantify and to gauge the effectiveness of its operations. The studies concentrate on party activity and organization in Detroit during the 1956 Presidential election, in the Stravanger area of southern Norway during the 1957 Storting (parliamentary) elections, and in Gary, Indiana, during the 1955 primary and 1956 general elections.

The Eldersveld and Valen-Katz studies are the most broadly conceived. They are also closely related in focus, research design, and analysis. Katz's association with the Detroit study, which included a joint report of direct relevance here, provides a connecting link between the two investigations. The findings of the Detroit study, in concert with a general knowledge of American party practices, are periodically introduced into the Norwegian report to provide a loose comparative perspective. Illustrating cross-national differences is understandably of secondary interest in studies that, while internally structured to permit comparative analysis, are confined to investigating party behavior within a specified community. The chief differences between the projects are in the lesser attention devoted to intra-organizational activities and the greater effort expended on describing electoral behavior in the Norwegian study, a concern not so pressing for Eldersveld, given the plethora of studies on American voting behavior. Each study achieves its immediate objectives, and each is a significant research contribution in its own right. Viewed together, they suggest the potential of related cross-national research on party operations.

The Rossi and Cutright explorations are more limited than either of the foregoing two studies. In a series of three articles, they report on efforts to devise candidate and party "input" measures and to isolate these as influences with discernible impact on the primary and general election vote. Measures of socioeconomic status and the ethnic composition of the population are constructed and employed to predict through multiple regression analysis "expected" primary and Presidential returns (Table 1). The extent to which party or candidate effort could account for the variance from the predicted vote constitutes the criterion of their impact, or effectiveness.

The party organizational measure at the local level was based on an assessment of the extent to which a "good" (active) precinct leader appears to influence the vote. The organizational indices intro-duced into the study include a profile of the precinct leader's involvement in elections and his investment in his work, as indicated by his politically relevant daily contacts and time devoted to his job. The gauge of intensity of precinct leader support for primary candi-dates ranges along a continuum from failure to do anything to personally approaching voters through precinct canvasses. The index of candidate input is a composite measure based on the total workers at his disposal and the number of home meetings held on his behalf within a precinct. Both variables are taken from estimates made by the precinct leaders.

Multiple correlation is employed to calculate the relationship between the activity patterns and the normal vote, which is derived from the socioeconomic variables. It was found that candidate and precinct activity does appear to influence the vote and that such other organization-related variables as patronage density, operationalized as the number of governmental employees within the precinct, corre-late positively with the election outcome and with the number of voters who could identify a candidate.

Katz and Eldersveld advance this strategy of investigation in their joint analysis of party operations in Detroit,[85] a report that preceded Eldersveld's more comprehensive publication and the one most directly comparable to the Gary study. The Rossi and Cutright elite (party leader) sample is based on a mail questionnaire. In addition, the analysis draws on a precinct sample and aggregate

TABLE 1. Two Studies of Party Organization

Study	Environmental (Predictor) Variables	Conceptualization of Party as Conversion Agency	Output Measure

Rossi and Cutright (Gary, Ind.), 1955, 1956
Data: aggregate socioeconomic and electoral data, mail-interview elite sample (precinct leaders), survey of precinct voters
	1. SES (Socioeconomic status)
	  a. Median rental
	  b. percent owner-occupied dwellings
	2. Ethnic
	  a. "Old" (those with English, Scottish, German, or Scandinavian names)
	  b. "New" (all other white immigrants)
		1. Determination of precinct leader effectiveness
		  a. median number of people contacted daily in precinct
		  b. time on the job, 21 hours or more per week during campaign period
		  c. proportion, over one-half, of precinct voters known personally
		2. Precinct-leader support for candidate
		  a. no support
		  b. minor support—told voters whom he supported if asked, distributed literature at polls
		  c. medium support—spoke on behalf of candidate to acquaintances
		  d. strong support—campaigned door-to-door for candidates
		3. Candidate activity measure
		  a. number of workers of candidate in precinct
		  b. number of house parties held on behalf of candidate
		4. Patronage deployment*
			1. Predicted vote, Presidential
			2. Predicted vote, primary
			3. Candidate "notoriety"; number of voters in precinct who knew candidate's name

Katz and Eldersveld (Detroit, Mich.), 1956
Data: aggregate socioeconomic and electoral data, extended-interview elite sample (142 precinct leaders), mass sample (596 voters in 87 precincts)†
	1. SES
	  a. Religion (percent Catholic)
	  b. Occupation (percent blue collar)
	  c. Race (percent Negro)
	  d. Education (percent completed eighth grade or more)
		1. Dimensions of party leader behavior
		  a. internal
		  b. representative
		  c. external
		  d. administrative
		  e. strength of motivational commitment
			1. Expected Presidential Vote

*Patronage consisted of the city administration's control over several hundred local government positions, not including police, firemen, and school crossing guards. The distribution of workers in the specific jobs by precincts was employed to determine the patronage density, or "heavy" and "light" patronage areas.

†Same data reported in more depth in Samuel Eldersveld, *Political Parties: A Behavioral Analysis.*

census and electoral data. The Katz-Eldersveld Detroit study includes
more reliable and inclusive elite data drawn from intensive interviews
with 142 precinct leaders and a mass sample of 596 voters in the
87 precincts randomly drawn for interviewing on a multistage probability basis.[86] The analysis also employs socioeconomic and voting
data. As in the Rossi and Cutright study, an expected vote is determined for each of the precincts, based on socioeconomic variables
(religion, occupation, race, and education); the variables, however,
have little overlap with those used to predict the expected vote in
the Gary study (see Table 1).

Katz and Eldersveld devise a more representative index of party-
leadership activity intended to include five dimensions of organizational behavior—internal, representative, external, administrative, and
strength of motivational commitment. A respondent is scored on each
variable in the index on the basis of his answers to questions as to
whether he kept records, registered voters, participated in fund
raising, and the like. The findings in this latter study are extensive.
Similarly to the Rossi and Cutright and other research,[87] it was
found that while socioeconomic variables are better predictors of the
vote, party organization and activity did influence electoral behavior;
that minority party activity appears to have greater effect on an
imminent election; and that the impact of one party is a product of
both situational conditions and the extensiveness of opposition-party
activities. When organizational effort of the two parties is roughly
equivalent, neutralizing each other, socioeconomic predictors come
within one percentage point of predicting the actual Presidential vote.
Among the precincts varying the most in party output, Katz and
Eldersveld are able to attribute as much as 10.5 percent of the
difference in the outcome to party activity—twice the maximum
Rossi and Cutright could account for.

All of the foregoing studies are broadly related; yet it is difficult
to generalize with confidence from one to the other. Each employs
its own conceptualization of the organization and of environmental
stimuli. For the most part, they remain carefully executed case
studies, each with its characteristic strengths and weaknesses. The
Rossi and Cutright findings, in particular, are restricted by the conception of the precinct captain as an entity virtually independent of
his immediate locality or broad social and organizational group forces.
As the authors themselves note, neither the distinctive attributes of
the party nor the horizontal or vertical aspects of party interactions
receive treatment in the analysis or are entertained as potentially
relevant dimensions of behavior in their conceptualization of this level
of party operations. The correlation between patronage and the vote
would indicate that a decision as to the deployment of a scarce
resource is an important organizational matter, and that a more
unified activist-in-group-context approach to the organization would

have improved their conceptualization of the party substantially. In general, the bureaucratic indices represent analytic conveniences more than valid, or theoretically determined, measures of organization.

Methodological shortcomings of each of the studies could be elaborated at length, but the studies modestly make no claims along these lines. They are best perceived as imaginative, exploratory ventures whose attraction for those interested in comparative parties lies in the research avenues explored. The studies break new ground, and represent, especially the inclusive studies of Detroit and Stravanger, significant additions to the literature. Yet even these only begin to tap the potential of the approach for intra-national or cross-national comparative analysis. They suggest ways in which to conceptualize and measure political parties as organizations reflecting diverse pressures, operating within restricted boundaries, and performing acts of consequence for the system. In a somewhat different vein, they contribute a series of propositions (some explicit as in the Valen and Katz report, others implicit in the research findings) that could be employed initially to guide related studies.

The immediate need is for a period devoted to complementary research undertakings: (1) building an empirical data bank on parties that will add to our limited understanding of the institution and its operations, and (2) experimenting with a series of different indices of party structure and output as they relate to chosen achievement and cultural measures. One major advantage of studies similar to the Rossi and Cutright research and the aspects of the Detroit study reported in the Katz and Eldersveld article, as well as those on county party organizations introduced earlier, is their flexibility and adaptability, qualities well suited to exploratory measurement ventures within limited populations. During experimental phases, such studies provide opportunities for devising gauges of performance and environmental interaction within reasonably narrow bounds, such as specified communities, and can be executed as exploratory works with no substantial commitments of manpower of financial resources. Whatever they contribute in addition to an understanding of parties is welcome.

Over-all, more broadly conceived measures of party organization and its output need to be developed. If voting is retained as a principal gauge of party impact, as it should be, multilevel and more discriminating measures of party performance as it affects the vote should be devised. Primary turnout and support for organizational candidates are superior indicators of party effectiveness. A reliance on Presidential returns is less satisfactory. The Presidential race is farthest removed from the immediate responsibilities and rewards of local party-unit activists and, conversely, the one of greatest interest and visibility to the voter. Community elections, on the other hand, are frequently nonpartisan in form or in practice. Between the two, there is a range of elections—county, district, and state—that could be employed in combination with the two polar types to construct a series of indices sensitive to party influence in a specific election or over time. In the latter regard, longitudinal analyses of party development and of shifts in personnel and emphases would be most helpful. However, presently there are no available data on the organization and its activities over time that can be analytically related to the more plentiful longitudinal aggregate information. More discouragingly, the possibilities for accumulating such information would appear long-range, following the general acceptance of the utility of organizational perspectives and the accumulation through cross-sectional research of descriptions of party operations.

VI. CONCLUSION

Political parties research has been particularly slow in capitalizing on the promise of comparative research. Duverger emphasized the point in 1951, and the situation is little improved today.[88] The need of comparative intra-national and cross-national research in acquiring reliable data on an important institution of modern society cannot be overemphasized. American state and local parties could be explored in a series of conceptually related ventures. Cross-national research is more demanding of time and sound financing. The continuing refinement of data collection and analytic techniques and the rapid advancements in computer technology provide tools needed for processing large quantities of materials. These tools should also assist in standardizing the conditions of data collection and evaluation. Difficulties that arise in comparative work are not be be minimized, as witnessed by the scarcity of research examples. The failure to engage in such research appears to result primarily from an unwillingness to confront fundamental methodological problems involved in conceptualizing the party in a manner conducive to related empirical investigations. This belief has served as an operating assumption for this chapter. In recognition of the problem, an attempt has been made to assess prominent theoretical alternatives to approaching research on political parties. Derivatives of systems theory and structural-functional analysis have been reviewed within a frame of reference employing empirical utility as the criterion. Downs's more formal deduction of a series of testable propositions from basic assumptions concerning democratic government and the value and present status of propositional inventories relevant to an understanding of political parties have also received attention.

In a related vein, the principal efforts to formulate comparative typologies[89]—Neumann's developmental models with different emphases, and the comparative sociological perspective of Lipset and Rokkan—have been assessed in terms of what they can contribute to an appreciation of contemporary party configurations. Consideration has also been given to the compatability of each approach with either an adaptation to field research or exploitation through the application of extant empirical data, either of which could serve to evolve more sophisticated, and powerful, explanatory theories. Finally, a perspective emphasizing the interrelationship of the political party with its setting and employing the concepts of organization and role as convenient focal points for integrating the many concerns of the parties researcher has been advanced. Over-all, the preference is for an inductive approach to theory, built up from studies sharing a common perspective and addressed to essentially related problems.

A concern with the conceptual problems of parties research can further such objectives and contribute to comparative research on political behavior generally. A consistent methodological attack on the problems of developing equivalent cross-cultural indicators and agreed-upon standards for the clarification and operationalization of widely applicable concepts relevant to the study of political parties as well as the acceptance of realistic criteria of significance for comparative work in general directly advance scientific inquiry on all fronts. Equally important, intra-national and cross-national comparative investigations afford an opportunity for bridging the troublesome distinction between micro- and macrolevel theories of political behavior, especially in focusing on institutions that perform linkage functions within the broader system. The political party is such an agency. Such research contributes to exploratory middle-range theories tied to empirical data, a base from which to construct the broader, more systematic, and more formal theories desired to explain political behavior.

NOTES

I appreciate the comments received on an earlier draft of this paper from Douglas S. Gatlin and my colleagues at Northwestern University.

1. For a discussion of recent voting studies and their interrelated development consult Peter Rossi, "Four Landmarks in Voting Research," *American Voting Behavior,* eds. Eugene Burdick and Arthur J. Brodbeck (New York: Free Press, 1959), pp. 5-54; Rossi, "Trends in Voting Behavior Research: 1933-1963," *Political Opinion and Electoral Behavior: Essays and Studies,* eds. Edward C. Dreyer and Walter A. Rosenbaum (Belmont: Wadsworth, 1966), pp. 67-76; and Robert T. Golembiewski, William A. Welsh, and William J. Crotty, *A Methodological Primer for Political Scientists* (Chicago: Rand McNally, 1968), Ch. XII.

2. Avery Leiserson develops the significance of parties research in his "The Place of Parties in the Study of Politics," *American Political Science Review,* LI (December 1957), 945-954; and in his *Parties and Politics: An Institutional and Behavioral Approach* (New York: Knopf, 1958). See also

Martin Grodzins, "American Political Parties and the American System," *Western Political Quarterly*, XIII (December 1960), 974-998.

3. Samuel J. Eldersveld, *Political Parties: A Behavioral Analysis.* (Chicago: Rand McNally, 1964).

4. Neil A. McDonald, *The Study of Political Parties* (Garden City: Doubleday, 1955); Bernard Hennessy, "On the Study of Party Organization," *Approaches to the Study of Party Organization*, ed. William J. Crotty (Boston: Allyn & Bacon, 1968), pp. 1-44; Joseph A. Schlesinger, "Political Party Organization," *Handbook of Organizations*, ed. James March (Chicago: Rand McNally, 1965), pp. 764-801; and *International Encyclopedia of the Social Sciences* (New York: Macmillan, 1968), XII, pp. 428-435. For a relevant development of one of the intellectual strains in parties research, see Golembiewski, Welsh, and Crotty, op. cit., Ch. X.

5. Talcott Parsons, "The Political Aspect of Social Structure and Process," *Varieties of Political Theory*, ed. David Easton (Englewood Cliffs: Prentice-Hall, 1966), p. 110.

6. Eugene J. Meehan, *The Theory and Method of Political Analysis* (Homewood: Dorsey, 1965), p. 130.

7. David Easton, "Alternative Strategies in Theoretical Research," *Varieties of Political Theory*, ed. Easton, op. cit., p. 9. Contrast this point of view with that in Morris R. Cohen and Ernest Nagel, *An Introduction to Logic and Scientific Method* (New York: Harcourt, Brace, 1934).

8. Merton writes: "Throughout this book . . . the term *sociological theory* refers to logically interconnected conceptions which are limited and modest in scope, rather than all-embracing and grandiose . . . what might be called *theories of the middle range:* theories intermediate to the minor working hypotheses evolved in abundance during the day-to-day routines of research, and the all-inclusive speculations comprising a master conceptual scheme from which it is hoped to derive a very large number of empirically observed uniformities of social behavior." Robert K. Merton, *Social Theory and Social Structure* (rev. ed.; New York: Free Press, 1957), pp. 5-6. The Merton approach is inductive, as is the principal emphasis in this chapter.

9. This position contrasts somewhat with that championed by Crowe and Mayo in their synthetic analysis of the party literature from a systemic perspective. They contend "that the discipline has been marking time, indulging in the repetition of not quite completely analagous studies for want of . . . a broad-range theory. Nor is this to say that there is no longer any need for the development of low-range and middle-range theory: this work must go on but in conjunction with the development of broad-range theory." Beryl L. Crowe and Charles G. Mayo, "The Structural-Functional Concept of a Political Party," *American Political Parties: A Systemic Perspective*, eds. Mayo and Crowe (New York: Harper & Row, 1967), p. 35. William Riker, in assessing the discipline as a whole, is in emphatic agreement with the need for formal, broadly conceived theories to push beyond the bounds of conventional wisdom. Riker, *The Theory of Political Coalitions* (New Haven: Yale University Press, 1962), pp. 6-7. The present discussion emphasizes grass-roots building of theory of a low-to-middle-range nature from investigations. Grander theories and useful formal theorizing of the kind Riker argues for appear farther off, although possibilities along these lines are discussed below.

10. The distinction between macro- and microtheories is elaborated in

Stein Rokkan, "The Comparative Study of Political Participation: Notes Toward a Perspective on Current Research," *Essays on the Behavioral Study of Politics,* ed. Austin Ranney (Urbana: University of Illinois Press, 1962), pp. 47-90.

11. In this regard, the comparative analysis of the dynamics of the party as an early and powerful socializing agent for the political system is a worthwhile focus. This perspective has developed most fully in the writings of Easton, Hess, Dennis, and Greenstein. See David Easton and Robert D. Hess, "The Child's Political World," *Midwest Journal of Political Science,* VI (August 1962), 229-246. Compare these findings on socialization for American parties with those for a French population in Philip E. Converse and Georges Dupeux, "Politicization of the Electorate in France and the United States," *Elections and the Political Order,* eds. Angus Campbell, Philip E. Converse, Warren E. Miller, and Donald E. Stokes (New York: Wiley, 1966), pp. 269-291.

12. See David Easton, *A Systems Analysis of Political Life* (New York: Wiley, 1965); Easton, *A Framework for Political Analysis* (Englewood Cliffs: Prentice-Hall, 1965).

13. The most relevant of Almond's work is found in his "Introduction: A Functional Approach to Comparative Politics," *The Politics of the Developing Areas,* eds. Gabriel A. Almond and James S. Coleman (Princeton: Princeton University Press, 1960), pp. 3-64; and, with G. Bingham Powell, Jr., *Comparative Politics: A Developmental Approach* (Boston: Little, Brown, 1966), pp. 99-127. Consult, in addition to Almond, William C. Mitchell, *Sociological Analysis: The Theories of Talcott Parsons* (Englewood Cliffs: Prentice-Hall, 1967); Mitchell, *The American Polity* (New York: Free Press, 1962); Talcott Parsons, "The Political Aspect of Social Structure and Process," op. cit.; Parsons, "Voting and the Equilibrium of the American Political System," *American Voting Behavior,* eds. Burdick and Brodbeck, op. cit., pp. 80-120; Parsons, "On the Concept of Political Power," *Proceedings of the American Philosophical Society,* CVII (June 1963), pp. 232-262.

14. Almond and Powell, ibid., p. 117.

15. Douglas S. Gatlin, "Toward a Functionalist Theory of Political Parties: Inter-Party Competition in North Carolina," *Approaches the Study of Party Organization,* ed. William Crotty, op. cit., pp. 217-246.

16. Marvin Harder and Thomas Ungs, "Notes Toward a Functional Analysis of Local Party Organizations," paper presented at the Midwest Conference of Political Scientists, 1963.

17. The problems in such an adaptation are illustrated by and, to an extent, discussed in Gabriel A. Almond and Sidney Verba, *The Civic Culture* (Princeton: Princeton University Press, 1963).

18. Anthony Downs, *An Economic Theory of Democracy* (New York: Harper & Row, 1957), pp. 11-12.

19. Ibid., p. 25.

20. Ibid., p. 21.

21. Ibid., p. 33. Emphasis added.

22. Donald E. Stokes, "Spatial Models of Party Competition," *American Political Science Review,* LVII (June 1963), 368-377. Also found in Campbell et al., op. cit., pp. 161-179. A work not discussed here but one that deals with similar concerns is Gordon Tullock, *Toward a Mathematics of Politics*

(Ann Arbor: University of Michigan Press, 1968).

23. Such an argument was put forward by the supporters of Barry Goldwater in seeking the 1964 Republican Presidential nomination. It is not clear, however, the extent to which this point of view was accepted as an explanation of those who did not turn out—certainly the balance of empirical evidence indicated that this point of view did not hold—and the extent to which it served as a tactical maneuver to enhance the candidates electoral "winability." The conservative Taft also used the same argument in attempting to gain the 1952 Republican Presidential nomination. For assessments of the 1964 nomination fight and Presidential campaign, see Charles O. Jones, "The 1964 Presidential Election—Further Adventures in Wonderland," *American Government Annual, 1965-1966,* ed. Donald G. Herzberg (New York: Holt, Rinehart & Winston, 1965), pp. 1-30; Philip E. Converse, Aage R. Clausen, and Warren E. Miller, "Electoral Myth and Reality: The 1964 Election," *American Political Science Review,* LIX (June 1965), 321-336; Theodore H. White, *The Making of the President: 1964* (New York: Signet, 1965).

24. Converse and Dupeux, op. cit., pp. 269-291.

25. Philip E. Converse, "The Problem of Party Distances in Models of Voting Change," *The Electoral Process,* eds. M. Kent Jennings and L. Harmon Zeigler (Englewood Cliffs: Prentice-Hall, 1966), pp. 175-207.

26. Ibid, p. 193.

27. Robert R. Alford, "Class Voting in the Anglo-American Political Systems," *Party Systems and Voter Alignments: Cross-National Perspectives,* eds. Seymour M. Lipset and Stein Rokkan (New York: Free Press, 1967), pp. 67-93; Alford, *Party and Society* (Chicago: Rand McNally, 1963), especially pp. 250-286.

28. Philip E. Converse, "The Nature of Belief Systems in Mass Publics," *Ideology and Discontent,* ed. David Apter (New York: Free Press, 1964), pp. 206-262.

29. Murray B. Levin, with George Blackwood, *The Compleat Politican* (Indianapolis: Bobbs-Merrill, 1962).

30. Riker, op. cit., pp. 149-158.

31. Charles Sellers, "The Equilibrium Cycle in Two-Party Politics," *Public Opinion Quarterly,* XXIX (Spring 1965), 16-37. Riker illustrates the possibilities, ibid., pp. 54-66. Another relevant example of a theory adapted from economics and directly related to party concerns would be Michael Leiserson's application of a modified Von Neumann-Morgenstern theory of coalitions to the study of Japanese political parties, "Factions and Coalitions in One-Party Japan: An Explanation Based on the Theory of Games," *American Political Science Review,* LXII (September 1968).

32. David Braybrooke, "Some Steps Toward a Formal System of Political Science" (New Haven: Department of Philosophy, Yale University, mimeographed, September 1957). A partial reproduction of Braybrooke's piece in modified form is found in Braybrooke, "An Illustrative Miniature Axiomatic System," *Politics and Social Life: An Introduction to Political Behavior,* eds. Nelson W. Polsby, Robert A. Dentler and Paul A. Smith (Boston: Houghton Mifflin, 1963), pp. 119-130.

33. Ibid., pp. 21-22.

34. Ibid., p. 22.

35. The man-hours of work involved in any sophisticated computer model building and the financial cost of such simulations create problems. An impressive computer simulation that deals with campaigning and opinion preferences and hence is of relevance to parties is Ithiel Pool, Robert P. Abelson, and Samuel L. Popkin, *Candidates, Issues, and Strategies: A Computer Simulation of the 1960 Presidential Election* (Cambridge: M.I.T. Press, 1964).

36. See Kenneth Janda, "Retrieving Information for a Comparative Study of Political Parties," *Approaches to the Study of Party Organization*, ed. Crotty, op. cit., pp. 159-216.

37. James S. Coleman and Carl G. Rosberg, Jr. (eds.), *Political Parties and National Integration in Tropical Africa* (Berkeley: University of California Press, 1966), pp. 655-691; Thomas Hodgkin, *African Political Parties* (Baltimore: Penguin, 1961); Frank J. Sorauf, *Political Parties in the American System* (Boston: Little, Brown, 1964), p. 161.

38. Sigmund Neumann (ed.), *Modern Political Parties* (Chicago: University of Chicago Press, 1966).

39. Ibid., p. v.

40. "Toward a Comparative Study of Political Parties," ibid., pp. 395-421.

41. Aristide R. Zolberg, *One-Party Government in the Ivory Coast* (Princeton: Princeton University Press, 1964); Richard L. Sklar, *Nigerian Political Parties* (Princeton: Princeton University Press, 1963); David Apter, *The Gold Coast in Transition* (Princeton: Princeton University Press, 1955), revised as *Ghana in Transition* (New York: Atheneum, 1963). A fine overview of this area is contained in Aristide R. Zolberg, *Creating Political Order: The Party States of West Africa* (Chicago: Rand McNally, 1966). Differences among one-party systems are discussed in Jerzy J. Wiatr, " 'One-Party' Systems—The Concept and Issue for Comparative Studies," *Cleavages, Ideologies and Party Systems: Contributions to Comparative Political Sociology*, eds. Erik Allardt and Krjo Littunen (Helsinki: Transactions of the Westermarck Society, Vol. 10, 1964), pp. 281-290. A discussion of problems in comparative analysis and a review of the literature for communist countries that has relevance for the present discussion is contained in Paul Shoup, "Comparing Communist Nations: Propsects for an Empirical Approach," *American Political Science Review*, LXII (March 1968), 185-204.

Examples of the principally historical treatment of parties in these countries would be Leonard Schapiro, *The Communist Party of the Soviet Union* (New York: Random House, 1960); M. K. Dziewanowski, *The Communist Party of Poland* (Cambridge: Harvard University Press, 1959); Richard F. Staar, *Poland 1944-1962: The Sovietization of a Captive People* (Baton Rouge: Louisiana State University Press, 1962). In general, there appear to be few comparative, empirical efforts in this area and a tendency in works to employ value-laden terminology and even to lapse into a disconcerting editorializing. Representative contributions to comparative social science inquiry are limited. Fleron evaluates the relevance of social science perspectives for communist studies in "Soviet Area Studies and the Social Sciences: Some Methodological Problems in Communist Studies," *Soviet Studies*, XIX (January 1968), 313-339.

An exploration of what can be done in analyzing parties in another area,

Latin American Studies, not noted for comparative research efforts, is Edward J. Williams, *Latin American Christian Democratic Parties* (Knoxville: University of Tennessee Press, 1967).

Finally, a review of the source materials available on communist nations, in particular Bulgaria and North Korea, from the project under the direction of Kenneth Janda to retrieve and code materials relevant to the study of parties, introduced below, indicates that there may be more usable documentary and interpretive data accessible than is realized. Curiously, the materials in English on a democratic country, Greece, are quite limited. Kenneth Janda, *A Microfilm and Computer System for Analyzing Comparative Politics Literature* (Evanston: International Comparative Parties Project, Report No. 3, November 1967), p. 12.

42. Joseph LaPalombara and Myron Weiner (eds.), *Political Parties and Political Development* (Princeton: Princeton University Press, 1966).

43. Two good beginnings along these lines are Leiserson, *Parties and Politics;* Austin Ranney and Willmore Kendall, *Democracy and the American Party System* (New York: Harcourt, Brace, 1956), pp. 83-154.

44. Joseph LaPalombara and Myron Weiner, "The Origin and Development of Political Parties," *Political Parties and Political Development,* eds. LaPalombara and Weiner, op. cit., p. 35.

45. Ibid.

46. Myron Weiner and Joseph LaPalombara, "The Impact of Parties on Political Development," ibid., pp. 399-435.

47. Seymour Martin Lipset, *Political Man: The Social Bases of Politics* (Garden City: Doubleday, 1960). See also Philips Cutright, "National Political Development: Measurement and Analysis," *American Sociological Review,* XXVIII (April 1963), 253-264.

48. Giovanni Sartori, *Parties and Party Systems* (New York: Harper & Row, forthcoming). Sartori's more comprehensive work was not available at the time of this writing. Hans Dadler also presents a fine discussion of cleavages that affect party systems and the oversimplifications in categorizations that can result in his "Parties, Elites, and Political Development in Western Europe," *Political Parties and Political Development,* eds. LaPalombara and Weiner, op. cit., pp. 67-69. Sartori's argument as to the causal implications of polarization for the party system has some relationship to the Downs-Stokes discussion earlier. The Downs model can account for and predict to the consequences of polarization for the parties depending on the dimension (Downs) or dimensions (Stokes) along which voter distribute themselves. The Downs model is adaptable to democratic multiparty as well as to two-party systems.

49. Seymour Martin Lipset, *The First New Nation* (New York: Basic Books, 1963). The two Chambers citations are "Parties and Nation-Building in America," *Political Parties and Political Development,* eds. LaPalombara and Weiner, op. cit., pp. 79-106; and *Political Parties in a New Nation: The American Experience 1776-1809* (New York: Oxford University Press, 1963).

50. Pye's elaboration reflects the thinking of the Comparative Politics Committee of the Social Science Research Council. Lucian W. Pye, *Aspects of Political Development* (Boston: Little, Brown, 1966), especially pp. 45-48.

51. Lipset and Rokkan, op. cit.

52. Lipset and Rokkan, "Cleavage Structures, Party Systems and Voter

Alignments: An Introduction," ibid., pp. 1-64. Similar problems specifically relating to the factors conducive to oppositions in Western Democracies are dealt with in Robert A. Dahl (ed.), *Political Oppositions in Western Democracies* (New Haven: Yale University Press, 1966). Dahl's concluding chapters provide a useful overview, pp. 332-401.

53. Lipset and Rokkan, "Cleavage Structures, Party Systems, and Voter Alignments: An Introduction," op. cit., p. 5.

54. Ibid., p. 25.

55. Ibid., p. 38.

56. V. O. Key, Jr., *Politics, Parties and Pressure Groups* (5th ed.; New York: Crowell, 1964), p. 200.

57. Fred W. Riggs, "Comparative Politics and the Study of Political Parties: A Structural Approach," *Approaches to the Study of Party Organization*, ed. Crotty, op. cit., pp. 45-104.

58. McDonald, op. cit., p. 6.

59. Almond and Powell, op. cit., p. 102.

60. Herbert McClosky, Paul J. Hoffman, and Rosemary O'Hara, "Issue Conflict and Consensus Among Party Leaders and Followers," *American Political Science Review*, LIV (June 1960), 406-429; McClosky, "Consensus and Ideology in American Politics," *American Political Science Review*, LVIII (June 1964), 361-379; Thomas A. Flinn and Frederick M. Wirt, "Local Party Leaders: Groups of Like Minded Men," *Midwest Journal of Political Science*, IX (February 1965), 77-98.

61. For examples of this strain and some assumptions of party functions subsumed from it, see Austin Ranney, *The Doctrine of Responsible Party Government* (Urbana: University of Illinois Press, 1962); James M. Burns, *The Deadlock of Democracy* (Englewood Cliffs: Prentice-Hall, 1963).

62. See, in order: Edward M. Sait, *American Parties and Elections* (New York: Century, 1927), p. 141; Ranney and Kendall, op. cit., p. 85; E. E. Schattschneider, *Party Government* (New York: Holt, 1942), pp. 35 ff; Bernard Hennessy, "On the Study of Party Organization," *Approaches to the Study of Party Organization*, ed. Crotty, op. cit., pp. 1-2.

63. Maurice Duverger, *Political Parties* (New York: Wiley, 1963), p. xv.

64. Eldersveld, op. cit., p. 1 ff.

65. The assumption of the two perspectives are treated in Howard A. Scarrow, "The Function of Political Parties: A Critique of the Literature and the Approach," *Journal of Politics*, XXIX (November 1967), 770-790. See Theodore Lowi, "Toward Functionalism in Political Science: The Case of Innovation in Party Systems," *American Political Science Review*, LVII (September 1963), 570-583; for an analysis of American party functions over time, Lowi, "Party, Policy, and Constitution in American," *The American Party Systems: Stages of Political Development*, eds. W. N. Chambers and W. D. Burnham (New York: Oxford University Press, 1967), pp. 238-276.

66. Examples of each, in order, are Flinn and Wirt, "Local Party Leaders: Groups of Like Minded Men," op. cit.; Herbert McClosky et al., "Issue Conflict and Consensus Among Party Leaders and Followers," op. cit.; McClosky, "Consensus and Ideology in American Politics," op. cit.; W. E. Binkley, *American Political Parties: Their Natural History* (New York: Knopf, 1943); Arthur N. Holcombe, *Our More Perfect Union* (Cambridge: Harvard University Press, 1950); Herbert Agar, *The Price of Union* (Boston: Houghton,

Mifflin, 1945); C. B. MacPherson, *Democracy in Alberta* (Toronto: University of Toronto Press, 1962).

67. Treatment of these topics, although their explicit relationship to the concern of the party researcher is not always clear, can be found in Campbell et al., op. cit.; Angus Campbell, Philip E. Converse, Warren E. Miller, and Donald E. Stokes, *The American Voter* (New York: Wiley, 1960); Donald R. Matthews and James W. Prothro, *Negroes and the New Southern Politics* (New York: Harcourt, Brace & World, 1966), pp. 369-404; Matthews and Prothro, "Southern Images of Political Parties: An Analysis of White and Negro Attitudes," *Journal of Politics*, XXVI (February 1964), 82-111; Almond and Verba, op. cit.; Lester Milbrath, *Political Participation* (Chicago: Rand McNally, 1965); Dwaine Marvick, "The Middlemen of Politics," *Approaches to the Study of Party Organization*, ed. Crotty, op. cit., pp. 138-199; Samuel H. Barnes, "Party Democracy and the Logic of Collective Action," ibid., pp. 105-138.

68. See the treatment in Angus Campbell et al., *The American Voter*, op. cit., and Campbell et al., *Elections and the Political Order*, op. cit. The most explicit treatment in principal voting studies of the party as an institution actively influencing voter behavior can be found in Bernard R. Berelson, Paul F. Lazarsfeld, and William N. McPhee, *Voting* (Chicago: University of Chicago Press, 1954), pp. 153-181.

69. Lipset, *Political Man;* Cutright, "National Political Development: Measurement and Analysis"; Gatlin, op. cit.; H. Eulau, "The Ecological Basis of Party Systems: The Case of Ohio," *Midwest Journal of Political Science*, I (August 1957), 125-135; Philips Cutright, "Urbanization and Competitive Party Politics," *Journal of Politics*, XXV (August 1963), 552-564; D. Gold and J. R. Schmidhauser, "Urbanization and Party Competition: The Case of Ohio, *"Midwest Journal of Political Science*, IV (February 1960), 62-75; V. O. Key, Jr., and Frank Munger, "Social Determinism and Electoral Decision: The Case of Indiana," *American Voting Behavior*, eds. Burdick and Brodbeck, op. cit., pp. 281-299; Richard E. Dawson and James A. Robinson, "Inter-Party Competition, Economic Variables, and Welfare Policies in the American States," *Journal of Politics*, XXV (May 1963), 265-289; Dawson, "Social Development, Party Competition, and Policy," *The American Party Systems: Stages of Political Development*, eds. Chambers and Burnham, op. cit., pp. 203-237; Richard L. Hofferbert, "The Relation Between Public Policy and Some Structural Variables in the American States," *American Political Science Review*, LX (March 1966), 73-82.

70. Donald R. Matthews and James W. Prothro, "Social and Economic Factors and Negro Voter Registration in the South," *American Political Science Review*, LVII (March 1963), 24-44; Matthews and Prothro, "Political Factors and Negro Voter Registration in the South," ibid. (June 1963), pp. 355-367.

71. Stanley Kelley, Jr., Richard E. Ayres, and William G. Bowen, "Registration and Voting: Putting First Things First," *American Political Science Review*, LXI (June 1967), 359-379.

72. Douglas Rae, *The Political Consequences of Electoral Laws* (New Haven: Yale University Press, 1967).

73. For relevant examples of such research, see Dawson and Robinson, op. cit.; Dawson, op. cit.; and the footnotes cited in each of the works.

.

74. Roberto Michels, *Political Parties* (New York: Dover, 1959). First published in English in 1915.

75. Daniel Katz and Robert L. Kahn, *The Social Psychology of Organizations* (New York: Wiley, 1966), p. 59. For examples of parties in traditional political systems, see Lucien W. Pye, *Politics, Personality, and Nation Building* (New Haven: Yale University Press, 1962), especially pp. 17-18; Robert L. Hess and Gerhard Lowenberg, "The Ethopian No-Party State," *American Political Science Review,* LVIII (December 1964), 947-950.

76. Lee Anderson discusses the possibilities for adapting perspectives and measurement indices from the conventional literature on organizations in "Organizational Theory and the Study of State and Local Parties," *Approaches to the Study of Party Organization,* ed. Crotty, op. cit., pp. 375-403. See also Stanley H. Udy, Jr., "The Comparative Analysis of Organizations," *Handbook of Organizations,* ed. March, op. cit., pp. 678-709; Theodore Caplow, *Principles of Organization* (New York: Harcourt, Brace & World, 1964).

77. William J. Crotty, "The Party Organization and Its Activities," *Approaches to the Study of Party Organization,* ed. Crotty, op. cit., pp. 247-306.

78. Thomas M. Watts, "Application of the Attribution Model to the Study of Political Recruitment: County Elective Offices," ibid., pp. 307-340. Robert A. Dahl employs a similar approach to studying political nominations in New Haven in *Who Governs?* (New Haven: Yale University Press, 1961), pp. 104-114.

79. Examples of the use of role theory in social science research are Neal Gross, Ward S. Mason, and Alexander W. McEachern, *Explorations in Role Analysis: Studies of the School Superintendency Role* (New York: Wiley, 1958), especially pp. 1-78; John C. Wahlke, Heinz Eulau, William Buchanan, and Leroy C. Ferguson, *The Legislative System* (New York: Wiley, 1962). An introduction to role theory can be found in Theodore Sarbin, "Role Theory," *Handbook of Social Psychology,* ed. Gardner Lindzey (Cambridge: Addison-Wesley, 1954), I, pp. 223-258; Bruce J. Biddle and Edwin J. Thomas (eds.), *Role Theory: Concepts and Research* (New York: Wiley, 1966); Talcott Parsons, *The Social System* (New York: Free Press, 1964).

80 Philip Selznick, *The Organizational Weapon* (Glencoe: The Free Press, 1960).

81. The gratifications from organizational involvement and their implications are treated in Dwaine Marvick, "The Middlemen of Politics"; Dwaine Marvick and Charles R. Nixon, "Recruitment Contrasts in Rival Campaign Groups," *Political Decision-Makers,* ed. Marvick (New York: Free Press, 1961), pp. 138-192. Various role conceptions relevant to this discussion can be found in Richard C. Hodgson, Daniel J. Levinson, and Abraham Zaleznik, *The Executive Role Constellation* (Boston: Harvard University Graduate School of Business Administration, 1965); Chris Argyris, *Personality and Organization: The Conflict Between System and the Individual* (New York: Harper, 1957).

82. A rough dichotomization of roles is illustrated in Samuel C. Patterson, "Characteristics of Party Leaders," *Western Political Quarterly,* XVI (June 1963), 332-352.

83. Unless otherwise defined in the text, a *party system* can be considered

as a collection, or set, of parties operating in any given country. A fine discussion of research questions of concern to party systems is found in Harry Eckstein, "Party Systems," *International Encyclopedia of the Social Sciences,* XII, pp. 436-453.

84. In order, these are Daniel Katz and Samuel J. Eldersveld, "The Impact of Local Party Activity upon the Electorate," *Public Opinion Quarterly,* XXV (Spring 1961), pp. 1-25; Eldersveld, op. cit.; Henry Valen and Daniel Katz, *Political Parties in Norway* (Oslo: Universitetsforlaget, 1964); Phillips Cutright and Peter H. Rossi, "Grass Roots Politicians and the Vote," *American Sociological Review,* LXIII (April 1958), 171-179; Cutright and Rossi, "Party Organization in Primary Elections," *American Journal of Sociology,* LXIV (November 1958), 262-269; Rossi and Cutright, "The Impact of Party Organization in an Industrial Setting," *Community Political Systems,* ed. Morris Janowitz (Glencoe: Free Press, 1961), pp. 81-116.

In an earlier study, Gosnell reviewed the resources at the disposal of the party organization, the shifting caliber of its personnel, and the activities conducted by precinct captains in Chicago. He also analyzed the vote for different types of elections, but made no systematic effort to trace the impact of organizational activities on voting. Harold F. Gosnell, *Machine Politics: Chicago Model* (Chicago: University of Chicago Press, 1937).

85. Katz and Eldersveld, "The Impact of Local Party Activity upon the Electorate."

86. The research design for the Detroit reports can be found in ibid., pp. 3-4, and Eldersveld, op. cit., pp. 24-44.

87. Crotty, "The Party Organization and Its Activities." See also the results from the index of candidates put forward for office as devised by Gatlin, op. cit., pp. 239-243.

88. Duverger, op. cit., p. xiii. For a more contemporary assessment, see Phyllis J. Peterson, "Political Parties: Problems of International Comparison," paper presented to the Annual Meeting of the Midwest Conference of Political Scientists, 1966, pp. 1 ff.

89. For an evaluation of Duverger's major contribution, see Golembiewski, Welsh, and Crotty, op. cit., Ch. X. A refinement of this typology is found in Janda, "Retrieving Information for a Comparative Study of Political Parties."

11 Urban Politics Research

WALLACE S. SAYRE, Columbia University

NELSON W. POLSBY, University of California, Berkeley

PRESCRIPTION BEFORE DESCRIPTION

The initial approach of American political science to its subject matter of government and politics shared the strong prescriptive tendencies of the nineteenth-century social sciences. Especially did the political scientists have a sharp sense of mission when they confronted the political and governmental institutions of urban America. In their view the urban condition was pathological, and they saw it as the proper task of the political scientists to prescribe the required remedies. This they did with vigor and eloquence, and their prescriptive mood was to endure among urban political scientists for at least a half century.

From Bryce to the Doctrines of 1915

When James Bryce in 1888 prepared the first edition of *The American Commonwealth,* there were no general systematic treatises to aid him. If one may judge from his bibliographical references, he was compelled to rely for his data concerning American cities, their government and politics, upon a few studies that had been published at Johns Hopkins University concerning individual American cities (studies that were largely historical and legalistic in content) and upon scattered articles in magazines of the decade. He also found occasionally helpful the reports of some official commissions and of several reform groups in the cities. With these materials in hand, Bryce wrote two general chapters—"The Government of Cities" and "The Working of City Governments." To these he added a chapter on "The Philadelphia Gas Ring," a chapter by Seth Low entitled "An American View of Municipal Government in the United States,"

■ Reprinted from "American Political Science and the Study of Urbanization," *The Study of Urbanization,* eds. Philip M. Hauser and Leo F. Schnore (New York: Wiley, 1965), pp. 115-156.

and a chapter by Frank J. Goodnow on "The Tweed Ring in New York City."

These five chapters not only set the stage but also determined the approach and tone for a long generation of American political scientists in looking at the government and politics of urban centers. It is therefore worth noting what Bryce and his colleagues in 1888 assumed and concluded about city government and politics.

Bryce began by declaring: "The growth of great cities has been among the most significant and least fortunate changes in the character of the population of the United States during the century since 1787." (There were thirty cities in the United States in 1888 with populations exceeding 100,000.) Bryce noted that "the history of American cities, though striking and instructive, has been short," and that although their governments

. . . have a general resemblance to those English municipalities which were their first model, their present structure shows them to have been much influenced by that of the State governments. We find in all the larger cities:

A mayor, head of the executive, and elected directly by the voters within the city

Certain executive officers or boards, some directly elected by the city voters, others nominated by the mayor or chosen by the city legislature

A legislature, consisting usually of two, but sometimes of one chamber, directly elected by the city voters

Judges, usually elected by the city voters, but sometimes appointed by the State.

What is this but the frame of a State government applied to the smaller area of the city?

After examining these arrangements in some detail, including special attention to the government of Boston (1880 population, 360,000), and after noting with disapproval the preeminent role of political parties in city elections, Bryce concluded his first chapter with the observation that

. . . The European reader . . . will contrast what may be called the political character of the whole city constitution with the somewhat simpler and less ambitious, though also less democratic arrangements, which have been found sufficient for the management of European cities.

Bryce then turned, in his second chapter, to more concrete matters.

Two questions may be applied to the government of a city: What does it provide for the people, and what does it cost the people? Space fails me to apply in detail the former of these tests, by showing what each city does or omits to do for its inhabitants; so I must be content with observing that in the United States generally constant complaints are directed against the bad paving and cleansing of the streets, the non-enforcement of the laws forbidding gambling and illicit drinking, and in some places against the sanitary arrangements and management of public buildings and parks. It would appear that in the greatest cities there is far more dissatisfaction than exists with the municipal administration in such cities as Glasgow, Liverpool, Manchester, Leeds, Dublin. . . .

The other test, that of expense, is easily applied. Both the debt and the taxation of American cities have risen with unprecedented rapidity, and now stand at an alarming figure.

Then came Bryce's famous indictment:

There is no denying that the government of cities is the one conspicuous failure of the United States. The deficiencies of the National government tell but little for evil on the welfare of the people. The faults of the State governments are insignificant compared with the extravagance, corruption, and mismanagement which mark the administration of most of the great cities . . . there is not a city with a population exceeding 200,000 where the poison germs have not sprung into a vigorous life; and in some of the smaller ones, down to 70,000 it needs no microscope to note the results of their growth. Even in the cities of the third rank similar phenomena may occasionally be discerned, though there, as some one has said, the jet black of New York and San Francisco dies away into a harmless gray.

Bryce was anxious to find an explanation:

For evils which appear wherever a large population is densely aggregated, there must be some general and widespread causes. What are these causes? . . . [The] party system . . . has, not perhaps created, but certainly enormously aggravated them, and impressed on them their specific type.

For more specific explanations, Bryce then turned to the report of the New York State Commission on Cities (1877), which had enumerated the following causes:

1. Incompetent and unfaithful governing boards and officials. . . .
2. The introduction of State and National politics into municipal affairs. . . .
3. The assumption by the legislature of the direct control of local affairs. . . .

Bryce added his own more pointed interpretation: the spoils system and the defects of the urban electorate were the central cause.

Now the Spoils system, with the party machinery which keeps it oiled and greased and always working at high pressure, is far more potent and pernicious in great cities than in country districts. For in great cities we find an ignorant multitude, largely composed of recent immigrants, untrained in self-government; we find a great proportion of the voters paying no direct taxes, and therefore feeling no interest in moderate taxation and economical administration; we find able citizens absorbed in their private business, cultivated citizens unusually sensitive to the vulgarities of practical politics, and both sets unwilling to sacrifice their time and tastes and comfort in the struggle with sordid wire-pullers and noisy demagogues. In great cities the forces that attack and pervert democratic government are exceptionally numerous, the defensive forces that protect it, exceptionally ill-placed for resistance. Satan has turned his heaviest batteries on the weakest part of the ramparts.

The remedies? Bryce adopted the recommendations of the New York Commission: (1) restrict the power of the state legislature to intervene by special legislation in the affairs of cities (the "home rule" doctrine); (2) hold municipal elections at a different period of the year from state and national elections; (3) vest the legislative powers of municipalities in two bodies—a board of aldermen, elected by the ordinary suffrage, and a smaller board of finance, elected by a limited, propertied suffrage, to have primary control over taxes, debt, expenditures; (4) limit the borrowing power of municipalities; (5) extend the powers of the mayor.

In summing up, Bryce was mildly hopeful:

City government . . . is admittedly the weak point of the country . . . Yet no one who studies the municipal history of the last decades will doubt that things are better than they were twenty years ago. The newer frames of government are an improvement upon the older. Rogues are less audacious. Good citizens are more active. Party spirit is less and less permitted to dominate and pervert municipal politics.

Bryce's American colleagues joined him in the general terms of his diagnosis and therapy. Seth Low wanted the European reader especially to understand some important differences between American and European cities:

(1) In the United States . . . no distinction is recognized between governing and governed classes, and the problem of government is conceived to be this, that the whole body of society should learn and apply to itself the art of government. Bearing this in mind, it becomes apparent that the tide of immigration into the United States is a continually disturbing factor. . . . In many of the cities of the United States, indeed in almost all of them, the population not only is largely untrained in the art of self-government, but it is not even homogeneous. (2) American cities as a rule have grown with a rapidity to which the Old World presents few parallels. . . . [This] has compelled very lavish expenditure under great pressure for quick results. . . . American cities have laboured under . . . inability to provide adequately for their needs,

while discounting the future so freely in order to provide their permament plant. (3) Charters were framed as though cities were little states. Americans are only now learning, after many years of bitter experience, that they are not so much little states as large corporations.

He pointed to the rise of the "strong mayor" in several cities (including Brooklyn, where Low had recently been mayor under a new charter) as evidence of the acceptance of the corporation model.

(4) The one organic problem in connection with the charters of cities, which apparently remains as far from solution as ever in America, is that which concerns the legislative branch of city government.... [T]hat it is so, illustrates with vividness the justice of the American view that it is a dangerous thing, in wholly democratic communities, to make the legislative body supreme over the executive.

Low concluded, echoing but going beyond Bryce:

The average American city is not going from bad to worse.... The general tendency, even in the larger cities, is toward improvement.... It may be claimed for American institutions, even in cities, that they lend themselves with wonderfully little friction to growth and development and to the peaceful assimilation of new and strange populations.

Frank Goodnow, with his more restricted focus on Tammany Hall, supported Bryce also.

The year 1957 [he noted] marks an important epoch in the history of the city of New York. It may be taken as the date of a great change in the character of the population of the city—a change which has vastly increased the difficulties of municipal government, and presented problems whose solution has unfortunately not yet been attained. The middle classes, which had thus far controlled the municipal government, were displaced by an ignorant proletariat, mostly of foreign birth, which came under the sway of ambitious political leaders and was made to subserve schemes of political corruption such as had not before been concocted on American soil.

The year 1957 is also [he continued] the date of a great change in the legal status of the city. Down to this time all charters, and almost all laws affecting the government of the city, were either framed or suggested by the municipal authorities or made to depend for their validity on the approval of the people. But in 1957, the legislature committed itself finally and definitely to the doctrine that it might change at will the city institutions, framing the municipal government and distributing the municipal powers as it saw fit.

The story of the Tweed Ring (1870-1871), Goodnow believed, was a natural consequence of these two factors. Looking back on that episode, Goodnow in 1888 concluded:

... [T]he old party system still remains and must, in a large city like New York with its great masses of ignorant voters, ever offer a great obstacle to the selection of the best men for office. The radical changes now advocated in the methods of elections, and the reform of the civil service by the extension of competitive examinations, can only serve as palliatives. Many of the evils which the city has experienced in the past may be expected to recur, until such time as its electors are more intelligent, their allegiance to party less strong, and their political leaders more pure.

These initial analyses by Bryce, Goodnow, and Low provided the main assumptions and conclusions that guided American political scientists for a half century and are still influential in the textbooks. The posture of these three early analysts may be summarized in the following attitudes:

1. Pessimism concerning urbanism and the institutions of urban society, a pessimism ranging from Low's moderation to the sharp dislike of Bryce and Goodnow.
2. Hostility toward political parties as instruments for the governing cities.
3. Indictment of the immigrant groups in the urban electorate as a central cause of urban political and governmental pathology.
4. Hostility toward the state legislatures as alleged violators of urban rights to self-government.

If Bryce and his colleagues had been writing their summaries a generation later (in 1919, let us say) they would have been able to use an enormously larger literature, but they would not have needed, on the basis of that literature, to change very much their posture of 1888. The optimism of the Progressive Movement, reflected in some degree in the literature on city politics and government, might have made them somewhat more moderate in their attitudes toward urban society, but their remaining assumptions would not have been directly challenged.

The 1890's and the early 1900's produced a flood of literature and action on the urban front. The 1894 Philadelphia Conference for Good City Government, a joint meeting of New York City and Philadelphia urban reformers held in January, led directly to the organization of the National Municipal League in May. In that same year Alfred R. Conkling published his *City Government in the United States,* a reformer's tract. In 1895 Albert Shaw introduced a broader dimension with his two volumes: *Municipal Government in Great Britain* and *Municipal Government in Continental Europe,* each of which seemed to buttress the reformers. In 1895 also, Frank J. Goodnow, who was to become the dominant intellectual figure for more than a decade in the field of urban government, brought out his *Municipal Home Rule: A Study in Administration,* and in 1897 his *Municipal Problems,* the first approach to a systematic textbook. These important beginnings were added to by William H. Tolman's *Municipal Reform Movements: The Textbook of the New Reformation* (1895), Delos F. Wilcox, *Study of City Government* (1897), and Dorman B. Eaton's, *Government of Municipalities* (1899).[1]

These urban political and governmental studies of the 1890's were crowned by the publication in 1900 of the doctrinal bible of municipal reform: the National Municipal League's *A Municipal Program.* Presenting its first Model Charter and Model General Charter Act, the League specified the goals of urban reform, urged on and supported generally by the political scientists of the day. These prescriptions, fully consistent with the assumptions of Bryce, Goodnow, and Low a decade earlier, may be paraphrased as follows:

1. Put no faith in political parties.
   a. Separate city elections from state and national elections
   b. Shorten the ballot (elect mayor and council only)
   c. Nominate by petition in a system of "free nominations" (not more than fifty signatures required)
   d. Make the ballot nonpartisan (list all candidates alphabetically under each office)
   e. Make appointive officials' terms indefinite: establish a "merit system" for all employees
2. Grant "home rule" to city governments of limited power.
   a. Restrict powers of state legislatures to enact special legislation affecting cities
   b. But restrain city governments by general legislation—for example by debt and tax ceilings
   c. Empower cities to frame and adopt their own charters
3. Concentrate power and responsibility in the city's chief executive, thus adopting for cities the model of the business corporation.
   a. The League spelled out this goal in terms of the "strong mayor" elected by the voters
   b. But Eaton and some others preferred a chief executive chosen by the council

These doctrinal prescriptions for the governing of cities in the United States were sustained and elaborated in the literature produced by the reformers and by the political scientists during the two decades following 1900. The most eventful episode of the period was provided by the National Municipal League's *New Municipal Program,* issued in 1915. In this revision of the bible of 1900, the council-manager plan (the council to be elected by proportional representation, the manager to be a professional executive) replaced the "strong-mayor" plan as a key item of structural doctrine. This modification gave to both the reformers and the political scientists a coherent program which represented, they believed, the optimum expression of their central values for urban politics and government: *separation of city government from state and national parties, non-partisanship in elections and appointments to office, minority representation in the city council, the business corporation as a model for the conduct of the city government, and the "merit system" in city employment.*[2]

The 1915 revision virtually completed the doctrinal evolution of municipal reform. Political scientists and urban reformers were to work in a close partnership based on the 1915 premises for more than three decades thereafter, with only a few of the former inclined to dissent. In this partnership the political scientists were primarily cast in the role of "social engineers," consultants to the reformers and to officialdom in achieving the goals prescribed in the *New Municipal Program.* In this respect they were not unlike their colleagues who were then and later prescribing national and state constitutional reform, executive and administrative reform, and political party reform. The difference was to turn out to be in the long duration of their role as "social engineer" in urban government and politics, and in their continuing and almost literal fidelity to the doctrines of 1915.

1915-1950: Doctrine and Dissent

The era of "social engineering" by urban political scientists in the United States was accompanied by the appearance of a large body of literature codifying and elaborating the prevailing prescriptive doctrines. The municipal government textbooks, which burgeoned in the 1920's and the 1930's especially, carried the main task of codification. All of them reflected rather uniformly the earlier attitudes and premises of Bryce and Goodnow, and presented with mild variation the prescriptions of the 1915 *New Municipal Program.* None of them dissented sharply from that platform of premises and remedies.[3]

As a key item of the established doctrine, the council-manager plan, with election of the council by proportional representation as an approved refinement, received the needed elaboration and support in the literature. The enduring popularity of the city manager idea and the steady rate of its adoption by additional cities each year provided eloquent testimony for the tracts and monographs which celebrated its virtues. The urban "social engineers" recognized the plan as their most saleable product. The National Municipal League was thus regularly reinforced in its inherently strong inclinations to retain the council-manager plan as the central feature in the successive revisions of its Model Charter, the continuing embodiment of the bible of 1915.[4]

But the shape of urban America was changing. The relatively self-contained cities of earlier decades were becoming, especially by the 1920's, surrounded by populous satellite cities and suburbs. Complex metropolitan regions were developing distinctive stresses and strains. At first the metropolitan region was perceived as simply another problem in "social engineering"; if annexation, city-county consolidation, intermunicipal cooperation, or special districts were not feasible "solutions," then the more drastic remedy of a fully integrated metropolitan government was required. As political scientists looked more closely at metropolitan regions, however, complexity and uncertainty became more apparent. For example, one of the prescriptions of 1915—home rule—was now seen as an ideological and strategic barrier to metropolitan integration. And each metropolitan region seemed to present some markedly unique conditions, resisting any single universal formula for governmental structure. Consequently, although the "social engineers" who surveyed and recommended solutions for metropolitan reform in the four decades after 1920 tended to follow a common pattern of prescriptions, no comprehensive, codified "Model Metropolitan Charter" achieved acceptance among urban political scientists.[5]

Other questions had also emerged by this time in urban political science in the United States. Political scientists interested in the study of political parties and political behavior had begun to turn their attention to urban politics, viewing urban party institutions and political processes more as clinical data for description and analysis than as opportunities for their indictment or for the prescription of remedies. This effort was especially centered (from 1925 to 1940) among the political scientists at the University of Chicago, where the sociologists also were attempting a broad analysis of urban life. The consequence was a new stream of political science literature about American cities which was, in due time, to play an important part in the reevaluation of the premises and methods of urban political science. In their day, however, these studies did not shake the doctrines of the textbooks.[6]

1950-1965: New Emphases on Description and Diagnosis

The municipal government textbooks remain largely inviolate even in the 1960's, despite some direct criticism by political scientists and occasional revisionist gestures.[7] All save a handful of the textbooks continue to carry forward the "social engineering" tradition of political science, defining the postwar urban problems of Negro in-migration, population explosion and dispersion, deterioration of physical plant, water and air pollution, and so forth, as difficulties to be dealt with by adjusting legal and governmental machinery. The problem, says one distinguished exponent of this approach to the study of urbanization, is not one of sheer size of cities:

[T]he problem is adjustment of management devices to the size which is forced upon us by events.... We have the organizational and managerial knowledge and tools. There is no reason for running away from scale.... The underlying problems become impossible of rational attack unless there is a single center for coordination analysis, planning, and action.[8]

Questioning Established Doctrine

There is little argument among political scientists that the scale of urban problems has increased with the increasing concentration of people in and near great central cities. But a growing number of political scientists are becoming impressed with the moral ambiguity of "engineering" solutions to municipal problems. Is the council-manager system the best form of city government? Should cities and suburbs combine under a unified metropolitan government? Are the nonpartisan ballot, the merit system, and zoning "good things"? The answers to these and other such questions, at one time an almost automatic "yes" among political scientists, are now much less obvious, especially when applied to communities with racially, ethnically, and economically diverse populations, which of course means at least all the larger ones.

Research on "nonpartisan" election systems, for example, has indicated that this "reform" tends to bring "better people" of high prestige into politics, to increase the influence of allegedly neutral organs of publicity, such as newspapers, and in some (perhaps most) cases to diminish the influence of the local political party organizations. Other consequences of depoliticizing urban electoral decisions appear to be the attenuation of the links between city officialdom and the low-income, low-status groups in the population, and the substitution of doctrinaire solutions for solutions resulting from continuous bargaining among visible subgroups in the city's politics.[9]

The council-manager plan has also confronted some explicit reappraisal. Why, it has been asked, do some state political systems seem to be more hospitable to the plan than others? Other questions center on the attractions of the plan for some types of groups in urban politics, the hostility which other groups display toward it. It has even been suggested that whether one prefers the council-manager plan to some other form depends on whose ox one wants gored.[10]

And home-rule doctrine, in its turn, has undergone some reexamination. The parallels between the strategic uses, frequently antigovernmental, of "states' rights" ideology and of "home-rule" ideology have been noted; the fictitious quality of proposals to seal off the governments of cities from those of the state and nation, in an era of increasing mutual involvement and interdependence of all three levels of government, has also been underscored. The simple myth of city virtue frustrated by rural villainy in unrepresentative state legislatures, it is suggested, is in need of revision in order to reveal the more complex reality of urban-state relationships.[11]

Some unanticipated consequences of merit-system doctrines, which aimed at depoliticizing the bureaucracies, have also begun to attract the attention of urban political scientists. The municipal bureaucracies, once they were emancipated from party organization control, became more and more active politically in their external environments. Especially when organized as interest groups, they have often become autonomous and potent actors in urban politics. As such, they have the same intrinsic interest for political scientists as do political parties, candidates, and officials, or other urban interest groups.[12]

The claim for the virtues of metropolitan integration has evoked questions, too. "Social engineers" have pointed to the proliferation of metropolitan "governments": counties, towns, cities, villages, police, fire, school and other special districts, independent boards and commissions, intermunicipal compacts, and so on. This "outmoded" array of governments should be replaced, it is argued, with an integrated metropolitan government which could not only take advantage of economies of scale in administration but which would also command the interest and involvement of citizens who are now thoroughly confused and frustrated by the multiplicity of governments having a claim on their attention.

But the uncertainties attending purely formal solutions to political problems in a metropolitan society have begun to impress political scientists. Why should central-city party leaders want to "unify" with suburban party leaders? Presumably because they feel confident of controlling the resulting consolidated government. But in that case, why should suburban leaders assent to this arrangement? On the other hand, if suburban leaders seem likely to win out, why should central-city leaders agree to consolidation? What are the inducements for collaboration between central-city and suburban interest groups? A few observers see the problem primarily as one of race. As Negroes increase in numbers in large cities and whites in the suburbs, the question of metropolitan centralization can be rephrased: will central-city Negroes choose to forfeit the election of their own political leaders to high public office by supporting proposals to consolidate with white suburban populations large enough to outnumber them? To these observers, the "solution" of metropolitan government, when exposed to the values and practices of the real world, creates "problems."[13]

Who Rules? A Return to Politics and Political Theory

One of the dilemmas confronting the urban political scientists in the 1960's is revealed by the tensions between the political scientist as adviser or consultant to reformers or officials—the role of "social engineer"—and the political scientist as clinical observer and analyst of urban political and governmental systems. Some find the two roles reasonably compatible and interchangeable, and mutually reinforcing. Others are impressed by the conflicts between the roles, and suggest a division of labor between political scientists and political engineers; they point also to indications that the professional journals of political science increasingly reflect one orientation, whereas the journals of activist groups (for example, the *National Civic Review*) reflect the other. The gap, it is suggested, is growing and will continue to widen. For the texts and the reformist literature have remained almost untouched by the work of political scientists who in recent years have begun to view urban communities as political systems capable of yielding answers to some of the enduring problems of political science as a discipline.[14] To a considerable extent, and notably since the mid-1950's, political scientists have turned from what Hugh Douglas Price has called " 'actor-defined problems' (actual subjects of metropolitan complaint, such as housing and transportation)" to " 'observer-defined problems' (such as the social scientists' interest in the abstract question of power structure)"; that is, to the study of cities and metropolitan areas because of their intrinsic interest as political systems and not primarily because they need a doctor's attention.[15]

This transition began, as we have noted, in the urban studies at the University of Chicago, especially in the 1930's. The influence of these studies was intensified and extended by the works of V. O. Key on political parties as national and state systems, and by the many studies inspired by his work.[16] Another contribution to the transition came from those political scientists interested in "case studies" for the teaching of public administration. Taking a "decision" by an administrator as their focus of attention, these political scientists sought to discover the actual conditions and influences present in the exercise of official power in explicitly identified situations. Decisions by city officials were included among their studies; the result was a new kind of urban political science literature.[17] To these eventually were added case studies of urban political party decisions.[18]

More recently, in this trend toward matters of description rather than prescription, urban political scientists have placed themselves in the debt of sociologists, with whom they have fallen into dialogue on the significant general question of "who rules" in American communities. The sociologist's answer typically has been couched in the vocabulary of the analyst of social stratification. In a series of field researches dating from the influential Middletown studies by Robert and Helen Lynd, forward into the present, sociologists have elaborated five key propositions about local community life, in American cities both large and small.[19] These propositions, stated baldly, hold that (1) an upper-class power elite rules, (2) politicians and civic leaders are subordinate to this elite, (3) there is only one elite in each community, exerting dominance on substantially all non-trivial community issues, (4) the elite rules in its own interests exclusively, and largely to the detriment of the lower classes, and (5) as a consequence, social conflict takes place primarily between the elite and the non-elite.

This pattern of community power has generally been held to exist whenever the social structure of the community is well formed and relatively stable. Deviations from the pattern have been accounted for by referring to apparent malformations, immaturities, or situations of flux in the community social structure, but that this was the "normal" pattern of power distribution, few sociologists seriously doubted. Many political scientists shared in the general satisfaction with these largely sociological findings; understandably, since the propositions were apparently buttressed and reconfirmed by consider-able field experience—experience of which political scientists then keenly felt a lack.[20] But as political scientists began to move into field research, dissatisfaction began to take hold. The literature shows a growing sense of skepticism toward both the methods and the findings of studies on community power.[21]

As James Thurber has said, "Skepticism is a useful tool of the inquisitive mind, but it is scarcely a method of investigation." As political scientists began to come in contact with American communi-ties in their new role as field researchers (rather than as consultants or reformers), they were forced to develop methods for viewing community politics and decision-making. In contrast with the socio-logical approach, political scientists recently concerned with the topics of power and influence in American communities have emphasized the examination of decisions and policies rather than the identifica-tion of alleged "influentials," of political decision-makers rather than economic or social elites, of observed behavior rather than reputations for influence.[22]

One consequence of these changes in methodological emphasis has been the rather persistent rejection of the five key propositions set forth in the sociological studies of community power. Political scien-tists have been compelled by this situation to state rather carefully the theoretical rationale for conducting research in the way they did, and to demonstrate its superior scientific utility to the approaches taken by sociologists. This has been necessary in order to establish grounds for rejection of the key propositions about community power asserted by sociologists.

Thus present-day political science literature on urbanism is increas-ingly concerned with two major problems: (1) stating the conditions and consequences of decision-making in various concrete situations, and (2) defending the methods used in arriving at conclusions about community policy-making patterns.

The rationale for conducting research in the way political scientists generally have proceeded has been developed principally in a series of papers growing out of an intensive study of New Haven by Robert A. Dahl and his associates.[23] Major points made in these papers have been: (1) that the concept "power," in order to have empirical meaning, should refer to observable changes in behavior brought about by the actions of one person upon another. In order to compare the power of actors, it seems necessary to refer to concrete decisions in the community where research observers have the opportunity to examine the changes in the probabilities of various outcomes taking place that follow from the initiatives, vetoes, and successes and failures of participants in policy-making. (2) The methods used by sociologists in studying community power bypassed the examination of behavior and of outcomes, relying instead upon samples of *belief about* power distributions. (3) Proffered confirmations of the five key propositions were often unconvincing because of (*a*) methods that did not adequately test the key propositions, (*b*) unexplained evidence that contradicted the propositions, and (*c*) repeated and varied attempts to save the propositions from contrary evidence by resort to *ad hoc, post-factum* explanations.

Although the research strategies of political scientists have been described and defended in a fairly comprehensive manner, the actual findings of research on community power and influence are just beginning to appear in the literature.[24] It is possible at this time only to sketch in some of the conclusions of these studies. A few such findings are outlined in the following paragraphs.

One of the most common patterns of behavior observed in American cities is that participation in the making of specific decisions is normally concentrated in the hands of a small proportion of the population. But this does not mean that the cities are ruled by a single, all-purpose elite, after the fashion suggested by stratification theory in sociology. At least three significant modifications of the finding of limited participation in decision-making must be made. First, different small groups normally make decisions on different community problems, and, likewise, the personnel of decision-making groups often change, even over the short run.[25] Second, the decisions made by small groups are most often considered routine or are otherwise ignored by most other members of the community. Third, when small groups undertake innovation, or decision-making, in cases salient or likely to become salient to many others in the community, they must achieve special kinds of legitimacy, and the strength acquired by competitive bargaining and meaningful accommodations among themselves, or risk the likelihood of failure.

The finding that participants in decision-making are largely specialized to certain *issue areas* has been confirmed by data gathered using a variety of methods prevalent in community power research. Thus, when citizens, or "experts," were asked to nominate leaders in specific issue areas, different leaders emerged in different issue areas.[26] This was also the finding when students used research techniques approximating a "total immersion" in the community. This latter method involved a combination of approaches, including such data-gathering devices as the examination of specific decisions and events in the life of the community, accompanied by lengthy, relatively nondirective interviews, participant observation, and the inspection of newspapers and other appropriate documents.[27]

One such study, by Norton Long in Boston, suggested the conclusion that important decisions in the community were made in a process which was largely decentralized. Insofar as different decision-making processes could be summarized by the observer seeking to characterize the total community, Long suggested the metaphor of "an ecology of games." This was defined as a territorial system in which a variety of "games"—banking, manufacturing, administering municipal government agencies, and many others—give structures, goals, roles, strategies, and publics to the players, the players in each game making use of players in the others for their own particular purposes. Long suggested:

At the local level [it is feasible] to look at the municipal government, its departments, and the agencies of state and national government as so many institutions, resembling banks, newspapers, trade unions, chambers of commerce, churches, etc., occupying a territorial field and interacting with one another. This interaction can be conceptualized as a system without reducing the interacting institutions and individuals to membership in any single comprehensive group.[28]

The first full-scale documentation of similar conclusions was provided in Wallace S. Sayre and Herbert Kaufman, *Governing New York City: Politics in the Metropolis* (1960). In this study political outcomes were viewed as a product of a contest in which there are stakes and prizes, contestants, and rules governing the strategies of the contestants. As Hugh Douglas Price describes its conclusions:

... [The contest] may have very high stakes, including ideological goals, public office and jobs, economic gains and losses, and provision of desired services. There are a variety of participants seeking various of these stakes, including party leaders, public officials, organized municipal bureaucracies, nongovernmental interest groups, officials of other governments, and ordinary voters. The contest is carried on by certain generally understood "rules of the game," some formal and some informal. . . . There are many varieties of strategies open to the various participants. They may seek to influence the nominations made, or the electoral outcome, or the appointments of nonelective officials, or the policies adopted by various officials, or the execution of policies after their adoption.[29]

The volume concludes that the governance of New York City takes place within a multicentered system, in which no single ruling elite can be identified; instead, the system is open, competitive, and fluid. Herbert Kaufman has summarized the conclusions of the New York City study bearing on the propositions of the stratification theory in these words:

> Decisions of the municipal government emanate from no single source, but from many centers; conflicts and clashes are referred to no single authority, but are settled at many levels and at many points in the system: no single group can guarantee the success of any proposal it supports, the defeat of every idea it objects to.[30]

Beyond issue specialization, other patterns of interaction also modify and constrain the rule of the few. One such pattern has to do with the grant of legitimacy made to these small groups, entitling them to make decisions. Careful examination of the evidence at hand seems to indicate that elites are freest in their power to commit the resources of the community when these decisions are relatively routine and innocuous; when any elite attempts other kinds of decision-making, of a nonroutine, unbureaucratized, or innovative variety, it seems to require special consent by other elites and citizens who fall outside the small decision-making group.

If this pattern is correctly identified, certain propositions might be seen to follow from it. We might reasonably expect, for example, that (1) a dominant "general elite," if one were found to exist, would place great emphasis on maintenance of sociability and contact with a wide range of citizens in the community, and less emphasis on "doing things," or innovation—in fact any such general elite would prudently seek to restrict its own activities in various ways; (2) an elite group wanting innovations in public policy would seek systematically to acquire consent from other elites and from nonelite members of the community; (3) an attempt by any one elite to put a program into effect without achieving in the community a legitimacy wider than its own sponsorship would fail; and (4) nonelite members of the community would seek to bring elites under control in areas of concern to them.

The evidence which has begun to accumulate on each of these points indicates that, in general, these propositions are all correct,[31] and hence we can say that in a wide range of community situations, participation in decision-making is limited to a relatively few members of the community, but only within the constraints of a bargaining process among competing elites and of an underlying consensus supplied by a much larger percentage of the local population, whose approval is often costly to secure.

At least three devices are available to nonelites in seeking to bring elites under control. Nonelites can withhold support at critical junctures in the decision-making process, by failing to support necessary referenda, for example. Or they can promote the creation of counterelites, as has happened, for example, in many communities with large unionized populations. A third device is simply to promulgate controversy, to "make an issue." As James Coleman has shown, this technique usually activates new participants in community decisions, and not uncommonly changes the decision outcomes drastically.[32]

Another area of interest to urban political science concerns the paths people travel in order to become involved in decision-making. Information concerning leadership recruitment is fragmentary in many community studies, but enough data exist for us to infer that few if any authoritative community decision-making groups are made up of participants whose backgrounds are entirely homogeneous. Contrary to the assumption in stratification theory to the effect that leadership recruitment is a process whereby the top leaders "pull" into their midst congenial new blood like themselves,[33] there is a good deal of evidence indicating that decision-makers become so by *self*-selection, "pushing" themselves into the leadership group by showing interest, willingness to work, and competence.[34]

Success in community decision-making evidently does not come automatically to possessors of great amounts of any one of the many possible resources available to actors in community life. Many resources in combination—time, knowledge, energy, esteem, wealth, legitimacy, and so on—must be applied with skill and diligence for actors to succeed in influencing community decisions in desired directions. This suggests that community power cannot be sensibly measured by noting the sheer amount and distribution of resources available in the community; rather, we have to know something about the rate and efficiency with which they are employed.[35]

Resources, skill, and diligence in exploiting them are three conditions that make for success in influencing community decisions. A fourth may often be the ability to choose goals that do not strain the compliance of others in the system. A fifth condition of successful participation is closely related to the fourth: capacity to form coalitions with other participants in order to achieve one's goals. This entails choosing goals which do not preclude the possibility of joining with others, and hence, like the fourth factor, implies that certain limits on the preferences of actors may be required for success. Another limitation this condition for success imposes is on the strategies available to actors for achieving their goals. In order to form coalitions with others successfully, it is necessary to pursue courses of action which do not conflict with potential allies.

Thus political science research over the last few years has vastly complicated our view of power distribution in American cities. As one observer has noted:

What began with Floyd Hunter and C. Wright Mills as a simple search for *the* power elite deepens into a study of a variety of powerful actors with different scopes of influence; but even this dissolves into a complex system where each actor is operating at partial capacity and can always muster more resources either by becoming more heavily involved or by diverting them from other enterprises. The simple logical model of how much A can influence B becomes largely irrelevant, for the outcome will depend on how far A goes in mustering his resources, and how far B goes in replying in kind. And since both A and B are usually involved with a wide range of other actors, we are inevitably pulled away from the relatively simple problem of partial equilibrium and faced with the necessity for explaining the general equilibrium among *all* the actors. Worse yet, this cannot be successfully done as a static analysis, but must be essayed in terms of dynamics. . . . If A is able to pyramid power over time then the whole system will change, but if A diverts resources under conditions of diminishing returns the change in power will be in the opposite direction.[36]

A RESEARCH AGENDA

The research priorities for urban political science in the next decade no doubt will include projects designed to test accepted doctrines, projects intended to be cumulative in relation to earlier research, and projects attempting to break new ground entirely. The central theme of all these endeavors will be the search for the political correlates of urbanization. The program of research suggested in the following pages is both eclectic and ambitious; its authors are aware, too, that the political scientists interested in the politics of the cities are autonomous and self-willed—to them an agenda is properly something to be departed from as often as it is followed. The intended function of this agenda, in a sense simply a list of preferences held by its two authors, is to stimulate urban research by political scientists. We have nominated our own somewhat subjective items as illustrating apparent opportunities, but they are set out in no firm order of priority and with no claim for inclusiveness.

Comparative Analysis of Community Power

The sheer number of case studies in depth describing power and decision-making in individual urban communities has begun to pose a formidable storage problem for the seeker of a more general view. Hence, high on the agenda would rank the comparative analysis of cities. The purpose of such a comparative analysis would be to aggregate findings so as to lay bare, if possible, the underlying conditions, processes and activities common to city life and politics. This may sound suspiciously like a counsel of perfection, for it does not answer a prior question: what is it about cities that we can profitably compare so as to arrive at general propositions—for example, about patterns of power and decision-making within them?

This question is more complicated than it appears. One source of complication is the fact that most descriptions of urban decision-making patterns attempt to demonstrate either that a ruling elite exists, or that it does not. Evidence arguing that the typical American community is run by a small, unified, multipurpose elite has now been discredited for the most part, and so we are left in the position of having to explain the existence virtually everywhere of "pluralistic" systems of decision-making. A clearly necessary first step, then, is the reexamination of urban pluralism, in order to sort out some characteristic types. Coalitions of elites are built on different sources of strength in different urban centers; the prevailing ideology or ethos differs from city to city, some being innovative, others static; the institutional patterns, formal and informal, range widely; the scope, frequency, and intensity of elite and nonelite participation in urban decisions differ widely among cities—criteria such as these might be used to construct a number of typical urban patterns of pluralistic decision-making, a typology of urban political orders.

Only after differentiating among different forms of urban pluralism can the next step be taken, a step that involves inspecting underlying social, demographic, economic, legal, institutional, and cultural patterns in search of determinants of the different forms of pluralism. This second step is what usually comes immediately to mind when one thinks of comparative analysis: the aggregation of cities by size, geographic location, economic diversification, age, and so forth, on the assumption that similarities in these basic characteristics will produce similarities in the prevailing political order, and differences in the independent variables will likewise produce differences in the dependent variable of politics.

This may turn out to be true, but at present our categories describing types of urban political orders are so insensitive as to make any such conclusion premature. If we are to pursue a broadly comparative analysis, we must first redefine our categories and, second, actually compare the political orders of cities, on the one hand, and the possible determinants of these types of political life, on the other.[37]

Political Parties in Urban America

Although the macroanalysis of political systems is currently the most fashionable way for political scientists to study urban communities, there are other attractive opportunities. There is, for example, the nature of the political party in urban America. The urban political party is perhaps our most maligned single political institution, and probably the least understood.

Many political scientists suspect that urban parties have been quite

drastically transformed in the last three decades. But most of the
literature is distressingly vague about how local parties are now
organized and led, how electorates are won or lost. In fact, the
picture appears to be quite complex. Within recent memory, for
example, City Hall has changed hands, and parties, in a number of
large cities—New York, Philadelphia, Detroit, and Los Angeles come
immediately to mind. In some cities—Baltimore, Chicago, and Boston
are three recent and notable examples—reform mayors coming from
"out" factions of the dominant political party have been elected.
This evidence suggests that urban party organizations are somewhat
more vulnerable than we are accustomed to admitting. And though
Northern cities may be more likely than rural areas to be governed
by Democrats, the major inroads made by Republicans in the Solid
South have been almost exclusively among voters in the urban areas.
The rulers of the large Northern cities are not all one kind of
Democrat; nor, for that matter, do urbanism and one-party rule
invariably go hand in hand. Different states have conflicting stories
to tell on this subject.[38]

One hypothesis which deserves elaboration and documenation
suggests that local parties have been "nationalized."[39] The melting
pot has done its work, and internal migration and the public school
system have sautéed the distinctiveness out of our urban neighbor-
hoods—so runs the logical extension of this hypothesis. Nowadays
city folk no longer congregate at various meeting places in the
neighborhood, but rather stay indoors and get their political gossip
from the television or the newspapers. The superior visibility of
national news in these media depresses the saliency of local issues,
and, come election day, voters respond to city elections by voting
the ticket they agree with nationally. Administrative types have taken
City Hall over from the great charismatic ethnic leaders of yore—so
this argument concludes.

There is a great deal of plausibility to the "nationalization"
hypothesis, but a casual examination of the urban political scene
suggests caution lest it be pushed too far. The examples of Mayors
Lawrence of Pittsburgh, Daley of Chicago, Tucker of St. Louis, Clark
and Dilworth of Philadelphia, and Lee of New Haven may represent
administrative adroitness of a high order, but they are political
leaders as well. In what ways, then, are their skills and situations
different from those of the men who presided over City Hall in
earlier days? Assuredly the times have changed: now mayors must
glue together local parties in ways more difficult and complex than
in the days before social security, state unemployment compensation,
and the merit system. But city governments still have indulgences
and deprivations to distribute, assessments and taxes to levy or to
vary, licenses to hand out or to lift, inspections to perform, rules to
enforce, construction, snow removal, and insurance contracts to let,

prestige to dispense or withhold, and so forth. One major change may be the extent to which new resources are available in the form of federal funds, for those cities mobilizing the technical know-how to claim their share. "Nationalization" of urban parties is a provocative hypothesis which invites testing.

Other questions about urban political parties present comparable research opportunities. Do urban party organizations share the tendencies toward "atrophy" which V. O. Key finds for state party organizations? What incentives, what sources of sustenance, leadership, and electoral followings, support the minority party or parties in the cities?[40] What strategies distinguish the minority party from the majority party? What conditions, incentives, resources, and strategies characterize insurgency within urban parties?[41]

Some urban political systems are greatly affected by the pivotal role their electorates have in statewide electoral contests for governor, senator, and president; in turn, they greatly affect their state political systems. Boston, New York City, Detroit, and Chicago represent examples of one such category. In other states a pair of cities share this role: Philadelphia and Pittsburgh, Cincinnati and Cleveland, Kansas City and St. Louis, Dallas and Houston, Los Angeles and San Francisco are illustrations. What are the dimensions of accommodation and competition, within and between the parties, in these situations? What are the consequences, for party organization, for electoral behavior, for public policy?

Groups within Cities

For a long time we have relied on rather crude designations of city political groups—as businessmen, or labor, or Negroes, or immigrants, or the professions, or rich, or poor, and so forth. It is now necessary to expand and enrich our view of these groups. For example, there are apparently several kinds of effective Negro political leadership in urban America.[42] Likewise, the term "businessmen" lumps together politically vulnerable retail merchants with insulated and apolitical managers of branch plants of large corporations, neighborhood merchants with downtown bankers, slum landlords with "civic" leaders, department store owners with real-estate men.[43] But the differences among these groups and among other large categories— in their political styles, their political interests, activities, and so on— are profound, and worth exploring.

Even a popular stereotype such as the monolithic qualities of the Roman Catholic Church must be set aside as an obstacle to straight thinking in research. Rather, factions representing parish and hierarchy, different orders, and diverse social philsophies within the Catholic Church, have their impact in political affairs.[44] So, of course, do national origins among communicants of the Catholic Church. In the industrial towns and cities of New England, Irishmen, arriving in the first wave of Catholic immigration, took over the Democratic Party. When their coreligionists from Italy arrived, the Irish did not voluntarily relinquish their grip, but rather drove the Italians into the wide-open spaces of the Republican Party, which, after years out of office, was in most cities glad to see them. To this day, working-class Italian Catholics tend to be Republicans in local politics in many New England cities.[45]

The smaller decision-making arenas often provide the research setting within which to discover the competition, the accommodations, and the alliances among the groups most relevant to urban politics. School boards are a pertinent example.[46] Despite the status similarities of school boards across the nation, the degrees of doctrinal division, of capture by superintendents, of susceptibility to party or business or other pressure, vary tremendously from case to case.

It would also be useful to capture and catalogue the various roles in the urban political systems played by information agencies, such as the newspapers. The communications media have significant multiple roles in urban politics: as reporters of the behavior of the other actors, as partisans of some actors and critics of others, and as "king-makers." The structure of competition among news media has for too long been allowed to dominate the discussion of their political behavior.[47] This is an understandable response in terms of democratic theory, but it does not exhaust our problems or our questions.

The urban bureaucracies, too, are worthy of additional attention as actors in the urban political systems. Their role in "routine administrative decisions" is now widely recognized in political science literature. Their electoral activities, their participation in crucial policy decisions, their alliances and competition with elected officials, high administrative officials, and other interest groups are as yet only beginning to be explored. Both their competition with each other and their tendencies to form alliances make urban bureaucracies significant urban political forces about which we know but little.[48]

Numerous groups are active in urban political systems. Political scientists are just beginning to learn their precise identity, their internal dynamics and governance, their resources and incentives, their individual strategies, and their capacities in building and rebuilding alliances. Their political roles are still more a matter of legend than knowledge.

External Political Forces

So far we have suggested research dealing primarily with trends and patterns of urban life as they affect the internal political workings and institutions of cities. Equally important is the web of relations tying cities to external political bodies. One persistent question concerns the sore point of equal representation in state politics. Despite the much-decried overrepresentation of rural areas, many state legislatures contain at least one house apportioned rather strictly according to population. This means that almost everywhere cities have some leverage in state politics even when they are not instrumental—as after all they usually are—in electing the governor. Rotten boroughs in one house are merely a predictable and rather stable element in what is in fact often an extremely complicated equation. Very little empirical consideration has been given to variables such as the numbers of different cities within the state and the extent to which they compete against one another, rather than against rural "interests," and the existence of coalitions involving the triad of rural, urban, and *sub*urban factions.[49]

The state legislature is only one of a series of external political bodies significantly linked to urban political systems. State constitutions provide a balance sheet and battleground of urban political relations with state political systems, as do the offices of the governors, the state administrative agencies, the state court systems, the state government bureaucracies. County governments and special districts provide another important category. The federal government institutions dealing with cities represent similarly significant foci for urban political research.[50]

One angle of approach to the external political forces which affect urban politics is to regard the city as a subsystem within the state political system, with some capacity and tendency to deal directly with the national political system and with other subsystems in the state. The relevant questions then include: what resources does the city system possess in its external relations; in what strategies and counterstrategies does it engage; how do resources and strategies vary over time and from one decision arena to another (for example, in the constitutional arena, the electoral, party, gubernatorial, legislative, judicial, administrative arenas)?

Conditions of Urban Life

Another aspect of urban political life which beckons the researcher must be approached with great circumspection. Much popular criticism in books and magazines holds that cities are becoming unfit habitations for mankind.[51] The responsible political science researcher, heeding the clarion call, might well ask himself: "What are the political prerequisites for making our cities more livable?"

The problem Coleman Woodbury describes as "the paradox of urban public finance" will serve as an example. The paradox, as Woodbury puts it, is this:

Although our urban localities today are the greatest aggregations of income-producing power the world has ever seen, the overwhelming majority of urban governments, from those of the new, lower and middle income suburbs and fringe areas to the mightiest central cities of metropolitan areas, are in financial stringencies that apparently are becoming more and more severe.[52]

At least some aspects of this situation can be assigned to the behavior of state legislatures gerrymandered so as to appear to be, from the standpoint of the cities, excessively sensitive to the preferences of "rural" constituencies. One result, as the President's Commission on Intergovernmental Relations has pointed out, "is that urban governments have bypassed the States and made direct cooperative arrangements with the National Government in such fields as housing and urban development, airports and community defense facilities."[53] But increasing demands on services traditionally provided by cities have on the whole far outrun municipal ingenuity in finding new ways of paying for these services.

To the extent that outside agencies cannot be depended on for relief, the problem becomes a classical political one of calculation and control—of deciding who is to pay, of determining which demands should and should not be met. As Woodbury says, researchers have already supplied information about the effects of some kinds of taxation on industrial and commercial location, but this hardly exhausts the possibilities. What are the factors predisposing communities to give different priorities to similar "needs" and demands? What governs who pays how much? What determines how much a city takes on in order to provide for its residents? The standard problem of politics in our cities—of heavy demands on scarce resources, and the resulting patterns of choice—remains largely unchronicled and unanalyzed.[54]

Who is entitled to define what the problems are? The researcher must be prepared to defend the legitimacy of the people whose problems he accepts as his own, or if he prefers, should be prepared to grind his own axes cheerfully, but without disguising the boundaries of his own "objectivity."

Although it is possible to define some of these "problems" in a way that avoids the necessity for taking sides among interested parties, some of the most compelling social criticisms of city life do not permit political scientists this luxury. Without arguing the merits of the social critics' positions, it seems manifest to us that political scientists, if they chose to do so, could describe some of the political prerequisites of abolishing the "tyranny" of motor cars, of curing the blight of obsolete physical plants, of controlling increases in densities of land use, and so on. The catalogue of critic-defined problems is a long one. So is the array of possible "solutions": subsidy of mass transit, urban redevelopment, zoning laws, and enforcement of certain kinds. The political scientist perhaps can contribute best not by formulating the particular panaceas to be applied locally, but rather by examining and discussing the political preconditions of getting various panaceas suggested by the social critics to work, and the political consequences of their success and failure.

Political scientists perhaps can make a valuable contribution to utopian criticisms of the qualities of urban life beyond the task of pulling utopians down to earth, beyond helping them to assess the social, economic, and political costs of achieving what they hope to achieve in cities. One of the major functions of political science has always been to formulate rationales for the prevailing social order. In some ways, the democratic "ideologies" of present-day America are more expressive of utopian ideals than are planned utopian cities themselves on the drawing board or in three-dimensional life.[55] Frank Lloyd Wright's Broadacres is an expression of a nostalgia for an agrarian social order which, as Louis Hartz has cogently argued, never was.[56] The various planned "new towns" here and abroad have often even in middle age retained the barrackslike qualities which proclaim them the work of hierarchical forces. To the casual reader of the news, Brasilia, the newest and most audacious hierarchically created combine-for-living, gives every indication of providing monotony where unity was sought, of having expunged variety in search of harmony.

We suggest the possibility that the failure in human terms of utopian city building (and the same possibly goes for gigantic "projects" *within* cities) is a failure to appreciate the qualities of social and political life which bind men together in peace yet do not efface their diversity. Utopian planners have often failed to mirror accurately the societies they were attempting to symbolize in their buildings, for lack of an adequate political theory. Clearly, the creators of Stalinist plaster castles in Eastern Europe are exempt from this criticism: in terms of symbolic values they doubtless built better than they knew. It is rather the large-scale planners of pluralistic societies who stand in greatest need of an appropriately pluralistic political theory, so that they may better look to the recently neglected values of variety and human scale in their attempts to symbolize and give a steel and concrete framework to the social order.[57]

Other problems, perhaps easier to keep within manageable focus and more overtly useful to scholars if not to citizens of most cities, can be posed as "scientific" questions. Answers to these kinds of questions can be used by all parties to disputes over the distribution of costs and benefits in cities. One series of "scientific" questions might be asked of urban renewal programs: Who initiates urban renewal programs? Who mobilizes for and against them? What techniques are used to mobilize the various sides? Who legitimizes renewal programs? Who vetoes them? Who prevails in cases of conflict? Which techniques and resources seem to be associated with winning and which with losing?[58] Fluoridation programs could be discussed using the same kinds of questions. The pertinacity and utility of questions of this kind seem obvious.[59]

Nor does this end the list of programs which might be similarly examined: air pollution control, water supply and sanitation, master plans, open-space programs, in fact the whole list of critic-defined or actor-defined "problems" of urban public policy are candidates for the useful application of such questions.

The Judicial Process in Cities

An area long neglected by political scientists is the judicial process in the urban setting. The tradition has been to envelop this process in studies of public law, and to treat it as a task of analyzing rulings of judges to test hypotheses about wise substantive rules of law, or as a problem in "depoliticizing" the judiciary. The courts, the judges, the police, the prosecutors, the bar associations, and closely related groups have seldom been studied as actors in the urban political system.

Several types of inquiry press for attention in this segment of urban politics. Judicial behavior in trial courts is one example. Studies applying quantitative techniques to decisions in discretionary, small-docket appellate courts have recently interested a number of political scientists; the method might also be productive at trial-court levels. Using the records in criminal courts for a time period, the pleas made by defendants, the appearances of various types of character witnesses, the ethnic, racial, and religious characteristics of defendants, and the types of sentences imposed might be studied to test relations between "discretionary justice" and the political system. Similarly, the disposition of civil suits, or the assignment of receiverships and bankruptcies, might be probed.

Another line of research is represented by possible comparative studies of the relation between "legal" issues and "political" issues. In some cities declaratory judgment procedures to test the validity of official actions are relatively easy to use; in other cities, tighter restrictions on test cases prevail. In the former, does this difference make more "political questions" into "legal questions"? What are the consequences for the judiciary's role in the urban political system? What groups in the city derive advantages, or disadvantages, under the alternative procedures?

The special role of lawyers in urban politics is a matter of general note by political scientists. But what are the politics of bar associations? How is their leadership recruited, what are their resources and strategies in the political process—for example, in the selection and advancement of judges, prosecutors, and the staffs of both; in the development of the formal and informal rules which guide judicial behavior? The roles of law schools, leading law firms, and other specialized groups in the legal profession in the political-judicial processes of cities are also worthy of research attention.[60]

Emerging Metropolitan Systems—and Suburbia

Political scientists, as we have seen, have so far confronted the "metropolitan problem" mainly as consultants required to prescribe remedies. Enough has been discovered, and sufficient disenchantment encountered, to support the suggestion that the most pertinent research efforts by political scientists might now be directed at discovering the political preconditions for various stages of metropolitan political integration. One set of questions for this purpose might inquire into the present perceptions of, and dispositions toward or against, metropolitan integration held by party leaders, elected officials, urban bureaucracies, interest group leaders, and the communications media in a particular metropolitan region. Another set of questions might ask: Who initiates proposals for metropolitan integration? Who supports and who opposes? With what resources and strategies? Which conditions produce acceptance, which rejection? Still another series of questions might seek to relate the prospects of each of the standard metropolitan proposals—annexation, consolidation, multipurpose or special districts, federation, and so on—to the variations in the political and governmental environment of metropolitan regions—one-party, two-party; one-county, multicounty; one-state, multi-state; international.

From such a program of research urban political scientists could develop not only a base of knowledge which would enhance their value as metropolitan consultants but, even more importantly, they would add appreciably to the understandings which political scientists have about the rudimentary or emerging metropolitan political systems.

Suburbia in the political process is a related but more neglected phenomenon. The numerous jurisdictional subsystems which flourish in the suburban counties have not been subjected to the kind of case analysis we now have for city political systems. As a consequence, knowledge about suburban politics is at best highly generalized, for the most part unabashedly impressionistic. There are quite obviously many different kinds of suburbs—old, new, homogeneous, hetero-geneous, Republican, Democratic, residential, industrial, populous, sparsely settled, upper class, middle class, restricted, unrestricted and others. Most current generalizations ignore or blur these variations. More valid generalizations about suburbia and its politics will clearly have to wait upon studies in depth of a sufficient number of the several types of suburbs and their political systems.[61] A few illustrative questions may serve to suggest points of entry for political science research in the world of suburbia: Is nonpartisanship a distinctive political style for local governments in suburbia generally, or only for certain types of suburbs? What conditions determine its incidence and distribution? Are the number and activities of interest groups in suburban politics proportionately greater or lesser than in central cities, or are the differences a function of visibility? Are suburban bureaucracies dependent on party leaders, or is their role relatively autonomous?

Urbanization and Democracy in Emergent Nations

American political science has reflected insufficiently the growing pains of cities in the United States. As we have attempted to show, much of the political history of urbanization in this country failed to capture the attention of the reformers and social engineers who dominated the early development of urban political science. Journalists and novelists took up some of the slack through the latter half of the nineteenth century and into the twentieth, during the violent expansion of industry and mass employment which underlay modern urbanization in America. But the political growth of cities is still only a partly told story.

Today throughout the world new nations are simultaneously restructuring their political, economic, and social systems. The relationship in these nations between urbanization and politics is intimate and difficult to describe. Gigantic political decisions have in modern times led to drastic redistributions of populations within nations—redistributions which formerly occurred by a concatenation of individual independent decisions by workers seeking employment and shelter, and employers seeking laborers. Nowadays, politics enters not only into the consequences of urbanization, but into its causes as well. But though political decisions can vastly promote and retard the process of urbanization, the internal political consequences of urbanization are seldom counted so heavily by new governments as are consequences relating to capital formation, economic development, and international prestige.

The newly emerging nations are unanimously seeking economic development; they are less unanimous and less energetic, on the whole, in their pursuit of democratic politics. American political scientists can generally agree on many of the attributes of political systems which would tend to promote human dignity, in the terms of Western civilization. They may well be doing their country and the free world a considerable service by attacking with energy and diligence the knotty problem of identifying and encouraging conditions necessary for democratic politics in the midst of economic development and accelerated urbanization.[62]

Certain hypotheses can be constructed outlining relations among independent variables such as literacy and education, income distribution and gross national income, ethnic homogeneity and variety, geographic mobility and stability, and other economic and social characteristics of populations, on the one hand—and the dependent variable of democratic politics on the other.[63] Rates and types of urbanization could function in such hypotheses as critical intervening variables. Marx long ago suggested, for example, that urban workers, because of their economic distress and spatial concentration, would be fertile soil for revolutionary activity. Today urban mobs in North Africa, the Middle East, and East Asia erupt into violence from time to time, on various pretexts.

The characteristics of urban groups in developing countries, and most particularly their links with the political system, are topics of research having obvious political significance. The foreign, economic, and domestic political policies of many countries depend greatly upon factual premises about the strengths and dispositions of these urban groups, but many of these premises— and the policies based on them—may be drastically if not disastrously out of date.

Political science is perhaps ready now to meet both the scientific and policy challenges posed by urbanization in the developing areas in ways it was not when America, West and Central Europe, Japan, and even Soviet Russia became urbanized. It is curious to reflect that the areas now emerging into political independence and economic ambition will in all probability be the last in history to undergo the massive changes in family structure, occupational and income patterns, and social organization associated with urbanization. How these changes affect and are affected by the pattern of politics and decision-making, the distribution of controls among leaders and nonleaders, the rights and privileges of citizens, and in some sense the dignity of men are topics which could easily and perhaps should imperatively engage the attention of the political scientist.

Urbanization is a process which continues long after cities replace villages and citizens replace tribe and clansmen. As people are drawn into cities and as cities grow into metropolitan areas, their political problems proliferate and intensify. As these problems increase and deepen, more resources are distributed intentionally and inadvertently, and more and more actors involve themselves in the political processes which affect the restriction and diffusion of valued outcomes. As the political problems of urbanization expand beyond state lines and leap beyond national borders, the scientific problems of *urban* political scientists merge with those of political scientists generally. These tendencies combine to discourage parochialism among political scientists and underscore the significance of urbanization as a focal point for research, for in many ways cities and urbanizing areas are the most dynamic elements in our political life.

NOTES

1. See, especially for this early period, Robert C. Brooks, "Bibliography of Municipal Problems and Conditions of City Life," *Municipal Affairs,* 5 (1903), a 300-page bibliography. For a recent and perceptive commentary and bibliography, see Robert T. Daland, "Political Science and the Study of Urbanism, A Bibliographical Essay," *American Political Science Review,* 51 (June 1957), pp. 491-509.

2. Goodnow provided the center of gravity for political scientists with two texts: *City Government in the United States* (1904), and *Municipal Government* (1909), which added comparative material on Great Britain and Western Europe. James A. Fairlie, *Municipal Administration* (1901); William B. Munro, *Principles and Methods of Municipal Administration* (1916); and Herman G. James, *Municipal Functions* (1917), extended the Goodnow and League premises into the discussion of city administrative agencies. Charles Zueblin, *American Municipal Progress* (1902); Delos F. Wilcox, *The American City: A Problem in Democracy* (1904); Lincoln Steffens, *The Shame of the Cities* (1904); L. S. Rowe, *Problems of City Government* (1908); Horace C. Deming, *The Government of American Cities* (1909); Charles A. Beard, *American City Government* (1912); Walter T. Arndt, *The Emancipation of the American City* (1917), all added confirmation.

Lincoln Steffens was enormously influential in this period as an essayist on urban politics. While confirming the image of urban life then held by reformers and most political scientists (he produced the classic literature on urban bosses and machines), and while anticipating the model of an ultimately controlling economic elite in the cities which some sociologists were to rediscover much later, he also expressed profound skepticism about the nostrums of the urban reformers. His indictment of misgovernment was accepted; his pessimism about reform doctrines was ignored. See R. V. Sampson, "Lincoln Steffens: An Interpretation," *Western Political Quarterly,* 8 (1955), pp. 58-67.

One deviant enthusiasm, the commission form of government, claiming for itself the maximum use of the business corporation as model, brought its spate of advocates: John J. Hamilton, *The Dethronement of the City Boss* (1910); Ernest R. Bradford, *Commission Government in American Cities* (1911); Clinton R. Woodruff, *City Government by Commission* (1911); Henry Bruère, *The New City Government* (1912); Oswald Ryan, *Municipal Freedom: A Study of Commission Government* (1915).

Two volumes in the period reflect hopeful premises about urban society. Richard T. Ely, *The Coming City* (1902), and Frederick C. Howe, *The City: The Hope of Democracy* (1906), welcomed the arrival of urbanization. Frank Parsons, *The City for the People* (1901), advocated municipal ownership of utilities. In other respects, none of these three studies departed greatly from the conventional reform prescriptions. Three relatively detached examinations of the urban scene, with minimum emphasis on prescription, also appeared during the period: Howard Lee McBain, *The Law and Practice of Municipal Home Rule* (1916); Tso-Shuen Chang, *Commission and City Manager Plans* (1918); Russell M. Story, *The American Municipal Executive* (1918). Less detached was Harry A. Toulmin's *The City Manager: A New*

Profession (1915).

3. Munro (1923), Maxey (1924), Anderson (1925), Reed, Hanford, Upson (all in 1926), MacDonald (1929), Kneier (1934), Hodges, Zink (both in 1939), Pfiffner (1940), MacCorkle (1942), Schulz (1949), Bromage (1950) indicate their growth in number; several appeared during the period in revisions or modifications.

4. Leonard White's *The City Manager* (1927) testified to the emergence of a profession. The International City Managers' Association was established, began the publication of its own journal, and in 1935 issued the first of its series of handbooks on municipal management. Charles P. Taft published *City Management: The Cincinnati Experiment* in 1933 and C. E. Ridley and O. F. Nolting, *The City Manager Profession* in 1934. In 1940, Harold Stone, Kathryn Stone, and Don K. Price issued their definitive and patristic document: *City Manager Government: A Review After Twenty-Five Years.*

5. Although Goodnow had devoted a chapter to "The Metropolitan City" in his text of 1897, and others (including Reed, as well as the authors of the *Regional Plan of New York*) had been concerned with metropolitan phenomena in the 1920's, the first systematic reconnaissance did not appear until Paul Studenski and others, under National Municipal League sponsorship, produced *Government of Metropolitan Areas* in 1930. This was followed by R. D. McKenzie, *The Metropolitan Community* (1933); C. E. Merriam A. Lepawsky, and S. Parratt, *The Government of Metropolitan Chicago* (1933); John A. Rusk, *The City-County Consolidated* (1941); and Victor Jones, *Metropolitan Government* (1942). Jones raised some searching questions about the causes and sources of resistance to metropolitan integration.

6. Robert E. Park, Ernest W. Burgess, and R. D. McKenzie, *The City* (1925); Charles E. Merriam, *Chicago: A More Intimate View of Urban Politics* (1929); Robert and Helen Lynd, *Middletown* (1929) and *Middletown in Transition* (1937); Harold Zink, *City Bosses* (1930); Harold Gosnell, *Negro Politicians: The Rise of Negro Politics in Chicago* (1933); Roy V. Peel, *The Political Clubs of New York City* (1935); J. T. Salter, *Boss Rule: Portraits in City Politics* (1935); David H. Kurtzman, *Methods of Controlling Votes in Philadelphia* (1935); Harold Gosnell, *Machine Politics: Chicago Model* (1937); National Resources Committee, *Our Cities: Their Role in the National Economy* (1937) and *Urban Government* (1939); Dayton McKean, *Machine Politics: The Hague Machine in Action* (1940); Robert A. Walker, *The Planning Function in Urban Government* (1941); Arthur H. Holcombe, *The Political Parties of Today* (1924) and *The New Party Politics* (1933); Charles E. Merriam and Harold F. Gosnell, *The American Party System* (1923).

7. See Lawrence J. R. Herson, "The Lost World of Municipal Government," *American Political Science Review,* 51 (1957), pp. 330-345; Robert T. Daland, *op. cit.;* Hugh Douglas Price, *The Metropolis and Its Problems* (1960); Charles R. Adrian, *Governing Urban America* (1955; revised, 1961). Finally, in 1963, major revision of the texts had begun to take hold. See Edward C. Banfield and James Q. Wilson, *City Politics* (1963); Herbert Kaufman, *Politics and Policies in State and Local Governments* (1963); and Duane Lockard, *The Politics of State and Local Government* (1963).

8. Luther Gulick, "Metropolitan Organization," *The Annals,* 314 (1957), pp. 57-59. See also, for example, Arthur W. Bromage, "Political Repre-

sentation in Metropolitan Areas," *American Political Science Review*, 52 (1958), pp. 406-418.

9. Duane Lockard summarizes much relevant material in Lockard, *op. cit.*, pp. 226-238. See also Oliver P. Williams and Charles R. Adrian, "The Insulation of Local Politics Under the Non-Partisan Ballot," *American Political Science Review*, 53 (1959), pp. 1052-1063; Charles R. Adrian, "A Typology of Non-Partisan Elections," *Western Political Quarterly*, 12 (1959), pp. 449-458; J. Leiper Freeman, "Local Party Systems: Theoretical Considerations and a Case Analysis," *American Journal of Sociology*, 64 (1958), pp. 282-289; Eugene C. Lee, *The Politics of Nonpartisanship: A Study of California Cities* (1960); Charles E. Gilbert and Christopher Clague, "Electoral Competition and Electoral Systems in Large Cities," *Journal of Politics*, 24 (1962), pp. 323-349.

10. "Leadership and Decision-Making in Manager Cities" (a symposium), *Public Administration Review*, 19 (1958), pp. 208-222; C. E. Ridley, *The Role of the City Manager in Policy Formulation* (1958); C. A. Harrell and D. G. Weidford, "The City Manager and the Policy Process," *Public Administration Review*, 2 (1959), pp. 101-107; Kent Mathewson, "Democracy in Council Manager Government," *ibid.*, pp. 183-185; Wallace S. Sayre, "The General Manager Idea for Large Cities," *Public Administration Review*, 4 (1954), pp. 253-358.

11. Morton Grodzins, "The Federal System" in President's Commission on National Goals, *Goals for Americans* (1960), pp. 265-284; Wallace S. Sayre, "Cities and the State" and "State-City Government Relations," in New York State-New York City Fiscal Relations Committee, *Final Report* (November 1956), pp. 55-65 and 281-288. See also Wallace S. Sayre and Herbert Kaufman, *Governing New York City: Politics in the Metropolis* (1960), Chap. 15.

12. William C. Thomas, Jr., *The Bureau Chiefs in New York City Government* (1962), unpublished Columbia University doctoral dissertation; Sayre and Kaufman, *op. cit.*, Chap. 11; Theodore J. Lowi, *At the Pleasure of the Mayor* (1964).

13. On the race factor, see especially Edward C. Banfield, "The Politics of Metropolitan Area Organization," *Midwest Journal of Political Science*, 1 (1957), pp. 77-91; Edward C. Banfield and Morton Grodzins, *Government and Housing in Metropolitan Areas* (1958); Morton Grodzins, *The Metropolitan Area as a Racial Problem* (1958); James Q. Wilson, *Negro Politics: The Search for Leadership* (1960).

14. See Herson, *op. cit.;* and Herbert Kaufman, "Emerging Conflicts in the Doctrines of Public Administration," *American Political Science Review*, 50 (1956), pp. 1057-1073.

15. Hugh Douglas Price, *op. cit.*, p. 25.

16. V. O. Key, *Southern Politics* (1949), *American State Politics* (1956); Allan P. Sindler, *Huey Long's Louisiana* (1956); Duane Lockard, *New England State Politics* (1958); Leon D. Epstein, *Politics in Wisconsin* (1958); John H. Fenton, *Politics in the Border States* (1958).

17. Harold Stein (Ed.), *Public Administration and Policy Development* (1952): "The Cambridge City Manager" by Frank Abbott, and "Gotham in the Air Age" by Herbert Kaufman. These were followed (1953-1955) by the case studies of the Inter-University Case Program: for example, "The

Gainesville School Problem" by Frank Adams; "The New York City Health Centers" by Herbert Kaufman; "The Promotion of Lem Merrill" by Chester and Valerie Earl; "Defending 'the Hill' against Metal Houses" by William Muir; "Closing Newark Airport" by Paul Tillett and Myron Weiner. The ICP published in 1964 a *Casebook in State and Local Government*, a collection of cases already published individually plus a number published for the first time. See also Richard T. Frost (ed.), *Cases in State and Local Government* (1961). Solon T. Kimball and M. Pearsall, *The Talledega Story* (1953), examining public health decisions in a Southern city, represented a more fully developed case study of the same genre, as did Martin Meyerson and Edward C. Banfield, *Politics, Planning, and The Public Interest* (1955), and Harold Kaplan, *Urban Renewal Politics: Slum Clearance in Newark* (1963).

18. See the Eagleton Foundation Series, *Case Studies in Practical Politics* (1958), and especially Paul Tillett (ed.), *Cases on Party Organization* (1963).

19. Much of the discussion in the following pages of this section is treated more fully in Nelson W. Polsby, *Community Power and Political Theory* (1963). See also, for example, E. Digby Baltzell, *Philadelphia Gentlemen* (1958); Ernest A. T. Barth and Baha Abu-Laban, "Power Structure and the Negro Sub-Community," *American Sociological Review*, 24 (1959), pp. 69-76; William H. Form and William V. D'Antonio, "Integration and Cleavage Among Community Influentials in Two Border Cities," *American Sociological Review*, 24 (1959), pp. 804-814; August B. Hollingshead, *Elmtown's Youth* (1949); Floyd Hunter, *Community Power Structure* (1953); Floyd Hunter, Cecil B. Sheps, and Ruth C. Shaffer, *Community Organization: Action and Inaction* (1958); Morris Janowitz (ed.), *Community Political Systems* (1961); Orrin E. Klapp and L. Vincent Padgett, "Power Structure and Decision-Making in a Mexican Border City," *American Journal of Sociology*, 65 (1960), pp. 400-406; Delbert C. Miller, "Decision-Making Cliques in Community Power Structures: A Comparative Study of an American and an English City, "*American Journal of Sociology*, 64 (1958), pp. 299-310; Delbert C. Miller, "Industry and Community Power Structure: A Comparative Study of an American and an English City," *American Sociological Review*, 23 (1958), pp. 9-15; C. Wright Mills, "The Middle Classes in Middle-Sized Cities," *American Sociological Review*, 11 (1946), pp. 520-529; Roland J. Pellegrin and Charles H. Coates, "Absentee-Owned Corporations and Community Power Structure," *American Journal of Sociology*, 61 (1956), pp. 413-419; Robert O. Schulze, "The Role of Economic Dominants in Community Power Structure," *American Sociological Review*, 23 (1958), pp. 3-9; W. Lloyd Warner et al., *Democracy in Jonesville* (1949); W. Lloyd Warner, *The Living and the Dead* (1947); W. Lloyd Warner and Paul S. Lunt, *The Social Life of a Modern Community* (1941); W. Lloyd Warner and Paul S. Lunt, *The Status System of a Modern Community* (1942); W. Lloyd Warner and Leo Srole, *The Social Systems of American Ethnic Groups* (1945); and especially, Robert S. Lynd and Helen Merrill Lynd, *Middletown* (1929) and *Middletown in Transition* (1937).

20. Kaufman and Jones, although sharply critical of findings in the field, have noted this lack among political scientists. Herbert Kaufman and Victor Jones, "The Mystery of Power," *Public Administration Review*, 14 (1954), pp. 205-212; see also Lawrence J. R. Herson, *op. cit.;* Robert T. Daland, *Dixie City: A Portrait of Political Leadership* (1956); William J. Gore and

Fred S. Silander, "A Bibliographical Essay on Decision-Making," *Administrative Science Quarterly*, 4 (1959), p. 106-121; Robert E. Lane, *Political Life* (1959); and Edwin Hoffman Rhyne, "Political Parties and Decision-Making in Three Southern Counties," *American Political Science Review*, 52 (1958), pp. 1091-1107.

21. Sociologists as well as political scientists have joined in this current reevaluation. See C. Arnold Anderson, "The Need for a Functional Theory of Social Class," *Rural Sociology*, 19 (1954), pp. 152-160; C. Arnold Anderson and Harry L. Gracey, "A Review of C. Wright Mills' 'The Power Elite,' " *Kentucky Law Journal*, 46 (1958), pp. 301-317; George M. Belknap, "A Plan for Research on the Socio-Political Dynamics of Metropolitan Areas," presented before a Seminar on Urban Leadership of the Social Science Research Council, New York, August 1957.

See also Robert A. Dahl, *Who Governs? Democracy and Power in an American City* (1961); Robert A. Dahl, "A Critique of the Ruling Elite Model," *American Political Science Review*, 52 (1958), pp. 463-469; Robert A. Dahl, "Hierarchy, Democracy and Bargaining in Politics and Economics," in Stephen K. Bailey et al., *Research Frontiers in Politics and Government* (1955), pp. 45-69; Robert A. Dahl, "Leadership in a Fragmented Political System: Notes for a Theory," presented to the Conference on Metropolitan Leadership of the Social Science Research Council, Evanston, April 1-3, 1960; Robert A. Dahl, "The New Haven Community Leadership Study," Working Paper No. 1, December 12, 1957 (mimeographed); Robert A. Dahl, "Organization for Decision in New Haven," presented before the meetings of the American Political Science Association, 1958; Robert A. Dahl, "Some Notes and Models for Political Systems," presented before a Seminar on Urban Leadership of the Social Science Research Council, New York, August 1957.

Morris Janowitz, *op. cit.;* Herbert Kaufman and Victor Jones, *op. cit.;* Reinhard Bendix and Seymour Martin Lipset, "Political Sociology," *Current Sociology*, 6 (1957), pp. 79-99; James B. McKee, "Status and Power in the Industrial Community: A Comment on Drucker's Thesis," *American Journal of Sociology*, 58 (1953), pp. 364-370; Nelson W. Polsby, "Power in Middletown: Fact and Value in Community Research," *Canadian Journal of Economics and Political Science*, 26 (1960), pp. 592-602; Nelson W. Polsby, "The Sociology of Community Power: A Reassessment," *Social Forces*, 37 (1959), pp. 232-236; Nelson W. Polsby, "Three Problems in the Analysis of Community Power," *American Sociological Review*, 24 (1959), pp. 796-803; Peter H. Rossi, "Community Decision-Making," *Administrative Science Quarterly*, 1 (1957), pp. 415-443 (but see Peter H. Rossi, "Theory and Method in the Study of Power in the Local Community," presented to the Social Science Research Council's Conference on Metropolitan Leadership, Evanston, April 1-3, 1960, where he reexamines his reexamination); Harry M. Scoble, "Yankeetown: Leadership in Three Decision-Making Processes," in Janowitz, *op. cit.;* Benjamin Walter, "Political Decision-Making in North Carolina Cities," *Prod*, 3 (1960), pp. 18-21; Raymond E. Wolfinger, "Reputation and Reality in the Study of 'Community Power,' " *American Sociological Review*, 25 (1960), pp. 636-644.

22. See, for example, Edward C. Banfield, *Political Influence* (1961); George M. Belknap and John H. Bunzel, "The Trade Union in the Political

Community," *Prod,* 2 (1958), pp. 3-6; Peter B. Clark, *The Chicago Big Businessman as a Civic Leader* (New Haven, September 1959), mimeographed; Robert A. Dahl, "The New Haven Community Leadership Study," *op. cit.;* Robert A. Dahl, "Organization for Decision in New Haven," *op. cit.;* Robert A. Dahl, "A Proposed Inquiry into Political Influences in an American Community" (New Haven, April 1956), mimeographed; Robert A. Dahl, *Who Governs?, op. cit.;* Herbert Kaufman, "Metropolitan Leadership: The Snark of the Social Sciences," presented at a conference on Metropolitan Leadership of the Social Science Research Council, Evanston, April 1-3, 1960; Norton S. Long and George M. Belknap, *op. cit.;* Murray Levin, *The Compleat Politician* (1962); James B. McKee, *op. cit.;* Martin Meyerson and Edward Banfield, *op. cit.;* Nelson W. Polsby, "Three Problems in the Analysis of Community Power," *op. cit.;* Hugh Douglas Price, "Research on Metropolitanism: Economics, Welfare, and Politics" (Columbia University, Summer 1959), mimeographed; James Reichley, *The Art of Government: Reform and Organization Politics in Philadelphia* (1959); Peter H. Rossi and Robert A. Dentler, *The Politics of Urban Renewal* (1961); Harry M. Scoble, *op. cit.;* James Q. Wilson, *Negro Politics, op. cit.;* James Q. Wilson, *The Amateur Democrat: Club Politics in Three Cities* (1962); Raymond E. Wolfinger, *The Politics of Progress* (1961), unpublished Yale University doctoral dissertation.

23. See the works by Dahl, Polsby, and Wolfinger cited above, and also Robert A. Dahl, "The Concept of Power," *Behavioral Science,* 2 (1957), pp. 201-215; Nelson W. Polsby, "How to Study Community Power: The Pluralist Alternative," *Journal of Politics,* 22 (1960), pp. 474-484.

24. See the works cited in note 22 above.

25. On this last point, see Donald Olmsted, "Organizational Leadership and Social Structure in a Small City," *American Sociological Review,* 19 (1954), pp. 273-281.

26. See Robert E. Agger, "Power Attributions in the Local Community," *Social Forces,* 34 (1960), pp. 322-331; Robert E. Agger and Daniel Goldrich, "Community Power Structures and Partisanship," *American Sociological Review,* 23 (1958), pp. 383-392; Robert E. Agger and Vincent Ostrom, "The Political Structure of a Small Community," *Public Opinion Quarterly,* 20 (1956), pp. 81-89; Robert E. Agger and Vincent Ostrom, "Political Participation in a Small Community," in Heinz Eulau, Samuel Eldersveld, and Morris Janowitz (Eds.), *Political Behavior* (1957), pp. 138-148; George M. Belknap and Ralph Smuckler, "Political Power Relations in a Midwest City," *Public Opinion Quarterly,* 20 (1956), pp. 73-91; Ralph Smuckler and George M. Belknap, *Leadership and Participation in Urban Political Affairs* (1956); Harry M. Scoble, *op. cit.;* Robert K. Merton, "Patterns of Influence: A Study of Interpersonal Influence and of Communications Behavior in a Local Community," in Paul F. Lazarsfeld and Frank N. Stanton (Eds.), *Communications Research, 1948-1949* (1949), pp. 180-219; A. Alexander Fanelli, "Extensiveness of Communication Contacts and Perceptions of the Community," *American Sociological Review,* 21 (1956), pp. 439-446; A. Alexander Fanelli, "A Typology of Community Leadership Based on Influence Within the Leader Sub-System," *Social Forces,* 34 (1956), pp. 332-338; and V. O. Key, Jr., *Southern Politics, op. cit.,* pp. 99-100.

27. See B. McKee, *op. cit.;* Herbert Kaufman, "Metropolitan Leadership . . . ," *op. cit.;* Wallace S. Sayre and Herbert Kaufman, *op. cit.;*

Nelson W. Polsby, "Three Problems . . . ," *op. cit.;* Robert A. Dahl, *Who Governs?* and "Organization for Decision . . . ," *op. cit.,* and "Leadership in a Fragmented Political System . . . ," *op. cit.;* C. W. M. Hart, "Industrial Relations Research and Social Theory," *Canadian Journal of Economics and Political Science,* 15 (1949), pp. 53-73.

28. Norton E. Long, "The Local Community As an Ecology of Games," *American Journal of Sociology,* 64 (1958), pp. 251-252. See also Norton E. Long, "Aristotle and the Study of Local Government," *Social Research* (Fall 1957); Norton E. Long, "The Corporation, Its Satellites and the Local Community," in E. S. Mason (Ed.), *The Corporation and Modern Society* (1960); and Norton E. Long, "An Institutional Framework for Responsible Citizenship," in *Nomos,* 3 (Annual of the Society for Legal and Political Philosophy), 1960. All of these, and other stimulating essays by Long, are reprinted in Charles Press (Ed.), *The Polity* (1962).

29. Hugh Douglas Price, *The Metropolis . . . , op. cit.,* pp. 25-26.

30. Herbert Kaufman, "Metropolitan Leadership . . . ," *op. cit.,* p. 5. More fully in Sayre and Kaufman, *op. cit.,* pp. 710 ff.

31. See Harry M. Scoble, *op. cit.,* p. 39; Robert K. Merton, *op. cit.;* Arthur J. Vidich and Joseph Bensman, *Small Town in Mass Society* (1958), pp. 98-99; Paul A. Miller, "The Process of Decision-Making Within the Context of Community Organization," *Rural Sociology,* 16 (1952), pp. 153-161.

32. James S. Coleman, *Community Conflict* (1957). See also W. Lloyd Warner and J. O. Low, *op. cit., passim;* James B. McKee, *op. cit.;* and Morris Janowitz, *op. cit.*

33. See C. Wright Mills, *The Power Elite* (1956), for the clearest statement of this position.

34. See Peter H. Rossi and Robert A. Dentler, *op. cit.;* Martin Meyerson and Edward C. Banfield, *op. cit.;* Edward C. Banfield, *Political Influence, op. cit.;* Wallace S. Sayre and Herbert Kaufman, *op. cit.;* Robert A. Dahl, *Who Governs?, op. cit.;* Raymond Wolfinger, *op. cit.;* and on New York City, the dissertations by Lowi and Thomas, previously cited.

35. See Robert A. Dahl, "Leadership in a Fragmented Political System," *op. cit.,* for the first and most elaborate statement of this point.

36. Hugh Douglas Price, *The Metropolis . . . , op. cit.,* pp. 27-28.

37. See David B. Truman, "Theory and Research on Metropolitan Political Leadership: Report on a Conference," Social Science Research Council *Items,* 15 (March 1961).

38. See David Gold and John R. Schmidhauser, "Urbanization and Party Competition: The Case of Iowa," *Midwest Journal of Political Science,* 4 (1960), pp. 62-75; Heinz Eulau, "The Ecological Basis of Party Systems: The Case of Ohio," *Midwest Journal of Political Science,* 1 (1957), pp. 125-135; Leon D. Epstein, *op. cit.,* pp. 151, 177; Robert T. Golembiewski, "A Taxonomic Approach to the State Political Strength," *Western Political Quarterly,* 12 (1958), pp. 494-513; Donald S. Strong, *Urban Republicanism in the South* (1960).

39. An eloquent presentation of the basic hypothesis, emphasizing the consequences of "nationalization" for national party structure, is E. E. Schattschneider, "United States: The Functional Approach to Party Government," in Sigmund Neumann (Ed.), *Modern Political Parties* (1956), pp. 194-215. See also E. E. Schattschneider, *The Semi-Sovereign People* (1960).

40. V. O. Key, Jr., *American State Politics* (1956); Marvin Weinbaum, *op. cit.;* Houston Fluornoy, *The Liberal Party in New York* (1960), unpublished doctoral dissertation, Princeton University.

41. For somewhat different questions, see Murray Levin, *The Alienated Voter: Politics in Boston* (1960); Scott Greer, "Urbanism Reconsidered," *American Sociological Review,* 21 (1956), pp. 19-25.

42. See James Q. Wilson, *Negro Politics, op. cit.;* Wilson, "Two Negro Politicians: An Interpretation," *Midwest Journal of Political Science,* 4 (1960), pp. 346-369; Hugh Douglas Price, *The Negro and Southern Politics* (1957); Oscar Handlin, *The Newcomers* (1959); Oscar Glants, "The Negro Voter in Northern Industrial Cities," *Western Political Quarterly,* 13 (1960), pp. 999 ff.

43. The case for differentiation among these groups is variously put in Robert O. Schulze, *op. cit.;* Warner and Low, *op. cit.;* Long and Belknap, *op. cit.;* Sayre and Kaufman, *op. cit.,* Chap. 13; Clark, *op. cit.;* Kenneth Wilson Underwood, *Protestant and Catholic* (1957); Rossi and Dentler, *op. cit.;* Meyerson and Banfield, *op. cit.;* Arnold Bornfriend, *Business Leadership in a Metropolis: The Commerce and Industry Association of New York,* doctoral dissertation in preparation, Columbia University.

44. See Rossi and Dentler, *op. cit.;* Underwood, *op. cit.;* and, for a fictional presentation of the theme, the stories of J. F. Powers.

45. See Dahl, *Who Governs?, op. cit.,* Chap 4; Elmer E. Cornwell, Jr., "Party Absorption of Ethnic Groups," *Social Forces,* 38 (1960), pp. 205-210; Nelson W. Polsby, "Three Problems . . . ," *op. cit.* See also Will Herberg, *Protestant-Catholic-Jew* (1960); Samuel Lubell, *The Future of American Politics* (1951).

46. See August B. Hollingshead, *op. cit.;* Robert A. Dahl, "Organization for Decision in New Haven . . . ," *loc. cit.;* Neal Gross, *Who Runs Our Schools* (1959); Thomas H. Eliot, "Toward an Understanding of Public School Politics," *American Political Science Review,* 53 (1959), pp. 1032-1051; W. W. Charters, "Social Class Analysis and the Control of Education," *Harvard Educational Review,* 23 (1953), 268-283; Sayre and Kaufman, *op. cit.,* Chaps. 8 and 11. Theodore Powell, *The School Bus Law, A Case Study in Education, Religion and Politics* (1960). See also the Syracuse University Press series on *The Economics and Politics of Public Education* (12 vols., paperback, 1962-1963), especially the studies by Bailey, Wood, Frost and Marsh, Martin, Munger and Fenno, Bloomberg and Sunshine.

47. As in, for example, A. J. Liebling, *The Press* (1961). Cf. Bernard C. Cohen, *The Press and Foreign Policy* (1963).

48. See Sayre and Kaufman, *op. cit.,* Chap. 11; and dissertations by Lowi, *op. cit.,* and Thomas, *op. cit.*

49. See especially Banfield, *Political Influence,* Chap. 6.

50. Paul T. David and R. Eisenberg, *Devaluation of the Urban and Suburban Vote* (1961); Gordon E. Baker, *Rural versus Urban Political Power* (1955); David R. Derge, "Metropolitan and Outstate Alignments in Illinois and Missouri Legislative Delegations," *American Political Science Review,* 52 (1958), pp. 1051-1065; Gilbert Y. Steiner and Samuel K. Gove, *Legislative Politics in Illinois* (1960); Vernon A. O'Rourke and Douglas Campbell, *Constitution-Making in a Democracy: Theory and Practice in New York State* (1943); Sayre and Kaufman, *op. cit.,* Chap. 15; Wallace S. Sayre, "A

Rejoinder . . . ," *The Annals*, 314 (1957), pp. 82-85; Robert C. Wood, "The Case for a Department of Urban Affairs," a paper delivered at 1960 Annual Meeting of the American Political Science Association.

51. Distinguished examples of this kind of criticism are contained in Percival and Paul Goodman, *Communitas* (1960); and Lewis Mumford, *The City in History* (1961).

52. Coleman Woodbury, *Urban Studies: Some Questions of Outlook and Selection*, Sixth Annual Wherrett Lecture on Local Government of the University of Pittsburgh (1960), p. 15.

53. The Commission on Intergovernmental Relations, *A Report to the President for Transmittal to Congress* (June 1955), p. 40. See also pp. 102-103.

54. Woodbury, *op. cit., passim;* see also Robert C. Wood, *1400 Governments* (1961); Lloyd Rodwin and Kevin Lynch (eds.), "The Future Metropolis," *Daedalus* (Winter 1961); Hugh Douglas Price, "Research on Metropolitanism: Economics, Welfare and Politics," Columbia University (1959) mimeographed; Anthony Downs, *An Economic Theory of Democracy* (1957); Robert A. Dahl and Charles E. Lindblom, *Politics, Economics and Welfare* (1953).

55. The terms "ideology" and "utopia" are used here in a manner similar to the usage presented in Harold D. Lasswell and Abraham Kaplan, *Power and Society* (1950), pp. 123-133.

56. See Louis Hartz, "Democracy: Image and Reality," in W. N. Chambers and R. H. Salisbury (eds.), *Democracy in the Mid-Twentieth Century* (1960), pp. 13-29.

57. We do not mean to carry the argument as far as Jane Jacobs seems to do in *The Death and Life of Great American Cities* (1961), but see Herbert Gans, *The Urban Villagers* (1962).

58. The Institute of Government and Public Affairs at the University of Illinois is currently collecting information from a variety of sources under headings approximately like these questions. See also Rossi and Dentler, *op. cit.;* Harold Kaplan, *op. cit.;* Raymond Vernon, "The Myth and Reality of Our Urban Problems," Stafford Little Lectures of Princeton University, Spring 1961 (unpublished); and Wolfinger, *op. cit.*

59. See James Coleman, *op. cit.* The Harvard School of Public Health has a research commitment in this area, which thus far has resulted in a number of mimeographed research papers. See also Thomas F. A. Plaut, "Analysis of Voting Behavior on a Fluoridation Referendum," *Public Opinion Quarterly,* 23 (1959), pp. 213-222.

60. For an early study of urban judicial processes, see Roscoe Pound and Felix Frankfurter (eds.), *Criminal Justice in Cleveland* (1922). See also: Walter F. Murphy and C. Herman Pritchett, *Courts, Judges and Politics* (1961); Jack W. Peltason, *Federal Courts in the Political Process* (1955); Sayre and Kaufman, *op. cit.,* Chap. 14, Clement Vose, *Caucasians Only* (1959).

61. See Robert C. Wood, *Suburbia: Its People and Their Politics* (1959); Edward Sofen, *The Miami Metropolitan Experiment* (1963); Forbes Hays, *The New York Regional Plan Association* (1965); Roscoe Martin et al., *Decisions in Syracuse* (1961); Henry J. Schmandt, P. G. Steinbicker, and G. D. Wendel, *Metropolitan Reform in St. Louis: A Case Study* (1961); Leo F.

Schnore and Robert R. Alford, "Forms of Government and Socioeconomic Characteristics of 300 Suburbs," *Administrative Science Quarterly*, 8 (1963), pp. 1-17; Charles S. Liebman, "Functional Differentiation and Political Characteristics of Suburbs," *American Journal of Sociology*, 66 (1961), pp. 485-490; Henry J. Schmandt, "The City and the Ring," *The American Behavioral Scientist* (November 1960), pp. 17-19; York Willbern, "Case Studies of Metropolitan Action Programs," *Western Political Quarterly*, 12 (1959), pp. 580-581; Frederick M. Wirt, "Suburban Patterns in American Politics," paper delivered at 1960 Annual Meeting of the American Political Science Association; Robert C. Wood, *1400 Governments, op. cit.*

62. See, for suggestive leads, William A. Kornhauser, *The Politics of Mass Society* (1959); Daniel Lerner, *The Passing of Traditional Society* (1958); Seymour Martin Lipset, "Some Social Requisites of Democracy," *American Political Science Review*, 53 (1959), pp. 69-105.

63. For an interesting attempt, see Phillips Cutright, "National Political Development: Social and Economic Correlates," in Nelson W. Polsby, Robert A. Dentler, and P. A. Smith (eds.), *Politics and Social Life* (1963). See also Russell H. Fitzgibbon, "A Statistical Evaluation of Latin American Democracy," *Western Political Quarterly*, 9 (1956), pp. 607-619, and Phillips Cutright, "National Political Development: Measurement and Analysis," *American Sociological Review*, 28 (1963), pp. 253-264.

VI

PUBLIC ADMINISTRATION AND ORGANIZATION BEHAVIOR

12 Administrative Behavior Research

WILLIAM J. GORE, University of Washington

> In a search for programs of activity to achieve goals, the focus of attention will tend to move from one class of variables to another in the following general sequence . . . (1) Those variables that are largely within the control of the problem-solving individual or organizational unit will be considered first . . . (2) If a satisfactory program is not discovered by these means, attention will be directed to changing other variables that are not under the direct control of problem solvers; . . . (3) If a satisfactory program is still not evolved attention will be turned to the criteria that the program must satisfy, and an effort will be made to relax these criteria so that a satisfactory program can be found.—*March and Simon*

I. INTRODUCTION

The structures of most governmental programs are creaking and groaning not from the weight of the massive claims we make against them, but from cracks in some of the timbers from which they are constituted. If the possibility of structural unreliability in the bureaucratic foundations of our great governmental programs is not yet a matter of general public concern, it has become the object of widespread professional concern. It has become the object of a professional dialogue among a number of scholars from a variety of disciplines.

What is central to this discussion is not the course and content of the dialogue itself, but some of the premises and several of its unexamined presuppositional underpinnings. Implicit in an open professional dialogue through which we seek agreement upon the nature and extent of structural deterioration of bureaucracy is a presumption central to our whole approach to governing—the belief that the ultimate function of politics is to facilitate the engineering of program mechanisms which embody (in the structures through which their costs and benefits are allocated) an accommodation of the competing claims for their goods and services among those clienteles which manage to substantiate a legitimate place for themselves in the policy-making arena.

The customary approach to program strain has been to assume that the source of strain—the "problem," to use the customary label—is a disjuncture between the allocation of values provided by the existing structure of a program and an emergent configuration of clientele (and other) interests, which implies another allocation of values. Attempts to resolve program strains by seeking new points of structural homeostasis have frequently only exacerbated program strains. This has led some students of administration and bureaucracy to consider reexamination of our regimes for achieving political accommodation. It is one prong of this reexamination that defines the focus of this discussion.

Fragmented Perspectives

Any attempt to reexamine the efficacy of our strategies for achieving political accommodation—"policy making" is the customary label—requires recognition of the existence of competing representations of policy making. These competing views exist not only between scholars in different disciplines, but there are also some sharp contrasts in the conceptions of the dynamics of policy making among political scientists. To reexamine the efficacy of governmental policy making in any depth raises the necessity for identifying the reasons for these competing perspectives.

Perhaps the most dramatic of the many developments in political science since World War II is the differentiation or fragmentation of the discipline into a multiplicity of fields. The initial impetus toward the proliferation of fields is clear; the constructs which emerged from the forties were too crass, too undifferentiated to sustain the research believed necessary to plumb the policy problems of the postwar polity.

That there has been benefit not only to the profession but also to society from the modest knowledge explosion resulting from the proliferation of fields into subfields needs no demonstration. Public administration, a field of most modest pretentions early in this century, illustrates what happened. It grew rapidly in the thirties, reaching proportions that led to subdivision into several subfields in the late forties. During the fifties several of these subfields were subdivided once again, and during the sixties this once unpretentious field has begun to establish itself as a separate discipline, an interdiscipline, as some of my colleagues have called it.

The emergence of interdisciplines in both the social and physical sciences reflects our need for knowledge in manageable packages. It may also reflect a need for more than one level of descriptive constructs. On the one hand, we need to increase our understanding of particular administrative processes, for example. Budgeting becomes differentiated as a sub-subfield, only to be followed by its further differentiation through nodes of literature dealing with performance

emergence of interdisciplines

budgets, programmed budgets, capital budgets, and so on. On the other hand, we have needs to understand such things as the legislative functions of budget reviews and the economic impacts of capital budgeting. Specialized theories providing high resolution and detail are not sufficient. The need for constructs of lower resolution but broader perspective is one kind of force fostering an interdiscipline, which is useful as a vehicle for fusing fragments of fields not only in one but in several disciplines. Certainly the Schools of Public Affairs that are emerging on many major campuses serve an important purpose when they facilitate these kinds of recombinations of theory fragments. Our capacity to plumb the dynamics of the policy process has been substantially extended by relating together components of decision theory, game theory, cybernetics, and theories of conflict and of innovation and change, not to mention managerial economics and political development.

Yet when one asks whether an ingenious fusion of these diverse perspectives into a synthetic construct has the potential (not capacity) of providing enough knowledge to ameliorate the structural deterioration affecting the efficacy of some programs, one may well answer in the negative. In fact, it may be that we are approaching a point in the accretion of structural deterioration where we shall have to question the adequacy of bureaucracy as we know it for the emerging challenges to self-government.

Man versus Environment

Governmental programs are collective mechanisms for producing goods and services. Typically they are extensive in their scope and of considerable impact upon the social scene because of their saliency. But any collective is also a social host for the specialized behavior it sustains, a man-made ambience designed so as to be uniquely supportive of seriously valued, carefully provided-for activities. In this latter role, governmental programs are intended to mediate man's relationships with his environment. The history of the development of every governmental program constitutes an attempt to turn man's interdependence with his environment in his favor. Invariably the development of a program becomes a succession of increasingly more effective attempts to shift the balance of rewards at its interface with environment in favor of those participating in the program.

The primary instrumentality through which this enterprise is carried on is not the program, however, but the complex organization. Programs are constituted of networks of organizations as carefully coordinated with one another as the machines on the floor of a factory or the independent components of a computer system.

Gradually, but at an accelerated rate, we tame one after another element of our environment. In the case of many programs (parks, for example), we have actually displaced a traditional and often indigenous or "natural" environment with a man-made ambience. Many complex organizations (hospitals, for example) can be conceived of as epi-environments that we insert between ourselves and an undisplaceable element of the "state of nature." So extensive and so comprehensive are these epi-environments that we have not only shifted the balance of the man-environment interdependency in favor of man, but by fashioning a nested set of epi-environments we have also begun to give man dominance, if not mastery, over certain of his environments (biophysical, for example).

That the balance has shifted into the zone of dominance (along a continuum from subjugation to mastery of the environment) if only recently is a truism. Historically, governmental programs have been focal in our struggle against the distressing disruption of our affairs by capricious environments. Our current policy-making processes presume—if only implicitly—that we expect only to improve our position vis-à-vis environment. Past some point the character of the dynamics of accommodation changes. A flood-control program based upon the construction of a series of expensive dams over a very long period of time comes eventually to a critical point where it is no longer a means of avoiding floods but an instrumentality for the virtual control of not only a river but also the hydrologic component of a whole river basin.

In the remainder of this discussion we shall examine several of the perspectives which articulate the dynamics of complex organizations in an attempt to identify some of the forces operative in the structural deterioration which threatens the efficacy of some governmental programs.

II. EVOLUTION OF ORGANIZATIONAL THEORY

If it is only a truism to assert that complex organizations are "man-made," it is nevertheless pertinent to another of our concerns. There is a widespread inclination toward the view that that which man has constituted is inherently understandable by him. Many of the theories and constructs that will be referred to below have been formulated in contradiction to this view. In fact, in some instances those persons who formed the instrumentalities for formally understanding complex organizations have felt that their efforts were necessary precisely because of the gross misunderstandings resulting from the then popular conceptions.

Origins of Complex Organizations

The evidence indicates that communities have existed for twenty-thousand years or more; associations linking traders together into traveling bands may have existed for twice that long. Man's reliance on collectives is of long standing indeed; but it is only relatively recently that he has undertaken a more positive and assertive posture toward them. Self-conscious manipulation of complex organizations is today the norm; it is what we expect from our commerce with them. This statement does not suggest that the ancients did not consider the possibility of molding social systems to serve their purposes. Plato had a good deal to say about a well-designed city-state, for example. However, the ancients did not seriously undertake to manage change in their collectives; and in this they were realistic, for successful management of organizational change can only be accomplished on the basis of reliable, empirically anchored knowledge. The ancients had only folklore available to them.

Successful managing of change in complex organizations requires not only analytic constructs but also normative and valuational formulations, for to determine the future course of collective activities successfully requires shared understandings of how they presently function and commonly accepted commitments as to where they ought to be heading. These conditions are merely necessary, not sufficient; for when there is a belief that the collective ought to be traveling a route it does not have the capability to traverse, strain is the inevitable result.

The ancients were not blind to the need for conceptual analogues for both latitude and longitude in setting a course for a collective. Aristotle's descriptive analysis of constitutional systems is only the most stereotyped example of an attempt to build a descriptive construct; and there are at least some who would credit Machiavelli with formally insisting upon the mating of descriptive and prescriptive constructs as the basis for making effective political decisions.[1]

With the reemergence of science in the sixteenth and seventeenth centuries, we came to see the desirability of a third kind of conceptual resource in casting stable, enduring policy decisions. Descriptive theories, we came to hold, describe the state of a collective at a given moment; prescriptive theories define future states of the collective we seek to invoke in place of what exists; analytic theories—in which inheres the capacity to anticipate the dynamics of a social system at some future date—are required to chart a course from the former to the latter.

At the time, and for some centuries thereafter, there was often ardent controversy as to whether scientists were not intent upon doing violence to the idealized conceptions through which philosophers identified how the collective should be brought to the point where they pronounced its having fulfilled its promise. Over the years many facets of the competition between normative and descriptive imperatives have been developed—some at length and others incompletely. New research technologies and vast research facilities seem to have conspired to reduce the preeminence that normative constructs once had in political science. Without asking what use the appropriate blend of these epistemological components will be if we are to maximize our capacity to manage the course of collective enterprises (perhaps a variety of "mixes" is needed), we shall posit—as a basis for discussion—the following as factors relevant to managing change in complex organizations:[2]

1. *Prescriptive theories* which identify in a coherent and internally consistent manner the kind of social environment we seek; and which elaborate these through concretized conceptions, presenting at least some aspects of the verbal ideal in actualizable form.
2. *Descriptive theories* which represent (with the requisite level of validity and reliability) the structures and processes of all of the elements of the polity.
3. *Analytic theories* which enable us to forecast the conditions under which political change will occur as well as the directions it can take.

We are suggesting, in short, that in order to be successful in managing the sequence of changes through which a collective develops, there must be a minimally extensive cognitive structure, constituted of prescriptive, descriptive, and analytic elements. The tremendous gain in our success in managing complex organizations in the past two decades, we would argue, is the consequence of the rapid development of the descriptive and analytic components of the cognitive structures undergirding our ability to project a collective goal object, engineer a social mechanism appropriate to its implementation, and then forecast the consequences (negative as well as positive) on the rest of the organization.

Origins of Social Theory

Durkheim and Comte are sometimes identified with the emergence of analytical social theories. In regard to complex organizations one titan's name stands out, however—Max Weber. Though it may not have been Weber's intention to give Western man the theoretical competence to enter into widespread manipulation of his social inheritance, this competence is unquestionably one—if only one—of the consequences of his work.[3]

It was Weber, more than anyone else, who first formalized our conceptions of complex organization which he labeled *bureaucracies*. His initial classifications of bureaucracies brought conceptual order to our understandings, introducing a presupposition of profound proportions, namely, that bureaucracies have elements in common with natural systems.

The unfolding of political philosophy brought formulations with an increasing emphasis on the social mechanisms required to effectuate idealized conceptions of government. By the seventeenth and eighteenth centuries much political philosophy had come to focus upon one predominant agent for governing—the nation-state. This step in the extension of the explanatory power of philosophically generated theories was important in that it concentrated energies on a single conceptual entity. Over time, crude analogues perscribing the character of democratic government were elaborated into formal, empirically oriented descriptions which provided ever more detailed conceptions of the relevant social machinery. Willy-nilly descriptive elements came to serve as woof to the warp of normative conceptions in the tapestry of political philosophy. There does not seem to be much basis for holding that, as the broad thrust of political philosophy moved from a concern with such dialectic issues as "the good life" and "justice" to a concern with the forms and elements of the state promising the most democratic quality of government, those forming these theories came to a self-conscious reliance upon empiricism, descriptive concepts, or statistical generalization. It is only to suggest that knowing—in the sense of knowing about reality in such a way that we can manipulate it—has probably become dependent upon the prior, and verbal, joint manipulation of prescriptive and descriptive conceptions.

This sum of a host of important developments suggests that, as we come into increasing capacity to mold (and hence exploit) environment through the interposition of more and more collectives between ourselves and "the State of Nature," pressures for ever more pertinent theories increased. Society—one way or another—has taken notice of developments in normative political theory, which have moved from exhortation to prescription.

Rousseau exemplifies those who "focused down" from exhorting men to live justly into prescribing a coherent set of specifications for the institutional mechanisms through which democracy could be realized in the political arena.[4] His concern with displacing the power to govern from the European aristocracy to a constituent citizenry, which was by definition "democratic," illustrates what we have in mind here. When he follows this through to the specification of the processes through which informed preferences (of the citizenry) are to be aggregated through the interplay of legislative politics, he relies heavily upon descriptive, empirically relevant, if not statistically based, conceptions.

It is not at all irrelevant to what we shall argue below to make explicit the genetic connection between exhortative, utopianist theories of democracy and the descriptive theories so central to our current attempts at building and rebuilding political mechanisms. Comprehensive, empirically anchored theories (such as Weber's) of political and bureaucratic processes were in large part a derivative, a logical extension of the ever more highly elaborated utopian theories of democracy. It is not merely that social theory has its lineage in political as well as social philosophy; political philosophizing provided the context, the epistemic substructure which was a requisite for a relevant and pertinent descriptive theory. Political philosophy provided both the focus and framework within which were raised theories devised self-consciously to allow man to manipulate the man-environment relationship.

Understandably, it was the particularistic problems of how to organize the legislature or how to monitor the flow of funds that first claimed the attention of those who sought to raise theories designed to facilitate the building of a more comprehensive social ambience. Perhaps this followed because the descriptive theories provided by social theorists were not entirely compatible with some of the premises implanted in prescriptive formulations.

Strains Between Prescriptive and Descriptive Theories

Prescriptive and descriptive theories were, and often still are, in strain over premises at two points. Much of what was written in behalf of democratic government took as its premise the desirability of substituting the collective reason of the citizenry for the tradition-based power of Europe's elites. The public interest, the general welfare, or the general will could—it was posited—be found through deliberation by the constituency and made the basis for public policy. While there have been some difficulties with the presupposition (a) that a general will or its equivalent can be evoked (especially in a crisis situation) or (b) that democracy is the appropriate device through which it can manifest itself, it is another aspect of the matter which interests us.

Public deliberation—efficacious, problem-based, issue-resolving public dialogue—does not flower as the necessary consequence of bestowing the franchise. Meaningful public dialogue is possible only when there are political parties and interest groups and a multiplicity of other social mechanisms appropriately linked within a comprehensive polity that channels preference-forming activities. Meaningful public dialogue is the product of relevant social structures.

Even more important, however, is the presence of an educational system through which the individual is socialized into roles appropriate to (and functional for) the democratic polity. Reason, to put the matter in the terms of the traditional dialectic, is merely a necessary, not a sufficient, condition for the existence of democracy. Again, in terms of the philosophical dialectic, reason becomes an actuality in our affairs through viable and relevant social structures. The rhetorician, at least, often presumed that to accept the preeminence of reason was equivalent to adopting it as the basis for one's behavior. Social theorists have made a place for themselves in our public affairs precisely because they have concerned themselves with the translation of ideals into action through appropriate structures, in which motivity is transformed—ultimately—into social income through the channeling that takes place in interpersonal relationships.

Specifying premises for the whole of a scholarly enterprise is a slippery business. Yet perhaps one could characterize much prescriptive theory as embodying the premise that men can mold and remold their social institutions according to their collective will. Perhaps it is endemic that this kind of theorizing underemphasizes the constraints placed by environment and the nature of man himself upon his molding of social institutions. In any event, the social theorist attempts to devise formal paradigms which describe the operation of these constraints to the free expression of will, in ever more detail.

Many of those concerned with perfecting democratic forms of government took it as an article of faith that democracy embodied the potentiality of enabling them to harness what they perceived as the vast power of reason to what they sensed as an immense capacity in complex organizations. If this implicit premise received little more than incidental consideration from those concerned with formulating the conceptions through which the idealized forms of democracy were translated into appropriate structures, perhaps it is because they felt hard-pressed merely to consummate the engineering of the ideal into credible blueprints of democratic structures. The larger potentiality—that these more complex institutions could be exploited to tip the balance in the man-environment interdependency—could only be seriously entertained after experience had shown that the viability of the remolded polity could be assumed.

It is this article of faith—that man can impose his design for his transactions with his environment by fusing Reason into complex organizations—that defines the thrust of many normative formulations about democratic government and virtually all early prescriptions for complex organizations. If characterizing them as concerned ultimately with providing regimes for a more rewarding *adaptation* to environment is simplistic, still it allows us to characterize the nature of an unstated goal.

More Recent Theories of Complex Organizations

The suggestion being made is that it is possible that we are witnesses to the breaking of a historical thread. From the beginning of human history man has viewed himself, in relation to his environment, as being somewhat disadvantaged. The theme of Man as an antagonist of Nature and the natural world is deeply embedded in much political philosophizing.

The natural world has neither been displaced nor transcended in the sense that these terms were used by those for whom Reason represented the ultimate manifestation of intellect. Yet in some important though as yet not sharply defined sense there is an implicit assertion in much of what is being said about complex organization that man is no longer the creature of his environment.

Quite obviously, man has not transcended his environment by evading or in some other way freeing himself completely from the constraints of Nature. And clearly, he has not left the familiar confines of this world for some never-never land. Still, he has been able to mobilize technology, harness innovation, mold expectations, and exploit resources so that, in developed societies, he is in fact largely free from such natural threats as epidemics, starvation, immobility, and ignorance. Environment is not—in the thinking of many social theorists—an inexorable referent against which the success of collective efforts must of necessity be gauged. The instrumentality of this transcendence without transcending is the complex organization— actually constellations of them—which we have interposed as a man-made environment between ourselves and Nature. And it is our growing capability to mold and remake these epi-environments that accounts for the ambiguity in regard to man's present capability in relation to Nature.

To repeat, Nature has not been displaced; however, its disruptive penetration into people's lives has been mitigated, often by the inter-positioning of a complex organization in the man-environment inter-dependency. Hospitals, fire departments, and flood-control agencies are obvious examples. Nor has man transcended limits imposed by the natural and life-giving processes of his physiology, though he has created new and sometimes mutationally different extensions to his social ambience which are remolding human nature. Whether we choose to affirm our transcending of certain environmental restraints, such a transcendence is taking place and shall continue at an increasing pace.

The proposition that man is modifying the context (environment) within which public policy is made introduces the need for more responsive policy-making regimes. We shall argue that there is an inherent self-defeating circularity in our practices for managing complex organizations that may place our public programs in some jeopardy.

III. SELF-CONSCIOUS DESIGN OF PRODUCTIVE MECHANISMS

If the gradual emergence of the factory and the displacement of the artisan are arbitrarily taken as marking the origins of the contemporary or complex organization, organizational theory can be said to have its roots in attempts to manage the developmental changes through which the factory was formed. And though it is nothing more than the folklore of management that the factory as a system of action was created in two phases, it is a useful point of departure to suggest that initially the factory was elaborated through the invention of machinery; it was only in a second stage of development, much later, that the need for social invention and later social engineering emerged. And it was only very much later, after the development of a social technology relevant to the factory as a social system had begun to prove its efficacy, that serious attention was given to the social engineering of public activities.

An important qualification ought to be made, however. We have been conceiving and building formal governmental mechanisms in Western societies for centuries. The whole technology of jurisprudence was used to conceive, form, and sanction public agencies. In fact, it was jurisprudence—with its elaborate rituals for the translation of Reason into rules of behavior—that served as the vehicle for the expression of the prescriptions of those who early concerned themselves with perfecting democracy. The process was forthright enough: define a social problem by identifying deviations in the practice of government from that specified in the constitution; examine the problem to ascertain why the deviation occurred; legislate additional laws to correct the deviancy by revising or extending the original legal arrangements. Jurisprudence initially served primarily as a means by which man sought to induce order into his environment, Nature being presumed to be inherently chaotic. Its intrusions into our affairs could be ameliorated if it were given some order. Eventually jurisprudence came to serve as a mechanism for imposing an orderly overlay of social action upon all of man's social ambience. So long as society consisted of relatively small enclaves of people living in collectives based upon affective or folk-culture relationships, and so long as there were vast social gulfs between almost all collectives (and their clienteles), jurisprudence was a serviceable device for regulating social relationships. If providing for relationships between collectives can be equated with maintaining the superstructure of society, then this assertion can be recast to indicate that so long as society was based upon *autonomous, affective-based* mechanisms—such as the traditional community—the legal mechanisms of jurisprudence were adequate for ordering social commerce.

The hallmark of the traditional community, a classic example of a folk-culture, was the strength of the ties between its members and their virtual isolation from the rest of their society (in terms of affective involvements). The village served as a mediating mechanism between the secondary social environments and virtually all of the members of the traditional community.

Factories are only the stereotyped example of the production-oriented, object-based, single-purposed social system, where the dependence relationships of the traditional folk-culture were displaced. Isolated from the intimate social commerce through which artisans working in shops sustained themselves, subjugated by the discipline of the machine in place of the naturally varying rhythms of an affective-oriented group, and subjected to not only multiple but sometimes conflicting external sources of authority in place of the benign, unitary authority of the traditional community, the industrial worker required very different social mechanisms to sustain him. These mechanisms were not provided for by those seeking to improve the complex organization as an instrumentality of production; and socially sustaining relationships were not legitimate within the terms of the legalistic bases upon which authority was dispensed.

The maturation of the nation-state as the vehicle for the active management of public affairs is matched by the emergence of the complex organization (of which the factory is only one example) as the mechanism of production. Kornhauser has suggested that it may be the conjunction between these two social instrumentalities that facilitated the rise to mass society.[5] Certainly, the mating of these two types of organization in a comprehensive societal mechanism—when joined by a third great social mechanism, the metropolis—led to irreversible changes in Western civilization.

For a metropolis to take its place in this emerging structure, the traditional community, with its deepseated claims against the individual, had to be displaced. But the traditional community was the social host for the family, and the family was the social host for civilized man. It was through the family as reinforced by the traditional community that Western man had channeled, tamed, and then calibrated his energies to the elaborate social mechanisms through which he sustained a burgeoning civilization.

The family, as sustained by the traditional community, was the mechanism for the socialization of the individual; inevitably this instrumentality of man's socialization assumed latent surrogate functions for him. Any direct threat to this surrogate was an implicit threat to his adequacy vis-à-vis his environment. The sounds of the collision of the tradition-oriented (rural) and the mass-oriented (urban) structures reverberate still. Western man could not reduce his dependence upon so salient a mechanism as the traditional community without jeopardizing his very identity.

Yet the potential trade-offs were attractive and to some extent imperative. Restrict the claims (as well as the functions) of the traditional community; increase the individual's psychological investment of himself in the complex organization; in place of the self-regulating, self-balancing social dynamic of the traditional community substitute self-conscious regulation of the commerce between complex organizations by the state. The result is a multilayered social system of incredible productive capability. Democracy came to imply not merely political equality; some undreamed-of redistribution of creature comforts providing for the physical security of the individual became embedded in what had earlier been only a political idealization.

Again, we are not suggesting that complex organizations in themselves were completely new in the eighteenth and nineteenth century. The church, the great mercantile companies, and many other social instrumentalities having something of this character had been in existence in Europe. What is new—in the past century—is their dominance in our society and the consequent displacement of most of the traditional collectives with their seamless structure in which each organization is meshed with all others; and where—as a consequence—the (social) environmental imperatives which come to bear upon the individual have an internal consistency. With the consummation of this displacement emerged an open society in which combines of complex organizations contend with each other for the privilege of legitimizing the values defining their particular (product) societal input.

The man on the street may not have understood why shoe factories could make more shoes and more kinds of shoes for very much lower prices than cobblers, but it was apparent that the great production mechanisms abuilding in the emergent metropolitan centers were somehow associated with the dramatically richer life-style developing there. Perhaps we are justified in claiming that complex organizations are the engines of our society, since they were the vehicles through which we accomplished the complementary developments which brought us to our current stage of development (or over-development, as the case may be).

IV. DEVELOPMENT OF ORGANIZATIONAL TECHNOLOGY

One of the first Americans to concern himself with formal analysis of the complex organizations was a man whose orientation was that of an engineer. Though Frederick Taylor is said to have begun his studies on bricklayers, his attention came finally to focus upon many elements of the firm. In contrast to those engineers who were interested in inventing machines and organizing factories to mass-produce a given item, Taylor was interested in a technology for perfecting factories as social systems. Given a firm comprehending a plant, the relevant machines, the necessary raw materials, and a corps of workers, how can these factors of production best be united in one mechanism so as to allow production at peak efficiency? Efficiency in this context is attained by maximizing positive achievement of one goal while concurrently maximizing negative achievement of another.[6] Taylor's formulations became the focus of increasing attention from the managerial elite that came to prominence early in this century and that sought to legitimize itself by demonstrating its prowess through impressive increases in profits. The eventual displacement of the ritualistic, legalistic managerial perspectives of the nineteenth century by the perspectives of Taylor's Scientific

Management movement is testimony to the extent to which our society accepted—if only implicitly—the trading (or reinterpretation) of social security for (or as) material affluence.

Scientific Management's preoccupation with "rationalizing" managerial decisions was important not so much because it gave managers a new regime for making decisions but because it provided new conceptualizations. Organizations could now be separated into components, each of which was to be understood in terms of its own functions in a larger and multifunctional social system, and each of which could be manipulated within a larger strategy of change. Taylor provided a technology which enabled managers to devise both the internal economies of scale that specialization allowed and the external economies that could be attained by manipulating the mix of production factors.

Scientific Management gave way to Management Theory in the second quarter of this century. Management Theory provided a much broader spectrum of concepts and a corresponding extension of the decisional competence of the manager. Central to Management Theory were formulations which provided still further differentiation of organizational processes. The procurement of resources, for example, was set off as an activity that could be distinguished from the mobilization of these resources; by considering the allocation of resources distinct from their transformation into goods and services, Management Theory introduced decisional regimes, which gave yet another quantum increase to the manager's already extensive control over organizational processes.[7]

Some years later Managerial Economics was to legitimize Management Theory's basic intellectual strategy of careful analysis of the factors of production and their interrelationships.[8] By this time, however, it was beginning to become clear that schedules, unit costs, rates of production and other indices dear to management were relevant dimensions, not of the total dynamics of production, but of the week-to-week flow of organizational activities.

Contradictory Imperatives

The cumulation of Scientific Management, Management Theory, and Managerial Economics provided the foundation for an organizational technology which gave managers effective control over the productive capability of the complex organization prior to World War II. But, even as this technology was achieving something approaching universal acceptance, it became apparent that a most profound dimension of the organization as a collective was being overlooked—its survival. Survival is not the term that was used, however. Management Theorists viewed complex organizations as production mechanisms; the market defined the environment within which these largely autonomous organisms were seen as operating. In the private sector of the economy competition between firms was posited as of ultimate value; it was not until after World War II that we began to examine carefully the social costs of competition. Perhaps it should be added that this delay was as much because of the centrality of competition in the market mechanisms of change as because of the limited perspective of Management Theory. In the end the contradictory imperatives of making, a profit and surviving led to severe reinterpretations of the role of profit making and then of competition within market mechanisms in our society.

In the public or governmental sector of our society, in that artificial social space presumably secured against competition for profit, public agencies were seen as benign mechanisms through which the "will of the majority" was implemented. Although the reasons why men would behave so differently from one sector to another were seldom drawn in detail, it was held that public agencies were creatures of the sovereign, bound to the will of the people's elected representatives, while the firm was constrained only by the forces of marketplace.

That both of these representations were so gratuitous as to be essentially misleading we have only now begun to demonstrate. Those dealing with the Theory of the Firm have begun to show that each firm is in fact locatable within interdependent grids through which every factor of a market is structured in intricate detail; only thus can a modest potentiality of survival be provided for.[9] And survival, we have come to postulate, is the primary dynamic of bureaucracies.

Since vast amounts of social capital must be invested to form the understandings which underlie programs, it is not surprising to discover potent forces behind extensive program-building demands. These forces are not difficult to find.

Profit maximization depends not on a single factor, but upon several interdependent dimensions of the market (resource unit costs, market fluidity, product substitutability, and so forth) which no agency or firm can hope to cope with effectively in terms of its own power base. For this reason it is more profitable in the long run to pour some surpluses into the maintenance of access to certain scarce resources (thus stabilizing unit costs of the whole resource "mix" of an agency), by participating in a mechanism through which market organization is maintained, than to "take" these surpluses immediately as profits. Agencies so arrange their relationships that competition which could result in product (or service) substitution is averted.

Mergers are—from at least one perspective—a potent device for intensively organizing so much of the environment for an organization that it can attain something approaching dominance over its ambience. Public programs serve this function in the governmental sector, for they provide a constituency large enough to insure the legitimacy of a domain. Logically, there comes a point of balance in the growth of a program where its reach and its grasp come into such a fine alignment that it becomes self-sustaining. In practice, this balance seldom occurs; and when it does, it cannot be sustained.

The difficulty seems to be that as the reach of an organization comprehends more and more of its environment, there is a very rapid increase in disruptive pressures that reflect penetration of the markets or resource bases into some domain perceived by another organization to be under its jurisdiction. Most programs are unable to maintain their grasp on the factors of production at the edges of their domain.

The result is a social mechanism characterized by high productive capability and low stability. Some argue that this arrangement is ideal, for when we take account of the political pressures which play against these unstable systems, their mercurial tendencies serve to make them very responsive to clientele and other claims.

It can be argued, then, that the succession of sociopolitical mechanisms we have experienced in this century has served us well. In place of the static and overly rigid traditional community, we have the metropolis with its multiplicity of open-end mechanisms; and in place of the highly rationalized, ritualistic, legalistic bureaucratic structures of the traditional government department, we have great programs which are loosely constituted constellations of clientele, production-oriented and facilitative and allocative groups. The shear between short-range imperatives pushing this system toward increasing productivity (by pouring all available resources into output) and the long-range imperatives toward strengthening the structure of the program (by pouring all available resources into building co-optative relationships) is said to insure that the whole system is highly adaptive. Adaptive capability is systemic, a consequence of the interaction of those dynamic forces within public programs which are largely beyond the control of its participants.

Management Science

We have yet made no mention of economic man, that hypothetical but nonexistent entity populating these abstract domains. Guided in all he does by profit-maximizing motives, he is presented as the vehicle through which the market is actualized. If his information is less than perfect, what happens to the self-regenerative dynamics we impute to the political "market system"? Even when he has full information, his preference structures have all the transiency of a pile of sand, and then to what does the conception of aggregated preferences refer? Does technology inevitably bias the structure of the market when it is intended only as a mechanical catalyst? These and many other issues tarnish the promise of our inheritance from a complex of disciplines rooted in the traditions of economics.

Still there is considerable conceptual power in this perspective toward complex organizations, and an interdiscipline of recent origin provides a label for much of this. Management Science embodies a fusion of electronic data processing, information theory, rational decision-making strategies, as well as several other technologies relevant to the exploitation of complex organizations.[10]

To return to an earlier theme, so long as we find ourselves in the role of stalwart and honorable antagonists of an inexorable environment, so long as the function of management is clearly unidimensional (to seek and maintain an ever more positive balance of payments vis-à-vis environment), Management Science provides a powerful regime for the management of our public affairs. The magnificence of our vast networks of complex organizations is testimony to this power.

V. SOCIAL THEORY AND SOCIAL INNOVATION

There is no well-recognized difference between the terms "social mechanisms" and "social system"; they are often used synonymously. We shall impute a distinction between them for purposes of this discussion, for there is a need to differentiate between two extensive bodies of knowledge and doctrine about complex organizations.

Let the label *social mechanism* mark those dimensions and the perspective discussed above; in terms of some of the metaphors used there, let this term refer to the technology which treats complex organizations as the engines (mechanisms) of our society. Then use the term *social system* to demarcate another constellation of dimensions constituting an alternative perspective toward complex organizations. Derived from another set of disciplines, anchored in another footing of presuppositions, and increasingly offering a valuational challenge to Management Science, social-systems conceptions deserve elaboration.

Some of the contrast between these perspectives can be seen in assumptions that they embody about the individual. Economic man, as invoked by management scientists, is not infrequently a largely self-sufficient, self-directing person, one who knows his own self-interest and pursues it in enlightened ways within the context of an open market. He is seen as having a relatively large as well as a diverse set of interests which, while not unique to him, are still divergent in some important respects from the interests of those he lives with as well as those he lives among. The maintenance of diversity is ultimately one of the primary functional justifications for the marketplace. The psychodynamics of rational choice-making against the criteria of enlightened self-interest is posited as the most efficacious mechanism for the organization of collective behavior. If the reduction of felt needs—clearly a universal claim against our energies—is posited as the object of behavior, there is much to be said in favor of the explanatory capacity of this formulation.

For such an individual, complex organizations—as "social markets"—are seen as optimal environments for the pursuit of need reductions. Collective behavior directed toward need reduction being mediated by enlightened self-interest, there is then a systemic mechanism for the aggregation of preferences which takes account of the diversity among individual needs.

Social man, to juxtapose one stereotype with another, is characterized somewhat differently. Finding not merely an identity, but a succession of identities (one for each of the seven classic stages in the lifetime of a man, for example), is not infrequently seen as his destiny. One of the inconveniences with this perspective is the lack of agreement on the ends of both individual and collectivized behavior. Only a generation ago the individual's need to find an adjustment (to his environment) was suggested as the ultimate object of his activities. One can choose from a full spectrum of representations; but whatever one's tastes, they all tend toward a common presupposition about man's ultimate interdependence with his own kind rather than his dependence upon a neutral, natural, biophysical environment implicit in many social-mechanism formulations.

Theories concerned with social systems invoke an individual who—while dependent upon this tiered structure of progressively more intimate, more immediate epi-environments—can be, and ultimately is, at once both dependent upon and autonomous with regard to his social ambience. It seems clear that one reason for this ambiguity in the representation of the individual in social systems theories stems from something approaching a contradiction in the human condition. A woman whose children have left home is still their mother; but she is a woman whose mothering is no longer needed and who no longer serves as a mother—only as one who was once so identified. Her needs as a mother are no longer likely to find adequate reduction nor effective expression in this circumstance; and yet the alternative—displacement of this role-based identity—does violence to the manner in which she has invested much of her life. A politician out of office, like an actor without a play, reflects the same kind of difficulty in matching the succession of external roles to internal conceptions of self.

Truncated Interaction Structures

Given the existence of an individual with a conglomeration of internally and externally dictated needs, there arises a secondary "need," a systemic imperative arising from the psychodynamics of the individual for some organization of these needs.[11] Identity has been used above to identify this crucial kind of concern; it may be little more than a play on words to refer to the individual's need to maintain his identity, but it makes clear the contrast between the relative survival values of immediate felt needs and the imperatives embedded in personality as a system of action through which the individual seeks to maintain a commerce with multiple environments (by means of which he achieves the reduction of his felt needs).

The relation between man and his environment was earlier broken down into a two-staged process wherein man provided himself with epi-environments which he then linked to the natural order of things. We can now add a third component to this chain of relationships if we differentiate between the "inner man" who seeks to maintain the integrity of his identity and the "public self" through which a personality relates to its multiple epi-environments. We now have man as a personality sustaining himself on a distinctly different level of experience from man as a complex of need-reduction-oriented, externalized roles. It is the latter, more immediate, more superficial, and distinctly more expedient layer of experience that is linked to epi-environments, which are in their turn linked to the classical State of Nature.

Quite in contrast to the ethical imperative of some political philosophers, social theorists posit man not as the would-be master of all he surveys, but man in interaction and interdependency with others, through this four-tiered structure. Choice-making on the part of the individual takes place within the dynamic context of these nested "environments," each of which levies constraints and demands against, as well as offering opportunities and benefits to, those adjacent to it.

Self-conscious, self-identified man—from his position in the center of this bullseye-like structure—must influence his epi-environments by manipulating his own needs. And if he would proceed beyond this manipulation to influence the natural order of things, he must be prepared to make proportionately larger traumatic manipulations of his felt needs as the price of penetration.

Interdependency, as manifest in these stages of transaction, has an immediate and patent implication for the policy-making process. In practice, the dialogues we consider as constituting the policy-making process are limited to the transactions which take place at the level of felt needs; accordingly, it is not difficult to understand the efficacy of managerial rationality as a device through which the policy decision is cast. However, if we add to this either of the other stages from this larger conception, there is the possibility of circularity being introduced into managerial-decision processes, for epi-environment is no longer a given but only another unknown in the man-environment equation when we somehow come to the enter-prise of changing our natural environment.

The phenomenon, while seldom recognized in the folklore of management, is not new to us. Its existence was first documented during a classic experiment in the Western Electric Corporation during the Hawthorne studies of Roethlisberger and Dickson some forty years ago.[12] Women in the bank wiring room responded to improved working conditions with increased productivity—as Management Theory forecast. When they then responded to experimentally induced deteriorating working conditions with still higher productivity, the forecasts of Management Theory were contradicted. The explanation often given is that to the women in the bank wiring room these changes came to be viewed as expressions of management's arriving at a new appreciation of what they could accomplish, of an expanded conception of their potentialities for identity-taking. So potent was this external penetration of their inchoate need for identity expansion that their overriding of the felt needs involved with working conditions was almost incidental.

The Hawthorne studies have been widely interpreted as demonstrating reciprocity inherent in the interdependence between man and his environment. The women engaged in wiring *imputed* an identity-affirming potentiality to their environment (or more precisely to the managerial component of the factory as an epi-environment). Their imputation persisted because of the systemic properties of their own personalities (in spite of themselves, so to speak), and in spite of their superiors' consistent failure to requite them. When they perceived this component epi-environment as having undergone an unexpected shift, one which seemed to them to indicate a thrust toward actualizing a higher potentiality in their self-concepts or identities, they adjusted themselves (including *ad hoc* modifications of extant felt needs) so as to take advantage of the apparent opportunity for identity-taking. This adjustment in turn led management to recognize the fact of their increased productivity, which reinforced the women's belief that management would continue to reward their identity extensions. A self-fulfilling prophecy was spawned, *experimentally*.

It is important to qualify this assertion of circularity in the transactions between man and his environment. Thirty years of research since this focal study indicate that the most frequently occurring and apparently normal flow of these transactions is consistently in one direction; the kind of reversal—the reversibility—that was evoked in the bank wiring room is now known to be an ubiquitous manifestation of the normal direction of this interdependency. When programs of action are operating as expected, environmental factors do not induce change in the individuals upon whom they impinge. In fact, the whole structure of normal programmed activities shields individuals from the intrusion of change. In psychological terms, these epi-environments serve as ego-defenses. These defenses range from active resistance, aimed at diverting the change, to misperception, which dispenses with any conscious encounter with change.[13]

This brings us not only to alternative views of the crucial relationships between man and the complex organization, but also to a conceptual issue generated by a conflict between them; the social-mechanism perspective posits a one-way, interactional relationship, while the social-system perspective posits a two-way, transactional relationship. What might be represented as competitive views might better be presented as two states of the man-environment relationship. The man-environment relationship may be interactioned under one set of conditions and transactioned under another set.

In one instance, an individual finds himself residing in a matrix of relationships in which he interacts with a stable, basically gratifying social mechanism. In the alternative case, the individual faces frustration, both of his felt needs and of his thrusts toward identity extension. There being no opportunity for any substantial substitute, the individual inevitably comes under considerable stress. In his desire to avoid the continued discomfort of stress, the individual becomes increasingly inclined toward change; and, increasingly, he becomes less and less particular as to how he accomplishes this change.

The question arises, What are the antecedents of the one and the other of these conditions? Quite obviously, the capacity to influence these conditions is relevant to the effective management of organizational change as well as to the actualization of an acceptable identity. The obverse of this statement is even more relevant; when change erupts without notice or fails to emerge following our best efforts, the promise of self-conscious management of change in complex organizations is unlikely to be fulfilled. And almost everyone is likely to have his identity-strivings dislocated. Some inscrutable dynamic within the organization would presumably run its natural course as an indigenous or systemic response to the threats such a prospect presents. It is the clear-cut challenge to our constellations of goals in regard to complex organizations that gives such importance to a reliable theory of organizational change.

Much has been said about the factors related to stability and change in the structure of the complex organization by those seeking to plumb its dynamics. Size, age, level of differentiation, and dozens of other factors have been explored. More purely social factors such as the mix of professional, skilled, and unskilled workers or the level of automation have also been examined. The papers in Cyert and March deal with all of these and many more factors in complex organizations.[14] Their formulations focus heavily upon utilities—specifically, marginal utilities—as the most prominent antecedents of systemic change. In general, falling utilities are associated with deterioration (and hence the potentiality of change), and gently escalating utilities are associated with not merely numerous economic factors (increasing resource costs, rising distribution costs, lower volume and/or increased product quality) but also with the interactions between these factors and with an equally complex network of social-psychological factors.

Starbuck examines the interactions among these kinds of factors against the background of alternative theories, and he interprets their interaction within the dynamic context of the decline and development of organizations.[15] His analysis suggests that while there are many regularities in the relationships between these factors, there is a great deal we cannot explain. Though we can only make an inferential leap to such a conclusion, it seems possible that reversibility (in man-environmental transactions) might be an antecedent of some of the unexplained variance.

Consideration of the individual in the complex organization has struck many social-systems theorists as a promising avenue of analysis. Chester Barnard identified some of the contributions of psychologists thirty years ago.[16] More recently, Chris Argyris's name is that most often associated with attempts to conceptualize the relationship between the individual and the organization.[17] One of the assumptions in the perspective of organizations as social systems—that the individual does not behave atomistically, does not act as if he were a social particle with internal unity based upon a presumed (logical) consistency of motives—became one of the recurring themes in Argyris's work. His work elaborates the not infrequently exotic psychodynamics introduced into behavior as role strain breaks past thresholds of identity, raising fundamental questions about self-efficacy.

Attitudes as Vehicles of Interaction

Attitudes, which can be considered as expressions of more deeply anchored motives, have been investigated extensively; they offer a powerful variable in analysis of individual behavior. Attitudes have been found (a) to vary over time, (b) to vary according to circumstance and/or situation, and (c) to reflect a multiplicity of motives that are typically inconsistent and often competitive. They serve the individual not only as vehicles for moving from one social domain to another, but also as devices for resolving the inconsistent behavioral directives implicit in diverse motivations.

Attitudes are of explanatory importance because of their influence upon individual behavior. They define propensities toward action—sometimes labeled the tendency toward action inherent in the cognitive structure of personality. In this context, individual activity in complex organizations can be seen as the consequence of a "staged response"; a response which evolves through a process in which it takes a succession of more sharply defined forms, each the product of a more "focused" set of structural imperatives.

Perception of either an internal need or an environmental opportunity for action is often the first stage in attitude formation and the first step toward a relevant action. Evaluating the pertinence of the situation to need fulfillment becomes a second stage, one which proceeds by cognitive manipulations traversing first the domain of felt needs, then the inner domain of identity, and eventually the epi-environment. Behavior is thus broken into a series of stages which we could label anticipatory, readiness, and manifest stages.

The behavior resulting from this formative mechanism, whether it is overt or merely verbal and vicarious, is held to be the product of the interaction of attitudinal and perception mechanisms in each of these stages. The succession of verbal mechanisms which bridge from inscrutable, unconscious motives on the one hand to completely overt behavior on the other provide the structural context within which the individual derives his personal preferences. These, in turn, become the raw materials that are processed through the means of a policy dialogue in order to provide an aggregation of preferences as a basis for collective response.

Individual behavior, as we have used that term here, is the resultant of the confluence of several streams of attitudes as mediated by several levels of cognitive as well as other personality structures. So far as the individual is concerned, an inclination toward action may culminate in internal or vicarious behavior (such as reading about an election) which is equally as satisfying to him as externalized behavior (campaigning for a candidate). Depending upon the difficulties externalizing behavior in action might present, vicarious behavior can be more satisfying; it frequently offers a preferred balance between costs and gratifications.

When behavior flows through a highly consistent, well-routinized (deeply internalized) structure, it cycles through to closure. That is, the social commerce resulting from behavior mounted in response to felt needs and channeled through the structures of a social mechanism comes, after an appropriate sequence of stages, to consummation in a transaction that has two levels of consequences. In the zone of felt need, it is need-reducing; and inside the eye of personality it is identity-affirming. These behaviors, in their turn, reinforce the efficacy of the existing structure, and the cycle tends to be self-sustaining. Should the sequence of action consummate unexpectedly in trauma, frustration, deprivation, or other social injury, there is at least the possibility that the individual will activate alternative response mechanisms, mechanisms of a higher order, more deeply seated in the personality than the habit patterns which channel behavior in relation to epi-enviornments. Given the nested structures suggested above, the individual has the capacity to remove himself from one domain and base his responses upon an alternative psychic instrumentality, one where he literally steps inside himself and examines his roles, his reference groups, his inputs and outputs into and from each role face, and accomplishes all of this with something like clinically dispassionate objectivity toward himself and his surroundings.

Depending upon his appraisal of the situation (which is heavily influenced by the cognitive perspectives he brings to the process), social man may decide to terminate his association with a p. ticular complex organization; or he may seek to modify the basis ` his transaction with it. He can, if he is so inclined, determine to seek a restructuring of some organization and/or his role(s) in relation to it.

We might earlier have noted that man structures himself into different relationships with different components of his environment. In relation to his biophysical environments the relationship is exploitive; a one-way transaction by means of which he seeks to benefit himself is typical. In relation to his psychosocial environments he makes provision for the investment of his wherewithal anticipating some kind of two-way or reciprocal transaction.

Social theorists have suggested that man's competence in relation to social systems is now so extensive that there is some basis for asserting that he has the capacity to structure his transactions with his environments in many different ways, and that he has a repertoire of change strategies he uses to accomplish this. Partly as a result of this competence he has so greatly increased his capacity to modify his felt needs that he can be said to have gained the capacity to deal self-consciously with each of the four domains of existence mentioned above (identity, felt need, epi-environment, Nature), as well as the capacity to modify the transactional mechanisms linking each of them to each other.

Several limiting factors exist; for example, the individual cannot make continuous changes in his role without reducing his effectiveness in it to such a level that the role becomes altogether unrewarding. The rate at which he makes these changes is one—though only one—apparently absolute limitation on what he can do. But within such limits as these there are many options which an individual and/or a collective may follow—if a reason is found for doing so.

VI. ALTERNATIVE POLICY PROCESSES

From what has been said above we can draw several conclusions:

1. By interposing complex organizations between himself and his natural environments, by creating epi-environments designed to sustain and to nurture highly civilized forms of behavior, man has been able to mitigate many of the crass elements of his nature, elements originally dictated by some primitive component of environment.

2. By devising self-conscious strategies for the initiation and management of change in complex organizations, man has begun to gain the capacity to influence the content of human nature in ways that

could never have been seriously entertained as recently as the last century.

3. The social technology from which this capability for managing change in complex organizations is derived was in turn of the genre of—though it was not derived from—philosophical formulations about politics. In many of the philosophical formulations it was presumed that man had ultimately to come to terms with environment in its primitive state; it was presumed, that is, that man's hopes and aspirations had always to be tempered by the mundane imperatives of an untamed environment. Social theorists introduced conceptions challenging this presumption.

4. Implicit in the gross political processes for democratic aggregation of preferences, as well as in the more refined goal-setting processes of policy-making, is the premise that environment provides the context, the field within which our decision making takes place. Even though we are no longer required by the pressures of our natural environment to behave as if it were an immutable antagonist, much policy-making runs its course as if this were the case, because of the presuppositional foundations of a democratic heritage in which the classic, philosophical premise is embedded.

Against the background of our emergent capabilities, Scientific Management becomes little more than a simplistic dogma. Once sophisticated and spawning regimes for making routine choices, it is now inadequate, even for making these choices. Managerial economics is an elegantly articulated doctrine which is relevant to a rapidly decreasing number of policy challenges. Management Science, which serves us widely and well, seeks to surmount many of the limitations of its antecedents: if it has yet to succeed entirely there is ample reason to await its fruition.[18]

Neither is there reason to suggest that social theory offers precepts that will necessarily allow us to initiate policy-making dialogues with the assurance that they will not become reversible. It appears that we are at a point where we have the conceptual technology to demonstrate the existence of a dysfunctionality in our polity, but where the theories available to us are not sufficient to support our forming a prognosis. Perhaps the most important prospect here is in what appears to be an increasing redundancy among descriptive theories, suggesting the possibility that we may move to a fully synthetic level of analytic theory in the foreseeable future.

The antecedents for the circularity of our policy-making practices which first contaminates program structures with virulent strain and then compounds it until structural deterioration reaches debilitating proportions, are not to be found in one or another of the theories available to us at this time. However there may be an alternative to waiting for the appearance of newer synthetic theories.

Early in this discussion three forms of theory were introduced as the conceptual foundations used to formulate the self-conscious strategies of change through which we manage complex organizations. Behind this classification is the presumption that there is not one "grand" theory implicit in them, but three strands of theory each with an independently identifiable epistemological and metaphysical character.

There is reason to argue that in developing the change strategies which now serve us so well, we have relied heavily upon scientifically derived descriptive theories, making modest use of such protoanalytic theories as we have. Prescriptive theories, while not infrequently discussed, have seldom played a central role in the formulation and development of policy-making regimes. Given what we have posited as the thrust of much public activity—the exploitation and/or buffering of environment—strategies with a heavy loading of descriptive theories have served us well. In most cases we are solving an equation with a given for an unknown. That is, given the nature of environment and a normative premise (posited long ago when a particular democratic practice was devised) regarding what we seek from it, we solve for what we can expect in the light of what we are capable of doing. This last qualifier—"capable of doing"—presupposes that our capability is always sufficiently limited in comparison to the constraints and imperatives of environment that the most we can hope for is accommodation to environment; usually a quantitatively similar accommodation to environment.

What we have argued, of course, is that quantum jumps in capability have begun to allow the possibility of our striking out for a quantitatively different kind of adaptation to environment, one based upon the potentiality of our manipulating the environment.

A social algebra based upon deducing the range of human nature in various types of environments will yield a more determinate solution. Once the flow of a great river has been controlled, it becomes irrelevant to socialize people who live along it to the possibility of its flooding. Once economic cycles are harnessed, it is no longer relevant to condition people to the prospect of depression. It appears that we are approaching a point where the social algebra upon which we have always relied is no longer sufficient. The outlines of an additional decisional dialectic can be sketched in terms of a revised "mix" of prescriptive, descriptive, and analytic theories as the basis for more sophisticated decisional logics.

An Alternative "Mix"

Characteristically, policy-making has relied heavily upon the knowledge provided by descriptive theories. Ours being a politics of accommodation (implicitly within the extant environment), one question is, What are the alternatives? We attach the label *policy making* to the process of choosing from among alternatives derived from a deductive system, taking environment as a given.

Ideals and aspirations are typically treated as points from which accommodation begins; normative postulates are expected to fall in the face of practicality. Equally important is the typical assumption that the dynamics of the program under consideration will not change in the foreseeable future.

Again, historically these decisional premises have served us well. It is only when the balance in the man-environment interdependency shifts permanently in man's favor that a qualitatively different decisional regime seems called for. What will it be like?

Initially there is probably a need for a predecisional choice: whether to activate the traditional accommodative decisional structure as a context for public dialogue or whether to activate a dialogue aimed at displacing some environmental intrusion in our affairs (polio, blight, riots, war) by reconstituting our social ambience.

If the displacement strategy is selected (and Management Science gives us elaborate procedures for examining the utilities of one or the other), normative conceptions might be the initial object of attention. While descriptively defined "reality" would not be disregarded, normative conceptions anticipating mutational levels of environmental change might well serve as the focus of analysis in the initiation of the displacement strategy. And since analytic theories can aid us in anticipating the course and consequences of mutational changes in a system of action, the second stage in the dialogue might well involve refining normative aspirations in terms of projected future states of the system, as the analytic analogues forecast these.

The alternatives in such a dialogue would not be alternative states of an existing program but instead future states of the polity extrapolated not from a simple regression line drawn through the past and the present, but from a curve self-consciously forecasting mutational changes. A third stage in the policy dialogue might seek to close the gap between what is and what we have decided ought to be through the extrapolation of sequential series of changes deduced from descriptive theories.

Summary

We have attempted to argue the need for a new class of policy-making procedures whose need arises out of the recent accumulative developments in our capacity to engineer complex organizations. Recognizing the efficacy of our existing regimes for securing accommodation, the need for a secondary, supplementary policy-making regime, designed to serve inherently different purposes, has been suggested as requiring a different "mix" of theoretical components. While it is difficult to encapsulate in a few words what might be involved, if the terms "adaptive" or "accommodative" are used to characterize current approaches, the words "innovative" or "transformational" seem to symbolize what we may require in the future.

NOTES

1. Aristotle, *The Basic Works of Aristotle,* ed. Richard McKeon (New York: Random House, 1941); see especially *Politica,* pp. 1127-1324. Niccolo Machiavelli, *The Prince and Other Discourses* (New York: Modern Library, 1940).

2. These are not universally regarded dimensions of theory; these three have been selected with the purposes of the present essay in mind.

3. Max Weber, *From Max Weber: Essay in Sociology,* trans. H. H. Gerth and C. Wright Mills (New York: Oxford University Press, 1958), pp. 196-264.

4. For those who feel that Plato (or some other ancient) did precisely this, this statement could be modified to suggest only that Rousseau and others reinterpreted man's political needs through the tailoring of ancient institutions to seventeenth-century Europe. Given Plato's epistemological strategies, I question this position.

5. William Kornhauser, *The Politics of Mass Society* (New York: Free Press, 1959).

6. Frederick W. Taylor, *Scientific Management* (New York: Harper, 1911, 1947).

7. Luther Gulick and L. Urwick (eds.), *Papers on the Science of Administration* (New York: Institute of Public Administration, 1937), is the classic source on Management Theory. However, Henri Fayol, *General and Industrial Management,* trans. Constance Storrs (London: Pitman, 1949) ought also to be included here. Contemporary statements of this perspective are reflected in Peter Drucker, *The Practice of Management* (New York: Harper, 1954); and in James D. Mooney, *The Principles of Organization* (New York: Harper, 1947).

8. Milton Spencer, with Louis Siegelman (rev. ed.; Homewood: Irwin, 1964) and Edwin Mansfield (ed.), *Managerial Economics* (New York: Norton, 1966) provide surveys of the current technology of the field as well as some insight into the course of its development.

9. Richard Cyert and James March, *The Behavioral Theory of the Firm* (Englewood Cliffs: Prentice-Hall, 1963) may still be the best source in this area. The first paper provides a succinct review of the literature dealing with the dynamics of the industrial organization.

10. The literature has not yet been neatly synthesized. Herbert Simon, *Models of Man* (New York: Wiley, 1957), and Simon, *The New Science of Management Decision* (New York: Harper, 1960) provide a sense of one interface of Management Science. Several journals are normal outlets for the mounting stream of reports on research in this area; among these, *Operations Research Management Science, Econometrica,* and *Behavioral Science* are representative.

11. Social-system theorists have provided a small but excellent literature on this critical problem. Chris Argyris, *Interpersonal Competence and Organizational Effectiveness* (Homewood: Dorsey, 1962); Fritz Heider, *The*

Psychology of Interpersonal Relations (New York: Wiley, 1959); George Homans, *The Human Group* (New York: Harcourt, Brace, 1950); and Elton Mayo, *The Social Problems of an Industrial Civilization* (London: Routledge, Kegan, 1949) all deal with some aspect of this problem.

12. F. J. Roethlisberger and W. J. Dickson, *Management and the Worker* (Cambridge: Harvard University Press, 1930).

13. One of the finest works on organization dealing with several aspects of this matter is James March and Herbert Simon, with Harold Guetzkow, *Organizations* (New York: Wiley, 1958). See also William F. Whyte, *Men at Work* (Homewood: Dorsey, 1961); Harold J. Leavitt, *Managerial Psychology* (Chicago: University of Chicago, 1964); and Victor A. Thompson, *Modern Organization* (New York: Knopf, 1961).

14. Cyert and March, op. cit.

15. William Starbuck's essay, "Organizational Growth and Change," *Handbook of Organizations,* ed. James March (Chicago: Rand McNally, 1965) must be the most profoundly analytic as well as the most extensive formulation of these factors to date.

16. Chester Barnard, *The Function of the Executive* (Cambridge: Harvard University Press, 1938).

17. Chris Argyris, op. cit.; Argyris, *Interpersonal Competence and Organizational Effectiveness* (Homewood: Dorsey, 1962).

18. The work of Herbert Simon must be considered by anyone interested in these developments. One could begin finding his way in Simon's manifold writings by locating the several places in which his work is cited saliently in March, *Handbook of Organizations.*

13 Organization Theory

ROBERT T. GOLEMBIEWSKI, University of Georgia

> Men can be free within wide limits in organizations, but almost every-where they are in unnecessary and ineffective bondage. This is a revolu-tionary tocsin, but it is more restrained than ringing pronouncements that men have only to break the chains of bondage. A great deal more, in point of fact, requires doing; and the doing requires a moral discipline and technical awareness beyond that of a simple call for unshackling man in organizations.—*Jean Jacques Rousseau**

I. DESCRIPTION AND PRESCRIPTION: TOWARD A SYNTHESIS

Scientific efforts must satisfy two basic conditions. First of all, *in the process of developing conclusions,* scientific work must avoid having its results determined by the values or opinions of researchers. In this sense, scientific effort must be value-free. And here logical positivists contributed an important theme to the early development of the field of public administration.

Second, scientific work also must be value-loaded in special ways, and here the logical positivists have encouraged considerable mischief in the study of public administration, for the values of science are the foundations of empirical research. More centrally for the present argument, *the use of* scientific results must be disciplined by explicit sets of values. It used to be fashionable to regard such applied work with moderate disdain, but it is now increasingly clear that applied work at least provides significant tests of basic research. Moreover, applied work is no longer necessarily the tail of the dog of basic research, even when it is possible to sharply distinguish the two.[1] Kurt Lewin's observation that "a good theory is one that works" implies the need of detailing how it is that we can achieve more of what we value by appropriately manipulating our environment.

In sum, scientific efforts profit from being viewed as both descrip-tion and prescription. Descriptively, *empirical theory* takes the form: A covaries directly with B. Prescriptively, *goal-based, empirical theory*

---

*Paraphrase from *The Social Contract* in R. T. Golembiewski, *Men, Management, and Morality* (New York: McGraw-Hill, 1965), p. 7.

takes the form: if you desire to increase A, manipulate B by varying x, y, and z. In the ideal case, each builds upon and contributes to the other.

Public Administration has at best come half-way in responding to these dual conditions of science. If I read the signs correctly, increasing attention is given to *description*, as in the behavioral approach,[2] but *prescriptive* aspects of the behavioral approach have been ignored.[3]

This essay seeks to correct this unfortunate imbalance by looking at the study of planned organizational change. Following Bennis, Benne, and Chin, this essay focuses on "the application of systematic and appropriate knowledge to human affairs for the purpose of creating intelligent action and change." Accordingly, the emphasis is on "conscious, deliberate, and collaborative effort to improve the operations of an [organizational] system . . . through the utilization of scientific knowledge."[4] Perhaps *the* most descriptive adjective is "collaborative," as distinguished from such approaches as that of Scientific Management. Defined in these terms, planned organizational change potently requires attention to two basic questions: What is related to what? How can we get what we want, based on a knowledge of what is related to what?

Despite the detail necessary to provide glimpses of planned organization change as a major emphasis in a behavioral approach to Public Administration, the analytical target and intent are uncomplicated. The focus of this essay provides three perspectives on planned change in organizations, all based on the laboratory approach. What Gore notes, in the preceding contribution to this volume, applies with equal force to the laboratory approach: ". . . quantum jumps in capability have begun to allow the possibility of our striking out for a quantitatively different kind of adaptation to environment; one based upon the potentiality of our manipulating [the] environment." The point of the manipulation is profoundly human, the goal being nothing less than to increase the gratification of man's needs in large organizations.

II. THE LABORATORY APPROACH: THREE BASIC LIMITATIONS

The following sections develop both the theory and some selected applications of the laboratory approach. As a preliminary, let us stake out some useful boundaries for that effort, keeping three points in mind. First of all, not every organization is a potential host to the laboratory approach. In other words, the cultural preparedness of the host organization is an issue of moment in any decision to begin a change-program via the lab approach. Warren Bennis has itemized several factors involved in testing for such cultural preparedness,[5] and his work is useful for those who want to avoid being licked before they start.

Second, the laboratory approach is only one of a family of possible approaches to organizational change. The histories and traditions of some organizations are not congenial to the approach; and not all organizational problems can be ameliorated by the laboratory approach. Indeed, the laboratory approach can aggravate some problems, though I have found it to be especially useful. Greiner's typology isolates seven such alternative approaches to organizational change:[6]

1. The Decree Approach. A person with high formal authority originates a "one-way" order to those of lesser authority.

2. The Replacement Approach. One or more officials leave or are replaced, and the new personnel trigger organizational changes.

3. The Structural Approach. Organizational relations are changed, presumably with effects on behavior.

4. The Group-Decision Approach. Group agreement is sought concerning the implementation of alternatives specified by others, as opposed to involving groups in isolating or solving problems.

5. The Data-Discussion Approach. Data are presented to a host organization by an internal or outside consultant, and organization members are encouraged to develop their own analyses of the data.

6. The Group Problem-Solving Approach. Problems are identified and solved in group discussions.

7. The T-Group or Laboratory Approach. The emphasis is on sensitivity to individual and group behavior, with improvements in interpersonal relations and in openness serving as a foundation for changes in organization structure and policies.

As in medicine, the success of therapy and accuracy of prognosis depend on the diagnosis of the organizational illness, so there is no single "magic bullet" organizational therapy. A highly authoritarian organization whose members have extreme personality constellations may usually find alternative 1 more useful and comfortable than 6 or 7, for example.

Third, a change-agent may intervene in an organization in a number of major ways, not all of which are always appropriate for a specific organizational problem and not all of which require or even use the laboratory approach. Blake and Mouton identify nine kinds of interventions:[7]

1. Discrepancy, by calling attention to contradictions in or between policy, attitudes, and behavior

2. Theory, by presenting research findings or concepts that enlarge the client's perspective

3. Procedure, by critiquing existing methods

4. Relationships, as by focusing attention on tensions between individual and groups

5. Experimentation, by encouraging comparisons of several alternative approaches before a decision is made

6. Dilemmas, by pointing up significant choice-points or dilemmas in problem solving, with attention to testing action-assumptions and seeking alternatives

7. Perspective, by providing situational or historical understanding

8. Organization Structure, by identifying problems as inhering in structure or the organization of work

9. Culture, by focusing on traditions or norms

The laboratory approach might be variously useful as a tool in each of the nine kinds of interventions, and particularly in types 4, 6, 8, and 9. But the laboratory approach is nowhere indispensable nor even necessarily useful.

III. THE LABORATORY APPROACH AS A FEEDBACK MODEL: NECESSARY SKILLS AND VALUES

The laboratory approach seeks to provide learning designs that maximize effective feedback. Using the cybernetic analogy, *feedback* may be defined as information concerning the efficacy of a data-processor's adaptations to his environment. To illustrate, a home furnace is linked with a temperature sensor so that the heating unit can approximate some desirable temperature setting. If that feedback linkage does not function, the furnace will reflect maladaptive behaviors as temperatures vary. Individuals and organizations, in analogous ways, will respond maladaptively to their environments if their feedback processes are inadequate. Hence the centrality of a laboratory approach.

A viable feedback linkage depends upon the nature of the "input" as well as the "throughput," in the vernacular of systems theory. As for feedback viewed as input, human beings and large organizations are alike in that they best adapt to environmental stimuli if feedback is timely, is presented in useful form, and validly reflects what exists. Figure 1 suggests the point in a generalized but useful way, schematizing a typical degenerative feedback cycle with attention to both interpersonal and organizational relations.

To comment upon the self-heightening features of such degenerating sequences, an *existential* reason to distrust A often will generate an *anticipatory reaction* that A is not to be trusted. Hence B is likely to be less open, and low trust in A is thereby reinforced. Further organizational elaborations of such feedback cycles could easily be made, and particularly in the case of line-staff relations.[8]

The crucial role of feedback is clearest in the *T group,* or a small unstructured training group which is the basic learning vehicle in sensitivity training.[9] Descriptive detail on the T group will be

FIGURE 1. Typical Degenerative Feedback Cycle with Some Typical Interpersonal and Organizational Outcomes

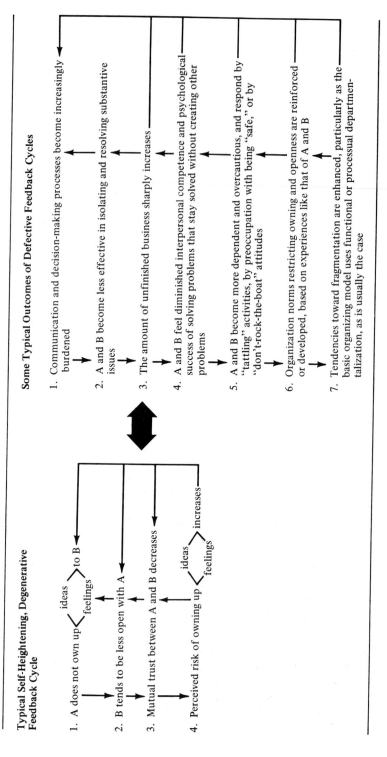

provided later, especially in Tables 1 and 2, but here we make only a narrow point. The question—How did I come across to you when I did that?—may be group member A's signal that he wants feedback. And other group members may respond by providing evidence on which they have a monopoly, their own reactions, feelings, and attitudes. The essential products are profoundly simple. Participants see how difficult but rewarding it is to risk sharing their ideas or feelings; they experience how much they limit themselves and others by not being open; they demonstrate for themselves the prime importance to others of their ideas and feelings and reactions; and they gain skill and insight in giving and receiving feedback, as well as in reversing degenerating feedback cycles.

Human beings and organizations will be *no better* in adapting to environmental stimuli than their feedback is timely, usefully presented, and valid; but human beings and organizations *can be much worse.* Like all servo-mechanisms, men-in-organizations must be appropriately programmed to provide and to process feedback. As with the furnace, the ideal is not providing just any feedback that is to be processed in just any way. How the feedback is given and how it is responded to—the style of the throughput—is patently of great significance. For our purposes, we consider *only two* throughputs—*skills* of giving and processing feedback, and *values* underlying these skills.

Table 1 attempts to do the complex job of sketching both the skills and the values appropriate to the laboratory approach. Column C, particularly, implies the skills required for the sensitive inducing and processing of feedback. "You are a stereophonic idiot, Charlie, and I'll bet it's because your father rejected you," illustratively, is not a skillful piece of feedback in a group situation. That is, the statement contrasts sharply with the ground rules for effective feedback in column 2 of Table 1. In summary, feedback:

1. is evaluative and judgmental, and leaves open only the options of accepting or rejecting the conclusion
2. rushes to "there-and-then" interpretations beyond the competence of perhaps anyone but the analyst of the target of the feedback
3. refers to the total person rather than to some act
4. is an outburst that does not encourage trust between the two individuals or between the initiator and other group members
5. does not contribute to a sense of the organic solidarity of the group, as could be done by an open invitation to group members by the speaker to cross-validate his reactions
6. paramountly does not indicate even remotely how an idiot can gain nonidiot status

TABLE 1. Some Values and Relevant Skills Underlying Laboratory Training[a]

Meta-Values [b]	Proximate Goals	Desirable Means	Consistent Organization Values[c]
1. An attitude of inquiry reflecting (among others): a. a "hypothetical spirit" b. experimentation 2. "Expanded consciousness and sense of choice" 3. The value system of democracy, having as two core elements: a. a spirit of collaboration b. open resolution of conflict via problem-solving orientation 4. An emphasis on mutual "helping relationships" as the best way to express man's interdependency with man	1. Increased insight, self-knowledge 2. Sharpened diagnostic skills (ideally) at all levels, that is, on the levels of the a. individual b. group c. organization d. society 3. Awareness of, and skill-practice in creating, conditions of effective functioning (ideally) at all levels 4. Testing self-concepts and skills in interpersonal situations 5. Increased capacity to be open, to accept feelings of self and others, to risk interpersonally in rewarding ways	1. Emphasis on here-and-now occurrences 2. Emphasis on the individual act rather than on the "total person" acting 3. Emphasis on feedback that is nonevaluative in that it reports the impact on the self of others' behavior, rather than feedback that is judgmental or interpretive 4. Emphasis on "unfreezing" behaviors the trainee feels are undesirable, on practice of replacement behaviors, and on "refreezing" new behaviors 5. Emphasis on "trust in leveling," on psychological safety of the trainee 6. Emphasis on creating and maintaining an "organic community"	1. Full and free communication 2. Reliance on open consensus in managing conflict, as opposed to using coercion or compromise 3. Influence based on competence rather than on personal whim or formal power 4. Expression of emotional as well as task-oriented behavior 5. Acceptance of conflict between the individual and his organization, to be coped with willingly, openly, and rationally

[a]From Robert T. Golembiewski, "The Laboratory Approach to Organization Change," *Public Administration Review*, XXVII (September 1967), 217.

[b] Adapted from Edgar H. Schein and Warren G. Bennis (eds.), *Personal and Organizational Change Through Group Methods* (New York: Wiley, 1965), pp. 30-35; and Leland P. Bradford, Jack R. Gibb, and Kenneth D. Benne (eds.), *T-Group Theory and Laboratory Method* (New York: Wiley, 1964), pp. 10, 12.

[c] Philip E. Slater and Warren G. Bennis, "Democracy Is Inevitable," *Harvard Business Review*, XLII (March-April 1964), 51-59.

A skillful piece of feedback might be phrased this way: "When you did x, Charlie, I got furious. I doubted your motives, and I believe I know one of the reasons why. I hope others can help, but at least I hear you sneering when you say 'Yes, sir.' I wonder if others in this group also feel that you were sneering at me? Do you want to make me furious? If so, keep saying 'Yes, sir,' just the way you did." The reader can measure this feedback against the ground rules above. For example, the feedback is quite specific about at least one of the behaviors Charlie can change if he wants a reaction other than "furious."

The other three columns of Table 1 apply more broadly to the value environment within which conditions are optimum for encouraging others to supply feedback, as well as optimum for increasing the probability that the feedback will be responded to effectively and efficiently. Such an environment is difficult to induce, but its main properties should be generally clear in Table 1.

The T group also clearly illustrates the significance of feedback viewed as throughput. Thus the T group ideal may be described as the development of a supportive environment within which group members feel it possible to share ideas and feelings, to test out their own perceptions against the perceptions of fellow group members, to judge the appropriateness of behaviors for attaining personal goals, and to experiment with new behaviors. The goal is to do all this, and to do it openly, with increasing honesty, and in a spirit that is increasingly helpful.

IV. THREE APPLICATIONS OF THE LABORATORY APPROACH

Diverse learning designs have been developed consistent with the brief characterization above of the laboratory approach as a feedback model. We can only sample that diversity of designs here, but even sampling suffices to demonstrate three uses of the laboratory approach:

1. to modify the problem-solving perspectives of individuals on work-related issues
2. to modify organizational styles by inducing changes in interpersonal and group behavior
3. to modify the attitudes of individuals in organizations so as to develop attitudes favorable to more effective performance

A Sensitivity-Training Design: Modifying Problem-Solving Perspectives of Individuals

The first learning design is the most simple of the three, and also the most modest in organizational terms. Its aim is to measure before-after changes in the ways individuals define work-related

problems.[10]   An orthodox week-long experience in T groups inter-
vened between two administrations of a questionnaire designed to
determine participants' perspectives on work-related problems. Each
participant chose his own reference-problem. Before their training
began, participants were asked to choose and describe a problem
they were having at work. Five criteria were to guide the selection
of the organizational problem:

1. The respondent was *directly* involved.
2. The problem was *unresolved.*
3. The respondent was *dissatisfied* with the lack of resolution and
wished to initiate some change.
4. The problem was *interpersonal,* that is, it involved the respondent's relation to some person or persons.
5. The problem was *important* to the respondent.

The problem chosen became the reference-problem for each participant on before and after administrations of questionnaire items.

Although the problems described by participants were not referred
to before or during the week-long experience in T groups, our
expectations were that a successful laboratory experience would
influence the ways in which a participant would view his reference-
problem "after" administration of the questionnaire. Our expectations
had two basic sources. First of all, many interpersonal problems at
work stem from a violation of such norms for the processes of
problem solving as those sketched in Table 1. A successful laboratory
experience would encourage participants to internalize the values in
Table 1, and consequently it should modify in predictable ways the
participants' definitions of their problem situations. Second, the
typical T group covers a wide range of learning opportunities. Table
2 attempts to provide some sense of this range of target data, of
kinds and levels of learning, and of basic outcome goals. Individual
T groups tend to vary widely in focus and extent of attention.
Since the laboratory experience is a simulation of life in these
various senses, however, consultants felt it very probable that participants would perceive analogs between their experiences in the T
group and their reference-problems. Moreover, a T group presents
sharp differences with life in what is discussed and how problems
are solved. Consequently, again, we expected that a successful laboratory experience would probably provide participants with success-
experiences in working with a framework of feedback values and
skills that could be generalized to the reference-problem of individuals
in back-home situations.

More specifically, Oshry and Harrison have developed nine scales
that permit testing before-after changes in the problem-solving perspectives of individuals.[11] Table 3 names and illustrates these nine scales.

TABLE 2. An Overview of Sensitivity Training[a]

Basic Approach of Laboratory Training	Kinds of Target Data	Kinds of Learning	Levels of Learning	Basic Goals for Outcomes
1. "Sensitivity training attempts to accomplish the end of behavioral change through a philosophy and technique of training which is best described as a concern with 'how'—how a trainee appraises himself, how a group behaves, how another would react in a given situation. In short, sensitivity training has as its purpose the development of an executive's awareness of himself, of others, of group processes, and of group culture."[b] The basic learning vehicle in any laboratory program is the T group. The T group is intended to help people:[c] a. explore the impact of their behaviors and values on others; b. determine whether they want to change their behaviors and values; c. test new behaviors and values, if individuals consider them desirable; d. develop awareness of how groups can both stimulate and inhibit personal growth and decision making.	1. The focus is on the public, "here-and-now" data—data available only to T group members. These here-and-now data include: a. the specific *structures* developed, such as the leadership rank order; b. the *processes* of group life, with special attention to getting a group started, keeping it going, and then experiencing its inevitable death; c. the specific *emotional reactions* of members to one another's behavior and to their experiences; d. the varying and diverse *styles* or *modes* of individual and group behavior, as in fighting the trainer or in fleeing some issue that has overwhelmed group members	1. Interaction in T groups generates three basic kinds of learning by participants, to varying degrees in individual cases: a. learning that is largely cognitive and oriented toward techniques, as for effective committee functioning; b. learning that highlights deep emotional needs of which the participant was variously aware, and that shows how such needs can be satisfied; c. learning that demonstrates the significance of unfinished business, and that illustrates how and with what effects the press against the consciousness of such matters may be relieved.	1. Laboratory programs typically try to touch on three loci at which learning can be applied; but the first level receives most attention: a. *personal learning*, when the person learns about himself in interaction in the T group; b. *transfer learning*, when personal learning is extended to external contexts (for example, a worksite) to increase understanding or to improve functioning; c. *environmental learning*, when the concern is to restructure some external context (for example, an organization) so as to make it more personally satisfying and rewarding while also enhancing the effectiveness of those involved.	1. Laboratory programs enhance authenticity in human relations by seeking to increase: a. individual awareness about self and others; b. acceptance of others; c. acceptance of self. 2. Laboratory programs seek to free individuals to be more effective while they are more themselves, both as persons and as members of organizations, by seeking to enhance the development of: a. sensitivity to self and others; b. ability to diagnose complex social situations and to conceptualize experience in behavioral science terms; c. action skills and attitudes required to capitalize on increased sensitivity and enhanced diagnostic skills.

a From Robert T. Golembiewski, "Theory in Public Administration: Defining One 'Vital Center' for the Field." Florida State University Lecture Series, November 17, 1967.

b From William G. Scott, *Organization Theory* (Homewood: Irwin, 1967), p. 332.

c Based on Chris Argyris, *Interpersonal Competence and Organizational Effectiveness* (Homewood: Dorsey, 1962), p. 156.

TABLE 3. Problem—Analysis Questionnaire of Oshry and Harrison [a]

Description of Scales and Possible Ranges of Scores	Test One			Test Two		
	Mean Initial Scores	Predicted Outcomes	Mean Outcomes	Mean Initial Scores	Predicted Outcomes	Mean Outcomes
1. Self: Rational-Technical (8-40) (Example: I have not let others know just where I stand on this problem.)	20.23	Sig. Higher	27.4[b]	17.33	Sig. Higher	27.4[b]
2. Self: Closed (8-40) (Example: I have been relatively difficult to approach.)	16.76	Sig. Higher	21.4[c]	12.72	Sig. Higher	18.88[b]
3. Organizational: Rational-Technical (6-30) (Example: The organization lets things go too far before taking action.)	15.35	Lower	11.35[b]	13.94	Lower	13.77
4. Organization: Closed (8-40) (Example: The organization has become inflexible.)	16.00	Lower	13.52[c]	16.47	Lower	18.00
5. Others: Rational-Technical (Example: The other person has not planned adequately.)	17.35	Insig. Change	17.35	16.94	Insig. Change	18.44
6. Others: Closed (8-40) (Example: Others resent outside suggestions or help.)	19.00	Insig. Change	20.05	21.64	Insig. Change	24.61
7. Self and Others: Rational-Technical (8-40) (Example: The other person and I have not tried hard enough to work this problem out.)	22.15	Sig. Higher	27.47[b]	15.06	Sig. Higher	23.83[b]
8. Self and Others: Closed (7-35) (Example: The other person and I really don't trust each other.)	15.58	Sig. Higher	19.94[b]	14.57	Sig. Higher	20.61[b]
9. Situational (5-25) (Example: Both the other person's job and my job are such that we must work toward opposing goals.)	10.00	Insig. Change	10.41	8.53	Insig. Change	8.38

[a]Data from tests of two populations of twenty each, based on Arthur Blumberg and Robert T. Golembiewski, "The PAQ and Laboratory Goal Attainment" (mimeograph, 1968).
[b]Designates a statistically significant difference at .01.
[c]Designates a statistically significant difference at .05.

Three types of outcomes were predicted for changes in participant responses to the scales after a successful laboratory experience. First of all, increases in scores were expected on Scales 1, 2, 7, and 8. That is, a successful laboratory experience should suggest to participants how both they and others had exacerbated their reference-problem by avoiding the expression of opinions or feelings (Scales 1 and 7), and by not being open (Scales 2 and 8). Second, significantly lower scores were expected on Scales 3 and 4 in the "after" administration of the questionnaire, as participants were less likely to scapegoat "the organization" as a contributor to their reference-problem. We did not expect statistically significant lower scores, if only because "the organization" was not specifically looked at. But we did assume that scores would trend lower. Third, insignificant before-after changes were expected on the other three scales, Scales 5, 6, and 9. On Scales 5 and 6, our rationale was that a participant in a successful laboratory experience would be less likely to place blame for his reference-problem on others, but the same participant also probably would be more sensitive to the manifold ways in which others can preoccupy themselves with the rational-technical and can be closed to feedback. On Scale 9, similar cross-pressures were felt to be at work.

As Table 3 shows, most predicted outcomes were realized; indeed 17 of the 18 paired scores changed in the predicted directions. Only Scale 4 on Test II is a deviant case. Of the 12 cases in which significant differences were expected, 10 reached usually accepted levels of statistical significance. The pattern of results reported in Table 3, in short, strongly supports the efficacy of the laboratory approach in modifying the perspectives from which organization members view problems. Although consultants could not arrange for a control group, there seem no reason to doubt that the observed effects were due to sensitivity training.[12] This is but one illustration of the potency of the laboratory approach.[13]

Additional data urge that the changes in problem diagnosis were more than attitudinal phantoms. Although it is too early to state the conclusion flatly, the changes seem to have remained stable over the interval of a year. Replications of the research design, most convincingly, have yielded similar patterns of results.[14] Hence it does not seem that respondents were simply giving the answers sought, even though their insights on their reference-problems were not deepened or sharpened or augmented by sensitivity training. We lack specific evidence that behavioral change has occurred, however.

The strength of the research design above is also its major weakness, to put the conclusion above in terms of the training design. The narrowness of the training intervention implies real shortcomings. Specifically, the goal was not change as such, but attitudinal change that would lead to behavioral change and to increased effectiveness in the back-home situation. But the training design touched only one part of the necessary organizational change process, which Mann notes "needs to be concerned with altering both forces within an *individual* and the forces in the *organizational situation* surrounding the individual."[15] The focus on the individual thus may have worked at cross-purposes with the ultimate purpose of inducing change in the back-home situation. That is, research concerned with back-home impact of laboratory training has yielded mixed results. Success stories exist, of course, but Bennis talks about the fade-out of attitudinal and behavioral changes when participants in sensitivity training return to organizations whose values were presumably different than the values of sensitivity training.[16] Similarly, Fleishman and his associates demonstrate the potency of the organizational situation.[17] Training did result in immediate changes, but changes were variously washed out if the trainee's back-home superior used a leadership style that was incompatible with the training.

Reactions to the mixed results concerning back-home changes often have been phrased in sharp terms. Bennis, Benne, and Chin observe of programs and technologies of planned change:

Isolating the individual from his organizational context, his normative structure which rewards him and represents a significant reference group, makes no sense. In fact, if it sets up countervailing norms and expectations, it may be deleterious to both the organization and the individual.[18]

In sum, an individual programmed for feedback consistent with Table 1 may find that his behaviors are maladaptive in an organization with different rules of the game. Frustration and/or rapid unlearning are likely consequences.

Consultants in the design above were aware of such back-home issues, but could not extend the learning design to the broader organization. As an alternative, we tried to be clear about the limits of the experience. Participants were told, to use the terminology of Table 2, that personal learning would be emphasized. We hoped that they would see opportunities for transfer learning, and we also noted that future cooperative environmental learning also was possible. That is, participants were "cousins" who came from the same organization and from similar levels, but who did not usually work together. Primarily, we stressed the vast difference between personal learning and environmental learning. Consultants noted that they hoped participants would become organizational crusaders for sensitivity training, if they saw value in it. As matters then stood, we felt it was appropriate to emphasize this lesson from the experience of the crusaders of old: more went than came back. Hence the watchwords were: experience, evaluate, and test for useful extensions. The organization's chief executive provided useful counterpoint to the theme, by stressing the developmental nature of the experience and by encouraging tests of extensions of the approach into the back-home situation. These structuring cues seem to have been accepted at face value.

A Sensitivity-Training Design: Modifying Organizational Styles

The basic design for sensitivity training sketched in Table 2 also has been used to induce a second type of organization development, namely, broad systemic changes in organizational styles. Two examples establish the efficacy of laboratory training for these broader purposes. One example derives from the work of a University of Michigan team on a change program at the Weldon Manufacturing Company;[19] and the other example comes from Friedlander's carefully controlled study at one of the armed services' largest research and development stations.[20]

The two examples complement as well as supplement each other. The macroscopic focus in Weldon is on the style of the total firm. This focus makes the Weldon effort an important one, for one of the fundamental criticisms of the laboratory approach to organization change is that it attempts the impossible or highly improbable job of inducing in large organizations processes and dynamics analogous to those that are rooted specifically in small-group behavior.[21] Friedlander's concern is with the style of a number of small, decision-making groups in a large organization. Both examples are complementary in testing the following basic premise:

Training which does not take the trainee's regular social environment into account will probably have little chance of modifying behavior. It may very well be that human relations training—as a procedure for initiating social change—is most successful when it is designed to remodel the whole system of role relationships . . .[22]

The organization change at Weldon was a massive effort to reorient a newly acquired company, in which change-agent specialties from industrial engineering to sensitivity training were used.[23] At the global level, it is difficult to isolate *the* significant interventions. Basically, the combined effects of these diverse inputs were such as to improve performance by technically and behaviorally changing the ways in which the firm went about its business, that is, by fundamentally changing the firm's style.

The style changes in Weldon were documented in part by Likert's 43-factor "Profile of Organizational and Performance Characteristics," which includes seven basic dimensions, variations in which can be described as composing different management systems. For example, "Manner in which motives are used" is one of the component scales of Likert's dimension "Character of Motivational Forces." Members of

FIGURE 2. Profile of Organizational and Performance Characteristics[a]

Illustrative Dimension	SYSTEM 1 *Exploitative, Coercive, Authoritative*	SYSTEM 2 *Benevolent, Authoritative*	SYSTEM 3 *Consultative*	SYSTEM 4 *Participative, Group-Based*
Character of Motivational Forces				
Manner in Which Motives Are Used	Fear, threats, punishment, and occasional rewards	Rewards and some actual or potential punishment	Rewards, occasional punishment, and some involvement	Economic rewards based on compensation system developed through participation; group participation and involvement in setting goals, improving methods, appraising progress toward goals

[a]From Rensis Likert, *The Human Organization: Its Management and Value* (New York: McGraw-Hill, 1967), pp. 190-199.

an organization can describe its systemic style by checking an appropriate descriptive point on a scale of 20 intervals, as illustrated in Figure 2. Likert's Profile has considerable value in organizational analysis. For example, respondents on the Profile can indicate where they perceive their organization to be and also where they would ideally prefer it to be. Reducing the real/ideal gap thus could be the goal of an organizational change program.

That the change program at Weldon succeeded in modifying the organization's style in profound ways also can be illustrated via Likert's Profile of management systems. To provide some necessary detail, managers completed the Profile three times in 1964, their instructions asking them in turn to describe the management system at Weldon from three perspectives: before its acquisition, the contemporary (1964) system, and the management system they felt was ideal.

Figure 3 shows the patent movement over time in Weldon's style, as rated by the firm's top management. The gap between the preacquisition scores and the ideal was diminished sharply. In other terms, Weldon in 1964 was seen by its top managers as a System 3 organization, moving toward its System 4 ideal; before the acquisition, it was seen as System 1 by its top managers. Top management was not alone in perceiving such change in their organization's style; ratings by other levels of management reflected a similar movement.

The movement in Figure 3 cannot all be attributed to sensitivity training, but its value seems undeniable in "building relationships of cooperation and trust in the Weldon organization" required to move toward a System 4 management system. Within the context sketched in Table 2, Gilbert David thus describes the learning strategy applied at Weldon:

A "family group" format would be used. That is, the training groups would be formed of people who were related in their normal work and who would bring their regular roles and relationships into the training sessions. This is probably the most difficult kind of group to engage in such training as the participants may well be reluctant to speak frankly with their superiors, and with colleagues with whom they must have future relations. It was felt, however, that this risk had to be taken as no other format would be likely to affect, in the short run, an internal organizational situation as critical as the one we had to deal with.[24]

That this learning strategy employing sensitivity training proved successful is implied in Figure 4, which graphically portrays the movement of some Weldon managers along continua that should be positively affected by a successful laboratory experience. For example, a laboratory experience should generally make participants more aware of the effects of their own behavior on others, and the figure shows that such an effect actually did occur after a sensitivity-training

410

FIGURE 3. Weldon's Progress toward System 4 Management[a]

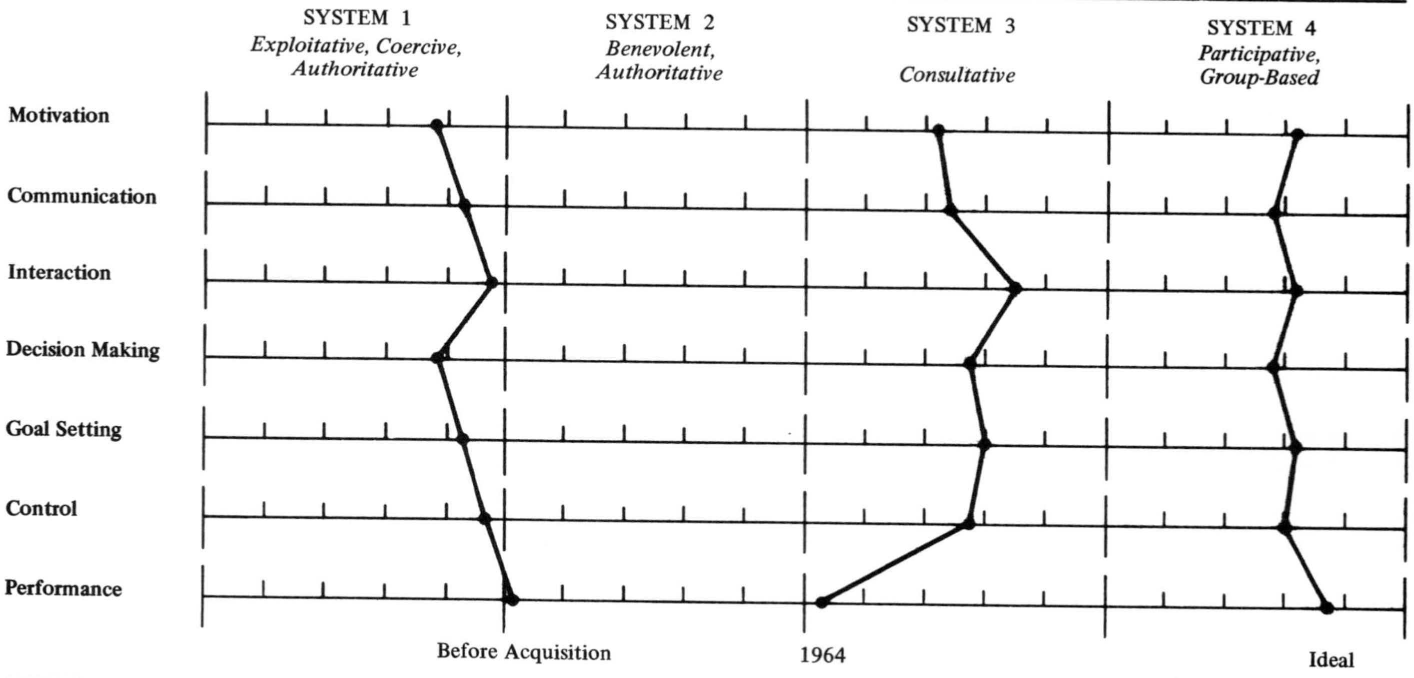

[a]Adapted from Alfred J. Marrow, David G. Bowers, and Stanley E. Seashore, *Management by Participation* (New York: Harper & Row, 1967), especially p. 219.

FIGURE 4. Self-Ratings of Managers in Weldon before, after, and Two Years after Training Seminars[a]

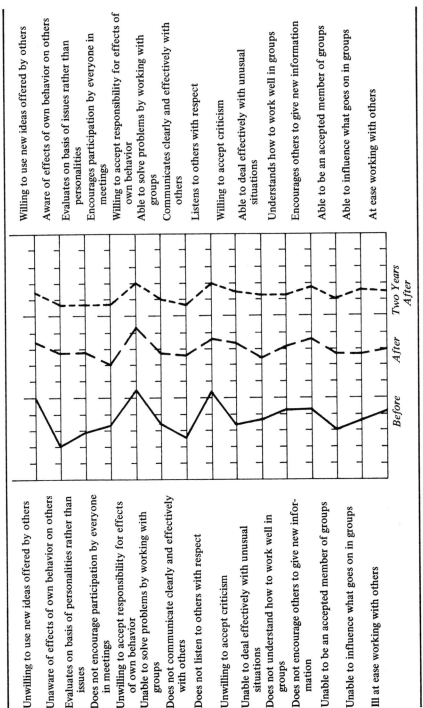

Unwilling to use new ideas offered by others — Willing to use new ideas offered by others

Unaware of effects of own behavior on others — Aware of effects of own behavior on others

Evaluates on basis of personalities rather than issues — Evaluates on basis of issues rather than personalities

Does not encourage participation by everyone in meetings — Encourages participation by everyone in meetings

Unwilling to accept responsibility for effects of own behavior — Willing to accept responsibility for effects of own behavior

Unable to solve problems by working with groups — Able to solve problems by working with groups

Does not communicate clearly and effectively with others — Communicates clearly and effectively with others

Does not listen to others with respect — Listens to others with respect

Unwilling to accept criticism — Willing to accept criticism

Unable to deal effectively with unusual situations — Able to deal effectively with unusual situations

Does not understand how to work well in groups — Understands how to work well in groups

Does not encourage others to give new information — Encourages others to give new information

Unable to be an accepted member of groups — Able to be an accepted member of groups

Unable to influence what goes on in groups — Able to influence what goes on in groups

Ill at ease working with others — At ease working with others

Before   After   Two Years After

[a]Retrospective self-ratings were made immediately before, immediately after, and approximately two years after training seminars. Note all Before-After and After-Two Years After differences are statistically significant at .05. Based on Alfred J. Marrow, David G. Bowers, and Stanley E. Seashore, *Management by Participation* (New York: Harper & Row, 1967), p. 210.

experience. Figure 4 also shows that a variety of other expected changes in perceptions of behavior occurred in response to the sensitivity training.

Several additional factors augment the present claim of the laboratory approach's potency in helping to modify the organizational style. Although the data in Figure 4 are retrospective self-ratings, they receive powerful support from the ratings of superiors and peers.[25] Data providing the latter support, which are not presented here, essentially establish that perceptions of behavioral changes reported by individuals were validated by their peers and superiors. If the retrospective self-ratings of how a person saw himself changing are fantasies, those fantasies are corroborated by both superiors and peers. Various tests of internal logical consistency also support the value of laboratory training in modifying the style at Weldon. Thus the data in Figure 4 are consistent with the movement toward a System 4 managerial style depicted in Figure 3; for instance, the greater willingness to accept criticism reported in Figure 4 is consistent with the movement toward a System 4 style.

One conclusion seems appropriate: sensitivity training patently aided various interventions designed to alter the organizational style at Weldon. Which intervention contributed how much defies an answer, but the data in Figure 4 demonstrate that the laboratory approach at least contributed its share toward inducing appropriate modifications in Weldon's behavioral system.

Friedlander similarly finds that a sensitivity training design can induce desired changes in the style of small decision-making groups in a public agency. Friedlander[26] uses factor-analytic techniques to isolate six dimensions accounting for most of the variance in member attitudes toward their groups. The six dimensions follow:

I. Group Effectiveness. This dimension describes group effectiveness in solving problems and in formulating policy through a creative, realistic team effort.

II. Approach Toward vs. Withdrawal from Leader. At the positive pole of this dimension are groups in which members can establish an unconstrained and comfortable relationship with their leader—the leader is approachable.

III. Mutual Influence. This dimension describes groups in which members see themselves and others as having influence with other group members and the leader.

IV. Personal Involvement and Participation. Individuals who want, expect, and achieve active participation in group meetings are described by this dimension.

V. Intragroup Trust vs. Intragroup Competitiveness. At the positive pole, this dimension depicts a group in which the members have trust and confidence in each other.

VI. General Evaluation of Meetings. This dimension is a measure of
     a generalized feeling about the meetings of one's group as good,
     valuable, strong, pleasant, or as bad, worthless, weak, unpleasant.

The success of a laboratory program of organization change was
estimated in terms of movement along these six dimensions, using
Friedlander's Group Behavior Inventory (GBI) which measures those
dimensions. The GBI was administered to twelve decision-making
groups to establish a base-line for descriptions of group styles. Four
"Trainee Groups" participated in laboratory training sessions; and
eight "Comparison Groups" did not. In order to determine any
before-after changes in the ways members viewed their groups, the
Trainee Groups took a GBI a second time six months after their
training; the Comparison Groups did so six months after the first
administration.

Friedlander's results support the success of the laboratory training.
Trainee Groups, to spell out some of the supporting data, markedly
improved on five of the six dimensions of the GBI (Table 4), and
three of these five positive changes reached the .05 level of statistical significance. The one deviant result—a small decrease in Leader
Approachability—did not reach statistical significance.

TABLE 4. Summary of Changes in Properties of
Small Decision-Making Groups [a]

GBI Dimensions	Trainee-Group Self Ratings			Comparison-Group Self Ratings		
	Before	After	Change	Before	After	Change
Group Effectiveness	2.08	2.31	.23[c]	2.35	2.28	-.07
Leader Approachability	2.46	2.37	-.09	2.78	2.62	-.16[b]
Mutual Influence	2.44	2.61	.17[c]	2.40	2.37	-.03
Personal Involvement	2.53	2.63	.15[c]	2.57	2.51	-.06
Intragroup Trust	2.13	2.25	.12	2.58	2.45	-.13
Evaluation of Meetings	2.04	2.08	.04	2.13	2.02	-.11

[a]Taken from Frank Friedlander, "The Impact of Organizational Training Upon the
Effectiveness and Interaction of Ongoing Work Groups," *Personnel Psychology,*
(Autumn 1967) especially p. 302.
[b]Designates a statistically significant difference at .01.
[c]Designates a statistically significant difference at .05.

Given the obvious difficulty of inducing change in any social
system, the data in Table 4 constitute solid proof of the impact of
sensitivity training on organization style. However, the environment
was also changing significantly. The data in the Trainee Groups are
all the more remarkable, given what was happening in the Comparison Groups, for relations in those groups had deteriorated between

the two administrations of the GBI. Negative changes occurred in the Comparison Groups on all six of the GBI dimensions, in sharp contrast to the marked positive drift of changes in the Trainee Groups. Apparently, the parent organization was undergoing some trauma that encouraged or reinforced the deterioration of relations among its members. The Trainee Groups, as it were, successfully swam against this tide of worsening relations.

The Confrontation Design: Modifying Attitudes of Individuals in Groups

Given the undoubted value of sensitivity training for organization change and development, a co-worker and I have been concerned with developing spin-offs of the technique.[27] These spin-offs attempt to take advantage of T-group dynamics while avoiding some features of sensitivity training that are limiting in specific cases. For example, an individual in a family group would certainly not reveal information about himself that might jeopardize his career. Moreover, sensitivity training requires considerable time and expense, and it is difficult to extend very far down an organization's hierarchy.

The confrontation design is one spin-off of the laboratory approach that seems to have considerable usefulness in organizations.[28] Seven properties of the design are most central:

1. Confrontation designs involve as participants individuals who are hierarchically and/or functionally involved in some common flow or work. The results at issue here concern four levels of the same marketing organization, and some nine of its component activities.
2. Confrontations involve two or more organizational entities whose members have real and unresolved issues with one another, for example, labor and management. In this case, the focus was on the relations between various headquarters activities and supervisors of a field sales force.
3. Confrontation designs involve the mutual development of images as a basis for attempting to highlight unresolved issues. "Three-Dimensional Images" are developed to answer these questions:
   a. How do we see ourselves in relation to the Relevant Other?
   b. How does the Relevant Other see us?
   c. How do we see the Relevant Other?
4. Confrontation designs provide for sharing 3-D Images between the involved parties.
5. Confrontation designs assume that significant organizational problems often are caused by blockages in communication.
6. Confrontations are short-cycle affairs. The one in question here took approximately 12 hours.
7. Confrontation designs typically are seen as springboards for organizational action. In this case, Core Groups were set up to work on

specific organization problems. The general theory is that confrontations can improve degenerating feedback sequences, which improvement leaves individuals with a sudden surplus of energy no longer needed to repress data. That energy can be applied to task.

The confrontation design attempts to encourage participants to join in a mutual escalation of truthfulness, so as to reverse such degenerative feedback sequences as the one schematized in Figure 1. A few details of the design imply how this is done. Learning groups are set up and asked to choose and to describe their relations with Relevant Others, that is, those in their organization with whom better relations are necessary in order for both to do a more effective job.[29] Each learning group then develops Three-Dimensional Images for each of the Relevant Others they chose, with results like those illustrated in Table 5. Willing Relevant Others then share their 3-D Images, with the focus being on understanding and illustrating individual items on the images and, perhaps, on beginning to work toward more desirable adaptations.

The confrontation design has a compelling internal logic. In terms of Figure 1, the design encourages owning and openness concerning organizational issues, with the goal of increasing mutual trust and decreasing the perceived risk of owning and being open. Owning and openness could be too radical, of course; but considerable reality-testing and disciplining seems to take place in the confrontation design. At one extreme, very hurtful feedback is made improbable because of consensual validation. Members of the learning groups know that they are going to have to live with whatever they communicate on their 3-D Image, and this obvious stake is an important disciplining feature in what gets communicated. At the other extreme, the confrontation design marshals significant dynamics that discourage safe blandness. The Images are formulated in isolation, and the design permits such complicated cross-checking of images that a learning group cannot take refuge in safe but spurious niceties; for while Group A is considering telling only the highly varnished truth, they know that Group B may be deciding to be more direct. Any obvious differences would be later targets for gleeful derision as the products of Group A's "fudge factory." Such processes induce an increase in truthfulness, as the participants see reality.

The available data suggest that the confrontation design does indeed induce dynamics analogous to those in a T group. The attitudinal changes from one application of the design support this conclusion with margin to spare. Pre- and post-confrontation administrations of a questionnaire solicited data about changes in a wide range of attitudes toward a number of units and positions in the

TABLE 5.   Three-Dimensional Image from One Application of the
Confrontation Design[a]

Attitudes of Regional Sales Group

In relation to Promotion Department, members see themselves as	Members believe Promotion Department sees them as	Members characterize Promotion Department as
1. circumvented	1. insensitive to corporate needs	1. autocratic
2. manipulated	2. noncommunicative upward, withholding ideas and suggestions	2. productive
3. receiving benefits of own efforts	3. productive in field saleswork	3. unappreciative of field
4. relatively non-participative	4. naive about Promotion efforts	4. competent with objects
5. defensive	5. unappreciative of Promotion efforts	5. industrious
6. used	6. lacking understanding of sales objectives	6. inflexible
7. productive	7. belligerent	7. unrealistic
8. instruments of own success	8. operating too independently	8. naive
9. never receiving a confidence from Promotion when a campaign fails	9. not qualified to evaluate promotion materials	9. progressive in promotion philosophy and programs
10. willing to help but cooperation must work both ways	10. evaluating opinions honestly	10. too competitive within own department
		11. plagiarizing field ideas at times

[a]From Robert T. Golembiewski and Arthur Blumberg, "Confrontation as a Training Design in Complex Organizations," *Journal of Applied Behavioral Science,* III (December 1967), 534.

parent organization. Three types of attitudinal questions may be distinguished:

1. Volitional Criteria Questions, which tapped attitudes the consultants viewed as relatively easy to change in a positive direction via the confrontation (for example, How much do you want to collaborate with Unit A?)[30]
2. Objective Criteria Questions, which tapped attitudes that might drift toward negative changes as people felt more free to be open about self and others, but which could not be changed in a positive direction by a confrontation (for example, What is the level of productivity of Unit A?)
3. All Criteria Questions, composed of eleven Objective and ten Volitional Criteria Questions, which consultants assume would show an over-all favorable drift in attitudinal changes

These attitudinal data were gathered for three types of organizational units:

1. Units that were deeply involved in the design, towards whom the most positive shifts in attitudes were expected
2. Units that had token or no representation in the design, towards whom (at best) only modest shifts toward more favorable attitudes were expected
3. Units which essentially reneged on full participation in the confrontation, towards whom the least favorable shifts in attitudes were expected

Roughly, then, consultants' expectations could be expressed in terms of a 3 x 3 matrix, as in Table 6.

TABLE 6. Predictions of Attitudinal Changes Following a Confrontation Design

Types of Criteria Questions	Unit I Involved	Unit II Underrepresented	Unit III New Business
Volitional	Most significant favorable shifts in attitudes	Moderate favorable shifts in attitudes	Least favorable shifts in attitudes
All	Favorable shifts in attitudes	Moderately unfavorable shifts in attitudes	Least favorable shifts in attitudes
Objective	Least unfavorable shifts in attitudes	Slight favorable shifts in attitudes	Most unfavorable shifts in attitudes

The pattern of attitudinal changes above was not only expected, but it was also the intended outcome of the learning design. This may seem paradoxical or even perverse. As was noted elsewhere, however, developing a design that induced "negative" or "unfavorable" shifts in attitudes on the Objective Criteria Questions was intended:

Basically, the learning design was a dilemma/invention model that characterizes much of the essence of the dynamics of T-groups. Let us simplify grievously. Consultants concluded that members of the host organization had entered into a mutual-defense pact expressed, for example, in terms of unrealistically-high but mutual public estimates of performance. The lack of openness, in short, obscured basic organizational dilemmas. The confrontation design attempts to induce the public recognition of such dilemmas by greater openness and risk-taking, by explicitly dealing with the "real reality" perceived by organization members. Hence negative changes in attitudes on the Objective Criteria-Questions do not signal a dangerous deterioration of "morale." Rather, such changes establish that dilemmas requiring attention have been acknowledged. During a confrontation, that is, organization members are encouraged to activate the "dilemma" part of the dilemma/invention learning model, as by seeing themselves and others as less productive than they were willing to admit previously. At the same time, however, the confrontation design encourages organization members to work harder on the "invention" aspects of the learning model. That is, the confrontation design is intended to favorably change the attitudes of organization members on the Volitional Criteria-Questions, e.g., toward greater desire to cooperate in coping with organizational dilemmas.

The matter may be summarized briefly. In its basic intent, then, the confrontation design proposes to raise to public attention unacknowledged dilemmas in an organization that must be dealt with. The confrontation design also intends to induce greater commitment and effort toward developing inventions capable of minimizing or eliminating the dilemmas, as in the Core Groups built into the confrontation design or in the back-home situation. These two intents are realized, in turn, as participants accept norms for giving and receiving feedback consistent with the laboratory approach [such as those sketched in Table 1 above].[31]

The pattern of a priori expectations proved to mirror the actual trends in the pre/post attitudinal changes, as Table 7 shows. Involved Units had fourteen times as many positive changes in attitudes toward them on the Volitional Items, comparing the results of the second administration of the questionnaire with the results of the first administration. In contrast, the New Business Units had less than two times more positive than negative changes. Statistically significant changes in attitudes toward the Involved Units were all

TABLE 7.   Changes in Attitudes toward Organization Units Following Confrontation Design[a]

Types of Criteria Questions	Unit I Involved +/- 14.00	Unit II Underrepresented 2.33	Unit III New Business 1.86
Volitional	ss+/ss- Infinity	4.45	1.67
Objective	+/- 1.65 ss+/ss- .25	.42 .00	.38 .18
All	+/- 1.86 ss+/ss- .25	.95 .82	.83 .58

[a]Positive/negative changes are based on questionnaires administered before and after confrontation, expressed as ratios. Based on Robert T. Golembiewski and Arthur Blumberg, "Confrontation as a Training Design in Complex Organizations," *Journal of Applied Behavioral Science,* III (December 1967), especially 538-539.

positive. The New Business units did only slightly better than to break even on such changes.

Other data not reported above also suggest the real, if necessarily limited, value of the confrontation design in programs of organization change and development. Although the focus above is on attitudes, we are quite certain that the confrontation design released new energies into work on task. A third administration of the questionnaire shows that the attitudinal changes remained roughly stable over a six-month interval. Impressively, this stability existed in the face of massive and unfavorable changes in the organization's external environment.

Conclusion

The illustrations above have been necessarily sparse and hurried, but they do support the basic premise of this essay. It would be useful to make efforts to affect planned organizational change central to a behavioral approach to Public Administration. Such an orientation change helps establish the effectiveness of existing behavioral theories; but the linkages are not clearly unidirectional, even on balance. *Applied* efforts at planned organization change, in short, not only profit from *pure* organization research, but they also vitally contribute to it. Indeed, the terms "pure" and "applied"—whatever their usefulness in other areas—misrepresent the complex linkages of concept and technique that alone can enrich our analysis of organizations.

Applications of the laboratory approach in public agencies have lagged behind those in business, and the most ambitious change program within government failed to mature.[32] The data reviewed above imply a real loss for the public sector on this score, just as those data support the value of the laboratory approach to planned organizational change as a major emphasis in a behavioral approach to Public Administration.

NOTES

1. Directly, there are areas in which theoretical and applied concerns are, or at least should be, ineluctably mixed. The study of organizations is one such area, as is (to chose only one example) international development. Fred W. Riggs expresses this comingling of concerns in the latter area in a useful way. "In discussing the aims of the Comparative Administration Group . . . it is not correct to speak of 'a synthesis of the theoretical and the practical,' if only because the line between theory and practice cannot be drawn in that way. It is most appropriate to speak of a synthesis of 'theoretical' and 'practical' *concerns* . . ." John D. Montgomery and William J. Siffin (eds.), *Approaches to Development: Politics, Administration and Change* (New York: McGraw-Hill, 1966), p. x.

2. Robert L. Peabody, *Organizational Authority* (New York: Atherton,

1964); and Robert Presthus, *Behavioral Approaches to Public Administration* (University, Ala.: University of Alabama Press, 1965).

3. This theme is the burden of my argument in *Men, Management, and Morality* (New York: McGraw-Hill, 1965).

4. Warren G. Bennis, Kenneth D. Benne, and Robert Chin (eds.), *The Planning of Change* (New York: Holt, Rinehart & Winston, 1962), p. 3.

5. Warren G. Bennis, *Changing Organizations* (New York: McGraw-Hill, 1966), especially pp. 131-152.

6. Larry E. Greiner, *Organization Change and Development* (Cambridge: unpublished Ph.D. Dissertation, Harvard University, 1965). See also Louis B. Barnes, "Organizational Change and Field Experiment Methods," *Methods of Organizational Research,* ed. Victor H. Vroom (Pittsburgh: University of Pittsburgh Press, 1967), especially pp. 58-77.

7. Robert B. Blake and Jane S. Mouton, "A 9, 9 Approach to Organization Development," *Organization Development: Theory and Practice,* ed. Dale Zand (forthcoming).

8. Robert T. Golembiewski, *Organizing Men and Power: Patterns of Behavior and Line-Staff Models* (Chicago: Rand McNally, 1967).

9. For detail on the laboratory approach, consult Robert T. Golembiewski, "The 'Laboratory Approach' to Organization Change: The Schema of a Method," *Public Administration Review,* XXVII (September 1967), 211-230, and especially the Bibliographical Note, pp. 229-230.

10. Arthur Blumberg and Robert T. Golembiewski, "The PAQ and Laboratory Goal Attainment" (Athens, Georgia: mimeo, 1968).

11. Barry I. Oshry and Roger Harrison, "Transfer from Here-and-Now to There-and-Then: Changes in Organizational Problem Diagnosis Stemming from T-Group Training," *Journal of Applied Behavioral Science,* II (June 1966), 185-198.

12. If anything, conditions in the host organization were such as to encourage contrary learning. The two training periods coincided with a massive and long-overdue shake-up of personnel and programs in the organization. Our best estimate is that the laboratory program had to weather the strong and hostile winds generated by these changes.

13. Generally, see Dorothy Stock, "A Survey of Research in T-Groups," *T-Group Theory and Laboratory Method,* eds. Leland P. Bradford, Jack R. Gibb, and Kenneth D. Benne (New York: Wiley, 1964), pp. 395-441; Lewis E. Durham and Jack R. Gibb, *A Bibliography of Research, 1947-1960,* and Eric S. Knowles, *Since 1960* (Washington: NTL Institute for Applied Behavioral Science, 1967).

14. Oshry and Harrison, op. cit., present generally parallel results, although their research design differs.

15. F. C. Mann, "Studying and Creating Change," eds. Bennis, Benne, and Chin, op. cit., p. 612.

16. Warren G. Bennis, "A New Role for the Behavioral Sciences: Effecting Organizational Change," *Administrative Science Quarterly,* VIII (September 1963), 125-65.

17. Edwin A. Fleishman, E. F. Harris, and H. E. Burtt, *Leadership and Supervision in Industry* (Columbus: Bureau of Educational Research, Ohio State University, 1955).

18. Bennis, Benne, and Chin, op. cit., p. 620.

19. Alfred J. Marrow, David G. Bowers, and Stanley E. Seashore (eds.), *Management by Participation* (New York: Harper & Row, 1967). See also Robert T. Golembiewski and Stokes B. Carrigan, "Planned Change in Organization Style Based on Laboratory Approach," *Administrative Science Quarterly* (in press).

20. Frank Friedlander, "The Impact of Organizational Training Laboratories Upon the Effectiveness and Interaction of Ongoing Work Groups," *Personnel Psychology*, XX (Autumn 1967), 289-307.

21. The theoretical nexus of laboratory dynamics is considered from the structural point of view in Robert T. Golembiewski, *The Small Group* (Chicago: University of Chicago Press, 1962). Herbert Thelen, *The Dynamics of Groups At Work* (Chicago: University of Chicago Press, 1954) emphasizes emotional dynamics.

22. Mann, op. cit., p. 608.

23. Marrow, Bowers, and Seashore, op. cit., especially pp. 63-139.

24. Gilbert David, "Building Cooperation and Trust," ibid., p. 98.

25. Marrow, Bowers, and Seashore, op. cit., especially pp. 211-212.

26. Frank Friedlander, "Performance and Interactional Dimensions of Organizational Work Groups," *Journal of Applied Psychology*, L (June 1966), 257-265.

27. Robert T. Golembiewski and Arthur Blumberg, "Confrontation as a Training Design in Complex Organizations: Attitudinal Changes in a Diversified Population of Managers," *Journal of Applied Behavioral Psychology*, III (December 1967), 525-547.

28. For some reservations about the confrontation design, see Stokes Carrigan, "A Plug for Non-T-Group Confrontation," and especially Donald Klein, "A Complex Process of Social Surgery—Or 'Technocrat, Don't Forget the Sutures,' " *Journal of Applied Behavioral Science,* III (December 1967), 548-555.

29. A confrontation design is most simple when it can be built around preexisting groups with a developed collective sense and with immediate shared interests. Thus labor and management in a collective bargaining situation could be both the Learning Groups and the Relevant Others. The situation underlying the present research was far more complex. For details of this complexity, consult Golembiewski and Blumberg, "Confrontations as a Training Design in Complex Organizations," op. cit. especially pp. 526-532.

30. "Positive" and "favorable" are shorthand for higher scores on such scales as "desire greater collaboration with." "Negative" and "unfavorable," similarly, are lower before-after ratings. The "direction" of scales for items on the questionnaire were varied so as to preclude the development of a "response set."

31. Robert T. Golembiewski and Arthur Blumberg, "Persistence of Attitudinal Changes Induced by a Confrontation Design," *Journal of the Academy of Management,* XII (September 1969), 309-318.

32. For one manifestation of Project ACORD (or Action for Organization Development) in the U.S. Department of State, see Chris Argyris, "Some Causes of Organizational Ineffectiveness Within the Department of State" (Washington: Center for International Systems Research, Occasional Paper No. 2, January 1967).

VII

INTERNATIONAL RELATIONS

14 International Behavior Research: Case Studies and Cumulation

BRUCE M. RUSSETT, Yale University

The best chef knows all dishes casually, and a few intimately.—
Marianne

I. RESEARCH STRATEGIES AND CLEAVAGES

It is now a tiresome cliché, and one with a good many unpleasant associations, that there are critical methodological and philosophical gulfs within the collectivity of scholars and practitioners of international politics. Certainly there are many different *foci* of attention, such as the five sets of variables identified by Rosenau for comparing the sources of foreign policy (systemic, societal, governmental, role, and idiosyncratic),[1] or Singer's labels for international linkages (structure, interaction, and behavior),[2] and numerous *methods* for examining each focus (for example, interviewing, survey research, and content analysis). Furthermore, each of the major methods can be further subdivided for the taxonomist's pleasure (for example, thematic vs. symbolic content analysis and computerized vs. manual content analysis), and the proponents of one approach will dispute violently over one method as compared with another. These disputes and divisions are expected and essential for the progress of understanding in a field as diverse as international relations, and especially one where our experience with large-scale research has yet to produce compelling results. No effort can or should be made to resolve all methodological conflicts or to impose a uniform research strategy.

While most professionals engaging in the analysis of international relations would doubtless agree with the necessity to maintain a pluralistic research community, many would nevertheless contend that certain *particular* cleavages in the collectivity are so deep and fundamental as to threaten the future of the enterprise. There are a few major characterizations which seem to cut the body squarely in two, and which seem to delineate groups that have little in common with one another. One of these cleavages is between the scholars

425

concerned with theory building and the practitioners, with not too many individuals possessing the skills and experience to talk knowledgeably and credibly on either side. But with the growth of mid-career programs which send policy professionals to academic campuses for interchange and with the great increase in the number of scholars who either serve as part-time consultants or who spend full-time periods of service in government agencies, this gap, while still productive of misunderstandings and even complete communication failures, is on the whole a manageable and tolerable one.

Much more serious is another cleavage which in part intersects with the first but also partially coincides with it—the gap between those who self-consciously think of themselves as social scientists, especially those who employ quantitative research methods, and those whose self-image and analytical style is more closely associated with historical analysis and the intensive study of particular cases. A case in this sense may be either a particular region or country, or a particular event, such as a decision or crisis. This cleavage intersects with the first because many scholars can be found on both sides, though in part of its course it runs along with the first because hardly any policy makers have firsthand experience with quantitative research or the background to understand it when presented with its full technical paraphernalia. Where cleavages coincide, the maintenance and stability of a system are endangered.

Furthermore, the communication failures become complicated by other sociological and psychological mechanisms. Quantitatively oriented scholars exude self-confidence and sometimes even arrogance—they look at the substantial development of their section of the discipline, which has grown up almost entirely within only the past decade, compare it with the similar but now much more extensive development of quantitative orientations in psychology and economics, and feel they are riding the wave of the future. For now they write for each other, train their graduate students at a number of the more prestigious universities, ignore their nonquantitative academic colleagues, and make little effort to convey to policy makers those of their findings which, if properly packaged, might be of considerable value. And a good many nonquantitative scholars sense both the arrogance, and behind the arrogance, a threat to their own influence. They are unsympathetic with the methods, cannot read the reports, see little of relevance in the findings, and sometimes deliberately close off potential channels of communication that do exist.

The consequences of protracted guerrilla warfare for the growth of a social system are seldom favorable, and it is clear that policy makers and scholars, both quantitatively and traditionally oriented, have suffered from their battles. They in fact do have a good deal to say to each other, and neither of their research approaches is complete without the other. Specifically, the so-called nomothetic-idiographic dilemma is an artificial one; neither the case study nor the general kind of systematic analysis I shall call correlational study can alone provide the basis for reliable and valid generalizations about international politics. I intend to suggest in this essay the *value of both types* and how the two must *complement* each other in critical ways.

II. THE USES AND AGGREGATION OF CASE STUDIES

Case studies abound in the literature of international politics. They are in fact far more numerous than are synthetic or broadly comparative examinations, and any list of their contributions to the study of foreign policy making, alliance formation, crisis behavior, and other areas would be incomplete and superficial. How can we explain the persistent popularity of this approach?

We are all aware that a case study cannot by itself establish propositions about uniformities in behavior. Practitioners of the approach, as well as its critics, agree about the idiosyncrasies of particular cases and the impossibility of deriving either deterministic or rigorously stated probabilistic laws from a single case. I shall show later how the case study nevertheless does have important value for the *scientist;* and despite its problems, there is no doubt in the mind of the *policy maker* that a case study has great utility to him. What is it, then, that he expects to learn from the intensive analysis of a single event, such as the Cuban missiles crisis of 1962 or the Quemoy crisis of 1958?

The policy maker is likely to be concerned with a relatively small class of events, with a few cases that resemble the Quemoy or Cuba crisis, but in which the consequences are major. His Monday-morning quarterback role is especially important under these circumstances; he is anxious to learn what *mistakes* were made—what was done wrong or left undone—so as not to repeat the error next time. Important lessons can, for example, be derived from communication or intelligence failures, whether human or technical.[3] Mistakes in judgment, in tactics, or in strategy also will be looked for avidly. For the policy maker it is important to know *who made the mistakes* so that the miscreant can either be corrected or prevented from having another opportunity. Who had a set of perspectives that turned out to be inappropriate? Who was unduly influenced by particular narrow interests within the nation? Who used the crisis for personal self-seeking?

For low-level decisions, of the kind that have many counterparts and can be delegated to subordinate levels in the decision-making process simply because comparable decisions are presented fairly often, it is fairly easy to tell what was a mistake and what was not. But such evaluations become harder to make the closer one comes to sweeping and unique decision nodes. Even if the mistake is clearly identified, it may be hard to know what to do about it.

Appropriate action can be taken against the perpetrator, but to apply the lessons of the mistake to further decisions is not so easy. It can be done only after deciding what other decisions fall within that general class, where a sufficient number of the relevant variables are similar. We may think we know the lesson of Munich, but the lesson of Sarajevo is the opposite. Which applies to Southeast Asia? About all that can be done solely from case experience is to use it to sensitize one to future situations that may be similar. But from the single case it is impossible to know *how often* such events are likely to occur, or under what particular *kinds of conditions* they may arise.

All the gains that may accrue from an intensive case study are relatively short-run accessions. With personnel turnover and changing conditions the lessons of earlier cases will be forgotten or thought not applicable and later ones will take precedence. The value of discrete cases for the cumulative building of information about experience is nil. We need controls, by observing many cases and accounting for the relevant varying factors, in order to establish causal relationships. But this does not mean that one case study has no value when rigorously combined with other cases or integrated with the findings from other modes of analysis. Case studies have at least four uses in building cumulated knowledge:

1. They can stimulate the production of *hypotheses* about possible regularities. This is essentially the sensitization function referred to above. It is important to note both that most hypotheses later investigated with correlational techniques are *originally generated* from case-study material, and that such generation is merely a *beginning,* not an end point, in the scientific process.[4]

2. Case studies can test in a different and more appropriate context the *inferences* made from suggestive but not fully appropriate correlational analyses. For example, there are now several cross-sectional (synchronic) studies, based on the examination of nearly 100 countries, which show a clear negative relationship between level of economic development and the frequency and/or magnitude of internal violence.[5] Rich countries evidence much less internal violence than poor or middle-income ones. Yet generalizing from such cross-sectional studies to scientific or policy statements about what may happen over time is full of obvious pitfalls. What we have is an interesting hypothesis that economic development, eventually at least, will produce more stable regimes in countries that are now poor. But the hazards of generalization demand an effort to move from the simulated "time" analysis implied by looking at several levels or "stages" of development to some actual time (longitudinal, diachronic) analyses of historical cases. Is there a discernible regularity in the relation between development and violence in eighteenth- and nineteenth-century England, for instance?[6] A single finding of such a

regularity would not verify a probabilistic hypothesis, nor would the absence of the regularity refute it. Repeated case studies, however, provide the new data base required for verification or rejection, and may, as tendencies emerge while the cases are being compiled, suggest important refinements.

3. Similarly, if the correlational pattern relating two variables, say violence and stability, is satisfactorily established, the case study provides an often unsurpassable means for pursuing a far more critical question, namely, What is the *causal* relationship between the two variables?

First of all, one looks at the *temporal* sequence. It might be that above the middle levels of development an improvement in economic conditions produces, through greater satisfaction, a decrease in the stimulus to violence. Or on the contrary, a decline in the frequency of violence may promote stable social and political conditions that make economic growth and controlled change possible. Whereas there are now available some statistical techniques employing correlational analysis for the investigation of causal propositions, those techniques are at best approximate procedures for eliminating certain possibilities without confirming the others, and at worst depend upon such restrictive assumptions about the data that they cannot even validly eliminate possible explanations.[7] Only a set of carefully dissected case studies can in the end do this job satisfactorily.

Second, case studies may be employed to *eliminate spurious* correlations. Again, the association between violence and development may be real enough but not necessarily causal in either direction; both may be the product of some third variable, or they may interact in a very complicated manner. Some of these findings too may be checked if one has a good deal of high quality cross-sectional data on a variety of potentially relevant variables, but the case-study approach is surer and more direct.

4. Finally, case studies are essential to the refinement and qualification even of a hypothesis strongly supported by high correlations. *Deviant-case analysis* here can provide an understanding of those instances that do not fit the general pattern of association.[8] Only by probing into the particular circumstances of the different behavior can one begin to distinguish limits of the empirical domain to which the hypothesis may be expected to apply. Most generalizations are more powerful when so restricted than as universal statements. Deviant-case analysis obviously requires first knowing what pattern the case deviates from.

All these uses of case studies, however, assume further correlational analyses at a later state. Without iteratively shifting back and forth, without later correlational analyses building upon the hypotheses suggested, or supported by the case studies, one is only a little better off than without any case studies at all.[9] A sequence of steps something like the following is essential:

a. The original case studies. All work on a particular class of phenomena, whether wars, democratic political systems, or whatever, begins with descriptive studies by those who are interested in a particular problem, with a dissection of the individual political system or an intensive study of the events in the conflict.

b. From the information provided by a variety of such case studies a taxonomy can then be constructed, consisting of a standard set of categories that attempt to identify the important variables and suggest hypotheses about their functional relationships. This taxonomic stage is crucial to the next step in the analysis. Though it may be done in conjunction with further analysis, it is a valuable step in itself, and even if done alone it is not to be deprecated as "mere description," as some quantitatively oriented scholars are occasionally prone to do.[10]

c. From the large number of cases, as classified by taxonomic procedures, it is then possible and necessary to move to *correlational analysis*. The hypotheses suggested by the individual case studies and taxonomy need to be tested systematically by rigorous techniques to determine the probabilities with which particular bivariate relationships will hold, the nature (such as linear or curvilinear) of the relationships, and their sensitivity to the effects of third variables. One moves from the original suggestion that two variables may be related to a detailed probabilistic statement. This statement may be extremely complex and based upon a very sophisticated manipulation of the material in what is simply referred to as "correlational" study. The satisfactory analysis of this material is seldom if ever a matter of simply performing one or two routine computations, but a *repetitive* process of sequentially performing similar but varying computations exploring various related but differentiable hypotheses until, figuratively speaking, the ground is littered with discarded hypotheses (and less figuratively, littered with discarded computer printouts).[11]

d. Once certain refined and carefully checked statements have been produced, however, it will be necessary eventually to *return to a case-study approach*. The statistical manipulations will reach a point where there still remain plausible alternative hypotheses that cannot be discarded on the basis of the material at hand. The data may be too contaminated by error, coded according to too gross a set of categories, or, despite great efforts to compile a large sample of cases, may in the end be based on too few instances to permit sufficiently refined multivariate analyses for discarding hypotheses. In particular, the multivariate analysis of data where the nation-state is the unit of analysis quickly begins to press against the limitations inherent in the fact that there are, by the most generous definition of the term, only about 130 sovereign states in the current world.[12]

Thus, using the taxonomy either as originally compiled or, more likely, as refined on the basis of the correlational studies, analysis shifts back to the identification and scrutiny of a particular case in order to winnow out some of the remaining alternative hypotheses and to suggest new ones.

e. But if one has, through a case study, raised the level of sophistication from what was produced by the correlational analysis, the process is still far from complete. If it is established that in this instance the temporal sequence was from A to B and not vice versa, one still needs to know how often—always, usually, rarely?—this happens, and further case studies, eventually feeding into second-stage correlational analyses, are essential.

The crucial point is that *both kinds of studies are critical to the development of scientific knowledge* either for its own sake or as reliable advice to the policy maker; neither one alone is satisfactory. Some scholars may prefer to work solely with one approach or the other. One may be better suited for a particular person's temperament, or he may have such a comparative advantage in the skills of one approach over the other that it is not productive for him to attempt both. Other analysts will find it easier to shift back and forth and may enjoy doing so. In any case, a recognition of the basic symbiosis between the two is essential to the long-run health of the research process.

Some of this may seem obvious, and other parts may be excessively vague and general. There are, however, plenty of illustrations from international politics research in recent years that show the limitations of both approaches when pursued separately. There are instances both of urgent needs for new case studies and of extant case studies that must now be brought together. There are even instances of case studies that employ a good many of the techniques of modern quantitative social science but that were undertaken prematurely, without first-order taxonomic and especially correlational analysis, and are hence of little or even negative value in the cumulative process. We will draw examples from the deterrence and escalation literature and from studies of political integration. The deterrence literature well illustrates the need for a judicious combination of the case study and correlational approaches, and research on international integration provides an excellent example of some quantitative case studies that were inadequately based upon theoretical and correlational materials, and whose policy conclusions were therefore rendered questionable.

III. CASE STUDIES OF POLITICAL INTEGRATION

The study of international political integration has been plagued with poorly articulated case studies. Though a great many writers are ostensibly concerned with the topic, it seems as though each has a different definition of integration and is concerned with a different set of dependent and independent variables. While many of these variables could be recoded to provide the basis for a correlational study looking for general patterns, the effort required would be substantial. To date the most notable effort at employing a common analytical framework in undertaking case studies specifically as inputs to a correlational analysis remains the 1957 Princeton study directed by Karl Deutsch.[13] This project produced some very important tentative generalizations about necessary and helpful conditions for successful integrative efforts, but it also left largely unexamined some of Deutsch's most stimulating hypotheses, such as those about transactions and communications flows.

For example, in several of his later works Deutsch has developed a null-model baseline for measuring an "expected" level of transactions in the absence of political, geographic, or other influences which would cause a nation to "prefer" transactions with a particular partner in excess of what its size alone would predict. The deviation of actual trade from this expected volume, expressed as an index of relative advantage (RA) is taken as an indication of possible political relevance for integration.[14] Although Deutsch and others have made fairly plausible deductive arguments about why greater-than-expected transaction levels should be conducive to integration, there have so far been *no* rigorous correlational analyses, and at best a very few case studies, which move in the direction of establishing the proposition.[15] Thus predictive studies, which would infer the likelihood of continued or further political integration on the basis of actual deviations from expected trade patterns, become extremely hazardous.

The hazards are well illustrated in a recent case study of the prospects for political integration in Western Europe.[16] Examination of the indices of relative acceptance within the region shows an increase throughout the early years following World War II, but, by 1957, a leveling-off onto a plateau, with few notable changes in either direction since then. What has happened is that both the actual and the expected volumes of commerce have themselves grown enormously over the same period, so that trade among the countries of the Six is four times what it was ten years ago. This growth is masked in the RA analysis because of a great expansion in the Six's total foreign trade (not just with each other), their consequent increased weight in all world markets, and the deliberate use of the RA model to control for such "size" effects. Nevertheless, the result is that for the typical country of the Six, the proportion of its national income that is derived from or spent on trade with the other members of the Common Market is more than *twice* what it was in 1957. Hence the conclusions drawn depend entirely upon which of the alternative analytical models one prefers. I have argued elsewhere that it is not the null model deviations that make most of the difference for political integration, but indeed the size of the impact that trade makes, relative to the domestic economy.[17] If one accepts the latter argument, then Western Europe has made great strides in developing the bases for a highly integrated political system.

In the end the analyst is reduced to weighing the relative plausibility of the arguments in which different conclusions are deduced from different premises. There have been no tests, performed on a variety of countries where the dependent variable of political integration is rigorously measured, to say which—high RA's or high trade/income volume—is more often associated with successful integration. Until such studies of the relationships between relevant independent variables and past integration are performed, case studies undertaken for *predictive* purposes raise a great many unintended questions.

Similarly, Deutsch makes other conclusions in his study of Western Europe which depend upon a choice between two alternative theoretical models with little empirical evidence as to which is the more powerful. For example, one table shows that the percentage of a national sample in France and West Germany with "good feelings" toward the other country rose from 11 percent in each to 30 percent and 37 percent respectively. These figures are juxtaposed against figures that show, for the same countries at the same time, an increase only from 6 to 21 percent and from 5 to 20 percent in the proportion who said they would trust the other nation in case of war. From these figures Deutsch draws the baleful consequence of a growing "trust gap."[18] But it is not clear why we should prefer the trust-gap interpretation, rather than one that stressed simply the growth in trust or its faster proportionate growth than the growth of mere liking. Again, evidence on which of the two variables has been more closely related to political integration in past cases is almost entirely lacking. Thus, while the Deutsch study was in many respects well-executed, and doubtless the need for predictive studies cannot always be postponed in favor of more basic research, the ultimate value of the study remains in some doubt. A clearly articulated set of hypotheses, to which further case studies could contribute, is needed.

If the variant of political integration in which one is interested happens to be the growth of supranational institutions, there are of course not many past cases which can be offered as candidates for intensive study. A number of writers have urged that conditions in underdeveloped countries are for these purposes sufficiently different from those in developed areas that generalizations about integrative processes cannot be transferred from one to the other.[19] If this conclusion is correct, then for finding a basis for predicting whether a full political union will develop from the EEC, one is virtually limited to those instances in which two previously independent nations joined or split apart in North America or Western Europe in the twentieth century. Even stretching the definitions, I can think only of Newfoundland-Canada and Yugoslavia as successes, and England-Ireland and Norway-Sweden as splits. Perhaps the universe could be expanded somewhat by going back into the nineteenth century or by adding unions formed of areas that had not previously been sovereign (for example, post-1918 Czechoslovakia), but even so the limits are easy enough to see.

The existence of such limits, however, does not necessarily indicate that the task is hopeless. Virtually all hypotheses of any interest about international integration specify not merely a causal relation between two variables, but also a specific mechanism or mechanisms by which the effect is produced. Where there are too few potential cases to produce an adequate basis for correctional procedures, or where such case studies would be far too expensive and time-consuming to replicate, one can look at the specific mechanism and shift levels of analysis. For example, Ernst Haas's famous study of the European Coal and Steel Community specified some hypotheses about spillover that could be tested on subgroups and individuals within various ECSC agencies.[20] Or in my own study of Anglo-American relations, in which the dependent variable of integration or responsiveness was extremely difficult to measure at the national level, I shifted at one point to an analysis of the behavior of particular legislators differentiated according to the number and strength of their personal or constituency ties with the other country. I then was able to determine the amount of behavioral difference that possessing such ties made, and could with a little more confidence return to inferences about the probable effect on national decisions of a decline in such ties at the aggregate level.[21] Often, in fact, the theoretical structure appropriate to an analysis may require correlational and case studies at a lower level even if the material at the aggregate level is plentiful and not too ambiguous.

Another aspect of the international integration literature that demands new case studies, with a view to eventual correlation analysis of those case studies, is the problem of sequence. Even where it is possible to identify certain regularities, such as the association at one time period between trade patterns and the existence of intergovernmental institutions, it is not possible with a snapshot to see which causes which or even, temporally, which leads which. Furthermore, the pace of movements in both such variables is normally so glacial that it is virtually impossible even with a ten-year interval to be very firm in causal inferences. Intensive examination of developments in particular geographically or politically defined areas, with frequent snapshots over a very substantial timespan and particular attention to the political consequences, is required.

IV. DETERRENCE AND ESCALATION

Some of my own experiences in strategic analysis indicate both the opportunities and the need for a synthesis of the case-study and correlational approaches.[22] Based largely upon individual case studies of international crises, generalizations about what factors contribute to the success of deterrent threats abound in the strategic literature. It has been alleged that successful deterrence requires over-all strategic superiority or at least parity or local military superiority, that the area to be defended must be of demonstrable intrinsic value, and that democracies where dissent is visible are less able effectively to demonstrate commitment; a variety of other propositions have been expressed either as laws or hypotheses. In a correlational study of seventeen instances of attempted deterrence between 1930 and 1961 I was able to show that the empirical evidence provides little support for any of these simple statements, and instead suggested, on the basis of further correlational evidence, that successful deterrence, or a decision to fight if deterrence failed, depends largely upon the strength and number of various ties between the would-be deterrer and the party he is attempting to protect.

Such a correlational study did not, however, demonstrate that deterrence succeeded or war resulted *because* of these bonds. To make such a demonstration requires not just the associational evidence, but a detailed look at the perceptions and decision-making process of officials in the government of the potential attacker and defender. Only if they perceived those ties and took them into account would the hypothesis be supported. In order to find evidence of such perceptions and calculations, I later looked in depth at a particular historical instance, the Japanese decision to attack Pearl Harbor in addition to escalating military activity within Southeast Asia. This evidence, however, does not close the matter. In the first place, the Japanese decided to attack *despite* the hypothesized perceptions and calculations; while this finding was not inconsistent with the basic formulation of the original model, some refinement was necessary. More importantly, the single case still does not establish the *probability* of such behavior or its interaction with other variables. Since few of us would subscribe to a completely deterministic model of human behavior, the need for gauging the probabilities demands a series of further case studies in which the relevant variables are measured rigorously by common definitions. From these further case studies can then come the second-stage correlational analysis.

To be useful, however, case studies have to be done in such a way that they can eventually be analyzed within a common framework, with the same variables, measured in the same way and studied in each. It is often helpful if such studies are undertaken *from the beginning* within such a framework, where the student of each case is consciously asking the same questions as is every other analyst, and where by a painstaking repetitive process of sharpening and refinement the coding and data-gathering procedures are made fully comparable. Few examples of such large-scale projects can now be found in international relations or political science. Perhaps the best in a related field is the set of country studies being undertaken by the Yale Economic Growth Center in response to a widespread dissatisfaction among economists with the quality and comparability of national-income accounts in developing countries. Very great resources are going into the compilation of fresh data by standardized categories, which eventually can be subjected to rigorous cross-national analysis.[23]

It is seldom essential, however, for such studies to be done originally within a common set of questions and definitions. A great number of valuable correlational analyses have been performed by a secondary coding of case studies originally undertaken for very different reasons. Here all the assets of good traditional case studies are of great value—the virtues of great detail, so that a wide variety of unanticipated questions can in fact be answered from the data by reordering the original information, and careful documentation, so that even where the case study does not itself contain the necessary information, the secondary analyst has good clues as to where he can himself dig it out from the primary materials with a minimum of wasted excavation. In fact, it is probably just as well for many correlational analyses to be done on preexisting case-study material. Given the primitive state of most international relations theory, a standardized descriptive framework might produce premature closure on a restricted and erroneous set of questions. But eventually the need for a common analytical model does arise. Further case studies cannot be undertaken to check on inferences from the correlational analysis unless the hypotheses are carefully articulated.

Certainly it is not exclusively the international-integration literature that is marked by disconnected analytical case studies and premature predictive case studies. One of the most obvious others is the effort to generalize about the stability or war-proneness of bipolar and multipolar international systems. Extremely few historical examples have been studied in depth, but this has not inhibited a good many authors from making rather sweeping generalizations based on a combination of deductive inference[24] and analogizing from historical instances. The available evidence on historical systems is rarely coded rigorously, and it is used in a fashion that is hardly more than anecdotal.

The situation becomes even worse with attempts to generalize from past cases to the contemporary international system. Such serious differences exist between both the abstract models and the available historical instances on the one hand, and the contemporary system on the other, that it becomes extremely difficult to decide whether the appropriate variables have been controlled and a "good" analogy produced, or whether the differences are critical. Desperately needed at this point are some correlational studies with a large number of cases, coded for a variety of variables that different theories regard as potentially relevant, with sophisticated multivariate quantitative analysis. Note the latter emphasis: I am specifically not implying that it will be enough simply to compare systems by the number of major actors and the number of war casualties in a bivarate correlation, though that is the necessary beginning. Technology, weapons systems, alliance aggregation, relative size and number of powers, the time elapsed since other wars, and many other variables will have to be taken into account. In this respect the current work of Michael Haas, Singer and Small, and Denton promises ultimately to be very important.[25]

It should be entirely clear from the preceding discussion that, though I have suggested a dichotomy between case studies and correlational studies, a case study can be systematic and may make use of a great many correlational materials from lower levels of analysis. The very intensive analyses to which the 1914 crisis has been subjected by the Stanford group illustrate well the degree to which sophisticated computerized content and aggregate data analysis can be employed. At the same time, the Stanford group has not limited its attention to the events of 1914, and has looked also, though so far less intensively, at the Bosnian crisis of 1908, the Cuban missile crisis, the deterioration of Sino-Soviet relations, and others.[26] Even a nonquantitative examination of other cases quickly brings home the limitations of a case-study approach taken in isolation. At least one noted writer on the 1914 events virtually attributes the outbreak of war to the military pressures produced by the war and mobilization plans prepared by the antagonists.[27] Comparative analysis shows, however, that essentially the same plans existed in three previous crises during which general war did not break out. One can quickly find instruction in the difference between necessary and sufficient conditions.

The World War I study and the case studies of the other crises, quantitative and nonquantitative, illustrate an area where the need for integrating the many case studies is especially apparent. There must be innumerable classified studies on the "lessons learned" in many of the crises in which the United States has been involved since World War II. Just a moment's reflection will bring to mind a great number of published studies—many of each set of events and using the full spectrum of analytical techniques—that have been done on the escalation and deescalation for the two Berlin confrontations, the Korean War, the Indochina conflicts in 1954 and more recently, the

Quemoy-Matsu crisis, the Cuban missile and Bay of Pigs affairs, and others. With all these intensive studies, combined with substantial speculation and deductive theorizing about escalation sequences, we have the basis for a very complex and sophisticated set of coding rules that could put those case studies within a common framework and begin to extract evidence for the support or disconfirmation of general hypotheses.

One could begin by trying to construct an empirical "escalation ladder," in which the goal would be to discover exactly which steps usually follow others—what is the "normal" sequence of events, up and down—so as better to single out the significance of deviations. Is "skipping a rung" more likely to result in further or more rapid escalation; or, as a demonstrative step, does it have important deterrent value in preventing counterescalation? Or, more satisfactorily, *when* and *for what steps* does "skipping" produce such results? And even more basic, is it even possible to construct such a ladder? Do sufficient uniformities exist to make it possible to say that, usually at least, a given sequence is followed? Or is the meaning of certain steps sufficiently different in threat—for instance, under some conditions troop movements may represent a higher stage of escalation than mobilization, and under others vice versa—that two or three intersecting ladders need to be constructed for distinct dimensions? Factor analysis, cluster analysis, or other inductive techniques, perhaps especially those which can operate merely on ordinal rather than interval data, should be of high potential use in sorting out the regularities in this large body of data.[28]

V. AN OPPORTUNITY FOR SYNTHESIS

The deterrence literature illustrates in especially poignant form the current doldrums of international politics research. It is no secret that strategic analysis has relied heavily, though hardly exclusively, on the case-study method. Nor is it any secret that many scholars in the field feel a certain malaise, a sense that the accomplishments of the past few years do not equal the contributions made during the "golden age" when such scholars as Kahn, Kissinger, Schelling, and Wohlstetter were most visible. Even if their assessment is correct, it by no means reflects on the intellectual quality of the men who continue to produce in the area. Partly it is a result of the shift of resources and concern to the Vietnam war. In part too it is the price of success: acceptance of the theory and policy consequences stemming from the principle of invulnerable second-strike forces has meant a revolution in military-political doctrine and practice, a tough act to follow in short order. But the need for some fresh approaches, both methodological and conceptual, is becoming apparent.[29]

The need is forced in part by behavioral questions about deterrence that the original approach could not answer. It also stems from changes in the international environment within which the major powers operate. The strategic-analysis community addressed itself largely to a bipolar world; that bipolarity has weakened greatly, though we are unsure how to describe the new one. Also, the analysts of strategy, perhaps in part because of their bipolar focus, concentrated too heavily on a perception of the international political process as dominated by conflict. Despite Schelling's contributions toward an understanding of the mixed-motive situation, I think this is the most telling indictment made by the critics of "strategic thinking."[30] To temper this emphasis on conflict, a broader attention to conflict resolution and cooperation is required. This leads to what I see as an escape from the present sense of letdown—an integration of the strategic field with an avowedly social-scientific search for the causes of war. It would be directed to historical as well as to contemporary information and would be less bound by the culture of the 1950's and the 1960's than the strategic field has been.

The chances for such an integration exist precisely because a parallel reassessment is appearing among some of those most firmly committed to a quantitative or systematic approach. A number of international relations scholars have remarked that they too sense a new mood among their colleagues, a felt need for the digestion and evaluation of the scientific achievements of the past decade. There is no doubt that reputations have risen and fallen sharply in the study of international relations; most of the major lights of the past decade are now in eclipse. Some approaches have faded because it turned out to be virtually impossible to put data into their imaginative theoretical systems; others (especially some simulations) are being looked at askance from a doubt whether their expensively accumulated data have enough to say about the "real" world. Still others have been more nearly institutional failures, where the resources necessary to build a self-nurturing organization proved lacking.

This new mood stems less from a change in intellectual convictions than from an evolution of the terrain being surveyed. It is not a matter of questioning the scientific enterprise *qua* science, but only a matter of doubts about particular techniques and procedures—a process that is in fact a requisite for a science. Ten years ago the discipline had hardly anything to show in the way of research achievements other than case studies. Now we have a substantial amount of theory expressed or expressible in formal symbolic terms and a large number of empirical studies using a spectrum of quantitative methods running from simple political arithmetic to the most complex multivariate statistical procedures for manipulating both numerical and verbal data. Some of the latter procedures will turn out to be overly complex for the relatively crude data to which they are applied; but despite the doubts all of us have about everyone else's manipulations, it is too early to rule out any path yet taken as merely leading to a cul de sac.

Thus it is important for the so-called traditional scholars to recognize the diversity achieved and the consequent inability to dismiss the entire enterprise as misguided or irrelevant. It can no longer be ridiculed as simply the product of a couple of simulations and the counting of postcards.[31] The variety is such that the traditional scholar could surely gain insight from applying some of the new techniques to any problem that interests him. On the other hand, both the data and the hypothesis-generating potential of the traditional materials will for the foreseeable future be essential (if occasionally exasperating) for those who seek to build a science. Precisely because of the quantitative advances, this need becomes apparent. But successful use of the case-study approach will require much careful winnowing of old material and designing research for new efforts.

N O T E S

This article reflects some of the research of the World Data Analysis Program of Yale University, under grant #GS-614 from the National Science Foundation and contract #N-0014-67-A-0097-0007 from ARPA, Behavioral Sciences, monitored by the Office of Naval Research.

1. James N. Rosenau, "Pre-Theories and Theories of Foreign Policy," *Approaches to International and Comparative Politics,* ed. R. Barry Farrell (Evanston: Northwestern University Press, 1966), pp. 27-92.

2. J. David Singer, "The Global System and its Subsystems: A Developmental View," *Linkage Politics: Essays on the Convergence Between National and International Systems,* ed. James N. Rosenau (New York: Free Press, 1969).

3. For example, Roberta Wohlstetter, *Pearl Harbor: Warning and Decision* (Stanford: Stanford University Press, 1962).

4. This function of case studies is of great value to the policy maker as well as to the scientist in expanding his intuitive base. For a useful essay see James W. Fesler, "The Case Method in Political Science," *Essays on the Case Method in Public Administration,* ed. Edwin A. Bock, et al. (Brussels: International Institute of Administrative Sciences, 1962), pp. 65-88.

5. See Ivo Feierabend and Rosalind Feierabend, "Aggressive Behavior Within Polities, 1948-1962: A Cross-National Study," *Journal of Conflict Resolution,* X (September 1966), 249-271; Bruce M. Russett, *Trends in World Politics* (New York: Macmillan, 1965), Ch. VIII; Robert S. McNamara, speech to American Society of Newspaper Editors, Montreal, May 18, 1966.

6. For a preliminary effort see Charles L. Taylor, "The Rise of Political Activity Among British Working Men, 1790-1850," paper presented to the annual meeting of the American Political Science Association, New York, September 1966.

7. See Herbert Simon, *Models of Man* (New York: Wiley, 1957), Ch. I-III; Hubert M. Blalock, *Causal Inferences in Nonexperimental Research* (Chapel Hill: University of North Carolina Press, 1964), and "Causal Inferences, Closed Populations, and Measures of Association," *American Political Science Review*, LXI (March 1967), 130-135; Hayward Alker, "Causal Inferences in Political Research" *Mathematical Applications in Political Science*, ed. Joseph L. Bernd (Dallas: Southern Methodist University Press, 1966), II, 7-43.

8. For a more extended discussion see especially Patricia Kendall and Katherine Wolf, "The Two Purposes of Deviant Case Analysis," *The Language of Social Research*, eds. Paul Lazarsfeld and Morris Rosenberg (Glencoe: Free Press, 1955).

9. In one prominent political science department regarded as behavioral, case studies have been declared unacceptable as dissertation topics. However, the rule has not been enforced when the role of the case study in theory building is carefully identified in the prospectus.

I am aware that no two cases are ever completely *identical*, and thus that all comparisons require careful controls to determine whether they are sufficiently similar to make the comparison profitable. Much of the art in political science lies in a good sense for penetrating behind verbal or other differences to identify similar cases where comparison will be productive, and in avoiding the verbal and other traps that misleadingly suggest relevant similarities. But I do assume that none of us rejects entirely the possibility of making such comparisons.

10. Arthur F. Wright, "On the Uses of Generalization in the Study of Chinese History," *Generalization in the Writing of History*, ed. Louis Gottschalk (Chicago: University of Chicago Press, 1963), p. 36, makes a distinction between "labelling" (or taxonomic) generalizations and "regularity" (correlational) generalizations. For a discussion of how some historians are coming to grips with the problems considered here see, of the other essays in the Gottschalk volume, those by Walter P. Metzger, Louis Gottschalk, Roy Nichols, William Aydelotte, and David Potter. Another useful reference on the comparative method in history is William H. Sewell, Jr., "Marc Bloch and the Logic of Comparative History," *History and Theory*, VI (#2, 1967), 208-218. See also Michael Haas, "Comparative Analysis," *Western Political Quarterly*, XV (June 1962), 244-303.

11. Factor-analytic studies come to mind here. There are several major decisions in any factor analysis—how to treat communalities, whether to normalize the data, how many factors to rotate, what kind of rotation to perform—that can change the final results. The analyst must decide which technical alternatives are compatible with his theoretical purposes and, of those that pass this test, try enough to be sure the results are not seriously affected by different technical decisions. A comparison of the factor-analysis results with those obtainable by other related techniques, such as nonmetric procedures or clustering techniques, may also be necessary. The principle of proceeding by strong inference to a single crucial experiment is a worthy ideal but often is not practicable.

12. The need for intensive case studies would in fact be a great deal less pressing if our universe were sufficiently large to permit much more reliable inferences from sophisticated multivariate analysis; but that need would not

be eliminated, as indicated by the continuing role of depth interviews concomitant with survey research.

13. Karl W. Deutsch et al., *Political Community and the North Atlantic Area* (Princeton: Princeton University Press, 1957).

14. Richard Savage and Karl W. Deutsch, "A Statistical Model of the Gross Analysis of Transaction Flows," *Econometrica,* XXVIII (July 1960), 551-572. Contrary to some assertions, Deutsch does not crudely argue that such deviations indicate the presence of integration, but merely that they indicate the presence of influences favorable to it.

15. Amitai Etzioni, *Political Unification* (New York: Holt, Rinehart & Winston, 1965) compares four cases with stimulating results, but the coding procedures are not fully replicable.

16. Karl W. Deutsch, Lewis J. Edinger, Roy Macridis, and Richard L. Merritt, *France, Germany, and the Western Alliance* (New York: Scribners, 1967).

17. Bruce M. Russett, *International Regions and the International System,* (Chicago: Rand McNally, 1967), Ch. VIII. For related doubts about this conclusion see Ronald Inglehart, "An End to European Integration?" *American Political Science Review,* LXI (March 1967), 102.

18. Deutsch, Edinger, et al., op. cit., p. 249.

19. For example, J. S. Nye, *Pan-Africanism and East African Integration* (Cambridge: Harvard University Press, 1965).

20. Ernst Haas, *The Uniting of Europe* (Stanford: Stanford University Press, 1957).

21. Bruce M. Russett, *Community and Contention: Britain and America in the Twentieth Century* (Cambridge: M.I.T. Press, 1963), Ch. X. Leon Lindberg is currently doing an interesting job of specifying the coding procedures for measuring the dependent variable of political integration. See his forthcoming book, *Europe as a Political System: Measuring Political Integration,* and also the work being done by Donald J. Puchala.

22. Bruce M. Russett, "The Calculus of Deterrence," *Journal of Conflict Resolution,* VII (June 1963), 97-109, and "Pearl Harbor: Deterrence Theory and Decision Theory," *Journal of Peace Research,* IV (#2, 1967), 87-104.

23. In international relations the most important efforts are still at an earlier stage. James Rosenau has been coordinating a group of comparative foreign policy studies around his set of categories for levels of analysis and gross characteristics of nations; the studies appeared in his *Linkage Politics,* op. cit. A second comparative study, concerning international organizations, is being sponsored by the SSRC. An important and promising effort to collect and analyze a large body of comparative data on nations' interactions, especially in establishing the common characteristics of crisis as compared with noncrisis periods, is directed by Charles A. McClelland. For an exploratory example see his "Access to Berlin: The Quantity and Variety of Events, 1948-1963," *Quantitative International Politics: Insights and Evidence,* ed. J. David Singer (New York: Free Press, 1968), pp. 159-186.

24. The major essays, of varying quality, probably are Morton A. Kaplan, *System and Process in International Politics* (New York: Wiley, 1957), Part I; Karl W. Deutsch and J. David Singer, "Multi-polar Power Systems and International Stability," *World Politics,* XVI (April 1964); Kenneth Waltz, "The Stability of a Bipolar World," *Daedalus,* XCIII (Summer 1964), 881-909; and

Richard N. Rosecrance, "Bipolarity, Multipolarity, and the Future," *Journal of Conflict Resolution*, X (September 1966), 314-327.

25. Michael Haas, "International Subsystems: Stability and Polarity," *American Political Science Review*, LXIV (March 1970); J. David Singer and Melvin Small, "Alliance Aggregation and the Onset of War," *Quantitative International Politics*, ed. Singer, op. cit., pp. 247-286; Frank Denton, "Some Regularities in International Conflict Behavior," *Background*, X (February 1966), 283-318.

26. The Stanford Studies on Conflict and Integration of the 1914 events are presently scattered in a great number of book chapters and journal articles, but will be gathered together in a forthcoming three-volume work by Richard A. Brody and Robert C. North. Materials by this group relevant to other interactions include Ole R. Holsti, "External Conflict and International Cohesion: The Sino-Soviet Case," *The General Inquirer*, ed. Philip J. Stone (Cambridge: M.I.T. Press, 1966), pp. 343-358; Holsti, Brody, and North, "Measuring Affect and Action in International Reaction Models: Empirical Materials from the 1962 Cuban Crisis," *Peace Research Society Papers*, II (1965), 170-189; P. Terry Hopmann, "International Conflict and Cohesion in the Communist System," *International Studies Quarterly*, XI (September 1967), 212-236; and M. George Zaninovich, "Pattern Analysis of Variables within the International System: The Sino-Soviet Example," *Journal of Conflict Resolution*, VI (September 1962), 253-268.

27. Barbara Tuchman, *The Guns of August* (New York: Macmillan, 1962), Ch. II-VI. I am indebted to Richard Brody for the example.

28. A major study of great promise for producing an empirically based taxonomy of escalations is Richard Barringer, *The Condition of Conflict: A Configural Analysis* (Cambridge: Center for International Studies, M.I.T., ACDA/WEC-98, Draft Technical Report, 1967).

29. My thinking on this has been notably influenced by Roy E. Licklider, *The Private Nuclear Strategists* (New Haven: unpublished doctoral dissertation, Yale University, 1968).

30. The principal critiques, containing a variety of trenchant, irrelevant, and mistaken points, are Anatol Rapoport, *Strategy and Conscience* (Ann Arbor: University of Michigan Press, 1964), and Phillip Green, *Deadly Logic* (Columbus: Ohio State University Press, 1966).

31. As evidence I would offer my own rather approximate survey of the academic political science and international relations journals published in the United States during 1966. About 30 percent of the articles either made use of mathematical formulations or had the equivalent of at least two tables. I recognize, however, that this survey of *publications* almost certainly exaggerates the number of quantitative *practitioners*.

15 International Relations Theory

MICHAEL HAAS, University of Hawaii

> Here is the world, sound as a nut, not the smallest piece of chaos
> left, never a stich nor an end, not a mark of haste, or botching, or
> second thought; but the theory of the world is a thing of shreds and
> patches.—*Ralph Waldo Emerson*

I. CHANGING SUBJECT MATTER AND FOCI

International relations began as a self-conscious field of study in the period immediately following World War I. Its emergence may be seen as related to the failure of the "old" diplomacy of secret deliberations and nonpublicized operations—as conducted by a professional class of diplomatic officials—to prevent the debacle of 1914. The use of "total war" in the course of the "war to end all wars" resulted in an effort consuming the energies and attentions of most citizens in the belligerent nations. A semblance of democratic consultation was needed to increase morale in the factories as well as in the trenches. When war veterans returned home, they began to assert views on foreign policy in a manner more vocal than had previously been the case. The "new" democratic diplomacy began,[1] and increasing public interest in international affairs was responsible for the introduction of international relations courses into the curricula of leading colleges and universities. Since the early part of the century the content of international relations coursework and research has remained responsive to trends in world affairs. Along with changes in international reality, in other words, there has been a shift in subject matter and foci among international relations specialists.

Starting with the early part of the twentieth century it is possible to trace four major eras in the development of the study of international relations.[2] The duration of each period has averaged fifteen years, and the location of productive scholars in the class structure of the times may account in part for the prevailing approaches. Before World War I the main students of international affairs were diplomatists. Because entry into the foreign service by and large was restricted to persons with aristocratic backgrounds, such matters as the upper-class interest in etiquette, rationality, honor, and the lessons of history pervaded writing on international relations. Diplomatic histories constituted the main fare for the small stratum that wished to acquire the patience, wisdom, and polish necessary for conducting the old diplomacy.

After World War I broke out, plans by academic scholars and idealistic legalists began to be formulated for the establishment of a consultative association of nations. When the League of Nations was formed after the war, academicians and international lawyers assumed prominence in the field of international relations. Coming from the professional middle class, oriented toward "hard work," such scholars felt that success in any venture can be guaranteed by making structural blueprints and then by pursuing concrete plans assiduously. A legal-institutional form of analysis was by far the most congenial for such an anti-intraceptive Victorian outlook. Institutional constraints on violent and reckless behavior of states were sought as a means for eliminating war, while "power politics" was debunked and ignored.

The breakdown of the League system in the 1930's indicated that dedication and hard work to achieve pious goals are insufficient to cope with realities of a world whose leaders are likely to revere self-interest much more than melioristic perspectives. The unparalleled prosperity of the 1920's had given rise to a vigorous entrepreneurial middle class, whose members tended to conceive of economics and politics as involving a struggle in which the best-organized and most powerful interests alone could count on large profits and slices of the public pie. When the economic depression of the 1930's brought severe social and economic crises to the capitalist world, socialist ideals were incorporated into the platforms of major political parties, while the conflict image of politics remained. The most socially just rule was believed to be a welfare state managed by a democratic elitist braintrust, members of which felt themselves entitled to prescribe solutions for social problems, while the "masses" most directly affected were not consulted. International relations was studied as an arena of power politics in which braintrusts, not the public, should exert pressures on governments to secure the adoption of wise policies. This scrappy orientation meshed best with an emphasis on the concept of power; an analysis of the moves of Hitler and Mussolini seemed most reasonable within such an entrepreneurial outlook, and a school of thought arose with power as the major concept.

Immediately after World War II the condition of tight bipolarity, characterized as the cold war, tended to reinforce the image of world politics as involving a continual struggle for power. But the increasing ambiguity of the world situation in the 1950's led to a questioning of the usefulness of a power-politics model. The bipolar confrontation became stalemated when each bloc developed nuclear-weapons systems capable of destroying any adversary almost completely in a second-strike retaliatory attack. Omnipotent as the United States and the Soviet Union have been, they have been unable to exercise their full power. It has been necessary instead to consider the psychological problem of how to deter first strikes. Because classical power analysis deliberately left out motivational elements, new types of approaches have been gaining currency, and an interdisciplinary study of international relations has seemed inescapable. The decision making approach, communication theory, and systems analysis have all drawn heavily from the social and even natural sciences. The newer approaches, which have been collectively given the label "behavioralism," have employed analytic and empirical procedures self-consciously and rigorously, with a view to transforming the discipline of international relations into the status of a theoretical science. Once again the academicians are in the forefront of international relations research, but they have tended to represent a lower-middle-class stratum that would have lacked the economic means to complete advanced schooling were it not for the success of two decades of welfare statism. Behavioralists in international relations, it may be argued, are likely to discount professions of omniscience on the part of braintrusts operating contemporary defense establishments and foreign ministries. Advocates of the newer approaches are more likely to want to bring about more complete democratic controls over foreign-policy processes; as the major beneficiaries of the welfare state, their confidence in a broader democracy often propels them to break policy matters down into questions of ends and means in which scientific operations are given more credence then the oracular wisdom of upper classes.

While the utility of the earlier approaches has been transcended in recent years by more complex theoretical efforts within the field of international relations, it is appropriate to note that the power school's concern over data and conceptual foundations probably contributed to a more theoretically oriented behavioralist revolution in international relations than has been possible in some of the other subfields of political science, which often succumb to a barefoot empiricism. So long as students of international affairs were preoccupied solely with providing mere descriptions of events, they were but chroniclers of diplomatic history. A bridge between historical description and scientific explanation in international relations was built by the exponents of the power school, who sought to present an insightful analysis of trends and patterns in international politics relevant to certain key concepts. Hence, the increase in specificity due to power analysis paved the way for an even more rigorous quest among the behavioralists for acquiring knowledge. Instead of looking for mere trends, the behavioralist defines knowledge as the sum of all tested propositions, while postbehavioralists are conscious of alternative paradigms and future states of affairs.

Although advocates of the earlier emphases are still active in the field of international relations, the behavioralist school is certainly the most important source of innovation today, though a multimethodological revolution (discussed in Chapter 16) is now in the offing. An appropriate question to ask, therefore, is how well behavioralists have fulfilled their own goal of advancing knowledge. It is the thesis of this essay that the behavioralist output of the 1960's has been disappointing, not just by traditional standards but in terms of scientific criteria. Some of the specific problems that behavioralists have been unable or unwilling to tackle are set forth in the final chapter in this collection of essays. But the underlying dilemma has been an abandonment of the very quest for theory that initially overturned the simplistic orientation of the power school. Whereas a *theoretical science* consists of a body of knowledge organized by analytical and conceptual frameworks, an isolation of research from the task of theory building has been developing in recent years. The highly self-conscious formulation of broad theories of international relations in the 1950's has been bypassed in the 1960's by scholars with solid methodological training, a strong commitment to operate on the frontiers of research, but with little theoretical sophistication or interest. Some "playing of the field" by theoreticians and methodologists may be useful in demonstrating the potentialities of behavioralism, but in the years to come it will be imperative to link theory and research much more intimately in order for the field of international relations as a whole to yield tested propositions that may be pyramided into the edifice of a theoretical science. But for such a marriage to occur as we enter the 1970's, alternative theoretical frameworks need to be enumerated and critiqued comparatively, a task that this essay seeks to perform.

II. THEORY: TYPES AND CRITERIA

The term "theory" conjures such a variety of possible meanings that it is necessary to qualify the particular manner in which it will be used here.[3] Accordingly, it is helpful to distinguish between levels of theory. At the lowest level of abstraction, we can speak of *narrow-gauge* theories, which are often called "hypotheses" or "empirical generalizations."[4] The finding that members of the middle classes in the United States are more informed about world politics than working-class persons is an example of this lower order of theory, which is rather limited in scope and predictive power. *Middle-gauge* theory attempts to explain a set of empirical generalizations at a somewhat higher level of generality. For example, we might account for the above finding by asserting that the degree of an individual's involvement in international affairs is a function of his socioeconomic status. Degree of involvement can be measured operationally by such indicators as the degree of salience that a person attaches to foreign affairs, his membership in groups that discuss world questions, the amount of media exposure he has to international news, as well as the amount of factual knowledge that he possesses. "Socioeconomic status" may be indexed by such variables as income level, the degree of mental versus physical work required in an occupation, and self-perception of membership in a particular social class. Since we have suggested four indicators of the dependent variable and three measures of the independent variable, there are at least twelve narrow-gauge hypotheses subsumed under our single middle-gauge theory, representing a substantial gain in the level of abstraction from the individual cases being analyzed. Continuing in this direction, we may desire to bring all middle-gauge propositions into the framework of a single, organizing theory. This higher-level theory purports to explain international affairs on the basis of a coherent set of omnipresent independent variables. Although the prospective content of *broad-gauge* theory, often labeled *metatheory*,[5] has been the subject of much debate, its desirability has been acknowledged generally throughout the field in international relations. Since a strictly *empirical science* would only consist of almanacs of raw data or isolated findings, in a *theoretical science* there must be an analytical structure capable of generalizing beyond data to predict relationships within as yet unexperienced situations. At the present time several unifying metatheories have been proposed,[6] but, for a number of reasons to be discussed below, no consensus on any one broad-gauge theory is likely to arise in the foreseeable future.

In order to assess each broad-gauge theory, we need criteria of some sort.[7] Perhaps the most obvious criterion is that of *parsimony* or economy. It is the essence of scientific theory to be simpler than reality.[8] Second, a metatheory should be *explicit* with respect to the meaning of concepts, hypotheses, and variables. Third, there must be a high degree of nomothetic *organizing power.* Metatheory should be internally consistent and combine middle-gauge theories within a coherent focus; nothing empirical should elude its grasp, and all boundaries or limitations to the scope of findings should be specified. The nomothetic character of theory is particularly crucial to international relations, for otherwise we could not generalize, speculate, or predict beyond our idiographic data; we would be prisoners of a reality that we would be unable to change or even describe meaningfully. *Rigor* goes hand in hand with organizing power, for if verbal explanations are supplied by the latter, we must have rigorous knowledge to specify the exact conditions observed at one time and predicted to occur in a future time. All variance in the dependent variables would ideally be accounted for in a truly rigorous theory. In short, metatheories must be *operational,* that is, capable of being tested with empirical data, as well as *correctible* when hypotheses and data are inconsistent with each other. The final two criteria are particularly relevant to recent developments in international relations. The requirement that metatheory must be *fruitful* beckons us to select formulations that heuristically stimulate a vast outpouring of empirical research. The most subtle criterion of all is that broad-gauge theory should be *relevant* to all aspects of international relations, especially to matters of policy. The final criterion is the most elastic because, as we have seen already, international relation-ists have felt quite free to redefine the scope of their interests during the present century.[9]

In assessing each major metatheory of international relations in terms of these eight criteria, the main purpose will be to point out differences in terminology, subjects of analysis, policy payoffs, and in methodological tools. What all metatheories share in common is a focus upon only one type of independent variable, which is advanced as a sort of deus ex machina for explaining various aspects of inter-national affairs. A secondary purpose of the overview will be to point out some of the shortcomings that beg for analytical work to render each metatheory more useful. In this second task the essay may appear to break with a tacit gentleman's agreement among inter-national relations theorists not to quibble too much with one another's problems in the pioneering stages of conceptualization, theory construction, and operationalization.[10] Yet after more than a decade of such pioneering, with a danger of theory diverging com-pletely from research in prospect, it seems urgent to attempt such a constructive critique.

III. THE ERA OF LATENT THEORY

The earliest theoretical writings on international relations are found in fugitive sections of Plato and Thucydides. Political philosophers have devoted so little attention to the subject that we are only now rediscovering that Kant was a field theorist and Rousseau, a system theorist.[11] For all practical purposes the discipline of international relations starts with diplomatic historians, whose main task it was to describe a sequence of events in a manner that would seem some-how reasonable, including and excluding materials as they saw fit. Their criteria of relevance were implicit, and their orientations had theoretical import only in a latent sense.

Cognitive Rationalism

The earliest and least well-articulated metatheory may be referred to as *cognitive rationalism*. Diplomatic historians since the time of Thucydides characterized international politics in terms of a quest by states to achieve particularistic objectives. Some of the main concepts of cognitive rationalist theory are goal, reason, means, action, event, justification, objective, plan, issue, dispute, agreement, and many legal terms referring to such devices as treaties, alliances, and ententes. The cognitive rationalist seeks to set forth reasons, both public justifications and private objectives, which prompt decision makers to act as they do. And the specific type of "reasons" on which they focus are manifest objectives, rather than psychological motivations. To use an illustration from the writing of David Jayne Hill, Prussia's aggression against Saxony in 1756 is explained as follows:

Frederick II had become convinced of the existence of a conspiracy for his overthrow and the dismemberment of the Prussian monarchy. Believing that the impending peril was inevitable, but that the moment for his enemies to strike had not yet arrived, he had resolved to invade Saxony . . . He had counted first of all upon proving by the capture of the Saxon archives at Dresden that a coalition had been formed against Prussia in which Saxony was a guilty partner, and then upon dissolving the hostile league by the force and rapidity of his military action.[12]

Cognitive rationalism is brought to bear when we weigh issues, pro and con, in a debate or an election campaign. The classic model of the Oxford debate is mirrored by the cognitive rationalist's emphasis on issues. Probes of cognitive rationalists consist of going behind the publicly stated rationale for foreign policy moves in order to ascertain "real" reasons for action. Hill's description of a mission undertaken in 1725 by the Spanish emissary Baron Ripperda is quite instructive on this point. Despite the manifest goal of concluding an alliance between Vienna and Madrid, Ripperda's "main object" is said to be to secure prestigious marriages for the sons of the Spanish queen, Elizabeth Farnese:

The only way was first to separate Austria from other alliances, to arouse the jealousy of Europe, and especially of the German princes, to bind the Emperor to Spain as his only friend, and then to extort from him what he would not otherwise bestow, his consent to the desired marriages.

If Ripperda was false to the real interests of Spain, he was at least true to Elizabeth Farnese, whose secret agent he really was; for his own fortune was linked with her success. Aside from this, Spain and Europe were nothing to him. Although the treaties were in reality hollow, the mere fact that a secret alliance between Spain and the Emperor had been concluded at the moment of the French rebuff was sufficient for his purpose.[13]

The research method employed by cognitive rationalists is nonfrequency content analysis; that is, support for their inferences consists of quoting or referring to official documentary sources for public objectives, and reliance on unofficial sources for private goals. A cognitive rationalist demonstrates that it is unwise for diplomacy to be conducted by individuals who are unable to juggle ends and means in such a way as to maximize state goals. Cognitive rationalism tends toward a "lessons of history" approach when it moves in a prescriptive direction.

Evaluating cognitive rationalism in terms of the criteria for broad-gauge theory, we find a most unsatisfactory state of affairs. History is retold with an abundance of detail, rather than parsimoniously; theory is not explicit; because a simplistic rational "diplomatic man" model is assumed, there is only a minimal degree of organizing power; rigor is nonexistent; operations are unspecified; the intellectual capital drawn from "lessons" does not allow for a correction process. In terms of numbers of volumes written, cognitive rationalism has been immensely fruitful, and the prose employing a cognitive rationalist orientation is a delight to read. Most of the cognitive-rationalists have been historians. In addition to Thucydides and Hill, we could mention such names as René Albrecht-Carrié, Samuel Bemis, A. J. P. Taylor, G. M. Trevelyan, Harold Vinacke, and C. K. Webster. When political scientists undertake cognitive-rationalist studies, they tend to engage in confidential interviews, rather than awaiting the publication of diaries or the opening of sealed archives. Allen Whiting and Herman Finer are the most recent insightful users of cognitive rationalism in international relations research.[14]

Genetic Theory

The second metatheoretical orientation may be called genetic theory. Historians engage in a genetic approach when they trace the flowering of trends over time. Key concepts of genetic theory are origin, genesis, development, decline, fall, rise, roots, evolution, death, birth, change, decay, growth, survival, precursor, organism, maturity, and other words reminiscent of Social Darwinist images. Some of the most celebrated genetic theorists title their volumes in the familiar jargon: *The History of the Decline and Fall of the Roman Empire* by Gibbon, and *The Origins of the World War* by Sidney Fay.

Genetic theory, which was most popular in the years immediately after World War I, is used in conjunction with legal-institutional analysis. Commentators on the League of Nations tended to employ genetic language in order to explain how that organization came into being and the progress it made during its existence. William Rappard, for example, axiomatizes:

The League, as all living organisms, cannot remain as it is. It must either die, or grow and change.[15]

Genetic theorists, who stress continuity of the present with the past, seldom find anything unique under the sun. Situations and structures are hypothesized to be based upon incrementally developed foundations. One of the central questions for genetic theory is what types of social arrangements are lasting. That which persists is said to have deep roots; ephemeral trends and phenomena lack genetic significance and will seldom be reported by genetic theorists, even though there may be much grist in such material for the cognitive rationalist's mill. The study of government is often viewed biologically as consisting of stages of development resembling the birth, childhood, adolescence, maturity, and death of living organisms.

The search for background conditions explaining the present involves a much more selective analysis than that undertaken by cognitive rationalists. If one wants to trace the development of the international secretariat, for example, it is obvious that the subject of alliances is peripheral as such, though one might go back to the councils of the Amphyctionic and other leagues of classical Greece to find models that have been influential in the thinking of statesmen and philosophers. Genetic theorists draw much material from international law in seeking to show that procedures or legal decisions lead to a growth or decline in functions and powers. An exegetic reading of legal documents, thus, is combined with a selective reporting of historical trends culled from chronicles written by the cognitive rationalists.

Genetic theory fulfills the eight criteria somewhat more fully than does cognitive rationalism. The universe of items to be studied is reduced to a more economical search for historical trends accounting for the persistence, growth, and decline in phenomena. Genetic theorists are self-aware concerning their own organic analogies, and are explicit concerning their research objectives. But conceptualization and hypothesis testing in genetic theory is far from sharp, in part because many believe that there are certain interdependent parts of an organism that are unknowable because it is impossible to measure without interfering with vital processes.[16] Organizing power, rigor, and correctibility are low. Observations about individual phenomena are seldom put together into a general theory of growth. Genetic theory is not very fruitful, for once a tracing has been completed, a second study may often fight very opposite trends, rather than leading to a cumulative body of knowledge about law and institutions.

Burke, Hegel, and Marx provide some of the best-known genetic interpretations of history, though their use of organic metaphors does not result in an explicit genetic theory. Within international relations, such writers as Sidney Fay and William Rappard enjoy company with Herbert Feis, Carlton Hayes, Gilbert Murray, Frederick Schuman, Harold Temperley, and Alfred Zimmern,[17] though such writers are more literary in their uses of genetic analogies in contrast with the writings of A. Lawrence Lowell.[18] Since World War II genetic theorizing has almost vanished.

Power Theory

Students of power conceive of world politics along the lines of Newtonian mechanical analogy. Factors accounting for the victory of one set of forces in an international confrontation are explained through the concept of power. Other recurrent terms are struggle, interest, preservation, monopoly, hegemony, resources, capabilities, settlement, balance of power, ideology, sovereignty, security, nationalism, imperialism, realism, and idealism. The underlying hypothesis is that the outcomes of disputes and contests is a resultant of a parallelogram of forces, in which the strongest vector triumphs. According to Hans Morgenthau, decision makers need resources in order to achieve objectives; man's desires are insatiable; therefore, they seek to accumulate as much power as possible, to achieve more goals. Morgenthau's so-called realist view came under attack in the early 1950's by so-called idealists, who asserted that under various conditions a decision maker may prefer a self-abnegating and altruistic solution, which may bring about a more respected and longlasting settlement of a problem than would the continual furtive and precarious jockeying for *modi vivendi* prescribed by Morgenthau.[19] Nevertheless, the same type of categories, terminology, and methodology employed by such "realists" as Kenneth Thompson and George Kennan has been espoused in the work of "idealists" Raymond Aron and Arnold Wolfers. The normative conclusions differ, but the realists and idealists belong to the same school of thought.

Power theory builds directly upon cognitive rationalism, for it treats policies and objective reality in much the same terms. The preoccupation with power as the dominant motive and the focus on capabilities as the ultimate predictive device are the unique contributions of power theory, even though such calculating statesmen as Frederick II and Baron Ripperda may fail to measure up to high standards of rationality. The main impact of power theory has been to transform the way in which political and military intelligence information is gathered and processed, whether by defense and foreign ministries or by such bodies as the Central Intelligence Agency. "Capabilities analysis," as urged by the power school, involves collecting data on resources of various countries in order to assess how to counter adversaries, and when to assist allies or even neutralist countries.

Power theory, in short, reduces problems of practical politics to questions of Clausewitzian cost/benefit ratios. As such the parsimony is remarkable, for one need not study motivations, structural elements, continuity with the past, the gap between real and public reasons, communication patterns between states, and the like. Although the variables tend to be explicit and the terms defined with much more precision than in earlier efforts, the notion that superior power leads to victory is in actuality an axiom that has not been fruitful in suggesting operationalizable hypotheses. After all, once one agrees with the initial axiom one would not dare undertake any research to disprove such a scholarly *raison d'être*. Power theory, thus, lacks built-in correctives. In the United States, capabilities analysis has been pursued quite rigorously as a short-range method for arriving at policy preferences. Without a complex theoretical framework to buttress the assembling of diverse yet relevant data, power theory has lacked organizing power, leading to the familiar criticism that American foreign policy only reacts but does not seek positive objectives.

Because the practitioners of power analysis deal with secret documents in making appraisals of the international scene, writings by men of experience seldom contain facts and figures. Instead, Morgenthau, Kennan, Wolfers, Aron and such writers as Inis Claude, Herbert Dinerstein, John Herz, Klaus Knorr, Harold Sprout, and Robert Strausz-Hupé tend to avoid studying concrete situations in their scholarly endeavors, except for illustrative purposes, though Zbigniew Brzezinski often has been current-events oriented.[20] Their focus is often prescriptive, sometimes polemical, but in the eyes of many behavioralists their main difficulty is a desire to let unsystematic insights guide policy applications, rather than respecting and building theoretically upon the very sort of data-gathering process that their approach has stimulated.

IV. MANIFEST THEORY: SYSTEMS ANALYSIS

Cognitive rationalist, genetic, and power theories constituted the only approaches to the study of international relations up to the middle of the present century. The majority of textbooks, documentary accounts, and analytical discussions in the field still retain one of these three outlooks. Between 1953 and 1957 a veritable storm broke loose in international relations with the publication of a number of ambitious and self-conscious metatheoretical essays; an age of "scientific revolution" dawned.[21] Although each formulation is based upon perspectives supplied by general systems theory, which seeks to achieve a unified theoretical framework for all of science,[22] there has been a divergence in terms of the levels of analysis studied. The decision making approach advocated by Richard Snyder focuses on the individual in an interpersonal setting. Karl Deutsch's application of communication theory examines states within a network of transactions. System theory, as sketched by Morton Kaplan, looks at the structure of international systems as a whole. We now turn to survey each of these initial metatheories and some derivative schema that may eventually supersede the three original formulations.

Decision Making Theory

If we desire to sort out interpersonal factors that differentiate decisions to go to war from decisions to avoid war, we are applying the decision making approach. A decision making analysis postulates that actions of nations proceed from decisions, which in turn depend upon the roles assumed by decision makers. Insofar as decisions are made in a bureaucratized setting, the role structure is highly complex. The American decision to enter the Korean War, for example, has been analyzed in terms of such factors as degree of surprise, deliberation, perceived threat, integration, directness, cruciality, urgency, programming, irrevocability, and compromise.[23] The variables of the decision making approach have been divided by Richard Snyder into three categories.[24] *Spheres of competence* is a label subsuming structural and organizational notions, such as specialization and division of labor, authority structure, bureaucratization, participation in decision making, professionalization, and decision latitude. *Communication and information* factors include foci of attention, feedback, primary versus secondary messages, competitive-role demands, and the formal and informal channels through which messages travel. *Motivation* deals with psychological states and energy, perceptual selectivities, group membership, socialization, tension-reduction mechanisms, attitudes, and opinions.

Dean Pruitt, Ralph Goldman, Charles Hermann, Glenn Paige, and James Robinson have tended to emphasize structural factors in their applications of the decision making approach, drawing upon organization theory.[25] Chadwick Alger, Richard Brody, Lloyd Jensen, James Rosenau, and Charles McClelland have paid particular attention to communication patterns.[26] Robert North, Dina Zinnes, and Ole Holsti have examined motivational states of decision makers, finding that in World War I there was much concern with matters of hostility and friendship in documentary statements, whereas the preoccupation with capabilities that one might expect on the basis of power theory was significantly absent.[27] If we include elite and public-opinion studies, as do most surveys of the decision-making approach,[28] the following names would be added to our roster: Bjørn Christiansen, Harry Grace, Daniel Levinson, Herbert McClosky, Ithiel Pool, Ross Stagner, and Kenneth Terhune.[29]

In examining such works as *Foreign Policy Decision Making* with respect to the various criteria suggested in Section II of this essay, one finds that Snyder and the adherents of the decision making approach have been espousing an orientation or a mode of thinking, rather than a carefully worked-out theory.[30] There is no doubt about the explicitness of concepts, building as they do upon empirical work in cognate disciplines of the social sciences; the explicit and implicit propositions, once tested, definitely would lead to a body of correctible knowledge, and the number of combinations between factors is so astronomical that the framework's potential fruitfulness in stimulating future research is undeniable. The crux of the problem has been a lack of operationalization, for to date such key notions as "irrevocability" and "crisis decision" are seldom specified in terms of statistical indicators nor examined in a comparative analysis of several decisions. Hence, the rigor of the decision making approach may appear to be a step backward from the capabilities-analysis methodology of power theory.

However, the empirical applications of decision-making analysis are now beginning to appear, moving from qualitative comparative studies to a more quantitative data base.[31] What is the status of the decision making approach as regards organizing power? At the conceptual level, decision making theory has been attacked for having too many terms, categories, and questions, thus violating the criterion of parsimony. Yet were we to have rankings assigned to about 100 decisions for each of the concepts, we might reduce the framework to a much more tidy set of dimensions by employing such data-sorting techniques as factor analysis and smallest-space analysis. The key analytical question, instead, is whether "actions can easily be isolated in time, pinned down like butterflies, broken up into distinct elements, and compared."[32] In other words, may we reduce all of international relations to decisions? It seems possible to conceive of anything as either an input or an output to a decision process of some sort; even aggregate data can be viewed as the composite results of many decisions. Cognitive rationalism, genetic theory, and the power school were all primarily interested in decisions. And, after all, how can knowledge about international relations be applied except in terms of decisions? The behavioralist aim has been to make intelligent policies more possible. The superficial view that the framework applies best to crisis, terminating, and self-conscious decisions is not addressed to the theoretical scope embraced by the most expansive decision making orientation. One can conceive of decision analysis eventually taking the content of messages into account, dealing with decisions that are made at a low level of consciousness, and even handling decisions not to decide and nondecision making processes, as a result of which the organizing power of the metatheory would be increased considerably. The concern for crisis may turn out to be a passing fad.

The most serious criticism is whether the approach is helpful for policy makers. For if we do have assurance that decision time is longer when decisions are made to avoid war, or that decision latitude varies inversely with structuredness of alternatives, how can we hope to bring about a different decision process in conformity with normative goals? Nearly all of the decision making variables deal with informal processes, with which it is difficult to tamper, especially in a crisis situation. If decisional characteristics do account for unwise policies, we may still be trapped. The technology for overcoming role constraints so far remains undeveloped.

Strategy Theory

A metatheory with a clearer policy focus, which in many ways could be regarded as a derivative of the decision-making orientation, is strategy theory. As developed by Herman Kahn and Thomas Schelling, the events and interactions of world affairs have been treated in terms of game theory.[33] Alternative means are assessed in terms of relative payoff by strategy theorists; bluffing and arranging to be caught bluffing are viewed as instrumental to certain goals, especially if the adversary has been estimated to become befuddled when confronted with seemingly randomized maneuvers. Strategy theory could be regarded as more theoretically rich and methodologically rigorous form of capabilities analysis. Nonmonetary and nonpower parameters are easily built into the structure of strategy theories, as well as the whole arsenal of role-theoretical concepts from Snyder.

Strategy theorists employ such terms as payoff, threat, perception, arms race, opponent, image, bargaining, goals, negotiation, saddle point, utilities, alternatives, player, stress, outcome, compromise, cooperation, zero-sum, communication barriers, choice, tacit understanding, optimality, tension level, and the familiar notion of the prisoner's dilemma. The research tool most often employed to test strategy theory is the small group experiment. When the experimental setting contains many features of real-world decision making it is referred to as a "simulation," especially when subjects are asked to pretend that they are decision makers of actual or imaginary states. Strategy theory, hence, almost entirely repairs the deficiencies of decision making theory. Indeed, the decision making school seems moribund in contrast with the rapid growth of theory and research on international strategy, all of which has a considerable impact upon deterrence policy.

The main criticism of strategy theory has come from within its own fold. The argument has been that the problems studied by strategy theorists have been hawk-oriented, rather than dove-oriented. Anatol Rapoport and Kenneth Boulding have attempted to treat the quest for peace more extensively in their writings,[34] transcending the early focus on zero-sum games. Indeed, the most self-conscious developers of strategy theory have gone far beyond the framework of military issues. Some of the other empirically oriented strategy theorists include Richard Brody, Malvern Lumsden, Charles McClintock, Thomas Milburn, Marc Pilisuk, Paul Smoker, and John Raser.[35]

Communication Theory

Decision making and strategy theorists tend to deal only with the level of the individual. But any truly comprehensive theory of international relations must take into account the fact that individuals and decision-making processes may differ from one state to another. Not only may cultural differences be significant in explaining state behavior, but the nature and structure of societies must also be taken into account. Attention to such questions is explicitly handled by Karl Deutsch and international integration theorists, who focus upon communication factors within and between countries.

Communication theorists deal less with the structural or gaming aspects of statements and behavior than with the gross flows of goods, persons, and messages across territorial boundaries. By constructing maps of mail flow, airline traffic, trade, exchanges of diplomats, and other instances of state interaction, one can observe communication modes, clusters, and isolates.[36] One of the major hypotheses of communication theory, which is in part based on cybernetics and electronic information theory, is that units interacting with each other at a very high level over a long period of time tend to develop positive affect for each other if mutual rewards for continued communication exceed costs and loads. Positive affect leads to a harmonization of foreign policy goals and to the development of permanent institutions for handling interstate problems; on occasion, two or more units constituting a very dense communication net will find it useful to unify politically. Deutsch uses "integration" to refer to the class of efforts between low-level harmonization of state goals and political mergers. Some of the most frequently used concepts are responses, loads, core, transmission, spillover, interdependence, amalgamation, security community, transaction, autonomy, assimilation, mobilization, value compatibility, and common way of life.

The parsimony of communication theory is one of its strongest features, inasmuch as it seeks to explain everything in terms of communication. Concepts, hypotheses, and variables have been spelled out in much detail, leading for example to the *World Handbook of Political and Social Indicators.*[37] The use of quantitative techniques has progressed from univariate descriptions toward multivariate analysis, so the degree of rigor has been increasing. Hypotheses have been framed to allow for self-correction should disconfirmation result. Many research undertakings have been stimulated by communication theory, but so far the theoretical import has been skimpy. Examining cases of national unification and integration, Deutsch's sample of ten and Amitai Etzioni's four instances have not led to definitive conclusions.[38] Bruce Russett explores several measures of integration between a pair of nations, the United States and Great Britain; but in order to substantiate his speculations some 5,000 additional dyads might have to be studied as well.[39]

Integration theorists might reasonably contend that everything in international relations consists of communications, for the entire process of decision making can be so conceived. But to date there has been little effort to expand the communication approach beyond the integration focus except in Deutsch's *The Nerves of Government.*[40] Instead, attention is concentrated on aggregated foreign state behavior as a function of patterns of communication within and among states. Because of a lack of pyramided theory, the prescriptive relevance of integration remains in doubt; only a very detailed series of quantitative and qualitative descriptions has been provided. The potential in organizing power has not been reached, yet seems reachable.

In contrast to the many persons using the decision making approach, the number of scholars using communication variables to test integration theory has been a small but influential stratum. In addition to Deutsch, Etzioni, and Russett, the only familiar names to add are Hayward Alker, Robert Angell, Alexander Eckstein, Richard Merritt, and Donald Puchala.[41] If we include scholars using more qualitative research strategies to study international organization as a focus for interstate integration, the list expands to include Lincoln Bloomfield, Ernst Haas, Werner Levi, and Richard Van Wagenen.[42]

Field Theory

Integration theory, particularly with its emphasis on aggregate indicators, encouraged the growth of a much more inclusive metatheory, which we may label *field theory*. Although Quincy Wright is probably the most authoritative founder, in various sections of his monumental *A Study of War* and his codificatory *The Study of International Relations,* as a metatheory this approach lacks a coherent sourcebook containing a statement of assumptions, definitions, and hypotheses.[43] Instead, philosophic field theory, social field theory, and mathematical field theory remain divergent.[44] Field theorists have proceeded to investigate domestic determinants of foreign state behavior on a comparative, cross-national basis. The main underlying notion has been that there are particular ways of structuring a society which tend to produce various levels of foreign conflict behavior. Domestic variables have been correlated with indicators of foreign behavior, but so far little attention has been directed to conditions intermediate between the two sets of variables, which assuredly must be part of the influences impinging upon states. Domestic variables range from measures of domestic conflict, such as strikes, revolutions, and riots, to indicators of economic development. Indices of international behavior include frequency of participation in war, membership and voting in international organizations, and trade habits. Communication factors usually show up on lists of variables in studies attempting to locate states within a field of vectors. As a result, field theory has tended to supersede integration theory in terms of quantitative operations. Conceptually, however, field theory has remained primitive—often deliberately so. The key terms have been dimension, factor, distance, asymmetry, cluster, attribute, pattern, space, coordinate, and similar words with a more statistical and mathematical than social-scientific origin. Most of the field theorists tend to be well versed in the philosophy of science or have a mathematical background of some sort. In addition to Wright, we may include in this category such researchers as Steven Brams, Ivo and Rosalind Feierabend, Michael Haas, Rauol Naroll, Rudolph Rummel, and Raymond Tanter.[45]

Field theorists attempt to locate actors within n-dimensional coordinates on the basis of empirical attributes. Intercorrelating variables describing nation-states, propensities to engage in international conflict can be assessed in terms of a state's position within an empirically derived set of dimensions, known collectively as a field. One task of field theory is to reduce the number of dependent as well as independent variables by intercorrelating all possible variables and thenceforward dealing with the major clusters that remain when spurious relations are factored out. "All possible" refers to in infinite quest, meeting the "fruitfulness" criterion, of course, but hardly supplying an analytically parsimonious perspective for research. The major problem in field theory has been to postulate in advance the types of clusters, or "dimensions," which are likely to be found universally. Following the example of dimensional analysis in physics, Michael Haas has attempted to postulate conceptual metadimensions that may lead to a master taxonomy for types of indicators.[46] Should this effect prove successful, field theory would move in the direction of much more parsimony, correctibility, and organizing power. The rigor of methods appropriate to field theoretical research, such as factor analysis, and the operationalizability of field theory are unquestioned. And, given the desire to measure everything, either quantitatively or by assigning a zero or one in the case of a qualitative dichotomy, field theory promises to pervade all facets of international affairs. Field theory is unique in having a well-developed technology but a weak conceptual and literary side. Its future rests on maintaining more balance between the two elements, for otherwise it will not be possible to draw policy implications.

System Theory[47]

Whereas the decision maker is the focus of decision making and strategy theories, and the state or society is examined as an empirical unit in communication and field theories, the structure and functioning of the international system as a whole are treated by system theorists. Starting in 1955 with a plea from Charles McClelland to look upon components of international relations as comprising a system of interrelated parts, in which structure to a considerable extent determines behavior,[48] users of systems analysis currently are about as numerous as decision-making theorists. The most familiar controversy has been whether bipolar systems are inherently more stable than multipolar systems, and a debate on this topic has engaged such scholars as Morton Kaplan, Richard Rosecrance, Kenneth Waltz, Karl Deutsch, and J. David Singer.[49] System theory concepts are quite abstract, because one of the aims of general systems theory has been to develop a language that would have identical (not merely analogous) meaning within all the sciences. For example, a system is said to have exchanges with environments, stimuli and responses, homeostatic mechanisms, performances, subsystems, levels of functioning, transformations from one state to another, structural channels for action, and inputs and outputs; systems may be characterized as open or closed, static or dynamic, containing high or low entropy, and stability or instability. Inasmuch as such terms could be used to describe not only international systems but also botanical, electronic, musical, geological, and even family systems, laws discovered about one level of analysis immediately suggest the utility of undertaking parallel studies at all other levels. When propositions true in one type of system are also true elsewhere, the body of general knowledge is increased; when no such isomorphism is found, it is necessary to formulate boundary conditions to explain limits to the scope of propositions, which further adds to the sophistication in distinguishing between types of systems and their comparative dynamics.

Systems analysts insist upon analytical precision at all levels, for one cannot begin to theorize about systems until the units of analysis are defined and enumerated fully; the boundaries separating the phenomenon under examination from its environment must be delimited firmly and justified on the basis of an explicit set of rules or assumptions. Only after these preliminary tasks are completed can a systems analyst begin to isolate appropriate variables and parameters for an inquiry.

One of the attractive aspects of systems analysis in international relations is that it can claim to subsume all of the metatheories previously discussed; McClelland has attempted to outline how such an effort would be conducted.[50] System theorists, thus, can simply proceed to reinterpret all existing studies, whether framed within the confines of a specific metatheory or not, and derive inputs into theoretical speculations at the highest possible level of analysis. However, what has been called "the international system" remains virtually unanalyzed empirically. Indeed, in light of the meager amount of research so far conducted on international systems, a superficial observer might conclude that theorizing about systems has been abandoned except as a form of catechism or poetic discourse. And one of the major reasons for this difficulty is that system theory has not been fully worked out in an operationalizable form. Definitions of "stability" are vague and vary considerably. Precise variables that might index such concepts as performance, channels, inputs, or even the dichotomy between open and closed systems have not been brought down from the clouds of general system theory, except in the qualitative *Action and Reaction in World Politics* by Richard Rosecrance, which has been followed up only by Michael Haas's empirical analysis of comparative international arenas in "International Subsystems: Stability and Polarity." Despite the promised organizing power, the explicitness of system theory has been low, even though its fruitfulness and potential relevance to all aspects of international relations seem undisputable. It seems to me, on the other hand, that a more specific derivation from general systems theory may tend to remedy this dilemma, and this metatheory will be discussed next.

Structural-Functional Analysis

Efforts to adapt systems analysis to the international level have tended to be phrased in a structural-functional style, though only one or two scholars have done so explicitly. As set forth by George Liska, George Modelski, Chadwick Alger, and Michael Haas,[51] there are two basic metaconcepts (concepts that subsume lower-level concepts) in a functional analysis of structures in international politics. The first notion is that of *function*, which is usually defined as a generic type of task that must be performed in order for a complete cycle in political activities to occur (Table 1).[52] The cycle consists of three stages—inputs into authoritative centers, withinputs, and outputs; the elites of international politics are generally regarded as the authoritative power centers. The second metaconcept is the *style* with which a function is performed. Such a function as "articulation of demands," for example, may be performed in a latent or manifest, diffuse or specific, universalistic or particularistic, or in an effective or instrumental manner by the actor in question (Table 2). Necessarily, the content of structural-functional analysis leads in the direction of a more precise yet unfamiliar vocabulary. Such scholars as Ralph Goldman and James Rosenau, who are not wholly committed to the level of international systems as a whole, have nonetheless contributed much to structural-functional analysis by suggesting increasingly refined categorizations for functional cycles and styles of function performance, respectively.[53]

An expansion of international relations terminology does not assist empirical research unless it is operationalized, and structural-functional analysis has been criticized for lack of operationalizability, both in

TABLE 1. Functions of a Political System

Behavioral Aspect	Temporal Aspect		
	Inputs	Withinputs	Outputs
Goal Attainment	aggregation	plan making	implementation
Adaptation	articulation	gate keeping	rule adapting
Pattern Maintenance	socialization	recruitment	enforcement
Coordination	support	supervision	direction

international relations and in the field of comparative government and politics. An encouraging sign, however, can be interpreted from the works of Rosecrance and Michael Brecher, who deal with regional international subsystems, the former implicitly in treating nine historical European subsystems, the latter explicitly in developing a schema for coding subsystems from the ancient Chinese multistate systems to the present Asian international subsystem.[54] Though the procedures for assigning ratings are purely judgmental and qualitative, the imagination of their efforts opens the path for collecting quantitative data relevant to such phenomena as wars, alliances, number of members in a system, and so forth. A study now underway on 21 subsystems, including European, Asian, and Hawaiian cases, attempts to operationalize in quantitative terms and to code each subsystem qualitatively in terms of some of the categories proposed by Brecher,

TABLE 2. Basic Styles of Function Performance

Pattern Variables	Level of Focus		
	Decision Making	Societal	Systemic
Manifest-Latent	unintended-intended	formal-informal	hyperactivity-hypoactivity
Diffuse-Specific	exogenous-endogenous	nonspecialized-specialized	polyarchical-hierarchical
Universalistic-Particularistic	macrocentric-microcentric	contract-status	multilateral-unilateral
Affective-Instrumental	ideological-pragmatic	preoccupied-routinized	turbulent-quiescent

Modelski, and Rosecrance, incorporating as well some concepts from Deutsch, Etzioni, and Gabriel Almond.[55] One value of the study is to demonstrate the operationalizability and potentiality for empirically developing a more parsimonious set of descriptive terms for analyzing systems, while preserving the broad organizing power that systems analysis provides. The development of an empirically correctible set of propositions on the middle-gauge theory can alone rescue system theory from its presently overabstract stalemate.

V. CONCLUSION

Returning to the question of whether it is possible to foster convergence amid the various broad-gauge theories of international relations, we can now see that many metatheories have in fact developed in isolation from each other. Cognitive rationalism looks only at issues and deliberations of decision makers, as if decision makers were members of debate squads. Genetic theory traces antecedents to present conditions, selectively bypassing that which is only incipient as lacking "deep roots." Power analysis explains the dominance of a state on the basis of its superior capabilities and rational calculations. Decision making theorists find that role factors determine decisional outcomes; strategy theorists focus on the use of bargaining and nonverbal devices for bringing about decisions. Communication theorists treat mergers and communication interchanges between states as subjects for analysis; field theorists seek to determine which basic ways of structuring polities militate toward particular types of international behavior. System theorists propose to explain equilibria in international stratification. Structural-functionalists pay most of their attention to the interaction between elites and nonelites. Each metatheory, in an effort to achieve parsimony, operates in accordance with a very different image of reality. Thus, the set of concepts for each metatheory constitutes a net that can catch only a restricted part of the universe of concepts; a partial picture of international affairs results.

According to Harold Guetzkow, the coexistence of several broad theories of international relations is a healthy sign in the development of a discipline. Although in the early stages each theory may constitute an island unto itself, as knowledge grows, islands become continents, and a superordinate metatheory capable of filling in the blank spaces is likely to arise.[56] But the danger of intermediate stagnation and overfragmentation is also an everpresent possibility.

Such forecasts, however, are to be contrasted with the view that metatheories are necessarily partial because reality is multiple, rather than singular in the cartographical sense implied by Guetzkow. This second position, as espoused by Richard Snyder, is grounded in the epistemology of Kant and his modern-day expositor, Alfred Schuetz.[57] The *multiple realities* thesis postulates that social phenomena can be grasped with a variety of analytical handles because the subject matter of the social sciences in principle has more dimensions than space and time, which have served so admirably to bound theoretical speculation in the natural sciences. Once one accepts an n-dimensional conception of international relations, it becomes clear that the models one chooses for examining international affairs will vary in appropriateness according to the subject of a particular study. We have seen in Section I of this essay that the subject matter on which international relationists have focused has changed in response to dramatically new directions in world politics. Similarly, researchers may find it entertaining to try out all possible models and research tools in an earnest attempt to come up with serendipitous results. The idealist perspective of Kant, based as it is on the premise that reality is not directly knowable but is interpreted and made meaningful only with reference to categories constructed by the mind, counsels the utility of embarking in all metatheoretical directions at the same time. Inevitably, each metatheory will develop its own language, its own favorite type of independent variable, its modes of translating research findings into policy prescriptions, and possibly will even prefer some research strategies over others. Rather than constituting discrete elements that will grow closer to each other, a set of metatheories interpenetrate one another insofar as they study identical phenomena, though from divergent analytical perspectives.

Does the notion of multiple realities mean that we are to witness a proliferation of metatheories in the future? The prevailing view has been that we have achieved a considerable degree of closure with existing metatheoretical alternatives. First of all, there is a tendency for each of the metatheories to deal with only one level of analysis. We have seen that cognitive rationalist, decision making, and strategy theories focus on the *individual* as a maker of a foreign policy decision. Similarly, power, integration, and field theories deal with the *societal* level; system, structural-functional, and to some extent genetic theory are concerned with the structure of *international* systems in the aggregate. Second, some of the later metatheories have tended to supersede earlier speculation, and there has been a trichotomization in foci: the three major levels of analysis, as specified by Waltz and Singer,[58] bound the number of possible innovations and permutations in metatheories. It has been such a consensus on research foci that probably has enabled international relationists in the 1960's to feel that a decade of prolific research would be the proper antidote for the hypertheoretical 1950's. In the process of contributing to balance, however, many researchers have been tempted to abandon theory entirely and to be overattentive to findings and data. As we have just seen, field theory has so far leaned in the direction of such a brute empiricism. But the difficulty with hyperfactualism and antitheoretical positivism is that one cannot rise above the data to assert anything that might apply to situations for which no data have been collected; a cross-sectional study conducted for one year, with some 80 countries, cannot be generalized to apply to any other years, to countries not represented in the sample, or to longitudinal situations. Only a well-developed theory will enable one to justify and affix significance to the choice of years and countries in such a way that results can be used to provide intelligible guides. Another way to state the same point is to say that a brute empiricist cannot by definition engage in replication: one can only replicate a tested proposition; if findings are the same in nontheoretical studies, no conclusions can be drawn, and one cannot really know whether they are "the same," which is a theoretical or logical notion, rather than an empirical one. A brute empiricist never knows what to study because he does not seek answers to theoretical questions. He can only collect data ad infinitum.

The researchers of the 1960's were reacting to what we may call brute theorizing, for some of the earlier statements of metatheories may have resembled a dream world, one of scholastic distinctions that make no difference in the "real world." Hypertheorists tended to be unaware of the lack of operationality of their formulations. The brute theorist who seems content to rely on his special form of revelation disengages himself from the very tested propositions that a metatheory is supposed to incorporate and subsume. Users of systems analysis have been the most inclined to become lost in this direction.

In view of the Scylla of naive empiricism and the Charybdis of ethereal theorizing, the sociologist Robert Merton has argued forcefully that much more emphasis should be placed on the middle-gauge level.[59] In applying his suggestion to the field of international relations, we can acknowledge yet another reason to expect existing metatheories to engage in a mutually supportive if analytically distinct enterprise; for the harvest of scholarship would be especially rich were all methods and metatheories employed to study subjects as alliance formation, conflict resolution, arms control, international organization, and international law. Middle-gauge empirical efforts would tend to be eclectic, in other words, thus providing all broad-gauge theorists with further tested propositions to pyramid. For the student of a particular problem area, a codification of studies based on different metatheories entails discovering linkages.[60] For example, an estimate of the probability that a particular country will go to war in a given year might be represented by an equation such as

$$W = aP + bS - cI$$

in which some sort of psychological factor (P) and societal factor (S) make positive contributions to the war propensity estimate (W), while an international systemic factor (I) is able to reduce war propensities. Multivariate analysis, in sum, goes hand in hand with multiple metatheoretical research foci in handling the problem of linkages between levels of analysis.

One of the strengths of decision-making and strategy theories has been the ability of their proponents to remain in the mainstream of sociological theory, which is highly middle-gauge-oriented, in part due to Merton's plea. At the same time, the somewhat disorganized "boxes within boxes" of the decision making metatheory and an unfortunate topsylike growth in strategy theory attest to yet another overemphasis: one can also be hyper-middle-gauge, for there is no inherent virtue in piling up empirical findings; it is essential to inventory findings on a particular subject from time to time, but were the entire body of scholars to follow this course, the yield would be a series of dry textbooks and lifeless codifications. In short, though individual scholars may choose to specialize in efforts on the broad- or middle- or narrow-gauge level, or perhaps on two of these levels, the profession as a whole must contain some balance among those playing the three roles in order for international relations to progress toward the goal of becoming a theoretical science.

Inasmuch as a theoretical science develops most evenly when all levels of theorizing are pursued in tandem, the hypotrophy of broad-gauge theory in recent years on the part of international relations researchers needs to be remedied. The history of scientific progress suggests that theory leads to research, findings from which are fed back to correct and to extend the original theory. It is the feedback loop in this process that has been neglected. All of the currently popular metatheories have been used only as preliminary guides and later abandoned, rather then being refined and worked out with more analytical precision. Even though no metatheory may ever become a grand theory, encompassing all of the field of international relations in an exhaustive manner, the more modest explanatory potentialities still remain unrealized. The task of the 1970's will be to juxtapose metatheorizing and empirical research in such a way that the protean character of a theoretical science of international relations will fulfill its ambitions.

NOTES

1. Harold Nicolson, *Diplomacy* (3rd ed.; New York: Oxford University Press, 1963). The following sociology-of-knowledge approach is admittedly impressionistic; the utility of such an ideal-typical presentation is to focus on

some of the factors that may underlie changes in focus over time. A fully documented case could doubtless be made in a manner similar to that suggested for the first section in Chapter I of the present volume.

2. See Kenneth W. Thompson, "The Study of International Politics: A Survey of Trends and Developments," *Review of Politics,* XIV (October 1952), 433-443; Richard C. Snyder, "Some Recent Trends in International Relations Theory and Research," *Essays on the Behavioral Study of Politics,* ed. Austin Ranney (Urbana: University of Illinois Press, 1963), pp. 103-171; Chadwich F. Alger, "International Relations: The Field," *International Encyclopedia of the Social Sciences* VIII, 60-69.

3. Anatol Rapoport, "Various Meanings of Theory," *American Political Science Review,* LII (December 1958), 972-988.

4. Strictly speaking, a *generalization* is a tested narrow-gauge hypothesis; a *law* is a tested middle-gauge proposition.

5. Broad-gauge theories, which are not themselves testable but instead are more or less analytically useful, consist of three distinct components—a frame of reference, an organized body of knowledge, and a conceptual scheme. *Working theories* are the more useful broad-gauge theories. "Usefulness" consists of meeting various criteria, which are enumerated in the next paragraph of this essay.

6. Cf. Stanley H. Hoffmann (ed.), *Contemporary Theory in International Relations* (Englewood Cliffs: Prentice-Hall, 1960); J. David Singer, "Theorizing About Theory in International Politics," *Journal of Conflict Resolution,* IV (September 1960), 431-442; William T. R. Fox (ed.), *Theoretical Aspects of International Relations* (Notre Dame: University of Notre Dame Press, 1959); Horace V. Harrison (ed.), *The Role of Theory in International Relations* (Princeton: Van Nostrand, 1964); Charles A. McClelland, *Theory and the International System* (New York: Macmillan, 1966); James N. Rosenau, "Games International-Relations Scholars Play," *Journal of International Affairs,* XXI (#2, 1967), 215-231; Klaus Knorr and James N. Rosenau (eds.), *Contending Approaches to International Politics* (Princeton: Princeton University Press, 1969).

7. See Quincy Wright, "Development of a General Theory of International Relations," *The Role of Theory in International Relations,* ed. Harrison, op. cit., pp. 20-27; Karl W. Deutsch, *The Nerves of Government* (New York: Free Press, 1963), pp. 3-21; Milton K. Munitz, *Space, Time and Creation* (Glencoe: Free Press, 1957), p. 58; Johan Galtung, *Theory and Methods of Social Research* (New York: Columbia University Press, 1967), p. 459.

8. Ernst Mach, *The Science of Mechanics,* trans. Thomas J. McCormack (6th ed.; La Salle, Ill,: Open Court, 1960).

9. One of the advocates of the power school, for example, prematurely chose to theorize only about "international politics," which is defined in the narrowest Weberian terms, as if it had no relation to international economics, communications, social relations, public opinion, personality factors, cooperative and integrative processes, and so forth. Hans J. Morgenthau, *Politics Among Nations* (3rd ed.; New York: Knopf, 1963), pp. 11-15. See also Kenneth W. Thompson, "The Internationalist's Dilemma: Relevance and Rigor," *International Studies Quarterly,* XII (June 1968), 161-173.

10. For one of the earlier critiques on the value of metatheories, see

Stanley Hoffmann, "International Relations: The Long Road to Theory," *World Politics*, XI (April 1959), 346-377. The more empirically oriented critiques so far include Herbert McClosky, "Concerning Strategies for a Science of International Politics," *World Politics*, VIII (January 1956), 281-295; Ernst B. Haas, "The Challenge of Regionalism," *International Organization*, XII (Autumn 1958), 440-458; Peter H. Rohn, "Testing Deutsch's Indices of Communication," *PROD*, III (September 1959), 7-9; Dina Zinnes, "The Requisites for International Stability," *Journal of Conflict Resolution*, VII (September 1964), 301-305; J. David Singer, "Data-Making in International Relations," *Behavioral Science*, XI (January 1965), 68-80; Anatol Rapoport, *Strategy and Conscience* (New York: Harper & Row, 1964); Richard W. Chadwick, "An Empirical Test of Five Assumptions in an Inter-Nation Simulation, about National Political Systems," *General Systems Yearbook*, XII (1967), 177-192.

11. Kenneth N. Waltz, *Man, the State and War* (New York: Columbia University Press, 1959); Waltz, "Kant, Liberalism, and War," *American Political Science Review*, LVI (June 1962), 331-340; Stanley Hoffmann, "Rousseau on War and Peace," *American Political Science Review*, LVII (June 1963), 317-333. Cf. Waltz, "Political Philosophy and the Study of International Relations," *Theoretical Aspects of International Relations*, ed. Fox, op. cit., pp. 51-67.

12. David Jayne Hill, *A History of Diplomacy in the International Development of Europe* (New York: Longmans, Green, 1914), III, pp. 533, 537.

13. Ibid., pp. 420-421.

14. René Albrecht-Carrié, *A Diplomatic History of Europe Since the Congress of Vienna* (New York: Harper, 1958), Samuel F. Bemis, *A Diplomatic History of the United States* (4th ed.; New York: Henry Holt and Co., 1955); Bemis, *Diplomacy of the American Revolution* (rev. ed.; Bloomington: Indiana University Press, 1957). A. J. P. Taylor, *The Struggle for Mastery in Europe, 1848-1918* (Oxford: Clarendon, 1954); Taylor, *The Trouble Makers* (Bloomington: University of Indiana Press, 1958). G. M. Trevelyan, *British History in the Nineteenth Century and After (1782-1919)* (London: Longmans, Green, 1922). Harold M. Vinacke, *A History of the Far East in Modern Times* (6th ed.; New York: Appleton-Century-Crofts, 1959). Charles Kingsley Webster, *The Foreign Policy of Castlereagh, 1812-1815* (London: Bell, 1925); Webster, *The Foreign Policy of Palmerston, 1830-1841* (London: Bell, 1951). Allen S. Whiting, *China Crosses the Yalu* (New York: Macmillan, 1960). Herman Finer, *Dulles over Suez* (Chicago: Quanrangle, 1964).

15. William E. Rappard, "The League of Nations as an Historical Fact," *International Conciliation*, CCXXXI (June 1927), 300.

16. Deutsch, op. cit., p. 32.

17. Sidney B. Fay, *The Origins of the World War* (2nd ed.; New York: Macmillan, 1930); Herbert Feis, *The Road to Pearl Harbor* (Princeton: Princeton University Press, 1953); Carlton J. H. Hayes, *The Historical Evolution of Modern Nationalism* (New York: Smith, 1931); Gilbert Murray, *From the League to the U.N.* (London: Oxford University Press, 1948); Frederick L. Schuman, *International Politics* (6th ed.; New York: McGraw-Hill, 1958); Harold W. V. Temperley, *The Foreign Policy of Canning 1822-1827* (2nd ed.;

Hamden: Archon, 1966); Alfred E. Zimmern, *The League of Nations and the Rule of Law 1919-1935* (2nd ed.; London: Macmillan, 1945).

18. A. Lawrence Lowell, *Essays on Government* (Boston: Houghton, Mifflin, 1889). Genetic theory is to a very large extent a precursor of modern structural-functional analysis. See Martin Landau, "Functionalism and the Myth of Hyperfactualism in the Study of American Politics: A Historical Note," paper presented at the American Political Science Association annual convention, New York, September 1966.

19. Arnold Wolfers, "Statesmanship and Moral Choice," *World Politics,* I (January 1949), 175-195; Wolfers, "The Pole of Power and the Pole of Indifference," *World Politics* IV (October 1951), 39-63; Thomas I. Cook and Malcolm Moos, "Foreign Policy: The Realism of Idealism," *American Political Science Review,* LXVI (June 1952), 343-356. See Morgenthau's rejoinder, "Another 'Great Debate': The National Interest of the United States," *American Political Science Review,* LXVI (December 1952), 961-998.

20. George F. Kennan, *American Diplomacy, 1900-1950* (Chicago: University of Chicago Press, 1951); Arnold Wolfers, *Discord and Collaboration* (Baltimore: Johns Hopkins University Press, 1962); Raymond Aron, "The Quest for a Philosophy of Foreign Affairs," *Contemporary Theory in International Relations,* ed. Hoffmann, op. cit., pp. 79-91; Inis L. Claude, Jr., *Power and International Relations* (New York: Random House, 1962); Claude, *Swords into Plowshares* (3rd ed.; New York: Random House, 1964); Herbert S. Dinerstein, "The Transformation of Alliance Systems," *American Political Science Review,* LIX (September 1965), 589-601; John H. Herz, *Political Realism and Political Idealism* (Chicago: University of Chicago Press, 1951); Klaus Knorr, *The War Potential of Nations* (Princeton: Princeton University Press, 1956); Harold Sprout and Margaret Sprout (eds.), *Foundations of National Power* (2nd ed.; New York: Van Nostrand, 1951); Robert L. Strausz-Hupé et al., *Protracted Conflict* (New York: Harper, 1959); Zbigniew K. Brzezinski, *Ideology and Power in Soviet Politics* (rev. ed.; New York: Praeger, 1967).

21. A *scientific revolution,* according to Kuhn, occurs when one set of paradigms or metatheories displaces another. Thomas Kuhn, *The Structure of Scientific Revolutions* (Chicago: University of Chicago Press, 1964).

22. Ludwig von Bertalanffy, *General Systems Theory* (New York: Braziller, 1968); James G. Miller, "Toward a General Theory for the Behavioral Sciences," *The State of the Social Sciences,* ed. Leonard D. White (Chicago: University of Chicago Press, 1956), pp. 29-65.

23. Glenn D. Paige, *The Korean Decision* (New York: Free Press, 1968).

24. Richard C. Snyder, H. W. Bruck, and Burton Sapin (eds.), *Foreign Policy Decision Making* (New York: Free Press, 1962), pp. 86 ff.

25. Dean G. Pruitt, *Problem Solving in the Department of State* (Denver: Social Science Foundation, 1966); Pruitt, "Definition of the Situation as a Determinant of International Action," *International Behavior,* ed. Herbert C. Kelman (New York: Holt, Rinehart & Winston, 1965), pp. 391-432. Ralph Goldman, "A Theory of Conflict Processes and Organizational Offices," *Journal of Conflict Resolution,* X (September 1966), 328-343. Charles Hermann, *Crises in Foreign Policy* (Indianapolis: Bobbs-Merrill, 1960); Charles F. Hermann and Margaret G. Hermann, "An Attempt to Simulate the Outbreak of World War I," *American Political Science Review,* LXI (June

1967), 400-416. Paige, op. cit.; James A. Robinson and Richard C. Snyder, "Decision-Making in International Politics," *International Behavior*, ed. Kelman, op. cit., pp. 433-463; Robinson, *The Monroney Resolution* (New York: McGraw-Hill, 1960).

26. Chadwick F. Alger, "Personal Contact in Intergovernmental Organizations," *International Behavior*, ed. Kelman, op. cit., pp. 521-547; Alger, "Decision-Making Theory and Human Conflict," *The Nature of Human Conflict*, ed. Elton B. McNeil (Englewood Cliffs: Prentice-Hall, 1965), pp. 274-295. Richard A. Brody, "Some Systemic Effects of the Spread of Nuclear Weapons Technology: A Study Through Simulation of a Multi-Nuclear Future," *Journal of Conflict Resolution*, VII (December 1963), 663-753; Brody, "Cognition and Behavior: A Model of International Relations," *Experience, Structure and Adaptability*, ed. O. J. Harvey (New York: Springer, 1966), pp. 321-348. Lloyd Jensen, "Soviet-American Bargaining Behavior in the Postwar Disarmament Negotiations," *Journal of Conflict Resolution*, VII (September 1963), 522-541; Jensen, "Military Capabilities and Bargaining Behavior," ibid., IX (June 1965), 155-163. James N. Rosenau, *Public Opinion and Foreign Policy* (New York: Random House, 1961); Rosenau, *Calculated Control as a Unifying Concept in the Study of International Politics and Foreign Policy* (Princeton: Center of International Studies, 1963); Rosenau, "Theories and Pre-Theories of Foreign Policy," *Approaches to Comparative and International Politics*, ed. R. Barry Farrell (Evanston: Northwestern University Press, 1966), pp. 27-92; Rosenau, "The Premises and Promises of Decision-Making Analysis," *Contemporary Political Analysis*, ed. James C. Charlesworth (New York: Free Press, 1967), pp. 189-212. Charles A. McClelland, "The Acute International Crisis," *World Politics*, XIV (October 1961), 182-204; McClelland, "Access to Berlin: The Quantity and Variety of Events, 1948-1963," *Quantitative International Politics*, ed. J. David Singer (New York: Free Press, 1968), pp. 159-186.

27. Robert C. North, Ole R. Holsti, M. George Zaninovich, Dina A. Zinnes, *Content Analysis: A Handbook with Applications for the Study of International Crises* (Evanston: Northwestern University Press, 1963); North and Holsti, "The History of Human Conflict," *The Nature of Human Conflict*, ed. McNeil, op. cit., pp. 155-171; Holsti, Brody, and North, "Affect and Action in International Reaction Models," *Journal of Peace Research*, I (#3-4, 1964), 170-190; Holsti, "The 1914 Case," *American Political Science Review*, LIX (June 1965), 365-378; Zinnes, "A Comparison of Hostile Behavior of Decision-Makers in Simulate and Historical Data," *World Politics*, XVIII (April 1966), 474-502; Zinnes, "The Expression and Perception of Hostility in Pre-War Crisis: 1914," *Quantitative International Politics*, ed. Singer, op. cit., pp. 85-119.

28. Robinson and Snyder, op. cit.; Snyder and Robinson, *National and International Decision-Making* (New York: Institute for International Order, n.d.); Robinson and R. Roger Majak, "The Theory of Decision Making," *Contemporary Political Analysis*, ed. Charlesworth, op. cit., pp. 175-188; Dean G. Pruitt and Richard C. Snyder (eds.), *Theory and Research on the Causes of War* (Englewood Cliffs: Prentice-Hall, 1969).

29. Bjørn Christiansen, *Attitudes Towards Foreign Affairs as a Function of Personality* (Oslo: Oslo University Press, 1959); Harry A. Grace, "Hostility, Communication, and International Tension," *Journal of Educational*

Psychology, XLI (March 1950), 161-172; XLII (May 1951), 293-300; Grace and Jack Olin Newhaus, "Information and Social Distance as Predictors of Hostility Toward Nations," *Journal of Abnormal and Social Psychology,* XLVII (April 1952), 49-54. Daniel J. Levinson, "Authoritarian Personality and Foreign Policy," *Journal of Conflict Resolution,* I (March 1957), 37-47. Herbert McClosky, "Personality and Attitude Correlates of Foreign Policy Orientation," *Domestic Sources of Foreign Policy,* ed. James N. Rosenau (New York: Free Press, 1967), pp. 51-110. Ithiel de Sola Pool, *Symbols of Internationalism* (Stanford: Stanford University Press, 1951); Pool, "Effects of Cross-National Contact on National and International Images," *International Behavior,* ed. Kelman, op. cit., pp. 104-129. Ross Stagner, "The Psychology of Human Conflict," *The Nature of Human Conflict,* ed. McNeil, op. cit., pp. 45-63; Stagner, *Psychological Aspects of International Conflict* (Belmont: Brooks/Cole, 1967). Kenneth W. Terhune, "Nationalism Among Foreign and American Students: An Exploratory Study," *Journal of Conflict Resolution,* VIII (September 1964), 256-270; Terhune, "Nationalistic Aspiration, Loyalty, and Internationalism," *Journal of Peace Research,* II, 3 (1965), 277-287.

30. See Snyder, "Introduction," *Foreign Policy Decision Making,* eds. Snyder, Bruck, Sapin, op. cit., pp. 1-13.

31. For some examples of comparative decision-making analyses, see Glenn Paige, "Comparative Case Analysis of Crisis Decisions: Korea and Cuba," *International Crisis,* ed. Charles Hermann (Indianapolis; Bobbs-Merrill, forthcoming); Bruce Russett, "The Calculus of Deterrence," *Journal of Conflict Resolution,* VII (June 1963), 97-109; Russett, Ch. XIV of the present volume; Michael Haas, *International Conflict* (Indianapolis: Bobbs-Merrill, forthcoming), Part II.

32. Hoffmann, "International Relations: The Long Road to Theory," op. cit., p. 364.

33. Herman Kahn, *On Thermonuclear War* (Princeton: Princeton University Press, 1960); Kahn, *On Escalation* (New York: Praeger, 1965); Thomas C. Schelling, *The Strategy of Conflict* (New York: Oxford University Press, 1963); Schelling, *Arms and Influence* (New Haven: Yale University Press, 1966). The foundations of game theory are contained in John von Neumann and Oskar Morgenstern, *Theory of Games and Economic Behavior* (3rd ed.; New York: Wiley, 1953). See also Morgenstern, *The Question of National Defense* (New York: Random House, 1966), and Glenn Snyder, *Deterrence and Defense* (Princeton: Princeton University Press, 1961).

34. Anatol Rapoport, *Fights, Games, and Debates* (Ann Arbor: University of Michigan Press, 1960); Anatol Rapoport and Albert M. Chammah, *Prisoner's Dilemma* (Ann Arbor: University of Michigan Press, 1965). Kenneth E. Boulding, "The Economics of Human Conflict," *The Nature of Human Conflict,* ed. McNeil, op. cit., pp. 172-191; Boulding, *Conflict and Defense* (New York: Harper, 1962). See also Phillip Green, *Deadly Logic* (Columbus: Ohio State University Press, 1966).

35. Richard A. Brody, "Some Systemic Effects of the Spread of Nuclear Weapons Technology: A Study Through Simulation of a Multi-Nuclear Future," op. cit.; Malvern Lumsden, "Perception and Information in Strategic Thinking," *Journal of Peace Research,* III (#3, 1966), 257-277; Charles G. McClintock et al., "A Pragmatic Approach to International Stability,"

International Stability, eds. Dale J. Hekhuis, Charles G. McClintock, Arthur L. Burns (New York: Wiley, 1964), pp. 1-26; Thomas Milburn, "What Constitutes Effective Deterrence?" *Journal of Conflict Resolution,* III (June 1959), 138-145; Marc Pilisuk and Anatol Rapoport, "Stepwise Disarmament and Sudden Destruction in a Two-Person Game: A Research Tool," *Journal of Conflict Resolution,* VIII (March 1964), 36-49; Pilisuk et al., "War Hawks and Peace Doves: Alternative Resolutions of Experimental Conflicts," ibid., IX (December 1965), 491-508; Paul Smoker, "Fear in the Arms Race: A Mathematical Study," *Journal of Peace Research,* I (#1, 1964), 55-64; Smoker, "Trade, Defence and the Richardson Theory of Arms Race: A Seven Nation Study," ibid., II (#2, 1965), 161-176; John MacRae and Paul Smoker, "A Vietnam Simulation," ibid., IV (#1, 1967), 1-25; John R. Raser, "Learning and Affect in International Politics," ibid., II (#3, 1965), 216-227; Raser, "Deterrence Research," ibid., III (#4, 1966), 297-327. A codification of research appears in Jack Sawyer and Harold Guetzkow, "Bargaining and Negotiation in International Relations," *International Behavior,* ed. Kelman, op. cit., pp. 433-463.

36. Karl W. Deutsch, *Nationalism and Social Communication* (Cambridge: MIT Press, 1953); Deutsch, *Political Community at the International Level* (Garden City: Doubleday, 1954); Deutsch, "Shifts in the Balance of Communication Flows: A Problem of Measurement in International Relations," *Public Opinion Quarterly,* XX (Spring 1956), 143-160; Karl W. Deutsch and Alexander Eckstein, "National Industrialization and the Declining Share of the International Economic Sector, 1890-1959," *World Politics,* XIII (January 1961), 287-299; Karl W. Deutsch, Chester I. Bliss, and Alexander Eckstein, "Population, Sovereignty, and the Share of Foreign Trade," *Economic Development and Cultural Change,* X (July 1962), 353-366; Phillip E. Jacob and James V. Toscano (eds.), *The Integration of Political Communities* (Philadelphia: Lippincott, 1964).

37. Bruce N. Russett, Hayward R. Alker, Jr., Karl W. Deutsch, and Harold D. Lasswell, *World Handbook of Political and Social Indicators* (New Haven: Yale University Press, 1964).

38. Karl W. Deutsch, et al., *Political Community and the North Atlantic Area* (Princeton: Princeton University Press, 1957); Amitai Etzioni, *Political Unification* (New York: Holt, Rinehart & Winston, 1965).

39. Bruce N. Russett, *Community and Contention* (Cambridge: MIT Press, 1963).

40. Karl W. Deutsch, *The Nerves of Government* (New York: Free Press, 1963). See also Robert C. North, "The Analytical Prospects of Communications Theory," *Contemporary Political Analysis,* ed. Charlesworth, op. cit., pp. 300-316.

41. Hayward R. Alker, Jr., "Supranationalism in the United Nations," *Peace Research Society, Papers,* III (1965), 197-212; Hayward R. Alker and Bruce N. Russett, *World Politics in the General Assembly* (New Haven: Yale University Press, 1965); Hayward R. Alker and Donald Puchala, "Trends in Economic Partnership in the North Atlantic Area," *Quantitative International Politics,* ed. Singer, op. cit. pp. 287-316; Robert C. Angell, *Peace on the March* (Princeton: Van Nostrand, 1969); Angell, "The Sociology of Human Conflict," *The Nature of Human Conflict,* ed. McNeil, op. cit., pp. 91-115. Deutsch and Eckstein, op. cit.; Deutsch, Bliss, and Eckstein, op. cit. Richard

L. Merritt, *Symbols of American Community* (New Haven: Yale University Press, 1966); Merritt, "Distance and Interaction Among Political Communities," *General Systems,* IX (1964), 255-264; Karl W. Deutsch, Lewis J. Edinger, Roy C. Macridis, and Richard L. Merritt, *France, Germany and the Western Alliance* (New York: Scribner's, 1967).

42. Lincoln Bloomfield, "The United States, The United Nations and the Creation of Community," *International Organization,* XIV (Autumn 1960), 503-513. Ernst Haas, op. cit.; E. Haas, *The Uniting of Europe* (Stanford: Stanford University Press, 1958); E. Haas, *Beyond the Nation State* (Stanford: Stanford University Press, 1964). Werner Levi, *Fundamentals of World Organization* (Minneapolis: University of Minnesota Press, 1950); Levi, "The Concept of Integration in Research on Peace," *Background,* IX (August 1965), 111-126. Richard Van Wagenen, *Research in the International Organization Field* (Princeton: Center for Research on World Political Institutions, 1952); Van Wagenen, "The Concept of Community and the Future of the Untied Nations," *International Organization,* XIX (Summer 1965), 812-827.

43. Quincy Wright, *A Study of War* (2nd ed.; Chicago: University of Chicago Press, 1965), passim; Wright, *The Study of International Relations* (New York: Appleton-Century Crofts, 1955), pp. 539-569. For an enumeration of middle-gauge conflict-theory propositions, which have applicability to field theory, see Raymond W. Mack and Richard C. Snyder, "The Analysis of Social Conflict—Toward an Overview and Synthesis," *Journal of Conflict Resolution,* I (June 1957), 212-248. The philosophic underpinnings of field theory are to be found in Percy W. Bridgman, *Dimensional Analysis* (New Haven: Yale University Press, 1922). See Michael Haas, "Dimensional Analysis in Cross-National Research," *Comparative Political Studies,* in press. One of the most recent attempts to survey field linkages is found in James N. Rosenau (ed.), *Linkage Politics* (New York: Free Press, 1969).

44. Social field theory is presented by Kurt Lewin, *Field Theory in Social Science* (New York: Harper, 1951), and a derivative, facet theory, by Louis Guttmann, "A Structural Theory for Intergroup Beliefs and Action," *American Sociological Review,* XXIV (June 1959), 318-328. Mathematical field theory is presented succinctly by Rudolph Rummel, "A Field Theory of Social Action with Application to Conflict Within Nations," *General Systems,* X (1965), 183-211. Rummel, a political scientist, makes no effort to establish a linkage with the Lewinian tradition. An interesting attempt to apply field-theoretic reasoning appears in Davis B. Bobrow, "Old Dragons in New Models," *World Politics,* XIX (January 1967), 306-319.

45. Steven J. Brams, "Transaction Flows in the International System," *American Political Science Review,* LX (December 1966), 880-898. Ivo Feierabend and Rosalind L. Feierabend, "Aggressive Behaviors Within Polities, 1948-1962: A Cross-National Study," *Journal of Conflict Resolution,* X (September 1966), 249-271; Feierabend and Feierabend, "The Relationship of Systemic Frustration, Political Coercion, International Tension and Political Instability: A Cross-National Study," paper presented at the American Psychological Association annual convention, September 1966. Michael Haas, "Societal Approaches to the Study of War," *Journal of Peace Research,* II (#4, 1965), 307-323; M. Haas, "Social Change and National Aggressiveness, 1900-1960," *Quantitative International Politics,* ed. Singer,

op. cit., pp. 215-244. Rauol Naroll, "Does Military Deterrence Deter?" *Trans-Action*, III (January-February 1966), 14-20; Rudolph J. Rummel, "Dimensions of Conflict Behavior Within and Between Nations," *General Systems*, VIII (1963), 1-53; Rummel, "Some Dimensions in the Foreign Behavior of Nations," *Journal of Peace Research*, III (# 3, 1966), 201-224; Rummel, "Dimensions of Dyadic War, 1820-1952," *Journal of Conflict Resolution*, XI (June 1967), 176-183. Raymond Tanter, "Dimensions of Conflict Behavior Within and Between Nations, 1958-60," ibid., X (March 1966), 65-73. See also Lewis F. Richardson, *Statistics of Deadly Quarrels* (Chicago: Quadrangle, 1960); Richardson, *Arms and Insecurity* (Chicago: Quadrangle, 1960).

46. Michael Haas, "Types of Asymmetry in Social and Political Systems," *General Systems*, XII (1967), 69-79; Haas, *International Conflict*, Ch. VI.

47. The distinction between *systems theory* and *systems analysis* is one between interdisciplinary general systems theory and applications at various levels of analysis. *System theory* refers to a metatheory at the level of an international system or international subsystem.

48. Charles A. McClelland, "Applications of General Systems Theory in International Relations," *Main Currents in Modern Thought*, XII (1955), 27-34; see McClelland, *Theory and the International System* (New York: Macmillan, 1966). The term "states system" was in vogue much earlier, though with no pretensions to linkage with systems analysis. See R. B. Mowat, *The European States System* (London: Oxford University Press, 1923). Morton Kaplan applies systems analysis in "Balance of Power, Bipolarity and Other Models of International Systems," *American Political Science Review*, LI (September 1957), 684-695.

49. Morton A. Kaplan, *System and Process in International Politics* (New York: Wiley, 1957); Morton A. Kaplan and Nicholas de B. Katzenbach, *The Political Foundations of International Law* (New York: Wiley, 1961). Richard Rosecrance, *Action and Reaction in World Politics* (Boston: Little, Brown, 1963); Rosecrance, "Bipolarity, Multipolarity and the Future," *Journal of Conflict Resolution*, X (September 1966), 314-327. Kenneth N. Waltz, "Stability of the Bipolar World," *Daedalus*, XCIII (Summer 1964), 881-909; Waltz, "Contention and Management in International Relations," *World Politics*, XVII (July 1965), 720-744; Waltz, "International Structure, National Force, and the Balance of World Power," *Journal of International Affairs*, XXI (#2, 1967), 215-231; Karl W. Deutsch and J. David Singer, "Multipolar Power Systems and International Stability," *World Politics*, XVI (April 1964), 390-406. Greater stability for bipolarity is reported empirically in Michael Haas, "Internation Subsystems: Stability and Polarity," *American Political Science Review*, LXIII (March, 1970).

50. McClelland, *Theory and the International System*, op. cit.

51. George Liska, *International Equilibrium* (Cambridge: Harvard University Press, 1957); George A. Modelski, "Agraria and Industria: Two Models of the International System," *World Politics*, XIV (October 1961), 118-143; Chadwick Alger, "Comparison of Intranational and International Politics," *American Political Science Review*, LVII (June 1963), 406-419; Michael Haas, "A Functional Approach to International Organization," *Journal of Politics*, XXVII (August 1965), 498-517. J. David Singer's analysis of prerequisites for inter-nation influence attempts may be viewed as a contribution to structural-functional theory as well: "Inter-Nation Influence: A Formal

Model," *American Political Science Review,* LVII (June 1963), 420-430.

52. A *function* may be defined formally as the intersection between two distinct categories—stages in behavior cycles and types of imperative meta-tasks. The *stages* are divided by Easton into inputs, withinputs, and outputs; the *imperatives* are presented by Parsons as goal attainment, adaptation, pattern maintenance, and integration. David Easton, *A Systems Analysis of Political Life* (New York: Wiley, 1965); Talcott Parsons and Neil Smelser, *Economy and Society* (Glencoe: Free Press, 1956).

53. Goldman, op. cit.; Rosenau, *Public Opinion and Foreign Policy,* op. cit.

54. Rosecrance, *Action and Reaction in World Politics,* op. cit.; Michael Brecher, "International Relations and Asian Studies: The Subordinate State System of Southern Asia," *World Politics,* XV (January 1963), 221-235.

55. See Gabriel A. Almond and G. Bingham Powell, Jr., *Comparative Politics* (Boston: Little, Brown, 1966). The subsystem study appears in M. Haas, *loc. cit.,* and in Haas, *International Conflict,* Part IV.

56. Harold Guetzkow, "Long Range Research in International Relations," *American Perspective,* IV (Fall 1950), 421-440.

57. Snyder, Bruck, Sapin, op. cit., p. 30; Alfred Schuetz, "On Multiple Realities," *Philosophy and Phenomenological Research,* V (June 1945), 533-576.

58. Kenneth N. Waltz, *Man, the State, and War* (New York: Columbia University Press, 1959); J. David Singer, "The Level-of-Analysis Problem in International Relations," *World Politics,* XIV (October 1961), 77-92.

59. Robert K. Merton, *Social Theory and Social Structure* (rev. ed.; Glencoe: Free Press, 1957).

60. Rosenau, *Linkage Politics,* op. cit.; Rosenau, *Of Boundaries and Bridges* (Princeton: Center of International Studies, 1967).

VIII

CONCLUSION

16 The Behavioral Revolution and After

MICHAEL HAAS and THEODORE L. BECKER,
University of Hawaii

> The man who sees two or three generations is like one who sits in the conjurer's booth at a fair, and sees the tricks two or three times. They are meant to be seen only once.—*Arthur Schopenhauer*

I. INTRODUCTION

The course of history, according to Hegel and Marx, tends to follow a dialectical path. At one point in time two contending processes, a thesis and an antithesis, vie for supremacy. When a synthesis emerges as the new theme, it is initially inchoate and molar; but as the synthesis grows, reaching maturer levels of development, internal contradictions become manifest and a new thesis and antithesis appear.

The development of the field of political science may be conceived of in terms of such a dialectical process. All fields of study once were lumped together as philosophy, but in time a division between natural and moral philosophy took place, one that still represents the pattern for educational systems in European countries. The humanities and social sciences subsequently parted company from the former common rubric of moral philosophy, and political science is a product of the gradual differentiation of autonomous fields within the social sciences, a process that is even now incomplete within American colleges and universities.[1]

However, the purpose of this essay is not to trace the incremental and dramatic aspects of broad sweeps in academic history. Instead, our focus is on the rise of a science of politics, which some in the profession believe to have reached such a towering level that the behavioral revolution of the 1950's constitutes a terminal or ultimate stage in the development of the field.[2] Though it is our view that in a broad sense behavioral political science was victorious in its confrontation with traditional modes of thinking, we are of the opinion that inner contradictions have appeared within an overly successful and smug circle of behavioralists, such that a new battle is taking shape.

479

The hypertrophy of behavioralism, in short, has led to debate within the ranks of its practitioners, one that resembles at least superficially, but should not be regarded as just a continuation of the old traditional-behavioral dispute of the 1950's, which was interpreted by most behavioralists as essentially a methodological debate consisting of a priori speculation about what science could and could not do for the study of politics. The new kind of argument involves a thoroughgoing assessment of the now well-established behavioral achievement. Exclamations concerning alleged inherent defects of behavioralism are far less raucous nowadays. But the fact that behavioralists continue to regard recent critiques almost wholly in methodological terms is instructive,[3] for the problem of an accumulation of methodological errors and false theoretical leads by particular behavioralists in their research is one that has yet to be faced. As many former traditionalists avidly read the behavioral output, becoming in the process converted to the quest for "a coherent, precise, and orderly body of knowledge,"[4] their misgivings have not been asserted in ignorance of what behavioralism is all about.

Instead, many former traditionalists have become convinced of the soundness of a behavioral creed in general. But their recent critiques, even when phrased loosely, rather than in the proper jargon, seem increasingly to consist of well-taken points. The newer attacks are brushed aside far too cavalierly—and too often in terms of the earlier debate. In our view, traditionalists who refused in the 1950's to adapt to the behavioral mood may be considered intellectually no less shabby than behavioralists who decided in the 1960's to spurn the traditionalist legacy and who refused to confess their guilt of what Morton Kaplan calls "crudities and errors," which have remained curiously resistant to the so-called "self-corrective techniques of science."[5]

The authors of this essay believe that the newer criticisms of behavioralism apply across all the various areas and subfields of study in the discipline of political science. However, instead of attempting a comprehensive survey providing details for such a broad charge, we intend to be selective. Actually, this essay is an outgrowth of a discussion between the two authors. This discussion led to the mutual discovery that although we both consider ourselves to be behaviorally oriented and trained, as recent graduates of Stanford and Northwestern universities respectively, we have substantially similar complaints and fears about the behavioral work being done in each of our main fields of study, international relations and judicial behavior. We feel that a collaborative effort, demonstrating the similarity of defects and dangerous trends in these two fields, will be of interest to the discipline at large.

Accordingly, we envision for ourselves a threefold task. First of all, we wish to review the major points of the now moribund behavioral-traditional dispute. Second, we wish to point out some recent valid criticisms of behavioral research, which, if not taken to heart, would result in behavioralists' impeding their own quest for science while contributing very little toward the improvement of political systems. Finally, we will sketch what seems to us to represent a synthesis that will arise in the 1970's as a result of the current debate. We wish to name this new attempt to transcend current stultifications within behavioral political science *multimethodologism*. We intend to document each point with illustrations from the present-day literature of political science. The aim, it should be made clear, is not to attack any of the individuals cited personally. Rather, the names involved will be relegated to footnotes, out of deference to convention and scholarly necessity. Our focus is neither on personalities nor on broad isms or approaches but, instead, on particular *practices* that have become fetishes in current behavioral research in political science. For it is our hope to incite a multimethodological revolution aimed, in William Bluhm's terms, at building a bridge over the chasm now separating traditional from behavioral political science.[6] It is our task to develop a convincing multimethodological plea.

II. TRADITIONAL THESIS AND BEHAVIORAL ANTITHESIS

David Easton's authoritative definition of behavioralism itemizes eight characteristics that distinguish traditional from behavioral political science.[7] His discussion provides a coherent summary of issues in the traditional-behavioral debate of the 1950's.

1. Regularities. In contrast with the traditional penchant for careful historical description and detail, behavioralists seek to uncover uniformities.
2. Verification. Behavioralists argue that knowledge consists only of propositions that have been subjected to empirical tests, which implies that all evidence must be based upon observation.
3. Techniques. In order to acquire knowledge concerning particular phenomena, a research tool or method that guarantees valid, reliable, and comparable data must be employed.
4. Quantification. Imprecise qualitative judgments need to be replaced by rigorous measurement and data manipulation procedures in order for us to obtain precise and accurate knowledge about the complexities of political life.
5. Value Neutrality. Facts and values are two separate realms of discourse that should not be confused. Scientific inquiry, to be objective, must be value-free. Values cannot be derived from facts.
6. Theory. Knowledge needs to be codified in a systematic manner. Testable hypotheses should be deduced from a logically interrelated structure of concepts and propositions, and theories are

to be corrected in the light of new evidence.

7. Pure Science. Not all research should be geared at the practical level for immediate application to policy: there is a need to generate knowledge for its own sake in order to provide firmer foundations for an applied science of politics.

8. Interdisciplinarism. Political scientists should liberate themselves from the confines of their own boundaries to integrate the methods, theories, and findings of other disciplines into their research.

Most of the above eight points were subjected to attack from traditionalists in the 1950's, but the behavioral creed remained unshaken by the counterarguments. For example:

1. Contrary to the "regularities" position, traditionalists have argued that political reality consists largely of unique elements. But such an assertion is in actuality a proposition that there is such a fundamental agglutination among observable traits that only the most trivial regularities are likely to be found. And the test of such a proposition lies in multivariate research rather than in speculating a priori about what one might expect to find.

2. In opposition to the "verification" argument, some traditionalists claimed that much of politics is beneath the surface and unknowable, whereas the past decade is filled with intensive studies of attitudes underlying voting behavior. The point that eluded traditionalists here is that behavioralists indeed prefer to know about subsurface dynamics but that epistemologically the only way short of revelation to learn about any level of reality is to collect data based on observational evidence, such as verbal responses to interviews and questionnaires.

3. Traditionalists scoffed at the idea that data can be objective in the social sciences, despite the fact that one of the most basic aspects of any data-collection operation is the specification of the amount of error and unreliability in a set of data, information which is subsequently used to assess the extent to which an investigator is confident of his findings.

4. Hayward Alker has answered in much detail the view that behavioralists "quantify the unquantifiable" and "measure the immeasurable" in referring to a variety of rigorous quantitative procedures for handling problems of an ambiguous qualitative nature.[8] That such techniques have long been available is yet another indication of the irrelevant musings with which many traditionalists attempted to quash the behavioral revolution.

5. The "value-neutrality" position is held to be untenable inasmuch as researchers have value preferences that allegedly creep into any attempt to handle reality. But the assertion that persons of different ideological persuasions will be unable to agree upon a common set of scientific canons is a hypothesis that has been tested in the past

decade. As the history of science attests, the possibility for replication and the availability of data for subsequent reexamination enable an investigator to check on the objectivity of any study and to draw contrary inferences based on his own fresh analyses. It is the lack of accessibility of the various intermediate steps in a traditional research project that has beclouded political science with an overly value-laden folklore.

6. The role of theory was downgraded by many traditionalists, who preferred to deal with matters of policy and substance, which they felt would ultimately and practically be the only meaningful points of reference. Contrariwise, behavioralists seek to predict behavior by extrapolating theoretically conceived conditions into the future, and behavioralists tend to agree with Kantian epistemology in conceiving that reality can only be grasped in terms of analytical models and categories, which need to be made explicit and thereby rendered testable. The seventh and eighth points have not been so seriously challenged by traditionalists, who have engaged in much pure research and have always had a healthy respect for the relevance of at least one other discipline—history.

However, it is not the purpose of this essay to trace rebuttals and counterrebuttals among traditionalists and behavioralists who have claimed exclusive utility for their particular approaches. Behavioralists have had no trouble in meeting superficial methodological objections. But the hyperbolic flourish with which behavioralists have often restated their case has of late brought many traditionalists sympathetic to the behavioral persuasion into greater juxtaposition with an entirely new generation, one trained behaviorally and committed to a science of politics, but one which fears considerable imbalance within political science in the years ahead. A growing group of scholars, which we are inclined to refer to as "multimethodologists," accept the need for all eight elements of behavioralism as set forth by Easton, but they find that overpreoccupation with any one of the eight facets, as has been the case among too many behavioralists so far, needs to be arrested as soon as possible in order to insure a balanced growth in the discipline of political science. The argument is combined with suggestions for specific remedies.

III. A MULTIMETHODOLOGICAL PLEA

If the three main elements within a science are agreed to consist of substantive knowledge, pyramided theory, and rigorous methods, then we may represent the first phase of behavioral political science as having an empirical and *quantitative* thrust (Figure 1). The behavioralists of the 1920's and 1930's, as best exemplified by Stuart Rice and Harold Gosnell, urged the introduction of quantitative methods then being used within related disciplines in the social

FIGURE 1. First Behavioral Movement

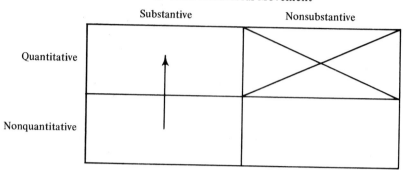

sciences.[9] Statistical tables of various sorts began to appear throughout writings in the field, though the methodological sophistication in analyzing such data was at a low level. But, as Lazarsfeld's definition of "methodology" implies,[10] the reason that early behavioralism was not revolutionary was that new methods were merely adapted to enable a somewhat more precise description and analysis of the prevailing and enduring paradigms of political science. Substantively oriented political scientists participating in this early quantitative movement urged a shift from the level of impressionistic description to the level of detailed factual description. Nonsubstantive political scientists, notably political theorists, did not join the early movement, and there were no nonsubstantive quantitative political scientists. Theoretical breakthroughs did not emerge until after World War II, though Harold Lasswell's use of content analysis and interest in psychoanalytic theory bridges the gap between behavioral generations.

The prime movers of the behavioral revolution in its second phase were *theoretical* innovators (Figure 2). The writings of Gabriel Almond, Robert Dahl, David Easton, Karl Deutsch, and especially Harold Lasswell called attention to the need to formulate and to test propositions. A spate of theoretical schemas, research designs, and pleas for theory building appeared in the 1950's, urging an end to the overly monographic character of the discipline. The systems approach, decision making theory, the focus on communication, and other theoretical innovations described in the Deutsch-Rieselbach essay led to a transformation within all of the subfields of political science, political theory itself moving toward an emphasis on empirical theory. The analytical edifices of the behavioralists of the 1950's have been so vast that progress in developing research techniques to test theory has only recently begun to scale the heights of such theoretical mountains. The initiators of the second behavioral revolution envisaged and encouraged quantitative advances, but only insofar as techniques were a means to theory building. Systematic case analyses, content analyses, surveys,

FIGURE 2. Second Behavioral Revolution

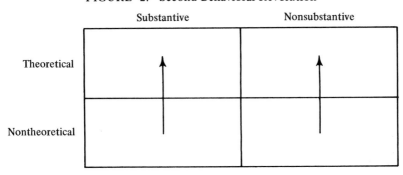

experiments, aggregate statistical analyses, and causal modeling have all blossomed as a result.

Although it is refreshing and exciting to find at last that mathematical techniques and multivariate analyses are being undertaken within political science, we feel that somewhat of a retrogression has taken place within political science in the 1960's. Quantitative strategies seem to have advanced far beyond the theoretical equipment on hand, whereas many theoretically innovative behavioralists have failed to keep abreast of the newer advancements in research technology. The result appears to be a fragmentation of behavioralists—who perhaps feel complacent because they are recognized as the more important corps of researchers within political science today—into parochial schools of thought and even occasionally into warring camps (Figure 3).

FIGURE 3. Current Divisions within Political Science

	Quantitative	Nonquantitative
Theoretical	**Multimethodologists**	**Theoretical Behavioralists**
Nontheoretical	**Positivist Behavioralists**	**Tradtionalists**

Some behavioralists continue to spin webs of theory, unchecked by substantive findings; this tendency we shall call *theoretical behavioralism.* The brute or barefoot empiricists, whose tinkering with methods seems unrelated to theory and even to political science, seem to deserve the label *positivist behavioralists.* The attraction of these orientations has been so strong that many nonbehavioralists have found themselves gravitating toward one of the two choices, leaving the *traditionalist* category as a residual for nonquantitative, nontheoretical scholars.

It is no secret that the polarizations of this third behavioral revolution have been associated with a wholesale movement of theoretically oriented traditionalists into juxtaposition with the theoretical behavioralists at professional conferences, in footnote references to scholarly papers, and in hiring practices within the academic marketplace. What is alarming is that positivist and theoretical behavioralists are so isolated from each other in intellectual stimulation and rapport. This new cleft appears to be much deeper than the behavioralist-traditional division of the 1950's, for the two new groups do not have a common idiom; instead of debating epistemology, they retreat to esoteric havens called "theory" and "research." In the final chapter, by David Easton, the consequences of this new cleft are delineated from a normative perspective.

The orientation that we herein refer to as *multimethodologism* is attempting to combine theoretical sophistication and advanced research technology. In the process of doing so, multimethodologism has been discovering that many charges against behavioralism made in the 1950's are being remade by theoretical behavioralists against positivist behavioralists—and with excellent justification. Multimethodologists find that theoretical behavioralists, who are under attack from the positivist-behavioral camp, have shortcomings as well. But it is not the purpose of this essay to focus on the adversaries and polemics in this great debate of the 1960's. Instead, we should like to focus on the issues which from the standpoint of a multimethodologist constitute monomanias and prejudices that need to be corrected by a more balanced approach in the years ahead. More specifically, our lack-of-balance argument implies that an overcommitment to only a few of Easton's eight behavioral characteristics has tended to undermine progress in some of the other seven. Accordingly, we intend to present five cross-cutting propositions for the consideration of the reader. Each proposition is phrased in a manner that captures the essence of current misgivings. We will proceed to separate sound from unsound implications in each proposition and finally will demonstrate how multimethodology constitutes a new synthesis which promises to overcome current parochialisms.

Proposition I. Political behavioralists are interested mainly in general or regular properties of human behavior.

The charge that behavioralists concern themselves excessively with regularities is used in the "uniqueness" argument: behavioralists are said to relegate unique occurrences and idiosyncratic factors, especially those upsetting the neat patterning of social phenomena, to the periphery. Behavioralists are attacked for being overly nomothetic, and it is claimed that integrated knowledge is facilitated by moving back and forth along the nomothetic-idiographic continuum in interpreting research findings. To date many behavioralists have overlooked idiographic research all too frequently, violating their own methodological canons in failing to do so.

In the behavioral study of the judicial decision making process there is a curious inclination to observe and interpret without an interest in explaining deviant or inconsistent behavior. In the proliferating scalogram analyses of the decisions of judges on a number of related cases, as described in Chapter 5, the main concern has been to reduce case decisions into one unidimensional scale, such as "libertarianism-conservatism," on which the judges may be ranked.[11] "Errors," that is, inconsistencies between an individual judge's responses and a hypothetical unidimensional pattern, are counted and expressed statistically as the "coefficient of reproducibility" for each scale. And the frequently high figure (usually over .90) is alleged to indicate that single psychological and sociological factors are related to judicial decisions, that is, that judicial behavior is motivated consistently by single variables. However, this consistency is an artifact of the attempt (à la Occam's razor) to find a single scale in which to collapse votes on a large set of cases. For instance, most of the judges analyzed actually appear quite inconsistent in their behavior. Judges rarely decide various types of cases completely in one direction, and they alternate their decisions on cases because they are not fully doctrinaire in their views. Moreover, since unanimous decisions do not differentiate between judges' preferences, they are not brought into scalogram analyses, with the result that many instances of "conservative" judges voting in unanimously "liberal" decisions—and vice versa—are neglected. Thus the scalogram method, because of its requirements, fails to come to grips with important deviant individual behavior.

A classic example of the disappearance of individual cases is repeated in a series of content-analysis articles in which perceptions of several decision makers are counted together. In one essay that studies conditions leading to the outbreak of World War I, perceptions of various kinds are summed across approximately fifteen decision makers from five different countries.[12] Although the data reveal rather sharp fluctuations from day to day, the authors inform us that hostility was increasing among decision making elites prior to the outbreak of war. The infrequent rise in quantities could as well have been accounted for if one British or French decision maker had spoken garrulously and intemperately on a few occasions, less aggressive belligerents' statements having been counted in the same omnibus pool with those of Germany and Austria. After failure to design the research so as to observe each individual separately, it is impossible later to generalize about the behavior of the class of decision makers. In another content analysis, a study of the 1962 Cuban missiles crisis, we find that five American decision makers and an unknown number of unidentified Russian and Chinese leaders are all treated as a single lump for purposes of counting statements and perceptions.[13] No control groups are present; there is no analysis of deviant and negative findings; and results do not satisfy requirements for a comparative study of decision makers, since the individual is not the recording unit in the analysis.

Sampling crudity prevents the researchers from generalizing about the various national decision making units in the aggregate: should one desire to build a theory about crisis decision making, one subsample of countries to study would be those entering war in a crisis; another subsample would consist of a control group of countries that do not experience a feeling of crisis; a third subsample would include states failing to go to war though exposed to somewhat similar crisis stimuli; and perhaps a fourth would be a nonwar noncrisis group of countries. If decision making processes are substantially different between aggregated perceptions of decision makers within each of the four categories, the comparative method will yield an answer. Instead, the 1914 case consists of a study of belligerent countries alone, whereas a much larger number of countries stayed out of the war or entered the conflagration later, during a noncrisis period. In ignoring the sampling question, the authors fail to supply data which are minimally necessary to any scientific enterprise: they do not test their own null hypothesis. This is not to say that the authors are unaware of such sampling difficulties. On the contrary, they would be among the first to agree that the level of univariate discription needs to be transcended in the years ahead, and they do have data at their disposal that could be analyzed case by case to determine which decision makers and countries depart from the over-all pattern.

Fortunately, the correlation between high methodological tinkering and low theoretical sophistication is not perfect. There are notable deviant cases, even among users of aggregate data, who have thus far demonstrated little interest in individual cases from which variables are extracted. Since no theory of human behavior can be comprehensively explanatory and highly predictive without being able to accommodate much deviant behavior, one can only be pleased to see the care which at least one user of factor analysis takes to explain cases that fail to conform to general patterns. In *International Regions and the International System* Bruce Russett devotes major sections of his discussion to the identification of countries exhibiting the most deviation in their membership within regions or in their over-all profile for a large number of variables over time.[14] And

Russett's ingenuity in Chapter 14 of the present volume in suggesting how to handle case analysis in conjunction with a cumulative, comparative theoretical point of view should encourage further multimethodological optimism, for the continuing use of multiple-regression techniques points toward the possibility of isolating the exact amount of variance in a variable that is due to idiosyncratic (nongeneral) factors.[15] Having located deviant cases and unexplained variance, the next step clearly is to sharpen theory so that it can take more and more cases into account. Meanwhile, much more precise content analyses are appearing,[16] and the research mentioned in nearly every essay in the present volume suggests the rise of a truly comparative science of politics from individual case studies.

Clearly, the abhorrence for deviant findings among some behavioralists is a fetish which neophyte users of exploratory theories and of newly adapted research techniques may be prone to adopt. So the answer to the first objection is not a return to traditional methods at all, for more rigor and a respect for the importance of deviation in pursuing behavioral methods of research will result in a more complete accumulation of knowledge concerning political behavior.

Proposition II. Behavioralists discount the utility and validity of impressionistic accounts of political phenomena.

One of the fears among many traditionally oriented political scientists is that they and their followers will be considered non-contributors to political knowledge because they are not inclined to undergo a "retooling" process. Unfortunately, there are many behavioralists whose words, deeds, and omissions give much substance to this fear, for their attitude toward the traditional literature is either one of hostility or of indifference. Such behavioralist behavior is not only crass, but it is also antitheoretical, insofar as it involves a continuation of current behavioralism's highly pervasive unwillingness to build upon previous insights and speculations in political science.

Scholarly inquiry can be pursued at a variety of levels. In the development of a science from lesser to greater levels of comprehension, false leads may be avoided by gaining an empathic and intuitive understanding of a subject before conducting research. In sociological research it is common practice before undertaking a massive research effort to conduct an "experience survey," in which the researcher becomes acquainted with, or even lives on a day-by-day basis among, the persons to be studied systematically. One of the best examples of the latter is described by W. F. Whyte in *Streetcorner Society,*[17] who set out to portray slum living in terms of the then popular notion that a slum is socially disorganized. Taking up residence in a Boston slum, the author was able to determine how a stable pattern of interactions could be maintained among persons lacking economic security.

In the field of international relations, there are some recent examples of model building on subjects in which the author failed to secure grounding in the existing literature. In an attempt to develop a general theory, one theoretically oriented author asserts, for example:

> The irreducible minimum objective of foreign policy is precisely to safeguard the integrity of the state so that the values of the surviving society can be determined by domestic political processes independently of external pressures. Where this objective is realized, the diminished role of domestic politics in foreign policy-making is compensated by an enlarged autonomy in all other matters.[18]

The implication of this statement is that decision makers would prefer not to be bothered by the ambiguities of international dealings; or, to use a somewhat milder notion of a prominent theoretical behavioralist, government leaders seek to routinize external inputs into national decision systems.[19] If the two theorists imply that decision makers are eager to reduce the problem of selecting among myriad possible responses to international situations by devising a small set of stock procedures, one searches in vain for empirical confirmation of such a proposition. It is true that isolationism and economic autarky have been policies of some states in the past, and some crises may evoke an amateurish diplomacy.[20] But the overwhelming trend in international diplomatic history has been toward a larger variety and volume of international dealings and a persistent quest for creative and flexible ways of solving problems. Events subsequent to Matthew Perry's "opening" of Japan reveal that the needs and rewards of participation in international affairs may often facilitate the resolution of internal conflicts. The extensive literature on supranationalism developed by Ernst Haas and others demonstrates that foreign policy decision makers often view the rationality of their opposite numbers in other countries as preferable to the narrow, nationalistic pressures of domestic constituents.[21] Again, we find that behavioralists, even those who are not positivist in inclination, spurn the use of case study material, emerging with hypotheses that contradict documented insights from the extant literature—and without an explicit acknowledgment or justification for such a departure from the traditional legacy.

It should be borne in mind that theoretical behavioralists are attempting to rise above the overly factual and normative character of the traditional literature to construct more general theory, which we agree emphatically is a desirable goal. Perhaps there is no direct reference to the traditional literature in the writings of some of the theoretical behavioralists because no quotable nugget is at hand, but the implicit theory in many explicit accounts of traditionalists contrasts with almost a total absence of illustrative examples in buttressing many new theoretical frameworks. The danger is that a behavioral solution is not likely to be impressive if it involves ascendance to the clouds, where case descriptive material may be forgotten and reality, so to speak, constructed from scratch. Codification of earlier writings should be a first step before rushing to research frontiers that remain unexplored.[22] The need for propositional inventories and literature, in fact, stimulated this volume.

Yet another aspect of the behavioralist disdain for studies lacking a rigorous or esoteric methodology is that the range of possible inquiries in political science is constricted. If we must have quantitative data before undertaking research, we have just excluded entire millennia of history from our attention. A behavioral theory based only on recorded votes or survey research will be limited largely to twentieth-century materials, and the result will be a time-bound conception of political affairs, rather than general theory.

Fortunately, there has been a refreshing trend within political science to pursue general systems theory and its derivatives as means for achieving a multimethodological synthesis. A critical commentator on several early theoretical efforts in international relations, Stanley Hoffmann, may perhaps be regarded as the first thinker to argue for a nomothetic use of case analysis in propagating the method of "historical sociology," namely, the systematic use of case materials in testing theories.[23] And a growing number of studies on such subjects as deterrence and escalation have compared historical cases along a number of qualitative dimensions with considerable theoretical payoff.[24] The historical data required for the examination of Riggs's framework in Chapter 8 of the present volume seems to require a similar strategy.

The situation is similar in the field of judicial decision making, perhaps because there has been such a vast gulf between modern social scientific work and fundamentalistic legal analysis, between judicial behavioralists and public-law men. Indeed, in the introductory essay to a book of readings published in 1963, its editor reveals upon an examination of the bibliography that

over 90 per cent of the items listed are less than five years old—as a result, let it be noted, not of the selective perception of the compiler, but rather of the almost complete absence of writing on judicial behavior until very recently.[25]

Nonetheless, the editor betrays academic provincialism by an apparent readiness to classify as writings on "judicial behavior" only a very few studies which employ certain types of statistical techniques and research designs, despite the fact that most libraries are well stocked with materials written by historians, sociologists, philosophers, jurisprudents, novelists, dramatists, and even poets who deal with judicial processes and judicial behavior. Potentially testable hypotheses fairly burst from their pages, but they are not considered to be worthwhile fare by most practicing, self-styled, contemporary judicial behavioralists. Fortunately, a few studies illustrate the intrinsic compatibility of the traditional, historical case study approach and aspects of behavioralism. In one of these studies, the author spends about two-thirds of his time portraying the history of the appointment of a Supreme Court justice—in living color.[26] It is an intensive and detailed description. Based on his analysis, he next develops a set of concepts and propositions which may well be of much assistance to those who wish to do future research on the politics of judicial appointment. It is a fitting marriage of traditional and behavioral techniques—but fairly unique and limited, in the main, to an understanding only of the American judicial system.

It seems apparent that much more legal-institutional data gathering and analysis is needed on nonwestern societies by contemporary political scientists if we are ever to develop a comparative theory of political behavior. Yet, even if this recommendation were implemented immediately by an army of researchers of all kinds, many gaps would appear and much overlap would occur. Comprehensive working theory and conceptual schemes are needed for guiding all manner of researchers into relevant areas of study.[27] Comparative politics and international relations seem advanced in this respect. Though starts in this direction have been made recently, researchers on the more specialized subjects of legislatures, political parties, and courts have been reluctant to cope with the need for reconceptualization of the field, partly because conventional ways have yet to be demonstrated to be useless in attempting to comprehend the role of these institutions outside America, Canada, and Europe. A rich case literature is essential in connection with a nonculture-bound adaptation of systems theory and structural-functional analysis urged by Crotty (Chapter 10 of the present volume) in the analysis of political parties and in the study of judicial behavior by Becker (Chapter 6).[28] Such a conscious concern with higher level theory will undoubtedly trigger a larger number of significant empirical studies.

To summarize the second plea, the behavioralist argument that certain methods of research yield sounder conclusions than traditional methods has won. There is considerable payoff to be derived in employing traditionally oriented case material in the systematic testing of theoretically oriented conceptual schemes. Multimethodologists, in other words, are not content to propose theoretical schemes; they wish to conduct cross-historical comparative studies in order to apply the most useful theoretical formulations. If occasionally the method consists of a very elementary coding of a case into one of a number of possible categories, much as Banks and Textor have placed countries into various categories of alternative conceptual schemes,[29] then it should be underscored here that the rigor of a particular mode of research is secondary to the theoretical and practical significance of a study.

Proposition III. Behavioralists impose procrustean models upon reality and thus delude themselves about the relevance of their research.

Although some traditionalists have argued that one should avoid using models and concentrate upon concrete reality instead, the fact remains that the selection of any aspects of a case under study constitutes an ordering of reality for analytical purposes. Such an ordering is a model, and modeling is an inescapable feature of any form of analysis. The multimethodological issue, on the contrary, is whether some political behavioralists are overly committed to the use of certain models, or more precisely whether an attachment to particular research tools has resulted in model-bound research, rather than a conscientious search for models that are more appropriate or more useful in comprehending particular phenomena.

As a culmination of the practices of the scalogram researchers in judicial behavior, one such researcher has recently presented a case for a "unidimensional model" to explain judicial decision making. Not only does he remain unconvinced that scalogram analysis creates artifacts and cannot be used to disconfirm multidimensional hypotheses, but he also argues that one need only know one variable to account for all judicial behavior. This long-sought variable is baptized as "attitude," by means of which one can consider that justices will

respond in case X to the stimulus of "civil liberty," and not to the separable component aspects of search and seizure, right to counsel, and cruel and unusual punishment. The unidimensional model is obviously simplistic and, admittedly, loses the asserted "richness" and "variation" of judicial decision making.[30]

In other words, he chooses to ignore the probable influence of many factors, such as conflicting attitudes, underlying values, and institutional and political elements. Indeed, one of the original workers in this area of research recently has abandoned the search for "the existence of a unidimensional continuum."[31] And even the most prolific user of the scalogram now admits the possibility that the bulk of the work along these lines may have conceptualized such "efforts in terms of a search for unidimensionality."[32] A more multivariate approach, as is being employed in other subfields of political science, seems to be the antidote for such a large dose of theoretically barren scalogram analyses.

Within international relations, however, the use of factor analysis has tended to be conceived of as some sort of ultimate deus ex machina. Whereas many factor analysts are frank in admitting the need to employ a variety of procedures other than factor analysis as parallel checks on findings of factor analysis studies, few have embarked upon such a path. Current forms of factor analysis assume that the distribution of variables is normal within the population under investigation and that relationships between variables are linear, rather than involving curvilinearities, thresholds, and the like. Moreover, there are many options in rotating a set of factors to achieve a meaningful solution, each of which is based upon a somewhat different model of reality: If reality is nonlinear, factor analysis would seem less appropriate; if factors in the real world are highly correlated with one another, one would be more correct in selecting an oblique rather than an orthogonal rotation. Indeed, more powerful techniques apply to more restricted segments of reality, and reality will continue to elude our attention unless we employ a battery of procedures in order to determine which model results in the best fit.[33]

Despite such obvious caveats, we find that one user of factor analysis, in comparing his own chosen technique with that of the calculus, refers to the latter—which is designed precisely to handle nonlinearities—as a "limited tool."[34] Indeed, the same author has ebulliently claimed that "factor analysis and the complementary regression model are initiating a scientific revolution in the social sciences as profound and far-reaching as that initiated by the development of the calculus in physics."[35] However, the researcher, in analyzing data that had been handled in an earlier study through the use of the calculus, proceeds to extract a set of factors but remains oblivious of the fact that his own results mesh well with those of the earlier study. Whereas the factor analyst gives the impression that all findings are novel, the significance of his study is that similar results emerge even when very different models are assumed to exist in the data. But in his replication no reference is made to the much richer findings of the earlier study, in which deviant cases are handled in much detail; interest in a research tool is stronger than a concern for developing a body of tested propositions about the subject of the study, international conflict.

However, if factor analysis leads sometimes to conclusions that would be drawn by other techniques, yielding the comforting inference that one's findings are independent of the procrustean beds which particular techniques assume, on some occasions a different tool has yielded entirely new results, though political scientists so far have been unwilling to seek out such situations.[36] It is our view that political science in the future not only will make allowances for more traditional-type data collection in accordance with the discussion in proposition II, but also will insist that multiple data analysis procedures be employed before any study is approved for publication in a scientific journal. Harold Guetzkow's use of simulation as a means for validating aggregate data analysis heralds an era in which propositions will only be taken seriously when they have been confirmed in a variety of settings and by a variety of research procedures, each of which will be employed less self-consciously and ethnocentrically.[37]

Proposition IV. Behavioralists invent a jargon that impedes communication and replication and renders prose tortuous and dull.

Excellence in style of writing is on the decline, a lamentable situation perhaps most eloquently described by George Orwell, who chose his examples from the writings of traditional political scientists.[38]

The charge that behavioral jargon represents a scholasticism that is excommunicating the intelligent layman from contact with the substantive output of current research is, on the other hand, a correct and unavoidable appraisal. Were modern chemistry limited in sophstication to concepts comprehensible to the nonspecialist, then it would not have progressed beyond alchemy; Lavoisier would have been exiled as a pernicious Thomist, and the possibility for scientific progress would have been arrested. If the popular lexicon is imprecise, it surely must be abandoned within the discourse of the profession. The specialist needs to know exactly what it is that he is describing and should be able to communicate with a high degree of fidelity. More nonspecialists are probably interested in the subject of politics than that of chemistry, so the gap in levels of understanding will have to be bridged at the secondary-school level as well as in university and college coursework. Still, these are arguments that found greater currency in disputes between behavioralists and traditionalists of the 1950's.

There is a further element in proposition IV that condemns behavioralist innovations in jargon on far sounder grounds. Traditional scholars are, after all, more than intelligent laymen; they are committed to the use of language for scholarly purposes. What they—as well as the newer generation of graduate students trained by behavioralists—encounter is a concatenation of fuzzily defined, inconsistently employed, and often theoretically confused terms. Rather than agreeing with the profession on the meaning of a particular term, each investigator has felt free to redefine any concept to suit himself. The result has been superficially related scholarship that has been noncumulative because the same terms are associated with different or ambiguous meanings by various researchers.

The terms "balance of power" and "integration" have been reviewed extensively by Ernst Haas and Werner Levi, respectively, as having been used in so many different ways that their technical character has been lost.[39] "Conflict" is used by some investigators to refer to verbal disagreement, while to others the term denotes physical opposition.[40] Similar confusions exist with respect to such terms as "stability," "cohesiveness," "consensus," and "system."

One practical consequence of a lack of an authoritative dictionary is that an indicator of concept A could be used as if it were an indicator of concept B without an awareness of the mistake on the part of either the researcher or his audience. In one classic of behavioral international relations, "integration" is defined as attainment of a "sense of community,"[41] although the two concepts do not appear to be related in any logically necessary way. "Integration" is used commonly to refer to structural linkage,[42] as when two formerly separate states merge into one; "sense of community," a concept left undefined by the author in question, seems to refer to an attitudinal notion of some kind. Certainly the distribution of a set of attitudes within a system is not the same thing as, nor a subtype of, a structural feature of a system's polity. Though indicators of the two concepts might be associated empirically with each other, a high correlation between two variables is not the sort of condition that would enable one to use them interchangeably conceptually. Germany, for example, annexed Alsace and Lorraine, a case of integration in the absence of a viable sense of community.

One could argue as well that many of the key concepts in political inquiry yield a wide range of empirical indicators. No single indicator can exhaust the meaning of such terms as "sovereignty," "power," "rationality," and "crisis."

In the judicial behavior field an example of bending concepts far beyond even their operational meaning is to be found in a study of "sociometric relations" between judges.[43] It has been conventional among sociologists to define "sociometric choice" as having a meaning commensurate with such primitive terms as "like" and "dislike" among members of a group. Subjects ordinarily are requested to rate their feelings of attraction or repulsion toward other members of a group. In other words, the operations utilized in determining "sociometric relations" have been confined to observational data, questionnaires, and interview responses. But that is not what "sociometric relations" means to some judicial behavioralists: although some researchers profess to study "sociometric relations," no such data have been collected. There is no study of the feelings of any judges towards any other judges; in cases decided at one time by a particular court there is simply an exhaustive tabulation of the subsequent reversals, distinctions, and upholdings by other courts. Data are derived from a tallying of the disposition of these cases from a number of volumes called "Shepard's Citations," which lists and chronicles the history of any case as it is subsequently cited by any other court in any other jurisdiction. How can such a set of volumes be a data source to discover "sociometric relations," as that concept has been used in sociology? Obviously it cannot. It seems very unlikely that sociologists who work in the field of sociometric relations would be enlightened by this particular usage of their conception.[44] Moreover, although it may be of substantial importance for us to understand judicial sociometric relations, such as how judges' feelings toward one another affect judicial decision making, so far no relevant studies have appeared. The serious theoretical question for us to raise is why any political behavioralist would feel compelled to study one court's historical record for being overturned by another type of court.

Other concepts in behavioral science literature have been pulled out of shape once they were applied to the study of judicial behavior. Indeed, one may be amazed at what inferences some researchers make from the mere tabulation and statistical analysis of votes of judges; for example, "attitudes," "values," "ideologies," "homeostatic tendencies," "personality," and "sociometric relations" all have been inferred from judicial voting data.

To illustrate further, one judicial behavioralist recently sought to measure "ideological" positions within a group of political scientists who study courts and law.[45] Essentially, each member of a panel was asked to rate himself in relationship to every other member of the group relative to perceived variation in their points of view in the study of judicial decision making. They had the choice of placing themselves and their colleagues somewhere on a continuum that was divided generally into three major categories—and most of them (32 out of 37) did so. On the basis of factor analysis and smallest space analysis, the author of the article feels justified in concluding that "The major findings are that there are three such ideological groupings: the traditional, the conventional, and the behavioral."[46] Yet is seems to us that the questionnaire could well be perceived by the respondents as simply asking for perceptions of one's own *approach* and the *approach* of others to the study of judicial decision making. The junior author of the present essay acted under such an assumption when he responded to the questionnaire. Are "approach" and "ideology" synonymous? It would not seem so.

The low level of concern with explication and the careless adaptation of social scientific concepts in the study of judicial behavior has had its exceptions. Perhaps the most obvious exception is in the study of judicial role, which promises to be an ever-increasing focus of research in the field.[47] For the concept of role in the social sciences has been developed, in an operational sense, mainly from an extensive utilization of questionnaires, small-group experimental and quasi-experimental situations.[48] Fortunately, much the same methodology has been employed in the initial studies of judicial role by political behavioralists. A good chance exists that all of social science will gain as our knowledge accumulates on the possible variations in judicial role and on the possible consequences of any such variations, provided that some care is taken in conceptual and operational explication.

Unfortunately, to date few serious attempts have been made to delineate coherent definitions for sets of words and to employ them consistently. That behavioralists have been playing a blind-man's-bluff game with words while proliferating ad hoc single-concept studies without a concern over consistency in indicators and definitions is probably the most serious indictment of behavioral research yet articulated. With the lone exception of the clarificatory conceptualizing of Fred Riggs and his colleagues,[49] the failure of behavioralists to establish communication with each other seriously impedes the growth of science. It is no wonder that many open-minded traditionalists cannot empathize with the behavioral persuasion in political science. Much conceptual underbrush remains to be cleared.

Proposition V. Behavioralists are unable to make useful policy recommendations.

There are two parts to this final criticism. One argument is that competence in methodological skills and sophistication with respect to theoretical schema cannot be useful to a political decision maker in any way. The second point is that, because behavioralists seldom focus on a subject directly relevant to policy, the policy advice of the otherwise scientifically oriented behavioralist is apt to be superficial and incomplete.

The first part of the criticism is probably correct insofar as a political leader is confronted with practical problems concerning moral alternatives and strategies for remaining in office, on which he must often decide within a short deadline and in the absence of complete information. Conditions surrounding policy choices, in short, hardly are conducive to meticulous consideration of a subject with a scholarly reflectiveness, whether traditional or behavioral. But because policy advising is perceived by some behavioralists to be precarious so long as the body of scientific knowledge is relatively small and largely unreplicated, one posture of the behavioralist has been to disdain the practical and moral implications of his research. The hope is sometimes expressed in private that political science eventually will be liberated from "political engineering."[50] Such an ostrichlike stance cannot change the fact that decisions do have to be made in Washington and elsewhere, and decision makers anxious to implement the soundest possible programs will on occasion seek to have policy alternatives studied by those who are recognized as competent in the field. Even though the political scientist may be called upon merely to rationalize or support policies previously agreed upon, a mass abdication from the role of policy adviser on the part of the behavioralist could have unfavorable consequences for policy and for political systems. In addition, a behavioralist who is entirely unconcerned about public affairs will be isolating himself from a major source of new ideas for research, even if he displays a conscienceless lack of interest in human problems.

But what kind of advice could the behavioralist give? We are all familiar with the tendency of even the traditional scholar not to see the total picture, to adhere dogmatically to one type of theory, or to be too preoccupied with narrow research interests.[51] Academic investigators usually concentrate their attention on areas of uncertainty; on the very matters that most absorb their interest they can provide only tentative answers so long as their work remains exploratory and inexhaustive.

We would like to know, nevertheless, how long new leaders are likely to remain in office in underdeveloped countries. Does foreign aid eventually undermine the donor's objectives by exacerbating disparities in wealth? How likely is revolution throughout Africa and what could be done to prevent or encourage it? Should there be a reduction in trade barriers? What aspects of deterrence posture need strengthening? What are the consequences of the spread of nuclear weapons to other countries? How likely is it that lower-court judges will follow the mandate of the Supreme Court in its decision? Will there be a serious attempt in Congress to overturn a Supreme Court decision? Will it succeed? What is the probable follow-up litigation that can be expected in the legal system? For such questions the political scientist is much more qualified than the country-desk functionary or higher-level official in the Department of State, or member of the administrative staff of a court. Public officials characteristically lack free time to engage in research relevant to such problems.

In choosing between traditionalists and behavioralists, the government official or judge has been increasingly inclined to ask specialized questions for which precise answers are expected. In view of the fact that behavioralists follow the canons of scientific inquiry, they appear to have received increasing attention, even though our discipline has not reached such an advanced stage where results of research will be so solid a basis for decisions as those in many branches of physics.

Having posited that behavioralists are more likely than traditionalists to render scientifically sound advice, we ask two questions: Have behavioralists been helpful in fulfilling research assignments on government contracts? Have behavoralists served a role as independent critics of unwise polities?

In answer to the first question, negative reactions to at least one effort by behavioralists to perform research on government contracts have appeared already. We refer, of course, to Project Camelot, which was terminated in 1965 when Chileans learned that their country was to be studied as part of a pilot project for a $6,000,000 investigation of insurgency and counterinsurgency operations, sponsored by the United States Army. Although behavioral scientists received a clean bill of health before Congress, and even a net gain in federal funding from agencies other than the Army, the whole episode reveals the extent to which academicians have become infected with a machiavellianism that could be fatal in the long run to foreign-area research, if not to academic life:

From a Chilean perspective it seemed incredible that social scientists could have given themselves, in the first instance, to a project under the auspices of the United States Army involving research into "the most intimate details" of Latin American institutions and personal lives; equally incredible that in their earliest communication with Chilean social scientists, American social scientists had camouflaged Army sponsorship by referring vaguely to private foundation and National Science Foundation support.[52]

That the well-known sensitivity of Latin Americans to Yankee meddling was laid aside as a consideration in the name of science suggests the presence of a nihilistic streak within the ranks of at least some behavioral scholars. The willingness of some professionals to wink at sources of their research funding casts further doubt upon whether the results of scientific inquiry will be used to create a better tomorrow or merely to maintain a status quo in which the United States, for example, professes democracy yet staffs an agency whose undercover paramilitary operations are unchecked by the citizenry.

Rather than serving a role as social critics, whose grasp of an empirically based knowledge permits the vision to conceive of new patterns of living, some behavioralists have become highly paid legitimizers of government policy. Many behavioralists are employed by agencies in Washington, or they are supported by government grants for research. A politically bland outlook that insures continuing employment or success at grantsmanship has too often been the result. Few political scientists have been prominent in such organizations as ABSSOP (the Committee for the Application of the Behavioral Sciences to the Strategies of Peace), and there has been a disquieting silence on the part of behavioralists on such subjects as Vietnam. Even though an occasional behavioralist has affixed his signature to a petition appearing in the *New York Times* and elsewhere,[53] the public debate on American policy in Vietnam between Professors Morgenthau and Brzezinski, though conducted at an extremely high level of sophisticated rhetoric, undoubtedly reinforces the popular image of political science as a breastbeating enterprise. It is very possible that behavioralists see more ambiguities in the international environment than do traditionalists; a more skeptical or middle-of-the-road position has an appeal for the thoroughgoing empiricist. The behavioral movement was indeed founded on the principle that questions of fact must be distinguished sharply from questions of value, and behavioralism has advocated rigor in the former realm. Nevertheless, one can be systematic and rigorous in one's thinking when approaching moral propositions. Until recently behavioralists had not yet devised a technique for making "ought" statements in such a way that they had a scientific flavor at the same time.

The first major crisis to confront behavioralists since their success in the 1960's has been the war in Vietnam. Accordingly, efforts by political behavioralists to conduct surveys of American attitudes toward Vietnam have constituted somewhat of a breakthrough: [54] marriage between the behavioral penchant for data and the traditional concern within political science over moral issues has resulted. The fact that a very large proportion of the American population would support peace negotiations with the Vietcong was not predictable on a priori grounds, and such information can be useful in arguing for a foreign policy more responsive to public opinion. Alternatively, one could use the same data to make a recommendation that more information needs to be communicated to the public about the Vietcong's somewhat anarchical leadership. Values are in no sense derivable from facts, so whether the behavioralist advises the public or the State Department, it should be kept in mind that he does not do so in his role as a political scientist if he actually prescribes a solution. Even in his role as disseminator of information relevant to political decisions, he must perhaps be quite modest in his pretensions. But he should be encouraged in any case to play multiple roles, as do his counterparts in the other social and natural sciences.

The behavioralist who might consider offering data and analysis to the judiciary, where the situation is much less urgent, would have to be equally cautious in making prescriptions; for it will be some time before lawyers or courts start seeking the advice of political behavioralists or, for that matter, from public law men. This does not mean that the legal profession is hostile to social science; that is far from the case. However, thus far, the political behavioralists interested in courts are able to predict future court decisions only a little bit more precisely than public law men. Such information could hardly be considered as useful "advice" to judicial policy makers, though it might aid attorneys in arriving at more objective methods for computing fees for each of their clients. Judges would hardly be amused by political behavioralists claiming to predict decisions on pending cases. In examining the judicial decision making process as one in which information is sorted, evidence weighed, and cases decided with a view to their probable effects upon society, it is clear that there is a much larger potential role for the judicial behavioralist than has been fully explicated and realized. Evidence and inference procedures in legal reasoning are not always up to the more rigorous standards of contemporary social science methodology, and behavioralists could perform an invaluable service in pointing out such deficiencies, particularly where political phenomena are concerned.

One area under current academic development possibly could be of interest to high courts in the future. When Supreme Court justices deliberate, one of the problems which is likely to concern them is the specific impact that various kinds of decisions will have on the economic, social, and political systems. This is what Justice Frankfurter had in mind when he asked, "Does anybody know ... where we can go to find light on what the practical consequences of these decisions [Sherman Act cases] have been?"[55] Though a theory of case decision impact is barely out of the anecdotal stage of academic evolution, there is substantial promise that it will be built systematically in the years to come.[56] It is not too precarious a stretch of the imagination to suggest that one day political scientists might hold positions on judicial staffs to help determine whether a unanimous vote is desirable; when precedent should be used as the main thread of a decision rather than socio-logical evidence; under what situations clarity in a decision is desirable over ambiguity and vice versa; or what time of the year it might be best to announce a certain type of decision.

The systematic study of the impact of Supreme Court decision making is indeed rather new, and behavioral studies are quite rare, but there has been an outburst of them recently.[57] A comprehensive and rigorous collection of data on the consequences of Supreme Court decisions has begun in earnest; within a decade enough data may be gathered to develop some reasonably useful theory concerning the societal effects of court decisions.[58] Political behavioralists studying the judicial process may well have an interesting set of policy questions to answer at that time and a unique competence to do so. The caveat about modesty in theory and method should be remembered, and questions on the role of the scientist in policy advising should be raised now in the field of judicial behavior.

Other Observations

Although we enumerate but five main propositions, our list could be expanded much farther. In a larger version of this plea, we would develop the criticism of a "validity gap"; that is, in many behavioral studies the variables merely scratch the surface without demonstrating whether such measures are valid indicators of a more general concept. Such an argument is stated in considerable detail in a recent essay by Robert Jervis, who notes that often one variable alone has been selected to stand for a single concept, without adequate logical linkage between the two.[59] Furthermore, among multimethodologists it is already standard practice to undertake multivariable operationalizations of the same concept.

Most importantly, our purpose in writing this plea should be clear. We do not seek to criticize for the sake of criticism or to be polemical even in an obscure or indirect manner. If we have seemingly joined forces with traditionalistic criticisms, it is because we have become increasingly aware of pressing social problems that have been ignored by behavioralists, while becoming exposed to a literature on the philosophy of science for which traditional scholars always had considerable respect, though they remained for a time out of touch with the behavioralist reconstruction of the logic of inquiry in political science. Individual empirical research undertakings must inevitably make arbitrary choices and be finite in scope; science provides no set of dogmas for attaining knowledge, but instead seeks to embrace the infinite insofar as it is fundamentally an analytic quest to make the multiple facets of the so-called real world comprehensible to men in an ever-changing universe.[60] Indeed, the points that we have raised have been argued long before, across generations of scholars in previous centuries, and we are merely suggesting a next step for the 1970's—multimethodologism—with the aim of liberating current political science from its fixations regarding measurement and stagnations in the development of theory. We do so in a manner that may seem strident to some members of the older "silent generation," but our actual demeanor is one of chivalry and humility. We welcome a new generation of antimethodologists in the 1980's, for we do not seek to set up our own Establishment.

IV. CONCLUSION

To conclude this five-pronged plea, we should like to admit that we, too, are guilty of some of the practices which we have criticized. Why, then, have we fallen into such obvious traps? If behavioralists in political science to date have failed to live up to their own methodology—to integrate insights from the traditional literature, to try out alternative models, to develop a technical language in which words are defined consistently, and to formulate a coherent tested theory of interest to the policy maker—the reason may be that such an effort cannot be achieved in a decade.

The older generation of political behavioralists, whom we have largely been criticizing, is a self-taught generation, and its main success of establishing the behavioral mood in political science was a very formidable task. It is perhaps natural to expect that, after an era overly concerned with theory and methodology for their own sake, it should now seem appropriate to turn toward—and beyond—achieving a behavioral-traditional synthesis. To resolve the inadequacies of the behavioral achievement in the future, political science will demand more methodologically sophisticated traditionalism and a behavioralism that is both theoretically more sound and practically more relevant. In the multimethodological future that we envisage, political scientists will be methodologically more rigorous though less self-conscious about research strategies. Their impressionistic accounts will receive a new respectability whenever demands of theory or policy relevance exceed the reliable data available. A battery of data analysis techniques will be used to fathom the appropriate models for describing reality. Conceptualization will be sharper and more consistent within a cumulatively improving body of tested propositions. Finally, political scientists will remember that as human beings in a democratic society they have a genuine opportunity to play the role of responsible social critics and proponents of political innovations. The achievement of multimethodological goals is within reach. Therein lies the challenge.

NOTES

The authors wish to acknowledge helpful suggestions on various earlier drafts from David Danelski, Henry Kariel, and Glendon Schubert. An earlier version, pertaining only to international relations, dealt only with the problem of bridging behavioral and traditional political science: Michael Haas, "Bridge-Building in International Relations. A Neotraditional Plea," *International Studies Quarterly,* XI (December 1967), 320-338. The present essay, which treats all of the discipline of political science, seeks to bridge recent clefts among behaviorally trained scholars.

1. See Frederick Pollock, *An Introduction to the History of the Science of Politics* (Boston: Beacon, 1890, 1960); Albert Somit and Joseph Tanenhaus, *The Development of Political Science* (Boston: Allyn & Bacon, 1967). Our use of the dialectical model is meant to imply neither an organismic process nor an inexorability to schismogenesis.

2. Robert A. Dahl, "The Behavioral Approach in Political Science— Epitaph for a Monument to a Successful Protest," *American Political Science Review,* LV (December 1961), 763-772. But see also Harold D. Lasswell, *The Future of Political Science* (New York: Atherton, 1963).

3. See Morton A. Kaplan, "The Great Debate: Traditionalism vs. Science in International Relations," *World Politics,* XIX (October 1966), 1-20.

4. Hedley Bull, "International Relations: The Case for a Classical Approach," *World Politics,* XVIII (April 1966), 367. Some of the other recent assessments of behavioral political science include Walter Berns, "The Behavioral Sciences and the Study of Political Things—The Case of Christian Bay's *The Structure of Freedom,*" *American Political Science Review,* LV (September 1961), 550-559; Herbert J. Storing (ed.), *Essays on the Scientific Study of Politics* (New York: Holt, Rinehart & Winston, 1962); Christian Bay, "Politics and Pseudopolitics: A Critical Evaluation of Some Behavioral Literature," *American Political Science Review,* LIX (March 1965), 39-51;

and various essays in two symposia organized by James C. Charlesworth, *The Limits of Behavioralism in Political Science* (Philadelphia: American Academy of Political and Social Science, 1962), and *A Design for Political Science: Scope, Objectives, and Methods* (Philadelphia: American Academy of Political and Social Science, 1966). See also Klaus Knorr and James Roseman (eds.), *Contending Approaches to International Politics* (Princeton: Princeton University Press, 1969).

5. Kaplan, op. cit., pp. 19-20.

6. William Bluhm, *Theories of the Political System* (Englewood Cliffs: Prentice-Hall, 1965). The term "multimethodology" is coined to refer to a higher-order synthesis between traditionalism and both types of behavioralism. Glendon Schubert, meanwhile, used the label "conventionalists" to refer to a group allegedly associated with neither the behavioral nor the traditional camps in "Academic Ideology and the Study of Adjudication," *American Political Science Review*, LXI (March 1967), 106-129. As we shall see below, multimethodologists are hardly conventional in any way, believing that the customary problems of political science should be treated by several methodological and theoretical strategies at the same time.

7. David Easton, "Introduction: The Current Meaning of 'Behavioralism' in Political Science," *The Limits of Behavioralism in Political Science*, ed. Charlesworth, op. cit., pp. 1-25. Cf. Evron M. Kirkpatrick, "The Impact of the Behavioral Approach on Traditional Political Science," *Essays on the Behavioral Study of Politics*, ed. Austin Ranney (Urbana: University of Illinois Press, 1962), pp. 1-30.

8. Hayward R. Alker, Jr., "The Long Road to International Relations Theory: Problems of Statistical Nonadditivity," *World Politics*, XVIII (July 1966), 623-655.

9. Somit and Tanenhaus, op. cit., Ch. IX.

10. "The methodologist is a scholar who is above all analytical in his approach to his subject matter." Paul F. Lazarsfeld and Morris Rosenberg (eds.), *The Language of Social Research* (Glencoe: Free Press, 1955), pp. 1-4, at p. 4.

11. For instance, see Sheldon Goldman, "Voting Behavior on the United States Court of Appeals," *The Federal Judicial System*, eds. Thomas P. Jahnige and Goldman (New York: Holt, Rinehart & Winston, 1968), pp. 201-210.

12. Dina A. Zinnes, Robert C. North, and Howard E. Koch, Jr., "Capability, Threat and the Outbreak of War," *International Politics and Foreign Policy*, ed. James N. Rosenau (New York: Free Press, 1961), pp. 469-482; Ole R. Holsti and Robert C. North, "The History of Human Conflict," *The Nature of Human Conflict*, ed. Elton McNeil (Englewood Cliffs: Prentice-Hall, 1965), pp. 155-171.

13. Ole R. Holsti, Richard A. Brody, and Robert C. North, "Affect and Action in International Reaction Models," *Journal of Peace Research*, I (#3-4, 1964), 170-190.

14. Bruce M. Russett, *International Regions and the International System* (Chicago: Rand McNally, 1967).

15. Hayward R. Alker, Jr., *Mathematics and Politics* (New York: Macmillan, 1965).

16. Dina A. Zinnes, "A Comparison of Hostile Behavior of

Decision-Makers in Simulate and Historical Data," *World Politics*, XVIII (April 1966), 474-502; Zinnes, "The Expression and Perception of Hostility in Pre-War Crisis: 1914," *Quantitative International Politics*, ed. J. David Singer (New York: Free Press, 1968), pp. 85-119; Charles E. Osgood and Evelyn G. Walker, "Motivation and Language Behavior: A Content Analysis of Suicide Notes," *Journal of Abnormal and Social Psychology*, LIX (July 1959), 58-67. See also Ole R. Holsti, "External Conflict and Internal Consensus: The Sino-Soviet Case," *The General Inquirer*, eds. Phillip J. Stone et al. (Cambridge: M.I.T. Press, 1966), pp. 343-358. It is interesting to note also that in response to the original "neotraditional plea" of the senior author of the present article, Professor North has initiated plans to study Sweden in 1914; this is another instance in the refreshing trend toward multimethodologism. See Robert C. North, "Research Pluralism and the International Elephant," *Contending Approaches to the Study of International Politics*, eds. Knorr and Rosenau, op. cit., p. 241.

17. William Foote Whyte, *Streetcorner Society* (2nd ed.; Chicago: University of Chicago Press, 1955).

18. George Liska, *International Equilibrium* (Cambridge: Harvard University Press, 1957), pp. 200-201.

19. Charles McClelland, "The Acute International Crisis," *World Politics*, XIV (October 1961), 182-204.

20. Herman Finer, *Dulles over Suez* (Chicago: Quadrangle, 1963); see Ole R. Holsti, "The Belief System and National Images: A Case Study," *Journal of Conflict Resolution*, VI (September 1962), 244-252.

21. Ernst Haas, *The Uniting of Europe* (Stanford: Stanford University Press, 1958); E. Haas, "The Challenge of Regionalism," *International Organization*, XII (Autumn 1958), 440-458.

22. See the excellent codifications of literature in Richard A. Brody, "Some Systemic Effects of the Spread of Nuclear Weapons Technology: A Study Through Simulation of a Multi-nuclear Future," *Journal of Conflict Resolution*, VII (December 1963), 663-753; and Andrew M. Scott, *The Functioning of the International Political System* (New York: Macmillan, 1967).

23. Stanley Hoffmann (ed.), *Contemporary Theory in International Relations* (Englewood Cliffs: Prentice-Hall, 1960), pp. 174-184. For a similar argument, see Alfred de Grazia, Ralph E. Juergens, and Livio C. Stecchini (eds.), *The Velikowsky Affair* (New York: University Books, 1966).

24. Richard Rosecrance, *Action and Reaction in World Politics* (Boston: Little, Brown, 1963); Bruce M. Russett, "The Calculus of Deterrence," *Journal of Conflict Resolution*, VII (June 1963), 97-109; Quincy Wright, "The Escalation of International Conflicts," ibid., IX (December 1963), 434-449. See also Shabtai Rosenne, "The International Court and the United Nations: Reflections on the Period 1946-1954," *International Organization*, XII (Summer 1958), 274-287; Leland M. Goodrich, "The United Nations Security Council," ibid., pp. 274-287.

25. Glendon Schubert (ed.), *Judicial Decision-Making* (New York: Free Press, 1963), p. 2.

26. David J. Danelski, *A Supreme Court Justice Is Appointed* (New York: Random House, 1964); see also Danelski, "Conflict and Its Resolution in the Supreme Court," *Journal of Conflict Resolution*, XI (March 1967), 71-86; and Kenneth Dolbeare, *Trial Courts in Urban Politics* (New York: Wiley, 1967).

27. More must be done than simply rephrasing old ideas in the jargon of systems or structural-functional analysis; a language that permits comparisons across large numbers of systems is only a means to an end. The end is a theoretical science that can permit clinical applications. See Walter Murphy, *Elements of Judicial Strategy* (Chicago: University of Chicago Press, 1964); Glendon Schubert, *Judicial Policy Making* (Chicago: Scott, Foresman, 1965); Joel Grossman, "Social Backgrounds and Judicial Decisions: Notes for a Theory," *Journal of Politics,* XXIX (May 1967), especially pp. 337-344.

28. Donald Kommers, "Professor Kurland, the Supreme Court, and Political Science," *Journal of Public Law* (#2, 1966), 230-252; Theodore L. Becker, "Judicial Structure and Its Political Functioning in Society: New Approaches to Teaching and Research in Public Law," *Journal of Politics,* XXIX (May 1967), 302-334; Becker, *Comparative Judicial Politics* (Chicago: Rand McNally, 1970); Glendon Schubert and David Danelski (eds.), *Comparative Judicial Behavior* (New York: Oxford University Press, 1969).

29. Arthur S. Banks and Robert B. Textor, *A Cross-Polity Survey* (Cambridge: M.I.T. Press, 1963).

30. Harold J. Spaeth, "Unidimensionality and Item Invariance in Judicial Scaling," *Behavioral Science,* X (July 1965), 298. See also Spaeth, *The Warren Court* (San Francisco: Chandler, 1966), especially Ch. I.

31. Joseph Tanenhaus, "The Cumulative Scaling of Judicial Decisions," *Harvard Law Review,* LXXIX (Summer 1966), 1594.

32. Glendon Schubert, "Ideologies and Attitudes, Academic and Judicial," *Journal of Politics,* XXIX (February 1967), 25.

33. For an inventory of procedures, each of which is treated in terms of underlying models, see Hayward R. Alker, Jr., "Statistics and Politics: The Need for Causal Data Analysis," *Politics and the Social Sciences,* ed. Seymour M. Lipset (New York: Oxford University Press, 1969), pp. 244-313; see also Dennis J. Palumbo, "Causal Inference," ed. Michael Haas (Evanston: Northwestern University Press, forthcoming), Ch. XIX.

34. R. J. Rummel, "Dimensions of Dyadic War, 1820-1952," *Journal of Conflict Resolution,* XI (June 1967), 176. In this study, the investigator reanalyzes data on international conflict presented and extensively examined by Lewis F. Richardson, *Statistics of Deadly Quarrels* (Chicago: Quadrangle, 1960). A "superiority" of factor analysis, as opposed to such multivariate techniques as cluster analysis, smallest space analysis, or causal modeling, remains unjustified methodologically as well as theoretically.

35. R. J. Rummel, "Understanding Factor Analysis," *Journal of Conflict Resolution,* XI (December 1967), 455.

36. One such effort is in the field of judicial behavior: Schubert, "Academic Ideology and the Study of Adjudication," op. cit.; for a smallest space analysis that challenges an earlier factor analysis in sociology, see Milton Bloombaum, "Tribes and Traits: A Smallest Space Analysis of Cross-Cultural Data," *American Anthropologist,* LXX (April, 1968), 328-333.

37. Address before the International Studies Association, Western Branch, Seattle, March 22, 1968.

38. George Orwell, "Politics and the English Language," *On Shooting an Elephant and Other Essays* (New York: Harcourt, Brace, 1945), pp. 77-92.

39. Ernst B. Haas, "The Balance of Power: Prescription, Concept, or Propaganda," *World Politics,* V (July 1953), 442-477; Werner Levi, "The

Concept of Integration in Research on Peace," *Background,* IX (August 1965), 111-126.

40. Robert C. North, Howard E. Koch, Jr., and Dina A. Zinnes, "The Integrative Functions of Conflict," *Journal of Conflict Resolution,* IV (September 1960), 356; Lewis Coser, *The Functions of Social Conflict* (Glencoe: Free Press, 1956), p. 8. A third formulation mixes the two without comment: Rudolph J. Rummel, "Dimensions of Conflict Behavior Within and Between Nations," *General Systems Yearbook,* VIII (1963), 4-5.

41. Karl W. Deutsch et al., *Political Community and the North Atlantic Area* (Princeton: Princeton University Press, 1957).

42. Amitai Etzioni, *Political Unification* (New York: Holt, Rinehart & Winston, 1965).

43. Stuart Nagel, "Sociometric Relations Among American Courts," *Southwestern Social Science Quarterly,* XLIII (September 1962), 136-142; see also Glendon Schubert, "Academic Ideology and the Study of Adjudication," op. cit., p. 121.

44. Refer again to Schubert's article on academic ideology (ibid.): the mere fact that a professor sees another professor's work as being immensely different from his own in approach or point of view need not constitute an immense difference in sociometric distance. One might well have a liking for an individual with a different approach; no evaluation of an ideology is implied in the perception of such a distance.

45. Ibid.

46. Ibid., p. 127.

47. Recently published studies on judicial role by judicial behavioralists include Bancroft C. Henderson and T. C. Sinclair, *The Selection of Judges in Texas* (Houston: Public Affairs Research Center, University of Houston, 1965); Theodore L. Becker, "A Survey Study of Hawaiian Judges: The Effect on Decisions of Judicial Role Variations," *American Political Science Review,* LX (September 1966), 677-680; Gene L. Mason, "Judges and Their Publics: Role Perceptions and Role Expectations," unpublished doctoral dissertation, University of Kansas, 1967; Kenneth Vines, "The Judicial Role in American States," *Frontiers of Judicial Research,* eds. Joel Grossman and Joseph Tanenhaus (New York: Wiley, 1969).

48. See Neil Gross et al., *Explorations in Role Analysis* (New York: Wiley, 1962). The most complete discussion of the concept as it is used in social science is in Bruce J. Biddle and Edwin J. Thomas, *Role Theory* (New York: Wiley, 1966).

49. Fred W. Riggs, *Administration in Developing Countries: The Theory of Prismatic Society* (Boston: Houghton Mifflin, 1964); Michael Haas, "Types of Asymmetry in Social and Political Systems," *General Systems Yearbook,* XII (1967), 69-79. See also the too often ignored volume by Harold Lasswell and Abraham Kaplan, *Power and Society* (New Haven: Yale University Press, 1950); and the excellent discussion of Martin Landau, "Due Process of Inquiry," *American Behavioral Scientist,* IX (October 1965), 4-10.

50. See Charlesworth (ed.), *A Design for Political Science,* pp. 114-142, especially the remark on p. 115 by behavioralist Heinz Eulau, as contrasted with the more multimethodological view of John G. Kemeny, "A Philosopher Looks at Political Science," *Journal of Conflict Resolution,* IV (September 1960), 301.

51. See Lewis Anthony Dexter, "On the Use and Abuse of Social Science by Practitioners," *American Behavioral Scientist,* IX (September 1965), 25-29.

52. Robert A. Nisbet, "Project Camelot: An Autopsy," *Public Interest,* V (Fall 1966), 51-52.

53. Whatever the merits of petition signing may be, of 781 signatures on a statement of the Greater Boston Faculty Committee on Vietnam, for example, we were able to recognize 17 political scientists, with only 2 behavioralists; *New York Times,* May 9, 1965. The Ad Hoc Faculty Committee on Vietnam, with over 1,000 supporters, similarly has few political science contributors, with only 2 behavioralists; *New York Times,* January 15, 1967. The proadministration American Friends of Vietnam lists 6 political scientists, including 1 behavioralist, out of 75 letterhead names. The ratio of traditionalists to behavioralists in the profession as a whole leans more heavily to the former, but the fact remains that political scientists score lower on the "professional representation index" than sociologists, anthropologists, and philosophers in Everett C. Ladd, Jr., "Professors and Political Petitions," *Science,* CXLIII (March 28, 1969), 1425-1430. See also Howard Schuman and Edward O. Laumann, "Do Most Professors Support the War," *Trans-Action,* V (November 1962), 32-35; David J. Armor et al., "Professors' Attitudes Toward the Vietnam War," *Public Opinion Quarterly,* XXXI (Summer 1967), 160-175.

54. Sidney Verba et al., "Public Opinion and the War in Vietnam," *American Political Science Review,* LXI (June 1967), 317-333. Theodore L. Becker, "Ibsen Revisited: The Mass Media and Public Support for Administration Vietnam Policy," paper presented at the Annual Meeting of the Southwestern Social Science Association, New Orleans, April 1966. See also Davis Bobrow, "Liberation Wars, National Environments, and American Decision Making," paper presented at the Conference on China, the United States and Asia, Center for Policy Study, University of Chicago, February 1967.

55. Quoted in Donald Reich, "The Impact of Supreme Court Decision-Making," (Oberlin: unpublished manuscript, 1966).

56. Several calls for such a theory have been made of late, perhaps the most eloquent plea belonging to a law school professor. See Arthur S. Miller, "On the Need for 'Impact Analysis' of Supreme Court Decisions," *Georgetown Law Journal,* LIII (Winter 1965), 365-401. And, promisingly enough, there have been several attempts at the formulation of conceptual schemes that are necessary if research is to be organized. See Samuel Krislov, *The Supreme Court in the Political Process* (New York: Macmillan, 1965), Ch. VI, on compliance.

57. A few of the more interesting ones include Richard Johnson, *The Dynamics of Compliance* (Evanston: Northwestern University Press, 1967); Michael Wald et al., "Interrogations in New Haven: The Impact of Miranda," *Yale Law Journal,* LXXVI (March 1967), 1519-1616; James P. Levine, "Constitutional Law and Obscene Literature," *The Impact of Supreme Court Decisions,* ed. Theodore L. Becker (New York: Oxford University Press, 1969).

58. Jack Peltason, *Fifty-Eight Lonely Men* (New York: Harcourt, Brace & World, 1961); Kenneth Vines, "Federal District Judges and Race Relations

Cases in the South," *Journal of Politics,* XXVI (May 1964), 337-357; Stuart
Nagel and Robert Erikson, "Editorial Reaction to Supreme Court Decisions
on Church and State," *Public Opinion Quarterly,* XXX (Winter 1966-1967),
647-655.

59. Robert Jervis, "The Costs of the Quantitative Study of International
Relations," *Contending Approaches to International Politics,* eds. Knorr and
Rosenau, op. cit., pp. 177-217. Validity can operate in both directions: if
simulation worlds do not correspond to findings based on data assembled
from the so-called real world, does it follow that the simulate world is wrong?
A postbehavioralist, Paul Smoker, argues that such incongruities can be
devices for constructing future worlds, where present problems can achieve a
more desirable resolution than has been the case in the past, wherefrom
nonsimulated data must inevitably come. See his essay "Simulation for Social
Anticipation and Creation," *American Behavioral Scientist,* forthcoming.

60. And, incidentally, our multimethodological "reconstructed logic" is
not meant to displace "logic-in-use," but merely to sketch a newer logic that
seeks to be a useful next stage for the discipline of political science. See
Abraham Kaplan, *The Conduct of Inquiry* (San Francisco: Chandler, 1964);
Thomas S. Kuhn, *The Structure of Scientific Revolutions* (Chicago:
University of Chicago Press, 1962).

17 The New Revolution in Political Science

DAVID EASTON, University of Chicago

I. INTRODUCTION

A new revolution is under way in American political science. The last revolution—behavioralism—has scarcely been completed before it has been overtaken by the increasing social and political crises of our time. The weight of these crises is being felt within our discipline in the form of a new conflict in the throes of which we now find ourselves. This new and latest challenge is directed against a developing behavioral orthodoxy. This challenge I shall call the post-behavioral revolution.

The initial impulse of this revolution is just being felt. Its battle cries are *relevance* and *action*. Its objects of criticism are the disciplines, the professions and the universities. It is still too young to be described definitively. Yet we cannot treat it as a passing phenomenon, as a kind of accident of history that will somehow fade away and leave us very much as we were before. Rather it appears to be a specific and important episode in the history of our discipline, if not in all of the social sciences. It behooves us to examine this revolution closely for its possible place in the continuing evolution of political science. Does it represent a threat to the discipline, one that will divert us from our long history in the search for reliable understanding of politics? Or is it just one more change that will enhance our capacity to find such knowledge?

II. NATURE OF THE POST-BEHAVIORAL REVOLUTION

The essence of the post-behavioral revolution is not hard to identify. It consists of a deep dissatisfaction with that kind of political research and teaching that is striving to convert the study of politics into a more rigorously scientific discipline modeled on the methodology of the natural sciences. Although the post-behavioral revolution may have all the appearances of just another reaction to behavioralism, it is in fact notably different. Hitherto resistance to the incorporation of scientific

■ Presidential address delivered at the 65th meeting of the American Political Science Association, September, 1969, Commodore Hotel, New York City.

method has come in the form of an appeal to the past—to classical political science such as natural law or to the more loosely conceived nonmethodology of traditional research. Behavioralism was viewed as a threat to the status quo; classicism and traditionalism were responses calculated to preserve some part of what had been, by denying the very possibility of a science of politics.

The post-behavioral revolution is, however, future-oriented. It does not not especially seek to return to some golden age of political research or to conserve or even to destroy a particular methodological approach. It does not require an adherent to deny the possibility of discovering testable generalizations about human behavior. It seeks rather to propel political science in new directions. In much the same way, behavioralism in the fifties, by adopting a new technology, sought to add to rather than to deny our heritage. This new development is then a genuine revolution, not a reaction; a becoming, not a preservation; a reform, not a counter-reformation.

Post-behavioralism is both a movement, that is, an aggregate of people, and an intellectual tendency. As a movement it has many of the diffuse, unstable, even prickly qualities that the behavioral revolution itself once had in its own youth. It would be a serious mistake, indeed a grave injustice, to confuse this broad, inchoate movement with any organized group either inside or outside the profession. Nor ought we to attribute any special political color to post-behavioralists in the aggregate. They range widely, from conservatism to the active left. Nor has this movement any particular methodological commitments. It embraces rigorous scientists as well as dedicated classicists. Neither does it appeal to any one age group alone. Its adherents include all the generations, from young graduate students to older members of the profession. This whole improbable diversity—political, methodological, and generational—is bound together by one sentiment alone, a deep discontent with the direction of contemporary political research.

Even though today the organized cleavages within our profession are writing most of the dramatic scenarios, in the end these cleavages may prove to be the least interesting part of what is happening. What will undoubtedly have far deeper meaning for us is the broader intellectual tendency that provides the environment within which current divisions have taken shape. It is on the purely intellectual components of post-behavioralism, therefore, that I shall focus.

New as post-behavioralism is, the tenets of its faith have already emerged clearly enough to be identifiable. They form what could be called a Credo of Relevance. I would describe the tenets of this post-behavioral credo as follows:

1. Substance must precede technique. If one *must* be sacrificed for the other—and this need not always be so—it is more important to

be relevant and meaningful for contemporary urgent social problems than to be sophisticated in the tools of investigation. For the aphorism of science that it is better to be wrong than vague, post-behavioralism would substitute a new dictum, that it is better to be vague than nonrelevantly precise.

2. Behavioral science conceals an ideology of empirical conservatism. To confine oneself exclusively to the description and analysis of facts is to hamper the understanding of these same facts in their broadest context. As a result empirical political science must lend its support to the maintenance of the very factual conditions it explores. It unwittingly purveys an ideology of social conservatism tempered by modest incremental change.

3. Behavioral research must lose touch with reality. The heart of behavioral inquiry is abstraction and analysis and this serves to conceal the brute realities of politics. The task of post-behavioralism is to break the barriers of silence that behavioral language necessarily has created and to help political science reach out to the real needs of mankind in a time of crisis.

4. Research about and constructive development of values are inextinguishable parts of the study of politics. Science cannot be and never has been evaluatively neutral despite protestations to the contrary. Hence to understand the limits of our knowledge we need to be aware of the value premises on which it stands and the alternatives for which this knowledge could be used.

5. Members of a learned discipline bear the responsibilities of all intellectuals. The intellectuals' historical role has been and must be to protect the humane values of civilization. This is their unique task and obligation. Without this they become mere technicians, mechanics for tinkering with society. They thereby abandon the special privileges they have come to claim for themselves in academia, such as freedom of inquiry and a quasi-extraterritorial protection from the onslaughts of society.

6. To know is to bear the responsibility for acting and to act is to engage in reshaping society. The intellectual as scientist bears the special obligation to put his knowledge to work. Contemplative science was a product of the nineteenth century when a broader moral agreement was shared. Action science of necessity reflects the contemporary conflict in society over ideals and this must permeate and color the whole research enterprise itself.

7. If the intellectual has the obligation to implement his knowledge, those organizations composed of intellectuals—the professional associations—and the universities themselves cannot stand apart from the struggles of the day. Politicization of the professions is inescapable as well as desirable.

No one post-behavioralist would share all these views. I have presented only a distillation of the maximal image. It represents perhaps a Weberian ideal type of the challenges to behavioralism. As such the credo brings out most of the salient features of the post-behavioral revolution as it appears to be taking shape today.

III. SHIFTING IMAGES OF SCIENCE

What has this developing new image of political science to offer us? In the United States behavioralism has without doubt represented the dominant approach in the last decade. Will post-behavioralism destroy the undeniable gains of the behavioral revolution or is post-behavioralism only a valuable addition that can and should be incorporated into our practices?

One thing is clear. In a rapidly changing world surely political science alone cannot claim to have completed its development. Only on the assumption that behavioral political science has said the last word about what makes for adequate research and an appropriate discipline can we automatically read out of court any proposals for change.

The history of the various theoretical sciences, like physics and chemistry, reveals that every discipline rests on certain fundamental assumptions. It is a captive of what has been described as a research paradigm.[1] Over the years political science has been no less prone to develop models of what constitutes a good discipline or adequate research and these models have undergone marked transformations.

The behavioral model of this century has been but the last in a long chain. It has shifted the balance of concern from prescription, ethical inquiry, and action to description, explanation, and verification. Behavioralism has justified this shift on the grounds that without the accumulation of reliable knowledge, the means for the achievement of goals would be so uncertain as to convert action into a futile game. The growing success of the scientific enterprise in political science cannot be denied.

New conditions of the modern world, however, force us to reconsider our image of what we want to be. Scientific progress is slow, and however more reliable our limited knowledge about politics has become in the last fifty years, social crises of unforeseen proportions are upon us. Fear of the nuclear bomb, mounting internal cleavages in the United States in which civil war and authoritarian rule have become frightening possibilities, an undeclared war in Vietnam that violates the moral conscience of the world, these are continuing conditions entirely unpredicted by political science, behavioral or otherwise. The search for an answer as to how we as political scientists have proved so disappointingly ineffectual in anticipating the world of the 1960's has contributed significantly to the birth of the post-behavioral revolution.

In this perspective the legitimacy of raising doubts about the adequacy or relevance of political science in the contemporary world of crises cannot be questioned. We can join the post-behavioral movement at least in asking: Must we be committed eternally to an unchanging image of the discipline, behavioral or otherwise? Is it not incumbent on us to take account of changing conditions and to be ready and willing to reconsider old images and modify them to the extent deemed necessary? Must political science continue to do what it has been doing over the last few decades, in the hope that some "normal" period will one day return in which time will be on the side of those who seek to develop a more reliable understanding of political processes?

The negative answer that many individuals from all generations of political scientists are giving is clear. One of the probable underlying reasons for this answer we can readily understand. Mankind today is working under the pressure of time. Time is no longer on our side. This in itself is a frightening new event in world affairs. An apocalyptic weapon, an equally devastating population explosion, dangerous pollution of the environment, and in the United States severe internal dissension of racial and economic origin, all move in the same direction. They move toward increasing social conflict and deepening fears and anxieties about the future, not of a generation or of a nation, but of the human race itself. Confronting this cataclysmic possibility are a knowledge of the enormous wealth and technical resources currently available in a few favored regions of the world, the spectacular rate of increase in man's material inventiveness and technology, and the rich potential just on the horizon for understanding social and political processes. The agony of the present social crisis is this contrast between our desperate condition and our visible promise, if we but had the time.

In the face of a human situation such as this, the post-behavioral movement in political science (and in the other social sciences simultaneously) is presenting us with a new image of our discipline and the obligations of our profession. It pleads for more relevant research. It pleads for an orientation to the world that will encourage political scientists, even in their professional capacity, to prescribe and to act so as to improve political life according to humane criteria.

We can respond by refusing to budge, much as the classicists and traditionalists once did in the face of the onslaught of the behavioralists. Or we can recognize the need for change and explore the best ways of reconstructing our conception of our discipline and of the related professional institutions of which we are part. It is the second course that I propose we consider.

IV. THE IDEAL COMMITMENTS OF POLITICAL SCIENCE

A decision to contemplate revising the image of our discipline and profession places the political scientist in a strange and difficult predicament. Fierce pressures are building up for solutions to immediate problems. Yet the nature of basic research is to shift the focus away from current concerns and to delay the application of knowledge until we are more secure about its reliability.

This dilemma of contemporary political science is perhaps best revealed in the ideal commitments of behavioralism. For example, according to the behavioral image of science, those very epistemological characteristics of political research to which the post-behavioralists so strongly object would seem to be unavoidable, indeed, highly desirable. Post-behavioralism deplores what it views as technical excesses in research. Yet no one could possibly deny that technical adequacy is vital. Without it the whole evolution of empirical science in all fields of knowledge in the last two thousand years would have been in vain. Despite some post-behavioral objections to scientific abstractness and remoteness from the world of common sense, by its nature science must deal with abstractions. No science could by itself cope with the whole reality as it is interpreted by the politician. Only by analysis, by chopping the world up into manageable units of inquiry, by precision achieved through measurement wherever possible, can political science meet the continuing need of a complex, post-industrial society for more reliable knowledge. Even to appeal to science to discard abstract theory and models as the test of relevance for research and to put in their place the social urgency of problems, is to ask it to sacrifice those criteria which have proved most successful in developing reliable understanding.

Furthermore, it appears that the use of the methods of behavioral science favors the very kind of sociological position for the political scientist to which post-behavioralism so strenuously objects. These methods help to protect the professional scientist from the pressures of society for quick answers to urgent if complicated practical problems. The history of the natural sicences shows us how slowly basic research moves. The overshadowing new ideas in the natural sciences—Newtonian mechanics, Darwinian evolution, Einstein's relativity, or modern cybernetics—come infrequently, on a time scale of centuries. But during the intervals between new ideas, great or small, science seeks to work out their implications with a passion for details, even if research seems to lead away from the practical, obvious problems of the day. These seemingly remote, often minute details about scales, indices, specialized techniques for collecting and analyzing data and the like, these details are the building blocks of the edifice in which more reliable understanding occurs. What is true about the slow pace of basic research in the natural sciences and its remoteness we can expect to apply with equal force to the social sciences. Indeed in social research we even have difficulty in agreeing on the great discoveries, so undeveloped are our criteria of adequacy.

In addition, even if the political scientist begins with an immediate social problem, as he so often does, in the process of investigation he will be likely to restate the problem in more researchable terms. This reconceptualization usually leads him back to the very kind of fundamentals that appear irrelevant to initial practical concerns.

The ideology of pure or basic research and its success in the better developed sciences in providing a reliable base of knowledge have seemed to justify this research strategy, slow and painstaking as it is. In helping to protect scholarship from the daily pressures of society for quick and ready answers, this ideology has freed science to pursue truth in the best way it knows how.

This same concern for generalized, verifiable understanding has forced social scientists to discriminate with extreme care about what we can and cannot do with our premises and tools. We can describe, explain, and understand but we cannot prescribe ethical goals. The value question is thus set aside, not because we consider it inconsequential, but only because we see it as unresponsive to the tools useful in analyzing and explaining the empirical world.

These then are some of the normal ideal commitments of science: technical proficiency in the search for reliable knowledge, the pursuit of basic understanding with its necessary divorce from practical concerns, and the exclusion of value specification as beyond the competence of science. It is these ideals that behavioral research in political science has sought to import into the discipline.

V. NEW STRATEGIES FOR SCIENCE

Today these traditional ideals of science are confronted with a set of social conditions which have no historical precedent. This extraordinary circumstance has created the predicament in which behavioral research now finds itself. It derives from the fact that we are confronted with a new and shortened time scale in the course of human events, one in which the future may need to be discounted more heavily than ever before. For many, nuclear war or civil strife, with authoritarianism as a credible outcome, are clear and present dangers, to be counted in decades at the most. For many, without immediate and concentrated attention to the urgent issues of the present day, we may have no future worth contemplating, however uncertain our findings or inadequate our tools. How then can behavioral research, with its acknowledged glacial pace and apparent remoteness, hope to meet the demands now being placed upon our discipline?

For some post-behavioralists, the fear of physical and political self-destruction has led to the abandonment of science altogether. For them science is simply incapable of measuring up to contemporary needs. Others, who have always considered science to be inherently defective, now feel justified in their convictions. But for those post-behavioralists who continue to place their hopes in modern behavioral science, the current crisis poses the issue about the wisdom of continuing our commitment to a "normal" strategy of scientific research. These kinds of post-behavioralists have been driven to conclude that we have no alternative but to make our research more relevant. For them we can do so only by devoting all our professional energies to research, prescription, and action with regard to the immediate issues of the day. In short, we are asked to revise our self-image by postponing the demands of slow-moving basic research and by acting in our professional capacity so as to put whatever knowledge we have to immediate use.

For all of us this plea poses some critical questions. Even in the face of the social crises of our time, do we really need to subordinate the long-run objectives of the scientific enterprise to the undeniably urgent problems of the day? Is there any other way in which we can cope with this transparent need for practical relevance? And if so, can we hope to retain those conditions of theoretical autonomy, precision, and relative insulation for political science so vital if we are to continue to be able to add to our capital stock of basic understanding?

I would argue that we do not need to abandon the historical objectives of basic science. There is a strategy that will enable us to respond to the abnormal urgency of the present crises and yet preserve these traditions. If we adopt this course, post-behavioralism need not be considered a threat to behavioral research but only an extension of it necessary for coping with the unusual problems of the present epoch.

To appreciate the strategy implied, we must remember one thing. Even if it *is* arguable that the time scale in terms of which we must think has been greatly shortened, mere projection cannot fully persuade us that the future needs to be counted in decades, not centuries. What little solace we may get from it, we know that our intuitions have been wrong in the past. We may still have centuries rather than only decades ahead of us.

This realistic possibility suggests that we ought to pursue an optimizing strategy in which there is some apportionment of resources for the long run as against the short run, just in case we are not in fact all dead. The cost of devoting our efforts exclusively to short-run crises is far too high. It might easily assure that if we do in fact survive the present crises, the failure to continue to add to our capital accumulation of basic social knowledge will see us tragically unprepared for even greater crises in the more distant future. We will then have lost every chance to prevent the self-annihilation of mankind or the collapse of those political institutions we cherish.

Is there any sensible way in which we can provide for some satisfactory use of our resources without distracting excessively from the attention and altered research orientations that the major issues of the country and the world require? It is to this question that those of us who still have some hope that we may survive the certain and greater crises of the near future ought to be devoting some of our energies. Various courses of action are possible, and we need to consider them as they apply to the discipline as well as to the profession.

VI. THE DISCIPLINE

Basic Versus Applied Research

For the discipline, the post-behavioral revolution suggests the appropriateness of revising our ideal image at least as it has been incorporated into behavioralism. It is vital to continue to recognize the part that basic research ought to play. But in the allocation of financial and human resources we must also consciously recognize that a shift in emphasis must occur at once to take into account the critical times in which we live.

In terms of any ideal distribution of our efforts, basic research ought to command a disproportionate share. Although socially useful results from such research are usually a long time in coming, they are in the end more dependable. But under the inescapable pressure of current crises the emphasis needs to be reversed. A far larger part of our resources must be devoted to immediate short-run concerns. We need to accept the validity of addressing ourselves directly to the problems of the day to obtain quick, short-run answers with the tools and generalizations currently available, however inadequate they may be. We can no longer take the ideal scientific stance of behavioralism that because of the limitations of our understanding, application is premature and must await future basic research.[2]

In truth this proposal represents less of a shift in our practices than a change in our ideological posture. The behavioral revolution has never been fully understood or absorbed into the discipline; we are still grappling with its meaning. Any casual inspection of ongoing research would reveal that, regardless of any ideal apportionment, at no time has pure research really consumed more than a very small fraction of the resources of the discipline. We have been only too ready to advise federal, state, and local agencies on immediate issues, and political parties and candidates about their campaigns. It is just that with the behavioral revolution the ideals of the discipline as incorporated in research ideology were beginning to change. This new image legitimated the kind of basic research, the payoff of which might not be immediately apparent, but the future promise of which was thought to be considerable. Today we need to temper our behavioral image of the discipline so that in these critical times we no longer see it as commanding us to devote most of our efforts to the discovery of demonstrable basic truths about politics. We will need to obtain more of our satisfactions from seeking immediate answers to immediate problems.

This kind of shift in disciplinary focus will call urgently for the systematic examination of the tasks involved in transforming our limited knowledge today into a form far more consumable for purposes of political action. Certain difficulties stand in the way of applying our knowledge. In the first place, contemporary social problems far outrun the capacity of political science alone or in concert with the other social sciences to solve them. Our basic knowledge is itself limited. What little we have is not necessarily directly applicable to practical issues.

In the second place, like medieval medicine, we may still be at the stage in which we are letting blood in the hope of curing the patient. Because of our low capacity for sorting out the complex causal connections between our advice and its social consequences, we have little assurance that we may not be doing more harm than good. Some efforts are currently under way to correct this situation. In the broadening quest for social indicators we are inventing techniques for isolating the outcomes of policy outputs[3] and for comparing these consequences with the presumed policy goals.[4] Thereby we shall have a measure of the effects of our intervention in the social processes. But the success of these efforts lies some distance in the future.

In the third place, political science alone is unable to propose solutions to social problems; these normally involve matters that call upon the specialized knowledge and skills of other social scientists. Yet seldom do policymakers seek the collective advice of comprehensive teams of social scientists.

These and many other difficulties have stood in the way of the application of our knowledge to specific situations. They have contributed to the low academic esteem of applied science, in comparison at least with basic research. Past efforts at application have experienced too little success to attract the best minds of the day.[5] In temporarily modifying the immediate priorities of the discipline, we will need to devise ways for elevating the self-conscious development of applied knowledge, inappropriately called social engineering, to the respectability that behavioralism has succeeded in acquiring for basic research.

To assign all of our research resources to the present, however, as some post-behavioralists seem to be suggesting, would be to discount the future far too heavily. We need to keep alive and active the legitimate long-range interests of all science. Social problem solving is not totally inconsistent with this objective. The line between pure and applied research is often very fine. Those of us who choose to adopt the long-run point of view, optimistically expecting the survival of mankind, will find much from which to profit in the research undertaken by those concerned with applied problems. Yet this cannot relieve us of the need to continue to devote specific attention to basic problems in the discipline—to the reconceptualization of our significant variables, to the continuing search for adequate units of political analysis, to the exploration of alternative partial and general theories and models about the operation of various types of systems, and to our basic methodological assumptions and technical requirements. Admittedly these persisting concerns often lead us far from the practical issues of the day. Yet without attending to these basic problems we cannot hope to add to our store of reliable knowledge, and thereby to prepare ourselves for equally critical political crises in the more distant future.

Value Premises and Research Interests

In addition to suggesting this temporary reallocation of our resources as between basic and applied research, we need to become increasingly aware of the fact that basic research is not without its own substantive deficiencies. This is the message underlying the constant post-behavioral complaint that our research is not relevant. It is argued that excessive preoccupation with techniques and with factual description has distracted us from the significant questions about the operation of the American democratic system in particular. We have learned a great deal about this system but all within a value framework that accepts the ongoing practices as essentially satisfactory and at most subject only to the need for incremental improvements. As a discipline we have proved incapable of escaping a commitment to our own political system. This research myopia, the post-behavioralists argue, has discouraged us from posing the right questions for discovering the basic forces that shape the making and execution of authoritative decisions.

Here the post-behavioralists are alerting us, once again, to what has been repeatedly revealed over the years, by Marx, Weber, and Mannheim, among others, namely, that all research, whether pure or applied, of necessity rests on certain value assumptions. Yet the myth that research can be value-free or neutral dies hard. We have continued to develop our discipline as though the subjects we select for research, the variables we choose to investigate, the data we collect, and the interpretations we generate have all some extraordinary pristine purity, unsullied by the kinds of value premises to which we subscribe, consciously or otherwise. We do not consistently ask the question, central to the sociology of knowledge: To what extent are our errors, omissions, and interpretations better explained by reference to our normative presuppositions than to ignorance, technical inadequacy, lack of insight, absence of appropriate data, and the like? Behavioralists have indeed failed to insist, with the same fervor we have applied to our technological innovations, that our operating values be brought forward for self-conscious examination and that their impact on research be assessed.

Today the hazards of neglecting our normative presuppositions are all too apparent. There can be little doubt that political science as an enterprise has failed to anticipate the crises that are upon us. One index of this is perhaps that in the decade from 1958 to 1968, the *American Political Science Review* published only 3 articles on the urban crisis; 4 on racial conflicts; 1 on poverty; 2 on civil disobedience; and 2 on violence in the United States.[6]

In some considerable measure we have also worn collective blinders that have prevented us from recognizing other major problems facing our discipline. For example, how can we account for the failure of the current pluralist interpretations of democracy to identify, understand, and anticipate the kinds of domestic needs and wants that began to express themselves as political demands during the 1960's? How can we account for our neglect of the way in which the distribution of power within the system prevents measures from being taken in sufficient degree and time to escape the resort to violence in the expression of demands, a condition that threatens to bring about the deepest crisis of political authority that the United States has ever suffered? How can we account for the difficulty that political science as a discipline has in avoiding a commitment to the basic assumptions of national policy, both at home and abroad, so that in the end, collectively we have appeared more as apologists of succeeding governmental interpretations of American interests than as objective analysts of national policy and its consequences? Finally, in even so recent a major research as political socialization, how can we account for the natural, effortless way in which inquiry has sought to reveal the contributions of preadult political learning to the stability of systems, virtually ignoring the equally significant function of socialization in bringing about political change?[7]

There is no single explanation for the narrow vision of our discipline. We can, however, at least go so far as to offer this hypothesis: Whatever the reasons, the failure to broaden the vision of our basic research may well be due in good part to a continuing hesitation to question our normative premises and to examine the extent to which these premises determine the selection of problems and their ultimate interpretations.

Creative Speculation

How are we to make those serious efforts necessary to break out of the bonds imposed on basic research itself by ongoing value frameworks? How are we to create those conditions that will help us to pose fundamental questions about the operation of political systems, that will lead us to pose those "outrageous hypotheses" about which Robert Lynd once chided us?[8] A new awakening to the part that our value commitments and other social influences play in limiting the range of our basic research may partly correct the errors of our ways. But this moral self-scrutiny may not be enough. If we are to transcend our own cultural and methodological biases, such self-awareness can carry us only part of the way. We may need to take stronger measures and find additional help by returning to an older tradition in political research but in a thoroughly modern way.

Many years ago, in *The Political System,* I argued for the urgent need to reconsider our approach to value theory at the same time as we began the equally critical task of constructing empirical theory.[9] The latter task is now under way in our discipline. The first one, creative construction of political alternatives, has yet to begin.

To enrich their own understanding and to give broader meaning to their own social reality, the great political theories of the past found it useful to construct new and often radically different conceptions of future possible kinds of political relationships. By formulating such broad, speculative alternatives to the here and now we too can begin to understand better the deficiencies of our own political systems and to explore adequate avenues of change that are so desperately needed. This, I would argue, must now be considered part of the task and responsibility of science if it is to retain its relevance for the contemporary world. Those philosophies that seek to revive classical natural law and that reject the possibility of a science of man have thereby forfeited their opportunity and put in question their fitness to undertake this creative task of theory. We require boldly speculative theorizing that is prepared to build upon rather than to reject the findings of contemporary behavioral science itself and that is prepared to contemplate the implications of these findings for political life, in the light of alternative, articulate value frameworks.

The significance for political science of this kind of creative speculation cannot be overestimated. For those who seek to understand how political systems operate, such speculation provides alternative perspectives from which to determine the salience of the problems they choose for research and analysis. If we take seriously the conclusions of the sociologists of knowledge, then our scientific output is very much shaped by the ethical perspectives we hold. In that event, by failing to encourage within the discipline creative speculation about political alternatives in the largest sense, we cannot help but imprison ourselves within the limitations of the ongoing value framework. As that framework begins to lose its relevance for the problems of society, its system-maintenance commitments must blind us to the urgent questions emerging even for the immediate future.

And this is precisely what has happened to political science. Both our philosophers and our scientists have failed to reconstruct our value frameworks in any relevant sense and to test them by creatively contemplating new kinds of political systems that might better meet the needs of a post-industrial, cybernetic society. A new set of ethical perspectives woven around this theme might sensitize us to a whole range of new kinds of basic political problems worth investigating. It might also point up the significance of inquiry into these problems with new or radically modified types of relevant empirical theories. Thereby we could perhaps be freed from that occupational myopia brought about by excessive attention to the facts as they are. We would perhaps be less prone to stumble into the pitfall of "empirical conservatism,"[10] or commitment to system-maintenance perspectives, of which political science has with justice been accused,[11] by post-behavioralists among others.

In these several ways then does our discipline need reordering. Basic research needs to be maintained as an investment for the future. But even *its* priorities need to be rearranged in the light of a better understanding of its own value assumptions. Applied, action-oriented research requires more systematic attention than ever before. We need greater awareness of the limits that our value premises have imposed on our research. And on the solid foundation of knowledge constructed by behavioral research, alternative possible rearrangements of our political relationships need to be seriously contemplated.

VII. THE PROFESSIONAL AND THE USE OF KNOWLEDGE

Not only our discipline, however, but our profession needs restructuring to bring it into harmony with the changing conceptions of social science. Our discipline refers to our intellectual enterprise; our profession, to the trained and expert scholars who participate in the discipline. Post-behavioralism suggests that behavioral commitments create not only a discipline but a profession that shows a declining relevance to the political world around it.

The Behavioral Image of the Profession

Two basic reasons account for this decline, it is in effect argued. First, professionalization of the discipline in behavioral terms has nourished an image of political science in which knowledge and action have been carefully separated and compartmentalized.[12] As scientists possessed of special skills, we see ourselves as purveyors of something called professional expertise. Our task as experts is to offer advice about means only, not about the purposes to which our knowledge might be put. As the well-worn adage puts it, we are on tap, not on top.

In fact, as post-behavioralism correctly asserts, the expert has never lived by this rule. In the discipline, as we have already noted, behavioral inquiry has not been able to attain any real measure of ethical neutrality. This has had serious consequences for basic research. In the profession too, the critics point out, ethical neutrality is no less spurious. In the application of his knowledge the political scientist explicitly or unwittingly accepts the value premises of those he serves. His posture of neutrality has the added consequence of undermining his will or capacity to challenge the broader purposes to which his knowledge is put.

A second reason accounts for the decline of professional relevance. Here post-behavioralism breaks sharply with the prevailing professional paradigm about the moral relationship between research and action. In the behavioral interpretation, the possession of knowledge imposes no special obligation on the political scientist to put his knowledge to use in the service of society. He remains free to choose whether or not he ought to step outside his scientific role for this purpose. This laissez-faire attitude toward political engagement has been an accepted moral premise of the profession. It has permitted if not encouraged withdrawal from political strife. Knowledge is divorced from action.

For post-behavioralism, however, the line between pure research and service begins to fade. Knowledge brings an awareness of alternatives and their consequences. This opportunity for rational choice imposes special obligations on the knower. The political scientist as a professional is the knower *par excellence*. It is therefore immoral for him not to act on his knowledge. In holding that to know is to bear a responsibility for acting, post-behavioralism joins a venerable tradition inherited from such diverse sources as Greek classical philosophy, Karl Marx, John Dewey, and modern existentialism.

Criteria for the Use of Knowledge

The implications of this post-behavioral shift in the image of the professional's role in society are considerable. If the political scientist is to evaluate the uses to which his knowledge is being put and if he is himself to bring his knowledge to bear on social issues, what criteria are to guide his choices? Here post-behavioralism returns to the humanist conception of the intellectual as the guardian of those civilized, humane values known to most men. It is incumbent on the professional to see to it that all society, not just a privileged part, benefits from his expertise. His obligations are met only if he takes into account the broadest spectrum of interests in society.

Many post-behavioralists scrutinize the activities of scholars in recent years and conclude that the talents of political scientists have been put in the service largely of the elites in society—in government, business, the military, and voluntary organizations. The professional is seen as having little communication and contact with those who characteristically benefit least from the fruits of modern industrial society—the racial and economic minorities, the unrepresented publics at home, and the colonial masses abroad. These are the groups least able to command the resources of expertise for which political science stands. The social responsibility of the political science expert is to rectify the imbalance.

In this post-behavioral view, the application of expert knowledge in the service of social reform becomes competitive with the pursuit of knowledge for its own sake. Reform becomes inseparable from knowledge.

Clearly there is in birth a new image of the professional, one in which science is not necessarily denied its place but in which the scientist is no longer free to divorce the life of the mind from the life of social action. Weber's differentiation between the vocation of the scientist and that of the politician no longer wholly suffices.

This new image leads to the politicization of the profession. If the individual professional is called upon to utilize his knowledge on behalf of society, those collectivities of experts that we call the professional associations are themselves equally culpable if in their corporate capacity they fail to challenge the purposes to which their expertise may be put or if they fail to act when their knowledge warns them of danger. Herein lie the moral and intellectual roots of the constant pressure on the professional associations to take positions on public issues about which their competence may give them special knowledge.

The Politicization of the Profession

This post-behavioral tendency to politicize the professional associations has met with great resistance. Objection arises less from principled argument than from the practical fear that our professional associations will no longer be able to fulfill their normal scientific purposes. Let us grant the plausibility of this practical consideration. Even so, do we need to reject entirely the new moral image being developed by post-behavioralism?

One fact is clear. The crisis of our times spares no group, not even the social sciences. The pressures to utilize all of our resources in critically evaluating goals as well as in providing effective means are too great to be denied. For increasing numbers of us it is no longer practical or morally tolerable to stand on the political sidelines when our expertise alerts us to disaster.

In accepting this new (but ancient) obligation of the intellectual, however, we need to recognize that the professional political scientist may engage in three distinguishable kinds of activity. These are teaching and research on the one hand and practical politics on the other. Somewhere between these the political scientist acts as a consultant and an adviser. Each of these kinds of activity—as a scholar, politician, and consultant—shapes and influences the others. Is it feasible to construct a single organization that will serve the collective purposes of the profession for facilitating all three of these kinds of activities? It seems highly unlikely. Can we provide some sensible division of labor among different organizations that will permit the fullest expression for all those activities into which these critical times are pressing the professional political scientist? This seems possible.

We can conceive of some professional organizations being devoted largely to that kind of action that helps to add to our store of basic knowledge and that eases communication among ourselves and among succeeding generations of political scientists. These we already have in our professional associations. They are designed to aid both teaching and research. We can, however, also conceive of other types of professional organizations that would be concerned with structuring the application of our expertise to ongoing critical social problems. This kind of organization we do not yet have in political science, or, for that matter, in the social sciences as a whole.

But here if we consider the matter only as political scientists we create insurmountable difficulties for ourselves. Social problems do not come neatly packaged as economic, psychological, political, and the like. Our crises arise out of troubles that involve all aspects of human behavior. Our professional associations are oriented toward the disciplines, and these are analytic fields. Of necessity they piece up reality into specialties that have meaning largely for the pursuit of fundamental understanding. For purposes of setting goals and determining means for solving social problems, however, we need to draw the discipline together again into a single organization, one that can mobilize the resources of all the social sciences and bring them to a focus on specific issues.

To this end it is time that we accept our special responsibility as students of politics. We must take the initiative by calling for the establishment of a Federation of Social Scientists, a proposal that has already been advanced by one of our colleagues.[13] The tasks of such a Federation would be to identify the major issues of the day, clarify objectives, evaluate action taken by others, study and propose alternative solutions, and press these vigorously in the political sphere.

Without collectively politicizing ourselves in this way, by the very act of standing by while the problems of the world continue to increase in number and intensity, we thereby uncritically acquiesce in prevailing policies. We in fact adopt a political position. By acting collectively in our professional capacities through a Federation of Social Scientists, we will have an opportunity to justify our policies intellectually and morally. Thereby we may begin to satisfy our growing sense of political responsibility in an age of crisis. At the same time we shall be able to preserve our historic institutions, the professional associations, for the continuing pursuit of fundamental knowledge.

Such a Federation would fail in its responsibilities, however, if it became merely an echo of national goals, an instrument of official policy, or a bland critic of things as they are. If Mannheim is correct in describing the intellectual as the least rooted of all social groups, the professional social scientist ought to view himself as committed to the broadest of humane values. These need to be the touchstone that brings to bear on social issues. Yet many barriers block the way. Of these identification with the goals and interests of one's nation is prominent. Political scientists have still to escape the crippling effects for scholarship of unwitting commitment to national goals and perspectives. Just as science as a set of disciplines has pretensions to being international in scope, so the social scientist himself needs to be denationalized. Someday, like the ideal international civil servant, the professional social scientist too may be permitted to achieve maximum freedom from national commitments by being obliged to carry an international passport and to conduct himself accordingly.

For the profession, therefore, the emerging post-behavioral phase is encouraging the development of a new norm of behavior. It sees policy engagement as a social responsibility of the intellectual, whatever the institutional form through which this may be expressed. Someday it may also require the release of the social scientist from bondage to the unique needs and objectives of his own national political system.

It is clear that changing times require radical rethinking of what we are and what we want to be both as a discipline and as a profession. Post-behavioralism is a pervasive intellectual tendency today that reveals a major effort to do just this. Its very pervasiveness prevents it from becoming the possession of any one group or of any one political ideology. It extends behavioral methods and techniques by seeking to make their substantive implications more cogent for the problems of our times. Post-behavioralism stands, therefore, as the most recent contribution to our collective heritage. For that very reason, as an intellectual tendency it is not the threat and danger that some seem to fear. Rather, in the broad historical perspectives of our discipline, the post-behavioral revolution represents an opportunity for necessary change. We may choose to take advantage of it, reject it, or modify it. But to ignore it is impossible. It is a challenge to re-examine fearlessly the premises of our research and the purposes of our calling.

NOTES

1. T. S. Kuhn, *The Structure of Scientific Revolutions* (Chicago: University of Chicago Press, 1962).

2. See D. Easton, *The Political System* (New York: Knopf, 1953), pp. 78ff.

3. For the difference between outcomes and outputs see D. Easton, *A Systems Analysis of Political Life* (New York: Wiley, 1965), p. 351.

4. For the literature on social indicators see R. A. Bauer (ed.), *Social Indicators* (Cambridge: M.I.T. Press, 1966); "Social Goals and Indicators for American Society," *Annals of the American Academy of Political and Social Sciences,* CCCLXXI (May, 1967); CCCLXXIII (September, 1967).

5. See H. W. Rieken, "Social Science and Contemporary Social Problems," *Items*, XXIII (1969), 1-6.

6. This undoubtedly reflects only the few articles on this subject submitted for publication rather than any editorial predisposition.

7. See D. Easton and J. Dennis, *Children in the Political System: Origins of Political Legitimacy* (New York: McGraw-Hill, 1969), Ch. II.

8. R. S. Lynd, *Knowledge for What?* (Princeton: Princeton University Press, 1939).

9. Easton, *The Political System,* op. cit., Ch. IX-X.

10. H. Marcuse, *One-Dimensional Man* (Boston: Beacon Press, 1964), Ch. IV.

11. See C. A. McCoy and J. Playford (eds.), *Apolitical Politics* (New York: Crowell, 1967), and Easton, *The Political System,* op. cit., Ch. II, XI.

12. See especially T. Rozak (ed.), *The Dissenting Academy* (New York: Random House, 1968), Introduction.

13. David Singer of the Mental Health Research Institute, University of Michigan, Ann Arbor, Michigan, in personal correspondence.

Index